P9-CKP-291

MAN IN THE ANDES

US/IBP SYNTHESIS SERIES

This volume is a contribution to the International Biological Program. The United States' effort was sponsored by the National Academy of Sciences through the National Committee for the IBP. The lead federal agency in providing support for IBP has been the National Science Foundation.

Views expressed in this volume do not necessarily represent those of the National Academy of Sciences or of the National Science Foundation.

US/IBP SYNTHESIS SERIES ▌1

MAN IN THE ANDES

A MULTIDISCIPLINARY STUDY OF HIGH–ALTITUDE QUECHUA

Edited by

Paul T. Baker

The Pennsylvania State University

Michael A. Little

State University of New York, Binghamton

Dowden, Hutchinson & Ross, Inc.

STROUDSBURG, PENNSYLVANIA

LIBRARY OF CONGRESS CATALOGING IN PUBLICATION DATA

Main entry under title:
Man in the Andes
  (U.S./IBP synthesis series / 1)
  Bibliography: p. 429
  Includes index.
  1. Quechua Indians—Physical characteristics.
2. Indians of South America—Andes—Physical
characteristics. 3. Altitude, Influence of.
4. Quechua Indians—Social life and customs. I. Baker,
Paul T. II. Little, Michael A. III. Series.
F2230.2.K4M36   301.45'19'8   76-17025
ISBN 0-87933-228-X

Exclusive distributor: Halsted Press
A Division of John Wiley & Sons, Inc.
ISBN: 0-470-15153-6

to the memory of

CARLOS MONGE M.
1884–1970

Oh perhaps my mother was the vicuña of the pampas
or my father was the mountain stag
to be wandering,
to walk without rest
through the mountains and the pampas
hardly wrapped by wind,
in the creeks and on the hills
clothed by wind and cold.

Segment of Quechua Song[1]

[1] Reprinted with permission from *The Singing Mountaineers: Songs and Tales of the Quechua People,* ed. by Ruth Stephan. University of Texas Press, Austin (1971).

FOREWORD

This book is one of a series of volumes reporting results of research by U.S. scientists participating in the International Biological Program (IBP). As one of the 58 nations taking part in the IBP during the period July 1967 to June 1974, the United States organized a number of large, multidisciplinary studies pertinent to the central IBP theme of "the biological basis of productivity and human welfare."

These multidisciplinary studies (Integrated Research Programs), directed toward an understanding of the structure and function of major ecological or human systems, have been a distinctive feature of the U.S. participation in the IBP. Many of the detailed investigations that represent individual contributions to the overall objectives of each Integrated Research Program have been published in the journal literature. The main purpose of this series of books is to accomplish a synthesis of the many contributions for each principal program and thus answer the larger questions pertinent to the structure and function of the major systems that have been studied.

Publications Committee: U.S./IBP
Gabriel Lasker
Robert B. Platt
Frederick E. Smith
W. Frank Blair, Chairman

PREFACE

More than 25 million people throughout the world today live at altitudes above 3000 meters. At these elevations and above, limits of human health, productivity, and even survival are approached because of the high-altitude stresses of low oxygen pressure and cold. The reduced partial pressure of oxygen characteristic of high terrestrial elevations produces a state of hypoxia that influences nearly all systems in the body. Human adaptation to such environmental stresses depends not only on physiological responses but also on an interacting complex of sociocultural, demographic, and biological factors.

Despite the unfavorable conditions that exist at high altitude, humans have inhabited the Andean zone of South America for millenia. At the time of the Spanish conquest in the sixteenth century, the central Andes of what is now Ecuador, Peru, and Bolivia was the site of a high civilization that supported a population numbering in the millions. Following the dramatic and tragic population decline during the sixteenth and seventeenth centuries, the Andes has now recovered to its prehispanic population level. Whereas Indigenous American Indians have become extinct or assimilated in many other parts of the hemisphere, in the Andes today the native Quechua and Aymara Indian populations are a distinct numerical majority. Twelve years ago, when the research reported in this volume began, this predominance of Quechua Indians in the Andes appeared as persuasive evidence that these populations had achieved a marked degree of adaptation to high altitude.

The material in this volume consists of contributions from seventeen scientists who participated in a multidisciplinary and integrated effort to investigate the biology of human populations at high altitude in the district of Nuñoa and other parts of southern Peru. The Peruvian research began as a pilot project in 1962 conducted in Pucallpa, Chinchero, Cuzco, and Nuñoa. The Fulbright Commission, particularly its Peruvian director, Dr. Edwardo Indocochea, were helpful in the pilot project and the early stages of the research that followed. A five-year project was initiated in 1964 in the district of Nuñoa, which had been identified as an appropriate site for continued research. Principal investigators for this project were P. T. Baker and E. R. Buskirk, both from The Pennsylvania State University. In 1967 the Pan American Health Organization, the World Health Organization with the aid of Dr. Francis N. Dukes-Dobos, and the IBP sponsored a conference to determine the primary needs in high-altitude research in relation to IBP. This conference was instrumental in designing the subsequent parts of the Peruvian study. In 1968, the ongoing research in Nuñoa was incorporated as one of the three integrated research programs of the Human Adaptability component of the International Biological Program in the United States. Although research in Nuñoa continued until 1972, the program was expanded in the late 1960s by the initiation of studies of downward migrants from the highlands to the coastal and tropical forest lowlands. Although the more than a decade of research reported in this volume certainly is beyond a first stage in attempting to understand how Andean Indians have adapted to high altitude, it by no means represents a final stage in our accumulation of knowledge in this area. Plans by several contributors to this volume are currently under way to continue the work.

The research project culminating in the results reported in this volume required enormous personal, institutional, and financial support. Numerous individuals provided invaluable services in the United States and in Peru at all phases of the research from data gathering to analysis, and from graphics and manuscript preparation to editing of scientific papers. They are: Robert F. Akers, Cynthia Beall, Edward Carson, Darna L. Dufour, Hedy G. Frisancho, Judy D. Garruto, Martin J. Gursky, Sharon F. Haas, James Haight, Gaby A. Hanna, Jorge Huayhuaca, Linda J. Huff, H. John Jacobi, Fruma Klass, James W. Larrick, Robert M. Larsen, Adrienne V. Little, Jeanne B. Mazess, Ann and Stephen McGarvey, Kay McKinley, Edward Prokop, Robert Riley, David Rimmer, Richard M. Spector, Shirley C. Thomas, and Velma E. Weitz. Among the many Peruvians who offered help of a varied nature, we should like to acknowledge the assistance of Antonio Santos Aragon, Atilio Barreda M., Louisa de Barreda, Juan Bravo, Tomás Bustinza, Melquiades Huayna, Carmen Murillo, Francisco Palomino, Julio Sotomayor P., and Carlos Zamora J. We are especially indebted to Victor Barreda M., who worked with the members of the research team in Nuñoa from the project's inception in 1964. It is well known by all those who worked in Peru that Victor's friendship, advice, and unique skills were major factors contributing to the success of the project.

The data presented in this volume represent the contributions of many scientists who worked in Peru. We wish particularly to acknowledge the contributions of Drs. Romulo Acurio V., Donald Austin, Gordon F. DeJong, Dale Harris, James Kollias, Richard B. Mazess, Jean P. McClung, Ivan G. Pawson, Edward Watt, and Charles A. Weitz and anthropologists Danilo P. Pallardel and Jorge Sanchez. The success of the Peruvian research was dependent, to a large degree, upon the coordination and organization provided by several field directors over the years. They were: M. A. Little (1964), R. B. Mazess (1965–1966), A. R. Frisancho (1966), J. M. Hanna (1967), R. B. Thomas (1968), C. J. Hoff (1969), and J. D. Haas (1971).

We should like to express our deep gratitude to the Peruvian government and the many institutions that provided support and services. We acknowledge warmly the officials of the schools, hospitals, cooperatives, and other institutions of Chinchero, Chucarapi, Cocachacra, Cuzco, Lampa, Lima, Macusani, Mollendo, Ollachea, Puno, San Juan del Oro, Tacna, and Nuñoa, and particularly students, faculty, and officials of the Universidad Técnica del Altiplano in Puno and the Universidad Nacional del Cuzco. The cooperation and support of the Instituto Biología Andina of the Universidad Nacional Mayor de San Marcos, under the past direction of Dr. Tulio Velásquez and present direction of Dr. César Reynafarje, is gratefully acknowledged.

Financial support was provided by many universities and other institutions. We wish to thank The Pennsylvania State University, Ohio State and Cornell universities; the universities of Hawaii, Michigan, and Wisconsin; the State University of New York at Binghamton; and the Universidad Nacional Mayor de San Marcos. Funds for various aspects of the Peruvian project were derived from the following sources: Wenner-Gren Foundation grant 2723; PHS grants or fellowships 5-T01-GMO-1748, 1R01-HD-01756, 1-F2-GM-36,780, and 1-F1-GM-32,913; NIH grants, fellowships, or traineeships HE-13805, GM-07325, 5-F02-GM-41,055, and 5-TI-GM-1250; U.S. Army Medical Research and Development Command Contracts DA-49-193-MD-2260 and DA-49-193-MD-2709. Of these various sources, those contributing the bulk of funds were derived from the Army Medical Research and Development Command and the traineeship grants of the National Institute of General Medical Sciences. NSF provided funds through the International Biological Program Human Adaptability Coordinating Office for the preparation of this volume.

Finally, we owe a special debt of gratitude to the people of the communities where we worked. We thank them, simply but sincerely, for their patient and sometimes impatient cooperation as subjects and informants. We also thank them for their friendship.

P.T.B.
M.A.L.

CONTENTS

Foreword   vii

Preface   ix

List of Contributors   xix

1: Evolution of a Project: Theory, Method, and Sampling
   Paul T. Baker   *1*

   Theoretical Background, 2   Preliminary Assumptions of the
   Study, 4   Original Objectives, 5   Study Design and
   Population Selection, 6   Planned Sampling and Methods,
   11   Culturally Imposed Modifications of Methodology,
   13   Theoretical Changes Derived from Data,
   14   Methodological Changes Derived from Revised Theory,
   16   Overview, 20

2: Physical and Biotic Environment of Southern Highland Peru
   R. Brooke Thomas and Bruce P. Winterhalder   *21*

   Physical Environment and Climate, 21   Environmental Stress
   and Adaptation, 36   Biotic Environment, 37   Effects of
   Human Groups on the Environment, 45   The Nuñoa
   Ecosystem, 46

3: Social and Political Structure of Nuñoa
   Gabriel Escobar M.   *60*

   Ethnohistorical Background, 61   Social Structure and
   Organization, 65   The Economy, 67   The Political
   Structure, 76   Religion, 79   Cultural and Social Change, 82

4: Child Care, Child Training, and Environment
   Thelma S. Baker   *85*

   Methodological Frameworks, 86   Child Care, 88   Child
   Training, 92

5: Genetic History and Affinities
   Ralph M. Garruto and Charles J. Hoff   *98*

   Ethnohistorical and Cultural Perspective, 98   General
   Research Design, 99   Factors Governing the Genetics of the
   Nuñoa Quechua Population, 112   Overview, 114

6: Population Movement and Gene Flow
   James S. Dutt   *115*

   Factors Isolating the Native Population, 116   Migration and
   Gene Flow, 117   Genetic Drift, 120   Gene Flow Within the
   District, 121   Historical Perspectives, 123   Summary and
   Conclusions, 126

7: Fertility
   Charles J. Hoff and Andrew E. Abelson   *128*

   Hypoxia and Reproductive Physiology, 128   Altitude and
   Fertility, 133   Summary and Conclusions, 145

8: Morbidity and Postneonatal Mortality
   Anthony B. Way   *147*

   Review of Other Studies, 148   Nuñoa Study,
   150   Conclusions, 158

9: Prenatal and Infant Growth and Development
   Jere D. Haas   *161*

   Prenatal Growth and Birth, 162   Postnatal Growth and the
   Infant, 165   Conclusions, 178

10: Growth and Morphology at High Altitude
   A. Roberto Frisancho   *180*
   Part I: Growth and Functional Development

   Growth in Body Size, 180   Pulmonary Function,
   185   Body Composition, 188   Skeletal Maturation,
   190   Determinants of Growth and Development,
   191   Discussion and Conclusions, 199

   Part II: Adult Morphology

   Methods and Materials, 200   Results and Discussion, 201

11: Nutrition
   Emilio Picón-Reátegui   *208*

   Food and Activity Patterns, 208   Food Production,
   Preservation, and Preparation, 212   Evaluation of the Diet,
   214   Effect of Coca Chewing, 233   General Comments, 235

12: Pulmonary Function and Oxygen Transport
   Tulio Velásquez   *237*

   Lung Volume, 237   Ventilation, 244   Alveolar–Arterial
   Gradient, 250   Lung-Tissue Oxygen Transport, 252   Total
   Oxygen Pressure Gradient, 257   Summary, 260

13: Hematology
   Ralph M. Garruto   *261*

   Sampling and Testing Procedures, 262   Hematological
   Responses, 264   Peripheral Blood Changes During Strenuous
   Physical Activity, 275   Overview, 281

14: Work Performance of Newcomers to the Peruvian Highlands
   Elsworth R. Buskirk   *283*

   Subjects, Methods, and Procedures, 284   Results,
   288   Discussion, 295

15: Work Performance of Highland Natives
Paul T. Baker   *300*

Earlier Studies, 300   Project Hypotheses, 302   Project
Results, 303   Evaluation, 313

16: Natural Exposure to Cold
Joel M. Hanna   *315*

Cold Stress in the Dry Season, 316   Cold Stress in the Rainy
Season, 318   Technological Approaches, 323   Conclusions,
330

17: Physiological Responses to Cold
Michael A. Little   *332*

Background to Cold Studies in Peru, 332   Laboratory
Procedures, 338   Cold Responses of the Andean Native,
340   Discussion, 360

18: Drug Use
Joel M. Hanna   *363*

Coca Leaf Use in Nuñoa, 363   Alcohol Use in Nuñoa,
375   Tobacco Use in Nuñoa, 376   Drug Interactions,
377   Conclusions, 377

19: Energy Flow at High Altitude
R. Brooke Thomas   *379*

Methods and Concepts, 380   Energy Flow Through the
Nuñoa Population, 383   Adaptive Responses to the
Energy-Flow System, 391   Discussion, 402

20: Environmental Adaptations and Perspectives
Michael A. Little and Paul T. Baker   *405*

Major Areas of Contribution, 405   Future Perspectives, 426

References   429

Appendix: List of Symbols   471

Index   473

LIST OF CONTRIBUTORS

Andrew E. Abelson
School of Cultural and Community Studies, University of Sussex

Paul T. Baker
Department of Anthropology, The Pennsylvania State University

Thelma S. Baker
Department of Anthropology, The Pennsylvania State University

Elsworth R. Buskirk
Human Performance Research Laboratory, The Pennsylvania State University

James S. Dutt
Department of Anthropology, The Pennsylvania State University

Gabriel Escobar M.
Department of Anthropology, The Pennsylvania State University

A. Roberto Frisancho
Center for Human Growth and Development and Department of Anthropology, The University of Michigan

Ralph M. Garruto
National Institute of Neurological Disease and Stroke, NIH, Bethesda

Jere D. Haas
Division of Nutritional Sciences, Cornell University

Joel M. Hanna
Department of Physiology, University of Hawaii

Charles J. Hoff
Department of Anthropology, University of Oregon

Michael A. Little
Department of Anthropology, State University of New York, Binghamton

xx   LIST OF CONTRIBUTORS

Emilio Picón-Reátegui
Instituto de Biología Andina, Universidad Nacional Mayor de San Marcos, Lima

R. Brooke Thomas
Department of Anthropology, University of Massachusetts

Tulio Velásquez
Instituto de Biología Andina, Universidad Nacional Mayor de San Marcos, Lima

Anthony B. Way
Department of Environmental Health, Texas Tech University School of Medicine

Bruce P. Winterhalder
Department of Anthropology, Cornell University

MAN IN THE ANDES

EVOLUTION OF A PROJECT: THEORY, METHOD, AND SAMPLING

Paul T. Baker

In the early 1960s the state of evolutionary theory and the level of knowledge about man's adaptation to environmental stress suggested that a major research project in human population biology might provide some new insight into how genetic selection operated on man and how men adapted to some of the specific stresses faced in our evolutionary history.

More specifically, at that time the following conditions existed:

1. The modern synthetic theory of evolution had been developed in a form which allowed the specific definition of how gene frequencies could be modified in populations (Dobzhansky, 1955; Simpson, 1949).

2. In several instances it had been possible to define how selection had operated to cause genetic variations between human populations (Livingstone, 1958; Neel, 1951).

3. It was known that many of the physical characteristics which vary between human populations correlated significantly with the physical and biotic structure of the inhabited world (Baker, 1958, 1960; Newman, 1953; Roberts, 1953; Schreider, 1957).

4. It had been demonstrated that many physiological traits varied between human populations, and in some instances it was possible to surmise that these variations improved the ability of the particular groups to survive in their environments (Dill et al., 1964).

5. Finally, a battery of measurement techniques had been developed which allowed the detailed study of gene systems of body morphology, population structure, and physiology (Weiner and Lourie, 1969).

Under these circumstances, first a panel of experts convened by the World Health Organization (WHO, 1964) and later the planners of the International Biological Program (IBP) strongly urged the development of a series of multidisciplinary studies devoted to understanding how populations living with a simple technology had biologically adapted to their environments (Baker and Weiner, 1966; Weiner, 1965).

The Nuñoa project, the concern of this volume, began in the early sixties in response to these considerations and was later modified and extended by the IBP stimulus. In this chapter I will try to elucidate the original theoretical base, the basic methods, and the original sample planning, showing how they were modified and in some instances improved by the information feedback that was generated in this rather long project.

THEORETICAL BACKGROUND

The choice of a high-altitude focus for the study was, of course, partially dictated by the fact that several of the investigators, including myself as project director, had previous experience working with the Quechua in the Peruvian highlands. However, there were also some strong theoretical and factual reasons for believing that a study of such a population was ideal for examining man's responses and adaptations to extreme environmental stress. Theoretically, genetic and physiological adaptation to an environmental stress is more likely to occur when men do not have cultural tools which can prevent them from being biologically stressed. High altitude thus provides one of the clear examples where culture can do little to modify the impact of decreased oxygen pressure in the atmosphere. As I will discuss later, we found that cultural definitions of expected work-load levels may have some effect on hypoxic stress, but even so it remains correct to say that cultural responses have reduced ability to ameliorate hypoxic stress compared to the impact on such stresses as undernutrition or even cold stress.

As a second theoretical postulate it may be stated that the more the environmental stress affects such fundamentals as work ability or reproduction and growth, the greater the probability that genetic and physiological adaptations will be evoked. By the early 1960s there was clear evidence that under sufficient hypoxic stress all low-altitude mammals showed a reduced oxygen-uptake ability, and even when the stress was low enough to permit survival, at least, some species were sterile as adults, while younger animals failed to grow normally (Van Liere and Stickney, 1963).

The information base concerning the adaptation of man to high altitudes was quite varied in quantity and quality. The problems of low-altitude people traveling to high altitudes had intrigued physiologists for a considerable time, and the literature on the physiological and psychological impact of upward movement was voluminous (Wulff et al., 1968). Somewhat less effort had been expended on the high-altitude native. From times as early as the Spanish Conquest lowlanders had observed that high-altitude natives were apparently less affected by the high mountains than they were. Thus, as quoted in Monge (1948, pp. 3, 32), Father Acosta in 1608 said "and so I am persuaded that the element of air there is so thin and delicate that it doesn't provide for human respiration which needs it to be thicker and more tempered, and that I believe to be the reason for the stomach's being so greatly upset and the whole man put out of balance. . . ." Father Cobo later noted, in relation to the differences between Indians and Spaniards:

But where it is most noticeable is in those who have half, a quarter, or any admixture of Indian blood; for these are all raised with the same loving care as the pure Spanish children and yet the more Indian blood they have, the better they survive and grow; so that it is now a common saying based on everyday experience that babes having some Indian in them run less risk in the cold regions than those not having this admixture.

For all of which I know of no other reason which one could give more suitable than that which I have said, namely, that the warm constitution of the Indians is very resistant to the rigors of external cold; and as the greater the share of this constitution a babe inherits through the blood of its parents, the more heat it will have, hence it comes about that those who are closest to the nature of Indians run less risk in their childhood of being finished off by the cold, as it does finish and take away the life of most of the pure-blooded Spanish children.

As part of his landmark efforts of the 1940s, C. Monge M. published a small book in which he collated the historical and physiological evidence then available concerning the adaptations of the highland natives (Monge, 1948). He argued that the highland natives were indeed biologically different from the lowlanders and had an adaptation to high altitude which lowlanders could not achieve. Study of the oxygen-transport system of natives continued and was comprehensively summarized by Hurtado in the early sixties (Hurtado, 1964b). Other investigators, particularly those from Peru, had begun studies on other biological characteristics of the high-altitude native (Arias-Stella and Recavarren, 1962; Kerwing, 1944; Rotta, 1947). Despite the comprehensive nature of these oxygen-transport studies, we were at the time bothered by two aspects of them which could affect the conclusions. First, many of the studies were performed on the assumption that the physiology of the highland native, when compared to that of lowlanders, was the result of acclimatization (Balke, 1964a). This assumption seemed dubious because acclimatization was usually, although not universally, defined as a short-term process (Hurtado, 1966), and lowlanders who had been at high altitude for as long as a year failed to achieve native high-altitude oxygen-consumption capacities (Velásquez, 1964). Second, most of the studies reporting on natives had used men from a mining community as test subjects. In most studies the test subjects were not miners as such but employees working in surface positions. Nevertheless, they might have worked harder than in traditional Quechua society and were certainly exposed to different environmental factors, such as atmospheric pollution, modified nutrition, and changed housing. These factors combined with the fact that most test subjects were migrants from other altitudes made us doubt that they were representative of highland Quechua biology.

While considerable information had been collected about the oxygen-transport system of the native, most of the other biological parameters which might be affected by the environmental characteristics of high altitude were only partially studied. The population was increasing in size, but whether altitude had any specific effects on fecundity, parturition, or mortality was mostly unknown. Most medical doctors working at altitudes above 3000 m believed that lowlanders had at least temporary fecundity problems when coming to high altitude and were more emphatic that pregnant women who moved to high altitude were likely to abort. However, they found nothing unusual about native fecundity and parturition (Hellriegel, 1967; Monge, 1948).

The growth of high-altitude Quechua had been examined by several small cross-sectional studies (Hurtado, 1932a; Quevedo, 1949; Schraer and Newman, 1958). Growth appeared slow compared to that of U.S. and European children, but not unusually slower for peasants who might have a poor diet. Some nutritional surveys had been made, with conflicting evidence on the adequacy of the native diet (Baker and Mazess, 1963; Collazos et al., 1954, 1960; Mazess and Baker, 1964), and some studies had been made on responses to nonhypoxic stresses such as cold (Elsner, 1963; Hanna, 1965) and coca chewing (Chambochumbi, 1949; Risemberg, 1944; Zapata Ortiz, 1944).

PRELIMINARY ASSUMPTIONS
OF THE STUDY

Given the theoretical and an abbreviated version of the information base, it is possible to see why we wished to begin an extended study on a high-altitude Quechua population who (1) lived in the highest part of the *altiplano,* (2) lived in a traditional fashion with minimal impact from modern Peruvian culture, and (3) contained a sufficiently large population to permit adequate samples even for demographic analysis.

What may not be clear are all of the basic assumptions and hypotheses underlying the study. It may be helpful to review these in light of the subsequent methods and findings.

1. The prime assumption was that the population was biologically adapted to its physical and biological environment, as shown by the fact that the high-altitude Quechua population had maintained its numbers over a considerable time.

2. It was assumed that the primary environmental stressor was hypoxia produced by the lowered oxygen pressure at high altitude.

3. It was assumed from previous findings on high-altitude Quechua that they were fully adapted to the hypoxic stress. This assumption was based on

reports that high-altitude Quechua achieved sea-level values in oxygen consumption (Velásquez, 1964), and there was no strong evidence that hypoxia affected the fertility, growth, morbidity, etc., of the native.

4. Based on previous studies it was believed that the native hypoxic adaptation was achieved by short-term acclimatization probably built on a gene system which produced better oxygen transport than could be achieved by men from a low-altitude heritage. The possibility of a growth and development acclimatization component was considered but had little basis in scientific evidence at that time.

5. Two previous studies and experience in the altiplano suggested that there was a significant cold stress (Baker, 1963a; Elsner, 1963; Hanna, 1965). It was believed that while cultural factors modified the stress, the population showed a biological adaptation which could not be explained by short-term acclimatization. Again a heritable base to the adjustment was suspected.

6. A small nutritional survey had been made by some of the investigators in this project prior to the initiation of the major study (Baker and Mazess, 1963; Mazess and Baker, 1964). It, along with other studies on stable peasant populations (Dubos, 1965; R. S. Harris, 1945), suggested that relatively undisturbed Quechua populations might not have unusual dietary needs or problems. This was not a firm assumption.

7. A final and major assumption was that by conducting an in-depth study on the biological responses of an integral and interdependent population unit it would be possible to obtain better insights than were possible from a series of disconnected individual studies. Thus by drawing all samples for analysis from the same population it was believed that intercorrelations could be made to gain new insights. Furthermore, it was hoped that by the diversified collection of physiological data on identical subjects the possible variety of causative answers to a particular result could be reduced.

ORIGINAL OBJECTIVES

Given the underlying assumptions and hypotheses, the original objectives of the study were rather obvious. It may still be of value to the reader if they are broadly described so that he may judge how adequately the sampling, methods, and succeeding chapters of results reflect achievement of the goals. These objectives can be subdivided into two categories: (1) the development of normative data on the environment and the biological characteristics of the population, and (2) the experimental testing of a series of postulates about the physiological characteristics of the population.

1. The intent in collecting the environmental data was to develop as comprehensive as possible a set of measures on the stresses to which the population was exposed. Thus it was planned that environmental measurement should not only include the external factors such as climate, soils, flora,

and fauna but also include a careful analysis of how Quechua culture helped structure and modify the individual interactions of the population with the physical and biological environment.

The biological parameters to be measured on the population included gene systems, external morphology, body composition, and fertility, mating, mortality, growth, nutrition, health, and behavioral patterns.

2. At the onset experimental testing was limited to two topics: oxygen transport and physiological responses to cold. Briefly stated, the following were the postulates of these studies: (a) representative native Quechua have a greater ability to extract and use oxygen at high altitude than lowland natives; (b) short-term acclimatization to high altitude will not produce in lowlanders the same level of work capacity found among natives; and (c) representative Quechua have a different response to cold exposure than nonhighland natives, and this response is of adaptive value in their environment.

STUDY DESIGN
AND POPULATION SELECTION

We wished to concentrate our efforts on a restricted high-altitude Quechua population unit. Yet it was important that the group be reasonably representative of the highland Quechua. Thus, it would be helpful if the population had some form of breeding and social unity in the sense of Wright's island population model (Wright, 1943). At the same time, if the population were severely restricted in its gene flow or socioeconomic interchange with other populations, it would not be representative. Because the effects of altitude on human biology may be in some instances difficult to measure, we desired an extremely high-altitude location. However, this wish was counterbalanced by the fact that traditionally the resource base limited Quechua land usage to around 5000 m and, the topography is such that significant-size population units do not exist until substantially lower elevations are reached. Finally, accessibility by modern transportation was a consideration since the studies required the construction of a laboratory with controlled-temperature rooms.

Location

Given the necessary compromises, the district of Nuñoa, Department of Puno, in southern Peru was chosen. The location and some significant features of the district are shown in the map given as Fig. 1.1. As no detailed map of the district existed, the one shown was prepared from aerial photographs and information collected over the life of the project.

Detailed information on the physical and biotic environment are presented in the next chapter, but some explanation here will help elucidate the

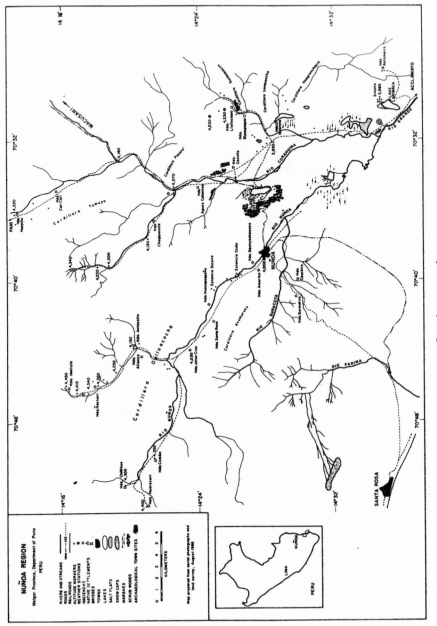

FIGURE 1.1 *Nuñoa district and its environs.*

FIGURE 1.2 *Views of the* puna *landscape. Native hut and stone-walled corrals in foreground; llamas grazing in centerground (upper left). View through a narrow valley (upper right). Distant view of the town of Nuñoa (lower left). Valley floor with small hacienda in left centerground (lower right). (Photos by M. A. Little.)*

choice of the district. This district is in the northeast corner of the large drainage basin surrounding Lake Titicaca. In the lower reaches of the river valleys there are broad plains of the true altiplano form which are characteristic of the large basin around the lake, but in the upper valleys the flat plain becomes quite small and disappears. The district is, in fact, somewhat like a basin itself, closed by hills and watersheds on three sides with only the southwest river opening reasonably flat.

The lowest part of the plain is approximately 4000 m above sea level. The elevation increases very slowly as one proceeds up the lower broad river valley but increases rapidly beyond such locations as the town of Nuñoa on the Nuñoa River. While the higher mountain slopes are used for animal grazing, permanent habitation ceases at the top of the tributary streams. These habitation sites do not exceed 4800 m and it is reported that during the rainy/snow season many are abandoned for temporary lower dwellings. Figure 1.2 gives several views of the Nuñoa region.

When the study was begun, only two roads provided regular access to the district. These are shown on the map as leading to Macusani and Santa Rosa. Most commerce was with Santa Rosa, which is on the main north–south road in southern Peru and on the Cuzco-to-coastal area rail line. At the beginning of the study all roads were suitable only for heavy-duty trucks and cross-country vehicles. Even for these vehicles the roads were frequently closed for long periods of time during the rainy season. Improvements during the mid-1960s on the Nuñoa to Santa Rosa road made car travel somewhat more feasible and permitted near-year-round use for trucks. Other roads shown on the map were unimproved dirt tracks. Vehicle transportation in and out of the district was at the beginning of the study limited to a few private trucks. While the number increased significantly over the life of the study, no public transport existed in 1972 when the last of the data presented in this book were collected.

For those familiar with the Andean region the preceding description will indicate that the Nuñoa district is somewhat higher than the majority of the highland regions and is at present somewhat more isolated than characteristic regions. However, the degree of isolation is probably representative of that found throughout the area only a few decades ago.

Population

A population pyramid based on the 1961 Peruvian census of the Nunoa district is shown in Fig. 1.3 (M.H.C., n.d., 1965). The total number of residents at that time was 7750, with 2137 of them residing in the town, which is also called Nuñoa. A first look at this population suggested that they were indeed living in a traditional fashion. Formal education, an indication of external influence, was low and mostly limited to the small upper classes. Medical care was traditional and had been only slightly affected by external influences. No medical doctor served the district, and modern medicines were

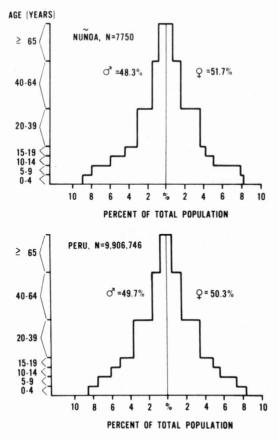

FIGURE 1.3 *District of Nuñoa and Peru; census,*
age, and sex distribution, 1961.

not generally available. Finally, the economy of the district was traditionally
based on herding and limited agriculture. At lower elevations the Quechua
economy is primarily agricultural, with less emphasis on herding (Flores
Ochoa, 1968). Thus, Nuñoa's altitude may produce a somewhat different
pattern in the population than a representative Quechua group, but the
structure allowed for several intrapopulation comparisons based on activity
patterns and exposure to varying socioeconomic structures.

Timetable

The Nuñoa study was originally envisioned as a four-year project beginning in 1964, and funding was on this basis. The scheduling of field research
was partially governed by the North American academic year and by the time
it would take to construct a suitable laboratory in Nuñoa. Timing was
planned as follows:

Advanced planning—January—June 1964

Collection of normative data—June—September 1964 and June—September 1965

Laboratory construction—June 1964—June 1965

Collection of experimental data—June 1965—June 1967

Collection of remaining necessary normative and experimental data—June—September 1966 and June—September 1967

Completion of data analysis and writing—January 1968

While the original timing was mostly adhered to, the Nuñoa project was reformulated in 1967 and 1968 under the impetus of the Human Adaptability Project of the International Biological Program, and with new funding continued without major interruption. The new formulation called for several projects to continue within the district as well as a series of studies requiring work in various parts of southern Peru. The Nuñoa laboratory served as a base for these studies through June 1971 and was again used for studies within the district during the period June—September 1972.

PLANNED SAMPLING AND METHODS

Because of our assumption that the collection of varied normative and experimental data on a unified population would allow a unique analysis our initial methodological consideration was population sampling.

From the beginning of the project it was recognized that two major factors were of prime consideration in the research strategy. The resources available in both money and manpower were limited, and therefore a careful sampling strategy was necessary to limit costs. Even so, it was immediately obvious that three factors—social class, altitude, and varying community social organization—were present and could operate to produce intrapopulation variability. The relationship of these variables to the approximate population distribution is shown in Fig. 1.4.

Thus the population sampling was outlined as shown in Table 1.1. It was not intended that the samples be random ones but rather that they be preselected so that the potential effect of altitude and community social organization could be determined. The upper or Mestizo class was not included in even the 100 percent samples since the goals of the study were concerned with the native Quechua. While some of the Mestizo class were of highland heritage, many were migrants from lower altitudes and most were either totally or partially of European ancestry. While the terms Mestizo and Indigena linguistically refer to genetic entities, it cannot be assumed in most areas of Peru that they conform to existing genetic systems. Instead they are popular social class designations based on the usual social class characteristics, such as wealth, dress, and speech (Schaedel, 1959).

In addition to the samples drawn from the Nuñoa district it was planned that for the experimental studies three other external groups would be

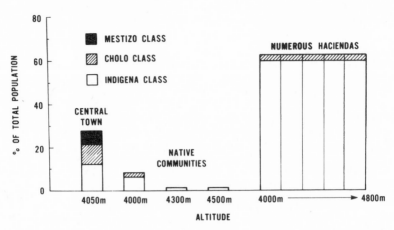

FIGURE 1.4 *Approximate distribution of the Nuñoa district population according to type of social unit, social class, and altitude.*

TABLE 1.1 *Proposed Population Sampling According to Category of Normative and Experimental Study*

Information	Population (%)	Source
Basic demographic structure	100	From Peruvian Census, 1940 and 1961
Fertility and mortality	100	District Registry, 1940–end of project
Questionnaire data on marriage—fertility, history, socioeconomic status, household structure	10	Collected by family unit, drawn from Cholo and Indigena families only; samples nonrandom; drawn to give adequate samples according to social organization and altitude
Biological data: gene systems, anthropometry, cursory medical exam, lung-function studies	10	Same as for questionnaire
Studies of exposure to cold	1	Samples based on altitude, family units, and type of housing
Nutritional surveys	1	Samples chosen to represent Indigenas living in contrasting social systems
Hypoxic responses and cold-tolerance tests	<1	Initially limited to young adult males whose body measurements were representative
Ethnographic data	—	Use of informants

introduced into Nuñoa for relatively short time periods in order to obtain comparative acclimatization data. These groups were all young adult males, the first to be representative of average U.S. men, the second a small group of highly trained lowland athletes, and the third a group of Quechua highland descendants who had been born and lived at low altitude.

The methods and techniques of the individual studies are described in the subsequent chapters, but these general perspectives on the original methodological approach have been outlined in order to point out how experience and results modified subsequent methods. In general it may be stated that a research strategy had been formulated whereby it was hoped that the detailed examination of the groups' responses to the environmental stresses one by one would permit the final integration of these responses into a coherent picture of how the population had achieved a successful adaptation to a series of environmental stresses which appeared difficult to the lowlanders.

CULTURALLY IMPOSED MODIFICATIONS OF METHODOLOGY

Although the district of Nuñoa was familiar to some of the initial investigators and the cooperation of the Nuñoans was generally quite good, numerous problems particular to the Nuñoa culture caused changes in aspects of the methods. Several ethnographers have documented the difficulties of working in cultures different from that of the investigator (Chagnon, 1974; Oberg, 1954), and it is not my intent to add to this literature. Instead, I wish to explain certain deficiencies and strange timings in the order of the studies.

An initial and somewhat unexpected resistance was found to the giving of blood samples. The population generally believed that the blood so removed was not replaced and that the procedure was, therefore, detrimental to their health. This aversion was so strong that it seemed unwise even to attempt subcutaneous temperature measurements with a needle probe. Somewhat later this problem even affected the measurement of blood pressure, apparently because the measure was called "blood pressure." It was suspected that the pressure cuff was designed to extract blood when inflated. The strong resistance to blood sampling meant that the initially planned study of gene systems and blood chemistry had to be drastically reduced in scope. Fortunately for the study, resistance gradually reduced over the time span of the project, and near the end it was possible to obtain some blood samples for genetic and hematological analysis.

Participation in any part of the study was on a voluntary basis, and participation seldom exceeded 50 percent in any of the community units. Even within families it was common for some members to volunteer while others refused. As a consequence it was not possible to entirely fulfill the sampling plan originally proposed.

A third major difficulty was an unexplained cycling in the degree of cooperation among the general populace. An initial high level of willingness to participate declined sharply after the first 2–3 months, reaching almost total resistance after 4–5 months of work. However, it was found that if no studies involving the general public were attempted for a period of 6 months or more, a willingness to participate often reappeared at a level higher than on the previous occasions. Although this phenomenon slowed data collection, it had the advantage of allowing for preliminary analysis and the rethinking of hypotheses as the project developed.

THEORETICAL CHANGES
DERIVED FROM DATA

Within a project as long as the Nuñoa one, the assumptions and hypotheses inevitably undergo change. Some of the change was caused by the introduction of new personnel, and some was the product of findings and theory changes outside the project, but a significant series of changes occurred because of the results emanating from the studies within the project. What follows is a partial list of how these results affected theory change.

General Theoretical Structures

Developmental Acclimatization.   At the onset there was little evidence that long-term growth and development changes were of significance in the physiological responses of Quechua adults to such environmental stresses as altitude and cold. However, our early studies suggested that preadolescent Quechua children appeared to be cold-stressed (Baker, 1966b), and that the effects of living in a more modern western culture affected at least the blood pressure of children by adolescence (Baker, 1969). We also failed to find major improvement in the oxygen-consumption capabilities of low-altitude adult men during relatively short (1–6 months) exposure to high altitude (Baker, 1969; Buskirk et al., 1967a, 1967b; Mazess, 1968c). All these individual findings began to suggest that while many of the differences which were found between the highland Quechua and lowlanders might be genetic, they might also be attributable to changes which occurred during the growth and development process. Therefore, it was apparent that we had to consider as a real possibility that the unique adaptive responses of the highland Quechua to cold and hypoxia might be the consequence of developmental acclimatizational responses.

Growth and Environment.   Although it was known that sea-level animals could be greatly affected in their growth by exposure to high-altitude hypoxia, no such evidence existed for man. As the initial data for growth in Nuñoa were analyzed it became increasingly apparent that growth in this district was slow as compared to that of populations at low altitude (Baker et al., 1966b; Frisancho and Baker, 1970). Indeed, in infancy not only growth but developmental variables such as tooth eruption and motor development seemed unusually retarded compared to U.S. standards (T. S. Baker et al., 1967a; Baker, 1969). Furthermore, even the small altitudinal variation within the district seemed to affect adolescent growth (Frisancho, 1969b). In a related study, not performed in Nuñoa, it was shown that full-term newborns had a lower average birthweight when born to Quechua mothers at high altitude than they did when born to Quechua migrant mothers at low altitude (McClung, 1969). All these findings in conjunction with nutritional surveys which failed to reveal significant nutritional problems in the Nuñoa district convinced most of us that altitude might indeed be slowing growth, even in native highland Quechua.

Fertility and Environment. While numerous historical references and recent experience suggested that the upward migrant might experience fertility difficulty due to altitude hypoxia, previous studies had failed to suggest that native highlanders might also be subject to some fertility reduction. The preliminary analysis of Nuñoa fertility based on questionnaires certainly indicated that fertility was more than adequate for population replacement (Hoff, 1968). However, the long child spacing, the high male ratio at birth, and the late onset of puberty all suggested that reproductive potential might be affected by altitude (Baker and Dutt, 1972). These data, combined with our ethnographic observations that the Nuñoans seem to have a culture designed to maximize fertility, convinced us that we should revise our assumptions to state that even high-altitude Quechua natives probably suffer reduced fecundity because of hypoxic effects.

Ecological Theory. As data accrued on the general ethnographic structure of the community, it became obvious that the population lived on a very tight energy budget. Thus, it was assumed that a study of the energy flow through the biotic and human community might provide significant new insights into the environmental stressors upon the community. Here was a first indication of how ecological theory might be applied with methodological rigor in order to understand the problems of population adaptation. Perhaps equally important, it showed that we should revise our theoretical structure so that system analysis modeling of the population functions were of prime importance.

Specific Hypotheses Changes

In addition to these rather general changes in theoretical base, specific discoveries led to the revisions or formation of specific hypotheses about how the high-altitude Quechua responded to specific environmental stressors. To list a few of these: (1) early studies indicated that the major uniqueness in the physiological responses to cold of the Quechua must be sought in their peripheral circulation (Baker et al., 1967); (2) an initial assessment of Nuñoa hematocrit and hemoglobin levels suggested that the high-altitude native did not necessarily have levels as high as is common to the upward migrant (see

Chapter 13); and (3) our original observations on the use of such drugs as alcohol and coca indicated that they might be significant to the Quechua responses in such parameters as work capacity and cold-tolerance tests (Hanna, 1970b). Thus, a number of subsequent studies were called for to test previously accepted assumptions.

METHODOLOGICAL CHANGES
DERIVED FROM REVISED THEORY

Evaluation of Research Strategies

In several previous reports I have referred to our early research method or research design as "a single-stress single-population model" combined with a "shotgun epidemiological approach" (Baker, 1968, in press a). By these terms I meant that at the onset we collected data with the intent of describing all the cultural and biological characteristics which improved a population's adaptation to an environmental stressor (cold, for example), not only in the hope that such a method could illuminate how a population survived in the presence of a single environmental stressor, but also because we hoped that by studying responses to more than one stressor we might discover some of the interactions. By a "shotgun approach" I meant that we hoped to achieve some insight into causation and interaction by collecting enough normative biological and cultural data on a single population so that statistical association could provide us with some hypotheses and even causal arguments on how high-altitude populations had adapted to their environment. As this chapter and the subsequent ones show, these methods did produce results but, as is so often the case, they raised more scientific questions than existed at the beginning of the project.

It seemed that new and more sophisticated research strategies were required to answer these questions. Some of the new methodology was generated by the project itself, but some undoubtedly grew from methods which were being advocated by other researchers. Thus, Harrison suggested in the planning stage of the International Biological Program that the comparative population approach used by animal experimentalists might be most useful to solving human adaptation problems if only the appropriate human population could be found (Harrison, 1966). Clegg reinforced the utility of such an analysis by showing in a review article that the comparison of the responses of the major high-altitude populations of the world could provide a new perspective on man's adaptive capacity (Clegg et al., 1970).

At the same time, social scientists (Vayda, 1969; Lee and DeVore, 1968) were discovering new ways to apply the system modelings of the ecologists to the problems of men. Particularly promising were the models of energy flow and infectious disease dispersion in human populations.

Thus, it was decided with the reformulation of this project that the addition of new research strategies were required. These strategies were divisible into three basic forms. One of these is the system model or the multiple-stress single-population strategy. The second is based on population comparisons. This form is derived from a single hypothesis tested by the measurement of similar populations living in varying environments. This research strategy might be labeled the single-stress multiple-population approach. Finally, an attempt was made to formulate a third, very elaborate, strategy in which populations migrant from various environments are studied in a similar environment. This might (rather inadequately) be labeled the multiple-population multiple-stress strategy.

To apply these strategies, numerous new populations and communities had to be sought and incorporated into the design. The communities and areas are located on the map presented as Fig. 1.5, and described as they appear in subsequent chapters; complete descriptions of each are unnecessary here except for one: the sea-level Valle de Tambo, where comprehensive research took place in 1970 and 1971.

The population had three components: (1) natives born at low altitudes, (2) migrants born below 2500 m, and (3) migrants born in the highland area above 3500 m. It seemed ideal for the application of our most elaborate research strategy: the three groups could be studied in depth for comparative adaptive models. The 1970 and 1971 studies in this valley were viewed as a pilot project (Baker, in press b). Nevertheless, the quantity of data collected was so great that analysis remains incomplete and a detailed description cannot be presented in this book.

Very briefly the Valle de Tambo may be described as one of the smaller irrigated coastal valleys of southern Peru. At the ocean end the flat, irrigated river plain is about 10 km wide but rapidly decreases in breadth upriver. There is virtually no rain, although there is substantial cloud cover during the winter period. The temperature range is moderate, with hot temperatures prevented by a cool ocean and cold temperatures ruled out by the tropical low-altitude location.

The population is somewhat larger than that of the Nuñoa district and is divided into three political districts. Regular transportation by automobile, truck, and bus connects the valley over good roads with the cities of southern Peru. Despite the numerous differences of the region from the Peruvian highlands, education, medical care, and income are on the average only slightly improved over Nuñoa conditions. Work patterns and social class structure are similar.

New Strategies

Systems Model. Continuing in Nuñoa beyond our original purpose of collecting normative and experimental data, we hoped that it might be possible to go to the next level of analysis possible on a single-population unit. This level involves the construction of working models on how given

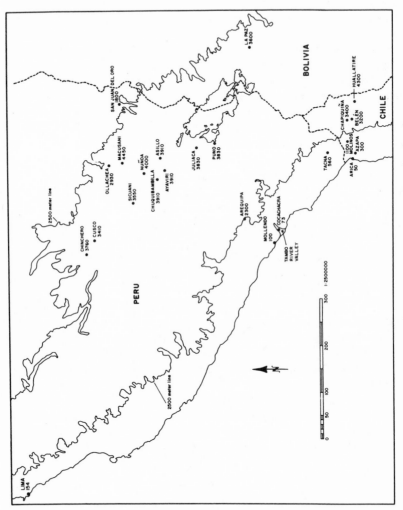

FIGURE 1.5 *Research locations cited in this book.*

systems function. At the individual level one might achieve a model of how the thermoregulatory, nutritional, or oxygen-transport system worked. At the population level one might construct models of adaptation to such potential environmental stressors as environmental temperature, infectious disease, inadequate nutrients, or low oxygen pressure. These models could be based on such measures as energy flow, population dynamics, health indicators, and genetic systems. Finally, such models could be descriptive, mathematically constructed from actual data or simulated to varying degrees.

All these optional modeling methods did not occur to us at the time the project was reformulated and, as will be apparent, not all have been attempted. While some modeling at the individual level was attempted, we viewed the real contribution of a depth project on a population as offering the opportunity for at least some forms of population modeling.

Single-Stress Multiple-Population Model. While the strategies described provided insights into functional relationships, they are not very satisfactory methods for testing specific causal hypotheses. For this purpose a comparative approach is most useful and to some extent such was used throughout the project. Thus the determination of Quechua work capacity—how it compared to that of other populations and the role of development in the physiological responses depended upon multiple-population comparisons. However, in the second phase of the project it was desired to test hypotheses about specific effects of hypoxia on growth and other factors. For this purpose the ideal comparison would have been between members of the same population living in identical environments except for one variable, such as oxygen pressure. Since this was not possible, several subprojects used a method that compared populations in sharply contrasting environments, thus hoping to either distinguish the relative impact of various environmental factors or cancel the effect of unwanted variables by randomizing them. Perhaps the most elaborate application of this design is found in the study of infant growth and development.

Multiple-Stress Multiple-Population Model. In theory it can be said that the study of natives, downward migrants, and lateral migrants all living in the same lowland environment should be a highly reliable method for determining the effects of altitude and migration on populations. This scheme will produce more dependable results according to the degree of similarity in life style at the lowland location and will be easier to interpret if the life styles of the migrants were reasonably similar prior to migration. In fact, the latter conditions did not exist to a high degree in our populations. To refine this strategy further and thereby increase the certainty of the conclusion, several steps were desirable. These steps included accurate definition of the pertinent biological and cultural data for each of the groups and development of samples large enough to subdivide and analyze for sources of internal variation. For example, if each population could be subdivided into those with and without modern medical care, the effect of this variable could be adjusted. To produce the maximum information and reliability for this kind of analysis it would, of course, be necessary to have system models such as those suggested for the high-altitude populations. When compared, such models could theoretically pinpoint the sources of variance for any population trait under study.

Although few of the design refinements were possible in this project, the results were often provocative and added to our body of evidence relative to hypotheses in such topics as health, fertility, and growth.

OVERVIEW

The reader who is accustomed to beginning a book with Chapter 1 and reading through will quickly find that the chapters which follow this one do not necessarily follow it in structure and content or even in theory and method. Scientific projects involving individuals from varying theoretical and disciplinary backgrounds can, after all, be no more unified than the composite of the individual interests and skills put into them. Some of the individuals participating in this project did so not because they were interested in all its objectives or even agreed with them. Rather, they had particular theories and hypotheses which could be pursued in the context of the project. This is perfectly appropriate to a project such as this one, as long as the information generated contributes to the overall goals.

In the formulation of this book we hoped to have presented in a concise fashion the various results produced by the total study. While the chapter of each contributor has been revised, based on the comments given by all the other contributors, no effort was made to develop a unanimity of interpretation. Thus while most of my fellow scientists in this project would agree with the statement on the project's general objectives, I suspect that most would not subscribe to all the theories, methods, and deductions which I have outlined. So I would like to make the rather obvious point that the success of the many individual research efforts reported in this volume should not be judged solely or even primarily on the theories, objectives, and methods set forth in this chapter.

2

PHYSICAL
AND BIOTIC ENVIRONMENT
OF SOUTHERN HIGHLAND PERU

R. Brooke Thomas and Bruce P. Winterhalder

The central Andes Mountains rise abruptly between the Pacific Ocean and the Amazon Basin. The west coast of the mountains, cooled by the north-flowing Humboldt Current, is a desert with a sparse loma vegetation. In contrast, the eastern escarpment with its equatorial warmth and rainfall is tropical forest. Between, in the mountains and intermontane valleys, is a patchwork of habitats ranging from the desert to the rain forest, and the coastal to the alpine. Two themes are essential to the Andes: the youth of these mountains, and their massiveness, both vertical and geographic. Immature soils and recent biogeographical development are given complexity by rugged topography and close proximity of diverse ecological zones. These conditions are set off by contrast with the long-stable Amazon Basin.

In this chapter the high-altitude, mountainous environment of southern Peru will be discussed, in terms of geology, climate, soils, and natural and domesticated biota. First described will be the central Andes as a region, and the complex gradients of climate and vegetation that cross this area, north-west to southeast and northeast to southwest. These gradients then provide the environmental context for more detailed treatment of a limited geographic area surrounding the town of Nuñoa. Nuñoa is treated as an example of the highland region, or altiplano, and specifically as the locality of the research described in this volume.

PHYSICAL ENVIRONMENT AND CLIMATE

Geology

The Andes are part of a larger mountain system, the New World Cordilleras, that traverses the western edge of the two American continents from Alaska to Antarctica. The Andes themselves are 7250 km in length; the larger Cordilleran system measures over 15,000 km. The Andes curve from the northern coast of Venezuela around the western margin of the continent, southwest through Columbia and Ecuador, southeast through Peru, and due south for the full length of Chile. Narrow in the north and south of the continent, the several chains of the Andes separate in central and southern Peru, eastern Bolivia, and northern Chile to accommodate broad high-altitude valleys and plateaus collectively known as the altiplano (Fig. 2.1). Following the definition of Pearson (1951), we consider the altiplano to be the treeless portions of the central Andes surrounding Lake Titicaca and Lake Poopó, above 3660 m of altitude. The Quechua term *puna*, meaning elevated earth, is also used for the area defined as altiplano, although some extend this term to cover broader areas or life zones (see Pearson, 1951).

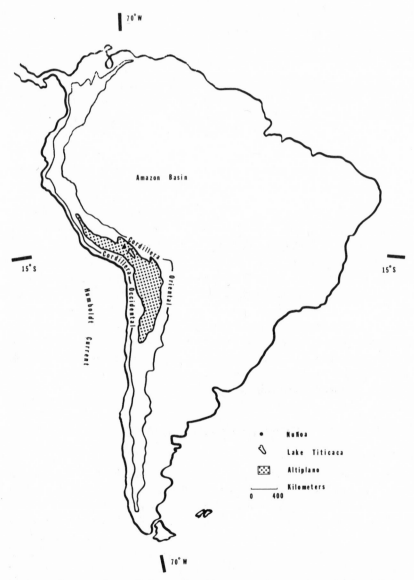

FIGURE 2.1 *Outline of the Andes Mountains (approximately the 2000-m isograph) and of the altiplano (shaded area).*

Jenks (1956) and ONERN/CORPUNO, Vòl. 2 (1965) have published general accounts of Andean geology; our description follows their approach.

Formation of the present mountains began with uplift during the Pliocene and Pleistocene. In central Peru the Andes were elevated to a general height of 4880 m, with monadnocks, mountainlike formations of material resistant to erosion, reaching as high as 6550 m. Peaks of comparable height in southern Peru are usually volcanoes built on flat lavas above a less strongly elevated puna surface. Normal thrust faulting and extensive folding during uplift of the Andes produced the Titicaca and other interior basins. During the lower Pleistocene the altiplano was covered by a vast lake (Lake Ballivian), which drained with final uplift of the Andes to form Lake Titicaca.

Jenks (1956) recognizes three "structural-morphological provinces" in the central Andes: the Cordillera Occidental (the western mountain system), the altiplano, and the Cordillera Oriental (the eastern mountain system). The Cordillera Occidental is composed of folded and mildly metamorphosed Mesozoic sediments. The altiplano, an undulating plain with dispersed monadnocks, is built of vast accumulations of Cretaceous deposits and Tertiary volcanic material which fill the Titicaca trough. The Cordillera Oriental, east of the Titicaca Basin, is formed predominantly of folded, faulted, and metamorphosed Paleozoic rock with Cretaceous and Tertiary intrusions of volcanic material. In general, the Andean geosyncline is now the site of a highly compressed mountain chain with strongly subdivided and differentiated igneous and stratigraphic rock units (Putzer, 1968).

The surface topography of these structural provinces is the result of more recent geological processes. Erosion and deposition, glacial and tectonic activity, faulting, and volcanics are all active processes. The Cordilleras are characterized by deep V- and U-shaped valleys, indicating strong alluvial and glacial erosion intensified by rapid uplift of the mountains and by faulting. Large mud and rock slides are a constant and sometimes tragic reminder of the tectonic instability of these mountains. Northeast of Lake Titicaca glacial valleys are recorded as low as 4000 m, and we have seen U-shaped valleys and glacial striation at about the same altitude near Nuñoa. Drainage from the eroding mountains into the intermontane basins and Lake Ballivian has leveled the altiplano with alluvial and lacustrine deposits. Rivers continue to fill Lake Titicaca with sediments. All these processes have combined to produce a rugged and youthful landscape, exposing a variety of stratigraphic rock types and igneous material that are undergoing strong erosion in mountains and deposition in the lower areas. These processes and the resulting topography have important influences on climate, soil formation, and the distribution of biota, including man.

Climate

Circulation patterns, astronomical position on the earth, and surface features such as altitude and exposure are the major variables affecting climate (Eidt, 1968). Related to these external factors are climatic elements such as temperature, precipitation, atmospheric pressure, and cloud cover. The central Andes, located at the division of two major air masses within the tropical latitudes, and composed of a rugged high-altitude topography, provide a unique situation for the interplay of the variables mentioned by Eidt. Our description in this section relies on background information provided by Eidt (1968), Garbell (1947), and ONERN/CORPUNO, Vol. 1 (1965).

The Andes reach high into the layer of atmosphere containing most weather phenomena (the troposphere), and for this reason the mountains sharply divide the major air masses of the western Southern Hemisphere (Schwabe, 1968). The asymmetrical distribution of precipitation on the east and west sides of the central Andes, and the seasonality of precipitation on the Peruvian altiplano, can be explained by the position of these air masses in relation to the mountains. On the coast, subsiding air from the eastern edge of the South Pacific anticyclone, and the Humboldt Current, which holds moisture in a cool sea-level inversion, act together to prevent storms. These two factors are responsible for the desertlike condition of this region (Sick, 1968). In contrast, the eastern escarpment of the Andes is an area of year-round rainfall. Moist air from the South Atlantic anticyclone is blown over the mainland, and cools and expands as it ascends the lower slopes of the mountains. Its capacity to retain moisture is thus reduced, and rainfall results. This same air, if it crosses the altiplano and moves down the western slopes of the Andes, has an opposite effect. As the air moves downslope its barometric pressure and temperature increase, and both of these factors increase its capacity to hold water. Consequently, precipitation is rare and these warm dry winds may actually increase dessication by evaporating moisture from plants and soil. The coastal desert then is an area of "rainshadow" with regard to the Atlantic anticyclone.

From April to September moist winds of the South Atlantic anticyclone are deflected inland by a small low-pressure area over the Gran Chaco of the Amazon valley, but do not penetrate to the altitude of the Andean intermontane basins. During this period, which corresponds to the highland dry season, the altiplano is dominated by a westerly flow of gusty, turbulent, subsiding air from the upper atmosphere over Brazil. Consequently, it receives little or no precipitation. This situation changes with southward displacement of the intertropical front (ITF) during the southern solstice season. Movement of the ITF and associated weather-front activity intensifies the spilling of cloud masses and precipitation through passes and gaps of the Cordillera Oriental and onto the altiplano (Garbell, 1947; Troll, 1968). Precipitation in the southern highlands reaches a peak in January and February, when the ITF is in its southernmost position, pushed against the Andes. Moving south along the Andes, away from continuous influence of the ITF, less moisture is available for convective storm formation. Annual precipitation decreases and becomes concentrated into a single wet season, as on the southern Peruvian altiplano.

Although distant from the central Andes the polar low off the tip of South America is an area for formation of weather phenomena that affect the continent far to the north. One of these phenomena important in the highlands is the friagem (Garbell, 1947). The friagem is an outbreak of cold, polar, maritime air that originates in the vicinity of the Antarctic Peninsula to the east of the polar low. This high-pressure air mass moves north across South America, causing intense frosts. A friagem will be discussed more completely under "Temperature."

Tropical latitude and high altitude are two other major variables that affect the climate of the central Andes. The influence of these two factors has been discussed by Troll (1968), who makes a distinction between "seasonal temperature climates" and "diurnal temperature climates." In the altiplano (a diurnal temperature climate), seasonal temperature variation is slight, as it is in other tropical regions; however, diurnal temperature variation is significant. Intense solar radiation through a thin atmosphere produces warm afternoon temperatures. Loss of heat at night, enhanced by low atmospheric density, low vapor pressure, and a general absence of clouds reduces night temperatures to freezing or below. The range of temperature variation is reduced somewhat during the cloudy wet season, but it is of major import to plant and animal life in the highlands that frosts can occur any time during the year, and in general are more likely the higher the altitude.

The major variables affecting climate of the central Andes, then, are the geographic massiveness and high elevation of the mountains interacting with large air masses, and second, latitude interacting with altitude. Decreasing precipitation gradients exist from northwest to southeast, and from northeast to southwest across the mountains. Seasonal temperature changes are modest, but diurnal temperature variation and the frequency of frosts are significant, and both increase with increasing altitude.

Precipitation. The seasonal distribution of rainfall on the altiplano is given in Fig. 2.2a, 2.3a, and 2.4a. The rains begin in September or October, reach a peak intensity in January or February, and end in April. The remainder of the year receives little or no precipitation. Total annual precipitation averages 830 mm on the northern region of the altiplano (Fig. 2.2a). In general, the annual cycles of plant, animal, and human activities follow this seasonal rhythm, but several kinds of variability induce deviations that are not evident in the mean figures. Droughts, which may last 1 yr or more, and which appear without predictable regularity (ONERN/CORPUNO, Vol. 1, 1965), are fairly common on the altiplano. Figure 2.5 shows weather data for 1 yr (1939–1940) of a severe drought sequence lasting several years: rainfall was reduced by 55 percent. Another kind of drought common to the altiplano does not involve a significant reduction in annual precipitation but is based on irregular monthly distribution of rainfall. In particular, insufficient precipitation during the months critical to plant growth can produce the effects of a year-long drought. September and October, the initiation of

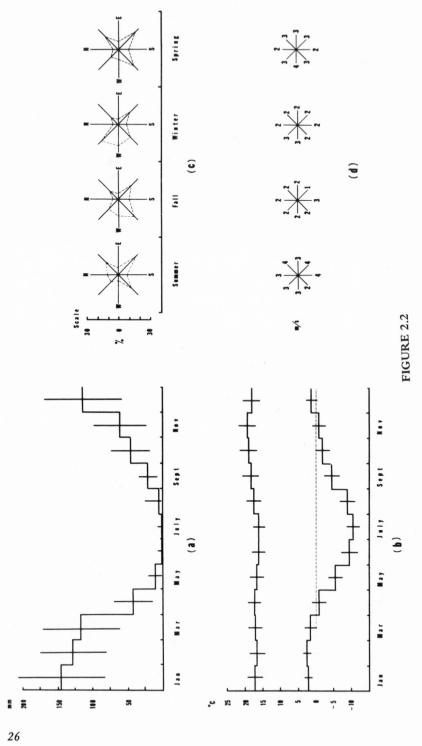

FIGURE 2.2

the growing season, are especially vulnerable in this respect. The vertical lines in Fig. 2.2a, which represent 1 standard deviation above and below the mean values, indicate the magnitude of this monthly irregularity.

The rugged topography of the high-altitude land surface introduces the variable of geography into the distribution of precipitation. Orographic precipitation, caused by movement of air up mountain slopes, is directly affected by local topography. Because of these factors, precipitation in one valley can be quite different from that of a neighboring valley, and both may vary independently from year to year or month to month (Thomas, 1973).

Although snow and hail can fall during any month of the year, they represent a small proportion of highland precipitation. Snow is most common in the transitional months between the solstice seasons. It generally occurs at night when air and ground temperatures are cool, and rarely reaches a depth of more than several inches. Because of the diurnal temperature cycle, nighttime snowfall melts the following day, usually by midmorning. Seasonal accumulation of snow below permanent snowfields, which is common in temperate-latitude mountain areas, does not occur in the tropical mountains (Troll, 1968). Hail, in contrast to snow, is common in the daytime, and hailstorms are frequent during the warm transitional months of the southern solstice.

Temperature.   Because the altiplano is located within the earth's tropical region there is a fairly constant change of mean temperature with altitude (Eidt, 1968), and a general absence of seasonal change in mean temperature. It is estimated that mean annual temperature for the Andes as a whole drops 0.5°C for each 100 m of elevation. On the altiplano between 4000 and 4500 m, Baker et al. (1968) have recorded a slightly greater drop of 0.8°C/100 m. Mean daily maximum temperature is nearly constant throughout the year. Mean daily minimum temperatures do show an annual cycle: lower in the clear months of the dry season, and higher during the cloudy months of the

FIGURE 2.2 *Climatic data for Chuquibambilla (Department of Puno, 70°43' W, 14°47'S, 3910 m), an altiplano station located about 100 km northwest of Lake Titicaca and about 35 km southwest of Nuñoa. (a) Mean precipitation by month for the period 1931–1972. Vertical lines represent 1 standard deviation above and below mean values. Mean annual precipitation is 830.4 mm. (b) Mean maximum and minimum monthly temperatures for the period 1931–1972. Vertical lines represent 1 standard deviation above and below mean values. Mean annual maximum temperature is 17.3°C; mean annual minimum, −3.0°C; range, 20.7°C. (c) The frequency of wind from a given direction in each of the four seasons. (d) The average velocity (meters per second) of the winds in (c). Both (c) and (d) are averages from 7 yr of observations. [Servicio Meterologico de la Granja Modelo de Puno, Chuquibambilla and ONERN/CORPUNO, Vol. 1 (1965).]*

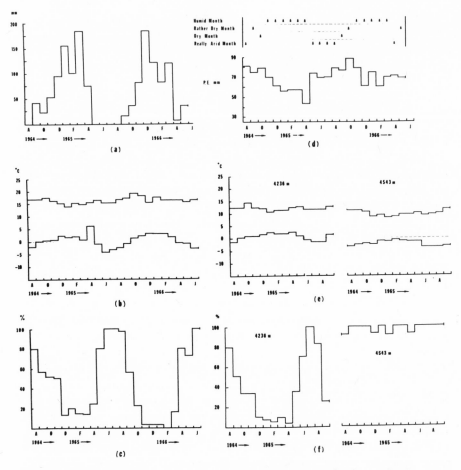

FIGURE 2.3 *Weather data for the district of Nuñoa (70°38'W, 14°28'S, 3974 m) for the period August 1964–June 1966. (a) Monthly precipitation. Mean annual precipitation is 710.3 mm. (b) Mean maximum and minimum monthly temperatures. For the 2-yr period, mean maximum is 16.4°C; mean minimum, 4.0°C. (c) The frequence of daily temperatures below 0°C in a given month. (d) Potential evaporation (P.E.) for the Nuñoa station, calculated by the method of Crowe (1971). This measure takes into account monthly precipitation, temperature, and changes of insolation by season and with lattitude. The relationship between potential evaporation and actual rainfall (P) determines the climatic characterization given in the upper portion of the graft (humid month P.E. < P; rather dry month P.E. ≥ P but < 3P; dry month P.E. ≥ 3P but < 6P; very arid month P.E. ≥ 6P). (e) Mean maximum and minimum temperature for Nuñoa weather stations at 4236 m and 4543 m above sea level. At 4236 m: mean maximum for the period, 12.2°C; mean minimum, 0.7°C; range, 12.9°C. At 4543 m: mean maximum for the period, 9.8°C; mean minimum, −2.3°C; range, 12.1°C. (f) The frequency of daily temperatures below 0°C in a given month at 4236 m and 4543 m. [Data from Baker et a. (1968).]*

28

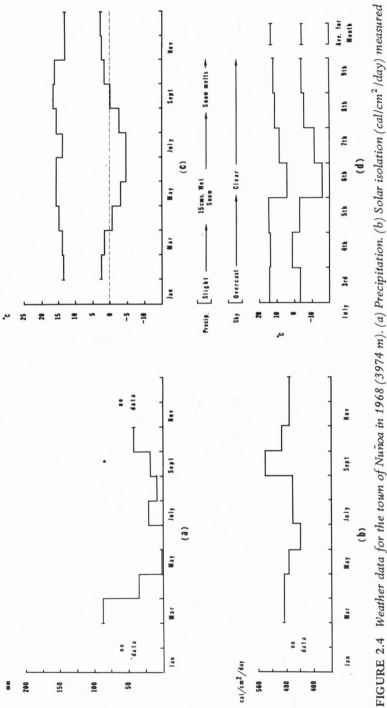

FIGURE 2.4 *Weather data for the town of Nuñoa in 1968 (3974 m). (a) Precipitation. (b) Solar isolation (cal/cm²/day) measured by a Belfort pyroheliograph. Mean annual insolation for the period shown is 468 cal/cm²/day. (c) Mean maximum and mean minimum temperature by month. (d) The week of July 3, 1968, representing a dynamic frost or frigem. Passage of the polar front (July 5 and 6) is accompanied by heavy snowfall and rapidly dropping temperatures. Unlike the normal highland pattern, ground snow persists for several days.*

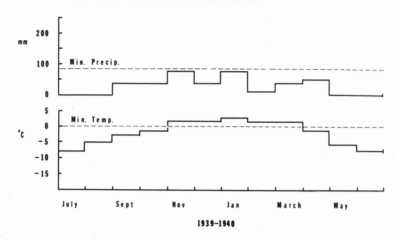

1939-1940

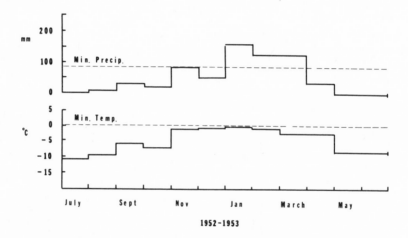

1952-1953

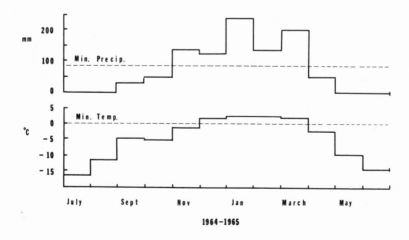

1964-1965

rainy season (Fig. 2.2b). Elevated minimum temperatures during the rainy season do not appear to be the direct result of increased insolation (see Fig. 2.4b and c), but are due to retention of heat through the night period. In addition, cloud cover inhibits reradiation of heat into space during the night. Seasonal changes in daily minimum temperature correspond to the seasonal pattern of cloud cover and precipitation.

Other aspects of highland temperature are apparent from Figs. 2.2b and 2.3b. This area has what Troll (1968) calls a "diurnal temperature climate," meaning that major temperature changes occur in a daily cycle. Strong insolation during the day produces a peak afternoon temperature of about 17°C. Rapid loss of this heat through a thin atmosphere, especially on clear nights, reduces night temperatures to near freezing or below. The mean range between maximum and minimum temperatures is over 20°C.

With minimum temperatures near or below freezing throughout the year, night frosts can occur in any season (see Fig. 2.3c). The frequency of night frost is a major factor (Fig. 2.6) influencing the vertical distribution of vegetation in the Andes (Troll, 1968).

Two types of frost occur on the altiplano. Most frequent is the static frost, caused by a rapid loss of lower air and ground heat at night. Cold air drains down slopes into basins and valleys, causing stable inversions of freezing air near the ground. Figure 2.3c and f compare the frequency of daily temperatures below 0°C on the valley floor (3974 m), the lower slopes (4236 m), and the higher slopes (4543 m). While freezing temperatures occur almost nightly on upper slopes, it is lower slopes and not the valley floor which have the fewest frosts. Of all highland frosts, 80 percent are static, and most occur during the dry season.

More severe is the dynamic frost caused by a northern eruption of a polar cold front followed by cold, maritime, arctic air. The cold air mass that

---

FIGURE 2.5 *Instability of annual precipitation and temperature. Each of these graphs represents 1 year of weather data, from the records of Chuqui-bambilla (3970 m). The year 1939–1940 is a drought year (total precipitation, 362.8 mm; mean minimum temperature for the year, −1.7°C), part of a drought that lasted about 3 yr and had severe local economic consequences. In the next year depicted (1952–1953), precipitation is nearer to normal (625.6 mm) but mean minimum for the year, −4.9°C). The third year, 1964–1965, is a good year for agriculture, with early and abundant precipitation followed by a continuously warm and wet cropping season (total precipitation, 955.9 mm; mean minimum temperature for the year, −4.0°C). The annual cycle is strongly developed, but monthly irregularities are slight. Minimum values for agriculture of highland crops have been established by ONERN/CORPUNO, Vol. 1 (1965) at 80 mm of precipitation per month and 0°C. (Data courtesy of Antonio Santos Aragon.)*

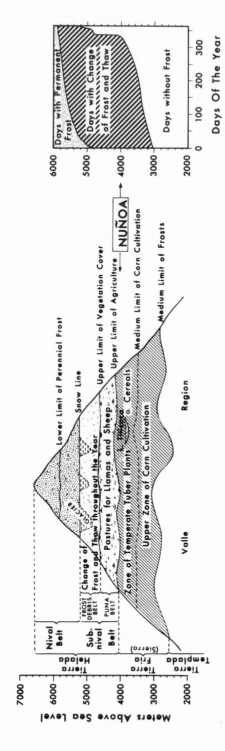

FIGURE 2.6 *Vertical zonation of agricultural vegetation types and frost climates in the Andes of southern Peru. The zonation of frost climates is based on information from Mt. El Misti in southern Peru. [Modified from Troll (1968).]*

follows the front and causes subfreezing temperatures may last for several days before breaking up. Dynamic frosts constitute 20 percent of all altiplano frosts; most also occur during the dry season (ONERN/CORPUNO, Vol. 1, 1965). It is the frosts, rather than the low mean annual temperatures themselves, that are limiting for highland plant communities (Mann, 1968). In general, the instability of the transitional seasons is the critical factor for vegetation development in the highlands (Schwabe, 1968).

We should comment on three other aspects of highland temperatures. The altiplano is not a "heat-deficient habitat" in the sense of Darlington (1965); the mean annual temperature of 8°C is equivalent to that of central New York. Rather, it is the strong daily cycle of temperature variation, the nightly interruption of physiological processes of plants, the similar interruption of animal activities, and the rapidity of temperature changes that are significant. Second, changes in temperature of biota, soil, or rock due to solar heating or loss of heat through radiation may be more rapid than changes in air temperature (Koford, 1957). Finally, because dampness, high humidity, and wind can increase the rate at which heat is lost from an organism, a wet or windy day may be "colder" than a dry or windless day with lower air temperatures. Thus, the relatively "warm" wet season on the altiplano may actually be a period of greater cold stress to animals than the somewhat colder dry season.

Other Climatic Elements. Uneven heating of rugged topography and associated movements of air are the most frequent causes of winds on the altiplano of southern Peru. These winds are variable in intensity and direction (Fig. 2.2c and d), and are seldom of sufficient strength to cause damage (ONERN/CORPUNO, Vol. 1, 1965).

Relative humidity (RH) follows a diurnal pattern opposite to that of temperature. Limited data (Larsen, 1973) suggest nighttime RH values of 40–60 percent with values of less than 10 percent for most of the daytime period during the dry season. Cloud cover and insolation are inversely related, and the fairly constant insolation values we have for Nuñoa (Fig. 4b) indicate an absence of seasonal full-day overcast. Clear skies predominate during the dry season, and during the rainy season a pattern of clear mornings with increasing cloudiness and formation of convective storms through the afternoon is common.

Finally, atmospheric pressure and the partial pressure of constituent gases, absolute humidity, and background radiation are all associated with altitude. At a representative altiplano altitude (4000 m) the barometric pressure averages 463 torr, the partial pressure of oxygen is 97 torr, and the partial pressure of carbon dioxide is 0.14 torr (Fig. 2.7a, b, and c), a reduction in all three measurements of about 40 percent from sea-level values (760, 159, and 0.23 torr, respectively). Absolute humidity decreases with decreasing temperature, and the air of the cool upper slopes and basins of the mountains is consequently dry.

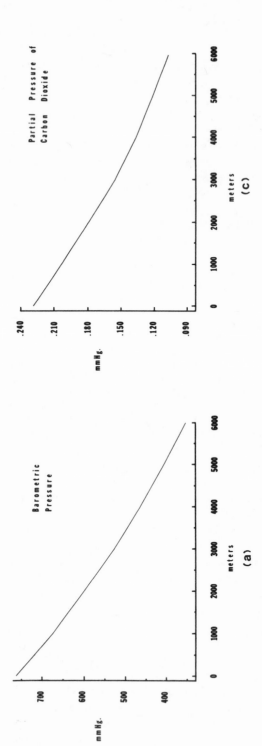

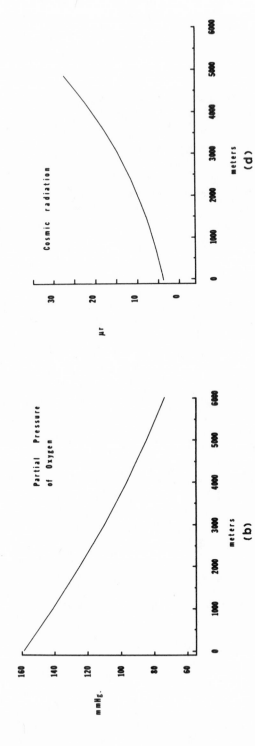

FIGURE 2.7 *Reduction in barometric pressure (a) and in the partial pressure of oxygen (b) and carbon dioxide (c) with increasing altitude, and the increase of ionizing cosmic radiation with altitude (d). [a, b, and c from Consolazio et al. (1963); d from Solon et al. (1960).]*

Background radiation is primarily of two sources: cosmic and terrestrial. Cosmic radiation increases with altitude, as shown in Fig. 2.7d. Cruz-Coke et al. (1966) estimate cosmic radiation on the altiplano of northern Chile at 22 μr/h, a value close to that given by Solon et al. (1960) for altitudes of 4000 m (see Fig. 2.7d). Terrestrial radiation depends on the exposure of different kinds of crustal material, but is generally greater in mountains, and greater near to granitic rock (Grahn and Kratchman, 1963; Hultquist, 1956).

Summary. The highland climate varies primarily because of sharp gradients of altitude, topography, and meteorological changes which occur daily, monthly, or annually. Additionally, one valley has different weather from the next, and valley floor is different from the slopes of the surrounding hills. Finally, marginal availability of moisture and of protection from frost make those small differences critical to plants and animals, and to human horticulturalists and herders.

Soils

Papadakis (1969) divides the soils of the southern Peruvian altiplano into two extensive subgroups, the recent brown soils and the chernozemic brown (Prairie) soils. The recent brown subgroup is made up of raw (undifferentiated) soils with a low degree of leaching and neutral pH, composed of unmodified or little modified parent material such as recent alluvium or consolidated rock. Chernozemic soils, also characterized by a low degree of leaching and neutral horizons, have a dark humic layer at least 25 cm thick formed under the influence of grassland cover. The mineral fertility of both subgroups is usually good; parent materials are geologically young and have not undergone intense leaching.

Within the regional subgroups given by Papadakis (1969) is a complex variety of local soils, reflecting the process of soil genesis in high mountains. Local soils are undeveloped (raw) for a number of reasons. Mechanical weathering (flake weathering) is intense in the diurnal highland climate (Schwabe, 1968), but cold and dryness, which inhibit chemical weathering and decomposition of organic matter (Cabrera, 1968; Weberbauer, 1936), can slow the evolution of soils. Solifluction, the downslope movement of surface material with the freeze—thaw cycle, is another climatic factor impeding soil development (Troll, 1968). Vegetation plays a more positive role. Plants enhance weathering, prevent erosion, and contribute organic material to upper layers of the soil.

ENVIRONMENTAL STRESS
AND ADAPTATION

One way of organizing our perception of the altiplano environment is to consider this environment's influence on plants and animals. We can delineate those conditions in the highlands, where any population of the biotic community must make some kind of adjustment in order to function and reproduce effectively. In the following list, potential environmental stressors of the southern Peruvian highland environment are grouped into five categories:

1. Reduced partial pressure of oxygen and carbon dioxide as a function of altitude. Low absolute vapor pressure; high background radiation.

2. Rugged topography and poorly developed soils, with marginal availability of certain nutrients.

3. Low temperatures with pronounced diurnal variation, and frequent and intense frosts that can occur in any season.

4. A lengthy dry season and irregular monthly distribution of precipitation; droughts that may last several years and are unpredictable.

5. A biotic community with limited productivity, spread over wide regions.

An environmental stressor will influence the kind and degree of biological adaptation through its frequency, intensity, duration, and regularity; "regularity" means that the stress varies in a predictable and repeated pattern. The lowered partial pressure of oxygen and carbon dioxide, and the low barometric pressure, are examples of stresses that are constant (regular and of indefinite duration) and vary in intensity uniformly with altitude. Topography and soils change over decades and have their major variability in space. Climatic stressors can be characterized by the seasonal or daily rhythms of moderate intensity, and by the sporadic and intense fluctuations of the stress, which vary in duration and are generally not regular.

All these physical stressors exert an influence on the spatial and temporal productivity of the biotic community, and on the flow of energy and materials between populations. Plants and animals must be capable of surviving the infrequent and rigorous environmental conditions as well as the more common ones. Some of the general adaptations made by altiplano biota are discussed below.

BIOTIC ENVIRONMENT

Flora

Mann (1968) points out that climax vegetation can be found only on relatively flat ground, such as areas of the altiplano or relic peneplains, and that a preponderance of pre- and postclimax vegetations is thus left on the larger areas of steeper slope. Competitive exclusion between plant species can sharpen divisions of vegetation along altitude gradients, divisions already influenced by climate and soils (Beals, 1969). All these factors interact to produce plant distributions.

Vegetation zones of the central Andes follow closely the gradients of temperature and moisture described under "Climate." As described by Troll

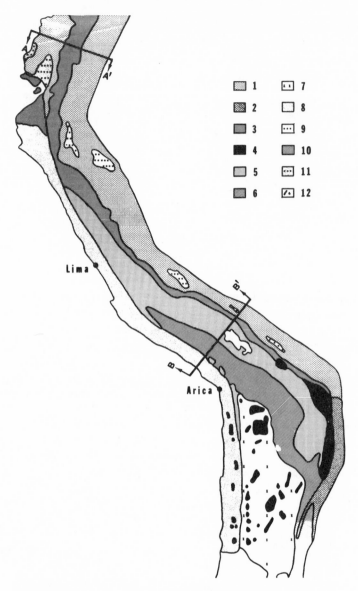

FIGURE 2.8 *Vegetation zones of the central Andes: 1, tropical rain forest (including montane forests); 2, tropical–subtropical semideciduous forests; 3, equatorial Paramo-belt and tropical-semievergreen high mountain grassland; 4, subtropical mountain meadows; 5, moist puna belt; 6, dry puna belt; 7, thorn and desert puna; 8, atacama desert; 9, open savannas within the rain forests; 10, moist savannas (deciduous forests and grassland); 11, thorn savannas (forests and grassland); 12, salt pans. [Modified from Troll (1968).]*

(1968) and Weberbauer (1936), the vegetation changes from northeast to southwest across the Andes of southern Peru, and northwest to southeast along the central Andes (see Figs. 2.8 and 2.9).

The Eastern Escarpment. East of the altiplano and approximately 4000 m below the snow-covered peaks of the Cordillera Oriental is the tropical forest and small areas of tropical savanna (Figs. 2.8 and 2.9). Despite its physiographic homogeneity the tropical forest is composed of a variety of plant associations (Weberbauer, 1936; Mann, 1968) that extend up the eastern slopes of the Andes to about 1000 m. Here the *tierra caliente* is replaced by the *tierra templada*, or zone of the lower montane tropical-evergreen forests, the *yungas*. Regular frosts begin at about 2500 m in the *tierra fria* (see Fig. 2.6).

Weberbauer (1936) describes the tropical-evergreen forest zone as constantly veiled with fog. The fog raises humidity, moderates light, and equalizes the cool temperatures. At higher elevations of the tropical-evergreen zone, trees become shorter and are replaced by a scrub formation with pockets of small moors and grass steppes. This scrub formation marks the transition to the *tierra helada* at 4000 m. The tierra helada is the area of a "microthermal grass steppe" (Weberbauer, 1936), also called the paramos. This steppe thins out and a frost desert forms between 4500 and 4900 m; permanent snowfields begin between 4900 and 5300 m.

The easternmost zone of the altiplano is the moist or grass puna; the western portion is the dry puna.

The Western Escarpment. West of the altiplano the dry puna is the predominant vegetation zone of the Cordillera Occidental above 4000 m. Stiff perennial bunch grasses and the tola shrub (*Lepidophyllum quadrangulare*) are common elements down to 3500 m. At lower elevations, vegetation becomes more open and xerophytic; trees are rare and grasses disappear. A zone of thorn and succulent shrubs and cacti (*Cerus*), with a few annual herbs and tuberous plants, reaches as far as the coastal desert, which begins at 2000 m. The desert, a zone without vegetation except where broken by narrow river valleys, is below the scant precipitation of the higher mountains and above the fogs of the coast. The last vegetation zone on the northeast to southwest gradient, the lomas, depends on seasonal fogs (*garuas*) for moisture.

The Altiplano. The three major vegetation zones of the altiplano are the moist puna, the dry puna, and the desert puna (Troll, 1968; Mann, 1968; Cabrera, 1968). These zones are long and narrow, reflecting both the topography of the mountains and the bands of decreasing precipitation, which run from northeast to southwest, each one more distant from the Intertropical Front (Figs. 2.8 and 2.9). Because the mountains become broader in southern Peru, the paramos and moist and dry puna zones are deflected eastward and tend to cross the Andes diagonally (Troll, 1968). In Ecuador, which receives rainfall on both sides of the relatively narrow mountains, the distribution of vegetation is nearly symmetrical (Figs. 2.8 and 2.9). As one moves southeast,

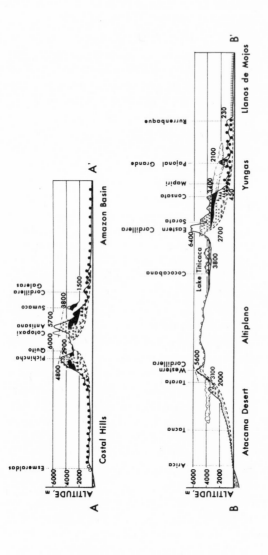

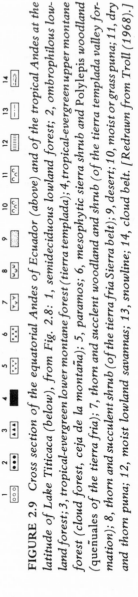

FIGURE 2.9 Cross section of the equatorial Andes of Ecuador (above) and of the tropical Andes at the latitude of Lake Titicaca (below), from Fig. 2.8: 1, semideciduous lowland forest; 2, ombrophilous lowland forest; 3, tropical-evergreen lower montane forest (tierra templada); 4, tropical-evergreen upper montane forest (cloud forest, ceja de la montaña); 5, paramos; 6, mesophytic sierra shrub and Polylepis woodland (quenuales of the tierra fria); 7, thorn and succlent woodland and shrub (of the tierra templada valley formation); 8, thorn and succulent shrub (of the tierra fria Sierra belt); 9, desert; 10, moist or grass puna; 11, dry and thorn puma; 12, moist lowland savannas; 13, snowline; 14, cloud belt. [Redrawn from Troll (1968).]

40

precipitation decreases and becomes concentrated in a single season, and the diurnal temperature range increases. The paramos are replaced by the moist puna and then the dry puna, along a transect down the interior of the mountains.

Our description of altiplano vegetation centers on the moist-puna zone outside the influence of Lake Titicaca, and on the dry-puna zone to the west, and is limited to southern Peru. The moist, or wet, puna is floristically more related to the western Cordilleras than to the eastern range (Weberbauer, 1936), and the moist and dry zones share many elements. Climatic data for both Nuñoa and Chuquibambilla are typical of the moist puna; on the dry puna, precipitation is reduced to 250–500 mm (Mann, 1968).

Weberbauer (1936) distinguishes five vegetation formations on the altiplano. First is the puna mat, occupying moist level areas with little rock. Densely packed mats of low herbaceous vegetation, cushion plants and rosettes, alternate with patches of bare ground. Few lichens, mosses, erect shrubs, or tall tufted grasses live in these mats. Hodge (1946) points out that cushion mats with *Azorella* sp. as the dominant species can be found over much of southern Peru between altitudes of 3800 and 5200 m. Second are the bunch or "tussock" grasses, which cover large areas of the altiplano. Tufts of these vigorous perennial grasses are surrounded with patches of open soil which support small numbers of dicotyledonous herbs and erect shrubs. The third formation is the *Distichia* moor. This formation requires constant ground humidity and is thus found near streams or small lakes on level, poorly drained ground. The dominant plant, *Distichia muscoides*, forms a closed, undulating surface firm enough to walk on, and broken by pools of water. Fourth is the vegetation found in rocky areas. Here one can find more abundant lichens, mosses, and ferns, in addition to erect shrubs, tall herbs, and tufted grasses. Vegetation in rocky areas can be found at higher altitudes than vegetation on bare earth, apparently because of the capacity of rock to retain heat longer than soil. Finally, there are the small and infrequent groves of *Polylepis*, a twisted, stunted tree that resembles mountain mahogany (Pearson and Ralph, 1974) and rarely grows taller than 3 m. Bunch grasses and herbs grow in the spaces between the trees; the ground beneath them is bare. These trees grow to altitudes of 4600 m (Troll, 1968), and their distribution is apparently independent of ground-water, slope, and soil conditions. Figure 10 illustrates some of the typical altiplano plants.

In general, altiplano vegetation is herbaceous, perennial, and dwarf (Hodge, 1946; Weberbauer, 1936). Bulberous or tuber plants and large shrubs or trees are scarce; the limited number of woody plants are evergreen (Hodge, 1946). Many of the cushion plants of the altiplano, as well as less specialized forms, are endemic (Weberbauer, 1936).

The Raunkaier system of vegetation classification is based on structural characteristics which are functionally related to adaptive requirements, particularly those of climate. A comparison of Andean life forms with

FIGURE 2.10 *Typical altiplano plants, illustrating the life forms found in the highlands of southern Peru: 1, Microphanerophyte:* (a) Polylepis tomentella; *2, Nanophanerophytes:* (b) Adesmia horrida, (c) Ephedra americana, (d) Baccharis serpyllifolia, (e) Lepidophyllum quadrangulare; *3, chamaephytes:* (f) Azorella multifida, (g) Pycnophyllum molle, (h) Lupinus microphyllus; *4, hemicryptophytes:* (i) Festuca scirpifolia, (j) Poa chamaeclinus, (k) Calamagrostis vicunarium, (l) Plantago lamprophylla; *5, geophytes:* (m) Perezia coerulescens, (n) Werneria pygmaea. [Redrawn from Troll (1968), Mann (1968), and Weberbauer (1945).]

— 1 meter

those of the Normal Spectrum (a randomly chosen composite of 1000 world species) reveals a disproportionate number of low and compact plants which protect important growth organs by keeping them from below to only slightly above the soil surface (Mann, 1968). These life forms rely on the warmth and microrelief of the earth to provide protection against drought, frost, and wind. Many altiplano species are, to greater or lesser extent, in the form of cushion plants (Hodge, 1946; Weberbauer, 1936), ranging from dwarf and involuted shrubs and the tough bunch grasses, which have the compactness of a straw broom, to *Azorella,* a plant that assumes the form of a small mound with a surface almost as hard as the soil that it resembles (Fig. 2.10f). These plants minimize external projections, reducing exposure. They tend to form closed surfaces, thus isolating much of their interior so that it is influenced by the relatively warm and moist soil environment. Cushion plants absorb water like a sponge (Hodge, 1946) and, aided sometimes by spines or sharp stiff branches, protect much of their structure from grazers.

Poor soils, drought, low nightly temperatures, and low partial pressure of carbon dioxide and oxygen probably limit altiplano productivity. On the other hand, the high insolation at tropical latitude and high altitude should be favorable for productivity. Schwabe (1968) has suggested that the diurnal temperature cycle also aids net productivity. Strong insolation with warm temperatures encourages photosynthesis during the day, and low or freezing night temperatures inhibit the consumption of the photosynthetic products in nighttime respiration.

Mann (1968) makes two estimates of altiplano productivity based on biomass data given in Pearson (1959). For the wet puna, Mann derives a standing crop of 7000 kg of dry matter/ha, which is calculated to provide an "annual harvest" of 80 kg of dry matter/ha/yr. The same values for the dry puna are 2000 kg of dry matter/ha of standing crop, and 3 kg of dry matter/ha/yr "annual harvest." For comparison, net primary productivity (mean) for temperate grasslands is 5000 kg of dry matter/ha/yr, and for dwarf and open scrub it is 900 kg of dry matter/ha/yr (Lieth, 1973). Mann's use of annual harvest may not be equivalent to net primary productivity, and his figures do appear conservative. Nevertheless, until productivity measurements are obtained for the altiplano, it appears that highland energy production is low (also low in relation to biomass), and it is dispersed over wide regions. Much of the productivity is accumulated beneath the soil surface.

Fauna

On the basis of environmental constraints we might expect to find a limited fauna on the altiplano. Herbivores, for instance, must cope not only with the rigors of climate and topography but also with the tough and energetically limited vegetation available as a food source. Many of the qualities of highland plants that enable them to survive cold, wind, and drought can also be viewed as adaptations that inhibit grazing or browsing. Included are subterranean growth or growth between rocks and in crevices; rosette or cushion form, stiff, short, and sometimes spiny branches; little foliage and few flowers; and no fruit. The oils, resins, and waxes found in highland plants, as well as their generally high content of cellulose and silica (Mann, 1968), also reduce their palatability.

In describing faunal diversity Fittkau (1968) states that the Andean–Patagonian region is extraordinarily poor in species number, compared with not only the tropical part of the same continent, but also the ecologically similar life zone of Holarctis. While reptiles and amphibians are fairly scarce, and live in and around lake habitats (Cabrera, 1968), the altiplano supports numerous endemic species of birds and mammals (Pearson and Ralph, 1974). Compared with other grassland habitats, the dry-puna *ichu* bunch-grass community supports an unusually high number of bird species.

The number of species of small mammals in the ichu bunch-grass community is similar to that of North American grasslands. Nevertheless, population density and biomass of small mammals is low. The biomass for small mammals is 115.0 g/ha, whereas that for birds is 463.6 g/ha, or four times greater (Pearson and Ralph, 1974). These data suggest that characteristics of birds enable them to more successfully utilize this altiplano community. An abundant number of carnivorous mammals (Mann, 1968) and birds (Olrog, 1968) are able to make use of the herbivore fauna, although some of the carnivores eat vegetable matter at certain times of the year (Mann, 1968). The diversity of mammals and birds on the altiplano arises from the faunal history (biogeography) of the region and from the adaptive flexibility of the animals involved.

Surprisingly, the low oxygen tension of the altiplano appears not to be an important limiting factor in the distribution of highland mammals. It is not because chronic hypoxia is an insignificant stressor; the importance of hypoxia is confirmed by observing the responses of lowland species to high altitude (Altland and Highman, 1971; Morrison, 1962). Rather, with few exceptions native highland mammals have successfully adapted to this ever-present and rather intense stressor.

Bullard (1972), in reviewing physiological responses to chronic hypoxia, divides mammals into two broad groups. One shows a typical normoxic response to hypoxia by increasing hematocrits or hemoglobin concentrations in the blood, and possibly shifting the oxygen dissociation curve to the right (indicating a lowered blood-oxygen affinity). This pattern of adjustment contrasts to that of the second group: the high-altitude native species. Genetically isolated highland mammals do not have elevated hematocrits and hemoglobin concentrations and tend to show a leftward shift in the dissociation curve (an increased affinity for oxygen). Other physiological characteristics of native high-altitude species have been summarized by Bullard (1972) and Folk (1974).

Unfortunately, the only highland mammals extensively studied, with the exception of man, have been rodents and camelids. It is possible that these animals possess special lowland characteristics which enabled them successfully to move into high-altitude regions (Bullard, 1972). In rodents, for instance, adaptations for burrowing (Darden, 1972) may be of value in adjusting to an hypoxic environment. Camelids as a family have small red blood cells and hence an increased surface area for oxygen diffusion, which accounts in part for their characteristic leftward oxygen dissociation curve, present in both high-altitude and lowland species (Chiodi, 1970–1971). One must, however, question the uniqueness of physiological characteristics in terms of a single environmental stressor (i.e., hypoxia).

EFFECTS OF HUMAN GROUPS ON THE ENVIRONMENT

The duration of human habitation and the size and economic organization of pre-Conquest human populations in the southern Peruvian highlands underlie the importance of considering man's role in shaping contemporary biota. Specific research on the effects of humans on the highland ecosystem is, however, limited and unsystematic. ONERN/CORPUNO, Vol. 1 (1965) reports that deforestation, degradation of pastures, and soil erosion are widespread in southern Peru. Ellenberg (1958) attributes a depression of altiplano tree lines, from a natural climax at 4600 m to the current and "artifically low" 4000 m, to biotic causes, specifically overgrazing. Because the vast puna grasslands were common at the time of Conquest, deforestation must have occurred much earlier. It is likely that the cutting of trees for construction and fuel contributed to the disappearance of highland forests (Budowski, 1968). Wickes and Lowdermilk (1938) suggest that one function of terracing was to check slope erosion following the removal of ancient forests. In recent times, shrubs and other woody vegetation have been removed from large, now-eroded areas to provide fuel for population centers and the railroad (Cabrera, 1968). Dourojeanni (1972) has noted with concern the continued cutting of what were once vast stands of *queñua (Polylepis)* and *quisuar (Buddeia)* trees, as well as the endangered status of many altiplano animals.

Browman (1974) indicates that overgrazing has been a problem of great antiquity. Evidence of severe erosion attributable in part to overgrazing dates back 2000 years in the Jauja-Huancayo Basin (Browman, 1970). He also notes that insufficient pasture in the Lake Titicaca area was reported prior to and during the Inca occupation (citing Diez de San Miguel, 1567). Koford (1957) and Mann (1968) mention that post-Conquest overgrazing by sheep might have led to soil erosion and invasion of weedy species, and that the present dominance of coarse and unpalatable bunch grasses might have resulted in part from the sheep's heavy utilization of more succulent plants.

Although none of these reports is detailed, they do indicate the kinds of major alterations of altiplano biota and soils which would have multiple ramifications throughout this simple and fragile ecosystem. As Billings (1973) has stated, although some alpine vegetations recover from severe disturbance, the majority do not.

THE NUNOA ECOSYSTEM

The district of Nuñoa (Melgar Province, Department of Puno) is approximately 950 km² in area and consists largely of the Nuñoa and Corahuina River drainage system. The district is located on the northeastern boundary of the Titicaca basin. The lower border of the district lies above and to the east of the adjacent Ayaviri valley. Elevation within Nuñoa rises in a northerly direction from 4000 m to 5500 m. Except for the southwestern sector, it is encompassed by a series of higher and frequently snow-capped ranges which make up the western flank of the Cordillera Oriental. To the west these mountains separate Nuñoa from the upper regions of the well-traveled Ayaviri valley, to the north from the headwaters of the Vilcanota River, and to the east from the precipitous and ecologically diverse Andean escarpment. While various passes permit access to these regions, the higher ranges act to some extent as natural barriers, especially to vehicular transportation, although less to travel on foot or by horse. One all-season road connects the town of Nuñoa with Santa Rosa in the Ayaviri valley. Consequently, the Nuñoa district occupies one of the higher and more remote areas within the southern Peruvian altiplano. Isolation allows us to consider the district not only as a political unit but as an ecosystem as well.

Landscape

The Nuñoa terrain reflects the drainage pattern of the Nuñoa and Corahuina Rivers and their tributaries. Both commence in permanent snow fields lying beyond the northern perimeter of the district. The snow fields serve as frozen reservoirs, providing almost continuous runoff, regardless of the rainfall pattern in the area below. Streams resulting from melted snow descend rapidly through steep-walled, narrow valleys to an altitude of approximately 4800 m. Thereafter, a definite valley floor becomes apparent and gradually broadens to 250 m across. The actual river bed frequently lies 25–50 m below this floor. Hills bordering the high river valleys are gently graded and rise smoothly, with catenary curves and interlocking spurs, approximately 200–400 m. Their mature slopes indicate extensive weathering and erosion. As the valley floor drops below 4050 m, its configuration becomes altered. The slopes are steeper and drier and the river descends more slowly over a flat valley floor which broadens to several kilometers. The valley reaches a maximal breadth of more than 10 km below the town (see Fig. 2.11). As the

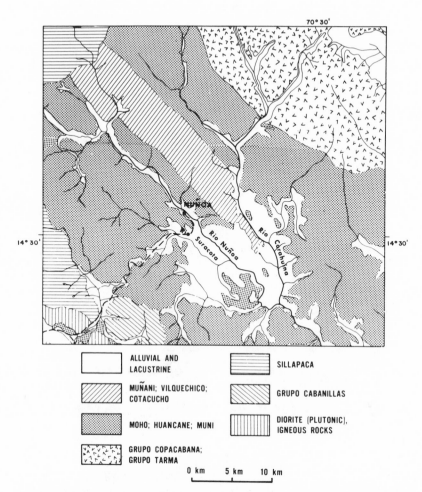

FIGURE 2.11 *Geology of the Nuñoa area. Alluvial and lacustrine: clay, sand, gravel, scattered fragments of ore, and transported material without consolidation. Muñani, Vilquechico, Cotacucho: sandstones, claystones, conglomerates, and red gypsum. Moho, Huancané, Muni: limestone, sandstones, and claystones. Copacabana, Tarma: black and gray bituminous slate, gray and blue-gray dolomitic limestones, sandstone, slate, and quartzite. Cabanillas: dark claystones with ferrous nodules, fossiliferous slates with strong intercalcation of quartzite, and sandstone. Sillapaca: outflows of basalts and andesites, calcareous tufa, and agglomerate. [Redrawn from ONERN/ CORPUNO, Vol. 2 (1965).]*

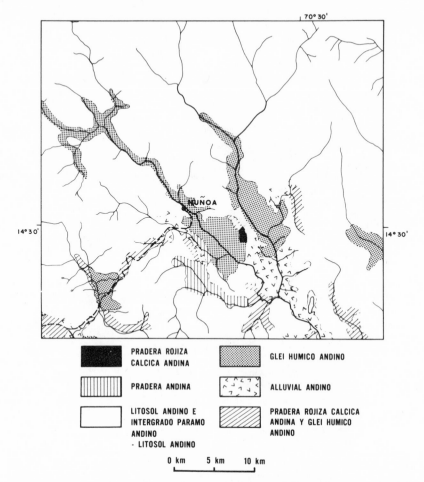

FIGURE 2.12   *Great soil groups (FAO System) of the Nuñoa area. Pradera Rojiza Calcica Andina: red calcareous meadow soils with good drainage. Pradera Andina: meadow soils with moderately good drainage. Litosol Andino e Intergrado Paramo Andino-Litosol Andino: lithosols and intergrade Paramo-lithosols with no clear morphology or definition. Glei Humico Andino: humid glei with a high organic-matter content. Alluvial Andino: alluvial soils with good drainage on gentle or flat relief. Pradera Rojiza Calcica Andina y Glei Humico Andino: a mixed soil group. [Redrawn from ONERN/ CORPUNO, Vol. 3 (1965).]*

two rivers converge, alluvial soils predominate (see Fig. 2.12), and this is one of the drier areas in the district (see Fig. 2.13). Water flow is restricted to a few isolated streams and the two rivers; there are also several marshes and two permanent lakes. Beyond these sources, vegetation on the lower valley floor is principally dependent upon precipitation as a water source.

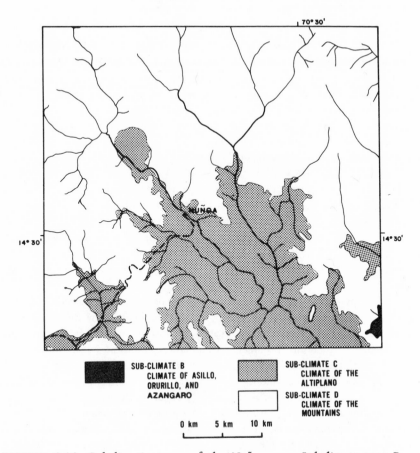

FIGURE 2.13 *Subclimatic types of the Nuñoa area. Subclimate type B: climate of Asillo, Orurillo, and Azangaro. Mean maximum daily temperature, 18.9°C; mean minimum daily temperature, 0.1°C; mean annual temperature, 10.4°C; mean daily temperature range, 18.8°C. Mean annual precipitation in this climate type, the most uniform in variation and distribution of the three types considered, is 88 cm. Subclimate type C: climate of the altiplano. Mean maximum daily temperature, 20.4°C; mean minimum daily temperature, -6.7°C; mean annual temperature, 6.6°C; mean daily temperature range, 27.1°C. Intense frosts occur in this zone. Mean annual precipitation is 64.4 cm. The variation and distribution of precipitation in some localities is not uniform. Mean annual atmospheric pressure is 472 torr. Subclimate type D: climate of the mountains. Extensive data do not exist for this type of climate; however, data gathered by Baker et al. (1968) for 14 months at an altitude of 4540 m provide the following information: mean maximum daily temperature, 9.8°C; mean minimum daily temperature, -2.3°C; mean annual temperature, 3.8°C; mean daily temperature range, 17.5°C. Temperatures below freezing were observed on 97.9 percent of the days recorded. [Redrawn from ONERN/CORPUNO, Vol. 1 (1965).]*

Climatic Characteristics

Little (1968) has reviewed meteorological information collected in Nuñoa between August 1964 and December 1965. Baker et al. (1968) added records extending up to August 1966, Thomas (1973) for 1968. Data are based on recordings from several weather stations placed at different altitudes on the valley floor and hillsides.

For the Nuñoa valley (4000 m) both precipitation and mean minimal temperatures are somewhat lower (Figs. 2.3 and 2.4) than for Chuquibambilla on the Ayaviri valley floor (Fig. 2.2). Minimal temperatures, especially when below freezing, greatly affect the kinds of vegetation that can be supported in the district (see Figs. 2.3 and 2.4). Although frosts can occur at any time throughout the year, they are most frequent at 4000 m in June and July, and least frequent from December to March. At 4500 m, frost occurs almost nightly. Nocturnal temperatures on the lower hillsides remain slightly above those of the valley floor, as a result of thermal inversion. It is on these lower hillsides that most horticulture takes place; the valley floor is cultivated only below 4000 m.

Precipitation may take a wide variety of forms. While hail and snow appear throughout the year, they are most frequent in the months directly before and after the cooler, dry season. It is estimated that frozen precipitation makes up about 10 percent of annual precipitation in lower areas of the district (Little, 1968), increasing curvilinearly with altitude.

In late September intermittent precipitation signals the outset of the rainy season. Significant rainfall generally begins in October, reaches a peak in December and January, and subsides in April. On a typical day, clear skies in the early morning become increasingly overcast toward afternoon, when most rainfall occurs. Despite the apparent uniformity in climatic pattern described above, considerable variation exists, both within the district and for a given area from year to year. It is not unusual, for instance, for one valley system to receive rain while adjacent ones remain dry. Climatic instability is greatest during the transitional period between the wet and dry seasons.

Accompanying local variation in the precipitation pattern are occasional, intermittent climatic disruptions that extend throughout the altiplano region. One such disruption is drought, which may persist for up to 3 years. In 1939–1940 (see Fig. 2.5) and 1956–1957 the district of Nuñoa, along with most of the Department of Puno, was exposed to such conditions. Effects were apparent along the entire food chain. Permanent water sources dried up, crops were lost, large numbers of livestock died, and many families were foced to migrate temporarily to lower ecozones. Since then, a number of less severe droughts have occurred. A second occasional disturbance is a dynamic frost or friagem. One such example was recorded in July 1968 (see Fig. 2.4d).

Wild Plants

Nuñoa is situated in the wet high puna, much of it falling within what Cabrera (1968) refers to as the *provincia altoandina*. Ecological formations,

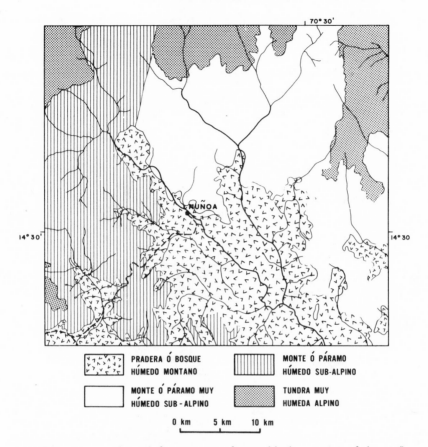

FIGURE 2.14 *Ecological formations (after Holdridge, 1967) of the Nuñoa area. Pradera o Bosque Humedo Montaño: agriculture and pasturage. Moist montane forest. Monte o Paramo muy Humedo Sub-Alpino: pasturage (sheep and camelids principally). Subalpine Paramo. Monte o Paramo Humedo Sub-Alpino: pasturage (sheep and camelids principally). Subalpine moist puna. Tundra Muy Humeda Alpino: pasturage (limited to camelids). Wet alpine tundra. [Redrawn from ONERN/CORPUNO, Vol. 4 (1965).]*

vegative associations, and land use capacity of the district are mapped in Figs. 2.14, 2.15, and 2.16. Among the natural flora of principal value to the human population, over twenty varieties of grass suitable for pasture have been identified within the district (Table 2.1). Of these, ecological dominants at lower elevations are the ichu bunch grasses (*Stipa ichu* and *Festuca dolicophylla*). Above 4250 m these grasses become less abundant and are eventually replaced by shorter bunch grasses. Ichu is one of the more important nonedible plants used by the human population. When cut, the long, rigid stems serve as roofing material on almost all rural dwellings. Ichu is employed in dehydrating potatoes, storing potato seed, and making twine. In view of its

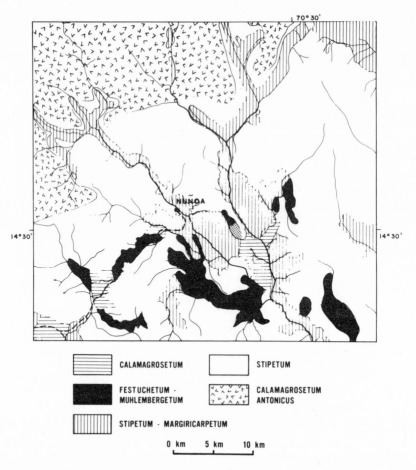

FIGURE 2.15 *Vegetation associations of the Nuñoa area. Calamagrosetum: supports 2.5–3 sheep, or the equivalent, per hectare. Festuchetum-Muhlembergetem: good to excellent pasture, supporting 3–3.5 sheep per hectare. Stipetum-Margiricarpetum: some degradation of pasture lands. The annuals are palatable, but they are ephemeral and of little importance. Stipetum: grasses that do exist are of low palatability and have little nutritive value. Camelids will, however, consume some species of Stipa. Capacity is 0.5 sheep per hectare, and is derived primarily from the annuals. Calamagrosetum antonicus: valuable solely for its protection of the soil. The vegetation is very fibrous, and contains abundant silica. Camelids will consume plants in this association, but prefer other pasturage. Capacity is the equivalent of 1.5 sheep per hectare. [Redrawn from ONERN/CORPUNO, Vol. 4 (1965).]*

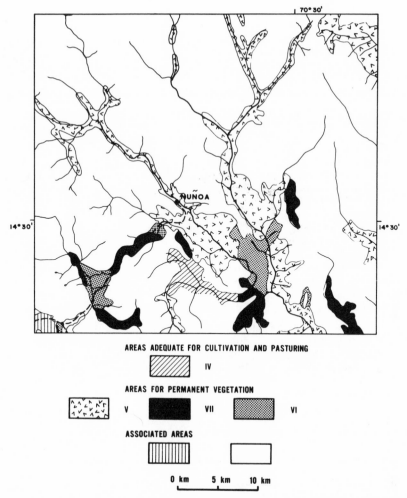

AREAS ADEQUATE FOR CULTIVATION AND PASTURING

IV

AREAS FOR PERMANENT VEGETATION

V   VII   VI

ASSOCIATED AREAS

0 km   5 km   10 km

FIGURE 2.16 *Land-use capacity of the Nuñoa area, following established* categories. Areas adequate for cultivation and other uses: *(IV) Land good for* *intense cultivation of high-altitude crops and pastures. Limitations are pri-* *marily those of soils.* Areas for permanent vegetation: *(V) Land good for* *limited cultivation of high-altitude crops and intense pasturing on cultivated* *or otherwise improved vegetation; (V) Land moderately good for pasture* *with improvement of the vegetation base. Limitations are superficial soils,* *excessive rockiness, poor drainage, and susceptibility to erosion. (VII) Land* *which can be used for extensive pasturing based on natural vegetation.* *Limitations are very superficial soils, excessive rockiness, poor drainage, and* *susceptibility to erosion.* Associated areas: *(1) Mixed area; land very good for* *intense cultivation of high-altitude crops and pasture (some soil limitations);* *mixed with type V. (2) Mixed area; land without agronomic use (limited by* *excess salinity, poor drainage, extreme topography, and rigorous climate);* *mixed with type VII. [Redrawn from ONERN/CORPUNO, Vol. 3 (1965).]*

TABLE 2.1   *Classification of*
Pasture Species
According to Quality[a]

Scientific name	Quechua name
High Palatability	
Alchemilia pinnata	Sillo sillo
Bromus unioloides	Cebadilla
Calamagrostis heterophylla	Sora sora
Distichia muscoides	K'unkuna
Festuca dolicophylla	Chillihua
Hypochoeris sp.	Pilli pilli
Hordeum muticum	Cola de ratón
Muhlembergia ligularis	Grama dulce
Cyperus sp.	—
Poa candamoana	Grama
Trifolium amabile	Trebol
Erodium	Auja auja
Gnaphalium sp.	Januncara
Moderate to Low Palatability	
Calamagrostis vincunarum	Ñapa pasto
Calamagrostis rigida	Mula pasto
Calamagrostis sp.	Huaylla ichu
Geranium sp.	Ojotilla
Muhlembergia peruviana	Llapa
Juncus sp.	Junquillo
Stipa sp.	Ichu
Plantago sp.	Llanten
Oxalis sp.	Añas cebolla
Gomphrena sp.	Pilli plateado
Scirpus sp.	Totorilla

[a]Adapted from Deustua (1971).

multiple usage in shelter as well as subsistence technology, access to a source of ichu is considered necessary by the Nuñoa rural native.

Although Nuñoa lies considerably above the present-day timberline, scattered pockets of small, slow-growing *queñua* trees (*Polylepis incana*) appear on protected slopes below 4250 m. While limited in distribution, these trees are used for roof supports, cooking utensils, stirrups, and spindle whorls. The *queñua* wood is generally not adequate for straight shafts needed in agricultural tools, which must be obtained from trees found outside Nuñoa. Finally, the queñua tree is only rarely used as a fuel source by the rural population, since dung is readily available. Dung is also used as the principal fertilizer throughout the ecosystem (Winterhalder et al., 1974).

More than 100 different plants of the Nuñoa area are used as either food or medicinal sources. Of these, approximately 20 are frequently relied upon and appear almost daily in the diet. Fresh herbs are most often used during the latter part of the rainy season; dried forms are utilized throughout the year.

Domestic Plants

Within the district of Nuñoa the principal cultigens are Andean-derived cereals and tubers. Their relative hardiness is indicated by the uppermost elevation at which they are effectively grown and productive (Fig. 2.17). Andean cereals of importance are *quinoa (Chenopodium quinoa)* and *cañihua (Chenopodium pallidicaule)*. Quinoa is generally restricted to below 4250 m, whereas cañihua cultivation has been observed as high as 4450 m. Although Old World grains (barley and oats) are occasionally grown by the rural population, they appear less resistant to environmental conditions, and their distribution is generally limited to a few well-protected lower slopes. These cultigens bend and frequently break under heavy snowfall, their grains have a greater tendency to become dislodged during a hailstorm, and they are more dependent upon moist soil conditions than the Andean cereals.

Five Andean tubers are grown within the district: *oca (Oxalis crenata)*, *ulluco (Ullucus tuberosa)*, *isaño (Tropaeolum tuberosum)*, and the *dulce (Solanum andigenum)* and *amarga* potato *(Solanum curtilobaum)*. Potatoes are hardiest and most extensively relied upon. The dulce potato produces best up to 4250 m, whereas the more frost-resistant amarga potato is grown as high as 4450 m. Both potatoes and the Andean cereals are cultivated within

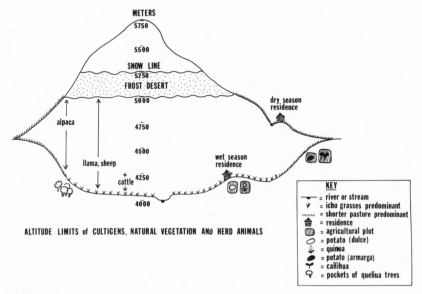

ALTITUDE LIMITS of CULTIGENS, NATURAL VEGETATION AND HERD ANIMALS

FIGURE 2.17 *Altitude limits of cultigens, natural vegetation, and herd animals in Nuñoa.*

altitude-specific microzones. Dulce potatoes and quinoa are concentrated at lower elevations; amarga potatoes and cañihua allow the extension of cultivation to a further 200 m. Within each microzone, varieties of each cultigen are planted, each with slightly different growing patterns, resistances, and qualities as food.

While altitude-associated variables impose a limit above which horticulture is not profitable, a number of other factors operate to further reduce the available arable land in the district: soil conditions, slope, exposure, water availability, drainage, and incidence and intensity of local frosts. For example, the dry, steep slopes adjoining much of the lower valley are not extensively used for cultivation. Western slopes are considered preferable to eastern exposures, since rapid thermal change caused by the intense morning sunlight on frost-exposed crops can result in considerable damage. Without irrigation, soil moisture content in much of the lower valley floor is inadequate for crops. Furthermore, on the valley floor frosts are more frequent than on the adjacent lower slopes. Areas best suited for agriculture are lower, less abrupt slopes which are watered well and have a western exposure. Surveys in the district have given estimates that less than 2 percent of the total land area is suitable for agriculture (Schaedel, 1959). This value does not reflect actual land under cultivation since a large portion must be left in fallow (from 2 to 12 years following 2 years of utilization). Finally, as a consequence of climatic instability, production from land under cultivation varies considerably from place to place and from year to year. Frosts in December can kill the new sprouts; hail directly before the quinoa and cañihua harvest may dislodge the ripe grain; insect attacks can result in extensive damage; too much rain can lead to rot and crop loss. In view of the limited arable land in Nuñoa and its productive inconsistency in a given area, it is expected that alternative subsistence patterns would be necessary to support the Nuñoa population. The natural flora do not appear to contribute significantly in this regard. It is therefore necessary to look beyond this trophic level to the natural and domestic consumers.

Wildlife

Humans do not appear to rely heavily on the natural fauna of the district (birds and small mammals), in part because of the widespread distribution of these species but also because of the absence of a suitable hunting technology. Rifles generally are not owned by rural natives, and their slings and slingshots are not effective enough to make hunting more than an amusement. Those families living near Lake Ututo occasionally seek waterfowl eggs. Trout are plentiful in most of the rivers and streams of Nuñoa, but serious fishing is infrequent. Gang hooks on the end of a nylon throwline are used for gigging, and in the course of several hours in the dry season a boy or man can usually catch enough fish to feed a family. Another technique employed during this season is blocking off a section of a stream with a series of dams, corraling the trout into a restricted area where they can be scooped onto shore. Fishing generally is terminated with the rising, turbid waters which accompany the rainy season. Although utilization of this food resource appears limited under normal conditions, fish might be an important food reserve. Under drought conditions, for instance, when land food is relatively scarce, fishing could provide an important food supplement. Low water levels would facilitate fishing.

Domestic Animals

There have been few attempts to introduce domestic fowl or small mammals into the rural areas. Exceptions have been the dog, the cat, and the guinea pig. All three may be viewed as playing a symbiotic role with the human group to which they are attached. The dog functions principally as a protector against crop thievery or animal loss, but also assists in herding. The role of the cat, if any, is to reduce the immediate rodent population and thus protect the stored grains. The guinea pig is used as a ceremonial food resource, as well as a food reserve. All three domesticates are fed on scraps (i.e., bones and potato peels, and, in the case of dogs, human excrement) and thus do not directly compete for human food resources.

Major alteration of natural animal populations in the district has resulted from placing domestic herbivores into the ecological niche formerly occupied by the *vicuña, guanaco,* and deer. Replacement herbivores are the alpaca, llama, sheep, cow, and horse. As was the case for cultigens, the importance of these domesticates is in part indicated by their distribution. Alpaca and llama herds, although found throughout the district, are concentrated at higher elevations (see Fig. 2.17). The major concentration of sheep is somewhat lower in an intermediate altitude zone, and cattle are usually found on the lower valley floors. This distribution appears to be related to differences in grazing patterns as well as in tolerance of climatic stress. Cattle, for example, have difficulty grazing effectively on the short grasses at higher altitude. In addition, cold stress probably produces a greater strain in these animals since the insulative value of their coats is considerably less than that of the camelids or sheep. Finally, the lower fertility of cattle and the low viability of their young in the upper altitudes of the district is a reason frequently given for their absence in these higher sectors. Horses are neither numerous, relative to other herbivores, nor do they appear in herds. Generally families in the more remote areas will have several to fulfill transportation needs. The horse is considered essential in this respect, which may account for its distribution irrespective of altitude. Because it is not a food source as are the other domesticates, its fitness at a given altitude is of less consequence. Horses may die more frequently at higher elevations, but they are just as necessary.

Given the limited capacity to practice cultivation, the people of Nuñoa rely on pastoralism as an alternative subsistence pattern. The advantages of domesticated herbivores in the high puna ecozone stem principally from the herbivores' efficient utilization of the environment and from the fact that they consume plants which have no utility to the human population, and can utilize pasture sources throughout the district. In doing so they are less influenced by local climatic disturbances and therefore constitute a more reliable human food source. Thus, although a moderate drought may destroy a large portion of crops, it is likely that the domestic herbivores would survive by relying upon mobility and their greater endogenous food reserves. They, in turn, would provide a food resource or a means for exchange for the human population under these conditions.

Land and pasture quality appear as important limitors to herd size. Animal-to-land ratios within Nuñoa vary from 0.5 to 3.5 sheep equivalents per hectare (a sheep equivalent is the amount of land necessary to support a 40-kg sheep per year; see Fig. 2.15). Pasture in the higher, well-watered areas of Nuñoa is generally considered good grazing for camelids. With a high composition of green, succulent herbs, these areas are especially important for alpaca grazing. A major limiting factor on herd size appears to be the availability of green pasture throughout the dry season (Koford, 1957). Herds converge on well-watered areas during this period and must be supported there for a minimum of 3 months. It is therefore the grazing potential of such areas which places limits on herd size and on pastoralism as a subsistence pattern. More detailed descriptions of pastoralism, as well as other subsistence practices in the Nuñoa area, are provided by Thomas (1973) and are further discussed in Chapters 3 and 19.

Summary

The general characteristics and constraints of the Nuñoa ecosystem conform closely to those discussed for the wet puna—an environment with microclimates that vary in both time and space. For the human population that depends upon the immediate ecosystem for its support, adaptive strategies reflect the environment's complexity. The population functions ecologically as an important primary, and dominant secondary, consumer, gaining access to material flows primarily through locally derived cultigens and domestic animals. These plant and animal species have been modified and regulated by human groups for centuries in an attempt to adjust them to diverse environmental conditions, as well as to human constraints. As a result, the range of cultivars utilized complement one another in tolerance, requirements, scheduling, and production. A similar complementary pattern exists between cultigens and domestic animals.

Cultivation in Nuñoa results in intensive utilization of small, dispersed areas up to 4450 m. Pastoralism, on the other hand, can be carried out throughout the ecosystem, extending up to the frost desert. The herd animals concentrate nutrients that had been thinly spread over wide spaces, as well as accelerate decomposition and the cycling of nutrients (dung from the animals is used as a fertilizer on newly prepared potato fields). A second-year crop

(Andean cereals) needs little additional field preparation and no fertilizer, since it can produce adequately with poorer soils.

Thus, a complex and interdependent mix of resources is utilized by the Nuñoa human group. The subsistence system appears to be effective in reducing environmental perturbation and increasing access to material flows of the biotic community. Reliance upon these resources is viewed as an adjustment to a variable and uneven environment, one entailing substantial modification of the biotic community. Modification, in turn, is a continuous process that requires biobehavior adjustments on the part of man.

3

SOCIAL AND POLITICAL STRUCTURE OF NUÑOA

Gabriel Escobar M.

Nuñoa is a district of the Province of Melgar in the Department of Puno. It has a population of a little more than 8000, according to the 1961 census. Of this population about 2000 live in the town of Nuñoa and the rest are spread throughout a large number of haciendas, a few Indian villages, and a scattered number of estancias and shepherds' huts. Ethnically, about 500 are Mestizos and Cholos, most of them living in Nuñoa and the rest distributed in the haciendas, mines, and estancias. In the town itself, there are about 200 Mestizos and an undetermined number of Cholos; the rest of the population are Indians, as is the bulk of the population of the district. Mestizos and Cholos are bilingual in Spanish and Quechua. The Indians speak only Quechua; a few speak Aymara as well. The bulk of the Indian population is relatively sedentary and fairly stable, but an unknown number of Indians and Cholos, from the town, the villages, and the estancias, travel within the district to the haciendas and mines, and migrate periodically to Cuzco, Puno, or Arequipa to work in road gangs, mines, and towns. Most of the Mestizo population in the district can be considered transient: in the town of Nuñoa there are a few families of impoverished hacienda owners; the wealthy merchants are usually from Arequipa and do not have strong roots in the area; and almost all the schoolteachers and government officers are outsiders recently settled in the area. The landlords, with few exceptions, reside in Lima, Arequipa, or Cuzco and come infrequently to the district.

The economic activities of the district are determined by the geographical and ecological characteristics of the area, and the main activities are herding and subsistence agriculture, with some mining exploitations. Herding is mainly of alpacas, llamas, sheep, and cattle. From the point of view of economic exchanges, alpacas and sheep are the most important for their wool, which allows their herders to participate in the money economy of the region. Subsistence agriculture is still carried out by simple pre-Columbian techniques. The main staples are Andean tubers (bitter potatoes, potatoes, *papaslisas, ocas añus*); two andean grains, *cañihua* and *quinoa;* and barley. Maize is imported from Cuzco. Figures 3.1A and 3.1B show some of the people of Nuñoa, including those engaged in some subsistence activities.

FIGURE 3.1A   *The people of Nuñoa. Two Quechua Indian children (upper left). Woman weaving on a hand loom (upper right). Woman grinding grain (lower left). A Quechua Indian family (lower right). (Photos by M. A. Little.)*

Most Indians travel on foot within the district and surrounding areas, following traditional paths in the altiplano. Indians in estancias and villages also have llama herds, mainly for the transportation of agricultural produce, firewood, and manure for fuel. Cholos and wealthy Indians in the estancias and haciendas also have horses; some have donkeys and mules. Most of the hacendados and some wealthy Mestizos in town have station wagons and trucks. Twice a week and on Sundays, trucks go by the main road to the large towns along the main transportation routes from Cuzco to Arequipa, and trucks to and from the mines cross the town rather frequently. Many Indians and Mestizos in the town and some of the villages own bicycles bought in Bolivia.

ETHNOHISTORICAL BACKGROUND

An ethnohistorical study of the area of Nuñoa and the surrounding districts is still a prospect for the future. This presentation is only an outline of the history of Nuñoa on the basis of standard references, and most of the statements are hypothetical. With the exception of the study made of the

FIGURE 3.1B   *The people of Nuñoa. Two men cultivating with foot plows (upper left). Two women and children from Nuñoa; the woman and child at the left are Cholo, the woman and child at the right are Indian (upper right). Man on horseback bringing a small herd of llamas through town (lower left). View in the town of Nuñoa adjacent to the main plaza (lower right). (Photos by M. A. Little.)*

Inca remains of Nuñoa by Luis Barreda, archaeological work has not yet gone beyond the stage of surface collections and observations. All we know at the moment is that the area contains evidences of preceramic occupation and that the area was well populated by the year 1000 A.D. The first historical reference in Nuñoa appears in a historical tradition of the Incas recorded by Father Bernabé Cobo (Cobo, 1956, p. 87) in 1653, in which Topa Inca lost the Province of Urcosuyo to one of his sons in a game of dice. The Province of Urcosuyo contained five pueblos: Nuñoa, Oruro (Orurillo today), Asillo, Azángaro, and Pucará.

According to other sources, this province is in the Colonial province and corregimiento of Urcosuyo and Hatuncolla (Vasquez de Espinoza, 1948, p. 658), which later was known as the Province of Lampa (Bueno, 1951, pp. 113–114). In 1901, this province was divided into two provinces, Lampa and

Melgar (Ayaviri), where Nuñoa is located. According to Rowe (1946, Map 3 and pp. 203–204) the Province of Lampa included most of what was the kingdom of the Colla, which extended to the northern shores of Lake Titicaca and bordered the province of the Canas on the south. The kingdom of the Colla was incorporated into the Inca empire by Inca Viracocha before 1438, when Pachacuti was crowned and started the career of expansion of the Incas.

For our present purposes, the most important references of Colonial times are those that refer to the population and the economy of Nuñoa, and there is hope that we will have more references to Nuñoa in future archival research. A document found in Seville by John V. Murra for the year 1558 (Archivo General de Indias, Contaduriá, 1824, 4-0) gives us evidence of the economy of the Indians in terms of the access of the population to the products of various ecological zones within the area (Murra, 1968). It also indicates that the economic standard of the Indians of Nuñoa was much better than it is today. According to this document, the Indians of Nuñoa paid rent to the Crown, both in taxes and in the coca production of the eastern slopes of the province in the montaña. The taxes were collected not only in money but also in sheep, llamas, *charki* (dried meat), pigs, lard, chicken, textiles, and *chuño*. The document also indicates that the Indians provided for the support of the priest and the church.

A later source, that of Vasquez de Espinoza for 1630 (Vasquez de Espinoza, 1948, p. 658), indicates a probable improvement in the economy of the district. According to him, in 1630 a total of 605 taxpayers paid 5449 pesos in taxes. Vasquez de Espinoza also gives the first figures of the population that we have. He divides the population into 605 taxpayers (roughly men from 20 to 50), 306 "old," 550 "*muchachos*" (probably children and adolescents), and 1269 women, for a total of 2730 people. Cosme Bueno, writing between 1763 and 1778 (Bueno, 1951, pp. 113–114), in his description of the Province of Lampa, mentions Nuñoa only as a parish, but his general description of the province seems to indicate that the economic condition of the province had deteriorated somewhat. He mentions that the province produces wool, fat, and *charki* or *chalona,* and he mentions that mining, although it is not very good, produces 15,000 marcos of silver.

Somewhat earlier, in a document found in Nuñoa, Doña Felipa Mamani Tapara (Instrumento . . . , copy made in 1872), in 1717 Cacica and Governor of "the town of Nunoa, of the ayllus included in it . . . and in the name of the Comun of Indians," petitioned the Crown for the confirmation of "possession and property of the lands in the name of this Our Comun." The document includes an ordered list of place names that mark the borders of the district, which indicates that the extension of the area was very much what it is today. She refers to the death of a cacique (chief) and to the poverty of the Indians and how hard it is for them to pay their taxes, and offers to pay 500 pesos for the legal costs of the visit.

None of these documents gives us any indication of what might have been the social and political organization of the district. Subject to later verification, we can assume that the organization of Nuñoa followed the pattern of dual organization established by the Incas, of which there are still evidences at present in Nuñoa and in all the highlands of Peru (Palomino, 1971). As early as 1567, Matienzo (1967) gives us a sort of "ideal model" description of this pattern:

> In each repartimiento or province there are two parcialidades or sectors: one is called *hanansaya,* the other *hurinsaya.* Each parcilidad has a principal cacique who leads the principales (those with some political power) and Indians of his parcialidad, and he does not meddle with the other, except that the curaca (religious leader) of the hanansaya is the principal for the whole province, to whom obeys the other hurinsaya curaca in all that he orders (Matienzo, 1967, pp. 20–21, my translation).

This model, with some modifications, still reflects Andean patterns of social organization as found, for instance, among the Lupaca, in the southern shores of Lake Titicaca (Murra, 1968).

Indian caciques (chiefs) and curacas (religious leader) became part of the Spanish administrative system, and their main function was that of collecting taxes for the Crown and for themselves and preserving order among the Indians. Within the district or pueblo, there were a variable number of *ayllus* (Indian communities), usually between 3 and 6, that were ruled by their principales. Each ayllu had to send the pueblo a principal and a number of Indians every year to attend the administration of the town and the church and to work for the Spaniards (if any) and the caciques. The town was divided into sections corresponding to the number of ayllus, and there was a house for the principal that came with the Indians. This kind of organization, with some modifications, is still operating in the town of Asillo, to the south of Nuñoa (Escobar M., 1959).

Caciques and curacas, the Indian principales, which constitute the civil–religious hierarchy of authority known as the *cargo* system in Mesoamerica (Cancian, 1965) and the *envarado* system in the Andes (Mishkin, 1946), eventually disappeared by the time of independence from Spain in 1824. In the Department of Puno, the system was eliminated in most of the communities around Lake Titicaca as a consequence of the Indian rebellions of the twenties (Escobar M., 1967), while it still survives in some of the very isolated communities in the higher punas. In Nuñoa, the last vestiges of the system disappeared by 1938 (Rodríquez, 1958).

The Republican history of Nuñoa cannot be well documented at the moment, and all the references we have found so far are fanciful or cautious (Stiglich, 1918; Romero, 1928) and the oral traditions in the town are contradictory. However, they adequately portray the present trend of gradual diminution of isolation and incorporation of the district into the Peruvian national political system. A large part of this history, from about 1850 to 1920, is one of progressive impoverishment, subjugation, and disorganization of the Indian population by violent means. According to the oral traditions of the Mestizos in Nuñoa, it was at this time that the Indian ayllus of Nuñoa were dispossessed of their lands, through legal chicanery and violent means, by a number of aggressive Mestizos who came from Cuzco and Arequipa, and the Indians were converted into serfs of the haciendas. Those Indians that escaped serfdom remained in the town and reorganized themselves in small refugee communities such as Sincata and in some of the estancias. Many of the new landowners maintained armed bands of blacks from Arequipa, and the fighting for pasture lands and cattle rustling amounted almost to civil war; the town itself was invaded many times. These activities diminished only when the Peruvian government established a number of army garrisons in the wake of the Indian rebellions of the times.

In 1901 the town was recognized as the capital of the district and the Mestizos were appointed as the political and municipal authorities; they have maintained their control up to the present. During the nineteenth century, the Indians also lost all their properties in the montaña, and whatever access they have now to the products of other regions is mainly through the market system and through migration. According to Stiglich (1918) and some oral traditions in Nuñoa, the Indian town was a set of Indian houses, not too well organized, surrounding the church and a plaza which was at the same time a cemetery. The present appearance of the town was established by the Mestizos, following a pattern of urbanization that has been called "early republican" by a geographer (Escobar M., 1967, personal communication), with some concessions to Indianness, like the houseroofs of ichu grass and the maintenance of the Andean dual pattern. The gilded altars and the paintings of the church were gradually stripped by the Mestizos to today's level of impoverishment.

SOCIAL STRUCTURE AND ORGANIZATION

Kinship, Marriage, and the Family

At the present state of research, we are not yet in a position to make definitive statements about the kinship structure of the population of Nuñoa. The information we have now tends to show that both Indians and Mestizos have a Spanish-type bilateral kinship system, similar to that of the Mestizos in the city of Cuzco (Escobar M., 1972), with some modifications due to economic status and stratification. However, such may not represent adequately the kinship system of the Indian population, because the patterns of reciprocity dominant among them tend to follow the pre-Columbian pattern.

Our analysis, based on information gathered in the community of Sincata, in the hacienda Chilíhua, and in the town of Nuñoa, tends to indicate that wherever you have a more or less permanent nucleus of population, the core of the community is made up of a number of extended families surrounded by a variable number of individuals and couples loosely related to this core. In Sincata, of 137 individuals counted in 1967, 93 belong to six extended families and the remaining 42 do not seem to be related in any fashion. Also, in Sincata, households tend to cluster in specific areas. In Nuñoa, extended families tend to be smaller and scattered throughout the town, but there is constant visiting between households. Most of the Indians in the town seem to have kinship relationships spread throughout the district, and frequent trips are made for purposes of work, trade, and ceremony, so relationships are established through individual kindred and through *compadrazgo* (god—parent bonds).

Ceremonial kinship or compadrazgo for marriage and baptism, although in many cases tending to reinforce family relationships, is mainly sought among wealthy Indians, Cholos, or Mestizos in terms of patron—client relationships.

Our observations about the marriage practices of Nuñoa tend to agree with the data and analysis of T. S. Baker (1966). Her assertion that Indian marriage in Nuñoa is a working institution leading to the formation of legitimate families, whether civil or religious ceremonies are performed or not, has been greatly reinforced by recent studies made in Bolivia and Peru (Albó, 1972; Carter, 1972; Bolton, 1972), all of them in the altiplano region. However, according to Carter (1972) and Albó (1972), the performance of the church ceremony is probably one of many other ceremonies that are performed throughout the life of the couple until the final bond of marriage has strengthened the links with the community.

In contrast with the Indian population, Cholos and lower-class Mestizos tend to have looser and more transient liaisons. In general, Cholo migrant workers tend to establish very brief links with women in the different places they work, while Cholo and Mestizo women tend to have a succession of consorts and children from them; helped by relatives, they form matricentric families.

Families in Nuñoa, while recognizing other relationships, tend to reside in nuclear units. Husband and wife share equal responsibilities in the economy and the management of the family. Children usually receive an equal share of whatever property the family has, with the exception of the house, which always goes to the youngest son. Until the age of six, all children wear a little skirt, which is taken away after the haircutting ceremony when children begin to learn their respective chores within the economy of the family.

Social Stratification and Social Mobility

Both Indians and Mestizos use ethnic and economic criteria in making social distinctions. Irrespective of economic distinctions Indians call Mestizos *misti* (connotation of power and foreignness); following economic criteria, all landlords are called *qhapaqh* (rich men), all estancia owners are called *askha uywayoqh* (cattle owners), and all poor people are called *wakcha*. "Wakcha" means not only economic poverty but also lack of relatives and compadres.

Mestizos call landlords and their families *gamonales* ("exploiters") or *clase alta* (upper class). Because most of them are related to middle-class families in Cuzco, Arequipa, Ayaviri, or Puno, they refer to themselves as *personas decentes, vecinos notables,* or some such term (proper people). They call Cholos all those members of the Indian population who are upwardly mobile to the Mestizo level, and Indios all the members of the Quechua-speaking population of the district. Cholos, in consonance with their upwardly mobile situation, adapt their references to the other strata.

Relationships between the strata follow strict patterns of subordination and superiority in terms of authority, paternalism, and patron–client relationships. In all cases Indians act with considerable restraint and obsequience toward Mestizos and landlords, who in turn always act overbearing and authoritarian toward Indians. Considerable hostility can be sensed behind the sometimes extremely formal behavior that characterizes their interactions.

For Indians, social mobility is related to migration, becoming a salaried worker in road gangs, mines, and cities, or becoming a merchant in the market networks from Cuzco to Arequipa. By learning Spanish and adopting the external symbols of the Mestizos, he becomes a Cholo and, if he is successful, his descendants may be considered Mestizos.

For Mestizos, social mobility is achieved through trade in cities, through commercial investments in stores, and through education. In most cases, improvement of economic or social position implies moving to the cities in the area and eventually to Lima, where the Mestizos blend into the middle class.

In the last five years, because of the Law of Agrarian Reform, many members of the upper class of landowners have descended to the level of the urban middle classes in Cuzco and Arequipa.

THE ECONOMY

Technology and Arts and Crafts

The economy of the peasant population of the district, Indians, Cholos, and a few Mestizos, is one of subsistence based on herding and agriculture, supplemented by commercial activities to dispose of small surpluses and provide food, clothing, and ceremonial necessities. The range of tools, occupations, and technological abilities of the peasants of Nuñoa corresponds to what Schaedel (1959) has called a "generalized mode of adaptation" to the ecological conditions of the area. The tools used in the different occupations are either locally produced or purchased in the hardware stores and markets of Ayaviri and Sicuani. Most peasants in haciendas, estancias, and communities own shovels and picks, axes, sickles, and knives for shearing and butchering, at an absolute minimum. Most women have a set of needles and pins, needles for knitting, and thread for sewing. Both men and women purchase their spindle whorls in stores in Nuñoa. Ropes are manufactured from raw hides and ichu grass, and can also be purchased in stores.

The only part-time specialists are probably curers and ceremonial practitioners, and distinctions in division of labor are based only on age, sex, and the energy a task may require. All men, women, and children spin wool or knit while they travel or tend cattle. All adult men and women know how to weave, and the difference is mainly in the kind of loom they use: women weave belts, blankets, ponchos, and bags on the pre-Columbian Inca loom, while men weave (when they do) on the Spanish loom the *bayeta* cloth that is still used for their clothing. All other occupations that we have been able to observe, such as shearing wool or butchering, wall building and house roofing, store tending and marketing, baking and knitting, were being carried out apparently without distinction as to sex and age. In Sincata, one distinction on the basis of age of women seems to be important; almost all herding is done by adolescent women before the age of marriage; after marriage, women settle at home, take care of the house, and weave.

In terms of survival, this generalized mode of adaptation gives the Indians better chances of earning a living than the Mestizos, because when they migrate, they can generally make a living by shifting from one occupation to another.

Peasant Agriculture and Herding

Around the town of Nuñoa, in the *haciendas* and in the communities, agriculture is practiced in small individual lots. The agricultural season begins in October and planting ends by November. After planting, the fields have to be weeded and furrowed, and care must be taken of the fields to prevent robbery, trampling by the cattle, or depredations by birds. Plowing is done with a metal hoe or with the Andean foot plow. Most of the lots can be planted by a man, his wife, and a helper in two or three days. When additional help is needed, it is secured either by the form of reciprocity known as *ayni* or by the *mink'a*.

Alpacas, sheep, and cattle are herded wherever there are adequate pastures and water resources. Within the haciendas, the best places are reserved for the herds of the landlord and his foreman, while the serfs are allowed to have only very small herds. In the communities the resources of pasture and water are very limited, probably because of the pressure of population. In the *estancias,* herding is the major economic occupation. A herd can be 200–400 alpacas but is usually smaller, for fear of rustlers. An estancia usually has two or three houses, a series of corrals fenced with fieldstones, and adequate extensions of grazing land for small herds of alpacas, cattle, and sheep. Scattered over the grazing land are small huts or *cabañas* for the livestock tenders. Estancias are usually owned by Indian, Cholo, or Mestizo families, who bring in additional labor by means of mink'a or ayni in times of need.

Indians in the communities also own llamas for transportation and wool, and estancia owners have llamas and horses, which they use for transportation and for tending their flocks, especially when they have cattle.

While all agriculture is mainly for subsistence, ownership of herds is a better indicator of wealth differences among the peasants. In the haciendas, the Indian workers have very small herds, if any, but most foremen have sizable herds and may even be considered wealthy by local standards. Estancia owners can be considered wealthy or well-to-do by Indian and Mestizo local standards. In general, they are well fed and dressed, most of them own bicycles and transistor radios, and most of them are also livestock and wool dealers.

Herding in Indian communities is mostly done by women and children, and it is usually of a limited nature. A good example of these communities is Sincata. Here, 153 people own small plots of agricultural land around a lake and grazing lands that go up to the surrounding hills. Each family has two or three plots of lands that are rotated every year and small herds of cattle, usually from 2 to 10 head, tended by all members of the family but especially by the women. The margin of subsistence seems to be low, and both men and women usually go to work on estancias and haciendas to supplement their livings.

No matter how small the herds a family may possess, herding seems to be the factor that allows it to acquire a surplus for supplementing its diet, purchasing coca and alcohol, and expending in ceremonial displays. Alpaca and sheep wool is sheared for home use and to sell or barter it to agents from Sicuani and Arequipa; cattle and sheep are also butchered regularly to be sold with a profit twice a week in the markets of Ayaviri and Sicuani; and manure is collected and sold in great quantities as fuel to the Mestizos of Nuñoa and other towns. During the months of July and August, meat dealers from Urubamba and Quillabamba in Cuzco take truckloads of alpaca meat from Nuñoa to the valley of La Convención.

Peasant and Hacienda
Land-Tenure Systems

Land-tenure patterns within the district have many variations still to be studied. Ownership of land for most of the peasant population is limited, but access to and utilization of grazing and agricultural land can be secured by a variety of arrangements. In communities like Sincata and Quitampari, peasants own individual lots; although the title to the lot is individual, the lot is used by the corporate unity of the family. Size of lots usually reflects on the number in the family, so wealth is usually measured by this double criterion. Peasants can have access to more land by renting some additional lots from other peasants, from estancias, or from haciendas, and by means of a form of sharecropping in which the harvest is divided in equal parts between the owner of the land and the sharecropper. Access to additional pastureland can be gained by paying a sum of money or an agreed-upon number of the calves to the owner of the land. The community of Orcorara, in the outskirts of Nuñoa, is somewhat atypical in that the land is the corporate property of the "Comunidad Indígena de Orcorara," an officially recognized Indian community that includes people living in the town and in the village. According to our informants, community members pay 10 Peruvian soles per year to the community for the right to cultivate an individual lot. In theory, the lots should return to the community and be realloted after abandonment or death of the previous user.

Estancias differ from haciendas in the fact that they are family estates of about 5–20 ha mainly devoted to livestock under the management of the owner. Haciendas are the large estates that were created by the Mestizos by seizure of Indian lands during the nineteenth century. There are about 104 haciendas in Nuñoa, which vary in size from 100 to 3000 ha, but the records are hardly adequate. Ownership of the hacienda is by individual title, but actual management and operation of the estates follow a variety of arrangements. In 1967, only four or five of the owners lived in their estates and came frequently to Nuñoa; about 10 others commuted frequently between their homes in Cuzco or Arequipa and their estates in Nuñoa; the others, some of them owning the largest estates, came to their estates only once or twice a year, leaving the management of the land to Cholo or Mestizo administrators, who took advantage of the situation to their own benefit.

The heyday of the hacienda system in Nuñoa and the rest of the altiplano was between the two world wars when the price of wool in the international market was very high. Even before 1945, the efficiency of the system was beginning to deteriorate because of litigation and mismanagement; the drop of the price of wool after 1945, which was due to the competition of plastic textiles, accelerated the deterioration to the point that in 1967 many hacienda-owning families had lost their properties or were renting them to more able administrators.

Partitioning of land through inheritance sapped the efficiency and profits of the system, invariably leading to endless litigation between relatives. In 1967, many of the smaller landowners had really given up administering their estates personally, and rented their shares to a few stubborn hacienda owners who attempted to improve the herds of the estates; a few others were entrusting their estates to the "Sociedad Ganadera del Sur," a large corporation in Arequipa that was formed by subsidies from the wool and cattle merchants of Lima and Arequipa.

In the traditional management of the hacienda, all operations are entrusted to a Cholo or Mestizo administrator; with the help of a variable number of Cholo or Indian foremen, the administrator supervises the daily work of the serfs, who are settled throughout the estate in groups of families near the foraging and watering places. The number of serfs varies with the size of the estate, usually between 30 and 300, according to a count made by Rodríguez (1958). The administrator and the foremen are sometimes paid a salary, but usually they are only allowed to maintain relatively large herds of livestock. Most of the serfs receive a place to build their houses and limited grazing rights; in exchange they owe the owner a number of days of work during the year, and they are under obligation to provide weekly services to the hacienda house or, in the city, and to provide fuel for the hacienda house. During times of hard and intensive work in shearing and butchering, they are paid a salary and given some food, and additional hands are hired from among the peasants that come from Nuñoa and other communities.

Patterns of Labor

Among the peasants of Nuñoa, labor exchange is secured by traditional Andean patterns on the basis of kinship, compadrazgo, and friendship. The most frequent form of exchange is that of *ayni,* in which individuals help each other for specific tasks of immediate need. When labor cannot be secured by ayni, individuals hire neighbors or peons by means of the mink'a, in which payment is made either in produce or money, without obligation to reciprocate. In both forms of work, additional expenses are incurred to provide the workers food, coca leaves, alcohol, and cigarettes. Occasionally some individuals are able to raise gangs of up to 15 or 20, and the work has a somewhat festive character.

Labor in the haciendas is invariably demanded by the administrator and it is always under the constant supervision of the foremen, for the peasant has a tendency to procrastinate because of the compulsive nature of the work. In cases of neglect, punishment is usually harsh; it may even entail losing one's livestock or being expelled from the estate.

Most of the Indians in Nuñoa and many in the communities hire themselves out as peons for a daily salary in the town and as migrant workers. In Nuñoa, the nominal salary is about $0.50 for a day, and they usually work in a variety of tasks such as house construction and roofing, butchering of alpacas, shearing, and carrying bundles or loading trucks.

Two traditional forms of labor taxation are demanded by the Mestizo authorities, in spite of the fact that they are not recognized by the law of the state. In the *faena* or *república,* which now is known euphemistically as "cooperación popular," about 10–50 peasants are forcibly requisitioned by the Governor and the police for road construction and repairing, or the maintenance and construction of public buildings. In the other form, called *tarea* (task), individuals are assigned to work demanded by the authorities for specific menial tasks in towns and communities.

Economic Exchanges

All economic exchanges in Nuñoa can be divided in the three spheres of reciprocity, barter, and commerce, with relatively easy conversion from one sphere to another. The three spheres function as a system in which the small surpluses of livestock, wool, agricultural produce, and animal manure is exchanged to supplement the subsistence economy with articles from the stores of Nuñoa. The most important articles, among others, are alcohol, coca, bread, noodles, sugar, and maize, needed not only for dietary supplements but also for ceremonial purposes. The nodal point of this system is the town, which relates the district through the dirt road leading to Santa Rosa, to the networks of transportation and market towns that go all the way from Cuzco to Arequipa.

Exchange reciprocity among the peasants, besides ayni for labor and the exchange of goods in terms of friendship and kinship in daily intercourse, is extremely important to secure additional goods for ritual celebrations and for patron—client relationships with the Mestizos of Nuñoa. All ritual celebrations, from haircutting to fiestas and funerals, demand elaborate displays of food, coca, and alcohol that very few individual sponsors would be able to provide by themselves. And in their dealings with the Mestizos, especially in terms of legal aid and influential patronage, presents have to be made in order to sustain the interest of the patrons.

Barter and money purchases in commerce operate throughout the district but are mainly carried out in the town of Nuñoa. In the town there are about ten large stores belonging to Mestizos who import alcohol, food (flour, maize, rice, sugar, salt, canned fish and fruit, biscuits, and candies), coca leaves, some clothing, cigarettes, Primus stoves, candles, and other urban conveniences. Additionally, Indians and Cholos have smaller stores that usually sell only alcohol, bread, rice, sugar, coca leaves, matches, and fruit in smaller quantities. While the stores of the Mestizos are regular capitalistic investments, most of the stores of the Indians and Cholos are only to supplement their living and to fill idle time.

Pending further verification, it can be said that about 20—40 percent of the trade is based on sugar-cane alcohol and coca leaves for the Indian population and beer for the Mestizos. The alcohol is imported from the coast, the coca leaves are brought from La Convención in Cuzco, and the beer is brought from either Cuzco or Arequipa, either by agents from these towns who come with their trucks to Nuñoa, or directly purchased by the merchants in trips to Sicuani, Ayaviri, and Juliaca. Most of the trade and barter is conducted in retail in small everyday quantities and usually paid for in small coins and bills, or bartered for eggs, small quantities of quinoa, cañihua, or potatoes. Most of the stores extend some credit to Indians or Mestizos in town on the basis of familiarity. The prices of sugar, alcohol, coca leaves, and rice are controlled by the government through the agency of the National Bank, but most other prices depend to a certain extent on supply and demand.

A brief comparison of prices in Nuñoa with those of Juliaca and Ayaviri shows that local merchants do not charge the Indians exorbitantly. Most of them overcharge from about ½ cent to 1½ cents per equivalent unit, although probably they cheat in the weights. Some goods, such as sporting shoes and balls, matches, leather jackets, bicycles, watches, and playing cards, are imported illegally from Bolivia through Indian and Cholo merchants; some of the store owners get these goods in Juliaca.

In an effort to increase commercial activities in the town, the municipal authorities of Nuñoa established in 1967 a Sunday market or fair in the main plaza of the town. In 1967, the number of Indian and Cholo merchants was still very small, but within 6 yr the market has grown to the point of filling the plaza, and it now conforms to the pattern of fairs of the area. Most of the retail products marketed are bread and sugar, fruits from the montaña and coast (oranges, bananas, avocados, apples, grapes) according to season, folk medicines, and peddler stands that sell needles, mirrors, wallets, dice, tire sandals, and other trinkets. Every two or three weeks, merchants from Puno or Juliaca come with their trucks bringing some special products from the coast: wine and *pisco* (brandy) from Tacna, molasses from Arequipa, dry yellow and red peppers from Arequipa and Cuzco, and maize and dry fish that are eagerly bought by the Indians.

Two other commercial activities are important in Nuñoa: baking and butchering. Baking is done with imported flour in about ten traditional ovens fired with cattle and llama manure. About 60 men and women rent the ovens from their owners and bake variable quantities of bread. While some of this bread is sold in stores in town, most of it is either bartered for the manure that is brought by the Indians, who sell the bread in the communities, or is sold or bartered by the bakers themselves in the countryside, by peddler merchants who also sell alcohol or coca leaves, salt, and sugar.

Butchering is done by Indians and Cholos, who have some livestock in the grazing lands around town but who also buy or barter animals from the haciendas or the estancias. According to Rodríguez (1958), a cow or horse equals 10 sheep, and an alpaca or llama equals 3 sheep. Animals are butchered twice a week to be sold to agents from Cuzco; the meat is used to make *chalona* (dried meat), and alpaca meat is sold as mutton in Cuzco and Quillabamba. The entrails are sold to the Indians or given as payment and are used mainly in their fertility rites in the rural areas.

From October to the beginning of the rainy season, commercial activities are very profitable for store owners. Almost daily, a large number of Indians come into town bringing small bundles of wool which are sold partly in barter for alcohol, coca, or sugar, and partly for money. All this wool is shipped either to agents in Arequipa or to the weavers and pelters of Sicuani and Juliaca, who work for the tourist trade.

In most houses in town and in the communities, all people have chickens, guinea pigs, and pigs, which are sold when a need for ready cash arises. Almost all Indians and some Mestizos use manure for cooking. Manure is bartered or purchased from Indians in the communities and estancias, who come two or three times a week to town with their packs of llamas or donkeys and take the manure directly to the house of the purchasers; a large quantity is traded for bread with the bakers.

THE POLITICAL STRUCTURE

Authority and Control
in the Indian Community

Since the liquidation of the civil—religious hierarchy during the 1930s, the only community that has a formal authority organization is the Comunidad Indígena (ayllu) of Orcorara, which was legally incorporated in 1953. The other two, Sincata and Chiriuno, have no formal organization and are related to the national political system through the *teniente gobernador* (intermediary), who mainly carries out orders from the governor and the police and does not exert any kind of initiative. At the local level, whatever authority or control exists is exercised informally by elder or mature men and women, who may or may not be wealthy but who have sponsored in the past one or two of the more important fiestas of the community. Next to them, curers and ceremonial practitioners exert some measure of influence.

The Comunidad Indígena de Orcorara is a local *sui generis* organization that was established in 1953 as a consequence of the struggle between two political factions among the Mestizos in their attempts to control the municipality. As a survival of Colonial times and the encroachment of the haciendas, the town of Nuñoa still had a large extension of commons land surrounding the town. These lands were used for the support of local authorities, as communal grazing lands in times of horse and mule transportation, and were under the control of the municipality. It is claimed that the faction in power in 1953, allegedly with urbanization in mind, was selling the land for its profit. The opposed faction of Mestizos agitated and organized the Indians, provided them legal help, and were able to register the community under the protection of the Law of Indian Communities, which had been passed in 1922 to prevent the encroachment of haciendas on communities and to avoid litigation between communities (Escobar M., 1967; Dobyns, 1964). Since its inception, the officers of the community are a group of Indians who know how to read and write Spanish. By law, they consist of a president, a legal representative, a secretary, a treasurer, and a number of members at large.

The community is *sui generis* because, in a certain sense, it is neither Indian nor a community. Theoretically, all the adult members of the town of Nuñoa, both Indian and Mestizo, are considered members of the community by paying a fee of about $0.25 per year to support the officers, but in practice the fee is paid only by Indians and Cholos. For this fee, the Indians establish their right to receive about a third of 1 ha of agricultural land in the outskirts of town, which they cultivate for their subsistence. Furthermore, the community owns the stone quarry west of town and charges small fees for its exploitation. During the 1950s the members of the community were persuaded to "donate" the site of the cemetery, the race course, and the soccer field to the town.

The control that the Mestizos exert on the community makes it a potential mechanism for further political developments, both in terms of improvements of services and political factionalism and as a way to tap labor for local works in terms of "popular cooperation."

The Hacienda System

Subject to further documentation, it is said that all the violence that existed in Nuñoa until the 1920s was due to the violent way in which outside Mestizos dispossessed and bought out the Indians and then quarreled among themselves over grazing lands and boundaries. In the past, under the pretext of defense from alpaca and cattle rustlers, every landowner maintained armed bands imported from Arequipa. This disappeared with the increased control exerted by the state by means of the army and police. Litigation and intermarriage between members of landowning families has replaced violence. Labor legislation and public attention to Indian problems militates against increased oppression of the Indians, most of whom can leave freely if they wish to migrate.

Whatever political influence the landowners may have at the local level, it is exerted at a second level by participation in national politics and influential patronage to prevent the passing of legislation and taxation that may affect their estates. Whenever they participate in the life of the district, they are usually paid homage and entertained by the local Mestizos, and they are cajoled to compete among themselves in making donations for public works and services. Some of the members of their families who cannot run their estates anymore are seeking other avocations, such as mining and commerce, and they incorporate themselves in the Mestizo group in town in influential positions. Through the new Law of Agrarian Reform the hacienda system of Nuñoa will eventually be eliminated; the Mestizo estates will return to the Indians and will probably be administered in terms of what Wolf (1966) calls "administrative domains."

The National Political Organization

Since 1901, Nuñoa has been a district within the Peruvian system of administration. As such, it ranks hierarchically below the provincial and departmental authorities. In 1963 to 1969, like the rest of Peru, it was briefly granted municipal autonomy, but since the revolution of Velasco Alvarado it has returned to the traditional dependence upon higher authority, although the new government is attempting to motivate greater local participation. Whether their officials are elected or appointed, local political systems like Nuñoa still conform tenaciously to traditional standards of political participation (Escobar M., 1967).

The Governor. The governor is, in theory, the main political authority of the district and is appointed from the provincial capital. The extent of tenure varies very much with the whims of national politics; the appointment is usually secured by influential patronage or is forced on individuals without pay. The only obvious function of the governor, who is always a Mestizo, is that of representing the national government in the locality. Whatever authority the governor had in the past, at present his importance has been undermined by the police and justices of the peace. As such, he has a measure of influence in maintaining public order and judging small complaints before the cases reach the justices of the peace.

At present, as in the past, the governor still exerts some arbitrary power over the Indians, and solves many small problems more through influential patronage than by official means. He is helped in his job by the teniente gobernadores, usually Indians or Cholos forced to serve as messengers and delegates.

The Police.   The police force in Nuñoa is appointed from Police Headquarters in Puno. It is usually composed of an underlieutenant, a sergeant, a corporal, and three or four policemen, all of whom are outsiders. Their main function is that of maintaining order. They have a post that houses the men, an office, a yard, and a jail, where mostly Indians accused of petty crimes are kept. The policemen are always accused of arbitrariness and violence to the Indians, but they obviously have fulfilled their function of maintaining order and reducing the violence in the district. They have been able to suppress large bands of cattle rustlers and frequent murders among the Indians and Mestizos. They are respected and feared and, in general, they maintain good relations with the Mestizos.

The Justices of the Peace.   Because of its large population, Nuñoa has three justices of the peace, who are appointed from the court in the departmental capital from a roster of experienced local citizens, always Mestizos. The appointment goes to no more than six people, who alternate as local legal experts when they are not in office. Although the appointment is honorary, they get a small fee for each case that is transacted and usually receive presents from litigants. They hold office in their homes, and the manner of holding court varies from extreme informality to extreme formality and complicated paperwork.

Most of the cases they judge are the settlement of quarrels, petty robbery, and other torts, and small land transactions. In theory, they follow a body of regulations provided by Peruvian law; in practice, they probably follow a code of informal and unwritten law that still needs to be studied, and that reflects the different degrees of sophistication of the individual judges. The judges are always Mestizos and are both feared and respected for their legal abilities and influential connections with lawyers and judges in provincial towns and cities. There is some evidence to believe that they are appointed through the influence of landlords in national courts, because of the importance of land litigation in the Peruvian highlands. In their functions they are usually helped by young scribes, sometimes relatives, who eventually train themselves for the major job.

The Municipal Council.   The council is composed of seven members: the mayor, the lieutenant mayor, and five councilmen, who are either elected or appointed for variable times. Each of the councilmen holds an inspection to distribute the tasks of administration of various services. In Nuñoa, these services include provision of drinking water, electric lights, markets, and sanitation, and control of butchering, breadmaking, and public relations. All records of births, deaths, and marriages are kept by the secretary of the council, who is a paid employee. Two other people are hired for cleaning the town hall and sending messages, usually Indians or Cholos. A representative of the comunidad indígena is also considered an honorary member of the council.

Theoretically, the mayor and the councilmen should be available for business every weekday morning and should meet in council every week, but in practice they operate in an extremely informal way. Most of the town business is transacted in informal conversations on a street corner, or a bench in the plaza, or in secret meetings at the dead of night, at which other influential members of the community and friends are accepted. Sporadically, wealthy landowners deal directly with the mayor or councilmen. The revenue of the municipality is relatively small. Data from 1967 indicate that it receives from the Peruvian government about $1250 a year, and it is authorized to collect a tax on breadmaking and butchering which amounts to about $500 a year, making a total of $1750 annually. It is a small amount, but it is always a bone of contention for political comment and accusations of mismanagement between political factions. Although this is part of the traditional pattern, there are some grounds for believing that some funds do actually filter out to the pockets of the mayor and councilmen.

As of 1967, the members of the council in Nuñoa constituted a tight faction of the Mestizos, who effectively control the political and economic life of the district; and their political functions go beyond the administration of public services. They have organized themselves as a musical group that has made itself famous in the area for winning a contest in Puno in 1964 and has recorded a long-playing record of the native music of Nuñoa. They are members of the "Club Juventud Nuñoa," and vigorously play basketball, volleyball, and soccer in local and regional competitions; they represent most of the political factions of the country, and are present at practically every ceremonial event in the community.

Sociopolitical Processes
and Ideology

Tentatively, we can postulate that political participation in Nuñoa serves three purposes: provision of local services, public works, and social control. The last purpose seems to be the most important, but the game of politics is manifestly played in terms of the other two. Factionalism and conflict, real and potential, depend on the way in which these two aspects are managed.

Symbolically, public works and services at the rural level in Peru are part of a progressivistic ideological orientation (Escobar M., 1968), and as such they constitute the only platform that is used at the local level. Probably since the time Nuñoa became a district, most of its public works have been constructed by means of the influential patronage that the appointed or elected authorities could garner from deputies, senators, and landlords, or by means of popular action and public charities organized for the purpose. In such a way, many new things have been added to the town in the last 50 years: a race track, soccer field, new cemetery, newly built town hall, piping of drinking water, electric motor donated by the government, secondary coeducational school, and the promotion of the Sunday fair as a way to attract commerce to the town.

The execution of any project of services or public works for the town usually takes a long time, even when the labor and funds for the project are available. This delay is because organization of the project, technical knowledge, and compliance with government regulations are usually haphazard and incomplete; there is mistrust about the use of funds and lack of confidence in outside help. It appears that, in fact, funds are sometimes embezzled, as in the case of the construction of the new stone tower of the church. The lack of trust is evidenced in the fact that in almost all cases opposing factions of Mestizos always accuse each other of misappropriation of funds. These accusations are not only verbal, but also written, in pamphlets and newspapers, and usually degenerate into long-standing quarrels and feuds between individuals, their families, and their friends.

The maintenance of social control and public order in the political life of Nuñoa has as its main purpose the avoidance of open conflicts between factions and across the social strata, and the maintenance of the relative isolation of the district by preventing the interference of outside elements that could conflict with the interests of the Mestizos or the security of the Indians. For these reasons, while factionalism may be intense and passionate to the point of degenerating into open violence, an effort is made to maintain order in social life by a kind of generalized ritualism and ceremonial in social relations, which expresses itself in everyday behavior in terms of very courteous forms of address, florid language, and conversation that emphasizes the superficial exchange of news and gossip. In most cases, whatever hostility there is is manifested in sarcastic joking and anecdotes about important individuals who are chosen as scapegoats. When, during fiestas and drinking parties, some individuals quarrel to the point of physical violence, every attempt is made to ensure that these quarrels do not develop into lawsuits and long-lasting quarrels between families or factions, which, according to local legend, in the past used to lead to civil war which would attract the attention of the national government.

Public ceremonials, whether political, religious, educational, or social, provide opportunities for entertainment and leisure, but also opportunities for social display and an indication of forced forms of reciprocity; when such patterns are broken, the public order and the quality of interpersonal relations may be upset. These ceremonials should be studied further; from what has been observed so far, they also serve as indicators of the kinds of changes that have been happening in the community in the last ten years. One good example is seen in the sporting events that usually accompany political ceremonials: teams in competition usually represent groups striving for social recognition and training grounds for potential leaders and organizers who wish to stand out individually (Escobar M., 1969).

In terms of intervillage or interdistrict relationships, the ideological orientation of the Mestizos of Nuñoa is ethnocentric and isolationistic. The most common phrases that an outsider hears from Nuñoans in conversation are usually, "Nuñoa, república independiente" ("Nuñoa, independent republic") and "Nuñoeno mata-gente" (Nuñoans are people-killers") as a proud and adequate description of their characteristics. The first phrase refers to the fact that, allegedly, their "progress" has been due mostly to their own efforts, and the second to the fact that during the nineteenth century they gained control of the lands of the district and the Indian population through bloody internal strife and successfully prevented further encroachment of outsiders. At present, this ethnocentrism manifests itself at every opportunity in which Mestizos from Nuñoa participate in sporting, musical, or educational events outside their town, which usually lead to hurt feelings, accusations of foul play, and a sense of frustration.

RELIGION

Peasant Folk Religion

The study of Andean religion is still neglected, and our observations will be very brief. The Indians of Nuñoa, in their practices and beliefs, combine pre-Columbian and Christian elements that in some cases are sincretic, while in others there is symbiosis. Pre-Columbian elements permeate their cosmology, their fertility rituals in relation to cattle and agriculture, and some of their curing practices. Magic and curing combines both Spanish and Andean elements. Catholic fiestas and rituals are related to the life crisis of individuals and to the validation of social position and social integration. Fertility rituals and Catholic fiestas are geared to the cycle of life of plants and animals and to the Catholic calendar. Although they are sometimes performed almost simultaneously, in most cases the Indians performing fertility rituals avoid any contact with Mestizo observers and participators.

Indian cosmology provides the rationale for the fertility rituals and usually explains in supernatural terms many of the aspects of their environment and some of the aspects of man. Great mountain peaks, rivers, caves, and valleys possess anthropomorphic spirits and supernatural beings, both good and evil. Mountain peaks have powerful owners (*apus*); they and the land, the *Pacha mama*, are both propitiated in relation to agricultural fertility.

Animals have fertilizing spirits called *illas,* which incarnate themselves in animals that visit the flocks at the dead of night and fertilize them. Illas also are contained in stones and pebbles which are collected and interred with coca leaves and the hair of animals to "tie" the illas to the corrals. Many sicknesses, such as *susto* or *wayra,* are produced by evil spirits contained in caves, the wind, isolated places. The *nak'aqh* is a blond being, dressed in a brown or white habit, who hypnotizes solitary travelers and steals their grease to lubricate mining machines. People attacked by them die of consumption.

Native performers of ritual and curing can also perform evil magic and they are usually feared and respected. Some of them travel widely between Cuzco and Puno and are jealously protected from the Mestizos for fear that they may be persecuted by the police. Fertility rituals are called *alcansos* or "payments." They involve the burial of a bundle containing fetuses of alpacas, llamas, or pigs with coca leaves, food, and pieces of clothing, amid the repetition of incantations, dancing, and entering a trance.

Besides the celebration of fiestas, the Indians believe in Jesus Christ and the Cross, the Virgin Mary in her many representations, and many of the saints: Santiago, Saint Francis, San Juan, and others; they generally pray to them, petitioning help in cases of crisis, and the saints' images are displayed prominently in their homes.

The Role of the Church and Priest

The Catholic Church in Nuñoa is represented by the priest and cult and celebrations are made in the church in town and in a relatively large number of shrines in haciendas and communities. Probably because of their relative isolation, the church and priest in Nuñoa hold a measure of political functions that have been lost in less-isolated places. The priest appoints a manager of church property and an overseer as attendants for the church building from among the Indian population, usually forcing these individuals to take the job. Performance of religious offices by the priest implies not only payment of fees but also traditional presents of sheep, chickens, and pigs, which are always demanded forcefully. Indians and Mestizos who make religious vows are required to record them with the justice of the peace and are fined in case they are not able to honor them. For the fiesta of the Patron Saint in October, these vows are posted on the church door a month in advance. Because of his clerical and urban connections, the priest is usually influential in local politics, although he is sometimes viewed with hostility. A great deal of his influence rests in the fact that, whether by supernatural pressure or by earthly force, he can potentially gain the support of the peasant population. The priest attends the rural shrines only when he is contracted by sponsors for the celebration of local fiestas, usually charges very high fees, often arrives late, and probably eats and drinks voraciously.

Rituals and Celebrations. Catholic rituals of baptism, marriage, and funerals are contracted for individually with the priest and usually involve family celebrations that may last for days. In most cases, to avoid expenses, the haircutting, baptism, and marriage are made to coincide on the same day.

The celebration of saints and patron saints is the most important form of participation of the peasant population in the Catholic religion. Since the disappearance of the politicoreligious hierarchy in Nuñoa, the Indians of Nuñoa have adapted a system that is different both from the *cargo* system found in Cuzco and from the religious sodalities of the Mantaro Valley in central Peru (Escobar M., 1968). The *alferado,* as the system is called, is the sponsoring of local fiestas of saints that are organized by relatively wealthy Indians and Cholos who can afford to invest huge sums of money and who can secure the additional help of relatives and friends. Those Indians and Cholos who cannot afford alferados usually celebrate some of the minor and more generalized fiestas of the Catholic calendar, such as Christmas, carnivals, Santiago, and the Holy Cross, usually in the form of family celebrations. Independent of the alferado sponsors, young men at the age of eighteen, more or less, "promise" to dance for three years, organize a group of dancers of one of the more than eight different dances, and join the celebrations, generally traveling to many places inside and beyond the district. They are accompanied by their wives and other relatives and usually have to provide their own food and alcohol.

The celebration of the fiestas follows the general Andean pattern, with some local variations. Vespers are celebrated, there is a mass on the day of the fiesta attended by the sponsors, which is accompanied by a band, and firecrackers are exploded. During the procession, the wife of the sponsor wears a large number of skirts, she wears a rich Manila shawl, and money is pinned to her dress.

After the procession, the sponsor invites his guests to a banquet, at which are served guinea pigs, roast beef or pork, and other delicacies. Drinking, eating, and dancing continues until night, and people become noisy and aggressive. Dancers go around the town and visit the house of the sponsor frequently. For the next three or four days, and sometimes longer, banqueting, drinking, and dancing continue, and frequently there are outbursts of violence. Mestizo observers claim that many of the guests, under the influence of alcohol, indulge in sexual promiscuity. Although such reports may be true, we were not able to observe this kind of behavior at the celebrations we attended, and probably some of these reports are exaggerated.

Given the fact that external pressures for the celebration of fiestas have disappeared, we can only surmise that the celebration of fiestas is due to strong traditional cultural compulsives for validation of individual status, accumulation of prestige, and integration of the Indian society. Although sometimes sponsors become impoverished, they tend to exert strong personal influence in their communities.

Native Religious Movements

Almost unnoticed by the Mestizos, but strongly discouraged by the church, in many Indian communities in the Department of Puno, local religious movements start when Indians see visions of Jesus Christ, the Virgin, or the saints. In 1967, a "prophet" appeared in Sincata. His name was Jesus Manuel, and he claimed to have received his message from Jesus Christ and Saint Thomas Aquinas. He was dressed in rags, was probably a Mestizo, and spoke both Quechua and Spanish. After staying in Sincata for a number of days he moved on to other communities. Although such events are usually very localized, they sometimes lead to the formation of new cults and they generally happen in very depressed and isolated communities such as Sincata.

In Nuñoa, the cult of Santiago, although related to cattle herding, seems to spread in this fashion. A new celebration starts when an Indian sees the image of Santiago on a rock in the fields. The rock is taken to the church in Nuñoa or to one of the shrines in the countryside, an image of the saint is purchased, and masses and fiestas are celebrated in its honor.

CULTURAL AND SOCIAL CHANGE

Acculturation and Social Change

Since the time of the Spanish conquest in the sixteenth century, Andean society has been undergoing a series of cultural and social changes due to the increased contact of the area with the rest of the world. Because Nuñoa is in the altiplano and is thus relatively isolated, social and cultural changes, although profound in many respects, have not been as widespread as in other areas of the Andes. A large proportion of the native Indian population has continued living in the area, and the process of Mestizoization did not begin until late in the nineteenth century.

Our ethnohistorical summary and the analysis of the economic and political structure of Nuñoa show that many new cultural elements—such as iron tools; cattle, sheep, and horses; or the Catholic religion—have been introduced, but it has been mainly in the area of political and economic changes that Nuñoa has been affected. The changes in these spheres can really be viewed as a process of deculturation. In the economic sphere, the measure of well-being and fine ecological adaptation that has evolved up to Inca times was broken; the Indian population became gradually impoverished and is reduced today to the level of subsistence. In the political sphere, while most changes have been imposed by forceful and violent means, they have in general reflected the instability and the inconsistency of the Peruvian political system. By political means, the patterns of social organization and settlement have been changed frequently and reorganized arbitrarily, and the population still lives under the threat of violence. Social deculturation and the exploitative economy of the Mestizos have disjointed the corporative nature of the pre-Columbian society and have more or less created the present relative isolation of the area and reinforced the isolationistic tendencies of the population.

Because of these changes, the culture of Nuñoa is, in my opinion, a very fragile and delicate system of adaptation to the ecological and social conditions of the area, in which latent hostility and the threat of violence are ever present; any internal or external element that disturbs this balance is feared as threatening, and there is a strong tendency toward the maintenance of the status quo. However, although this tendency is predominant, the inhabitants of Nuñoa cannot prevent natural changes, such as the drought of 1956, nor can they stop the effects of changes happening in the social, economic, and political structure of the country, and in fact many changes are happening in Nuñoa.

These new changes, although they are relatively small, can best be described by the name of modernization, and can be dated back to the 1920s. By this time, intrusive Mestizos had gained control of the district and the hacienda system was in slow decline. Perhaps the first step in modernization was the extension of sanitary measures that prevented the spread of epidemics, led to the growth of population and outmigration, and finally to the establishment of fiscal schools in the town. The "Comunidad Indígena de Orcorara" was formed, and the Mestizos of Nuñoa, adopting the progressivistic ideology of the country, launched a series of projects to provide the town with more modern conveniences. These projects were carried out by means of the "popular action" of the Indians, by donations of the landlords, and with some help from the government. By means of popular action, they have constructed a new cemetery, a soccer field, and a race track; the bullring was constructed by donations from the Mestizos and landowners; drinking water was piped into town with contributions from the Mestizos and Indians and by the government; the equipment of a vocational school was purchased with money collected in benefit-performance dances (Rodríguez, 1958).

The construction of the road through Nuñoa was a government project completed around 1950. It has somewhat affected the economic and migration patterns and, together with the establishment of the Sunday fair, has increased the market participation of the Indian population. There are still more projects in the imagination of the Mestizos. While these activities are more or less traditional, they represent modernization in the sense that they spread urban patterns to previously entirely rural areas.

During the time that the American personnel of the biocultural research project were resident in Nuñoa, a note of novelty was introduced into the tone of the native population's everyday interaction and their relations with the Mestizos. The close interaction of the members of the project with Quechua-speaking informants and test subjects probably aroused somewhat the suspicions and anxieties of the Mestizos, especially with regard to the salaries being paid and the purchases of eggs, textiles, and other local items. Although the economic effect of the local expenses of the project might have affected the price system temporarily, it was probably neutralized in the long run by the opening up of the market system and the general rise of prices in the area due to other external circumstances.

Education, Sports, and Communication. These three aspects deserve special mention because they probably will have widespread effects on the total population and may accelerate the process of Mestizoization and social mobility. The creation of a secondary coeducational school in Nuñoa early in the 1960s has attracted to town a number of outside Mestizo teachers and is influencing the population of the district in a number of subtle ways. For one thing, regardless of what the students learn, most of them are adopting the patterns of the Mestizos. Some of the new Mestizo teachers openly advocate some of the radical ideologies of Cuzco and Arequipa and are mildly critical of the conservatism of the locals. They are also strongly influential in spreading the national ideology of the state as the main organizers of the secular celebrations of the National Day at the local level and as the main organizers of sporting events.

The playing and organization of sports and sporting events, at present, may have the very important functions of breaking local isolation and may affect in important ways the patterns of leadership and social participation. A district league has been organized by the local Mestizos and the teachers, and tournaments are celebrated every Sunday. Communities like Orcorara and Sincata, and haciendas like Kitampari, Chilíhua, and others, participate in them. Two or three times during the year, a team representing Nuñoa is invited to play in such towns as Ayaviri, Santa Rosa, Sicuani, and Marangani (Escobar M., 1969).

Prospects of Future Change

Two important changes, both sponsored by the state, loom in the near future of Nuñoa. The application of the Law of Agrarian Reform of 1969 will expropriate the large estates, will distribute the lands to the Indian population, and will eventually organize production cooperatives. The state will purchase and market the production of the cooperatives. SINAMOS, a government organization similar to the Peace Corps and to the Cooperación Popular of President Belaunde Terry, will "mobilize" the Indian population for higher participation and integration in the social, economic, and political life of the country. The consequences of these changes cannot be predicted at this time.

4

CHILD CARE, CHILD TRAINING, AND ENVIRONMENT

Thelma S. Baker

The high-altitude Quechua represent a "quite obviously successful and unusual example" of the adaptation of a human population to its environment (Baker, 1969). For survival the adaptive structures of a population must be particularly responsive to the critical period in human development of birth and early infancy, when the newborn organism responds to the stresses of the extrauterine environment. In Chapter 9 Haas discusses the biological components of this response. In this chapter I propose to describe the cultural mechanisms—the child-care and child-training practices—of the Nuñoa Quechua population and to discuss the function of these cultural practices in the adaptive response.

For a population to ensure survival, there must be provision for the continuing biological and cultural replacement of the adult population. Because of the long biological and social dependence of the human infant, child-care practices have developed in all cultures to meet the minimum requirement: the survival of an adequate number of maturing individuals to ensure population continuity. Immediate postnatal care, nutrition, thermo-regulation, excretory waste disposal, sensory stimulation, and socialization are the minimal components of most cultural child-care systems.

In populations with average morbidity and few constraints on fecundity the survival of a maximum number of children is not of critical importance to population replacement. However, in a population facing special environmental stresses, such as our study population, cultural systems that maximize survival may be a necessity. As described elsewhere in this volume (Chapters 7 and 8), reduced fecundity and high infant mortality are consequences of the particular environment of the Nuñoa population, and therefore survival of a large number of children is necessary for population continuity.

What are the child-care practices of this population that might reduce or restrain morbidity? The sources of high morbidity have been tentatively identified as the stress of hypoxia, low temperatures, and high aridity (Chapter 8). In addition, nutrition and disease stress do contribute to high infant mortality in peasant populations (Puffer and Serrano, 1973, p. 125). We will, in this study, first examine child-care practices that specifically might mediate the effects of lowered oxygen pressure, low temperatures, high aridity, nutritional insufficiency, and disease.

To ensure cultural continuity, children must be trained to accept the values and behavior patterns and acquire the skills that will help them grow into productive adult members of the society. Dutt (Chapter 6) shows that there is a high rate of emigration from the district, particularly among young adults: 3500 people had migrated in one 21-yr period studied, a potential stress on cultural replacement. In the second half of this study, therefore, we shall examine Nuñoa child-training practices that could support cultural continuity.

METHODOLOGICAL FRAMEWORKS

Most of the information on child care in technologically simple societies has been collected in one of three ways. The first, and the least frequent, provides descriptions of child-care and child-rearing practices in a culture. Such studies are best exemplified by Sister Inez Hilger's monographs on American Indian child life (Hilger, 1950). Although Sister Hilger says that the purpose of her studies was "to record the customs, beliefs and traditions of the primitive Indians of the United States as found in the development and training of the child" (1950, p. 1), no theoretical analysis was applied to the comprehensive descriptions published in her monographs. Data for these studies were collected through informants and interpreters.

In a second type of study, the most frequent, data are collected on child-care practices as part of the description of the life cycle in a culture, in the context of ethnological theory, the life-cycle information is usually collected from informants or by observation and is an important component of ethnographic studies. Bernard Mishkin, for example, in his ethnography of "The Contemporary Quechua" (1946), describes Quechua child-care practices as part of the general life cycle of the Quechua. The Human Relations Area Files in this context has a category called "Infant Care," which contains cross-cultural information derived from this kind of approach.

The third, and most recent approach, is the collection of these data in the context of a specific theoretical approach and with precise methodological guidelines (Whiting et al., 1966). The theoretical base is derived from the subdiscipline of psychological anthropology. The basic premise for Whiting et al. was that ecology and maintenance systems set the parameters for the chief agents of child care and socialization, and that the resultant child behavior sets the structure of child personality and later adult personality. However, the series of studies inaugurated under the aegis of the Whiting et al. hypothesis selected out of the paradigm only those areas which related child care and child training to personality. I know of only two cross-cultural analyses in the potentially productive aspect of the paradigm to the present study—the relationship of ecology and maintenance systems to the development of culturally idiosyncratic rearing practices. In one, Whiting (1964) explored among other variables the relationship of climate to family sleeping arrangements and found that these arrangements are used as a method of temperature control. The other study (Barry et al., 1959) explored the relation of child training to subsistence economy.

While Whiting et al.'s paradigm has merit, the present data on child care and child training were collected from a different theoretical base. In Chapter 1 P. T. Baker elaborated on the interrelationship of theory and data collection for the overall project, and this applies specifically to the data on infancy, early childhood, and adolescence in the Nuñoa population. The first studies, establishing descriptive norms of growth and development for children from age 5 to adulthood, were based on the assumption that physical growth and development were significant in successful adaptation to environmental variety and stress through genetic selection and developmental plasticity. When it was found that there seemed to be a distinctive pattern of growth in this population (see Chapter 10) the investigations were then expanded to investigate the growth of infants and young children, which had not previously been studied. Since evidence from other populations showed population differences not only in physical growth but also in motor development, this new area of study was added to our infant and early childhood investigations. The results of these investigations are reported in Chapter 9.

In the first study of growth and motor development, conducted in 1965, a mother-recall questionnaire was administered to the mothers of the 80 Nuñoa infants in the sample by a Quechua-speaking investigator, asking for information on child-care practices related to postnatal care, thermoregulation, nutrition, and disease. A modified form of the protocol was administered to mothers of infants studied by Haas in 1971. The reliability of mother-recall age-specific information in this peasant society is open to question. We therefore attempted to validate the recall information by observation of behavior during the study period and by observation of other members of the Nuñoa community. At the same time, other investigators in the Nuñoa project were collecting data on nutrition and thermoregulation, and in the course of these studies, specific information on children, both in response to these stresses and in child-care practices related to these stresses, were collected.

Data on the daily life and activity patterns and child-care practices of the Nuñoa population were derived from the ethnographic work of Escobar M. (Chapter 3), the Thomas analysis of energy flow (1973), and my own ethnographic observations during the period of the Nuñoa project. Additional ethnographic information on the socialization of the Quechua child and the daily life of the Quechua Indian were obtained from the reports by Mishkin (1946) and Bolton and Bolton (1972).

CHILD CARE

Thermoregulation and Child Care

It has been shown (Chapter 16) that infants and young children are biologically the most severely cold-stressed age group in the Nuñoa population. Cultural responses to reduce cold stress include the use of clothing and fire, and maximizing the use of solar radiation to raise body temperature. Hanna also discusses in Chapter 16 the insulative qualities of Indigenous clothing. The Nuñoa infant from birth is usually dressed in three layers of clothing. The first layer consists of a diaper of homespun material and an undershirt, both secured in place by a wide cinching belt. The second layer consists of a homespun dress for both females and males, and sometimes legging and socks or booties. The outer layer is usually one or more sweaters and a knitted hat. The number of garments may vary with the economic resources of the family. No seasonal variation in clothing was reported or observed. If the economic position of the family permits, there may be some variation in clothing for ceremonial occasions. Since we provided Polaroid photographs of families participating in the study, we would occasionally note female babies who were dressed in lighter-weight western-style dresses. The neonate and young infant up to about 3 months of age are additionally wrapped in a small rectangular blanket and then placed in a carrying cloth which is made of tightly woven material (3 m by 12 cm). One fold of the carrying cloth covers the child's head and face, and up until about 3 months of age no part of the child's body is exposed except during feeding, diaper changing, and bathing.

At home, during the day, the child is placed in the sunniest area adjacent to the house. Older siblings play in this area also. At mealtimes and when the infant is being nursed, the mother usually sits next to the fire with the child. When the mother or caretaker leaves home, the infant is carried on the back in the carrying cloth. Except for the very early months of life the infant sleeps separately from the parents, either alone or with other siblings on a bed made of sheep hides, somewhat thicker than those used by the rest of the family, and covered with layers of heavy blankets. The youngest children are placed closest to the fire.

Prior ethnographic reports had suggested that Quechua mothers bathed the child every day and then doused it with cold water "for protection against the rigors of the Andean temperature" (Mishkin, 1946, p. 488). All the mothers of the Nuñoa sample reported using only warm or tepid water for bathing infants and, further, that they bathed the children only when the ambient temperature was favorable and the child was well.

Nutrition and Child Care

Both Picon-Reátegui (Chapter 11) and Thomas (1973) suggest that this population is in caloric balance, despite the low values recorded for caloric intake. In the 1965 sample, we found only one example of nutritional deficiency disease among young children. The majority of mothers in our sample nursed their neonates and young infants on demand, for an average of about 8 min per feeding. The frequency of the feedings decreased with age. The signal for nursing was usually the crying of the infant. The breast was also offered as a pacifier since mothers were observed nursing their infants as many as two or three times during the course of a 1-hr examination period. When mothers were questioned as to when they first placed the neonate to the breast, the range of responses varied from a few hours after birth to 3 or 4 days after birth. When questioned about milk substitutes in the absence of mother's milk, a small percentage of mothers suggested powdered, canned, or cow's milk substitutes, tea, coffee, or broth. A large percentage of mothers indicated they did not know because their milk supply had always been adequate. The median reported age of weaning was about 18 months, with first-born children being weaned some months later. Observational verification of these data seemed to indicate that weaning took place some months later than the reported time, since many of our infants of 20 months and older were observed nursing. Hoff has reported that for one sample of postmenopausal mothers there was an average of 3 yr between children. Based on these figures, age of weaning is probably related to the occurrence of subsequent pregnancies. Mothers reported applying strong spices to the nipples and breasts to discourage suckling, and the consumption of highly spiced foods to reduce the milk supply. Solid foods were introduced to infants by dipping mothers' fingers into the food and feeding the baby. Soft foods such as pureed mashed potatoes were usually introduced first. Most babies were eating adult foods at about 13 months but dietary intake was supplemented with breast milk for some months thereafter. Aside from nursing, children were fed at family mealtimes but usually served last. There seemed to be limited knowledge about nutritional content of food except for the increased protein needs during lactation and infancy.

Disease, Sanitation, and Child Care

Although Nuñoa mothers were not sophisticated about nutrition, they had a large compendium of knowledge on herbs and curing, and offered specific herbal remedies for a variety of infant diseases. In addition, aspirin and "injections" (of antibiotics) were specifically mentioned as the cure for respiratory infections. Mothers reported that the most frequent infant complaints were tonsillitis and constipation. Nuñoa mothers reported that their children were rarely ill, which in view of the high infant mortality rate must reflect the fact that only the health status of surviving infants was being reported. Many mothers suggested that cause of illness was related to bathing the child, particularly washing the hair, in intemperate weather. Another important cause of illness and death was reported as "susto," or fright. This is a residual category and the symptomology has not been extensively investigated. Mazess (1968b) has reported that the hot—cold designations of food commonly found in Latin American countries were also found in Nuñoa. These concepts were related to concepts of illness as well as nutrition. Both foods and herbs were thermally categorized, but only herbs were seen to have curative effects.

There was a medical post in the town of Nuñoa, but we have no data on how much the facilities were used. Mestizo storekeepers sold injections of antibiotics in cases of severe illness, and several times the resident physician of the project was called upon to dispense medicine for infants with severe respiratory symptoms.

Toilet training was started on the average at about 16.9 months and completed at about 17.4 months, closely correlated with age of walking. Toilet training, as defined by the mothers, means voiding in the right place, since there are no indoor or outdoor toilet facilities available. Toilet training is facilitated by the fact that the children do not wear underpants and thus need little adult assistance in toilet training. Infants who have defecated are usually cleaned by wiping the perineal area with the diaper. Diapers are not changed with any regularity.

Discussion

In view of the lability of the thermoregulatory systems of infants and young children, child-care practices in Nuñoa seem to center on reducing cold stress to the infant and young child. Whiting (1964) reports that in a sample of 136 societies, a significant association between sleeping arrangements and ambient temperature was noted. In 67 percent of the societies where the temperature falls below 50°F, the sleeping arrangement was mother—father sleeping together and infant sleeping apart or with other siblings, as we found in our sample. Whiting suggests that this "is a more effective means of insuring an appropriate body temperature for the infant than taking him into the parental bed" (1964, p. 516). The microclimate of the infant is thus controlled in relation to his own thermoregulatory needs, or the needs of siblings similar in body-fat distribution and body size, rather than those of the parents. Placing children in the sun to absorb maximum solar radiation, or next to the fire, is another way of increasing body temperature.

The complete wrapping of the young infant in the carrying-cloth envelope has been reported for another society, the Zinacanteco Indians in the highlands of Chiapas Mexico (Braselton et al., 1969). The village studied in the Chiapas highlands is located at an altitude of 7000 ft and is also characterized by a very low level of humidity. As in the case of Nuñoa, this type of wrapping combined with infrequent diaper changing would seem to provide a warm, humid envelope which would protect simultaneously against the stresses of low temperature and high aridity. Various attempts were made to measure the temperature and humidity inside the infant's envelope, but we could not develop a measuring device which would record temperature and humidity under those conditions. However, numerous instances of diaper rash and heat rash were observed on the test-subject infants, suggesting that temperature and humidity were elevated in the infant's microenvironment. In addition, the clothing and bedding of young infants and children served to elevate body temperatures.

Demand feeding, which is characteristic of most nonliterate societies, seems to serve two functions: to stimulate, increase, and maintain the supply of maternal milk, and to ensure adequate nutrition for the young. Since maternal milk substitutes are available in industrialized societies, either breast feeding is not practiced or weaning takes place at an early age. In Nuñoa, where these substitutes are not available, infants were not weaned even after they were eating adult foods, thus ensuring adequate nutritional intake into early childhood. There are, however, no data showing nutritional content of maternal milk at high altitude. The prolonged period between births and the extended nursing period thus interact to reduce the nutritional deficiency disease found in similar nonliterate societies.

Our data, showing an absence of nutritional deficiency diseases, are corroborated by the evidence of a World Health Organization (1971) survey on protein–calorie malnutrition, which showed that children up to the age of 5 in the Puno district has the lowest incidence of malnutrition of any population surveyed by WHO in South America or Asia. Colostrum, the fluid secreted by the breasts immediately postpartum, is high in carotene, but the data show that most mothers do not nurse their infants until the colostrum is replaced by milk. This pattern would seem disfunctional in view of Picón-Reátegui's suggestion of a low dietary intake of vitamin A for this population (Chapter 11). However, he found no symptoms of vitamin A deficiency disease. Maternal milk, in addition, contains antibodies to some diseases, some of which confer immunity on nursing infants. Also, maternal milk does not have the contaminants usually found when milk substitutes are used in nonliterate societies (Wade, 1974). This finding might partially explain the low incidence of gastrointestinal infections in the morbidity pattern of our population, as compared to the high incidence in other nonliterate populations (see Chapter 8).

Except for serious childhood diseases, most Nuñoa mothers felt that they had adequate knowledge of herbal medicine to deal with the common infectious diseases of infancy and childhood. When modern medicine was available and inexpensive or free they availed themselves of the opportunity to use it. Data from urban Quechua populations (Haas, 1973a) indicated that when modern medical facilities in other areas were available, Quechua Indian mothers modified the Indigenous patterns of disease treatment. Thus 79 percent of urban Quechua babies under 6 months and 66 percent of those over 6 months had been vaccinated against smallpox.

There seemed to be no practices which stressed the principles of modern sanitation in relation to drinking water or excretory waste disposal. It has been suggested, however, that the vectors for gastrointestinal infections related to these conditions are inhibited by the high-altitude environment.

To summarize, we may suggest that the Indigenous child-care practices which have evolved through a long cultural history in this area tend to reduce cold and aridity stress and nutritional stress. When new disease vectors are introduced into the area, contagious diseases for example, the child-care practices are flexible enough to incorporate other forms of non-Indigenous curing to reduce morbidity and mortality.

CHILD TRAINING

The primary agents of early child training are a function of the residence patterns of the family. In our sample we have two residence patterns: (1) the semi-isolated nuclear family living in neolocal habitations dispersed throughout the district; and (2) families living in native settlements such as Sincata or in Indigenous sections of the town of Nuñoa. For the first type of residence pattern, the primary agents are the members of the nuclear family, which include both parents and other siblings. Any other resident members of the household, such as aged parents, may also take responsibility for the socialization. In the settlements, although the nuclear family is primarily responsible for early socialization, other members of the extended family who live in the community as well as other community members may also serve to enculturate older children. If children from outlying settlements are sent into Nuñoa to work or to attend school, the *compadre* or *commadre* also assumes this function. In addition, for those children who attend school the teacher also fulfills this role. However, in all families the mother assumes the primary responsibility during infancy since during most seasons she is the person most frequently at home. Young siblings soon take on the role of caretaker of younger siblings and they also have a role of primary importance during infancy. The function of all the agents is to pass on their skills, as well as values and altitudes, to the children.

Informal Training

The child-training practices we are concerned with in this study are those related to training the child for two kinds of activity patterns, household maintenance and energy production. Table 4.1 shows the distribution of these tasks according to the age and sex of individuals who perform them. As can be seen from the age distribution, children of less than 5 years are allocated very few tasks in household maintenance and only occasionally perform tasks that require a minimum of skill and physical ability. From 5 yr of age on children participate in most of the household tasks. Tasks that require little training and skill in herding, such as pasturing, are usually performed by children 5 yr of age and older, either singly or in groups. The more highly skilled tasks and those closely related to the economic well-being of the family, such as curing, lambing, and slaughtering, are usually an adult

TABLE 4.1 *Age and Sex Distribution of Task Performance in Nuñoa, Peru*

Task	< 5 yr		5–12 yr		Adult	
	M	F	M	F	M	F
Household maintenance						
Child care and child training	R[a]	R	O	F	O	F
Food, water, fuel procurement	R	R	F	F	F	F
Fire making			F	F	F	F
Cooking and serving meals			R	O	O	F
Making and caring for clothes			O	F	O	F
Herding[b]						
Pasturing			F	F	F	F
Curing			R	R	F	F
Lambing			R	R	F	F
Slaughter			R	R	F	F
Storage			O	O	F	F
Agriculture[b]						
Field preparation			O	O	F	F
Planting			R	R	F	F
Weeding			O	O	F	F
Harvesting			O	O	F	F
Storage			O	O	F	O

[a]R, rarely; O, occasionally; F, frequently; no designation indicates that task is never performed by that age–sex group.

[b]After Thomas (1973).

task. All members of the family older than 5 participate in the agricultural tasks. The tasks that require a high level of energy expenditure and endurance are usually performed by adults, but all the agricultural tasks have some portions that are less arduous than others and are performed by children, such as removing stones from the field and carrying light loads. Infants and young children are usually carried to the field during peak work activities.

Division of labor according to sex is rarely observed in this population, as is evident from Table 4.1. Adults of both sexes perform all the tasks listed, except that of nursing children, which is sex-specific, Thomas suggests that there are some additional tasks which are sex-specific. Weaving on the ground loom is usually done by women, and men usually use the Spanish loom. The more strenuous tasks in field preparation are also usually done by males. Intrapopulation variability in the assignment of these tasks to specific members of a family is usually a function of family size and composition and the annual agricultural and herding cycle of activities. Thus in a small family with few children, all members of the family will participate in all the activities. In a family with a large number of children, household tasks will increasingly be taken over by women and girls and herding and agricultural tasks by men and boys unless the demands of planting, plowing, threshing, shearing, or harvesting require an extensive labor force for a prolonged period of time, in which case all members of the family participate in all the tasks.

Thus, after infancy, the child is differentiated from the rest of the family only in terms of relative capacity and participates in family activity according to his/her stage of physical and cognitive development. The child is not prohibited from participating in any of the events of family life.

Child training in Nuñoa, as in all peasant societies, is accomplished not by formal methods of instruction by specially designated agents but by observational learning on the part of the children (Scribner and Cole, 1973). This learning occurs in the course of all the mundane activities of daily family life in which the young take part. Since very little technological change has been introduced into the culture, the parents and older sibs are competent behavioral models for the child. Fortes (1938) has suggested that this type of informal or observational learning is accomplished by imitation, identification, and cooperation. Daily occasions for acquiring, developing, and practicing skills are also part of the training. The primary mode of learning is not through language as in formal education but by demonstration, and in the context of actual situations with very few verbal instructions or generalizations. To illustrate, I observed the behavior of a Nuñoa woman and her two daughters, aged 5 and 12, weaving on a ground loom. A small orange and white rug, 3 m by 1 m, was being woven. The tasks included carding, spinning the wool (on a spindle whorl), rolling the yarn into balls, dying the wool, designing the pattern, and weaving.

The weaving was done by the mother for 3 or 4 hr each afternoon for about a 3-week period. During this period neither of the children asked any questions about the weaving process other than establishing for whom the rug was being woven. When the rare verbal instructions were given, they were associated with fetching and carrying items associated with the weaving or food for the mother. The 5-yr-old performed the very simple tasks of bringing or retrieving the yarn balls and bringing snacks from the kitchen, close by. The child sat for the most part either by her mother or older sister's side, watching the weaving or playing with nearby farmyard animals. The 12-yr-old, on the other hand, helped to spin the wool into yarn, checked independently on the boiling dye solutions, anticipated some of her mother's needs for different-colored yarns, but did not actually work on the loom. The remainder of the time she sat by the loom watching her mother or caring for the 5-yr-old.

Formal Education

Formal schooling is mandatory in Peru between the ages of 7 and 16. However, because of lack of supervising personnel and the lack of schools, these laws are not enforced rigidly in the highlands. Thus participation in the national education system of Peru is to a great degree voluntary in the isolated highland areas. There are three school locations in the district. There is a primary school that was established by a hacendado for the Indian children living on his hacienda. In the 1960s a primary school was established in the Indigenous community of Sincata at the request of the local population. Since the 1920s the town of Nuñoa has had a primary school, and more recently (in the 1960s) a secondary coeducational school was established. Descriptions of formal education are based on the Nuñoa primary school.

The major agents of socialization in these schools are Mestizo teachers who are imported into the district. Although there is a formal school day, hours of instruction are irregular and frequently interrupted. The curriculum, organization, and administration of the Peruvian school system of which the Nuñoa school is a representative have been extensively studied and described by many authors (Baum, 1967; Paulston, 1971; Epstein, 1971). They agree that the primary national goal is to effect social change by teaching the Indian the skills and behavior necessary to participate in an urbanizing national political—economic system or by improving his economic skills and rendering him less dependent on Mestizos in his own community. The method of instruction is formal and didactic, and the language of instruction is Spanish. The curriculum focuses mainly on courses in reading and writing, arithmetic, Peruvian history and geography, deportment, and religion (taught by the local priest). Extracurricular activities center on an extensive sports program. Parents participate in an organization roughly similar to parent—teachers associations in the United States, whose chief function is to raise money for the repair and maintenance of the school.

An estimated school population derived from the 1961 census (M.H.C., 1965) shows a total of 580 persons attending school, with approximately 70 percent of the enrollment in the first grade. Also, only 30 percent of the school population was between the ages of 6 and 14. Indian children normally start school at a much later age than Mestizo children and rarely complete the 5 yr of primary school.

Discussion

Clearly, two patterns of socialization or child training coexist in the community. The informal pattern successfully trains Quechua children to take their place in the economic and cultural matrix of the traditional Indigenous community. On the other hand, the formal system of socialization is specifically directed toward another and totally different cultural pattern, that of integration into the national culture. All current analyses of these two systems are based on the assumption that the goals of Indigenous socialization and formal education are mutually antagonistic. One analyst suggests that the formal schooling system has one or more of the following effects: (1) "reinforcement of the defensive cultural adaptive pattern of the Indian or his community; (2) a negative or biased outlook toward school . . . and/or (3) acceptance of Mestizo culture and gradual rejection of all things Indian" (Paulston, 1971). Epstein conducted a study in Puno in 1966 to investigate the results of the schooling on the attitudes of the Indian population in the altiplano. He studied fifth-grade students at 19 government schools in the Puno district. The schools were located in towns having 5000 or more inhabitants, villages (population between 1000 and 5000), and parcialidades (1000 inhabitants or less). The students were asked to respond to questions on attitudes toward acculturation, preferred residence, and national or Indigenous identification. Epstein found that students who came from the parcialidades had the most positive identification with Mestizo culture and were most likely to identify with the national culture. The general trend of the results may be seen to confirm the hypothesis that schooling is antagonistic to the maintenance of the Indian way of life and that schools have been successful in changing the values and attitudes of Peruvian Indigenous children. Other studies have shown that the schools were not successful in teaching the skills necessary to improve Indigenous economic conditions in the home communities (Baum, 1967; Paulston, 1971).

Baum has also suggested that in the altiplano increased education leads to increased emigration (Dutt has calculated an annual migration rate for the total Nuñoa sample of 2.5 percent). Although there is a high level of emigration in Nuñoa, we have no data from Nuñoa that will support this hypothesis.

It has been assumed by those national regimes who concerned themselves with the economic condition of the highland Indian that education could be a resource for ameliorating economic conditions in Indigenous communities in the highlands. However, research on other communities has shown that the better educated the Indian is, the more willing he is to acculturate and leave his traditional way of life, and thus the net effect of education is to reinforce rather than change the traditional Indigenous pattern.

We might speculate that another way to view this process and the function of the two systems in this area is to view education, either formal or informal, as a cultural adaptation to the biocultural energetic needs of the community. Thomas (1973) has shown that in the Nuñoa community by the age of 6 yr the child becomes an energetic asset and thus produces more than he consumes. This remains true for the period from 6 to 18 yr of age. Our data show that very few Indian children enter school until much later. After the age of 18 the energetic cost of the adult increases, but so does the productive efficiency of the family. However, as Thomas has demonstrated, the carrying capacity of the Nuñoa system is severely limited and the largest drain on the population's energy-flow balance is that of young adult males who do not have their own landholdings. It is postulated therefore that this excess of young adult males approaching 18 or 19 years of age who are sent to school may be preparing themselves either for permanent or temporary migration to urban centers, thus decreasing the stress on the carrying capacity of the Nuñoa system.

Thus the traditional informal socialization process is adequate to maintain the population necessary for cultural continuity, and the formal system can serve as a mechanism for socializing—into the larger society—one segment of the population that could be a stress on community continuity.

5

GENETIC HISTORY
AND AFFINITIES

Ralph M. Garruto and Charles J. Hoff

The Quechua-speaking natives of South America at present form the largest single linguistic population native to the New World. Aggregates of Quechua speakers are distributed over an area that corresponds roughly to the Andean portions of the ancient Inca Empire (*Tawantinsuyu*) at its zenith of military expansion. This area covers all of modern Peru, the Andean areas of much of Ecuador and Bolivia, and the northern Andean sections of Argentina and Chile. Although these various populations share a common language and a large number of cultural traits, it has not been established that the Quechua (particularly those groups widely separated geographically) can be considered a single "racial" group.

According to population genetics theory, it cannot be presumed prima facie that two or more human groups derived from a common ancestral breeding population, speaking the same language and culturally similar, possess similar gene pools. If there has been even partial isolation and the habitats of the populations are dissimilar, there is the possibility that significant genetic differentiation at some loci may occur due to differential selective pressures, gene flow from other gene pools, selective migration, and stochastic processes, that is, sampling error in migrants and genetic drift in subpopulations (Wright, 1931, 1948).

Since there are few genetic data, with the exception of blood-group gene frequencies, for modern Quechua populations, a survey was undertaken, during the course of the IBP/HA Andean study, of the genetic characteristics of the focal population Nuñoa, and several other Quechua populations in southern Peru. The survey was done to establish the genetic affinities of control populations living in different portions of the altiplano and at lower altitudes.

ETHNOHISTORICAL AND CULTURAL
PERSPECTIVE

There are a number of hypotheses concerning the peopling of the South American continent (Cruxent, 1968), but most anthropologists contend that

98

it resulted from a series of southward movements of populations descended from migrants who had crossed the Bering Straits thousands of years before. It might have occurred between 40,000 and 100,000 years ago, since there is evidence of big-game hunting in the Peruvian altiplano by 22,000 B.P. (MacNeish, 1971). Whether these hunters represented populations native to the altiplano or coastal groups practicing seasonal transhumance is difficult to determine. However, there is ample evidence of cultural contact between the Peruvian altiplano and coast from 10,000 to about 2000 B.P. (Engel, 1960, 1971; Lathrop, 1969). By the end of this period more efficient exploitation of the two ecological zones through the development of agriculture and harvesting of seafoods on the coast caused the establishment of more sedentary groups (Lanning, 1967; Price, 1971), which might have led to a reduction in genetic contact between the two populations.

By the time of the major expansion of the Inca Empire, contacts with the coast and other parts of the altiplano were reestablished through conquest. Since the Incas would customarily transfer segments of conquered populations to other parts of the Empire (similar ecological zones), greater cultural and genetic contacts are likely to have resulted (Monge and Monge, 1966). Another important factor that might have affected the genetic relationships of high- and low-altitude populations is the vertical control of diverse ecological zones by the Quechua and Aymara populations inhabiting the Lake Titicaca area (Murra, 1970). There is evidence that many of these communities had extensive lands in the eastern Andean mountains and western Andean foothills where various crops were grown, thus possibly fostering further gene flow between high- and low-altitude populations.

After the conquest the Spanish forced many of the scattered rural populations to move to areas where they could be utilized for labor purposes (*reducciones*) (Bennett, 1946; Steward and Faron, 1959). At least initially this move might have augmented the hybridization of populations previously isolated. However, one possible result of this and other colonial Spanish policies was the disruption of the native culture and a decline in the size of the Andean population (Kubler, 1946; Smith, 1970). Since the nineteenth century the native Andean population has increased in Peru and Bolivia, and commensurate with this growth it has begun to take an increasing part in the highland market economy (Kubler, 1946). Furthermore, modern means of transportation have been made available, leading to greater communication and movements between traditional communities and large urban centers. As a result, gene flow is probably now occurring between communities that formerly were relatively isolated.

GENERAL RESEARCH DESIGN

In order to broaden the genetic perspective on the Nuñoa Quechua population, comparative data on Nuñoa Mestizos and the Quechua populations of Macusani, Acllamayo, Ollachea, San Juan del Oro, and Mollendo, situated at different altitude gradients from sea level to 4400 meters in the southern Peruvian Andes, were also included in the general research design (Table 5.1; see also Fig. 1.5). A detailed description of the Nuñoa population, including area ecology, culture, and biology and general methodological considerations, has been presented in other sections of this volume, while descriptions of the remaining populations have been presented in a number of recent publications (Garruto, 1973; Garruto et al., 1975; Hoff, 1972b; Plato et al., 1974a).

To assess the genetic affinities of Nuñoa and the surrounding Quechua populations, several gene-marker systems were examined in accordance with the suggestions and guidelines of the World Health Organization and the International Biological Program (Weiner and Lourie, 1969; WHO, 1968). These examinations included an extensive analysis of digital and palmar dermatoglyphic patterns, ABO and Rh blood groups, PTC-tasting ability, lingual rotation, and digital interlocking frequencies. The results will be interpreted in the light of pertinent demographic information and broad ethnohistorical data, together with the implications for microevolution in Nuñoa and other southern Peruvian Quechua populations.

Dermatoglyphic Patterns

Digital and palmar prints were collected from 362 male Quechua Indians of five populations resident in varying ecozones, representing the altiplano, tierra templada, and ceja de la montaña. Fingerprint patterns, main-line terminations, palmar patterns, accessory triradii, and width of the atd angle were analyzed as well as the simian and sydney palmar creases. The reading and reporting of the prints were based mainly on the established notations of Cummins and Midlo (1943), while the C-line classifications, R/U ratio, and interdigital pattern types followed the format established by Plato and

TABLE 5.1 *Ecological Summary of the Study Populations*

	Mean altitude		Population		
Community	Meters	Feet	(1961 census)	Ecological zone	Area economy
Macusani	4,400	14,400	1,601	Altiplano	Pastoralism
Nuñoa	4,000	13,100	2,157	Altiplano	Horticulture/pastoralism
Ollachea	2,680	8,800	903	Tierra templada	Horticulture
San Juan del Oro	1,340	4,400	1,767	Ceja de la montaña	Subtropical agriculture
Mollendo	Sea level		12,483	Coastal	Irrigation agriculture

coworkers (Plato, 1970; Plato et al., 1972; Plato and Wertelecki, 1972). The detailed comparisons between the five Quechua populations were reported in an earlier paper (Plato et al., 1974a), and thus only a summary of the results is presented here. Comparisons are also made with the only other complete study of dermatoglyphic patterns on Quechua Indians, that of Newman (1974) on 230 Vicos Quechua males from the central Peruvian Andes. It should be noted that all the comparisons reported are based on the analysis of the right hands only: left-hand prints, with the exception of Nuñoa, were not collected because of time and personnel limitations.

Initial comparisons of digital and palmar dermatoglyphic patterns indicated no significant differences among the Macusani, Acllamayo, Ollachea, and San Juan del Oro populations (Plato et al., 1974a). Consistently significant differences, however, were found between the Nuñoa Quechua and most of the other Quechua groups in palmar patterns, although not in digital pattern frequencies. In view of these initial findings the populations of Macusani, Acllamayo, Ollachea, and San Juan del Oro were combined to form the Quechua "pooled" sample.

Digital pattern frequencies for the Quechua pooled, Nuñoa Quechua, and Vicos Quechua groups are summarized in Table 5.2 and Fig. 5.1. No significant differences between the three groups were noted. The fingerprint frequencies are in close agreement with the other published data on South American Indians, with about 50–60 percent loops and 3–8 percent arches. The pattern intensity indexes (PII) of all three groups (right hands only) are well within the reported range of 4.9–7.8 for South American Indians. It should be noted, however, that the degree of variability in digital pattern frequencies among South American Indian groups is very high, a trend not observed in North or Central American Indians or among Europeans, Australians, or Asiatics (Coope and Roberts, 1971; Plato, 1974; Plato et al., 1974b).

In Table 5.3 and Fig. 5.2 the palmar main-line terminations have been summarized and expressed as modal types of the D and C lines, the main-line index, and the 11/7 and R/U ratios. The D-line modal types and the main-line indices indicated a moderate degree of transversality of the palmar ridges, with approximately 50–60 percent of the terminations type 9 and 14–20 percent type 7. The C line is absent in over 15 percent of the Quechua, a percentage that is quite high but consistent with most American Indian populations (Plato et al., 1974b). Overall, the frequency of the C-line modal types among the Nuñoa Quechua was significantly different from that of the Quechua pooled and Vicos Quechua groups. The Nuñoa Quechua demonstrated unusually high frequencies of ulnar types and consequently a very low R/U ratio. These values fall outside or on the fringe of the distributional range for other American Indians and appear closer to the distribution for Orientals and Pacific Islanders (Plato, 1974; Plato et al., 1974b).

Frequencies of the hypothenar and interdigital palmar patterns, accessory triradii, and palmar creases are presented in Table 5.4 and Fig. 5.2. Significant

TABLE 5.2 *Distribution of Digital Patterns and Pattern Intensity Index (PII) in Peruvian Quechua Populations, Right Hands Only (%)*

Population	N	Digit	Whorls	All loops	Ulnar loops	Radial loops	Arches	PII[a]
					Digital patterns			
Quechua pooled	251	All	44.2	51.9	47.3	4.6	3.8	7.0
Nuñoa Quechua	106	All	44.0	52.3	47.0	5.3	3.8	7.0
Vicos Quechua[b]	230	All	37.3	57.3	53.5	3.9	5.3	6.6

[a] Average number of triradii per hand.
[b] From Newman (1974).

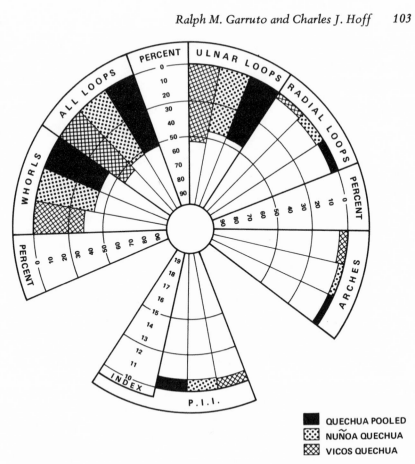

QUECHUA POOLED
NUÑOA QUECHUA
VICOS QUECHUA

FIGURE 5.1 *Cyclogram summarizing the digital dermatoglyphic pattern frequencies of Quechua Indian populations.*

differences were noted when the Nuñoa Quechua were compared with the Quechua pooled and Vicos Quechua groups, in both the thenar/I and IV interdigital pattern areas. The thenar/I pattern frequency for the Nuñoa Quechua (right hands) was quite low when compared with that for other Amerindian populations, and the overall frequency mean for both hands, 10.8 percent (5.9 percent for the right and 15.9 percent for the left), falls within the range of the Caucasian distributions of 9–15 percent (Plato, 1974; Plato et al., 1974a). In the IV interdigital area the differences stem from the higher frequency of loops found among the Nuñoa Quechua, although there appear to be no differences in regard to the specific type of loops present (Plato et al., 1974a). The frequency of palmar patterns in the III interdigital area showed the Quechua pooled sample to have a significantly higher frequency of pattern types than either the Nuñoa or Vicos Quechua. Yet frequencies for all three groups fall near or beyond the upper range of South

TABLE 5.3 *Comparisons of Modal Types of Lines D and C, Main-Line Indices, and R/U Ratios in Peruvian Quechua Populations, Right Hands Only*

Population	N	Modal type of line D					Modal type of line C				
		7	9	11	11/7 ratio	Main-line index	Ulnar	Radial	Proximal	Absent	R/U ratio
Quechua pooled	255	13.7	49.0	37.3	2.7	7.8	43.9	25.5	11.0	19.6	0.6
Nuñoa Quechua	106	20.6	58.9	20.6	1.0	7.6	61.7	13.1	8.4	16.8	0.2
Vicos Quechua[a]	230	17.6	52.9	29.5	1.7	8.2	49.1	24.3	4.0	22.5	0.5

[a]From Newman (1974).

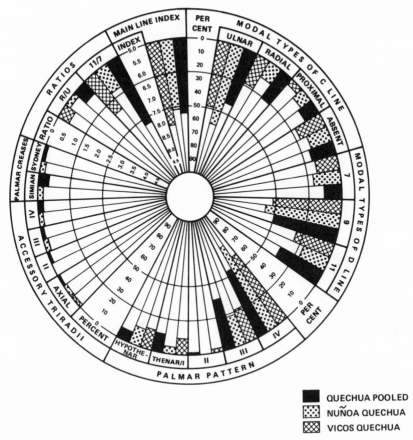

QUECHUA POOLED
NUÑOA QUECHUA
VICOS QUECHUA

FIGURE 5.2 *Cyclogram summarizing the palmar dermatoglyphic pattern frequencies of Quechua Indian populations.*

American Indian populations as described in a current review (Plato et al., 1974b). This discrepancy probably results from the fact that only right-hand frequencies are given; generally the frequencies of the III interdigital patterns are anywhere from two to five times as high for right hands than for left hands. Finally, all groups showed low frequencies of accessory triradii in the axial as well as the interdigital areas, and while the simian and sydney line frequencies were not available for the Vicos Quechua, the Nuñoa Quechua and Quechua pooled samples demonstrated no significant differences.

In summary, we note that no significant differences were found in digital pattern frequencies between the three groups, while in palmar pattern frequencies the Nuñoa Quechua appeared to be quite different from the Quechua pooled and Vicos Quechua groups, especially in regard to the modal types of the C line and the frequency of patterns in the thenar/I and IV

TABLE 5.4 *Distribution of Palmar Patterns and Accessary Triradii in the Palmar Configurational Areas and Palmar Creases in Peruvian Quechua Populations, Right Hands Only (%)*

Population	N	Palmar pattern					Accessary triradius				Palmar creases (complete only)[a]	
		Hypothenar	Thenar/I	II	III	IV	Axial	II	III	IV	Simian	Sydney
Quechua pooled	255	8.2	14.1	0.4	38.0	55.3	0.4	0.4	1.2	2.4	6.4	0.9
Nuñoa Quechua	106	14.0	5.6	0.0	24.3	73.8	0.9	0.0	1.9	1.9	2.7	2.7
Vicos Quechua[b]	230	14.3	13.7	1.3	26.0	61.9	0.8					

[a]For Quechua pooled, N was 235; for Nuñoa Quechua, N was 110.
[b]From Newman (1974).

interdigital areas. All groups, however, demonstrate enough similarity to be included in a single Mendelian population.

Phenotypic Variation
in Other Gene-Marker Systems

To further investigate the genetic affinities of the southern Peruvian Quechua populations in general, and Nuñoa in particular, we examined 493 Quechua males and 33 Mestizos for phenotypic variation in a number of other marker systems, most of which have a strong and well-known genetic base. Blood typing for ABO and Rh blood groups was carried out in the field by means of the slide coagulation method. The blood-group genetic studies were severely limited because of the difficulty in obtaining venipunctures and thus adequate amounts of blood for typing. Phenylthiocarbamide (PTC) tasting ability was determined with sensitized paper, indicating only the gross categories of tasters and nontasters, while lingual rotation and digital interlocking markers were collected according to standard techniques. The usefulness of these traits lies in the fact that they are genetic polymorphisms which are expressed independent of environmental factors (such as altitude), and their mode of inheritance, with the exception of digital interlocking, is generally well established (Cavalli-Sforza and Bodmer, 1971; Sturtevant, 1940). Furthermore, they have been recommended for collection on non-Western populations by the World Health Organization and the International Biological Program (Weiner and Lourie, 1969; WHO, 1968).

Two samples, in addition to those found in the dermatoglyphics section—from one highland Mestizo and one coastal Quechua—were added to further broaden the genetic perspective. The phenotypic distributions of all traits for the one Mestizo and five Quechua groups are summarized in Table 5.5 (Garruto, 1973; Garruto et al., 1975). In the ABO system, phenotypic frequencies were found to be very similar between the five Quechua groups but quite different for the Nuñoa Mestizos. The highest frequency of blood type O was found among the Indians, with an average of over 90 percent, followed by A and B with total frequencies of less than 10 percent. No type AB individuals were detected. The Mestizos had equal O and B frequencies at 32.4 percent each, followed by A and AB with frequencies of 26.5 and 8.8 percent, respectively. The Mestizo distribution, however, might have been affected by the smallness of the sample. In the Indian groups, 99–100 percent of the individuals were Rh positive. The Mestizos had a similar frequency, with 97.1 percent Rh positives.

The frequency of PTC tasters among the Indians was above 95 percent; the Mestizos had a slightly lower frequency, 90.9 percent. With respect to lingual rotation, ability to roll the tongue is the highest among the San Juan del Oro Indians and lowest among the Nuñoa Indians; the latter was the only case where nonrollers predominate, with a frequency of 53.7 percent. The

TABLE 5.5 *Summary of Discrete Phenotypic Variation in Quechua Indians and Mestizos (Frequency Distribution)*

Variable	Macusani Quechua (4400 m)		Nuñoa Quechua (4000 m)		Ollachea Quechua (2680 m)		San Juan Quechua (1340 m)		Mollendo Quechua (sea level)		Nuñoa Mestizos (4000 m)	
	N	%	N	%	N	%	N	%	N	%	N	%
ABO Blood-Group System												
A	11	9.3	16	9.7	4	6.9	5	5.0	2	3.8	9	26.5
B	3	2.5	5	3.0	0	0.0	1	1.0	0	0.0	11	32.4
O	104	88.1	144	87.3	54	93.1	94	94.1	50	96.2	11	32.4
AB	0	0.0	0	0.0	0	0.0	0	0.0	0	0.0	3	8.8
Rh Blood-Group System												
Positive	118	100.0	164	99.4	58	100.0	100	100.0	52	100.0	33	97.1
Negative	0	0.0	1	0.6	0	0.0	0	0.0	0	0.0	1	2.9
PTC												
Taster	110	95.7	166	96.5	58	100.0	88	98.9	55	100.0	30	90.9
Nontaster	5	4.3	6	3.5	0	0.0	1	1.1	0	0.0	3	9.1
Lingual Rotation												
Roller	60	52.2	81	46.3	33	55.0	54	60.0	30	55.6	22	66.7
Nonroller	55	47.8	94	53.7	27	45.0	36	40.0	24	44.4	11	33.3
Digital Interlocking												
Right/left	64	55.7	96	55.2	35	58.3	52	57.8	29	53.7	13	39.2
Left/right	51	44.3	78	44.8	25	41.7	38	42.2	25	46.3	20	60.6

range of frequency distributions among rollers in the Indian groups was between 46.3 and 60.0 percent, while Nuñoa Mestizos had the highest frequency of rollers at 66.7 percent.

Finally, frequency distributions for digital interlocking patterns, where a person clasps his hands in either of two ways (right-hand digits over left, or vice versa) indicated that in the Quechua groups the frequency of right-hand digits over left predominated with a frequency range between 53.7 and 58.3 percent. The Mestizos, however, had the lowest frequency, 39.4 percent.

Overall, the results of discrete phenotypic variation based on these five gene markers indicate a high degree of similarity among the Quechua populations studied; and, furthermore, that this pattern is different from that observed in the Nuñoa Mestizo sample. The ABO and Rh blood group frequencies are in close agreement with other, much more detailed and complete blood studies on Quechua Indian populations (Allen, 1959; Matson et al., 1966; Quilici, 1968). These previous studies found a frequency of the O phenotype of about 90 percent with nearly 100 percent of the individuals Rh positive. South American Indians, however, are almost universally blood type O; and blood types A and B, where encountered, probably indicate admixture (Fitch and Neel, 1969; Matson et al., 1966). Comparative data on other Quechua populations were not available for PTC taste sensitivity, lingual rotation, or digital interlocking patterns.

Genetic Distance

For an overview of the genetic relationships between Nuñoa and the other groups surveyed, Cavalli-Sforza and Edwards's (1967) genetic distance test (D) was performed on (1) the gene frequencies of the four gene marker traits: ABO and Rh blood groups, PTC-tasting ability, and lingual rotation (with the exception of digital interlocking, which was not used because of its questionable genetic base), and (2) the phenotypic frequencies of seven of the dermatoglyphic characters: digital patterns (arches, loops, whorls), main-line index, R/U ratio, hypothenar area, thenar/I, and interdigital areas III and IV. Dendrograms were then generated from the D-matrices by ordering pairs of populations into progressively larger clusters through an iterative process using average linkage (Sokal and Sneath, 1963). Since the actual distance between one group and another in a cluster is obscured by the average linkage procedure, single groups and/or clusters were arranged vertically to reflect differential affinities. For example, the Nuñoa Mestizos are farthest genetically from the Ollachea-Mollendo cluster and within that cluster their greatest genetic similarity is with the Ollachea Quechua (see Fig. 5.3). Phenotypic frequencies were used for the dermatoglyphic characters, and the relationships demonstrated by this dendrogram are phenetic rather than genetic (Fig. 5.4). However, it is expected that this represents an approximate genetic relationship because of the strong genetic effect on the phenotypic expression of dermatoglyphic traits (Holt, 1968).

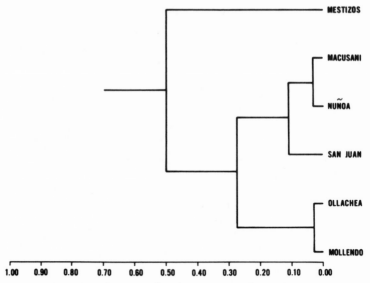

FIGURE 5.3   *Dendrogram showing genetic relationships between the one Mestizo and five Quechua groups for four gene markers. Based on Cavalli-Sforza and Edwards's (1967) D-test.*

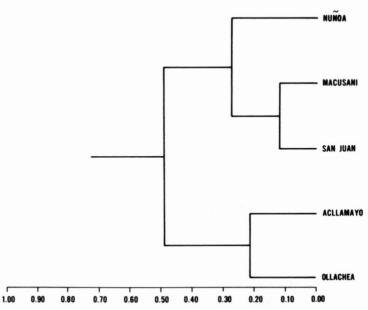

FIGURE 5.4   *Dendrogram showing phenetic relationships between the five Quechua groups for seven dermatoglyphic traits. Based on Cavalli-Sforza and Edwards's (1967) D-test.*

TABLE 5.6   *Pariwise Genetic Distances Between the Six Samples for the Gene-Marker Systems*

| | Quechua | | | | |
| | | | | | Mestizos |
Quechua	Nuñoa	Ollachea	San Juan	Mollendo	(Nuñoa)
Macusani	0.028	0.307	0.110	0.310	0.421
Nuñoa		0.295	0.112	0.300	0.424
Ollachea			0.215	0.031	0.591
San Juan				0.214	0.470
Mollendo					0.601
Quechua pooled					0.502

The results of this technique (dendrograms) imply that there are close genetic affinities between the Nuñoa, Macusani, and San Juan del Oro Quechua groups (Fig. 5.3 and 5.4, Tables 5.6 and 5.7). However, the two dendrograms are not consistent in the models of genetic relationships they present. The discrete gene markers imply a closer genetic affinity between Nuñoa and Macusani, while the dermatoglyphic traits imply closer affinities between Macusani and San Juan del Oro.

The comparison of the Nuñoa Mestizos with the Quechua pooled sample (gene-marker analysis) shows that the resultant distance is about 80 percent greater than that between the two major Quechua clusters (Nuñoa–Macusani–San Juan del Oro vs. Ollachea–Mollendo) (Table 5.6 and Fig. 5.3). The closest affinities with the Nuñoa Mestizos are demonstrated by the Nuñoa and Macusani Quechua groups (Table 5.6).

TABLE 5.7   *Phenetic Distance[a] Between the Five Samples for Seven Dermatoglyphic Traits[b]*

Sample	Acllamayo	Ollachea	San Juan	Nuñoa
Macusani	0.456	0.474	0.121	0.242
Acllamayo		0.214	0.459	0.533
Ollachea			0.451	0.570
San Juan				0.310

[a]The term "phenetic distance" is used because phenotypic rather than gene frequencies are being compared.
[b]Based on Cavalli-Sforza and Edwards's (1967) D-test.

FACTORS GOVERNING THE GENETICS
OF THE NUÑOA QUECHUA POPULATION

Through the use of the comparative approach for the study of the Nuñoa Quechua population, we have found that moderate to strong genetic affinities appear to exist between all the Quechua populations studied. These results were based on the study of digital and palmar dermatoglyphic patterns and simple genetic markers, as well as through the use of dendrograms in assessing the overall genetic (and phenetic) distances between the various populations. In addition, through a brief overview of the ethnohistorical and cultural perspective of Andean populations, we noted a number of factors that might have influenced the genetic history of these populations. As in other Mendelian populations, it can be assumed that factors such as degree of isolation, breeding patterns, selection pressures, demography, and random events have operated jointly to affect both the genetic structure of the Nuñoa population and its genetic affiliation with other Quechua groups in this area of Peru.

Recently, mathematical models in which demographic parameters are used to assess the effects of evolutionary forces have been gaining increasing usage in human population genetics (Schull and MacCluer, 1968; Cavalli-Sforza and Bodmer, 1971). Although these models do not allow precise quantification of real evolutionary events, they can be used to make estimates or discern modal tendencies in some of the directed and stochastic processes occurring in human populations. Since the pertinent demographic data have been collected in Nuñoa, a number of these estimates have been calculated in order to intensify the focus on the genetics of this population.

The size of a population and especially its effective breeding size (N_e) are influential in affecting a number of genetic parameters. The smaller the N_e, the more the population is subject to (1) the decay of genotypic variability as a result of a reduction in mate choice leading to inbreeding, and (2) stochastic processes such as genetic drift which tend to reduce the genetic variability over time. This factor may not be significant in affecting (at least in the short term) the genetics of the Nuñoa population, since Dutt (1969) has shown that the amount of gene flow into the district appears to be more than sufficient to counteract genetic drift (see Chapter 6).

If differential fertility and mortality are partially determined by genetic factors, it is possible to estimate the upper limits of postnatal selection intensity through the use of Crow's (1958) formula, the index of opportunity for selection (I) (Table 5.8). Spuhler (1962), Neel and Chagnon (1968), Johnston and Kensinger (1971), and Salzano (1972) have computed this index for a number of populations at varying levels of sociocultural, technological, and economic complexity. If the results of these studies are representative, it would appear that selection intensities tend to be higher (although there is much variation) in nonwestern peasant and pastoral societies than in hunting and gathering groups.

TABLE 5.8 *Fertility, Mortality, and Estimates of the Index of Opportunity for Selection (Crow, 1958) in Nuñoa and Two Other Andean Communities*

Variable	Nuñoa	Chapiquina	Huallatire
Mean progeny number, $\overline{X}_s$	6.7[b]	8.5[c]	7.3[c]
Variance, V_x	9.0	5.6	9.9
Fertility index, $I_f = V_x/\overline{X}_s$	0.200[a]	0.077[b]	0.185[c]
Proportion offspring surviving to adulthood, P_s	0.657[a]	0.751[a]	0.459[a]
Mortality index, $I_m = (I - P_s)/P_s$	0.522	0.331	1.178
$I_{f_s} = I_f/P_s$	0.305	0.232	0.403
Total index, $I = I_m + I_{f_s}$	0.827	0.563	1.581

[a]Based on data from Cruz-Coke et al. (1966).
[b]For women over 45 yr of age.
[c]For women over 35 yr of age.

The selection intensity index (I) and its two components, I_m (mortality) and I_f (fertility), were calculated from the demographic statistics of Nuñoa and contrasted with the values for Chapiquina and Huallatire (Table 5.8) (Cruz-Coke et al., 1966). The results of this comparison show that Nuñoa is intermediate between the two Aymara communities in the degree of selection intensity it is experiencing, and the greatest contributing factor to selection in all three communities appears to be differential mortality. As a consequence, it is possible that this phenomenon is consistent in other native Andean populations inhabiting the altiplano. This is somewhat unusual, since it is customary to find a larger fertility component in populations at the peasant socioeconomic level (Spuhler, 1962; Neel and Chagnon, 1968; Johnston and Kensinger, 1971; Salzano, 1972). Compared to other such societies, Nuñoa, Chapiquina, and Huallatire have a moderate to high degree of postnatal selection. Likewise, prenatal selection also appears to be intensive, since the evidence, although somewhat contradictory, suggests that stillbirths, miscarriages, and abortion rates are high in Andean populations (Hoff, 1968; see Chapter 7).

Finally, we noted a number of differences between Nuñoa and the other Quechua groups in palmar dermatoglyphic patterns while phenotypic frequencies for simple gene markers indicated close genetic affinities between all groups. Similarity in blood groups and other simple genetic markers may be interpreted either as a result of homogeneity of gene pools, recent intensive gene flow throughout the altiplano, or as an areawide set of consistent selection pressures resulting in high frequencies of certain simple genetic traits in all groups, even though partially isolated or subject to Founder's effect. Dermatoglyphic traits, however, are phenotypic characters under polygenic control. As a result, they are probably less susceptible to the effects of isolation, migration, and genetic admixture and more useful in determining old and persistent similarities and differences as well as sorting out ethnohistorical relations between populations than are simple gene traits (Plato et al., 1974a).

OVERVIEW

If the results of the genetic analysis are representative of the true genetic situation, it can be assumed that the southern Peruvian Quechua are a relatively homogenous population. As Dutt has pointed out for Nuñoa (Chapter 6), this may be at least partially the result of the gene flow that occurs between the Quechua communities in this area of Peru and the increase in the last several decades in migration rates from the altiplano into the communities in the tierra templada and ceja de la montaña. Also, another factor that may be important in many altiplano Quechua populations is the moderate to strong selection pressures produced by high mortality rates in the young. If these are the result of hypoxia, cold, malnutrition, and the other environmental factors associated with life at high altitudes, there may be strong directional selection pressures in all altiplano Quechua populations, for and against specific genotypes. Therefore, it is possible that the genetic communication between Quechua communities and the typology of selection pressures have led to a reduction in the amount of genetic and genotypic variability in this population, resulting in a maintenance of group similarities.

We have discussed in general some of the major factors thought to affect the population genetics of the Nuñoa Quechua and, more specifically, their genetic affinities with surrounding Quechua populations. Much of our interpretations of the results of this study have been speculative, and probably more questions than answers have been generated by our discussion. Although no detailed and concrete hypotheses have been established in this investigation, it has shed some light on the genetics of this population and may further provide the basis for continuing genetic research on the Andean Quechua.

6

POPULATION MOVEMENT
AND GENE FLOW

James S. Dutt

The district of Nuñoa is located at the northern edge of the Peruvian altiplano in an area of rugged terrain close to the Cordillera Real. The major proportion of the population of the district, native Quechua Indians, appear to be isolated from surrounding Indian populations because of a combination of environmental and social factors which limit interpersonal contact. Such isolation may affect the genetic structure of the population.

Studies of small populations have shown that when populations or sub-populations become genetically isolated (as the Indian population of Nuñoa appears to be), the genetic structure of such populations may gradually become distinct from that of surrounding populations, owing to the joint effects of local selection pressures and genetic drift, unless these forces are counteracted by a significant amount of gene flow between the populations (Wright, 1951). The process of gene flow enables semi-isolated breeding populations to share genetic material and, thus, maintain genetic continuity. If, in the present case, the native population of the district of Nuñoa is a true isolated breeding population, as it appears to be, and has been so for a number of generations, it is possible that its genetic structure will differ from that of other neighboring Quechua populations of the southern Peruvian Andes.

The ideal method for determining whether the Indian population of the district differs genetically from other Quechua populations of the Department of Puno would involve the comparison of the frequencies of a number of different genes between the population of the district and the surrounding populations. Unfortunately, such an approach cannot be used in the present instance. Although there are some genetic data (see Chapter 5) for a small number of populations in the southern Peruvian Andes, including Nuñoa, the information is limited to a few gene-marker systems and the results are inconclusive. Analysis has shown no major differences between the Nuñoa Indian population and that of surrounding areas with regard to ABO or Rh systems and most dermatoglyphic characteristics. However, as there is very little variation in the ABO and Rh systems among New-World Indians, the absence of differences in these traits does not necessarily imply that the populations being examined have identical genetic structures. In the absence of more detailed genetic information, other types of data can be utilized to further examine genetic relationships between the Nuñoa population and its neighbors. Although not as exact as gene frequencies, the study of human movement and mating patterns can provide much useful information from which deductions about gene flow and genetic drift, and thus genetic continuity, can be made.

FACTORS ISOLATING
THE NATIVE POPULATION

The Quechua population of the district is isolated from neighboring Indian populations through a combination of environmental and cultural factors (Dutt, 1969). Mountains bound the district to the west, north, and east, while to the south a series of smaller, very sparsely populated mountains and hills separate Nuñoa from the district of Orurillo. While there is some movement over these mountains, most travel both within and out of the district is funneled along the valley floors. As a result, except for people who live in the southeastern sector where the Rio Grande leaves the district or near one of the few gaps in the mountains surrounding the district, movement out of the district is both time- and energy-consuming.

Vehicular transportation within the district is minimal. Although Nuñoa is connected by rough dirt roads to the towns of Santa Rosa, Orurillo, and Macusani, the roads are quite recent, built in the 1950s, and only the main road to Santa Rosa is passable year-round. The vehicles using these roads are owned by Mestizos and a few Cholos who either operate small businesses in the town of Nuñoa or own haciendas within the district. Although it is possible to travel from the town of Nuñoa to several nearby towns for weekly markets, such transportation is quite limited. Other than local trucks there is no regularly scheduled vehicular transportation.

Travel by the Indian population is either by foot or horseback, which limits their mobility somewhat. Trips outside the district or even to the town of Nuñoa usually require the expenditure of much time and are rare events for many natives, particularly women and residents of some of the more remote haciendas. The limited mobility of the Indian population and the lack of any great amount of movement through the district by nonresidents strongly suggests that contacts between much of the Indigenous population and residents of other districts are fairly infrequent.

The structure of the local economy and social system also tends to isolate the native population. Although there is a small amount of mining done within the district, the herding of alpacas, llamas, and sheep along with subsistence agriculture forms the economic base of the district. While originally land was controlled by native communities, during the past century or so a small number of Mestizo families have gained control over most of the land within the district and simultaneously, because herding requires large land holdings, over the local economy. The majority of the Indigenous population lives on haciendas or estancias, working for the owner in return for the right to herd their own animals and cultivate small plots of land. Most live at or slightly above the subsistence level and many have become indentured to the landowner. The small surpluses which are produced can be bartered or sold in one of the *tiendas* or the weekly market in Nuñoa for the few essentials not produced locally. As a result, many natives feel little need to leave the district. Escobar (personal communication) reports talking to several older natives who had never ventured outside the boundaries of the district. It should be noted that this pattern is beginning to break down in the last decade as many young men are migrating seasonally from the district to seek work in larger towns in the altiplano.

There appears to be little in the way of economic opportunities within the district to attract nonresidents, particularly Indians. The main economic activity, herding, requires large acreages, and all land within the district has already been acquired. Agriculture, because of the local environment, is limited to the raising of marginal crops, tubers and a small number of grains, and its productivity is quite low. Furthermore, the growth of the local population has already saturated the labor market. As a result, few outsiders, especially Indians, have taken up residence within the district.

MIGRATION AND GENE FLOW

The results of a study of the birthplaces of a sample of Quechua residents of the district indicates that this isolation affects the composition of the gene pool. In my 1969 study of the birthplaces of 154 couples residing within the district, I found that of the 308 adults interviewed (who had children residing within the district and, thereby, where presumably contributing to the gene pool), 40 (13 percent) were immigrants. Similar results were obtained when the birthplaces of the parents of those individuals who had been born within the district were studied. Birthplaces were obtained for 176 individuals; of these only 19 (11.4 percent) had been born outside the district. These figures suggest that the local Quechua population is a semi-isolated breeding population and that the rate of gene flow into the gene pool is between 10 and 15 percent per generation.

An examination of the source of the immigrants indicates that the great majority (60 percent) are from districts either bordering or very close to Nuñoa, which have altitudes and environments similar to that of Nuñoa. Only 9 percent were born in districts with an altitude of less than 3000 m and farther than 200 km from the district. It should be noted, however, that it was impossible to determine the exact district of birth of 16 percent of the individuals.

The previous analysis may underestimate the amount of gene flow into the population, as several factors which may lead to the introduction of genes from other populations have not been considered. It is likely that there is some influx of genes from the Mestizo, upper-class, segment of the residents of the district, approximately 5 percent of the total population. Most of these individuals are not native to the district, and many have some European ancestry. Mestizos choose marital partners from among the Mestizo residents of the district or from other towns or cities and rarely from the Indian population. As a result, members of the Mestizo class, although residents of the district, are not part of the local breeding population. However, while there are few formalized unions between Mestizos and Indians, Mestizo men do occasionally father children of Indian women. This pattern was much more common several decades ago than it is today (Escobar, personal communication). In addition, there are about six major fiestas held in the town of Nuñoa each year. These fiestas may last a week or more and attract participants, spectators, and vendors from outside the district as well as from within. According to the common folklore of the altiplano, during such fiestas the normal moral code breaks down and a great deal of sexual promiscuity results. Furthermore, there is a custom that the sponsors of a fiesta will provide important male guests with female partners for their sexual amusement. Definite evidence is lacking, but it is possible that as a result of these fiestas, nonresidents of the district father children of local women. It is impossible to measure the amount of genetic material introduced into the gene pool from the upper classes or from fiestas, and in either case it is probably not great. However, such factors should not be overlooked, as they do act to reduce the genetic isolation of the local population.

The departure of individuals from a population will affect the genetic structure of the population if individuals with certain genotypes have higher probability of emigrating than do others. There is considerable evidence that a large number of residents have left the district of Nuñoa during the past two decades. A preliminary study conducted by DeJong (1967) noted that while the total population of Peru had increased by nearly 60 percent from 1940 to 1961 the population of the district had increased only 20 percent. These figures suggest a substantial amount of out-migration from the district.

Examination of the vital statistics for the period of 1940 to 1961 and the 1940 and 1961 censuses of the district strengthens this conclusion. According to the official records, there were a total of 8037 births and 2693 deaths during the 21-yr period. However, Spector (1971) suggests that there was a considerable amount of underreporting of deaths, particularly for infants, during the period 1940–1950. For a more realistic estimate of the number of deaths during the total period, the average number of deaths per year was calculated for the period 1950–1961 and the figures for 1940–1950 were corrected to give similar yearly averages. On this basis the number of deaths from 1940 to 1961 was estimated to be 3290. As the population size was increasing during this period, it is likely that the new estimate of total deaths is slightly high. Thus the vital statistics for the district indicate a population increase of 4747 based on 8037 births and 3290 deaths. On the other hand, the 1940 census reports the population of the district to be 6470 while the 1961 census reports a population of 7740, an increase of only 1280 (M.H.C., 1942, 1965).

Comparison of population figures from these two sources shows that while the vital statistics show an increase of 4747, the census data report an increase of only 1280, a difference of 3464. There are three possible explanations for these differences: underenumeration of the population in the 1961 census and overenumeration in 1940, massive underreporting of deaths, or a high rate of out-migration. Although underenumeration is a possibility, it is more likely that underenumeration took place in 1940, suggesting that the increase in population is not as great as reported. Although there might have been underreporting of deaths in the death records, a correction has already been made and it is highly unlikely that unreported deaths account for more than a small percentage of the surplus. The most probable explanation for the differences in figures reported above is out-migration. The results suggest that in a 21-yr-period approximately 3500 people migrated out of the district. Assuming that migration has taken place at a fairly uniform level through the past two decades indicates a yearly out-migration rate of about 2.5 percent.

Other supporting data come from a study conducted by McGarvey in 1972, who was reexamining children previously studied in 1965. He reports that of the 80 families in the initial survey, 31, or 39 percent, had left the district by 1972 (McGarvey, 1974). For this sample of 80 families, the data suggest a yearly emigration rate of nearly 5 percent, further suggesting that during the period 1940–1961 the rate of emigration was not constant but increased.

McGarvey (1974), using informant sources, reports the areas to which the 31 families had migrated. The majority, 71 percent, were still living at relatively high altitudes in southern Peru but had moved to larger urban locations, such as Sicuani, Cuzco, Arequipa, Ayaviri, and Juliaca. A smaller percentage, 22 percent, were living in low-altitude areas either on the coast or in the jungle, while the remainder had moved to distant high-altitude locations. These data correspond to migration patterns reported for Peru. In general, migration in Peru is characterized by a movement from rural to urban areas and from higher to lower altitudes (Schaedel, 1967).

Although there is a considerable amount of emigration from the district, it is not known what effect, if any, out-migration has on the genetic structure of the gene pool. At present it is not known if the emigrants differ genetically from those who remain. McGarvey (1974) does note, however, that for his limited sample, families with a higher socioeconomic status have a greater probability of migrating. If differences in socioeconomic status are correlated with an individual's genotype, it is probable that emigration will have some effect on the genetic structure of the population.

GENETIC DRIFT

Genetic drift is the sampling process by which gene frequencies in a later generation may differ purely by chance from those frequencies in a previous generation. The probability of drift occurring is inversely related to population size; thus it becomes an important factor when small populations are being studied. Li (1955) gives the following formula for genetic drift:

$$^{\sigma}\delta q = \sqrt{q(1 - q)/2N}$$

in which $^{\sigma}\delta q$ represents the random drift per generation, q the gene frequency, and N the effective population size. The effective population size of the Nuñoa breeding population has been estimated to be about 1800 (Dutt, 1969). Using this estimate and a gene frequency of 0.5 (drift has the greatest effect on genes with frequencies of 0.5), the random genetic drift per generation for the Nuñoa gene pool would be approximately 0.0083.

The probability of genetic drift having an important effect on the genetic structure of a population is also related to the degree to which the population is genetically isolated. A high rate of gene flow from a genetically related population will decrease the importance of genetic drift. Lasker and Kaplan (1964) have suggested that the coefficient of breeding isolation, a product of the effective population size and the effective immigration rate, is a useful indicator of the importance of genetic drift. A coefficient of less than 5 suggests that drift may have a significant effect on the genetic structure of the population, while a coefficient of more than 50 indicates that drift is not an important factor.

In 1969 I calculated an estimate of the coefficient of breeding isolation for the local breeding population, reporting a coefficient of 237 for the population in 1968, and approximately 144 for the previous generation. Survey data on the birthplaces of individuals were used to determine the immigration rates while data from the 1940 and 1961 Peruvian national censuses were used to estimate the effective population sizes. Table 6.1 compares the sizes, immigration rates, effective population sizes, and coefficients of breeding isolation of a number of peasant populations with those of Nuñoa. The figures indicate that Nuñoa has a low immigration rate compared with other Peruvian and Chilean populations. However, the effective population size is great enough and gene flow is adequate, so that genetic drift probably has little effect on the genetic structure of the population.

TABLE 6.1   *Comparison of Immigration Rates, Effective*
Population Sizes, and Coefficients of Breeding
Isolation for a Number of Different Populations

Population	Size	Immigration rate (%)	Effective population size	Coefficient breading of isolation
Nuñoa (Peru)				
(1968)	7,300	13.0	1,816	236
(1940)	6,470	11.4	1,260	144
Azapa (Chile)[a]	384	77.5	80.6	62.4
Belen (Chile)[a]	177	32.6	51.6	16.8
Monsefu (Peru)[b]	10,000	13.0	2,900	377
San Jose (Peru)[b]	1,500	24.7	435	107
Mochumi (Peru)[b]	1,200	29.2	348	102
Paracho (Mexico)[c]	4,593	20.2	967	193
Providencia (Columbia)[d]	2,146	8.1	517	41
Dinka Village (Sudan)[e]	375	50.0	109	55

[a]From Cruz-Coke et al. (1966).
[b]From Lasker and Kaplan (1964).
[c]From Lasker (1954).
[d]From Wilson and Buettner-Janusch (1961).
[e]From Roberts (1956).

GENE FLOW WITHIN THE DISTRICT

In addition to isolating the district from neighboring areas, mountain ranges also cut through the district and minimize contact between the inhabitants of different parts of the district. While the ranges are often traversed, most movement is along the valley floors. As a result, most personal contacts are most likely to take place between residents of the same valley system. Thus it is possible that isolated breeding populations exist within the district.

Geographically, the district consists of two major diverging river valleys surrounded by steep-sided mountains, and a broad, flat plain located below the juncture of the valleys (see Fig. 1.1). The population of the district can be characterized as concentrating in four district subunits: two river valleys, the plain, and the town of Nuñoa, which is located near the juncture of the Nuñoa river valley and the plain. In order to determine if any one or more of these areas was genetically isolated from the others, I studied in 1969 the area of birth of 154 couples. The results of this study are given in Table 6.2, which shows the area of birth of the man and the woman, and the expected

TABLE 6.2   *Composition of Families According to the Birthplaces of Mates: Observed and Expected*

| | Birthplace of female | | | | | | | | |
| | Nuñoa Valley (24) | | Pueblo (29) | | Corahuina Valley (38) | | Plain (45) | | Outside district (18) | |
Birthplace of male	Ob.	Ex.	Ob.	Ex.	Ob.	Ex.	Ob.	Ex.	Ob.	Ex.
Nuñoa valley (19)	6	3.0	1	3.6	6	4.7	4	5.6	2	2.2
Pueblo (26)	5	4.1	9	4.6	6	6.4	5	7.6	1	3.0
Corahuina valley (36)	5	5.6	8	6.8	13	8.9	7	10.5	3	4.2
Plain (51)	4	7.9	8	9.6	8	12.6	23	14.9	8	6.0
Outside district (22)	4	4.3	3	4.1	5	5.4	6	6.4	4	2.6

frequency if mating were random between areas. Examination of the table indicates that matings between individuals born within the same area take place more often than expected if matings were to take place randomly between areas; the difference between the observed and the expected is significant at the 0.05 level (Dutt, 1969). Although more unions than expected were composed of individuals born within the same area, it is important to note that in almost two-thirds of the couples surveyed, the man and woman were born in different areas of the district. This indicates a great amount of population mixture between the various geographical regions of the district, and that the residents of the different areas are all members of the same breeding population.

In further analysis it was determined that only the subpopulation residing in the plain was significantly endogamous (Dutt, 1969). This appears to be the result of the fact that almost one-half of the couples interviewed from the plain resided in Sincata, an Indian community located at the extreme southeastern edge of the district (see Fig. 1.1). Of the 34 men and women interviewed who resided in Sincata, 26 were born in the plain area (of these 14 were born in Sincata itself), while only 8 were from other parts of the district. The reasons for this difference are not readily apparent. It is probably partly due to the fact that Sincata is located at the edge of the plain, farther from Nuñoa and both river valleys than most parts of the district; it also may relate to preferential mating patterns or to the social organization of the community. If mates were normally chosen from Sincata or from the remainder of the plain which was also endogamous, it is probable that the population of the community would become highly inbred. However, the data suggest considerable mixture between the rest of the plain and the other parts of the district, and little evidence of a high rate of inbreeding within the community. Furthermore, Sincata has probably been in existence no more than 200 years, or seven or eight generations (Escobar M., personal communication), so that it is unlikely that the genetic structure would differ greatly from that of the remainder of the Nuñoa gene pool.

It is important to note that while genetic contact with neighboring populations is minimal, mixture within the population (internal gene flow, so to speak) is very high. One major reason is the location and importance of the town of Nuñoa. Nuñoa is the only urban center within the district and serves as the center of social and economic activity for the population. Furthermore, its location near the juncture of the three major physiographic areas, the two river valleys and the plain, makes it accessible to people from all over the district. As such, it serves as the one point within the district where people congregate at regular times.

The native system of marriage appears to increase the movement of people within the population and, thus, increase internal gene flow. The Quechua marriage system is characterized by the establishment of a union which gradually becomes more stable and permanent as time passes. During the first years of marriage, unions are often dissolved. As a result, women often have children by two or more men. In a study conducted in 1968, 22 of 89 women (24 percent) reported having had children by at least two different men (Dutt, 1969). A similar rate was obtained from data gathered in a 1964–1965 biocultural survey. Of the 175 women interviewed, 39 (22.3 percent) had had children by at least two different men (Dutt, 1969). Such a pattern increases the amount of genetic mixture within the population and may act to slightly increase the effective population size.

The fiesta system also may help to prevent the formation of population isolates within the district. There is the possibility that temporary unions formed during a fiesta will lead to pregnancy. Second, fiestas bring people together from all over the district, increase the amount of personal contact, and provide individuals who live in different parts of the district with the opportunity of meeting potential mates. Seven women (10 percent) of a sample of 70 reported first meeting their marriage partner at a fiesta.

HISTORICAL PERSPECTIVES

While the Nuñoan Indigenous population is somewhat isolated, the size of the population is sufficiently large and the rate of gene flow is great enough so that genetic continuity with surrounding populations should be maintained. However, it is possible that in the past the population was much smaller in size and more isolated and that only recently have mates been selected from surrounding populations. If such is the case, the genetic structure of the Nuñoa population might have been affected by drift and may still be much different. For a more definitive statement, it is necessary to examine the history of the population.

Unfortunately, there are very little quantitative data available on the population of the district for either historic or prehistoric periods. It is almost impossible to obtain accurate figures on the size of the breeding population and the amount of gene flow into or out of it. However, various types of information do exist from which deductions can be drawn concerning the dynamics of the population in the past, to a degree, and the amount of genetic contact with neighboring populations.

Archaeological evidence indicates that the area now comprising the district of Nuñoa has a long history of habitation. I have found projectile points which have tentatively been dated from 3000 to 7000 B.C. (Lynch, personal communication). Although no detailed study of local archaeology has been undertaken, a survey of the Ayaviri valley system, which includes the district of Nuñoa, was conducted by Luis Barreda (an archaeologist presently with the University of Cuzco). Barreda (unpublished) notes the location of a number of sites within the district which range from small preceramic sites to larger middle or late horizon settlements. This finding suggests that the general area has been inhabited for a relatively long period of time, perhaps as much as seven or eight thousand years.

The ruins of a fairly large settlement are located several kilometers from the town of Nuñoa. Furthermore, local sources indicate that two similar sites (which have since been destroyed by individuals seeking stone for construction purposes) also existed within the district. Although no excavations have been conducted, the location of the sites on ridges and the type of building construction suggest that they date from the later intermediate period (1000 A.D. to 1436 A.D.). The size of the sites indicate that as long as 800 yr ago the general area now comprising the district supported a population of 5000 or more.

It is difficult to state with much certainty the linguistic affiliation of the population of the area during the late intermediate period or middle horizon. Since agriculture has a relatively low productivity in the region at present, the size of the population suggests that the area was part of a larger sociopolitical unit. Information from the middle horizon indicates that at that time the area may have been under control of Tiahuanaco, probably an Aymara-dominated political unit. Furthermore, early Spanish chronicles report that the area around the northern part of Lake Titicaca, including the altiplano, was under the control of the Colla Kingdom, a people who also might have been Aymara speakers. It is reported that when the Spanish arrived in Nuñoa around 1540, the local population spoke Quechua (Escobar M., personal communication). Although the present evidence is scanty, it is possible that there was some population displacement in the area during the period of Inca expansion between 1400 and 1500.

There is somewhat more information available on the region for the colonial period. The Spanish arrived on the altiplano about 1535 and in Nuñoa shortly thereafter (Escobar M., personal communication). Although the original records have been destroyed, it is reported that the church in Nuñoa was constructed in the 1540s (Escobar M., personal communication).

Nuñoa seems to have been of some importance within the northern sector of the altiplano during much of the colonial period. Important trade routes, which were probably of precolonial origin, ran through the district connecting mines and the eastern escarpment to Cuzco and other locations on the northern altiplano. There is also evidence that the church in the town of Nuñoa became an important religious center for the surrounding area during the early colonial period and that large numbers of people attended the annual religious festivals (Escobar M., personal communication). As a result, it is likely that there was a continual flow of people through the district.

A document dating from 1558 found by Murra (1972) in the archives in Seville indicates that the district had ties with areas located in the *selva* to the east. According to the document, the Indian population paid rent to the Crown, both in money and in coca produced in the eastern slopes of the province. Murra (1968) feels that such ties between different ecosystems were probably continuations of precolonial patterns. Trips by foot to the selva from the district require a minimum of several days' travel, and it is possible that there was a small permanent population of Nuñoans living there. Such verticality might have increased gene flow into the population by giving local residents the opportunity of traveling and making contact with individuals from other areas.

The first population figures for the district are for the year 1630. Vasquez de Espinoza (1942) reported that in 1630 the district had a population of 605 taxpayers (men from 20 to approximately 50), 1269 women, 550 "muchachos" (probably children and adolescents), and 306 old (presumably men and women over 50), for a total population of 2730. This population would be about one-third the size of the present population, and considerably smaller habitation than estimates made for the population of the area during the late intermediate horizon. It is possible that the size of the population might have been somewhat underreported, particularly as it evidently was calculated for tax purposes. Or there might have been a substantial decline in the population after the arrival of the Spanish. Smith (1970) has examined the depopulation of the central Andes Lake Titicaca area and estimates that the population decline of the province of Chucuito declined by a factor of three from 1520–1525 to 1571. If these estimates are accurate, it is probable that the population of the district suffered a similar decline during the sixteenth century.

There is evidence that during the latter part of the colonial period the economic condition of the district began to deteriorate (Bueno, 1951). As the mines to the east gradually became depleted, it is likely that there was less movement along trade routes passing through the district. This fact, along with a reduction of the importance of the Church in the district, suggests that contact between Nuñoans and residents of other areas declined. It appears that conditions remained fairly stable until early in the republican period, when two events took place which further isolated the district. The first was the development of the hacienda system, which placed the local economy under the control of a small number of Mestizo families, most of whom came from outside the district. The second was the completion of the Cuzco–Puno railroad about 1870, which greatly reduced the importance of the trade routes that passed through the district. Both events reduced contact with the populations of surrounding districts, and it is likely that as contacts decreased, so did the amount of gene flow into the breeding population. The situation appears to have remained fairly stable for the last 90–100 yr.

SUMMARY AND CONCLUSIONS

From this brief survey of data, it can be stated that the present Quechua population of Nuñoa is isolated from the Indian populations of surrounding districts because of the joint effects of a topography and an economy that limit personal contacts between the native residents of the district and those of other districts. The rate of immigration into the population and, thus, the rate of gene flow, is between 10 and 15 percent per generation, the majority of these immigrants coming from neighboring districts. There may be some additional gene flow from the Mestizos and Cholos, who reside in the district but who are not members of the breeding population, and during the fiestas, which attract many outsiders into the district. The rate of emigration out of the population is quite high, about 2.5 percent per year, but it is not known at the present time if the outward flow has any affect on the gene pool. The combination of a fairly large effective population size and the immigration rate greatly reduce the probability of genetic drift being an important factor affecting the genetic structure of the population.

There is a high level of population mixture within the district. Although mountains cut through the district, over half of the couples sampled had been born in different parts of the district. This finding probably relates to the central location of the only town within the district and to the marriage system, which facilitates the dissolution of marriages, particularly within the first few years. With the possible exception of Sincata, there is no evidence of isolated subpopulations within the district.

An examination of the data available for the historical and prehistorical periods indicates that the district has become more isolated in the past hundred years than it was in the previous thousand or more. Until the completion of the Puno–Cuzco railroad, important transportation routes passed through the district, ensuring contact with other populations. Furthermore, during the colonial period mines were located within the district, and the church in the town of Nuñoa was one of the more important churches in the general area. Under these conditions, the amount of gene flow into the population was probably greater than it is today.

As a whole, the information available indicates that, while the native population of the district is somewhat isolated, the isolation is relatively recent and is not great enough for genetic drift to be an important factor influencing the genetic structure of the population. If the genetic structure of the population does differ significantly from those of surrounding populations, the differences are probably due to the effects of local differences in selection pressures or genetic differences in the populations that originally settled the areas.

7

FERTILITY

Charles J. Hoff and Andrew E. Abelson

An adequate reproductive performance is a prerequisite for adaptation in any environment. At high altitude, where hypoxia may act directly to reduce fecundity, reproductive performance is of critical importance. Andean populations have demonstrated their capacity to adapt to this stress; and over many hundreds of generations they have been able to maintain and even increase their numbers. By contrast, the experience of the Spanish seventeenth-century colonists was reportedly one of infertility, inability to carry the fetus to full term, or, in the event of live birth, neonatal death (Monge, 1948).

In human populations reproductive capacity is also often curbed by cultural factors. In order to explain how human populations may be affected by hypoxia and how they may adapt to this stress, it is necessary to understand the physiological factors of importance in determining levels of fertility, as well as behavioral and cultural factors. It may then be possible to explain the roles of biological variables, and the way or ways in which biological and cultural variables interact. This interaction of biological and cultural factors in the short term is important not only for adaptation to the immediate environment, but also for the long-term survival of the population.

HYPOXIA AND REPRODUCTIVE PHYSIOLOGY

Hypoxia may act to affect the process of reproduction at several stages: during gametogenesis, by exerting an effect on the ovarian cycle, and by acting as a stress on the maternal and fetal environments during pregnancy. Any one of these stages may represent a critical phase, but in general studies show that there are multiple risks involving the whole process of reproduction.

Here we review the way in which hypoxic stress can affect gametogenesis, the ovarian cycle, and pregnancy. Studies of both experimental animals and human populations are included. While caution is necessary in extrapolating from nonhuman animals to man, the studies are largely complementary, indicating both ways in which hypoxic stress may affect reproductive physiology and some sources of adaptation to this stress.

128

Gametogenesis

The effect of hypoxia on gametogenesis has been considered from the point of view of histological damage to gonadal tissue, spermatogenesis, oogenesis, and ovulation. There are some conflicting results reported in these studies, which may reflect in part differing experimental conditions, and in part the different ages and sexes of the experimental animals. But overall the results are largely consistent.

A relationship between hypoxia and histological damage to gonadal tissue, and morphological and physiological changes in the anterior pituitary gland, has been shown by Gordon et al. (1943). Adult male rats were exposed for 18–20 h daily to hypobarometric pressures simulating altitudes between 7600 and 8500 m, for 2–3 weeks. The major changes observed were hypertrophy of the interstitial tissue of the testes and of the epithelial tissue of the seminal vesicles. Similar findings have been reported for rats (Sundstroem and Michaels, 1942), for cats and rabbits (Monge and Mori-Chavez, 1942), and for guinea pigs (Guerra-Garcia et al., 1965). On the other hand, Altland (1949a, 1949b) found no evidence of damage to the gonads of male or female rats exposed to hypobarometric pressures for the period of 1 yr from the age of 14 days on. A possible explanation for the differing results may be that the animals adapt to the stress over a longer time period. Further studies (Moore and Price, 1948; Nelson and Burrill, 1944; Altland and Highman, 1968; Timiras, 1964) have also failed to confirm gonadal tissue damage. Although they did report little disturbance of the ovarian cycle, this last finding is not confirmed in later studies.

Spermatogenesis appears to be affected by hypoxia, but only on a temporary basis (Altland, 1949a; Altland and Allen, 1952; Altland and Highman, 1968; Chiodi, 1964; Johnson and Roofe, 1965) in rats, and in domestic farm animals (Monge and Monge, 1966). Observations on men normally resident at low altitude but transported to high altitude have shown temporary reductions in sperm counts and an increased proportion of abnormal sperm (Donayre, 1966; Donayre et al., 1968; Sobrevilla, 1967). For natives to high altitude, Sobrevilla (1967) found that sperm production was normal. It would appear, then, that tissue damage and abnormal sperm production are probably temporary phenomena, and not of lasting importance. These findings are paralleled by the changes seen in testosterone secretion in males. In those transported to high altitude there is a temporary fall in the amount of testosterone excreted in the urine, followed by recovery to normal levels (Guerra-Garcia et al., 1965). These same workers found no differences between those normally resident at high and at low altitudes.

Oogenesis occurs at a very early stage during mammalian growth and no studies of the effect of hypoxia appear to have been reported. With respect to ovulation the more recent studies show that changes occur with exposure to hypoxic stress. Fernandez-Cano (1959) found a lower rate of copulation among rats exposed to high-altitude stress, from which he inferred a lower rate of ovulation. Donayre (1966) stimulated the shedding of ova in mice by the administration of pregnant mare's serum and human chorionic gonado-trophin. After 5 days of hypoxic stress the number of ova shed decreased significantly, and this effect was intensified by cold. Weihe (1964) observed a prolongation of the anestrous phase of the menstrual cycle under conditions of hypoxic stress. It has further been observed that ova may fail to implant or be reabsorbed (Fernandez-Cano, 1959; Sundstroem and Michaels, 1942; Altland, 1949b; Chiodi, 1964). For women moving to high altitude, distur-bance of the menstrual cycle has been observed in Peru (Sobrevilla, 1967; Donayre, 1966) and in the United States (Harris et al., 1966), but not in Ethiopia (Harrison et al., 1969). Little information exists on the regularity of the menstrual cycle of high-Andean natives, but Moncloa (1966) found no difference in the excretion of pregnanediol between natives to high and to low altitude.

The implication of these studies for human populations are that male fecundity may be temporarily impaired in the short term. Low-altitude women transported to high altitude do experience some difficulty in adapta-tion, at least with respect to menstruation, but women native to high altitude do not provide evidence of impaired fecundity. But at the present we lack information on the process of ovulation and implantation in women normally resident at high altitudes.

Gestation and Parturition

The physiological effect of hypoxia on the fetal environment is poorly documented. As early as 1936 Barcroft described the supply of oxygen to the fetus as similar to an ascent of the Himalayas. However, in pregnant ewes at high altitude, Barron et al. (1964) found no evidence of hypoxic stress. In human populations the oxygen tension of the fetus at high altitude has not been found to be reduced (Sobrevilla, 1971). Similarly, there is no apparent reduction in the oxygen tension of the capillary circulation of the high-altitude neonate (Howard et al., 1957).

Despite the lack of direct evidence of hypoxic stress on the fetus, there is reason to believe that such stress does exist. Hytten and Leitch (1971) point out that energy requirements are increased during pregnancy. Changes also occur in the respiratory pattern of women pregnant at low altitude. Vital capacity is reduced and there is hyperventilation. In the third trimester the position of the fetus will also restrict the expansion of the diaphragm. These effects at high altitude are yet to be investigated in detail, but the limited data available suggest that they should not be overlooked.

In experimental studies of animals, Moore and Price (1948) found that litters were less frequent and smaller in rats exposed to hypobarometric pressures; and Fernandez-Cano (1959) reported resorption and also rejection of embryos in rats. In human populations there is evidence of hypoxic stress with respect to rates of conception and the products of conception. There is also some indication of possible mechanisms of adaptation to hypoxia and of interpopulation differences.

The reported effect of almost total infertility among Spanish colonial women moving to high altitude (Monge, 1948) appears to have been particularly drastic. In Ethiopia, low-altitude-born women moving to high altitude have experienced successful pregnancies (Harrison et al., 1969). But among such subjects there was a higher rate of reported miscarriages than at low altitude. In the United States there is also anecdotal evidence of a greater risk of fetal loss, especially in the third trimester (Johnson and Roofe, 1965; McClung, 1969; Van Liere and Stickney, 1963).

In high-Andean natives the reported rate of abortion is extremely low. Rates of less than 10 per 1000 live births have been reported (Cruz-Coke et al., 1966; Cruz-Coke, 1967; Hoff, 1968; Buck et al., 1968), and of 49 per 1000 by Way (1972) and 60 per 1000 (CISM, 1968). In the low-altitude community of Arica, Chile, Cruz-Coke (1967) estimated an abortion rate of between 17 and 30 percent. It has been suggested by Clegg et al. (1970) that at high altitude abortions may occur too early to be recognized as such.

There is, however, evidence of a different nature that the rate of intrauterine survival differs at high altitude, among the Indigenous Andean populations. The sex ratio at birth (secondary sex ratio, or SSR) has been found to be unusually high, between 110 and 130 (M.S.P.A.S., 1965; Hoff, 1968; Baker and Dutt, 1972), at least in the Puno area of the Peruvian altiplano. Indeed, Clegg and Harrison (1971) point out that under stressed conditions male mortality is usually increased. As Ciocco (1938) showed for seven states in the United States, for all months of pregnancy the rate of fetal loss of males was greater than of females. At the present the reported SSRs of the southern altiplano are an anomaly. Both genetic and environmental factors remain as possible explanations; and gametic selection cannot be ruled out.

With respect to the physiology of pregnancy at high altitude, several changes have been observed. Placental size is increased, in the llama (Meschia et al., 1960) and in the ewe (Barron et al., 1964), at high altitude. Placental sizes and weights in human populations were found to be increased in Cuzco at high altitude (McClung, 1969); birth weights were decreased, compared with those measured at Lima at low altitude. The larger placental size relative to birth weight is adaptive in that there is a greater capacity to deliver oxygen and nutrients to the fetus. McClung also found morphological changes in the placentas of the high-altitude Indian sample that favored the delivery of blood to the fetus. Similar findings with respect to increased placental size and decreased birth weight at high altitude have been made by Kruger and Arias-Stella (1970) and Sobrevilla (1971).

The decrease in birth weight with altitude has also been observed in the United States by Lichty et al. (1957) and Grahn and Kratchman (1963), and it appears that the decrease observed in the United States is greater than that seen in Peru (McClung, 1969; Haas, 1973a). Concerning the reduced birth weights at high altitude in Peru, McClung was able to eliminate factors such as maternal size, parity, and smoking, and Haas was able to eliminate factors such as nutrition, rural—urban differences, and socioeconomic and cultural factors. When altitude was controlled the birth weights were greater for Indians than for both Caucasians and the interethnic group, Mestizos. It is possible that the smaller reduction in birth weight among Amerindians at high altitude may be related to genetic factors, as McClung has suggested; but the issue is complicated by the fact that Amerindian birth weights in general are larger than in all other ethnic groups (Roberts, 1969). These ethnic differences may then be unrelated to any altitude effect.

The reduced birth weights at high altitude are accompanied by reduced secretion of estrogens in the maternal venous system, the amniotic fluid, and the urine (Sobrevilla, 1967; Sobrevilla et al., 1968). The reduction of these estrogens, particularly estriol, appears to be a function of metabolic changes in the fetoplacental unit.

Last, with respect to physiology, hyperventilation and reduced vital capacity, seen at low altitude, have also been recorded at high altitude at Cerro de Pasco at 4600 m (Sobrevilla, 1971). There was marked respiratory alkalosis and a blood pH of 7.432 in these subjects. Although it is uncertain that further stress is imposed on the fetus per se, there is evidence that increased alkalinity of the uterus is associated with an increased SSR, at least in mice (Weir, 1953, 1955).

The low birth weights seen at high altitude are accompanied by an increase in neonatal and infant mortality (Grahn and Kratchman, 1963; Mazess, 1965; Cruz-Coke et al., 1966). Of these infants with low birth weights, a greater proportion than usual were male (Acosta Chavez, 1964); and Spector (1971) found that the differential mortality between males and females in infancy was increased at high altitude. In the United States Grahn and Kratchman found that the increase in infant mortality was almost entirely attributable to low birth weight induced by hypoxia. As Frisancho and Cossman (1970) have shown, the increasing use of incubators has led to a secular decline in infant mortality in the mountain states of the United States. In Peru, infant mortality at high altitude is further complicated by cold and poor rural medical facilities (Frisancho and Yañez, 1971). In Ethiopia, Harrison et al. (1969) found an elevated perinatal mortality, which might indicate an inadequate intrauterine environment. In general, the biological characteristics of highland Ethiopian populations differ somewhat from those of Andean populations (Clegg et al., 1970), possibly reflecting differences in adaptation to hypoxia.

In summary, there is evidence that hypoxia acts as a stress during pregnancy and parturition. For women not normally resident at high altitude, there is a greater risk of fetal loss. Birth weights are lower at high altitude and infant mortality is increased. High-Andean populations show some differences with respect to rates of abortion and SSR, and there is some circumstantial evidence relating the latter to physiological intrauterine changes. Adaptation to the stress of hypoxia may occur by increased placental size, but the extent to which populations vary in their capacity to adapt to hypoxic stress during pregnancy is not known.

ALTITUDE AND FERTILITY

The assessment of the effect of hypoxic stress at high altitude on fertility poses several problems. In particular, fertility is affected by many cultural, social, and behavioral factors. Thus, measurement of the effect of hypoxia on fertility, even within a single homogeneous community, is difficult. Where many populations are studied under the broad heading "Altitude and Fertility," further complications are introduced, by cultural and social variation between communities, between nations, and between continents. In addition, it is not entirely irrelevant that populations vary in their genetic composition. However, starting from the broad level of analysis based on national census data, more specific hypotheses and methods of analysis have been developed. This approach has led to the study of fertility at the community level, and to the analysis of the reproductive performance of individual women within the communities. From these investigations it has been possible to assess the relative role of hypoxia within the context of the community. Such studies also provide some understanding of the importance of social and cultural factors in fertility.

National and Regional Studies
in the Andes

Census Studies. Studies utilizing census data from Peru, Ecuador, and Bolivia show that fertility is reduced at high altitude. At the same time this level of analysis only allows workers to postulate that one or several of a variety of factors are of importance. Measures of fertility were taken from the 1940 census of Peru (total number of children born) and the 1950 censuses of Ecuador and Bolivia (child/women ratios).

First observations by Stycos (1963) related fertility differences to behavioral and cultural differences between Indian- and Spanish-language speakers. Heer (1964) found that the ethnographic literature did not support such a relationship; he suggested that fertility differentials were functional effects of socioeconomic and demographic structure, demonstrated by a negative correlation of the fertility of women with their proportion in the labor force, and a positive correlation of fertility with the adult sex ratio. But when altitude was introduced as a variable, James (1966) found it to be the most important factor. On reanalysis, Heer (1967) confirmed this result for Peru, but not for Ecuador or Bolivia. But as Baker and Dutt (1972) observe, altitude is positively correlated with both Indian-language speaking and the proportion of women in the labor force. Altitude is negatively correlated with the adult sex ratio, where migrants are preponderantly men moving from high to low altitude. Complications are found in Ecuador and Bolivia, where the capital cities are at high altitude.

Problems of a different nature are raised by Whitehead (1968) and Bradshaw (1969). The effect of high infant mortality rates, especially at high altitude, renders the use of the child/woman ratio unreliable as a measure of fertility (see Robinson, 1963). In addition, Bradshaw has suggested that there may be underreporting and underenumeration of births, particularly in poorer rural areas at high altitude. The result that Mazess (1965) obtained, showing that infant mortality is greater at high altitude and increased in rural areas, does cast serious doubt on the validity of the use of the child/woman ratio as a measure of fertility. On the other hand, the force of the criticism of inadequate census data collection in Peru is reduced where "children ever born" was used as the measure of fertility. Infant mortality is computed in relation to live births, and it seems unlikely that the births of those that survive are reported less frequently than those that die. However, Mazess' study was based on vital-statistics data, which are not directly comparable to census data.

Reviewing these results, doubt must remain as to the accuracy of the data used. A basic relationship between higher altitude and reduced fertility is demonstrated (Fig. 7.1), but a variety of explanations of this relationship is possible at this level of analysis. For this reason, both DeJong (1970) and

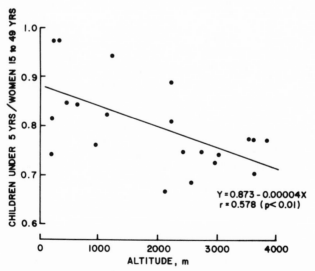

FIGURE 7.1 *Fertility and altitude in 21 Peruvian provinces. [From Instituto Nacional de Planificacion (1964).]*

Baker and Dutt (1972) find that the interpretation of results derived from the use of aggregate statistics is difficult.

Vital Statistics Data. Detailed information on the fertility of populations in the Andes is limited. Baker and Dutt (1972) have reviewed these data. Lack of demographic detail rather than the level of analysis prevent any direct conclusions concerning how fertility varies with altitude. On the other hand, with respect to biological and social characteristics of reproductive life, it was possible to suggest that certain aspects of fertility at high altitude were atypical of low-altitude peasant populations.

The data presented in Table 7.1 are taken from studies at Vicos, Peru (Alers, 1965), at Cerro de Pasco in Peru (CISM, 1968), from highland Chilean communities (Cruz-Coke, 1967; Cruz-Coke et al., 1966), and from Nuñoa in Peru. The data on crude birth and death rates are largely uninformative. These rates are high, and paralleled by high death rates. The high-altitude community of Lauca in Chile has exceptionally high birth and death rates. The very high crude birth rate here may simply be a function of the interaction of fertility with infant mortality; but in the absence of data on the age—sex structure of the populations, no conclusions can be reached.

Despite the lack of demographic detail, Baker and Dutt were able to identify three ways in which the high-altitude communities might differ from other populations in their pattern of fertility. The use of contraceptive methods in Cerro de Pasco is extremely limited (CISM, 1968). In conjunction with this, Baker and Dutt suggest that the marital pattern of serial monogamy and changes of mates during reproductive life probably does not act to reduce fertility. They found that at Nuñoa the proportion of children ever born among postmenopausal women was greater in second unions than in first unions. It may be that the infertility of a union acts to disrupt the union; and as we shall see, there are some substantial advantages to be gained from larger family size. On the other hand, temporary emigration of a seasonal nature provides ample opportunity for the formation of liaisons with other partners. There appears, then, little reason to suspect that mate change acts to reduce fertility. Similar conclusions were reached with respect to high-altitude Ethiopian populations (Harrison et al., 1969).

The pattern of growth and development at high altitude differs from that at low altitude. Several observers (Frisancho and Baker, 1970; Sobrevilla, 1967; Cruz-Coke, 1967) have found that the age at menarche is delayed at high altitude. In general, growth is slower and adult size (which is smaller than at low altitude) takes longer to reach in highland Peru (Frisancho and Baker, 1970; Hoff, 1972b), and in highland Nepal (Pawson, 1972). Ethiopian highlanders form an exception, where those living at high altitude may suffer less stress during growth from disease and nutritional factors than lowlanders (Clegg et al., 1972).

While nutritional and disease factors may certainly affect growth, it is unlikely that these factors have any effect directly on fertility. Only gross

TABLE 7.1 *Comparative Fertility and Mortality Rates for Various Andean Communities*

Place	Mean altitude (m)	Year	Size of population	Crude birth rate (births/1000)	Crude death rate (deaths/1000)	Infant mortality rate (deaths/1000 < 1 yr)
Arica, Chile[a]	100	1965	No data	47.9	6.9	24.0
Belen, Chile[a]	3,200	1965	No data	46.0	20.7	175.0
Lauca, Chile[a]	4,300	1965	No data	82.4	50.0	388.0
Vicos, Peru[b]	2,800	1952	1,798	45.6	14.5	122.0
	2,800	1963	2,118	56.2	24.6	142.9
Cerro de Pasco, Peru[c]	4,600	1967	30,000	53–54	No data	100.0
Nuñoa, Peru	4,200	1940	6,470	56.6	—	—
	4,200	1961	7,750	48.6	23.5	164.10

[a]From Cruz-Coke et al. (1966).
[b]From Alers (1965).
[c]From CISM (1968).

nutritional insult appears to affect fertility (Stein and Susser, 1973); and for a sample of high-Andean altiplano communities near Puno, nutritional intake was more than adequate (Mazess and Baker, 1964; ICNND, 1959). With respect to disease, at high altitude in Peru upper-respiratory-tract infections predominate (Buck et al., 1968; Spector, 1971). Such diseases apparently are not of importance to fertility (Sever, 1966).

Nor does this growth pattern seem to reduce fertility by shortening the length of reproductive life. Mean ages of mothers at first live birth are similar for those living at different altitudes (Cruz-Coke, 1967; Abelson et al., 1974). But Baker and Dutt (1972) did observe that for postmenopausal women in Nuñoa, fertility had been highest in the fourth decade of life. A similar observation was made for Huallatire at high altitude in Chile, by Cruz-Coke (1967). This differing pattern of fertility with age seen at high altitude parallels the observation of greater fertility among second unions. In the absence of evidence for nutritional and disease effects on fertility at high altitude, the unusual pattern of age-related fertility may most easily be explained either in terms of culturally mediated modifications or, possibly, adaptation to hypoxic stress during reproductive life.

Concerning age at menopause at high altitude, there are no reliable data. Estimates by Cruz-Coke (1967) and Hoff (1968) give figures in the range 45–50 yr, which are not abnormal by low-altitude population standards.

Baker and Dutt (1972) found that for 9920 births over a 25-yr period from 1940 to 1964, the mean SSR was 110.9. They were unable to discover any practices of differential reporting of births by sex of child, or any evidence of female infanticide.

This survey by Baker and Dutt did not provide any answer to the question: Why is fertility lower at high altitudes? It did, however, find that some characteristics of the fertility of high-altitude populations are unusual, and pointed to the necessity of detailed study of individual women in communities. It also emphasized the need to use an integrated approach, considering not only one set of variables, social, cultural, or biological, but also how these variables interact.

The Study of Individual Women in Communities

Nuñoa: A High-Altitude Community at 4200 Meters. The study of fertility in Nuñoa has been an integral part of the IBP Andean biocultural study, since the earliest stages of this research project (Baker, 1965a). Individual life histories, together with socioeconomic and cultural data, were collected during the 1964–1965 field sessions, comprising a 10 percent sample of the population. A further small sample was collected by Way (1972).

The Nuñoan population are primarily Quechua in origin. Their marital patterns and reproductive life style have been studied by T. Baker (1966), and the relevance of these factors to reproductive performance has been assessed by Hoff (1968). Escobar M. (Chapter 3 of this volume) and Thomas (1972) have considered the importance of the resulting family sizes for social and economic implications.

Unions are formed by trial marriage, consensual union, or formal marriage through civil registration and/or religious ceremony. These categories are not mutually exclusive, the tendency being that consensual unions, should they last, are later formalized (T. S. Baker, 1966). Consensual unions are often of shorter duration than formal marriages, but after separation, remarriage usually occurs.

The existence of a union does not define the period of exposure to risk of pregnancy. Hoff (1968) found that the formation of first union most often followed first pregnancy. Similarly, it does not follow that a woman is not at risk of pregnancy between unions. This pattern of frequent mate change is termed "serial monogamy," and acts to include almost all the women into the breeding population. Hoff (1968) found that only 3 women out of his sample of 136 had not given birth to a child, all 3 being under 26 yr of age.

The reproductive performance of Nuñoan females, by Western standards, is high, with a completed fertility of 6.7 (Hoff, 1968). Age at inclusion into the reproductive community and reproductive performance of Nuñoans are compared to those of other Andean communities in Table 7.2. Completed fertility in Nuñoa is slightly less than in Huallatire (7.3) and Cerro de Pasco (7.7), but by peasant society standards these values are not high. Henry (1961) has compiled data on the fertility of populations that do not practice contraception, and found a distribution of completed fertility ranging from 6.2 to 10.9. The high-altitude populations considered here are in the lower part of the range.

Considered in the context of environment and community, Hoff (1968) suggested that despite the stress of hypoxia, with cold superimposed, Nuñoa women reach high fertility levels. These levels were achieved by incorporating almost all women into the breeding population, combined with cultural and behavioral factors that act to maximize fertility. As Clegg and Harrison (1971) state, these high levels of fertility result from a reduction in unused reproductive capacity.

Surveys of preference for family size, at Cerro de Pasco (CISM, 1968) and in Nuñoa (Thomas, 1972), indicate desired family sizes of six or more children. Social demographers have claimed that social norms of fertility are, in fact, major determinants of the numbers of children born (Freedman, 1961–1962; Hawthorn, 1970). In Nuñoa it is possible to point not so much to desired family size as an explanation of high fertility, but rather to its practical advantage in terms of subsistence, at least to the parental generation.

The staple diet in the high Andes is based on the potato, with grain crops playing a secondary role. Therefore, potato production is of primary importance. Thomas (1972) has shown that the energetic efficiency of the prepara-

TABLE 7.2 *Fertility Statistics for Individual Women in Communities*

| Community | Altitude (m) | Sample size | Mean age (yr) | | | Completed fertility at 45 yr |
			At time of sample	At first pregnancy	At first marriage	
Nuñoa[a]	4000–4500	136	36.2	19.5	19.7	6.7 (N, 31)
Cerro de Pasco[b]	4400	642	ca. 33	–	–	7.7 (N, 58)
Huallatire[c]	4300	30	31.8	18.7	–	7.3 (N not given)
Tambo valley[d]	100					
Nonmigrants		63	37.63	19.77	19.81	8.29 (N, 14)
Low-altitude-born migrants	Born below 3000	57	39.56	19.12	19.09	–
High-altitude-born migrants	Born above 3000	121	31.75	19.45	19.57	–

[a]From Hoff (1968).
[b]From CISM (1968).
[c]From Cruz-Coke et al. (1966) and Cruz-Coke (1967).
[d]From Abelson et al. (1974).

tion of fields for cultivation is optimal for three workers, two men and one woman. A man and his wife can extract more energy from the crop than they expend in its preparation. For the individual working alone, the energy expended in production is hardly covered by the caloric value of the resulting crop. This provides a strong incentive for the formation of unions in adult life. Social ties, primarily with biological kin, make it possible to form the optimal group in potato production. Such kin are available as a result of larger family sizes. These larger family sizes are also important in relation to herding activities. Here Thomas has shown that it is energetically more efficient for lower-calorie consumers (i.e., children) to perform this activity. In order to provide this labor for the length of adult life, optimal family size is seven children spaced at about 3-yr intervals. Finally, certain dietary components are obtained by trading with those living in other ecozones in the Andes—"vertical adaptation." Trading partners may be kin who have married into these other communities. Escobar similarly points out that the social system of an extended family within the community, and kin relations both within the community and outside the community, performs social functions that act to reinforce the network of relationships necessary to meet subsistence requirements.

The Tambo Valley: Low-Altitude Communities at 100 Meters. As we have indicated, considerable evidence exists to show that hypoxia acts as a stress that reduces fertility at high altitude; but the fertility of Nuñoan women is high. Therefore, a comparative study of fertility at low altitude was undertaken to investigate the role of hypoxia (Abelson et al., 1974). This study utilized a research design that would illustrate the effects of a high-altitude environment on a phenotypic characteristic of a population (Harrison, 1966).

The subjects of the study were natives to low altitude, born in the Tambo Valley; migrants to the valley born at low altitude; and migrants to the valley born at high altitude. Environmental effects were illustrated by comparing the fertility of nonmigrants resident at different altitudes, and by the change in fertility with change in residence from high to low altitude. Specifically, the effect of downward migration from high altitude allows the measurement of the effect of the removal of the hypoxic stress on fertility. The effect of migration on fertility was controlled for by examining the fertility of low-altitude-born migrants to the Tambo valley. These effects were measured by the use of a series of dyadic comparisons. Aspects of reproductive life style and sociocultural variables uncontrolled in the dyadic comparisons were examined in an analysis of intrapopulation variation.

The sample used was approximately 10 percent of the adult female population of the communities of Cocachacra, Chucarapi, Arenal, and La Curva. In addition to the fertility and sociocultural questionnaires administered in Nuñoa, data on migration and contraception were also collected. [For details of these questionnaires, see Abelson (1972).] The measure of fertility used was the number of children born in a 5-yr age interval. Thus it was possible to measure the fertility of the subjects according to the environment in which they lived at that time.

As in Nuñoa, it was found that almost all women enter the breeding population; only one subject over the age of 25 yr, a low-altitude-born migrant, had not given birth to a child. Reproductive life style was also similar to that of Nuñoa, age at first marriage generally being later than age at first pregnancy; consensual unions and remarriage were common. There was some variation with respect to social, economic, and cultural characteristics. Migrants were in general of lower socioeconomic class and less well educated than nonmigrants. Literacy and length of schooling were less for those born at high altitude. The first language learned by those born at low altitude was Spanish, while those born at high altitude first learned to speak either Quechua or Aymara. These high-altitude-born migrants were derived mainly from the Puno–Lake Titicaca region of the altiplano.

Length of reproductive life for all groups was similar, and age at first pregnancy and at first marriage for Tambo valley subjects are almost identical to the values for Nuñoa (Table 7.2). Contraceptive practice was not well understood and exceedingly limited. Completed fertility for 14 nonmigrants living in the Tambo valley was 8.29, which is higher than for Nuñoa, Cerro de Pasco, and Huallatire (Table 7.2). The measure of completed fertility was not appropriate for the migrants, who were exposed to the risk of pregnancy in more than one environment. Abortions were reported by those at risk of pregnancy at low altitude, but not with the frequency of 17–30 percent that Cruz-Coke (1967) reports for the low-altitude community of Arica, Chile. Rather interestingly, the downward migrants reported high SSRs among live births, of over 120, both before and after migration, but sample sizes were small.

Rates of fertility by 5-yr age interval and place of residence are given in Table 7.3. For migrants prior to migration, data are incomplete, because migration occurs during reproductive life. Total fertility for the Tambo valley nonmigrants was 8.04, giving rather more confidence in their calculated completed fertility of 8.29.

Figures 7.2 and 7.3 were extrapolated from the data in Table 7.3, and from Hoff (1968). The number of children born, by age, give very similar slopes for the downward migrants before migration and for the Nuñoa population. Since these slopes represent rates of fertility, the data from the downward migrants before migration to the Tambo valley were used in statistical comparison. The original data from Hoff (1968) were presented in a slightly different form, making direct comparison difficult. The downward migrants at risk of pregnancy at high altitude were significantly less fertile (calculated with Student's t-test) than Tambo valley nonmigrants (ages 15–19.9, $p < 0.02$; ages 20–24.9, $p < 0.01$), and also when compared to the fertility of high-altitude-born subjects at risk of pregnancy in the Tambo

TABLE 7.3 Births by 5-Year Age Intervals, According to Altitude of Birthplace and Migrant Status: From Reproductive Histories of Subjects Living in the Tambo Valley[a]

| | Low-altitude-born | | | | | | | | | High-altitude-born | | | | | |
| | Nonmigrant Tambo valley | | | Migrant before migration | | | Migrant after migration | | | Migrant before migration | | | Migrant after migration | | |
Age group	N	X	S.D.	N	X̄	S.D.	N	X̄	S.D.	N	X̄	S.D.	N	X̄	S.D.
15–19.9	56	0.79	1.02	36	0.44	0.65	19	0.95	0.91	57	0.37	0.69	23	1.08	0.99
20–24.9	54	1.87	1.23	18	1.28	1.13	30	1.70	0.99	33	1.12	1.11	39	2.00	0.75
25–29.9	44	1.89	1.20	—			34	1.65	1.07	17	1.41	1.12	38	1.76	1.10
30–34.9	34	1.53	1.37	—			29	1.34	0.97	—			31	1.84	1.03
35–39.9	28	1.21	1.37	—			24	1.00	1.14	—			21	1.14	1.01
40–44.9	16	0.75	0.86	—			19	1.05	1.47	—			14	0.64	1.09
Total	8.04						7.69						8.46		

[a]From Abelson et al. (1974).

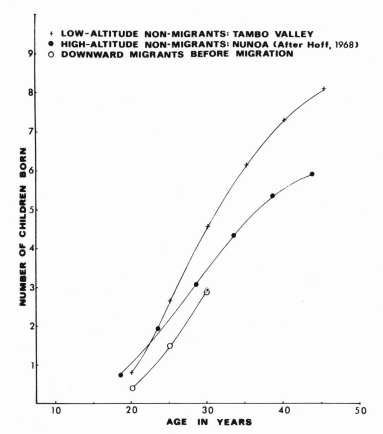

FIGURE 7.2 *Cumulative fertility of high- and low-altitude non-migrant populations. [Reprinted from Abelson et al. (1974).]*

valley (ages 15–19.9, $p < 0.01$; ages 20–24.9, $p < 0.01$). Low-altitude-born migrants did show an increase in fertility for the age group 15–19.9 years ($p = 0.05$), but for other groups of the same age, no further statistically significant differences in fertility were found.

Migration may act to increase fertility, in cases where fertility before migration is low. But this increase did not result in a level of fertility greater than that of nonmigrants living at the same altitude and under similar socioeconomic conditions (Table 7.3). In contrast, the increased fertility of downward migrants is not only greater than that of nonmigrants living at high altitude, but also greater than that of nonmigrants living at low altitude (Table 7.3). These results do then provide evidence that the stress of hypoxia does act to reduce fertility at high altitude.

An analysis of intrapopulation variation, and interpopulation variation for those at risk of pregnancy in the Tambo valley, showed no significant

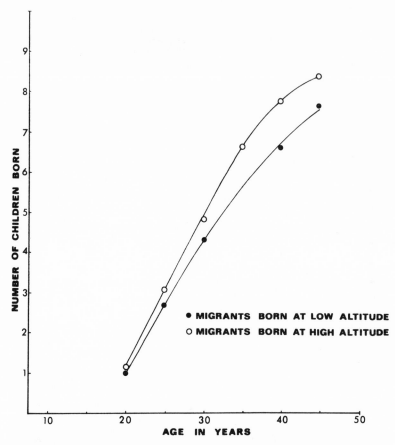

FIGURE 7.3 *Cumulative fertility of migrant populations after migration. [Reprinted from Abelson et al. (1974).]*

differences in fertility with respect to sociocultural-, economic-, migration-, or community-of-residence-related variation. However, as a group those born at high altitude were significantly more fertile, at the 0.05 level, than those born at low altitude. Considering fertility changes with migration, the studies of Goldberg (1959) and Iutaka et al. (1971) indicate that migrants tend to retain the fertility characteristics of their place of birth for at least one generation. Mejia Valera (1963) has also pointed out that downward migrants tend to remain unacculturated at low altitude. So, if those living at high altitude attempt to maximize their fertility, retention of this reproductive life style may account for the downward migrants having higher fertility than those born at low altitude in the Tambo Valley.

Hypoxia, which acts to reduce fecundity, appears to be the major component of reduced fertility at high altitude. This effect is seen in Table 7.4. The populations described are based on synthetic cohorts, and parity intervals

TABLE 7.4   *Parity Intervals, Based on Population
Differences Between Ages at Each Parity Level[a]*

| Interval | Nonmigrant populations | | Migrant populations after migration to Tambo valley | |
	Tambo valley	Nuñoa	Low-altitude born	High-altitude born
1–2	3.0	4.5	3.0	3.0
2–3	2.5	4.0	3.0	2.5
3–4	2.5	4.0	3.0	2.5
4–5	3.0	5.0	3.5	2.5
5–6	3.0	7.5	4.0	3.0
6–7	3.5	—	5.0	3.0
7–8	6.0	—	—	5.0
1–6	2.80	5.00	3.25	2.70
1–7	3.08	—	3.54	2.75
1–8	3.50	—	—	3.07
No. of years, first birth to last	23.5	25.0	21.5	21.5

[a]From Abelson et al. (1974), interpolated from Figs. 1 and 2.

are calculated as the number of years between the successive numbers of children ever born. The description of parity intervals in this way reduces bias that results where individual women differ in their ages at each parity, and in cases where higher fertility is associated with more infant deaths. It also allows comparison of migrants and nonmigrants. While the number of child-bearing years, from the first birth until the last, is similar for all the populations, the spacing between births is always greater in Nuñoa at high altitude. This is consistent with the explanation that hypoxia acts to reduce fertility throughout reproductive life.

SUMMARY AND CONCLUSIONS

In this review we have attempted to show how hypoxia acts as a stress that reduces fecundity in both animal and human populations. In human populations, men normally resident at low altitude may experience temporary infertility on moving to high altitude; it does not seem to be of lasting importance. Low-altitude women moving to high altitude experience menstrual disturbances and risk of fetal loss, especially in the third trimester. Birth weights are reduced at high altitude, but this reduction is less for the Indigenous populations of the high Andes. Removal of the hypoxic stress by migration to low altitude results in increased birth weights and in increased fertility.

Adaptation to the stress of hypoxia occurs by means of an increased placental size, giving rise to a more favorable fetal environment. For native Andean women living at high altitude, decrease in birth weight and increase in placental size are accompanied by changes in endocrine secretion. Concerning live births it is not impossible that the altered intrauterine environment is related to the reported high secondary sex ratios found in a rather localized area of the Peruvian altiplano.

High-Andean populations also report a very low rate of fetal loss. If this report is indeed true, there may be an implication of more rigorous rejection of zygotes at early stages in pregnancy. Zygotes may conceivably be malformed through hypoxia-induced stress, or maladaptation of the maternal environment may be indicated. The long spacing between births at high altitude in the Andes is suggestive of fetal loss, despite the fact that only negative evidence is available in support of this statement.

Considered in the context of their community, social activities, and subsistence requirements, Nuñoans attempt to maximize their fertility. The necessity to meet the requirements of these interrelated activities places a premium on large family size and high reproductive performance, which must be achieved in the face of the combined stresses of hypoxia and cold, stresses that act to reduce fecundity.

Three mechanisms of adaptation may be identified:

1. Cultural and behavioral modifications of the breeding structure.

2. Maximum use of the reproductive life span.

3. Physiological changes during pregnancy. Such changes appear largely to be the result of plastic responses, but genetic factors remain to be ruled out.

These responses of high-Andean natives, which are necessary for their immediate short-term requirements, have important implications for their long-term survival, especially with respect to their reproductive capacity.

8

MORBIDITY AND POSTNEONATAL MORTALITY

Anthony B. Way

There is often confusion about the concept of adaptation. Some of this confusion arises, as Mazess (personal communication) points out, because different types of adaptation can apply to a variety of levels of biological organization: molecular, cellular, tissue, organ, physiological, individual, familial, social, species, and ecological. Some confusion also arises because in English the word may refer either to the process of adapting or to the result of adapting.

The characteristic of greatest importance in biological evolution is the ability of a population to maintain itself from generation to generation. This population characteristic may be thought of as encompassing a variety of processes for adapting to the environment. In order to have an effect of evolutionary significance, each adaptive process must have an effect on fertility or mortality (Crow, 1958; Fisher, 1958) which may be considered to be the result of adapting.

Mortality, therefore, may be an indicator of the adaptive state of a population. In most cases, populations with a lower mortality in a given environment than other populations may be considered to be better adapted. Populations with a mortality consistently in excess of fertility are clearly in danger of extinction and therefore may be called "maladapted."

Mortality is closely related to fertility when one considers prenatal and neonatal deaths, but since Hoff and Abelson discuss fertility in Chapter 7, this chapter will generally be limited to postneonatal mortality. While mortality, as an indicator of adaptation, may be studied directly, in some circumstances it is easier to study an indicator of mortality. Morbidity, or the level of illness, may be an indicator of mortality if one assumes that, in general, sick people are likely to die sooner than healthy people. This assertion seems reasonable if one considers that all people must eventually die of either disease or trauma. Thus, morbidity may be an indirect indicator of a population's adaptive state.

Nontraumatic morbidity may be divided into two categories: chronic illnesses and acute illnesses. Chronic illnesses are defined as those that persist through time and worsen progressively. Many chronic diseases lead either to death or increased susceptibility to death. The prevalence of chronic disease therefore should be a predictor of the mortality rate.

Acute illnesses, however, are defined as being intermittent. The end result of an acute illness will be either death or recovery. Often it is an acute illness that produces death during a chronic illness. The incidence of acute illnesses, therefore, should also be a predictor of the mortality rate.

REVIEW OF OTHER STUDIES

Prior to and concurrent with the Nuñoa project, a number of other studies have provided information about mortality and morbidity at high altitude. Mazess (1965) presented data on the crude death rate of Peruvian departments (political subdivisions) and the altitudes of the departmental capitals. If one accepts Mazess' (1965) assumption that the altitude of the departmental capital reflects the altitude of a major portion of the departmental population, analysis of the data reveals no significant correlation between these altitudes and mortality rates. This finding is true even though medical care, as measured inversely by the number of medically unassisted births, declines significantly with altitude. Cruz-Coke et al. (1966) did find that the crude death rate is higher at 3200 and 4300 m above sea level than at 100 m in Chile. However, the crude death rate at 4300 m is surprisingly high, being more than two times greater than the highest crude death rate reported by Mazess (1965). Even so, these three death rates are not significantly correlated (statistically) with altitude.

Chronic Disease

The prevalence of chronic disease in high-altitude populations is reported to be different from that in low-altitude populations. A chronic disease unique to high-altitude populations is chronic mountain sickness (Hurtado, 1955, 1960; McFarland, 1952; Monge, 1937; Monge and Monge, 1966). This disease is characterized by relative hypoventilation, tissue hypoxia, and polycythemia. Buck et al. (1968), in a study of four Peruvian villages at 150, 730, 1870 and 3500 m, found that the highest community had a high prevalence of polycythemia. This polycythemia was often associated with chronic lung disease and therefore probably represented chronic mountain sickness.

Other chronic illnesses reported to be increased or exacerbated at high altitude are: keloid formation, bleeding tendency (Hurtado, 1955); peptic ulcer (Hurtado, 1955, 1960; Monge and Monge, 1966); cholecystitis, cholelithiasis (Hurtado, 1960); tuberculosis (Hellriegel, 1967); and chronic nephritis (Monge and Monge, 1966). Chronic illnesses reported to be decreased in high-altitude populations are: tertiary syphilis (Hultgren and Spickard, 1960); leukemia (Hurtado, 1955); hypertension (Hurtado, 1960); and arteriosclerosis (Hellriegel, 1967, Hurtado, 1960). Unfortunately, as Krüger and Arias-Stella

(1964) pointed out, reports such as these are often just anecdotal and not well documented.

There are, however, some documented reports on chronic illnesses in high-altitude populations. Garrido-Klinge and Peña (1959) and Hellriegel (1967) found a higher incidence of gastric ulcers in the Peruvian Andes. Hellriegel (1967) also reported a higher incidence of gall-bladder disease at high altitude.

Alzamora et al. (1953) and Hellriegel (1967) reported an increase in atrial septal defects and patent ductus arteriosus with altitude in Peru. Calderón et al. (1966), Forbes (1936), and Picón-Reátegui (1962, 1963) all found lowered serum glucose levels during a glucose tolerance test at high altitude in the Andes. Picón-Reátegui et al. (1970) confirmed that altitude is the deter-mining factor in the low blood glucose concentrations in both sea-level and high-altitude natives.

Ruiz-Carillo (1973) documented lower blood pressures and serum choles-terol levels, less hypertension, and fewer signs and symptoms of cardiac ischemia in high-altitude natives than in low-altitude natives living in similar socioeconomic conditions. Watt et al. (1973) also reported low serum choles-terol levels and blood pressures. Buck et al. (1968) similarly found lower systolic pressures at high altitude.

On the other hand, Morton et al. (1964) and Morton (1966) could find no relationship between altitude and arteriosclerotic or hypertensive deaths in Colorado. Furthermore, Buck et al. (1967) found no regular change in the total number of radiologically visible cardiac and aortic lesions at 730, 1870, and 3500 m.

Infectious Diseases

From animal experiments there is evidence that at high altitude, resis-tance to acute viral infections is increased while resistance to acute bacterial infections is decreased (Berry et al., 1955; Ehrlich and Mieszkuc, 1962; Highman and Altland, 1964; Tengerdy and Kramer, 1968; Trapani, 1966, 1969). In man, Glenn (1959) found no change in serum proteins on acute exposure of two men to 3300 and 5600 m. Buck et al. (1968) did find a decrease in anthropod-borne viral infections and an increase in typical tuber-culosis infections with altitude in Peru. However, their epidemiological data may best be interpreted as showing that environmental factors other than hypoxia might account for the distribution of acute infections with altitude.

Other data on acute illnesses at high altitude include Hellriegel's (1967) and Puffer and Serrano's (1973) reports of very high incidences of respiratory infections at high altitude. Interestingly, Beall (1972) has shown that this high incidence of respiratory illnesses persists in high-altitude natives who have migrated to sea level. Hellriegel (1967) also reported a high incidence of postoperative hemorrhage and a low incidence of postoperative phleboth-rombosis, as well as a high incidence of intestinal volvulus.

High-Altitude Diseases

There are also data on health problems unique to people migrating to or from high altitude. Acute mountain sickness is a disease found in people who have just arrived at high altitude (Carson et al., 1969; Forwand and Landowne, 1968; Hecht, 1967; Pugh, 1964; Roy and Singh, 1969; Shields et al., 1969). This disease is characterized by hyperventilation, alkalosis, and, in extreme cases, pulmonary edema (Menon, 1965; Nayak et al., 1964). In high-altitude natives who descend to low altitude, Monge (1948) believed there is more tuberculosis. Reynafarje et al. (1959) and Reynafarje (1966a) also found that high-altitude natives have a lower than normal erythrocyte mass at sea level. On the other hand, Watt et al. (1973) found that high-altitude natives retain their low blood pressures, low serum cholesterol levels, and adiposity at low altitude.

On the basis of the mortality data cited above, one might conclude that populations native to high altitude may be as well adapted to their environment as populations at low altitude. The morbidity data cited, however, do not permit any generalizations along this line. Although it seems likely that altitude does have an effect on the pattern of morbidity, it is difficult to predict on the basis of this pattern what the indirect effect might be on mortality.

NUÑOA STUDY

Mortality

Crude death rates were calculated directly from the district of Nuñoa registry of vital statistics from 1950 to 1969 (Baker and Dutt, 1972; Spector, 1971). For a total of 3081 deaths over these 20 yr, the annual crude death rate varied from 15 to 25 deaths per 1000 population, except for 1957 when the death rate reached a maximum of 33.3. The 20-yr average was 20.11 ± 1.06 (S.E.).

TABLE 8.1   Crude Death Rates for Various Andean Communities[a]

Location	Altitude (m)	Period	Deaths/1000 population
Vicos, Peru[b]	2800	1952	14.5
Vicos, Peru[b]	2800	1963	24.6
Belen, Chile[c]	3200	1965	20.7
Nuñoa, Peru	4000	1950–1969	20.1
Laura, Chile[c]	4300	1965	50.0

[a]Adapted from Spector (1971), Table 1.
[b]From Alers, cited by Spector (1971).
[c]From Cruz-Coke et al. (1966).

TABLE 8.2 *Crude Death Rates*
for Selected Populations
(weighted Average
for 1950–1966)[a]

Area	Deaths/1000 population
Nuñoa (1950–1969)	20.1
India[b]	19.5
Guatemala[b]	19.0
United Arab Republic[b]	17.2
South Africa (Colored)	16.4
Ecuador	14.8
Chile	12.3
Mexico	12.2
Peru	11.2
Sweden	9.8
United States	9.5
Venezuela	8.6

[a]After Spector (1971), Table 6, as adapted from United Nations Statistical Office (1967).
[b]Estimated by Spector (1971).

This average death rate is approximately the same as the 20.9 found for the Province of Melgar (which includes the district of Nuñoa) in 1961. However, it is much higher than the 14.4 deaths per 1000 people reported for the Department of Puno (which includes the Province of Melgar) in 1961 or the 11.2 for Peru as a whole in 1967. As may be seen in Table 8.1, the 20-yr average crude death rate for Nuñoa is similar to the death rates from other high-altitude areas. Hoff (1968) found no significant differences in mortality between 369 offspring of 82 women from 3960 m and 239 offspring of 54 women from 4270 m. Table 8.2 presents estimated average crude death rates of 11 countries for comparison with Nuñoa. The death rate in Nuñoa is similar to that of countries with large peasant populations. However, Garruto and Hoff (see Chapter 5) calculate that unlike the case in other peasant populations, differential mortality contributes more to potential natural selection than does differential fertility. Also, as Spector's (1971) data show, the death rate in Nuñoa shows no regular change from 1950 to 1969, while the death rate of most of the countries, including Peru, clearly declined.

Spector (1971) also calculated 20-yr averages for each monthly death rate. He noted that the death rate reached a maximum from November to January, when it was about 60 percent above the minimum from April to June. He noted that the annual maximum coincided with the height of the rainy season, while the minimum occurred about harvest time.

The crude death rate is a unique characteristic for each population because it depends entirely upon the death rate of each specific age and sex group, and upon the age and sex distribution of the population. Baker and Dutt (1972) calculated age- and sex-specific death rates (Fig. 8.1) from the registry of vital statistics in the district of Nuñoa and from the age and sex composition of the Province of Melgar for the years 1940 to 1961. These results are virtually identical with those reported by Spector (1971) for 1950 to 1969. From these results (Fig. 8.1), it can be seen that mortality drops rapidly from a high in infancy to a low in the 10- to 14-yr-old age group. Mortality then rises slowly until there is a jump to a second maximum in the over-65 age group.

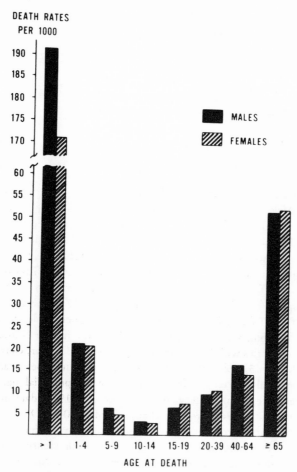

FIGURE 8.1 *Age- and sex-specific mortality rates for district of Nuñoa. Based on provincial census and district registry data, 1940–1961. [From Baker and Dutt (1972).]*

The population pyramid, based on the 1961 census for the district of Nuñoa (Fig. 1.3) also suggests that the mortality is highest up to the 10- to 14 yr-old cohort. Baker (1965b) presented a similar-appearing population pyramid for 476 subjects from randomly chosen families. This high mortality in the first 15 years of life is slightly more pronounced than for Peru as a whole (Baker, 1965b; Spector, 1971). Hoff (1968), in a study of the 608 offspring of 135 living women, also found that about 90 percent of the deaths in these offspring occurred before the age of reproduction (mean age of first pregnancy, 19.5 ± 3.5 S.D.). He also noted a mortality of about 30 percent in the first 5 years of life, which compares with a world average of about 13 percent.

Baker and Dutt (1972) calculated a survival curve from their age-specific mortality rates for comparison with the United States in 1965 and India in 1911. As may be seen from Fig. 8.2, mortality in infancy and childhood exceeds that of the United States but is only slightly less than for 1911 India. However, in adulthood, mortality in Nuñoa is similar to that of the United States and slightly less than for 1911 India.

Spector (1971) further broke down the deaths in the first year of life (Table 8.3). It can be calculated that, based on the same unit of time for

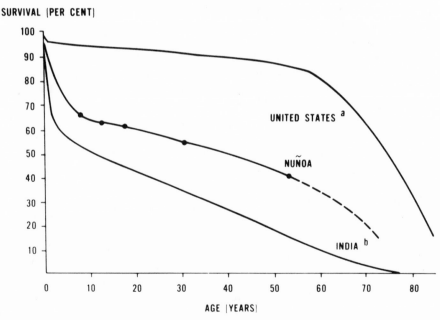

FIGURE 8.2 *Survivorship estimates for district of Nuñoa compared with other selected populations. (a) Estimate for 1965 U.S. population, Bogue (cited by Baker and Dutt, 1972). (b) Estimated from 1911 Indian census, United Nations (cited by Baker and Dutt, 1972). [Adapted from Baker and Dutt (1972).]*

TABLE 8.3   *Age-Specific Death Rates (Per*
1000 Live Births, Under 1
Year, for District of Nuñoa,
1950–1969[a]

Week of age	Number of deaths		
	Total	1000 per live births	Death rate per week of age
0–1	198	24.2	24.2
1–4	348	42.5	14.2
4–52	563	68.7	1.4

[a]Adapted from Spector (1971), Table 12.

deaths to occur, mortality drops by 41 percent from the first week to the next 3 weeks of life. It then drops again by 90 percent for the last 48 weeks in the first year of life.

As with the crude death rate, Spector (1971) found no clear decline in infant (under 1 yr) mortality, from 1950 to 1969. He also noted that seasonal variation in infant mortality is less marked than for older age groups and is probably related to the seasonality of births.

Baker (1965b), Baker and Dutt (1972), Hoff (1968), and Spector (1971) noted various differences in the mortality rates of males and females. However, few of these differences are shown to be statistically significant. Hoff's (1968) data show that female mortality (438/1000 population) is significantly greater ($p < 0.025$) than male mortality (273/1000 population) for a sample of 207 offspring of 31 living women who were over the age of 45. Spector's (1971) data also show that the mortality of women (8.4/1000 population) is significantly greater ($p < 0.025$) than the mortality of men (6.4/1000 population) in the age range of 20–30. This pattern is unlike that in either Peru as a whole or the United States (Fig. 8.3). However, in the 40- to 64-yr age range the men's mortality of 18.1 is significantly greater ($p < 0.05$) than the women's of 14.5.

Spector (1971) also divided his data into 300 pastoralists and 242 nonpastoralists (largely village dwellers) over the age of 15. Over the age of 15, the average age of death is 34.5 yr for pastoralists and 39.9 yr for nonpastoralists. A higher mortality for the pastoralists than the nonpastoralists, which is not marked in the 14–24 age group, persists until over the age of 64, for the years 1940–1949 and 1965–1969. Throughout the year the deaths in each of these groups seem not to be well correlated with each other, and appear to set a more irregular annual pattern than for the population as a whole.

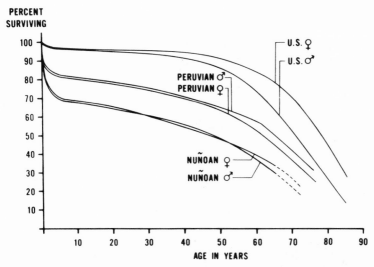

FIGURE 8.3 *Survivorship estimates for district of Nuñoa compared to life-table survivorship for Peru and the United States. [After Spector (1971), as adapted from United States Statistical Office (1967) and Direccion Nacional de Estadistica y Censos (1966).]*

In 1972 I compared the offspring mortality experience of Nuñoa area residents with that of high-altitude migrants to the Hacienda Chucarapi in the Tambo valley on the southern Peruvian coast (Way, 1972). I found no significant difference in the mortality of the offspring of these high-altitude men and women living at high and low altitudes. Furthermore, there was no significant change in offspring mortality with length of residence at low altitude. Looking at the mortality of 120–148 men and women, at both high and low altitudes, and correcting statistically for various factors, including age and estimated number of years of fertility, I found the combined prenatal and first-week mortality to be 8 ± 2.9 percent (S.E.) of all pregnancies. This value is not significantly different from Spector's (1971) first-week mortality rate of 2.4 percent. From 1 week to 5 yr of age, the mortality of the offspring was 24 ± 5.9 percent (S.E.), which together with the preceding perinatal mortality is similar to Hoff's (1968) 30 percent mortality by 5 years of age. The total mortality for all ages was 42 ± 5.5 percent (S.E.).

Morbidity

Spector (1971) also collected data on 3081 reported causes of deaths between 1950 and 1969. These are causes of death as determined and recorded by various medically untrained people. The five most common causes of death are given in Table 8.4. The paramount importance of

TABLE 8.4   *Five Highest Reported*
Causes of Death for
District of Nuñoa,
1950–1969[a]

Cause	Percentage of deaths (3081)
Respiratory	59.1
Other infectious diseases	16.5
Old age	7.1
Gastrointestinal	6.6
Degenerative	2.1

[a]Adapted from Spector (1971), Table 15.

respiratory deaths shown (Table 8.4) is confirmed by Hoff's (1968) data on causes of death in 608 offspring of 136 women and by Baker's (1969) casual observations of morbidity in living subjects. These results support Hellriegel's (1967) and Puffer and Serrano's (1973) reports. The peak in the crude death rate from November to January is preceded by a peak in respiratory deaths from October to December (Spector, 1971).

The Department of Puno, and Peru as a whole, had more gastrointestinal and degenerative disease (e.g., heart disease, cancer) deaths than did the district of Nuñoa (Spector, 1971). Hoff's (1968) data also show a relatively low mortality due to gastrointestinal as opposed to other causes. On the other hand, the district of Nuñoa has more deaths due to infectious disease (e.g., whooping cough, measles) than the Department of Puno or the nation as a whole (Spector, 1971).

As noted earlier, it is suspected that cardiovascular disease may be less common at high altitude (Hurtado, 1960; Ruiz-Carillo, 1973). Only about 1.8 percent of the deaths in Nuñoa are attributed to cardiovascular causes (Spector, 1971). Baker (1969) also reported no observed cardiovascular disease. Measuring casual blood pressures on both male and female subjects, he found no blood pressure over 150/90 torr. From his data, Baker (1969) believed that something associated with lower altitude, such as acculturation, may be the important factor contributing to a significant rise in blood pressure with age. These results are consistent with those of mine in 1972: blood pressures were measured on 150 men and women in the Nuñoa area and at sea level in the more acculturated Hacienda Chucarapi. Systolic blood pressures, adjusted for age, sex, and sex–altitude interaction, were found to be 7.0 torr lower ($p < 0.001$) at high altitude than at low altitude. Diastolic pressures were similar at both altitudes. No significant association with age was seen. At high altitude, the mean systolic pressure was 105.8 torr, and the mean diastolic pressure was 71.0 torr. Hoff (1972b) similarly found that

blood pressure is lower in Nuñoa than in comparable low-altitude populations. Watt and coworkers (1973), however, found no significant difference in
blood pressure in high-altitude natives at both high and low altitudes. Also,
unlike Watt et al. (1973), I found in 1972 that adiposity significantly
increased in high-altitude natives living at low altitude.

Breaking the population down into age groups, Spector (1971) showed
that respiratory causes of death predominate in all age groups. This finding is
true even in infancy in the district of Nuñoa, the Department of Puno
(Spector, 1971), and La Oroya, Peru (Hellriegel, 1967). However, Peru as a
whole attributes most of its infant deaths to gastrointestinal causes (Spector,
1971). In childhood, other infectious diseases (e.g., whooping cough, measles)
are more common causes of death than in adulthood (Spector, 1971). Baker
(1969) also reported finding many heart murmurs in Nuñoa children.

Spector (1971) asserted that during the period of reproduction, childbirth
accounted for 20 percent of the deaths of women. Comparing 303 pastoralists with 249 nonpastoralists over the age of 15 from 1940 to 1949 and from
1965 to 1969, Spector's (1971) data show that the pastoralists had significantly more ($p < 0.0005$) infectious-disease (e.g., typhus, typhoid fever)
deaths than the nonpastoralists.

These data on the incidence or prevalence of specific diseases provide a
good description of the health experience of the high-altitude population in
Nuñoa. However, it is often difficult to find data on a comparable low-
altitude population. It is probably not correct to compare any health (or
vital) statistic of a small, homogeneous community with that of a large,
heterogeneous population. Furthermore, it is difficult to draw conclusions
about a population's overall adaptation to the environment, when one disease
is more common and another is less common.

In an attempt to solve some of these problems, I collected health data
from 37 Quechua men and 39 Quechua women in the Nuñoa area, and from
38 Quechua men and 36 Quechua women who had migrated from high
altitude to work at low altitude on the Hacienda Chucarapi (Way, 1972). The
data consist of the number of symptoms and signs of chronic illness ascer-
tained by 179 questions and by physical examination for 158 findings, on
each subject. These frequencies of symptoms and signs are an indicator of
general health if one assumes that people with more symptoms or signs are
likely to be sicker than those with fewer symptoms or signs.

The high-altitude residents give a mean of about 21 more ($p < 0.02$)
symptoms each on the questionnaire than the low-altitude migrants (Table
8.5), after adjustment for a variety of disturbing variables, including age and
sex (Way, 1972). The symptoms were then broken down into 16 subcate-
gories. In a reanalysis of that data, 7 show significantly more chronic
symptoms at high altitude (Table 8.5).

The larger number of chronic hemolymphatic symptoms at high altitude
(Way, 1972) may reflect Hurtado's (1955) and Hellriegel's (1967) report of a

TABLE 8.5 *Categories with Significant Differences in Number of Reported Symptoms Between Quechua Subjects at 4000 Meters and at Sea Level*

Symptom category	Difference (high − low altitude) ± S.E.	Significance[a]
All chronic symptoms	21.2 ± 8.97	0.02
Ear and nose	1.8 ± 0.63	0.005
Hemolymphatic system	1.8 ± 0.62	0.005
Nervous system	4.6 ± 1.81	0.02
Skin	1.7 ± 0.70	0.02
Urinary	2.8 ± 1.21	0.025
Eye	2.1 ± 0.96	0.05
Allergic	1.7 ± 0.86	0.05

[a]Degrees of freedom, 136, except for "urinary," 135.

strong bleeding tendency at high altitude. On the other hand, the similarity in chronic respiratory symptoms suggests that, in line with Beall's (1972), Hoff's (1968), and Spector's (1971) data, the high-altitude native may suffer from a high incidence of respiratory illnesses, which is not altered by the altitude of residence in adulthood.

On physical examination for signs of chronic illness, no significant difference was found between high and low altitude after adjusting for age and sex (Way, 1972).

CONCLUSIONS

The long time that Quechua Indians have been at high altitude—300 or more generations (Hurtado, 1969; Monge, 1948)—suggests that they may have had time to develop measurable genetic adaptations to high-altitude hypoxia. If so, one might expect to find the mortality and morbidity rates at high altitude to be similar to those of comparable non-Quechua populations at low altitude. If they have also been relatively isolated from low altitude during the 300 generations, it is possible that genetic changes have proceeded to the point where mortality and morbidity rates of the Quechua would be lower at high altitude than those of Quechua who have recently migrated to low altitude.

Comparative data on the mortality of populations native to high and low altitudes by Cruz-Coke et al. (1966) and Mazess (1965) suggest that the high-altitude natives may be as well adapted to high altitude as the low-altitude natives are to low altitude. The data from Nuñoa (Baker and Dutt, 1972; Spector, 1971) make it clear that the mortality in this high-altitude area is similar to that of some other rural high-altitude communities (Table 8.1). Furthermore, my finding of similar mortalities in high-altitude natives at both high and low altitude suggests that they are at least equally well adapted to both high and low altitude. The Nuñoa mortality data, therefore, at least do not contradict the evidence that high-altitude natives could be genetically adapted to high altitude.

Otherwise, the Nuñoa data (Baker and Dutt, 1972; Hoff, 1968; Spector, 1971) suggest a mortality pattern similar to that of other populations lacking western health care (Table 8.2 and Fig. 8.2). Mortality is high during infancy and childhood, dropping to a low by adolescence. The mortality of women is high during the reproductive years (Tables 8.3 and 8.4; Fig. 8.1, 8.3, and 1.3). The only difference Nuñoa shows from other areas is a failure to participate in the decline in mortality commonly associated with inroads of western health care, likely reflecting a static health-care level in Nuñoa.

Reports from outside the Nuñoa area suggest that morbidity at high altitude may be different from that at low altitude. It is particularly clear that high altitude is associated with acute and chronic mountain sickness (Carson et al., 1969; Forwand and Landowne, 1968; Hecht, 1967; Hurtado, 1955; McFarland, 1952; Menon, 1965; Monge, 1937; Monge and Monge, 1966; Nayak, 1964; Pugh, 1964; Roy and Singh, 1969; Shields et al., 1969), more gastric ulcers (Garrido-Klinge and Peña, 1959; Hellriegel, 1967), lower blood pressure (Buck et al., 1968; Ruiz-Carillo, 1973; Watt et al., 1973), lower blood glucose levels (Calderón et al., 1966; Forbes, 1936; Picón-Reátegui, 1962, 1963; Picón-Reátegui et al., 1970), and probably more congenital heart defects (Alzamora et al., 1953; Hellreigel, 1967).

The Nuñoa data provide comparisons for some of these well-documented illnesses. Baker (1969), Hoff (1972a), and I (Way, 1972) confirmed that blood pressures are indeed low at high altitude. Baker (1969) also suggested a high incidence of congenital heart defects.

Although the evidence from other studies for less cardiovascular disease at high altitude is contradictory (Buck et al., 1968; Hellriegel, 1967; Hurtado, 1960; Morton, 1966; Morton et al., 1964; Ruiz-Carillo, 1973), the Nuñoa data are at least consistent with less cardiovascular disease (Baker, 1969; Spector, 1971). The Nuñoa data (Baker, 1969; Hoff, 1968; Spector, 1971) also support a high incidence of respiratory deaths at high altitude (Hellriegel, 1967; Puffer and Serrano, 1973) (Table 8.5). My recent data on chronic respiratory illnesses at high and low altitude (unpublished) suggest that the high incidence of respiratory illnesses at high altitude (Buck et al., 1968; Hellriegel, 1967; Hoff, 1968; Puffer and Serrano, 1973; Spector, 1971) may persist after downward migration (Beall, 1972; Monge, 1948). These data from Nuñoa may even support Hellriegel's (1967) and Hurtado's (1955) suspicion of an increased bleeding tendency at high altitude (Table 8.5). There may also be less gastrointestinal illness and more of some infectious disease in Nuñoa (Table 8.4) than elsewhere (Hoff, 1968; Spector, 1971), which is consistent with either some immunological (Berry et al., 1955; Ehrlich and Mieszkuc, 1969; Highman and Altland, 1964; Tengerdy and

Kramer, 1968; Trapani, 1966, 1969) or some microbial (Buck et al., 1968) alteration at high altitude.

Again, as with the mortality data, there are few comparable morbidity data from a community of similar low-altitude natives. Also, it is difficult to know how to combine these various data to draw conclusions about the overall adaptation of the high-altitude natives to high altitude. However, the specific morbidity data shown in Table 8.5 do point to a better adaptation to low than to high altitude.

In conclusion, the mortality data are at least consistent with some degree of genetic adaptation to high altitude by high-altitude Quechua Indians. The morbidity data, however, neither confirm nor deny the possibility of genetic adaptation, but merely emphasize that the pattern of morbidity changes with altitude. Further studies to clarify these issues are therefore warranted.

9

PRENATAL AND INFANT GROWTH AND DEVELOPMENT

Jere D. Haas

Human growth at high altitudes in Peru may be affected by many environmental stresses, including hypoxia, cold, nutritional deficiency, and disease, as well as genetic variation within the high-altitude populations. Previous investigations dealing with growth and development of children under environmental stress indicate that stress affects children most at ages when they are growing fastest and cellular division (hyperplasia) is most active (Tanner, 1962). From conception through the second postnatal year is a period of extremely rapid growth. Considering the rapid growth and high mortality rate for this age group compared with that at other stages of the life cycle, prenatal and early postnatal stages may be the most critical to examine in a study of a population's biological adaptation to its environment.

The period of embryonic and fetal growth represents a stage of rapid cellular differentiation and hypertrophy. The end result of growth and development during this period is observed in the newborn infant. The biological status of the newborn is the expression of the interaction of genetic and environmental factors operating directly on the fetus and indirectly through the mother during gestation and delivery. From the studies of Penrose (1961) it is apparent that the genetic constitution of the mother and the fetus, and the interactions of these two genotypes with their respective environments and with each other, create the phenotype we observe at birth in the human infant. This interaction is most apparent during gestation, but may also operate before conception. The mother's level of biological adaptation to her physical environment, as well as her nutritional status, health history, activity pattern, and genetic endowment may all influence the development of her unborn child (N.A.S., 1970; WHO, 1970).

Infancy represents a critical stage of the life cycle when the human organism is first faced with the task of responding to the stresses of its extrauterine environment. After birth the infant no longer benefits from the mother's biological buffering capacity to aid in the maintenance of a warm intrauterine microenvironment, with its fairly constant supply of oxygen and nutrients. The biological integrity of an infant born into the extreme conditions of a cold and hypoxic high-altitude environment is severely tested at a very young age when many of his physiological controls are not fully developed. During the period of infancy one observes the first opportunity for postnatal selection to operate by differential mortality.

The process of physical and motor development during infancy should represent to some degree the biological status of surviving offspring living at high altitude. The following data collected in southern Peru demonstrate some of the biological responses of the Peruvian Quechua infant to his high-altitude environment, specifically to high-altitude hypoxia.

PRENATAL GROWTH AND BIRTH

The biological status of the newborn infant is, at present, the best measure we have of the effects of high altitude on prenatal growth in Peru. Studies of the effects of high altitude on human birth weights as a measure of the biological status of the newborn are the most prevalent and are sum-

TABLE 9.1 *Summary of Mean Birth Weights at Various Altitudes in Peru*

Source	Location (altitude in meters)	Lowest weight in sample (g)	N	Mean (g)	S.D.
Vilchez (1954)[a]	Lima (203)	2500	440	3612	**425**
Jara Velarde (1961)[a]	Lima	1500	100	3297	511
Cuellas Huapaya (1962)[a]	Lima	1500	100	3540	550
McClung (1969)	Lima	1000	100	3300	544
Sobrevilla (1971)[b]	Lima	2500	38	3505	495
Kruger and Arias-Stella (1970)	Lima	2500	118	3489	—
Haas (1973a)	Tacna (568)	2500	45	3482	431
Haas[c]	Tacna	1500	1920	3620	550
Haas[c]	Arequipa (2363)	700	5605	3263	536
McClung (1969)[d]	Cuzco (3416)	2500	571	3213	380
McClung (1969)[d]	Cuzco	1500	619	3127	472
McClung (1969)	Cuzco	700	100	3074	514
Haas (1973a)	Puno (3870)	2500	27	3264	343
Haas[c]	Puno	1800	63	3033	402
Jara Velarde (1961)[a]	LaOroya (3880)	1500	186	3039	420
Sanchez Kong (1963)[a]	Cerro de Pasco (4340)	1500	100	2730	350
Sobrevilla (1971)[b]	Cerro de Pasco	2240	43	2955	454
Kruger and Arias-Stella (1970)	Rio Pallanga (4660)	2500	84	2946	—
Macedo Dianderas (1966)[a]	4860	—	10	2720	337

[a]Reported by McClung (1969), p. 59.
[b]Recalculated for this study.
[c]From unpublished hospital data and records.
[d]Recalculated by McClung from unpublished data by Acurio (1965).

marized in Table 9.1. A more extensive review of the topic can be found in McClung (1969).

It is apparent from these studies that birth weight is significantly low at altitudes above 3000 m when compared to sea-level values for Lima and Tacna. The difference in mean birth weight between matched high- and low-altitude samples varies from 218 to 550 g, or 6.3–15.7 percent reduction at high altitude. In addition to the lower mean birth weight at high altitude, the percentage of low-birth-weight babies (under 2500 g) is greater at high altitude than at low altitude. McClung (1969), in her review of Peruvian birth-weight statistics, reports frequencies of low-birth-weight infants at 2.6–7.0 percent for Lima (203 m) and 7.9–26.0 percent for various high-altitude communities above 3400 m.

The major shortcoming of most of the studies reported in Table 9.1 is that they generally do not specify variation in birth weight according to ethnic group, socioeconomic class, sex, or mother's parity. They also are limited to reporting only birth weight and seldom report other measures of biological development, such as crown-heel length and thickness of adipose tissue. Two studies, which attempted to control for several of the factors noted above and therefore give a more complete profile of the biological status of the newborn, were conducted by McClung (1969) and Haas (1973a). Although the research protocol for the two studies is very similar, the McClung study dealt with newborns from Cuzco and Lima, while the Haas study included newborns from Puno and Tacna as part of a larger study of infant growth in southern Peru. Since the results of the two studies were in many ways similar, only the data from the Haas study will be presented here.

The newborn infants (birth to 5 days) were divided into two altitude groups: Puno at high altitude (3830 m) and Tacna at low altitude (568 m). Each altitude group was further subdivided for two-way analysis of variance into Indians and Mestizos or subdivided by sex. Sample size limited subdivision for three analyses of variance for differences due to altitude, ethnic group, and sex. The results of the various two-way analyses of variance are presented in Table 9.2 for weight, crown-heel length, and subscapular skinfold thickness. Altitude differences are observed for all measurements, with the low-altitude values being greater than the high-altitude values. However, statistical significances ($p < 0.05$) of these altitude differences are observed only for weight and crown-heel length when the total sample is considered.

When altitude differences are analyzed for each sex, males are more affected than females, in that the differences in weight and crown-heel length between altitude groups is statistically significant for males but not for females. This interaction between sexual dimorphism and altitude differences is statistically significant for crown-heel length.

When altitude differences in birth weight are analyzed separately for Indians and Mestizos, Mestizos at high altitude are significantly smaller than Mestizos at low altitude. Although high-altitude Indians are over 200 g lighter

TABLE 9.2 *Altitude, Sex, and Ethnic Differences in Body Weight, Crown-Heel Length, and Subscapular Skinfold Thickness for Peruvian Newborn Infants*

Group	Low altitude			High altitude			Significance (p)[a]
	N	Mean	S.D.	N	Mean	S.D.	
Weight (kg)							
Males	21	3.53	0.49	17	3.24	0.45	<0.05
Females	24	3.44	0.42	10	3.28	0.19	N.S.
Indians	22	3.55	0.49	15	3.32	0.43	N.S.
Mestizos	23	3.42	0.40	12	3.18	0.27	<0.05
Total sample	45	3.48	0.43	27	3.26	0.34	<0.05
Crown-Heel Length (cm)							
Males	21	50.7	2.2	17	49.0	1.8	<0.05
Females	24	49.5	2.0	10	49.6	1.0	N.S.
Indians	22	50.2	2.5	15	48.9	2.0	N.S.
Mestizos	23	49.9	1.8	12	49.6	0.9	N.S.
Total sample	45	50.1	2.0	27	49.2	1.6	<0.05
Subscapular Skinfold (mm)							
Males	21	3.7	1.0	14	3.6	0.9	N.S.
Females	24	4.0	0.8	10	3.4	0.8	N.S.
Indians	22	4.0	1.0	13	3.7	0.9	N.S.
Mestizos	23	3.7	1.1	11	3.4	0.9	N.S.
Total sample	45	3.9	0.9	24	3.5	0.9	N.S.

[a]Significance is for altitude difference; sex and ethnic differences were not significant.

at birth than their low-altitude counterparts, the difference is not significant. The interaction between ethnic group affiliation and altitude as they affect birth weight approaches statistical significance at the 0.07 level of probability.

The exact cause of the depressed birth weight at high altitude is not entirely clear. From the studies of McClung (1969) and Sobrevilla (1971), it appears as if newborn gestational age at high altitude is normal, thus ruling out prematurity as a cause for low birth weight. The studies of McClung (1969) and Haas (1973a), carefully controlled for socioeconomic class, as well as maternal smoking, parental stature, and maternal parity, so that these factors could not confound their results. Fetal hypoxia as a result of maternal tissue hypoxia at high altitude would appear to be a plausible explanation for the reduced weights at high altitude. However, studies by Sobrevilla (1971) and Howard et al. (1957) indicate that the oxygen tension and saturation of the umbilical-cord blood may not differ between low- and high-altitude pregnancies. This suggests that the fetus in utero is under no more hypoxic stress at high altitude than at low altitude. However, these studies analyzed cord blood during labor and delivery, and their values may be subject to error through placental leakage and the trauma of labor.

If maternal uterine tissue hypoxia is a factor in retarding prenatal growth, the placenta at high altitude may respond with a potential adaptation to fetal hypoxia. The enlarged placental surface area and greater placental weight/ fetal weight ratio observed at high altitude has been suggested as a mechanism by which the fetal oxygen supply is maintained at a constant level (Kruger and Arias-Stella, 1970; McClung, 1969).

The fact that subtle Indian–Mestizo differences exist for the relationship between altitude and birth weight suggests a potential genetic factor in the control of birth weight among the Quechua. McClung (1969) notes that birth-weight depression at high altitude is less severe in Peru than in the United States. She reports that not only are birth weights at high altitude in Peru (Cuzco, 3416 m) about 400 g greater than birth weights at comparable altitudes in the United States (Lake County, Colorado, 3200 m), but the frequency of low-birth-weight infants at high altitude in Peru is less than half the frequency reported for comparable altitudes in the United States (10 percent in Cuzco versus 23.7 percent in Lake County). These differences are more profound if one considers the better prenatal care and higher socio-economic status of the U.S. population. McClung further suggests two possible explanations for this difference: "racial differences or a more complete altitude adaptation of the Peruvian population" (p. 60).

The latter explanation for the population differences in birth weight at high altitude may deal more with the general level of response of the highland Quechua female to the hypoxic environment. Biological response acquired as a result of lifelong residence at high altitude or as a result of genetic selection may predispose the Quechua women to provide a better intrauterine environment in which to carry her fetus.

The relationship between neonatal mortality and altitude is covered in Chapter 8. However, a few words should be said here in reference to low birth weight. The association between neonatal mortality and birth weight has been well documented (WHO, 1961, 1970). Regardless of what causes the reduced birth weight at high altitude, it is an observable phenomenon that creates real health problems for a population with limited medical facilities. To reduce the high neonatal mortality observed among the Andean peasants, it is necessary to take into account the cumulative risks to the low-birth-weight infants who are born into a cultural environment that may not adequately protect them from the environmental agents of disease, cold, and hypoxia.

POSTNATAL GROWTH AND THE INFANT

Since the high-altitude environment is characterized by multiple stresses, all of which may affect postnatal growth during infancy, it is necessary to

TABLE 9.3 *Characteristics of Six Samples of Southern Peruvian Infants*

Characteristic	Nuñoa Indian	Puno Indian	Puno Mestizo	Tambo Indian	Tacna Indian	Tacna Mestizo
Community type	Rural	Urban	Urban	Rural	Urban	Urban
Altitude (m)	4050	3870	3870	51	568	568
Population size	2200	27,000	27,000	3100	32,000	32,000
Medical facilities	*Posta medica,* no physician	Fully staffed hospital, free well-baby clinic		*Posta medica,* one physician	Fully staffed hospital, free well-baby clinic	
Nutritional supplement	None	Free milk and vitamins		Very limited	Free milk and vitamins	
Sample size						
Neonates	0	15	12	0	22	11
7–820 days	75	132	67	63	67	81
Parity of neonates' mothers	—	3.3	2.9	—	2.9	2.0
Ethnic group	Quechua	Quechua/ Aymara	Mestizo	Quechua	Quechua/ Aymara	Mestizo
Parents birthplace (altitude)	High	High	High	High	High	Low
Socioeconomic class	Lower	Lower	Middle	Lower	Lower	Middle
Sample code	NI	PI	PM	CI	TI	TM

determine to what degree the single most pervasive stress, hypoxia, is affecting the population. To do so requires that the effects of nutritional and disease stress, as well as genetic variation and ethnic differences in child rearing, be adequately controlled. It is possible to isolate the single effect of hypoxia on infant growth by comparing six samples of infants living in southern Peru. The important characteristics of these six samples are presented in Table 9.3. The rationale for this sampling procedure is based on three criteria. First, a high altitude/low altitude dichotomy permits comparisons for the effect of high altitude on infant growth. Second, a rural—urban dichotomy conveniently contrasts rural infants who have limited access to medical facilities and a marginal diet to urban infants who attend hospital well-baby clinics, where nutritional supplements and medical care are administered free of charge. Third, an Indian—Mestizo dichotomy permits a comparison between infants from an Indian population with a long ancestral history of high-altitude residence and a Mestizo population with a short ancestral history of high-altitude residence. In addition, the Indian—Mestizo comparison may also reveal socioeconomic and ethnic differences in child care and subsequent differences in infant growth.

The important dyadic comparisons between two matched samples that may answer specific questions about infant growth at high altitude are:

1. Nuñoa Indian vs. Tambo Indian: altitude differences between genetically similar rural Indians who have little benefit from modern health care or nutritional supplementation.

2. Puno Indian vs. Tacna Indian: altitude differences between genetically similar urban Indians who have equal benefits from a free well-baby clinic with nutritional supplements. This should isolate the effect of hypoxia on infant growth while controlling for disease and nutritional stress in a population that has a very long ancestral history of high-altitude residence.

3. Puno Mestizo vs. Tacna Mestizo: altitude differences between genetically similar Mestizos who have a short history of altitude residence and benefit equally from the free well-baby clinic as well as a middle-socioeconomic-class standard of living.

In addition, two statistical interactions can be tested to reveal (1) how rural—urban residence affects altitude differences in the growth of Indian infants, and (2) how ethnic (genetic) group affiliation affects altitude differences in infant growth for urban residents. These sample comparisons and interactions are represented schematically in Figure 9.1.

The data on infant growth to be analyzed within this research design were collected in Nuñoa (4050 m) by T. S. Baker et al. in 1965 (T. S. Baker et al., 1967a, 1967b) and in Puno (3780 m), the Tambo valley (100 m), and Tacna (568 m), by me in 1971 (Haas 1972, 1973a, 1973b). The measurements discussed here will be crown-heel length (cm), body weight (kg), and subscapular skinfold thickness (mm): all determined according to the protocol described by Weiner and Lourie (1969) for infants from birth to 2 yr of age.

TABLE 9.4 *Age-Group Distribution of Body Weight (kg), Crown-Heel Length (cm), and Subscapular Skinfold Thickness (mm) for 6 Samples of Infants*

| | Indian | | | | Mestizo | |
| | Low altitude | | High altitude | | | |
Age group (days)	Tambo	Tacna	Nuñoa	Puno	Tacna	Puno
7–91						
N	7	18	9	22	15	8
Body weight	4.85 ± 0.83	4.60 ± 0.95	4.72 ± 1.16	4.12 ± 1.00	4.93 ± 0.85	4.40 ± 0.93
Crown-heel length	54.9 ± 2.9	54.7 ± 3.1	53.6 ± 3.0	52.3 ± 4.0	56.2 ± 3.1	54.1 ± 4.3
Skinfold thickness	7.8 ± 2.6	5.7 ± 2.1	6.5 ± 2.6	5.1 ± 2.1	6.6 ± 2.4	6.3 ± 3.1
92–182						
N	10	15	9	24	21	13
Body weight	7.69 ± 0.89	7.48 ± 1.21	5.91 ± 1.07	6.60 ± 0.90	7.20 ± 0.93	7.19 ± 0.95
Crown-heel length	64.9 ± 2.3	64.3 ± 3.2	59.3 ± 3.1	61.3 ± 2.5	62.4 ± 2.4	62.9 ± 2.8
Skinfold thickness	7.7 ± 1.7	8.0 ± 2.7	7.7 ± 1.4	6.8 ± 2.1	8.7 ± 2.9	7.9 ± 2.0

183–273

N	10	8	11	17	8	9
Body weight	8.68 ± 0.66	8.89 ± 0.83	6.97 ± 0.48	7.68 ± 1.35	8.71 ± 0.31	8.05 ± 1.10
Crown-heel length	67.2 ± 1.3	67.5 ± 4.5	62.1 ± 3.3	65.9 ± 2.6	68.4 ± 1.9	67.6 ± 2.4
Skinfold thickness	7.1 ± 1.6	8.3 ± 3.0	5.7 ± 1.0	6.3 ± 1.9	6.9 ± 1.6	6.5 ± 2.5

274–365

N	13	3	7	11	10	4
Body weight	9.39 ± 1.39	9.76 ± 1.12	8.25 ± 1.06	8.47 ± 0.96	9.83 ± 2.07	8.82 ± 0.94
Crown-heel length	70.0 ± 3.9	70.0 ± 2.4	68.2 ± 1.7	69.3 ± 4.2	71.6 ± 4.3	70.7 ± 3.4
Skinfold thickness	8.2 ± 2.4	7.0 ± 1.7	6.1 ± 2.3	6.2 ± 2.5	7.5 ± 2.9	5.7 ± 1.2

366–548

N	10	11	20	27	7	11
Body weight	10.73 ± 1.01	10.94 ± 1.26	8.01 ± 1.17	9.27 ± 1.08	11.95 ± 1.62	9.77 ± 1.02
Crown-heel length	74.9 ± 1.7	75.2 ± 2.5	72.3 ± 3.5	72.1 ± 3.0	76.9 ± 2.6	73.3 ± 2.5
Skinfold thickness	5.9 ± 1.6	7.2 ± 3.1	4.5 ± 1.3	5.5 ± 1.2	7.1 ± 1.4	6.3 ± 1.5

549–820

N	13	5	19	16	9	10
Body weight	12.50 ± 1.89	11.79 ± 2.23	9.37 ± 1.07	9.97 ± 1.27	13.19 ± 1.14	11.33 ± 0.69
Crown-heel length	80.1 ± 4.3	79.6 ± 5.5	76.5 ± 3.3	74.8 ± 2.6	83.3 ± 3.3	79.0 ± 2.6
Skinfold thickness	5.9 ± 1.5	5.2 ± 1.4	4.0 ± 0.8	5.0 ± 1.6	6.0 ± 2.1	7.5 ± 2.1

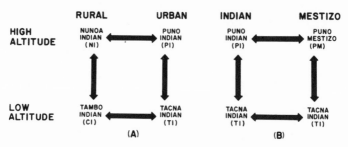

FIGURE 9.1 *Schematic representation of various altitude comparisons and interactions of altitude with (A) rural—urban residence and (B) ethnic group affiliation.*

Subjects over 1 month of age were also tested for motor development according to the protocol of Bayley (1969). All subjects were examined once in the cross-sectional studies, and additional information on parental birthplace, occupation, ethnic group, and education, as well as infant care practices, nutrition, health history, and maternal reproductive history, was obtained through questionnaires. Analysis of data utilized Student's *t*-test, analysis of variance for grouped data, and analysis of covariance for age trends for the anthropometric data.

Body Size and Composition

Table 9.4 presents age-group values for mean weight, crown-heel length, and subscapular skinfold thickness in the six samples of Peruvian infants. Figure 9.2 illustrates the age trends in weight and crown-heel length for the combined high-altitude and combined low-altitude samples as they are divided into males and females. The growth trends are interpreted from regression lines fitted to the age and measurement data for two age groups: 1 week to 6 months, and 6–27 months. Analysis of covariance indicates that the age trends for both measurements are significantly different between high- and low-altitude groups, and that at any age the high-altitude infant is lighter and shorter than its low-altitude counterpart. When altitude differences are considered in relation to sexual dimorphism, males are more affected by the high altitude than are females, although the altitude difference for either sex is statistically significant. Sexual dimorphism is considerably reduced at high altitude when compared to the pattern of sex difference observed at low altitude. This differential effect of altitude on males and females results in a statistically significant interaction between sex and altitude when the weights of 15-month-old infants are compared (see Table 9.5).

Figure 9.3 presents the age trends in weight for three controlled high altitude/low altitude comparisons. These three comparisons analyze altitude differences by matching each high-altitude sample with a low-altitude sample

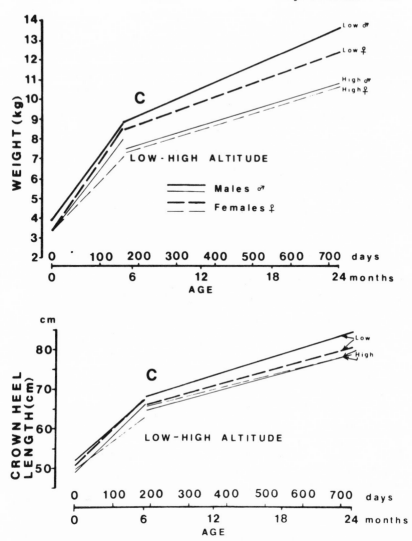

FIGURE 9.2 *Sexual dimorphism in age trends for weight and crown-heel length in high- and low-altitude Peruvians.*

that is similar in life style, access to medical facilities, and ethnic affiliation. Analysis of covariance indicates that for both rural and urban Indians, the high-altitude samples at all ages are significantly smaller ($p < 0.001$) than their matched low-altitude counterparts. However, altitude differences for the urban middle-class Mestizo infants are significant only after 6 months of age. The difference between the three comparisons is observed as early as the first

TABLE 9.5 *Altitude and Sex or Rural–Urban Differences in Weight for 15-Month-Old Peruvian Infants (kg)[a]*

Altitude	Sex				Residence[b]			
	Male	Female	Mean	Signif. of diff.	Rural	Urban	Mean	Signif. of diff.
Low	11.16	10.32	10.80	<0.01	10.58 (CI)	10.32 (TI)	10.63	N.S.
High	9.09	8.86	8.95	N.S.	8.23 (NI)	9.27 (PI)	8.73	<0.001
Signif. of diff.	<0.001	<0.01	<0.001		<0.001	<0.001	<0.001	

[a]Weights were computed from regression equations for weight vs. age relationship, and significances from covariance analyses. Interactions are significant at the $p < 0.05$ level.
[b]For sample codes, see Table 9.3.

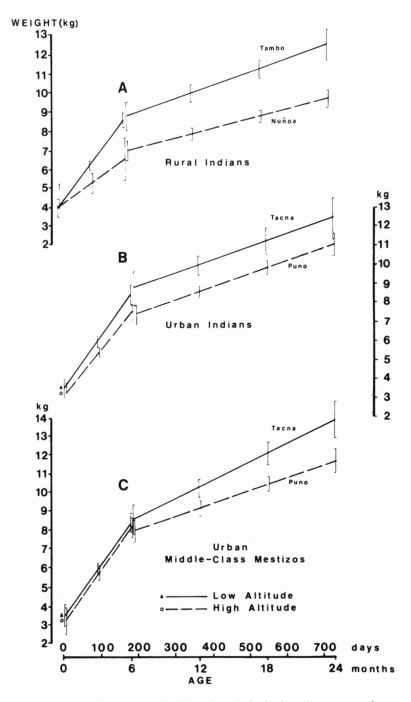

FIGURE 9.3 *Three controlled low altitude/high altitude contrasts for age trends in weight of Peruvian infants. Brackets indicate 95 percent confidence intervals.*

6 months. Altitude difference became apparent earliest in the most stressed group (Nuñoa Indians) and latest in the least stressed group (Puno Mestizos).

The relationship between rural—urban residence and altitude is also demonstrated by the comparisons of weights for 15-month-old infants (Table 9.5). While altitude differences in weight are significant regardless of rural or urban residence, the rural high-altitude infant is most affected. This low body weight of the Nuñoa infant also results in a greater, and significant ($p <$ 0.001), rural—urban difference at high altitude than is observed between rural and urban infants at low altitude. The interaction between rural—urban residence and altitude as it affects the weight of Indian infants is statistically significant ($p < 0.05$). Indian or Mestizo ethnic affiliation appears to have no differential effect on the relationship between altitude and weight in urban residents.

Data on subscapular skinfold thickness (Table 9.4 and Fig. 9.4) indicate altitude-related differences similar to those observed for weight and crown-heel length. Skinfolds are greater at low altitude than at high, and males are more affected by the altitude than females. Also, of the three highland samples, Nuñoa Indians have the least amount of subcutaneous fat and Puno middle-class Mestizos have the most fat.

Other measures of physical growth were examined in the two infant studies: head circumference, brachial fat, brachial muscle, cortical bone thickness in the humerus, and the number of hand—wrist ossification centers present. All showed significantly greater values at low altitude than at high altitude. Deciduous tooth eruption was similar between high- and low-altitude groups. The only measurement of physical development that showed greater values at high altitude was the size of the marrow cavity in the humerus. Both absolute size and size of the cavity relative to size of the total bone were greater in the high-altitude urban samples than in comparable low-altitude groups.

Hypoxia as an explanation for the reduced growth of infants at high altitude is plausible, especially if one considers that even middle-class Mestizos in Puno are smaller and lighter than their Tacna counterparts. However, similar patterns of retarded growth have been linked to undernutrition. Certainly the pattern of infant growth observed for all three high-altitude populations would fit the description of a population under nutritional stress. The role of nutritional stress in retarding growth indeed may apply to the Nuñoa population, which has no supervised nutritional supplementation to their marginal and seasonally fluctuating diet (Thomas, 1973). The pattern of infant growth in Nuñoa is the most retarded of the six samples and probably reflects the effects of the multiple stresses of hypoxia, poor nutrition, disease, and perhaps cold.

However, the nutrition and health situation in Puno is quite different from the situation in Nuñoa. Samples of both Puno Indians and Puno Mestizos were examined at the regional hospital's well-baby clinic, which offers free medical care with a monthly checkup and dispenses daily dietary

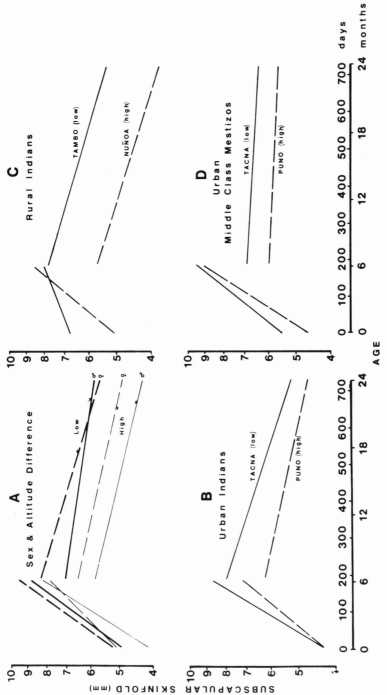

FIGURE 9.4 Age trends in subscapular skinfold thickness for various controlled low altitude/high altitude contrasts.

supplements of milk and vitamins if the situation warrants. In addition, the middle-class Mestizo infants examined in Puno benefit from their parents' secure financial status in that their normal diet is probably adequate. Further support for a nonnutritional argument to explain the small size of the infants in Puno is offered through evidence of a World Health Organization survey on protein–calorie malnutrition (WHO, 1971). It reports that of 3313 Puno children between the ages of 1 and 4 years, only 0.5 percent were classified as severely malnourished and 4.4 percent as moderately malnourished. These are the lowest incident figures reported for any South American, Asian, or African site surveyed by WHO.

Sociocultural questionnaires dealing with child care and infant feeding practices indicate that the high-altitude mothers from Nuñoa and Puno wean their infants at 20 and 13 months, respectively. This timing is about 6 months later than the weaning ages of 13 and 7 months, for the respective samples in Tambo and Tacna (Haas, 1973a). Considering the trend in developing countries toward migration, urbanization, early weaning, and increased incidence of malnutrition (Jelliffe, 1968), it would appear as if the high-altitude Indians are under less nutritional stress than their low-altitude counterparts. From these findings it appears as if the retarded growth observed at high altitude, at least in Puno, is the direct result of hypoxia.

The decreased sexual dimorphism in crown-heel length and weight observed at high altitude simulates a condition observed by Stini (1969, 1972a) for a population under severe nutritional stress. It has been demonstrated that in a population under stress, boys will be more disrupted from their genetically disposed growth curve than girls (Tanner, 1962), which may result from the greater "canalization" of the female. If the alteration of the normal patterns of sexual dimorphism is any measure of the degree to which a population is suffering from a biological stress, then it can be suggested that the highland Peruvian population faces rather severe stress during infancy.

The capacity of a population to respond favorably to stress is a good measure of the population's adaptability. The exact nature of that response may be seen in the end result of infant growth, that is, an individual who, because of his small body size, requires less nutrients in times of nutritional stress. The reduced metabolic demands of this type of growing child have been suggested by Thomas (1973) as a means by which the traditional Quechua population may adapt to a limited energy-flow system. Frisancho et al. (1973a) support this argument by demonstrating an increased survivorship of offspring born to smaller mothers than to larger mothers in Cuzco, Peru. Their assumption is that smaller women tend to have smaller offspring, and that under poor socioeconomic conditions the smaller offspring will require less food to sustain them.

Motor Development

In addition to studying physical growth, the two infant studies included an examination of the development of motor function. Table 9.6 presents the

TABLE 9.6 *Standardized Psychomotor Scores for Six Samples of Infants*

	Age group						
	2–12 months			13–27 months			Significance of age-group diff. (*t*-test)
Sample	N	Mean	S.D.	N	Mean	S.D.	
Nuñoa Indian	33	89.4	21.5	24	94.5	29.3	N.S.
Puno Indian	60	103.7	20.5	37	85.2	20.4	<0.01
Puno Mestizo	31	104.3	16.3	15	100.5	25.9	N.S.
Tambo Indian	33	106.9	23.8	19	94.1	29.9	N.S.
Tacna Indian	35	110.8	18.6	14	88.0	22.1	<0.01
Tacna Mestizo	94	100.0	17.7	24	102.5	20.1	N.S.

results of analysis of motor development sequences for each of the six samples. The values reported here are standardized psychomotor scores derived from the standards of Bayley (1969) and based on a mean score of 100 for U.S. children with a standard deviation of 16 points. Scores are reported for two age groups in each of the six samples: infants from 2 months to 1 yr, and infants from 1 to 2 yr of age. Age-group differences in motor scores are significant for the two urban Indian samples, Puno and Tacna, where the scores drop from the first to the second year. A similar trend exists for the Tambo Indian, but the difference is not significant. Mestizos do not demonstrate statistically significant changes in scores from the first to the second year.

The results of selected two-sample comparisons for controlled ethnic, rural–urban, and altitude differences are presented in Table 9.7. It is apparent from the comparison of specific samples that the greatest difference in motor

TABLE 9.7 *Results of Two Sample t-Tests for Difference in Psychomotor Scores*

	Age group	
Samples compared	2–12 months	13–27 months
Indian vs. Mestizo (all samples)	<0.01	<0.01
Puno Indian vs. Puno Mestizo	N.S.	<0.05
Tacna Indian vs. Tacna Mestizo	<0.01	<0.05
Rural vs. urban (all samples)	N.S.	N.S.
Nuñoa Indian vs. Puno Indian	<0.01	N.S.
Tambo Indian vs. Tacna Indian	N.S.	N.S.
High vs. low altitude (all samples)	N.S.	N.S.
Nuñoa Indian vs. Tambo Indian	<0.01	N.S.
Puno Indian vs. Tacna Indian	N.S.	N.S.
Puno Mestizo vs. Tacna Mestizo	N.S.	N.S.

development scores is between ethnic groups. The general pattern is for slight Indian–Mestizo difference in scores in the first year, but for a significantly greater Mestizo score in the second year. High altitude does appear to depress the motor scores, especially in Nuñoa, where the Indians in the first year of life have the lowest scores reported. In contrast, the urban low-altitude Indian, in Tacna, has the highest motor score reported for the first year of life.

Analysis of individual psychomotor skills such as age at which head is lifted, hands are held open, partial and complete thumb opposition is achieved, finger prehension is achieved, and sitting, standing, and walking skills are accomplished indicates no difference between high- and low-altitude infants. However, significant Indian–Mestizo differences are observed. Indians are advanced over Mestizos in the early skills achieved before 1 yr of age; then the trend reverses, and Mestizos advance past the Indians in the later skills achieved in the second year. This trend in individual skill achievement parallels the Indian–Mestizo difference in normalized scores reported in Table 9.6.

From this preliminary analysis it is difficult to ascribe the observed Indian–Mestizo differences in motor development to genetic factors or to ethnic differences in child rearing. Both arguments have been reported in the literature of motor development in different ethnic groups (Malina, 1973). A combination of genetic, cultural, and biological factors may be operating in this Peruvian population to determine the pattern of motor development.

For example, small body size may account for the delayed development of the Nuñoa sample relative to the other Indian and Mestizo samples. It is interesting that the group that is most retarded in physical development in the first year is also the most retarded in motor development in the first year; perhaps an adequate physical substrate of muscle and bone must be laid down before certain early motor skills can be learned. However, one cannot discount the importance of culturally prescribed child-rearing practices to the early learning experience of the infant. The life style of the traditional rural Quechua society may be sufficiently altered through acculturation to the national Mestizo life style in the cities or coastal haciendas. The traditional modes of child care may be replaced by subtle Mestizo practices. The fact that Indian and Mestizo infants do differ in their motor patterns does suggest that either ethnic differences in child care practices or perhaps genetic differences between groups may be affecting the timing of motor development sequences.

CONCLUSIONS

As indicated by these most recent findings, the association between hypoxia and retarded growth at high altitude is apparently well established. However, by pinpointing hypoxia as the major growth-retarding stress affecting the Peruvian Quechua, we introduce an entirely new set of questions to be answered.

The role of maternal adaptation to high altitude, especially as it relates to child bearing, should not be overlooked. Further research should be concerned with the relationship of maternal constitution with fertility, neonatal constitution, and early infant development. In particular, does the level of a mother's adaptation to her high-altitude environment significantly affect the course of her pregnancy? And to what extent is birth weight and neonatal mortality, as well as early postnatal development and infant mortality, influenced by the maternal environment during gestation? Many factors affecting infant development and mortality should perhaps be viewed in terms of maternal fertility and reproductive success.

Considering the critical nature of the period of infancy in the population's adaptation to its environment, and given the severity of the high-altitude environment, further research should probe into the significance of biological response by the infant to such stresses as hypoxia and cold and how they interact with nutrition and disease. Such research may lead us one step closer to an understanding of the mechanisms by which man has been able successfully to inhabit such a unique environment.

10

GROWTH AND MORPHOLOGY AT HIGH ALTITUDE

A. Roberto Frisancho

Part I:
GROWTH AND FUNCTIONAL DEVELOPMENT

It is a basic principle that internal and external environmental factors significantly influence growth and development, and that the physiological and morphological profile of the adult results from both genetic and environmental interactions. The environmental factors include nutrition, temperature, hypoxia, radiation, drugs, and so forth. These features are constantly conditioning and modifying the expression of inherited potentials at all stages of life. Indeed, one of the basic characteristics of life is its capacity to adapt to a changing environment. The environmental influences, however, are quite variable; they depend on the type of stress encountered, especially on the age of the individual at the time of the stress. Generally, the younger the organism, the greater the environmental influence. Therefore, the interaction of the developmental, genetic, and environmental factors defines the competence with which the individual responds and adapts to environmental challenge.

Within this conceptual framework, the present chapter summarizes our findings on the development of body size, pulmonary function, body composition, and skeletal maturation based upon a cross-sectional and semilongitudinal sample of 1204 subjects aged 2 to 35 yr, derived from the rural and urban sections of the district of Nuñoa. The findings are interpreted along with experimental studies on animals and analytic studies on human growth in the Peruvian central Andes and Bolivia.

GROWTH IN BODY SIZE

Sample

The data to be presented here were collected from June 1964 to August 1966, and are reported in Frisancho and Baker (1970). The method of data collection included both cross-sectional and semilongitudinal samplings.

180

The cross-sectional sample consisted of 1204 subjects, 702 male and 402 female, between the ages of 2 and 22 yr. They represented 30 percent of the total population under 25 yr of age. The adult reference sample was comprised of 52 men and 50 women between the ages of 25 and 34 yr.

The semilongitudinal sample consisted of 300 subjects, aged 2 to 22 yr, 140 of whom were remeasured after 12 months and 160 after 27 months.

The ages of the subjects in both samples were verified by birth records provided by the municipal council of Nuñoa district and the town school officials. These records covered 98 percent of those between 2 and 22 yr of age.

Measurements

Standard anthropometric measurements included weight, height, sitting height, biacromial diameter, chest depth, chest breadth, chest circumference, and arm circumference. In addition, measurements of skinfold thickness at the upper arm, scapula, and waist were also obtained. All these measurements were taken, according to the "Recommendations Concerning Body Measurements for the Characterization of Nutritional Status" (1956). Weight was recorded to the nearest quarter-pound and converted into kilograms. Height was recorded to the nearest millimeter. Sitting height was taken with the subject seated on a firm, flat stool with the knees flexed and trunk in contact with the anthropometer at both scapular and sacral regions. Chest circumference at the xyphoid level was measured at maximum inspiration and expiration, from which the midchest circumference was calculated. Biacromial diameter, chest width, and chest depth were measured with the anthropometer's sliding calipers. With a flexible steel tape, upper-arm circumference was measured midway between acromion and olecranon with the arm hanging freely. All measurements were taken in centimeters.

Skinfold-thickness measurements were made with a Lange caliper having a pressure of 10 g/mm^2 of contact surface area. All measurements (in millimeters) were taken on the right side: at the upper arm on the same site as that of the circumference; and also at the waist, calf, and lower end of the scapula. All these measurements were added to give the sum of skinfolds. Three readings were taken at each site and the average was used to represent the subcutaneous fat (plus skin) at that site. The upper-arm diameter of muscle was derived from the upper-arm circumference and triceps skinfolds by computation (Brožek, 1961).

Patterns of Growth

As shown in Fig. 10.1, growth in stature and weight appears to continue until the twenty-second year. On the other hand, growth in chest width and depth stops increasing at about the age of 19 yr. Sexual dimorphism in

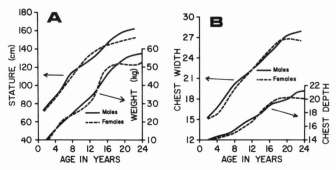

FIGURE 10.1 *Development of stature, weight, chest width, and chest depth of Nuñoa Indigenes. [Reprinted from Frisancho and Baker (1970).]*

stature, weight, and chest size is not well defined until about the age of 16 yr.

The growth increments of stature derived from the semilongitudinal data are presented in Fig. 10.2. On the basis of the Fels Growth Data, Nuñoa males and females have (1) a late and poorly defined adolescent growth spurt, and (2) a very prolonged growth period.

Intrapopulation Differences

Rural–Urban. For analytical purposes a sample of 388 boys, ages 7–22 yr, and 216 girls, ages 7–16 yr, has been divided according to residence into (1) urban, comprising those who live in the central town capital of the district of Nuñoa and attend the school, and (2) rural, comprising those who live in the native communities and privately owned ranches (haciendas) and who do not attend the central school in the central town.

Figures 10.3 and 10.4 illustrate the development of stature, weight, sum of skinfolds, and upper-arm muscle diameter of the rural and urban male

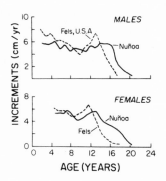

FIGURE   10.2 *Stature growth rate of Nuñoa Indigenes, compared with U.S. Fels standards (U.S.). [Reprinted from Frisancho and Baker (1970).]*

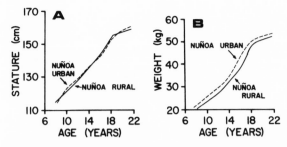

FIGURE 10.3 *Stature (A) and weight (B) of Nuñoa boys residing in the urban and rural areas of the district. [Reprinted from Frisancho and Baker (1970).]*

samples. The urban groups are heavier than the rural samples, but age for age, both groups attain nearly the same stature. The urban groups are also considerably fatter (about 20 percent more than the rural samples), while they appear to have nearly the same upper-arm muscle diameter.

Altitude. Since the population of Nuñoa lives at altitudes which range from 4000 to 5500 m, the sample was divided according to the altitude of residence into a lower-altitude group, those who live at 4000 m (13,150 ft), and a higher-altitude group, those who live at altitudes above 4500 m (16,000 ft).

Both groups attained nearly the same values for body size and composition in stature, weight, sitting height, biacromial diameter, sum of skinfolds, and upper-arm diameter. On the other hand (Fig. 10.5), the higher-altitude group, especially between ages 14 and 18, attained a significantly larger ($p <$ 0.01) chest circumference at maximum inspiration than those residing at lower altitudes.

Interpopulation Differences

The development of stature and chest circumference of the Nuñoa cross-sectional sample is plotted in Fig. 10.6, in comparison with data derived from the United States (Stoudt et al., 1960) and with data on Peruvian samples from sea level and moderate altitude (Preto and Calderón, 1947). As shown, the Nuñoa boys are absolutely and relatively smaller than the American and Peruvian people of the sea-level samples as well as those from moderate altitude of 2300 m (7500 ft); they also attain a lower percentage of the adult values. Figure 10.7 also shows that despite these smaller statures, the high-altitude Nuñoa boys develop systematically greater chest circumferences, averaging about 8 and 10 percent above Americans and other Peruvians,

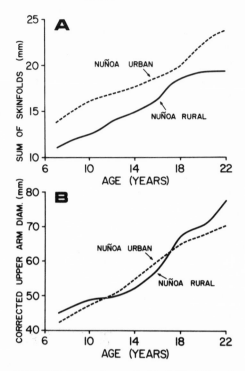

FIGURE 10.4 *Sum of skinfolds (A) and corrected upper-arm diameter (B) of Nuñoa boys residing in the urban and rural areas of the district. [Reprinted from Frisancho and Baker (1970).]*

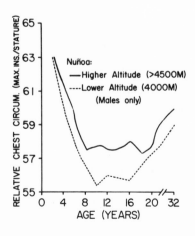

FIGURE 10.5 *Comparison of relative chest circumference at maximum inspiration of male Nuñoans residing at around 4000 and above 4500 m. [Reprinted from Frisancho and Baker (1970).]*

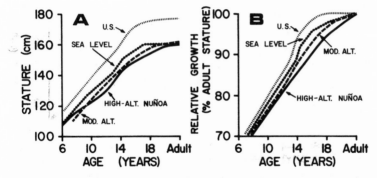

FIGURE 10.6 *Comparison of (A) absolute and (B) relative development in stature of Nuñoa boys and Peruvians from sea level and a moderate altitude of 2300 m. [Reprinted from Frisancho and Baker (1970).]*

respectively. In other words, the chest size of Nuñoa boys shows accelerated rather than slowed growth.

PULMONARY FUNCTION

Sample and Measurements

The subjects were a cross-sectional sample of 150 Quechua boys aged 11 to 20 yr, part of the student population of the school of the central town of Nuñoa. Standard anthropometric measurements were obtained on all subjects as described above.

Forced expiratory volumes were measured according to standard procedures (Comroe et al., 1955; Consolazio et al., 1963; Cotes, 1965) with a dry spirometer (Jones-Pulmonor). Each subject was carefully instructed in

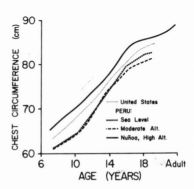

FIGURE 10.7 *Comparison of chest circumference of Nuñoa boys and Peruvians from sea level and moderate altitude of 2300 m. [Reprinted from Frisancho and Baker (1970).]*

Spanish and Quechua, the maneuvers were practiced several times, and recordings were made of several attempts to ensure precision. The readings were obtained from the highest values. All measurements were obtained in the standing position. In order to get records of the best quality, the subjects were stimulated to compete with each other and were rewarded with a photograph of themselves.

Results

Figure 10.8 illustrates the development of forced vital capacity of Nuñoa boys compared to that for Peruvian samples (Preto and Calderón, 1947) and U.S. norms (Bjure, 1963). The Nuñoa boys show an accelerated growth in forced vital capacity, so that by the age of 20 years, their values for FVC are nearly twice those attained at 11 years. The Nuñoa boys, age for age, attain a significantly higher value than the other Peruvians and U.S. sea-level norms. In other words, the growth in forced vital capacity follows the same rapid developmental pattern of the chest (Frisancho, 1969a; Frisancho and Baker, 1970). These findings confirm the earlier studies of Hurtado (1932a).

Figure 10.9 illustrates the results of the studies on highland (Nuñoa) and lowland (Mollendo) Quechua samples studied with the McDermott dry spirometer by Rimmer and recently analyzed by Boyce et al. (1974). These data show that the forced vital capacity (FVC) and forced expiratory volume

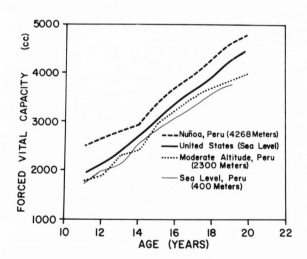

FIGURE 10.8 *Forced vital capacity (FVC) of Nuñoa boys, and Peruvian boys from ICA (sea level) and Huanuco (2300 m), as compared with U.S. norms. [Reprinted from Frisancho (1969a).]*

FIGURE 10.9 *Development in forced vital capacity (FVC) and forced expiratory volumes in 1 min (FEV) of highland Quechua natives from Nuñoa and lowland Quechua natives from Mollendo. [Adapted from Boyce et al. (1974).]*

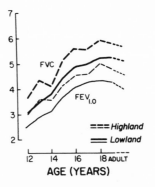

(FEV), adjusted for height and weight, of the highland Quechuas is greater than those of lowland Quechua counterparts.

As shown by the multiple regression analyses presented in Table 10.1, of all the variables used to characterize body size (height, weight, surface area) and chest size (chest depth, chest width, chest circumference), the chest circumference at maximum inspiration appears to be the best predictor of FVC, thereby explaining about 81 percent of the variance. As indicated by the standard partial regression, the next important variable that predicts FVC includes chest volume and sitting height. Figure 10.10 depicts the relationship between chest circumference at maximum inspiration and forced vital capac-

TABLE 10.1 *Correlation Coefficients and Regression Equation of Prime Predictor of Forced Vital Capacity (FVC), as Determined by Up-Rank, Multiple Regression of 150 High-Altitude Peruvian Quechua Boys, 11–20 Years of Age[a]*

Forced vital capacity vs.:	r	Equation	Standard and partial regression coefficients
Chest circumference at maximum inspiration	0.90	$Y = -6113.10 + 117.56X_1$	$b_1 = 0.90$[b]
Chest circumference at maximum expiration and sitting height	0.91[c]	$Y = -6801.10 + 920.80X_1 + 358.00X_2$	$b_1 = 0.70; b_2 = 0.50$[d]
Chest circumference at maximum expiration, sitting height, and chest volume	*0.91c*	$Y = -5412.90 + 729.86X_1 + 291.26X_2 + 859.92X_3$	$b_1 = 0.55; b_2 = 0.18$[d] $b_3 = 0.20$

[a]From Frisancho (1969b).
[b]Standard regression coefficient.
[c]Multiple regression coefficient.
[d]Partial regression coefficient.

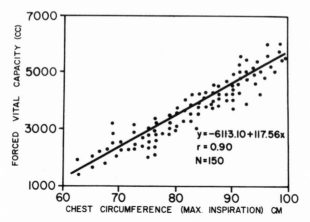

FIGURE 10.10 *Relationship between chest circumference at maximum inspiration and forced vital capacity (FVC) of Nuñoa boys. [Reprinted from Frisancho (1969a).]*

ity. It shows that among Nuñoa boys, the greater the chest circumference, the greater the forced vital capacity. This relationship holds even after corrections for age (see Table 10.3).

BODY COMPOSITION

Skinfold Thickness

The sample and protocol for the measurements of skinfold thickness were the same as those for measurement of body size. The median values for the triceps, subscapula, and muscle diameter (Frisancho and Baker, 1970) are illustrated in Fig. 10.11.

These data show that in females the skinfolds at the scapula from childhood to adulthood increase steadily, but the triceps skinfolds after the age of 16 years decline markedly. On the other hand, in males the increase in the subscapular skinfold thickness is very slow, while the triceps skinfolds after the age of 10 yr and through adulthood decline drastically. In other words, the distribution of subcutaneous fat during growth follows a centripetal pattern. This means that while trunk fat increases steadily during the middle teens and early twenties, limb fat decreases in females but not in males. It would follow that "fat gain" and "fat loss" in the body may take place simultaneously in different locations over the same time span. Thus, as in western populations, the adult pattern of subcutaneous fat among Nuñoans is the result of a developmental rearrangement of adipose tissue.

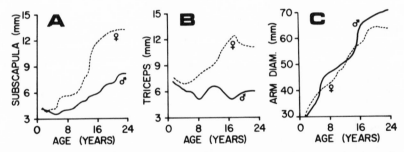

FIGURE 10.11 *Skinfold thickness (A and B) and upper-arm muscle diameter (C) of Nuñoa Indigenes. [Reprinted from Frisancho and Baker (1970).]*

Brachial Tissue Areas

Sample. The data were drawn from both cross-sectional and semilongitudinal samples (Baker et al., 1966b; Frisancho, 1969b). The cross-sectional sample consisted of 300 subjects, ages 2–35 yr. The semilongitudinal sample consisted of 110 subjects, ages 2–22 yr, who were measured after 27 months.

Measurements. Standardized lateromedial radiographs of the right brachium were taken at a focal distance of 91.5 cm, with a portable X-ray machine of 15 mA. The protocol for the measurement of radiographic shadows of fat, muscle, bone, and marrow cavity was according to that of Baker et al. (1958). The tissue diameters were converted into areas of cross section according to the formula

$$A = \frac{\pi}{4} d^2 \qquad (1)$$

where A represents the area of cross section in mm^2 and d is any of the brachial diameters listed above.

Results

Figure 10.12 illustrates the development of the brachial tissues in Nuñoa compared to data of U.S. samples (Baker et al., 1958). These data show that in girls the deposition of fat proceeds at a rapid and steady rate until the age of 14 yr, and between 15 and 18 yr of age has a marked spurt. In this manner, by adulthood women have about twice as much fat as at an age of 2 yr, while in men the trend of fat deposition proceeds at a slow and irregular pace so that by adulthood they have nearly the same amount of fat as during childhood. In Nuñoa, a clear sexual difference in fat deposition occurs after the age of 14 yr, while in the U.S. samples, it occurs by the age of 8 yr.

The development of muscle proceeds at a steady and regular pace in both sexes until about the age of 18 yr. In boys, the adolescent spurt in muscle size

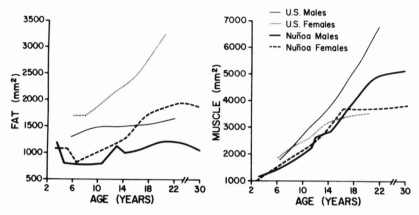

FIGURE 10.12 *Development of brachial tissue areas in Nuñoa and U.S. norms.*

occurs between the age of 15 and 19 yr; in girls it occurs between 14 and 17 yr of age. In Nuñoa, the sexual dimorphism is well defined after the age of 18 yr; in the United States it occurs after the age of 14 yr.

The growth in compact bone proceeds at a steady and regular pace until the age of 12 yr in both sexes. The adolescent spurt occurs between the age of 15 and 18 yr in boys and between 13 and 15 yr in girls. In Nuñoa the sexual dimorphism is well defined after the age of 18 yr.

The development of marrow cavity proceeds at the same rate until the age of 12 yr in males and females. Unlike that of the brachial tissues, the development of the marrow cavity does not show an adolescent spurt. In Nuñoa, the sexual dimorphism is well defined after the age of 14 yr; in the United States, boys exceed girls at the age of 12 yr.

SKELETAL MATURATION

Sample and Measurements

Sample. As before, both cross-sectional and semilongitudinal samples were studied. The cross-sectional sample consisted of 270 subjects aged 1 month to 24 yr. The semilongitudinal sample comprised 110 subjects aged 2–22 yr who were remeasured after 27 months.

Measurements. For assessments of skeletal age, the Greulich and Pyle atlas (1959) was the standard for reference. These evaluations excluded the round bones of the carpal area.

Results

As shown in Fig. 10.13, the Nuñoa children are markedly delayed in skeletal maturation for their chronological ages, in comparison with U.S.

norms. Regression equations describing the relationship between skeletal age
(y) and chronological age (x) yield y values of $-0.165 + 0.910x$ for boys, and
$-0.168 + 0.881x$ for girls, indicating that the rate of maturation in boys and
girls tends to be about equal. Furthermore, the negative value for the y
intercept suggests that the average Nuñoa child is 0.168 yr (i.e., 2 months)
behind U.S. children in maturation age at birth.

DETERMINANTS OF GROWTH AND DEVELOPMENT

For an understanding of the dynamics of the physical and functional
development of the high-altitude native, this section will be concerned with
environmental and genetic factors that may affect growth at high altitude. In
addition, functional requirements and growth as it pertains to the development of lung volumes and marrow cavity at high altitude are discussed.

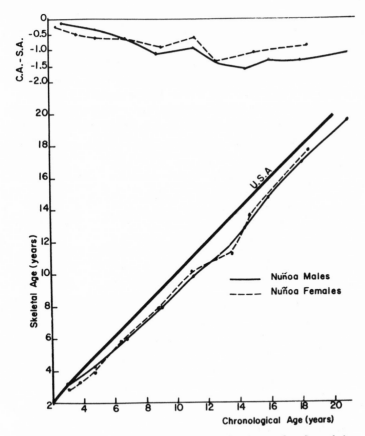

FIGURE 10.13 *Chronological and skeletal age of Nuñoa children, and U.S. norms.*

Nutrition

In Chapter 12, Picón-Reátegui, based upon the dietary surveys of Mazess and Baker (1964), Gursky (1969), and Thomas (1972), concludes that the dietary intakes of Nuñoa meet U.S. dietary recommended allowances.

In order to clarify the role of nutrition on growth of Nuñoans, I have calculated partial correlation coefficients (adjusted for age) between dietary intakes and height of Nuñoa subjects. As shown in Table 10.2, the reported caloric and protein intakes by both boys and girls during childhood and adolescence are not significantly related to height. The lack of relationship between dietary intakes and growth in Nuñoa is probably due to the fact that evaluations of dietary intakes in any population, because of the technical and field difficulties and because of wide daily, monthly, and seasonal variations, do not give a true picture of actual food consumption. Indeed, as pointed out by Picón-Reátegui, in Chapter 11, the various dietary surveys show great variability in both quantity and quality of dietary intakes. For these reasons, and in view of the fact that the height of a child reflects the cumulative effect of his developmental history, it is not surprising that in Nuñoa the dietary intakes show little relationship to growth.

Bouloux (1968) conducted a study among two selected Aymara samples from La Paz, Bolivia. One sample of adolescents was derived from a population living in the outskirts of La Paz (Comunidad de la Garita de Lima), and the second sample was derived from an orphanage of La Paz (Orfelinato de Mindes Arcos). According to the evaluations of Bouloux (1968), the orphanage provided the children with conditions of nutrition (not quantified),

TABLE 10.2 *Correlation Coefficients Between Calorie Intake and Height, and Protein Intake and Height, Partialing Out the Effect of Age*[a]

| | Age group (yr) | | | | | |
| | 1–12 | | 13–19 | | 20–80 | |
Variable	N	r	N	r	N	r
		Males				
Calories–height	25	0.29	15	−0.03	15	0.32
Protein–height	25	0.28	15	0.15	15	0.35
		Females				
Calories–height	28	−0.19	7	0.26	24	0.30
Protein–height	28	−0.26	7	0.61	24	0.02

[a]Calculated from individual values given by Gursky (1969).

TABLE 10.3 *Maturation and Body Size of Two
Groups of High-Altitude Aymara
Adolescent Indian Boys Studied in
La Paz, Bolivia*[a]

Characteristic	Community (N = 31)		Orphanage (N = 24)	
	Mean	S.D.	Mean	S.D.
Age (yr)	15.9	0.3	16.0	0.3
Height (cm)	157.1	6.1	157.6	5.0
Weight (kg)	49.1	5.7	51.5	5.2
Chest circumference (cm)	81.3	4.0	82.5	1.5
Chest depth (cm)	20.2	1.9	21.0	1.1
Arm circumference (cm)	21.6	1.8	23.0	1.7
Leg circumference (cm)	31.5	1.8	32.8	1.7
Skeletal age (yr)	15.0	0.6	15.5	0.3

[a]Adapted from Bouloux (1968).

health, hygiene, and housing that were better than those of the community. In Table 10.3, data from that study are summarized. These data show that the adolescents living in the orphanage are slightly heavier in weight and attain slightly greater values for chest circumference, chest depth, arm circumference, leg circumference, and skeletal age than those living in the community. However, it is important to note that both the orphanage and the community subjects attained the same height.

The intrapopulation comparisons in Nuñoa indicate that the urbanized groups are slightly heavier and considerably fatter than their rural counterparts. These differences are probably related to differences in activity and dietary intake. In any event, whatever the factors responsible for the greater fat deposition of the urbanized group, they did not appear to be reflected in taller statures. In other words, it appears that in Nuñoa, greater calorie reserve as reflected by the increased fatness and weight is not associated with increased dimensional growth. This finding is contrary to those found among sea-level populations, where increased fatness and weight is associated with advanced maturity and growth (Reynolds, 1960; Garn and Haskell, 1960; Lloyd et al., 1961).

Hypoxia

Studies on experimental animals have been particularly fruitful to our understanding of the mechanism underlying the myriad effects on the development of the organism under hypoxic conditions. Several studies have shown that rats and guinea pigs born and raised at high altitude and under favorable conditions of nutrition and temperature have a lower body weight at birth and slower postnatal growth at all ages than their sea-level counterparts (Gordon et al., 1943; Hale et al., 1959; Krum, 1957; Timiras, 1965; Timiras and Wooley, 1966; Naeye, 1966; Cheek et al., 1969; Delaquerriere-Richardson et al., 1965; Burri and Weibel, 1971a, 1971b; Bartlett and Remmers, 1971). As demonstrated by the investigation of Timiras (1965) and illustrated in Fig. 10.14, the growth retardation at high altitude continues even after the second generation of exposure to hypoxia.

Cytological studies under conditions of hypoxia and undernutrition indicate that the cellular pattern associated with retarded growth in hypoxic conditions is quite different from that associated with malnutrition. The

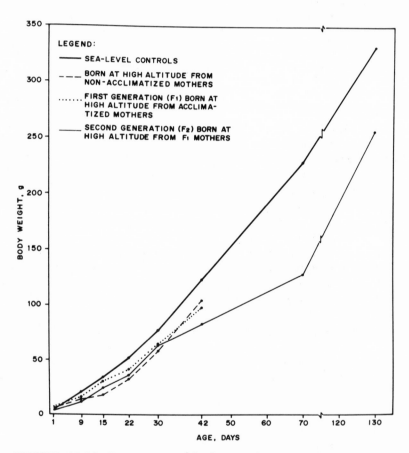

FIGURE 10.14 *Comparison of body growth, measured in terms of body weight, between rats born and raised at sea level and rats born and raised for two generations at high altitude (3800 m). [Adapted from Timiras (1965).]*

TABLE 10.4 *Percentage of Dietary Intakes Among High-Altitude (Huancayo, 3000 m) and Sea-Level (Lima, 147 b) Girls at Menarche[a]*

Residence	Mainly protein	Protein/calorie mix	Mainly carbohydrates	Low-Calorie
Sea level	30.5	42.0	24.0	3.5
High altitude	28.5	34.0	33.5	4.5

[a]Adapted from Peñaloza (1971).

research of Naeye (1966) demonstrates that the growth retardation under hypoxic conditions is because of a low number of cells, while the growth retardation under nutritional deficiency is because of a low mass of cytoplasm.

Recent studies conducted by Peñaloza (1971) demonstrate that growth in the Peruvian central Andes (Cerro de Pasco, 4200 m) during childhood and adolescence is markedly retarded when compared to growth at sea level of people from comparable socioeconomic conditions and with similar dietary intakes (see Table 10.4). These findings are confirmed by the studies of Llerena (1973). Furthermore, Llerena (1973) points out that the pubertal growth spurt, as in the Quechua population of Nuñoa and in boys and girls of Cerro de Pasco, is poorly defined.

The studies of Donayre (1966) indicated that menarche among high-altitude girls occurred at a later age than among sea-level girls. Recently, Peñaloza (1971) pointed out that the mean age at menarche in Cerro de Pasco is 13.58 yr, while at sea level it is 11.58 yr. These findings are in close agreement with those for Nuñoa Quechua girls (13.72 ± 0.50 yr) and Aymara girls (13.58 yr) reported by Bouloux (1968).

Table 10.5 summarizes the ratings of secondary sexual maturation among high-altitude and sea-level samples derived from the data of Llerena (1973). These data show that within the age range 7–15 yr, about 76 percent of the boys at high altitudes were in the prepubertal stage (stage I), while at sea level only 39 percent were prepubertal. Consequently, the proportion of boys in the second, third, fourth, and fifth pubertal stages was lower at high altitude than at sea level. Indeed, none of the boys at high altitude were in the fourth and fifth stages. In the same manner, at sea level about 60 percent of the girls were already in the fourth pubertal stage, while at high altitude, there were only 30 percent. In other words, in both males and females the age at which the secondary sexual characteristics is attained at high altitude is markedly delayed. Furthermore, measurements of luteinizing hormones indicate that the adult values in girls are attained by the age of 11 yr at sea level and 12 yr at high altitude (Llerena, 1973). It is also important to note that according to

TABLE 10.5   *Comparison of Sexual Stage Among Sea Level (Lima) and High-Altitude (4200 m) Children Aged 7–15 Years, in Central Peru[a]*

				Secondary sexual maturation stage (%)				
		Mean age		Prepubertal	Pubertal			
Residence	N	Mean	S.D.	I	II	III	IV	V
Males								
Sea level	105	11.1	2.2	39.3	23.4	18.7	16.8	1.9
High altitude	96	11.2	2.4	76.0	15.6	8.4		
Females								
Sea level	89	12.2	2.0	22.5	13.5	4.5	59.6	
High altitude	44	12.7	1.7	34.1	29.6	6.8	29.6	

[a]Adapted from Figs. 10–13 of Llerena (1973).

the studies of Guerra-Garcia (1971), the excretion of urinary testosterone in adults is lower at high altitude than at sea level.

Genetics

In an attempt to assess the influence of genetic factors on growth of Nuñoa, I have calculated the parent–offspring correlations in height. These results are compared in Table 10.6 with similar (unpublished) data derived

TABLE 10.6   *Parent–Offspring Correlations Among Two High-Altitude Samples: Quechua from Nuñoa and Impoverished Quechua from Cuzco*

	Father				Mother			
	Son		Daughter		Son		Daughter	
Age group (yr)	N	r[a]	N	r	N	r	N	r
Quechuas from Nuñoa								
1–4.9	24	0.12	25	0.08	20	0.18	21	0.10
5–10.9	115	0.31[b]	98	0.29[b]	96	0.36[b]	86	0.32[b]
11–16.9	80	0.40[b]	60	0.42[b]	60	0.48[b]	50	0.52[b]
Impoverished Quechuas from Cuzco								
1–4.9	54	−0.23	52	−0.28[c]	80	−0.18	57	−0.46[c]
5–10.0	85	0.10	71	0.08	99	0.30	78	0.21
11–12.0	16	−0.05	19	0.40[c]	12	0.50	20	0.24

[a]Weighted mean r is from Z-transformed age-specific values of r.
[b]$p < 0.01$.
[c]$p < 0.05$.

from a sample of impoverished Quechua Indians from Cuzco (Frisancho et al., 1973a). In Nuñoa, as shown in Table 10.6, the parents' height is significantly correlated with the stature of the offspring. In contrast, among the impoverished Quechua from Cuzco, the parents' height is *not* correlated with the height of the offspring, except during earlier childhood. These findings suggest that the environmental conditions for both parents and offspring are more uniform in Nuñoa than in the squatter settlement or *barriada* of Cuzco.

The parent—offspring correlations in Nuñoa range from 0.08 to 0.48; among western populations, they range from 0.36 to 0.60 (Tanner, 1962). Thus it would appear that the genetic contribution to phenotypic variation in growth in height is less in Nuñoa than in Western populations. This finding is supported by the investigations of Rothhammer and Spielman (1972) among Aymara Indians living at various altitudes in Chile. They note that altitude difference makes the largest contribution to anthropometric variation, while geographic and genetic distance contribute considerably less.

Functional Demand and Growth

Lung Growth. In terms of pulmonary function, the Nuñoa children showed rapid and accelerated development in forced vital capacity. In view of the fact that at sea level during childhood, growth in lung volume is associated with proliferation of alveolar units and alveolar surface area (Dunnill, 1962), the rapid growth in forced vital capacity seen among high-altitude children is probably also associated with an increase in alveolar units and alveolar surface area. Since there is a direct relationship between alveolar quantity and diffusion capacity (Cotes, 1965), the accelerated development in lung volume almost surely has adaptive significance in facilitating the diffusion of oxygen. Several studies, after adjustment for variations in body size, have demonstrated that adult highland natives have an enlarged lung volume (Hurtado et al., 1956a; Hurtado, 1964b; Frisancho, 1969b; Frisancho et al., 1973c; Garruto, 1969; see also Chapter 12). It is through this rapid pattern of growth that the high-altitude native attains his enlarged lung volume.

In a recent investigation designed to determine the mechanisms of functional adaptation to high-altitude hypoxia (Frisancho et al., 1973b), we measured the forced vital capacity of sea-level and high-altitude natives (see Table 10.7). The results of this study, after adjustment for variations in body size, demonstrated that sea-level subjects who were acclimatized to high altitude during growth attained the same values of forced vital capacity as the high-altitude natives. In contrast, sea-level subjects (Peruvian and U.S. whites) acclimatized as adults had significantly lower vital capacity than high-altitude natives. On the basis of these findings, we have postulated that the enlarged lung volume of the high-altitude natives is the result of adaptations acquired during the developmental period.

The hypothesis that the enlarged lung volume at high altitude is probably

TABLE 10.7   *Covariance Adjustment of Forced Vital*
Capacity (FVC) Among Subjects Tested
at High Altitude[a]

Test altitude (m)	N	Group	FVC, adjusted for age, weight, and height (ml)		F- ratio
			Mean	S.E.	
3840	40	High-altitude natives	4830.3	69.9	
3840	13	Sea-level subjects acclimatized as adults	4504.6	122.1	
					5.19[b]
3400	20	High-altitude natives	4990.3	128.6	
3400	21	Sea-level subjects acclimatized as children	5055.0	121.5	
					0.36
3400	10	U.S. whites acclimatized as adults[c]	4573.9	231.6	
					5.53[b]

[a]From Frisancho et al. (1973c).
[b]$p < 0.02$.
[c]Compared with high-altitude natives at both altitudes.

developmental in nature is supported by experimental studies on animals. The studies of Burri and Weibel (1971a), Bartlett and Remmers (1971), and Bartlett (1972) demonstrate that young rats with prolonged exposure to high-altitude hypoxia (at 3450 m) show an accelerated development in the proliferation of alveolar units, alveolar surface area, and growth in lung volume. In contrast, adult rats with prolonged exposure to high-altitude hypoxia did not show changes in alveolar quantity and lung volume (Burri and Weibel, 1971b). These findings together suggest that in experimental animals and man the development of an enlarged lung volume at high altitude is probably mediated by developmental factors.

Growth in Marrow Cavity.   During postnatal life the red blood cells are produced exclusively by the marrow of all bones. Although after about the age of 20 yr the marrow of the long bones diminishes in hematopoietic function, its continuing activity and growth depends entirely on the organism's requirements for oxygen (Wintrobe, 1967). Therefore, the growth or hyperplasia of the bone marrow is regulated by the demands for increased functional activity. X-ray measurements of marrow cavity at high altitude indicate a continued growth through the age of 22 yr in men, and 18 yr in women, as compared to 10 and 16 yr at sea level (Baker et al., 1958; Johnston and Malina, 1966; Frisancho et al., 1970).

In view of the importance of red blood cells in oxygen transport at high altitude, the differences in the pattern of growth in bone marrow and in marrow space are probably related to the increased demand for functional activity. Through experimental studies, Hunt and Schraer (1965) demonstrate that under hypoxic conditions the bone marrow of rats is increased by about 20 percent. Studies on man (Merino and Reynafarje, 1949) indicated that in the bone marrow the ratio of nucleated red-cell elements to granulocytes in high-altitude natives is 1:1, while at sea level there is 1 nucleated red-cell element for 3 granulocytic cells. These indications suggest that at high altitude the increased requirements for O_2 result in increased hematopoietic activity of the bone marrow.

DISCUSSION AND CONCLUSIONS

The following conclusions appear justified from this investigation:

1. Physical growth of the high-altitude Nuñoa Quechua Indian is unquestionably slow.

2. Sexual dimorphism in the development of body size and muscle size appears to occur after the age of 16 yr.

3. The growth rates show a slow and poorly defined adolescent spurt for both sexes.

4. Distance curves indicate a very prolonged body-growth period, and termination of growth in stature appears to occur by the age of 22 yr in men and 20 yr in women.

5. Assessments of skeletal maturation and skeletal development indicate a slow maturation and delayed mineralization. Studies on skin reflectance by Conway and Baker (1972) demonstrate that the prepubescent darkening in skin color which occurs at sea level prior to the age of 10 yr takes place after the age of 13 yr among Nuñoans. Thus, adolescent maturation by any criteria is delayed among Nuñoans.

6. The reported protein and calorie intakes among selected samples in Nuñoa are not correlated with stature during either the period of growth or adulthood. Similarly, rural—urban differences in weight and subcutaneous fat are not parallel with differences in growth in height.

7. As inferred from parent—offspring correlations, in Nuñoa the genetic contribution to phenotypic variation in growth in height is less than in western populations.

8. In view of the experimental evidence derived from animals reared under hypoxic conditions, and human data derived from studies in the central regions of Peru and Bolivia, the role of high-altitude hypoxia on growth of man at high altitude cannot be ruled out. Although the data on dietary intakes of Nuñoa do not show meaningful relationships to growth, in explaining the growth delay at high altitude, the role of nutritional factors must also be taken into account. For these reasons, it is suggested that the slow growth

and development of Nuñoa children reflects the synergic influence of high-altitude hypoxia, hypocaloric stress, and genetic factors.

9. The study of pulmonary function and body size indicates a rapid and accelerated development of forced vital capacity and chest size. Since the development of lung volume during childhood at sea level is associated with increases in alveolar units and alveolar surface area, the rapid development in forced vital capacity of Nuñoa children is probably also reflected in greater alveolar quantity and area. Since there is a direct relationship between alveolar area and diffusion capacity, the rapid growth in forced vital capacity probably has an adaptive capacity in facilitating the diffusion of O_2.

10. As derived from analytical studies on sea-level populations, the enlarged forced vital capacity of the high-altitude native is probably developmental in nature.

11. Since high-altitude populations also have accelerated growth in heart size, along with the rapid growth in lung volume (Peñaloza et al., 1960), the rapid development in chest size of Nuñoa subjects probably forms an integrated part of this system. The implications that the enlarged thorax of high-altitude natives is not adaptive per se but is, rather, a by-product of their enlarged lung and heart volumes.

12. The continued growth in marrow space at altitude is probably related to the demand for increased hematopoietic activity at high altitudes.

Part II:

ADULT MORPHOLOGY

In this section, the characteristics of the adult Nuñoa Quechua native are compared with those of highland and lowland populations. Changes in morphology with age among Nuñoa subjects were studied also.

METHODS AND MATERIALS

The sample included a total of 106 men and 140 women ranging in age from 20 to 70 yr. The measurement methods used were outlined in Part I.

Nuñoa subjects were compared in body size with highland and lowland populations from Peru, Bolivia, Ecuador, and Brazil. The comparison was limited to measurements of height, weight, sitting height, and cormic index. More ample comparative data of Latin-American Indigenous populations can be found in Comas (1971).

RESULTS AND DISCUSSION

As shown in Table 10.8, the Nunoa men in terms of height, weight, sitting height, and cormic index are indistinguishable from other highland Andean populations. The average adult height for Nuñoa is 159.2 cm, which is equal to the average highland height (159.8 cm). In contrast, the lowland populations on the average, at 162.0 cm, are about 3 cm taller than those of the highlands.

In body weight, the highland populations, at 56 kg, are about 3 kg lighter than the lowland populations, at 59 kg. However, this difference is negligible when one takes into account the differences in stature.

The Nuñoa Quechua sample and the other highland populations have a larger sitting height than does the lowland population I recently studied. This finding is interesting in view of the fact that sitting height has been assumed to be under genetic control (Greulich, 1957).

Tables 10.9 and 10.10 give the means and standard deviations for the measurements of body size of Nuñoa men and women, divided into 10-year age groups. The data on height and weight are compared in Fig. 10.15 with those derived from the U.S. Ten-State Nutrition Survey (1972) and Mexican Indigenous samples (Lasker, 1953). From this information it is evident that the height of Nuñoans does not show changes associated with aging. In contrast, in both U.S. and Mexican samples, the decline in height amounts to about 1.5 cm per decade.

Among Western populations, the decline in height associated with aging is generally assumed to be due in part to reduction in intervertebral space, increased curvature of the spinal column, and the occurrence of the secular trend in stature in younger populations (Miall et al., 1964). It is quite possible that among Nuñoans the decline in stature occurs at the same rate as in the United States, but it is not shown because of the small number of old subjects. This lack, coupled with the lack of secular trend in stature in this population, may make it difficult to determine major changes in height associated with aging.

In Nuñoa men, the increase in weight follows the same pattern as in the United States. In populations after the age of 40 years, weight declines by 2.5 kg per decade. Among Nuñoa women, weight continues to increase until about the age of 40 years, while in the United States it continues until about the age of 60 years. However, despite this difference, the rate of weight decline with age is about the same in both populations (2.5 kg per decade).

The subcutaneous fat of Nuñoan and U.S. men, as shown in Fig. 10.16, changes very little with age. The Nuñoa women show declines in subcutaneous fat after 20 years of age. In contrast, U.S. women have a continued deposition of subcutaneous fat through the age of 50 years, after which declines take place.

The muscle diameter appears to increase until about the age of 50 years in

TABLE 10.8 Selected Anthropometric Measurements of Highland and Lowland Latin American Adult (30–50 Years) Indigenous Populations

Population location	N	Height (cm)		Weight (kg)		Sitting height (cm)		Biachromial breadth (cm)		Cormic index		Reference
		Mean	S.D.	Mean	S.D.	Mean	S.D.	Mean	S.D.	Mean	S.D.	
Highlands												
Quechua												
Nuñoa, Peru	95	159.2	5.7	55.5	5.4	85.1	3.5	35.3	2.3	53.5	1.8	Present study
Anta, Peru	53	160.7	5.1	57.1	5.0	86.2	3.3	38.5	—	53.7	—	Quevedo (1960)
Apurimac, Peru	124	158.3	—	—	—	83.6	—	38.1	—	51.8	—	Ferris (1916)
Morococha, Peru	478	159.0	—	55.4	—	—	—	—	—	—	—	Hurtado (1943a)
Imbabura, Ecuador	134	156.5	5.7	—	—	82.5	—	36.4	2.0	52.6	1.6	Gillin (1941)
Uros-Chipayos												
Lake Titicaca, Peru	33	160.5	—	—	—	84.8	—	37.2	—	52.8	—	Vellard (1972)
Aymaras												
La Paz, Bolivia	104	157.0	—	—	—	87.0	—	—	—	55.4	—	Chervin (1907)
La Paz, Bolivia	132	161.9	—	55.8	—	86.8	—	36.1	—	53.6	—	Sacchetti (1964)
Lake Titicaca, Bolivia	69	161.1	—	—	—	85.7	—	36.7	—	53.2	—	Vellard (1961)
Lake Titicaca, Peru	112	161.1	—	—	—	85.3	—	36.4	—	52.9	—	Vellard (1961)
Lake Titicaca, Peru	33	161.8	—	—	—	84.7	—	33.5	—	52.3	—	Vellard (1961)
Lake Titicaca, Peru	100	159.9	—	—	—	—	—	—	—	—	—	Vellard (1961)

Lowlands

	n											Reference
Quechua												
San Jose, Chiclayo, Peru	44	156.6	6.2	—	—	—	—	39.8	1.6	—	—	Lasker (1962)
Peru; Lamas, S. Martin, Peru	59	163.1	5.5	55.1	5.5	84.5	3.3	—	—	51.8	—	Frisancho[a]
Arawakan												
Eastern Peru	42	161.5	3.8	—	—	—	—	—	—	—	—	Farabee (1922)
Panoan												
Eastern Peru	22	157.8	2.8	—	—	—	—	—	—	—	—	
Cashinahua												
Eastern Peru	24	155.3	—	61.0	—	—	—	—	—	—	—	Johnston et al. (1971)
Xavantes												
Mato Groso, Brazil	42	170.2	5.3	69.8	5.2	—	—	—	—	—	—	Niswander et al. (1967)
Caiapos												
Mato Groso, Brazil	110	165.0	4.9	61.9	5.9	—	—	—	—	—	—	Da Rocha (1971)
Yanomamo												
Northeast Brazil	69	154.8	5.3	49.9	5.9	—	—	—	—	—	—	Da Rocha (1971)
Bororo												
Mato Groso, Brazil	20	173.7	5.8	—	—	—	—	—	—	—	—	Ehrenheich (1897)

[a]Unpublished data.

TABLE 10.9 *Anthropometric Characteristics of High-Altitude Nuñoa Quechua Men, by Age Group*

Characteristic	20–25 Mean	20–25 S.D.	26–35 Mean	26–35 S.D.	36–45 Mean	36–45 S.D.	46–55 Mean	46–55 S.D.	56–70 Mean	56–70 S.D.
N	41		40		30		14		11	
Age (yr)	21.6	1.6	30.0	2.9	39.5	3.0	49.7	3.4	63.0	4.1
Weight (kg)	52.9	5.5	55.2	5.2	56.8	5.4	57.1	5.4	52.8	5.8
Standing height (cm)	158.1	5.6	158.9	5.3	159.1	5.7	159.3	5.6	157.9	5.8
Sitting height (cm)	83.7	5.3	85.8	3.2	85.1	3.5	85.7	3.0	84.4	2.0
Biachromial diam. (cm)	34.8[a]	3.7	35.2	2.3	36.3	2.3	35.0	2.1	31.6	9.6
Chest width (cm)	27.6	2.0	27.6	1.8	28.8	3.7	28.2	0.9	27.4	1.7
Chest depth (cm)	20.5	2.0	20.6	1.7	21.4	2.2	21.5	1.2	21.7	1.5
Chest circum., max inspiration (cm)	91.9	4.8	93.9	3.7	95.1	4.2	94.8	4.1	94.7	7.1
Chest circum., max. expiration (cm)	83.7	4.0	85.5	8.8	88.5	4.2	88.9	4.5	87.7	4.5
Arm circum. (mm)	240.0[b]	16.8	246.5	14.6	251.6	16.3	251.2	10.8	239.7	15.6
Arm muscle diam. (mm)[c]	71.1[b]		75.2		74.4		76.6		71.1	
Upper-arm skinfold (mm)[c]	4.5[a]		4.0		4.0		3.0		4.0	
Subscapular skinfold (mm)[c]	7.0[d]		7.3		8.0		6.8		6.3	
Waist skinfold (mm)[c]	5.7[d]		5.0		5.2		5.0		4.7	
Calf skinfold (mm)[c]	6.3[a]		4.0		4.0		3.3		4.0	

[a]N, 34.
[b]N, 32.
[c]Fiftieth percentile values.
[d]N, 33.

TABLE 10.10 Anthropometric Characteristics of High-Altitude Nuñoa Quechua Women, by Age Group

Characteristic	20–25 Mean	20–25 S.D.	26–35 Mean	26–35 S.D.	36–45 Mean	36–45 S.D.	46–55 Mean	46–55 S.D.	56–70 Mean	56–70 S.D.
N	34		41		40		14		11	
Age (yr)	22.3	1.6	30.7	2.9	39.6	3.0	50.8	2.9	64.4	5.4
Weight (kg)	48.8	5.8	50.3	6.5	51.0	6.9	48.7	6.5	46.6	6.3
Standing height (cm)	147.5	5.9	148.0	4.7	148.0	4.9	148.1	4.9	146.6	3.3
Sitting height (cm)	80.9	3.4	81.7	3.1	82.3	3.8	81.4	4.1	80.7	1.3
Biachromial diam. (cm)	32.5	7.3	32.9	3.3	32.1	2.7	31.8	1.6	32.2	2.2
Chest width (cm)	26.9	2.2	26.4	4.1	27.0	1.7	27.0	1.7	24.0	7.5
Chest depth (cm)	19.5	2.7	19.2	3.2	19.8	1.4	19.5	1.0	19.1	3.5
Chest circum., max. inspiration (cm)	88.6	5.1	88.9	5.6	88.2	7.2	88.9	4.3	87.3	4.6
Chest circum., max. expiration (cm)	81.6	5.0	82.3	5.7	82.4	6.5	83.5	3.6	81.5	3.8
Arm circum. (mm)	230.9	17.4	231.7	15.1	232.3	18.0	223.3	14.2	223.2	20.4
Arm muscle diam. (mm)[a]	64.2		64.0		64.6		62.1		63.9	
Upper-arm skinfold (mm)[a]	9.7		8.3		7.7		6.0		4.7	
Subscapular skinfold (mm)[a]	12.0		10.0		11.0		8.0		6.0	
Waist skinfold (mm)[a]	8.3		7.3		7.0		6.0		4.3	
Calf skinfold (mm)[a]	8.0		7.0		7.0		3.0		4.7	

[a]Fiftieth percentile values.

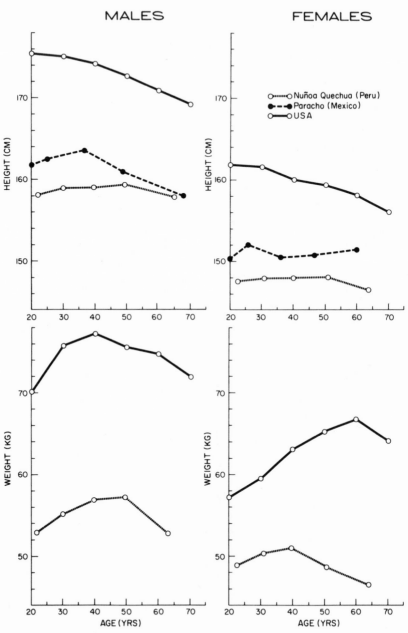

FIGURE 10.15 *Change in height and weight with age, in Nuñoan, Mexican, and U.S. samples.*

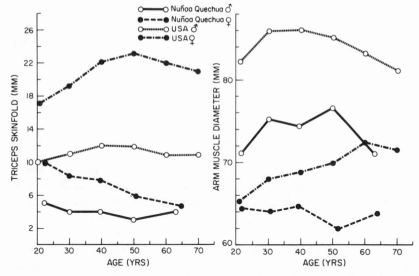

FIGURE 10.16 *Changes in subcutaneous fat and estimated upper-arm muscle measurements with age, in Nuñoan and U.S. samples.*

Nuñoa men and until about the age of 40 years in U.S. men. Afterward, in both populations, the muscle diameter declines by 5 mm per decade. In both Nuñoa and U.S. women, the muscle diameter does not show any systematic changes associated with age.

11

NUTRITION

Emilio Picón-Reátegui

The Peruvian Andes may be divided into two well-defined food zones. The *sierra* includes lands from close to sea level up to elevations of 3200 m. At this range of altitudes, weather conditions allow the cultivation of a variety of cereals, tubers, and legumes, and in the lower valleys, sugar cane, coffee, cacao, and bananas. Such food diversity is one of the principal reasons why the sierra zone has a long history of dense population settlement in Peru. The contemporary natives of this zone are largely engaged in agricultural labor as well as cattle and swine husbandry.

The puna zone can be divided into two subzones: (1) the *jalca* of the northern Peruvian Andes, which begins at about 3200 m and where only natural pasture grows; and (2) the *true puna* of the central and southern Peruvian Andes, which begins at about 3800 m and where environmental temperatures are lower than in the jalca. Because of the harshness of the environmental conditions and terrain, only tubers and cereal-like goosefoot plants of the *Chenopodia* genus can be cultivated. The main economic activities in this subzone are mining and llama, alpaca, and sheep herding, with agriculture as a subsidiary activity.

Since environmental temperature, which is tied to altitude, affects both caloric requirements and food production, it is understandable that food habits will differ according to the food zone where people live.

FOOD AND ACTIVITY PATTERNS

The daily activities of natives in the district of Nuñoa have been described by Little (1968). The activities commence at about 5:00 A.M., when one member of the family gets up to light the stove and prepare the breakfast. Other members of the household arise a little later.

After a hot breakfast, the flock is moved from the corral to the grazing areas by one or two members of the family. The grazing areas ordinarily are situated about half a mile from the settlement. Activities during herding consist of keeping watch on the herds, spinning wool into thread, and knitting. All members of the family, including children, participate in herding activities, which are carried out on foot and over very harsh terrain. This routine ends at between 4:00 and 6:00 P.M., when the animals are led back to the corral. At home, female members of the family spend the day weaving, spinning, knitting, and preparing skins.

The stove is lighted again at about 5:00 P.M., in order to prepare the evening meal, which is usually served at about 7:00 P.M. The preparation of meals is a somewhat lengthy process at high altitude because water boils at temperatures below 100°C. For example, at 4500 m above sea level (barometric pressure of about 440 torr) water boils at 85°C.

After the evening meal, the activities are limited to conversation within the house structures. All family members retire at 8:00 or 9:00 P.M. This cycle of activities, with little variation, is carried out daily during the year by families living above 4000 m. However, this basic activity pattern is altered in late November or early December with the shearing of the wool-bearing animals as well as during the season of agricultural labor. At altitudes where climatic conditions permit plant cultivating, all members of the family devote from 4 to 5 weeks of the year to heavy agricultural labor. Planting begins in late August or early September when cañihua and quinoa are sown. In September or October, potatoes are planted. The grains are weeded once or twice during the growing season. Harvest takes place in early April for cañihua, late in the same month for quinoa, and in May for potatoes. The total time spent in harvesting does not usually exceed 2 weeks.

Other important activities, according to energy expenditure, are trips made on foot to other communities and to fiestas for purposes of trade and social exchange. Small children frequently are transported on the backs of their mothers during such trips, which may cover distances of up to 50 km. During fiestas and trade fairs, the natives may spend about 4 or 5 days dancing and drinking alcohol. The town of Nuñoa has about three fiestas yearly, although many others are held in adjacent districts. Since the main occupations are performed out of doors, all members of the family are together inside settlement structures only during morning and evening meals and during retiring hours.

Because of lack of roads, poor transport facilities, and the socioeconomic characteristics of the communities in the district of Nuñoa, food habits have been tied for ages to local food production. The studies of Mazess and Baker (1964) showed that natives were incorporating maize and wheat into their diet. However, these products represented only 2.5 percent of the bulk of foods eaten (see Fig. 11.1). Later studies (Gursky, 1969) showed an increase in the consumption of foreign foods (foods not native to the Nuñoa or altiplano district) by the natives of the district, although the proportion of these products in the daily native diet appears to be related not only to patterns of agricultural production but also to the degree of isolation of the population. The survey on food consumption, carried out by Gursky (1969), is very instructive in this respect. It shows that in the town of Nuñoa, with access to the railroad that links Cuzco with the commercial center of Juliaca, foreign products covered about 53.5 percent of the bulk of food consumed.

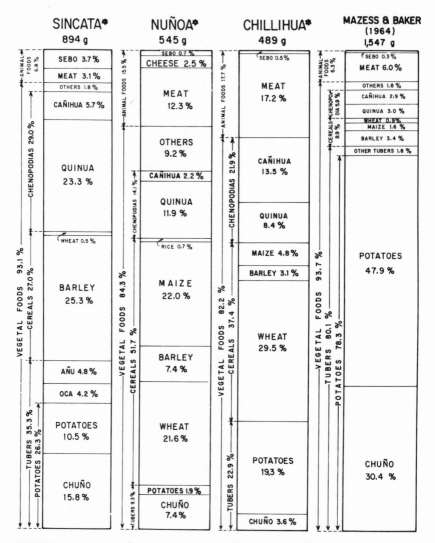

FIGURE 11.1 *Food consumption in the district of Nuñoa. The several foodstuffs are given as percentage of total bulk. Asterisk indicates data from Gursky (1969).*

Among these food products, white flour, bread, wheat kernels, maize, corn meal, rice, white sugar, oil, and fresh fruits were reported to be consumed. Products derived from wheat and maize constituted about 43.6 percent of the bulk of food ingested. Twenty-five different food products were reported in the diets of Nuñoa town residents.

In Sincata, a small native community situated at 4000 m at a distance of 20 km from the town of Nuñoa and having a traditional peasant agricultural system of subsistence, only about 3.5 percent of the bulk of food ingested was identified as a foreign product. Products derived from wheat and maize made up about 1.7 percent of food consumed. Twenty-three food products were available to this community.

Another community studied, the hacienda Chillihua, is situated at an altitude of 4300 m, where the daily morning frosts throughout the year make it impossible to grow plants. At some 23 km from the town, members of this community have an economy derived from herding llamas, alpacas, and sheep, and have incorporated only white wheat flour, wheat kernels, and maize into their daily diet. However, these products comprised about 34.3 percent of the bulk of food consumed. Products derived from wheat made up 29.5 percent of the bulk ingested. Twelve food products were available to this community.

Figure 11.1 is a comparison of the data from the surveys of Mazess and Baker (1964) and Gursky (1969). This comparison suggests that in the 5 or so years between the two surveys, tubers were practically displaced from the daily native diet of the district of Nuñoa by cereals and *chenopodias*. It must be remarked that both surveys were carried out at the same time of year and only 1 or 2 months after the harvest of potatoes. However, as a justification for the discrepancy between the results of these surveys, Gursky (1969) points out that the harvest of potatoes which preceded his survey was unusually small.

It is worth noting that even in communities where altitude limits or prevents cultivation and where 100 percent of the economy is derived from herding, vegetal products still are the most important part of the native diet. The survey on food consumption carried out by Gursky (1969) showed that food of vegetal origin provided about 82.2 percent of the bulk of food consumed in the herding community of Chillihua and 93.1 percent in the agricultural community of Sincata. This last figure agrees with that reported by Mazess and Baker (1964) for food consumed in the district of Nuñoa (see Figure 11.1). In addition to cattle, llamas, alpacas, and sheep, many people from these communities maintain some domestic fowl and nearly all families raise guinea pigs. Furthermore, the rivers of the district are rich in fish (largely trout). However, neither Mazess and Baker (1964) nor Gursky (1969) reported consumption of eggs, chicken, or fish by the natives of the district, although the former investigators observed that milk is occasionally consumed from December to May. A possible explanation for the absence of such items in the diet is related to the practice of wages commonly distributed in the form of agricultural products (Little, 1968). Moreover, products such as eggs, chicken, or fish are sold in order to purchase cheaper, more energetic foods, as well as tools for general use at home.

As may be supposed, meat consumption was higher in the herding community of Chillihua and much less in the agricultural community of Sincata. Meat consumption reached a daily average of 89.5 g per person in Chillihua, 68.7 g in the town of Nuñoa, and only 26.0 g in Sincata (Gursky, 1969). Meat of sheep, llama, or alpaca is consumed in the district. Dried meat of llama or alpaca (*charqui*) is a common source of protein.

Another common animal product is rendered sheep or alpaca fat (*sebo*). Its daily consumption reached, according to Gursky (1969), 30.7 g per person in Sincata, 4.2 g in the town of Nuñoa, and 2.5 g in Chillihua. It is of interest to note that sebo consumption was higher in families in which meat consumption was low. Apparently, sebo is frequently consumed instead of meat or when meat is not readily available (Mazess and Baker, 1964).

FOOD PRODUCTION, PRESERVATION, AND PREPARATION

Of the approximately 158,183 hectares occupied by the district, only 0.2 percent, or 340 ha, are cultivated; 99.6 percent, or 157,535 ha, are used for pasturing herds of llamas, alpacas, sheep, and cattle; and 0.2 percent, or 308 ha, are unused (Baker et al., 1965). With this view of land utilization, it is understandable that herding constitutes the basis of the economy in the district. Agriculture constitutes a subsidiary occupation in places where climatic conditions permit the cultivation of potatoes, quinoa (*Chenopodium quinoa*), cañihua (*Chenopodium pallidicaule*), and, in lesser proportion, barley, ollucos (*Ullucus tuberosa*), oca (*Oxalis crenata*), and isaño (*Tropaeolum tuberosum*).

Since the potato constitutes the food staple, the greater proportion of the land is devoted to its cultivation. Part of the cropped potatoes is consumed fresh, but a larger proportion is processed to make *chuño negro* or *moraya,* which, as Mazess and Baker (1964) point out, enables not only a long-term preservation but also the concentration of nutrients in an edible bulk of potatoes. The potatoes processed in this form can be kept for 10 yr if stored in a closed room. Chuño negro and moraya are prepared by methods that have been employed for ages by the natives of the district.

To prepare chuño negro, small potatoes are placed in one layer over grass and exposed to heavy frost for 4 or 8 nights. Then, they are walked and stamped upon to squeeze out the water through small fissures in the skin. The processing of 4 nights gives a light and tender product which is stored for home consumption. The 8-night processing produces a totally dessicated and somewhat bitter potato which is used for trading.

To prepare the leached form of dehydrated potatoes, moraya, *tunta,* or *chuño blanco,* the potatoes are placed in one layer over grass and exposed to a heavy frost for one night only. On the following day, the potatoes are picked up before the sun shines, placed in the bed of a stream, and covered by straw and sand. The potatoes are removed from the water after 4 weeks, placed in one layer over grass, and exposed again to a heavy frost for one additional night. They are then dried and peeled. Common potatoes or *papas dulces (Solanum andigenum)* are used to prepare moraya, and bitter potatoes or *papas amargas (Solanum curtilobaum)* for tunta preparation.

The natives of the district of Nuñoa customarily take two or three meals a day. Gursky (1969) showed that 90 percent of the families in the town of Nuñoa, 30 percent in Sincata, and only 2 percent in Chillihua took three meals a day. The rest of the families took only two meals per day. In this last case, supplementary foods, such as boiled potatoes, toasted maize, or toasted barley, were usually eaten. This habit of supplementary food intake is common in people who must work out of doors away from the settlement (in agricultural or herding labor), and is usually not recorded in food-consumption surveys.

Breakfast is generally taken between 6:00 and 8:00 A.M., lunch between 12:00 noon and 2:00 P.M., and the evening meal from 6:00 to 8:00 P.M. When hot meals number only two, the evening meal is also served between 6:00 and 8:00 P.M. A very hot herb infusion is sometimes drunk early in the morning.

The diet in these communities is very monotonous. However, the diet does show some variation according to seasonal availability of foodstuffs. The thick soups (*masamora*) constitute the daily dish and are ordinarily served at all meals. Soups are prepared using either only one food product, generally chuño negro and sometimes moraya, or two or three products, such as quinoa, barley, wheat flour, and occasionally meat of alpaca or sheep. Two typical Nuñoa soups are prepared as follows:

Soup 1

Ingredients: chuño negro, quinoa, sebo, onions, and salt.
Preparation:
1. Boil quinoa in water for 2½ h.
2. Soak chuño negro in water for 1 h and then wash it.
3. Sauté the onions in sebo, add 1 tablespoon of pepper, and add to the boiling quinoa.
4. Add chuño negro to the boiling quinoa ½ h before serving.
5. Add salt and more water.
6. Stir until ready.

Soup 2

Ingredients: moraya, barley, meat, salt, and onions.
Preparation:
1. Soak moraya for 10 min. Then peel off remaining skins and soak for 1 h more.

Broth for soup:
2. Cook meat, onions, and salt in water for 2 h.
3. One-half hour before serving, mix barley with cold water and add it together with moraya to boiling broth.

Since soup with dehydrated potatoes is the basic dish, it is clear that potatoes, processed in this form, constitute the staple food in the district. Fresh potatoes are consumed for about 3 months after harvest and are served after boiling with the skin, although the skin is removed before eating. Maize and barley are of limited consumption at home, but their consumption increases during periods of outdoor labor.

Every 8 or 15 days, two delicacies, *parara* and *catahui lahua,* are prepared and consumed (generally at breakfast) by the majority of the families in the district. The preparation of these two dishes is as follows:

Parara
Ingredients: wheat flour, onions, sebo, and salt.
Preparation:
1. Mix wheat flour with enough water to form a dough.
2. Add salt and chopped onions.
3. Shape like doughnuts.
4. Fry in sebo for 10 min.

Catahui Lahua
Ingredients: quinoa, cañihua or maize (ground), sebo, salt, and *cal* (calcium oxide).
Preparation:
1. Boil quinoa and cañihua (or maize) with sebo for 1 h.
2. Add cal 5 min before serving.

EVALUATION OF THE DIET

Table 11.1 shows the composition of the diet consumed in the district of Nuñoa. From a general point of view, proportions of carbohydrate, protein, and fat are similar to those described for developing countries and agree with

TABLE 11.1 *Composition of the Diet in the District of Nuñoa*

			Caloric intake (%)		
Place	Altitude (m)	Reference	Carbo-hydrates	Protein	Fat
Nuñoa	4000	Mazess and Baker (1964)	87.8	8.7	4.5
Nuñoa	4000	Gursky (1969)	76.7	12.6	10.8
Sincata	4000	Gursky (1969)	80.3	10.7	8.9
Chillihua	4300	Gursky (1969)	71.0	16.1	13.0

those reported for other Andean populations by Collazos et al. (1960) and Picón-Reátegui (1963). It can be seen that about 79 percent of caloric intake is covered by carbohydrates, 12 percent by proteins, and 9 percent by fat. Whether this dietetic pattern is a consequence of socioeconomic conditions or an adaptive selection to life at high altitudes is not known. From a theoretical point of view, it can be postulated that a carbohydrate-rich meal may be the most adequate for a hypoxic environment, since carbohydrates use less oxygen in their metabolism than either proteins or fats.

Calories

The survey of Gursky (1969) shows that about 90 percent of the caloric intake came from foodstuffs of vegetal origin in the three communities of the district surveyed. The kind of economy of the community had no influence on this value, which is somewhat lower than that reported by Mazess and Baker (1964) for the same area. The main difference in the findings of the two studies is in the identification of the staple food in the district. According to Mazess and Baker (1964), tubers were the staple food, providing about 74.2 percent of the total caloric intake. Further, 49.5 percent of the caloric intake was provided by chuño negro and 23.5 percent by fresh potatoes. In the survey of Gursky (1969), however, a preponderance of cereals was noted, with tubers consisting of only 22.2 percent of caloric intake in Sincata, 11.8 percent in Chillihua, and 8.4 percent in the town of Nuñoa. The potatoes, fresh or dehydrated, as the staple food in the district were displaced in Chillihua by products derived from wheat, which made up 38.6 percent of the caloric consumption, and in the town of Nuñoa by products derived from wheat and maize, which contributed about 23.9 and 24.0 percent, respectively, to caloric intake. Neither wheat nor maize were produced in this geographical area; most of these products constituted surpluses sent to Peru by the United States (Gursky, 1969).

The influence of these products on food intake was minimal in the agricultural community of Sincata. In Sincata grain foodstuffs such as quinoa and barley produced locally contributed 28.0 and 29.2 percent to total caloric intake. It is surprising that Chillihua and the town of Nuñoa have not resolved their food problems in the same way. Foreign food products covered about 48.7 percent of total caloric intake in the town of Nuñoa. If it is true that the unusually small harvest of potatoes which preceded Gursky's survey explains the small consumption of fresh potatoes, it still leaves unexplained the small consumption of dehydrated potatoes. Whatever the reason may be, this fact may explain the difference in caloric intake reported for these communities by Mazess and Baker (1964), on the one hand, and by Gursky (1969), on the other. However, differences in caloric intake were apparent not only between the results of these two studies but also among the communities surveyed by Gursky (1969). According to Mazess and Baker (1964), mean daily caloric intake in the district of Nuñoa was 3110 kcal per person. Gursky (1969) gives a mean caloric intake of 1784 kcal for the town of Nuñoa, 1376 kcal for Chillihua, and 2544 kcal for Sincata. Not only did the people of Sincata consume the highest amount of dehydrated potatoes among the communities surveyed by Gursky, but also, almost 100 percent of their caloric consumption was covered by food produced locally. If the data of Gursky give the real picture of food consumption in these communities, they would verify the contention of R. S. Harris (1945) on the pitfalls of an unplanned introduction of foreign food products into the diet of populations with well-established food habits.

In 1972, Thomas reported the results of another survey on food consumption carried out in a small number of the same families studied by Gursky (1969). His results show a lower caloric intake than that reported for Sincata, but comparable for the town of Nuñoa (Gursky, 1969), especially for those between 16 and 35 years of age. Thomas (1972) thinks that the caloric intake reported for Sincata is too high, yet explainable by the fact that during the survey of Gursky, the community was engaged in a road construction and, thus, earning wages that might have been used for food. Table 11.2, taken from Gursky's data, shows that 66.7 percent of the subjects whose caloric intake was 30 percent or more above recommended allowances

TABLE 11.2 *Survey of Subjects Whose Caloric Intake was 30 Percent Above Recommended Allowances[a]*

Subject	Sex	Age (yr)	Weight (kg)	Height (cm)	Intake (kcal)	Recommended allowance[b] (kcal)	Deviation from recommended allowance (%)	Survey site
35	F	3	11.3	78.6	1751	1250	+ 40.1	Sincata
34	F	6	17.0	105.3	2320	1600	+ 45.0	Sincata
55	F	6	17.7	101.3	2144	1600	+ 34.0	Chillihua
42	F	8	21.8	109.5	2732	2000	+ 36.6	Sincata
33	F	27	42.6	143.8	2786	1904	+ 45.9	Sincata
54	F	27	49.4	139.1	3509	2128	+ 64.9	Chillihua
20	F	35	53.1	156.2	3236	2073	+ 56.1	Sincata
27	F	36	45.8	143.3	3013	1861	+ 61.9	Sincata
45	M	39	57.6	155.7	5064	2711	+ 86.8	Sincata
2	F	44	60.6	154.4	3137	2282	+ 37.5	Sincata
1	M	45	62.0	169.6	3618	2629	+ 37.6	Sincata
68	F	60	55.8	148.1	1422	1801	+ 66.1	Chillihua
52	M	70	51.2	152.3	5289	1884	+180.7	Chillihua
53	F	70	41.7	138.3	2657	1316	+101.9	Chillihua
21	F	80	43.2	146.4	2992	1205	+148.3	Sincata

[a]From Gursky (1969).
[b]Recommended allowances from Food and Nutrition Board NRC-NAS (1968) standards.

were from Sincata; the rest were natives from Chillihua. This supports the statement of Thomas. However, 80 percent of those individuals from Sincata with a high caloric intake were female, and one-third of this sample were children 3–8 yr of age. One individual with a caloric intake of 148.3 percent over her recommended allowance was a women of 80 yr whose actual body weight fell within ±10 percent of her standard weight. In the study of Gursky there were 5 subjects, aged 60–80 yr, whose actual weight fell within ±10 percent of their respective standard weights, but whose caloric intake ranged from 25.4 to 180.7 percent above recommended allowances.

Table 11.3 surveys the subjects of Gursky whose caloric intake was 30 percent or more below recommended allowances. It can be seen that 54.5 percent were natives from the town of Nuñoa, 42.4 percent from Chillihua, and only 3.0 percent from Sincata. These percentages are oddly similar to the proportion of caloric intake coming from foreign sources: 48.7, 45.1, and 2.0 percent for Nuñoa, Chillihua, and Sincata, respectively. It must be noted also that 60.6 percent of the group with low caloric intake were male and that 72.7 percent were younger than 18 yr of age. However, the differences in caloric intake in the three communities seem not to be influenced by differences in age or sex composition of the sample. Age composition was similar for the three communities. Males made up 43.1 percent of the sample in Sincata, 42.9 percent in Chillihua, and 58.3 percent in the town of Nuñoa.

It is surprising that neither high nor low caloric intake had an effect on actual body weight (see Fig. 11.2 and Tables 11.2 and 11.3). Actual body weight of the majority of the people surveyed fell within ±10 percent of their standard weight (Fig. 11.2). The few cases that fell outside this limit do not appear to constitute pathological cases of underweight or overweight. It is true that body weight is not a good indicator of caloric intake. There are, for example, pathological conditions where water retention may give a blurred picture of a true caloric inadequacy. However, such must not be the case in the samples surveyed by Gursky, since no mention is made of edema, which would have been easy to detect with skinfold measurements.

Figures 11.3 and 11.4 show, in percentiles, the arm skinfold distribution in the population surveyed by Gursky (1969). The figures for the male samples fell within the tenth and seventy-fifth percentile of the values reported for a Canadian male population (Pett and Ogilvie, 1956). The larger proportion, for male subjects 3 to 18 years old, were distributed within the twenty-fifth and seventy-fifth percentiles. The survey of Gursky (1969) showed that a higher percentage of subjects with a caloric intake 30 percent or more below recommended allowances belonged to this same age and sex group.

In spite of the fact that the survey of Gursky (1969) showed a higher percentage of subjects with a caloric intake at or above recommended allowances were female, the figures for upper-arm skinfolds for the female

TABLE 11.3   *Subjects Whose Caloric Intake was 30 Percent Below Recommended Allowances[a]*

Subject	Sex	Age (yr)	Weight (kg)	Height (cm)	Intake (kcal)	Recommended allowance[b] (kcal)	Deviation from recommended allowance (%)	Survey site
79	M	1	8.2	69.8	202	816	−75.2	Chillihua
109	M	1.5	5.4	64.8	585	1100	−46.8	Nuñoa
17	F	2	10.4	74.7	661	1100	−39.9	Sincata
59	F	2	9.3	71.2	645	1100	−41.4	Chillihua
100	M	2	8.8	70.0	639	1100	−41.9	Nuñoa
112	M	2	8.6	69.4	523	1100	−52.5	Nuñoa
66	M	3	13.2	85.9	494	1250	−60.5	Chillihua
78	F	3.5	13.4	89.6	445	1400	−68.2	Chillihua
108	M	4	11.8	80.3	629	1400	−55.1	Nuñoa
107	M	6	15.9	95.3	901	1600	−43.7	Nuñoa
101	F	7	17.2	101.7	1031	2000	−48.4	Nuñoa
64	M	8	22.7	114.3	1136	2000	−43.2	Chillihua
98	M	8	23.1	113.8	1099	2000	−45.0	Nuñoa
74	F	9	27.8	118.7	742	2200	−66.3	Chillihua
75	F	9	27.2	125.7	678	2200	−69.2	Chillihua
105	F	10	22.2	116.0	1013	2200	−54.0	Nuñoa
83	M	11	24.0	117.3	1585	2500	−36.6	Nuñoa
63	M	12	32.6	128.6	936	2500	−62.6	Chillihua
106	M	12	27.2	126.0	1461	2500	−41.6	Nuñoa
82	M	13	30.6	132.4	1803	2700	−33.3	Nuñoa
73	M	15	48.1	151.0	1284	3250	−60.5	Chillihua
104	F	15	41.3	138.5	1203	2400	−49.9	Nuñoa
72	M	16	46.2	147.2	1545	2753	−43.9	Chillihua
97	M	18	58.0	158.6	1231	3396	−63.8	Nuñoa
62	F	20	61.7	144.5	853	2549	−66.5	Chillihua
77	F	20	44.9	142.7	1125	2066	−45.6	Chillihua
96	M	25	23.5	157.0	1652	2643	−37.5	Nuñoa
69	F	26	52.6	138.5	1173	2227	−47.3	Chillihua
94	F	26	50.3	145.3	1403	2156	−34.9	Nuñoa
95	M	26	54.4	155.4	1700	2811	−39.5	Nuñoa
60	M	38	62.6	152.4	1775	2880	−38.4	Chillihua
93	F	40	53.5	146.1	1316	2085	−36.9	Nuñoa
103	M	42	54.8	154.3	1759	2616	−32.8	Nuñoa

[a]From Gursky (1969).
[b]Recommended allowances from Food and Nutrition Board NRC-NAS (1968) standards.

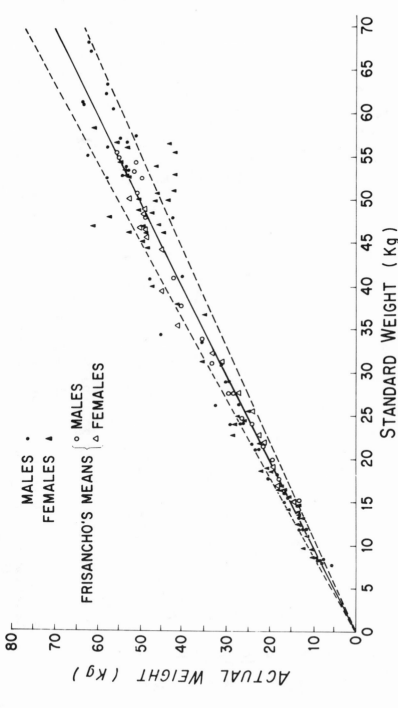

FIGURE 11.2 *Actual body weight versus standard weight relationship in the Nuñoa population surveyed by Gursky (1969). Data from Frisancho (1966) are also included. Solid line represents the mean standard body weight for age, sex, and height (Metropolitan Life Insurance Co., 1943; Wilder, 1941). The dashed lines are ±10 percent deviations from the mean.*

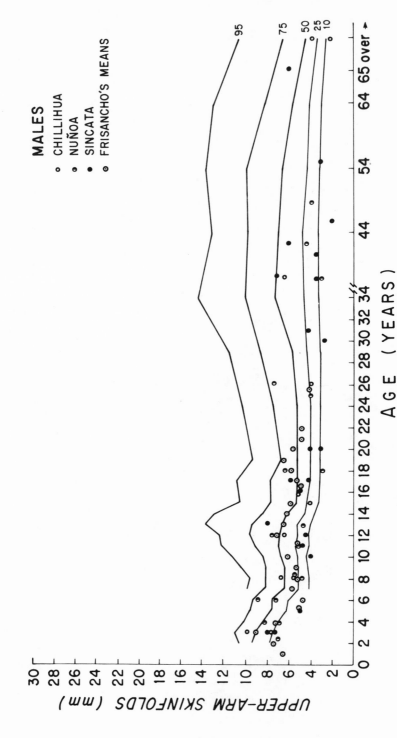

FIGURE 11.3 *Upper-arm skinfolds: percentile distribution in Nuñoa male population surveyed by Gursky (1969) and as reported for the Canadian population (Pett and Ogilvie, 1956). Frisancho's means (1966) for the male Nuñoa population are also included.*

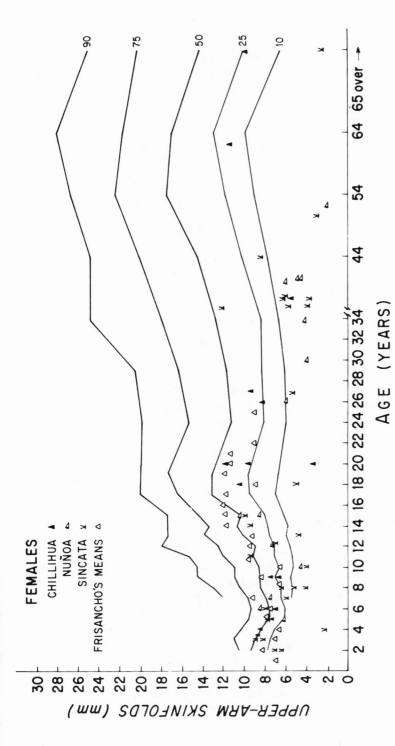

FIGURE 11.4 *Upper-arm skinfolds: percentile distribution in Nuñoa female population surveyed by Gursky (1969) and as reported for the Canadian female population (Pett and Ogilvie, 1956). Frisancho's means (1966) for the female Nuñoa population are also included.*

samples in my survey (Fig. 11.4) showed a distribution that fell within the tenth and fiftieth percentiles reported for a Canadian female population (Pett and Ogilvie, 1956).

The discrepancies between caloric intake and actual body weight or skinfolds might have had their origin in a quantitative and qualitative alteration of the usual food habits during or some time before the Gursky survey was carried out. This pattern of behavior is common in populations during food consumption surveys. In the case of the natives of the district of Nuñoa, this behavior might have been motivated by their desire to qualify for supplementary aid. For example, while Gursky was carrying out his survey, the resident priest was distributing surplus food products among the native population (Gursky, 1969). These products appeared in the native diet of the town of Nuñoa and Chillihua, covering a great deal of the caloric intake of these communities. It should be noted, however, that the question of who received these products is unresolved since much of the food appeared to be diverted to nonnative members of the community (Escobar M., personal communication).

The results on caloric intake, reported by Thomas (1972), are only comparable to those of the town of Nuñoa in Gursky's survey and, in this case, only for females 16–19 and 20–55 yr of age and for males 13–15 and 20–55 yr of age. Moreover, actual body weights were higher for every age group in the sample of Thomas. Thomas reports that these data suggest that segments of the Nuñoa population have caloric intakes considerably below their recommended allowances during the period when food energy resources are most abundant in the annual cycle. In spite of this fact, seasonal variations in skinfold measurements suggest a period of fat deposition, or positive caloric balance. Thus, according to Thomas, these facts and the absence of apparent deficiency diseases could be associated with seasonally low activity levels in the Nuñoa population.

As a support to his statement that "low caloric intake does not necessarily place an individual in negative caloric balance," he cites the case of a women of 38 yr, residing in the town of Nuñoa, who, in spite of an extremely low caloric intake throughout 10 months, showed a dramatic increase in skinfolds. No mention is made about changes in body weight. Thomas states that "assuming that skinfold increase is, in part, associated with an increase in body fat, this would indicate that positive caloric balance may exist at levels considerably below recommended values." The data of Gursky (1969) as well as those of Thomas (1972) do not show a logical relationship between caloric intake and body-weight maintenance. Although the methodology used by these investigators is reliable, there must be some error in their data, probably related to food consumption. Table 11.4, derived from Gursky's data, shows caloric intake per age groups. Most of the groups had a lower caloric intake than their recommended allowances. Despite low caloric intakes, actual body

Table 11.4   Caloric Intake for Age Groups in the District of Nuñoa[a]

Age (yr)	Number of subjects	Body weight (kg)	Height (cm)	Intake (kcal)	Recommended allowance[b] (kcal)	Intake X 100 allowance (%)
½–1	1	8.2	69.8	202	816	24.8
1–2	7	8.7	70.5	719	1100	65.4
2–3	6	12.7	82.5	1142	1250	91.4
3–4	5	13.5	88.2	1057	1400	75.5
4–6	10	15.6	96.6	1621	1600	101.3
6–8	8	20.2	109.0	1648	2000	82.4
8–10	5	26.1	121.5	1257	2200	57.1
			Males			
10–12	5	28.3	125.8	1639	2500	65.5
12–14	3	27.6	129.0	2295	2700	85.0
14–18	6	46.2	148.7	2020	2900	71.3
18–22	1	52.6	161.1	3181	2973	107.0
22–35	3	57.1	159.9	2216	2867	75.9
35–55	9	58.1	160.3	3000	2678	112.3
55+	2	57.1	156.8	4019	2038	203.0
			Females			
10–12	3	29.9	124.4	2149	2250	95.5
12–14	1	34.8	143.3	2063	2300	89.7
14–16	3	45.8	143.0	2008	2400	83.7
16–18	2	52.6	146.1	2344	2266	103.7
18–22	3	51.8	143.4	1416	2282	63.2
22–35	10	49.8	143.9	2060	2142	96.2
35–55	8	48.8	146.2	2181	1930	112.2
55+	3	46.9	144.3	2357	1442	205.4

[a]Derived from Gursky (1969).
[b]Recommended allowances from Food and Nutrition Board NRC-NAS (1968) standards.

weights were in accord with their respective standard weights, after adjustments for age, sex, and height.

With the available data, it is not possible to make an accurate calculation of energy expenditure for the native of the district of Nuñoa, but attempts can be made to establish some limits to judge these surveys. With this objective in mind, let us take as an example an adult man whose main labor is herding and whole life habits are the same as those described for a resident of the district of Nuñoa. The physical characteristics of this "reference man" correspond to those of the average adult male studied by Thomas (1972), i.e., height 158.7 cm, body weight 57.6 kg, body surface area 1.585 m^2, and body weight maintained at a constant level. Table 11.5 has been derived by using data on energy cost of different activities in the district (Thomas, 1972) and

TABLE 11.5 *Energy Expenditure in a Standard Man from the District of Nuñoa[a]*

Activity (hr)	Expenditure (kcal)
Sleeping, 8	531
Lying in bed, 1½	124
Personal occupation, 2	360
Standing, 2	194
Walking slowly, 2½	527
Herding, 8	983
Total (24)	2719

[a]Derived from the data of Thomas (1972) and Mazess et al. (1969).

on basal metabolic rate in adult male native residents of Nuñoa (Mazess et al., 1969). In order to maintain actual body weight, without modifying body composition and while maintaining usual physical activity, this "reference man" must have a daily intake of about 2719 kcal. Assuming an error of ±400 kcal, any report giving a daily caloric intake below 2319 or above 3119 kcal must be suspect. Caloric requirements for this same "reference man," predicted by extrapolation from the "standard man" of FAO/WHO (1957), was 2930 kcal/day. Caloric requirements for the standard woman, from the sample of Thomas, is estimated to be about 2136 kcal/day. Comparing these figures with those for the 22–35 age group in Table 11.4, it can be concluded that actual caloric intake for this age group should be enough to meet caloric requirements in adult women, but it may be about 25 percent below requirements for adult men.

The thesis of Thomas would not appear to hold, for the following reasons. (1) Basal metabolic rate is slightly higher in natives of Nuñoa than in sea-level residents (Mazess et al., 1969). (2) There is no discernible change in physical activity in people from 20 to 40 years old (Thomas, 1972). (3) Energy cost of physical activity in Nuñoa natives is not lower than that reported for sea-level residents (Thomas, 1972). (4) The resident of Nuñoa is exposed to a mean annual environmental temperature of about 8°C.

A study of metabolic balance was carried out on six adult male native residents of Nuñoa who consumed a native diet. (Picón-Reátegui, unpublished data). The results suggest that in order to maintain actual body weight without modifying body composition, an active adult man residing at an altitude of 4000 m must increase his caloric intake by about 14.8 percent over the requirements of a man with his same physical characteristics who resides at sea level.

Figure 11.2 suggests that for subjects aged 1–70 yr, caloric intake is adequate for body-weight maintainance. It shows that actual body weight falls within ±10 percent of standard weight adjusted for age, sex, and height. However, as Fig. 11.5 suggests, it is possible that from weaning to 18 years of age, caloric intake might not be sufficient to promote adequate growth. It is

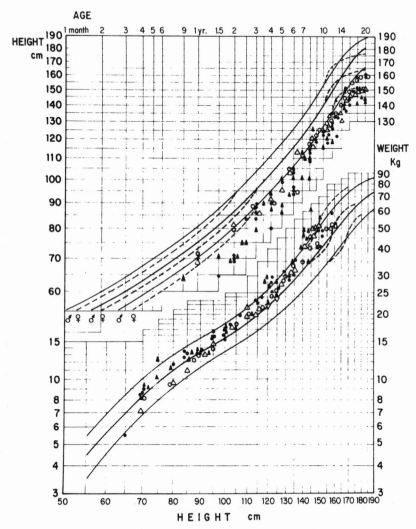

FIGURE 11.5 *Body weight for height and height for age in the Nuñoa population surveyed by Gursky (1969) and Frisancho (1966), compared with U.S. (Stuart et al., 1956), Swedish (Karlberg, 1955), and Swiss (Heimendinger, 1958) populations from 9 to 20 yr of age. Nuñoa females are indicated by triangles, males by circles.*

also suggested that caloric intake may not be adequate either for pregnant or lactating women.

Proteins

According to Mazess and Baker's survey (1964), mean protein consumption was about 69 g/person/day—i.e., somewhat more than 1.0 g/kg of body weight for the standard adult of Nuñoa. About 21.9 percent of the total protein ingested was of animal origin, 49.7 percent came from tubers, 10.9 percent from cereals, and 17.0 percent from *chenopodias*.

According to the data of Gursky (1969), mean protein consumption was 63.9 g/person/day in the agricultural community of Sincata. Barley and chenopodias made up 26.8 and 47.3 percent, respectively, of total protein consumed. Only 12.6 percent came from tubers and 10.7 percent was of animal origin. From the same study, protein consumption was similar for the town of Nuñoa at 53.4 g, and for the herding community of Chillihua at 53.8 g/day/person. The proportion of animal proteins in the protein mixture was 30.2 percent for Nuñoa and 32.0 percent for Chillihua. However, differences were found in vegetal sources of protein. In the town of Nuñoa, 22.3 percent of the total protein intake came from wheat, 19.2 percent from maize, and 17.6 percent from chenopodias. In Chillihua, wheat and chenopodias made up 27.5 and 28.3 percent, respectively, of protein intake.

Protein consumption, as reported for these communities, meets the recommended allowances of the Food and Nutrition Board, NRC-NAS (1968), as well as those of the Instituto de Nutricion, Institutos de Salud of Peru (1973). However, Gursky (1969) remarks that this statement is true for the adult population, but not for children under 3 years of age nor for girls 9–12 yr of age.

In the 1965 metabolic balance studies (Picón-Reátegui, unpublished data) subjects had a native diet whose composition was 583 g of carbohydrates, 53 g of protein, and 16.8 g of fat, and protein intake was about 1.0 g/kg of body weight. Although animal protein made up only 17.5 percent of total protein intake, the subjects maintained a positive nitrogen balance. Since no allowance was made for nitrogen lost throughout the skin, it is more correct to say that they maintained nitrogen balance. This observation is not a new one, since the subjects of Hegsted et al. (1946), with a mean body weight of 70 kg, were maintained in nitrogen balance with a diet containing 30–40 g of protein. About 50 percent of this protein mixture was derived from white bread, 12 percent from other cereals, 30 percent from vegetables, and 8 percent from fruits.

In our experiment, the apparent digestibility coefficient of the protein mixture of the diet was 76 percent. This coefficient is similar to what was reported for vegetable proteins (Swaminathan, 1967), which suggests that high altitude has no effect on protein absorption in natives.

These data suggest that the adult population was receiving a protein mixture that was quantitatively and qualitatively adequate for maintenance.

It does not mean that this protein mixture was also adequate in cases of physiological stress, such as pregnancy, lactation, and growth. In this respect, it is worth noting that children below 3 years and girls from 9 to 12 yr of age had a protein intake below recommendations for these ages (Gursky, 1969).

Fats

Table 11.1 shows the contribution of fats to caloric intake in the district of Nuñoa. These data agree with those reported for other Andean communities (Collazos et al., 1960; Picón-Reátegui, 1963). Mazess and Baker (1964) reported a fat intake of 16.0 g/day/person in the district of Nuñoa. According to Gursky's survey (1969) it ranged from 16.3 g in the herding community of Chillihua, to 23.0 g in the town of Nuñoa, to 45.6 g in the agricultural community of Sincata.

The data of Mazess and Baker (1964) show that animal food products, *chenopodias*, and tubers were the main sources of fat in the native diet. They made up 39.9, 25.8, and 24.1 percent, respectively, of the fat content of the native diet. Sebo constituted about 22.9 percent of fat intake. Foods of animal origin were also the main sources of fat in the groups surveyed by Gursky (1969). They made up, respectively, 45.4, 47.0, and 54.4 percent of the fat content in the diet of Chillihua, Nuñoa, and Sincata. Sebo constituted 11.7 percent of the fat content in the diet of the herding community of Chillihua, 13.9 percent in the town of Nuñoa, and 50.9 percent in the agricultural community of Sincata. In general, sebo consumption was inversely related to meat consumption in the three communities, which agrees with the observation of Mazess and Baker (1964) that sebo is usually consumed instead of meat. It is possible that either sebo or meat is used to give flavor to prepared dishes.

Fat intake is low in the district of Nuñoa in comparison with common American or European diets. Although there are no recommended allowances for fat recorded, fat is important in the daily diet because it provides a concentrated source of calories, gives flavor to foods, is a source of essential fatty acids, and constitutes a vehicle for the transportation of fat-soluble vitamins.

In the Nuñoa metabolic balance study noted above (Picón-Reátegui, unpublished data), fat content of the daily diet was 16.7 g/person. In spite of this low fat intake, fat absorption was only about 55.7 percent of intake. It is not known whether this low fat absorption was because of the type of fat consumed or if it was an effect of the high-altitude environmental conditions. These communities use rendered sheep or alpaca fat for food preparation, which is a hard fat with the appearance of wax.

There appear to be no studies on the effect of chronic hypoxia on fat tolerance in human beings. There is some disagreement with respect to fat tolerance during processes of acclimatization to high altitudes. Pugh (1962), for example, observed fatty feces and a low tolerance to fat among the members of the British expedition to Mount Everest. On the other hand, Siri (quoted by Consolazio et al., 1968) affirms that the members of the American expedition to Mount Everest had a typical American diet and there apparently was no ill effect from a moderate fat intake.

Calcium

Calcium consumption was of the order of 441 mg/person/day, according to Mazess and Baker's survey (1964). The main sources of calcium were chuño negro and chenopodias, which supplied 47.0 and 25.4 percent, respectively, of the total calcium intake. In Gursky's survey (1969), calcium intake ranged from 243 mg in Chillihua, to 334 mg in the town of Nuñoa, and to 464 mg in Sincata. Calcium consumption was different among these communities not only in the amount ingested, but also in the main sources of calcium. In Chillihua, wheat and chenopodias contributed 22.7 and 58.0 percent, respectively, to total calcium content of the diet. In Sincata, barley and chenopodias made up 24.5 and 58.5 percent, respectively. In the town of Nuñoa, maize made up 25.9 and cheese 38.7 percent of calcium content of the diet. Gursky (1969) remarks that the calcium-intake patterns were rather erratic and that this intake falls below the recommended allowance for men under 18 and for women under 35 years of age. These are the ages when an adequate calcium intake is especially needed to combat normally stressful conditions, such as growth, pregnancy, and lactation.

Although adequate minimum calcium requirements have not yet been established for human beings, calcium consumption as reported for these communities, in particular for Chillihua (Gursky, 1969), may not be sufficient even for maintenance of calcium balance in adult men. However, the natives of the district of Nuñoa consume some products very rich in calcium, which are not commonly recorded in dietary surveys. They are *catahui lahua*, whose preparation has already been described, and coca leaves with *llipta*. Llipta is prepared by mixing the ashes of the stalks of quinoa and cañihua with water to form a paste which is dried in the sun into small cakes. Catahui lahua is consumed once a week to once every 15 days by all the members of the majority of the families in the district. According to Baker and Mazess (1963), catahui lahua may add about 300–1200 mg of calcium to the usual diet. Coca leaves and llipta are used every day by the majority of the adult native population of both sexes from about 15 years of age. Calcium content in coca leaves is about 484 mg/100 g (Picón-Reátegui, unpublished data), and about 12 mg/100 g in llipta (Baker and Mazess, 1963).

In a controlled experiment carried out in the town of Nuñoa (Picón-Reátegui, unpublished data), coca leaf consumption ranged from 12 to 22 g/person/day. Calcium intake, from this source, should range from 57 to 107 mg. The amount of llipta consumed ranged from 250 to 3500 mg/person/day; thus, calcium intake from llipta should theoretically range from 30 to 450 mg/person/day. However, coca leaves are not swallowed. Hence coca leaves and llipta do not constitute an important source of calcium from a nutritional point of view. In this study, only a daily average of 3.0 mg of calcium was available from these sources.

In the experiment on metabolic balances carried out in the town of Nuñoa (Picón-Reátegui, unpublished data), about 632 mg of calcium was available from the daily individual ration of the native diet. There was a positive balance of 424 mg, and 527 mg was absorbed. No correction was made for the amount of calcium lost throughout the skin. These data confirm the statement of Hegsted et al. (1952) that it is possible to maintain calcium balance in adults where the intake is below recommended dietary allowances.

Phosphorus

Although phosphorus takes part in more physiological processes than any other mineral element, there appear to be no cases of phosphorus deficiency described in human beings. The reason is that phosphorus content of common diets is almost always sufficient to meet the requirements of an active person.

According to Mazess and Baker (1964), phosphorus content in the diet of Nuñoa natives was 2119 mg. In the survey of Gursky (1969), it ranged from 973 mg in the town of Nuñoa, to 1074 mg in Chillihua, to 1718 mg in Sincata. Food products consumed with high phosphorus content were chuño negro and chenopodias, which contributed 45.1 and 17.1 percent, respectively, to the total phosphorus content of the diet (Mazess and Baker, 1964). According to Gursky (1969), wheat and chenopodias made up 27.8 and 25.7 percent, respectively, of the phosphorus content of the diet in the town of Nuñoa, wheat made up 31.9 and chenopodias 37.5 percent in Chillihua, and barley 31.1 and chenopodias 44.9 percent in Sincata.

The phosphorus/calcium ratio was rather high in these diets: 4.1 for the Mazess and Baker survey; and 2.9, 4.4, and 3.7 for the town of Nuñoa, Chillihua, and Sincata, respectively, in the survey of Gursky (1969).

In the diets consumed during metabolic studies (Picón-Reátegui, unpublished data), the phosphorus content of the ration was 1366 mg. Despite a phosphorus/calcium ratio of 2.2, there was good calcium absorption. Phosphorus absorption averaged 351 mg, giving a positive balance of 145 mg/day. No allowance was made for phosphorus lost through the skin.

Iron

Both studies (Mazess and Baker, 1964; Gursky, 1969) agreed that the iron content of the diets consumed in the communities of the district of Nuñoa met recommended dietary allowances (Food and Nutrition Board, NRC-NAS, 1968). Gursky (1969) remarks that iron intake was higher than recommended for every age group, except for children below 3 yr of age. Iron intake was higher for men than for women over the age of 15 yr.

The diet reported by Mazess and Baker (1964) for the district of Nuñoa had an iron content of 22 mg/individual ration. About 36.7 percent of this amount was supplied by tubers and 44.1 percent by chenopodias. According to Gursky's survey, the iron content in the diet of the town of Nuñoa was 18 mg/individual ration, 21 mg in Chillihua, and 34 mg in Sincata. About 30.9 percent of the iron intake came from wheat and 26.6 percent from chenopodias in the town of Nuñoa; 33.4 percent from wheat and 45.6 percent from chenopodias in Chillihua, and, about 44.0 percent each from barley and chenopodias in Sincata. It can be noted that iron intake was higher the less the foreign food consumed.

If it is true that there is a 25 percent increase in iron utilization and a more rapid turnover in adult men residents to an altitude of 4540 m above sea level (Reynafarje et al., 1959), it is also true that there is a balance between blood production and destruction. This fact and the fact that climatic conditions do not induce any abnormal excretion of iron throughout the skin suggest that the iron content of these diets meets the requirements for every age group, including those ages where some physiological stresses, such as pregnancy, are common.

In our metabolic-balance study, carried out in six adult native male residents of Nuñoa (Picón-Reátegui, unpublished data), iron consumption from the native diet used during the experiment was 46.9 mg/man/day, which produced an absorption of 18.4 mg and a positive balance of about 17.0 mg. No allowance was made for iron lost through the skin.

Vitamin A

All the studies on food consumption carried out in Andean populations agree that vitamin A intake is very low. According to Mazess and Baker (1964), vitamin A intake in the district of Nuñoa was 102 IU per person per day. Gursky (1969) reports means and standard deviations of 4501 ± 10,076, 1.5 ± 5.8, and 5542 ± 5962 IU for Chillihua, Sincata, and the town of Nuñoa, respectively. Gursky remarks that vitamin A intake was quite variable and that its content in the native diet was related to liver consumption. Since liver was only consumed by three families in the district, it is understandable that a great majority of the population must have shown vitamin A deficiency. This situation may be aggravated by the low fat content of the diet. Gursky (1969) showed that daily vitamin A intake ranged from zero to 44,000 IU/person. However, no case of hypo- or hypervitaminosis A was reported. The signs of vitamin A deficiency may also be produced by the environmental cold, environmental dryness, and patterns of personal hygiene. To clarify these apparent discrepancies, it will be advisable in the future to carry out some chemical determinations of vitamin A and carotenes in the dietetic mixtures as well as in the blood of these populations. Moreover, since chili peppers are used as a seasoning in the native diet, it is possible that their carotene content was not recorded when computing vitamin A intake. A variety of chili, Capsicum sp., which is commonly used in its dry form, has a vitamin A activity of 3410 mg/100 g of edible portion (INCAP-ICNND, 1961).

Thiamine

According to the results of Mazess and Baker (1964), daily thiamine consumption was 1.8 mg/person. Thiamine content of the diet in the town of Nuñoa was 1.8 mg; it was 2.4 mg in Chillihua and 4.2 mg in Sincata (Gursky, 1969).

The main sources of thiamine were chuño negro and fresh potatoes, which supplied 33.6 and 25.6 percent, respectively, of the total thiamine content of the diet in the district of Nuñoa (Mazess and Baker, 1964). Chenopodias supplied about 63.9, 72.1 and 85.8 percent of the total thiamine content in the diets of the town of Nuñoa, Chillihua, and Sincata, respectively (Gursky, 1969).

On the basis of 0.5 mg of thiamine/1000 kcal, as recommended to maintain satisfactory thiamine nutriture under normal conditions (Food and Nutrition Board, NRC-NAS, 1968), it is calculated that the standard man of Nuñoa (studied by Gursky, 1969), with a 52.6-kg body weight and a calorie requirement of 2743 kcal/day, may have a thiamine requirement of 1.4 mg/day. Therefore, the diet consumed by the population of the district of Nuñoa generally meets the requirements for thiamine. In addition, the thiamine content of the diet of these communities was higher the greater the consumption of locally produced foods.

Riboflavin

Riboflavin content of the diet in the population from the district of Nuñoa was 2.1 mg/individual ration (Mazess and Baker, 1964). Fresh potatoes, chuño negro, and chenopodias supplied, respectively, 35.8, 28.2, and 20.3 percent of riboflavin to the diet. The diets of the town of Nuñoa, Chillihua, and Sincata had, respectively, 1.0, 1.2, and 2.5 mg of riboflavin/individual ration (Gursky, 1969). The main sources of riboflavin in these diets were barley and chenopodias, which made up, respectively, 21.2 and 31.0 percent of the riboflavin intake in the town of Nuñoa, and 42.9 and 39.7 percent, respectively, in Sincata. In Chillihua, chenopodias supplied about 57.9 percent of the total riboflavin content of the diet.

The recommended parameter to calculate requirements for riboflavin is metabolic body size, represented as kilograms of body weight taken to the 0.75 power (Food and Nutrition Board, NRC-NAS, 1968). According to this recommended allowance, the standard adult man of the district of Nuñoa, studied by Gursky (1969), has a daily requirement of 1.4 mg of riboflavin. Hence, intake in the town of Nuñoa (1.0 mg) and Chillihua (1.2 mg) may not meet the recommended allowances for riboflavin.

Niacin

The survey of Mazess and Baker (1964) shows a niacin equivalent of 41.0 mg for the individual ration of the diet in the district of Nuñoa. The main sources of niacin were fresh potatoes and chuño negro, which supplied about

39.7 and 33.2 percent, respectively, of the niacin content of the diet. The survey of Gursky (1969) shows a daily intake of 13, 18, and 31 mg of niacin for Chillihua, the town of Nuñoa, and Sincata, respectively. In Chillihua, wheat and meat supplied 32.5 and 19.3 percent, respectively, of the total niacin intake. In the town of Nuñoa, wheat contributed 19.6, barley 22.7, and maize 31.2 percent of the niacin intake. In Sincata only barley covered 65.5 percent of the niacin content of the diet. According to Gursky (1969), niacin content of these diets meets the recommended allowances, except for children aged 6–9 yr and for girls aged 9–12 yr. Since recommended allowances for niacin are 18 mg for adult men and 20 mg for pregnant women (Food and Nutrition Board, NRC-NAS, 1968), it is our feeling that the niacin content of the diet in Chillihua does not meet the recommended allowances for any age group, and that of the town of Nuñoa must be adequate for the adult population only under conditions of minimal stress.

Ascorbic Acid

The survey of Mazess and Baker (1964) showed a daily intake of 114 mg of ascorbic acid/person in the district of Nuñoa. Daily intake was 8.0 mg in the town of Nuñoa, 23 mg in Chillihua, and 65 mg in Sincata (Gursky, 1969). The difference in the results may have to do with the consumption of fresh tubers. Gursky suggested that the low consumption of fresh potatoes in his survey was due to a poor harvest of potatoes just before his survey was carried out, although the potato yield was not indicated. Since his survey was carried out about 1 month after the potato harvesting season, it must be assumed that the crop loss must have been of such a magnitude as to induce the population to shift from potatoes to another staple food. In Sincata, where few foreign food products were consumed, the consumption of tubers provided enough ascorbic acid to meet the recommended allowances for the native population. Such was not the case for the town of Nuñoa or Chillihua, where U.S. surpluses might have temporarily constituted the staple food.

In Mazess and Baker's survey (1964), 89.3 percent of the ascorbic acid intake was supplied by fresh tubers. However, fresh tubers are seasonal foods, in that they are consumed in high quantities during and for several months after harvesting. For example, fresh potatoes are consumed in high quantities from April to August, and años, ollucos, and ocas from April to June. During the following months, tuber consumption decreases. Thus ascorbic acid intake must be high from April to August, and then it must decrease according to the amount of tubers stored for late consumption, as well as according to the amount of ascorbic acid lost during storage.

It is of importance to note the differences in ascorbic acid content of the tubers consumed: fresh potatoes contain 20.5 mg/100 g of edible portion, and chuño negro contains 1.7 mg (Collazos et al., 1957). Since freezing alone and storage in the frozen state produce only a small loss of ascorbic acid, it is clear that the processing of chuño negro (according to native technology) and its subsequent storage contributes to a substantial loss in ascorbic acid when compared with the content in fresh potatoes.

EFFECT OF COCA CHEWING

The natives of the district of Nuñoa, like the great majority of people who live on the Peruvian and Bolivian Andes, chew coca (*Erythroxylon coca*). This habit is practiced both by men and women after about 15 years of age. It has been speculated that coca mastication has an effect on the nutritional status and physical fitness of members of the population who engage in this practice. From a theoretical point of view, cocaine (the active constituent of coca leaves) could have a dual function in coca chewers. On one hand, by acting locally through the oral mucosa, it may somehow produce a decrease in food intake by curbing the appetite. On the other hand, cocaine may impose increased food requirements mediated by its action on muscular activity and, perhaps, on the temperature-regulating center (Ritchie et al., 1966). The interaction of these two mechanisms may result in both under-nutrition and low work performance. However, the general action of cocaine may be qualitatively different in coca chewers. It is well known, for example, that use of cocaine produces drug addiction (*cocainism*), whereas there is evidence suggesting that chewing coca leaves (*coquism*) is not habit-forming to any greater extent than tobacco smoking. It is also possible that the local anesthesia produced by cocaine on the oral mucosa facilitates the consumption of the monotonous diet of the highland native.

The results of the study on metabolic balance in the town of Nuñoa (Picón-Reátegui, unpublished data) suggest that coca mastication does not affect food intake, nor does it modify protein, fat, calcium, iron, phosphorus, sodium, and potassium absorption. Moreover, protein, fat, and mineral requirements are unaffected by the practice. However, caloric requirements appear to be increased by about 12.9 percent (see Table 11.6). The lower

TABLE 11.6 *Caloric Balance in Six Adult Male Residents of Nuñoa*

Energy (kcal)	First period, 4 days (no coca)		Second period, 4 days (coca)		Significance (t-test)
	Mean	S.E.	Mean	S.E.	
Intake	11,401	12	10,982	15	<0.01
In excreta	741	16	741	30	N.S.
Available	10,660	17	10,241	30	<0.01
Dissipated	12,336	171	13,720	182	<0.02
Balance	−1,676	550	−3,479	572	<0.01

TABLE 11.7 *Effect of Chewing Coca Leaves on Several Parameters*

Measurement	First period, 4 days (no coca)		Second period, 4 days (coca)		Significance (*t*-test)
	Mean	S.E.	Mean	S.E.	
Skin and Body Temperatures (°C)					
Upper arm	31.2	0.2	32.1	0.3	<0.01
Chest	32.5	0.1	33.0	0.2	<0.05
Back	31.8	0.2	32.7	0.2	<0.05
Thigh	31.0	0.2	31.9	0.2	<0.05
Calf	30.3	0.2	30.9	0.3	N.S.
Oral	36.6	0.2	36.6	0.1	N.S.
Rectal	—	—	36.5	0.1	—
Water Excretion (g)					
Urine	7,771	280	7,113	246	N.S.
Stool	592	7	654	62	N.S.
Insensible	5,110	228	5,701	243	<0.02
Coca residue	—	—	277	30	—
Total loss	13,473	192	13,744	184	N.S.
Balance	+912	265	−250	221	<0.01

caloric intake during the period when subjects were chewing coca leaves resulted from a daily reduction of 25 g of carbohydrates during the period of coca mastication. This action was taken under the erroneous assumption that the increases in body weight, recorded in subjects during the period without coca, were due to an excess caloric intake. Experimental results indicated that water retention produced the body-weight increase, a common finding in studies on metabolic balances.

An increase in skin temperatures with no change in body-core temperature was recorded during the period of coca mastication (Table 11.7). Since when there is no change in body temperature, heat loss keeps pace with heat production, it is assumed that there must have been an increase in heat production to maintain constant core temperature when subjects were chewing coca. Moreover, it is likely that excess water was liberated through insensible water loss associated with higher skin temperatures. An increase in water loss via the avenue of insensible sweat was recorded during the period when subjects were chewing coca (Table 11.7). There is a direct relationship between skin temperature and the amount of insensible water loss (Pinson, 1942), and about 24 percent of body heat is removed by vaporization of water (Newburgh et al., 1931).

GENERAL COMMENTS

The surveys of Mazess and Baker (1964) and Gursky (1969) were conducted on members of the same population, during the same season of the year, and separated by a space of 5 yr. Despite these similarities, the results were at variance, not only in the amount of energy and nutrients ingested, but also in the identification of the food staple of the native population. Gursky (1969) attributes the difference to a low potato harvest which immediately preceded his survey. An examination of Gursky's data on caloric intake and energy requirements (adjusted for body size, environmental temperature, physical activity, sex, and age) suggests that there must have been errors introduced, probably in the collection of data on food consumption. Such errors are common even in the hands of the most skilled investigators. It is well known that the usual food consumption pattern, both quantitative and qualitative, may be modified in the course of a survey, according to the goals of the surveyed people. For this reason, results of surveys on food consumption must be interpreted very cautiously. During the survey of Gursky (1969), food intake of natives might have been intentionally altered so that the natives would qualify for supplementary aid. At this time, the local priest was distributing surplus food (Gursky, 1969). These products constituted the staple food in the town of Nuñoa and in Chillihua, but not in Sincata, where almost 100 percent of the caloric consumption was covered by locally produced foodstuffs. In this last community, the consumption of fresh tubers made up 22.2 percent of the total caloric intake. Among the communities surveyed by Gursky in the district of Nuñoa (1969), Sincata registered the least percentage of subjects with a caloric intake lower than recommended. It was also in Sincata where protein, mineral, and vitamin intake (except of vitamin A) met the recommended dietary allowances of the Food and Nutrition Board, NRC-NAS (1968). Such was not the case for the town of Nuñoa and Chillihua, where foreign products constituted the primary food staples. In general, caloric, protein, mineral, and vitamin intakes were higher when foreign foodstuffs contributed minimally to the local diet. These facts recall the admonitions of R. S. Harris (1945), who stated that the habits of people with long-established food cultures should be regarded as inviolable until they have been most carefully analyzed, and that food habits should not be altered until one is certain that the substituted food will supply the quantities of all nutrients formerly provided.

In summary, it is my feeling that when foodstuffs produced locally in the district of Nuñoa are used in the daily diet of the native population, the dietetic mixture provides sufficient calories, proteins, minerals, and vitamins to meet the recommended dietary allowances of the Food and Nutrition Board, NRC-NAS (1968). However, it is probable that they are not, either quantitatively or qualitatively, sufficient to meet the additional requirements imposed by needs of pregnancy, lactation, and growth.

The problem of vitamin A intake requires a special study in order to clarify the discrepancy between the results of food consumption and clinical health surveys. It may be advisable to carry out chemical determinations of vitamin A activity in specific foods in the district, as well as in food composites of the common diets consumed. Analysis of vitamin A content in blood, liver biopsies, and postmortem liver studies in the native population may also be productive ways to approach the problem.

Finally, despite the high ultraviolet radiation at high altitudes, elongation or attenuation of physical growth, slow motor development, and late deciduous tooth-eruption processes (T. S. Baker et al., 1967a) suggest a deficiency in vitamin D. Such a deficiency may be conditioned because of the moderate degree of skin pigmentation in the native and, mainly, by the native habit of keeping children away from sunlight at least up to 2 years of age (see Chapter 4).

12

PULMONARY FUNCTION
AND OXYGEN TRANSPORT

Tulio Velásquez

Two major purposes are fulfilled by the respiratory-function and oxygen-transport systems in the process of high-altitude adaptation: (1) preventing an excess oxygen-pressure drop during oxygen transport to the tissues, and (2) increasing the amount of oxygen available to the tissues in the systemic capillaries at any given pressure. Both are certainly two facets of the same phenomenon, but some of the complex interrelated factors of the system will serve mainly the first purpose, and others, the second. The ability of the respiratory function to achieve both objectives can be assessed (1) by measuring the overall oxygen conductance of the system and the pressure drop at different levels where resistances to oxygen flow are located, and (2) by measuring the quantity of the gas reaching the capillaries in a given time with any prevailing pressure.

To accomplish these adaptive objectives, physiological and morphological changes are required both in the function itself and in its control. Numerous studies have provided insights into the mechanisms of respiratory changes during the process of adaptation to high altitude as well as in the final representation of this process, the high-altitude native.

What follows in this chapter is a short summary of research on respiratory function among high-altitude natives of the Peruvian Andes.

LUNG VOLUME

It is well known that total lung capacity in high-altitude natives is greater than in lowlanders. The reason is largely due to a significant increase in residual volume, but also to a slight increase in the other components that constitute total lung volume. During growth, as in adulthood, the lung volume of highlanders is proportional to chest size, especially to thoracic circumference (Frisancho, 1969a). Thus growth of the lung follows the same general developmental pattern of the chest as described by Frisancho and Baker (1970). Effectively, Nuñoa natives, from 11 to 20 yr of age, have a greater vital capacity than lowlanders and middle-altitude (1990 m) boys of similar age, despite the smaller stature of the highlanders (Frisancho, 1969a).

These findings, confirming the earlier observations of Hurtado (1932a) on Indian boys from 7 to 19 yr of age and resident at 4540 m, are illustrated in Fig. 12.1 and Table 12.1. In these studies comparisons were made of both European-derived and Andean Indian boys. Hence the amount of these differences that can be attributed to altitude adaptation and the amount that can be attributed to racial variation remains uncertain.

Lack of data on residual volume during childhood and adolescence prevents the drawing of conclusions on hyperinflation of the lung during the early stages of life, as is suggested by growth of the chest (Frisancho, 1969a; Hurtado, 1932a).

Part of the process of accommodation to high altitude during acute and subacute exposures involves changes in lung volume. In general, these changes do not affect total lung capacity; rather, residual volume increases while vital capacity decreases. This enlargement of residual volume then produces a further decrease in vital capacity. The considerable individual variations in the amount and duration of the changes and, in some instances, even an enlargement of total lung capacity (Tenney et al., 1953), as well as the elusive factor of changes in thoracic blood volume, are obstacles that limit our understanding of the mechanisms involved.

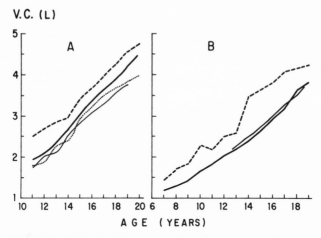

FIGURE 12.1 *Vital-capacity development in relation to age. At left (A), data from Frisancho (1969a): Nuñoa boys (dashed line); U.S. sea-level boys (heavy solid line); Peruvian boys at 2300 m (dotted line); Peruvian boys at sea level (light solid line). At right (B), data from Hurtado (1932a): Peruvian boys born at 4540 m (dashed line); Peruvian boys at sea level (solid lines). Hurtado's data were not corrected for BTPS.*

TABLE 12.1   *Vital Capacity of Children and Adolescents
Native to High Altitudes*

Age (yr)	Hurtado (1932a)[a]			Frisancho (1969a)[b]		
	N	VC (ml)	VC (ml/m²)	N	VC (ml)	VC (ml/m²)
7	16	1466	1833			
8	32	1653	1922			
9	14	2050	2228			
10	21	2114	2273			
11	12	2294	2271	10	2545	2520
12	22	2312	2181	10	2638	2512
13	8	2444	2185	20	2808	2576
14	8	2914	2449	15	2876	2501
15	3	3050	2421	19	3368	2652
16	13	3462	2455	23	3644	2761
17	21	3708	2649	18	3909	2853
18	64	3817	2629	11	4260	2958
19	94	4024	2680	12	4832	3310
20				12	5033	3330

[a]Values from the work by Hurtado, conducted at 4540 m, are not corrected for BTPS.
[b]The studies by Frisancho were conducted at 4000 m.

One of the first experiments in immediate effects of altitude exposure on vital capacity (Hurtado, 1928; Hurtado and Guzmán-Barrón, 1934) showed a definite and constant decrease in all experimental subjects. Immediately after the subject ascended to 5356 m, his vital capacity decreased to a value 528 ml lower than at sea level. Upon return to sea level, recovery was complete. Tenney et al. (1953), in four subjects sojourning 7 days at 4340 m, found that vital capacity decreased during the first 3 days and then progressively increased to sea-level control values in two subjects and to values above those at sea level in the other two subjects. Moreover, residual volumes at the end of the exposure period were larger than those of controls in three of the subjects and equal to the initial value in the remaining subject. In simulated flights of up to about 5000 m, Hurtado et al. (1934) found increases in residual volume, decreases in vital capacity, and no change in total lung capacity.

In Nuñoa, Garruto (1969, 1970) reported on two groups that were tested: U.S. whites (athletes and nonathletes) and sea-level Indians during sojourns of 8 and 4 weeks, respectively. In the first group, vital capacity decreased, following individual patterns, but at the end of the period it was almost 500 ml lower, with the lowest value reached on the first day. In contrast, sea-level Indians did not show changes in vital capacity, corroborating an earlier observation by Hurtado and Guzmán-Barrón (1934).

No satisfactory explanation has been given for these sharp changes. Congestion of the pulmonary vascular tree was suggested by Hurtado (1932a), but the experiments of Tenney et al. (1953), incorporating positive pressure breathing, failed to show an increase in the depressed vital capacity. Moreover, the greatest change took place immediately after climbing; thereafter, vital capacity tended to recover its initial value. Thus, since congestion increases with time at altitude, it is difficult to see how it could explain the described changes in vital capacity.

Inhalation of oxygen does not change the decreased vital capacity, which seems to prove that hypoxia alone is not the direct cause, although some other factor may be hypoxia-dependent. The fact that vital capacity decreases while residual volume increases suggests, at least in part, that the increased inspiratory muscular tonus (A. S. Harris, 1945) will produce an inbalance in thoracic cage-lung forces so that the lung will inflate to a larger residual volume while diminishing vital capacity (Velásquez, 1966).

In adult high-altitude natives, lung volume follows the same trend as in children and adolescents. Data collected from various studies at different altitudes are presented in Table 12.2 and Fig. 12.2. Lung volumes are closely related to body characteristics and affected by wide individual variations, so

TABLE 12.1 *Lung Volume at Sea Level and at Different Altitudes*

Reference	Altitude (m)	Subjects	N	Vital capacity ml	Vital capacity ml/m²	Residual volume ml	Residual volume ml/m²
Hurtado (1928)[a]	S.L.	Mestizos	22	4625	2506		
Hurtado (1928)	2300	Indians	100		2600		
Hurtado (1928)	3870	Indians	29		2331		
Hurtado (1928)	4540	Indians	478	4240	2683		
Garruto (1969)[a]	S.L.	Indians	10	5185	3162		
Garruto (1969)	S.L.	White (U.S. nonathletes)	6	5578	2860		
Garruto (1969)	S.L.	White (U.S.)	11	5591	3022		
Garruto (1969)	4000	Indians	23	4448	2815		
Boyce et al. (1974)	4000	Indians	92	5290	3210		
Boyce et al. (1974)	S.L.	Indians	31	5020	3070		
Frisancho (1970)	4000	Indians	12	5033	3330		
Frisancho et al. (1973c)	3400	Indians	40	4990	3043		
Frisancho et al. (1973c)	3840	Indians	20	4830	2916	1585	0.957
Velásquez (1972)	S.L.	Mestizos	112	4900	2920	1390	0.830
Velásquez (1972)	4540	Indians	185	4970	3220	1920	1.250

[a]Data by Hurtado were not corrected for BTPS; in Garruto's work there is no statement about this correction. Correction for BPTS: a 4.5-l volume of gas at sea level will expand about 200 ml at high altitude, temperatures being equal.

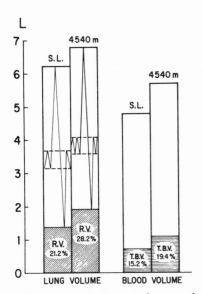

FIGURE 12.2 *Lung volume and subdivisions, residual volume (RV) and thoracic blood volume (TBV), in high-altitude and in sea-level natives.*

direct comparison between individuals and populations is inappropriate without a common unit of measurement. Such controls for body size are even more important when comparing two human groups as dissimilar in many morphological features as are sea-level and high-altitude populations. Lowlanders and highlanders have well-established anatomical differences, for example, those of body and chest size and shape of the chest which are most closely related to lung volumes. Although there is no complete agreement on the characteristic that correlates best with lung volume, either at high altitude or at sea level, it is necessary to find as common a unit as possible for population comparisons.

There are few studies on the subject at high altitude. Hurtado (1932a) found that in the young, high-altitude adult vital capacity is most closely related to body surface area (BSA) and secondarily to chest circumference. In childhood and adolescence, relationships were found with height, body-surface area, and chest size. Frisancho (1969a) found a better correlation with chest circumference and chest expansion as well as BSA. Garruto (1969) observed that the best predictive factor for vital capacity is chest expansion; the second, body height; and the third, body weight. In a more recent study, Frisancho et al. (1973c) described an equally good correlation with chest size and BSA. At sea level there are numerous studies demonstrating the highest correlation of vital capacity with height and BSA (West, 1920; Kory et al., 1961; Needham et al., 1954; Baldwin et al., 1948; Boren et al., 1966; Hart et al., 1963; Grimby and Soderholm, 1963). On the other hand, residual volume has been found to be highly correlated with BSA at sea level and at high altitude, although in high-altitude natives the greatest correlation appears to be with chest size. Since BSA appears as the first- or second-best correlation choice at altitude and at sea level, it seems suitable to control for individual and group differences in body size by reducing lung volumes to comparable units of BSA (m^2).

Despite the obvious group differences in parameters associated with body size, it does seem clear that vital capacity per unit of BSA is greater in high-altitude natives than in lowlanders. Data by Hurtado follow the same direction but with lower values; less-sophisticated instrumentation and lack of correction for lung gas to body temperature and saturated pressure (BTPS) would explain his results. Garruto (1969) has found the opposite: the group of Nuñoa natives tested at high altitude show significantly lower values than did the three lowland groups observed at sea level; the size of the sample would affect his results in a function so widely influenced by individual variations. Boyce et al. (1974), in a similar population of Quechua Indians at high altitude, found 5290 ml for highland residents and 5020 for highlanders living at sea level.

Residual volume (RV) per square meter in natives at 4540 m is 50 percent larger than in lowlanders and represents 28 percent of total lung capacity (TLC) (Velásquez, 1966, 1972; Hurtado, 1937). At lower altitudes (3870 m), RV is smaller (Frisancho et al., 1973c) but still greater than in the lowlands. These values in young adults indicate a moderate hyperinflation of the lungs, which had been observed directly in autopsies by Campos and Iglesias (1957). They describe their findings this way: ". . . two things were particularly noticeable: the large volume of the lungs and the partial absence of retraction. . . ." It has not been determined, then or since, if there is an increase in the number of alveoli.

Moreover, it is not known if the enlarged TLC and chest size are racial characteristics or acclimatizational responses to high altitude; or further, if they are an inherited adaptive response. Frisancho et al. (1973c) support the idea of a developmental adaptation of lung characteristics in such a way that if the exposure to high altitude begins early in life, the individual can attain the same volumes the natives have. However, hyperinflation of the lungs is a constant finding at high altitude, either in short-term or chronic exposure of newcomers and in natives. This fact alone forces us to assume that it is adaptive in itself or a result of some other adaptive change.

The mechanisms involved in the increment of RV with larger RV/TLC ratio are not well defined. One of the main factors should be the diminished elasticity of the lungs due to both the greater amount of blood in the pulmonay vessels (Monge et al., 1955) and the increased number of interstitial reticular cells (Campos and Iglesias, 1957). This altered elasticity will determine a different level of equilibrium between the mechanical forces of the thoracic cage and the lung and produce chest expansion.

Whether lung hyperinflation assists in respiratory adaptation to altitude is still a subject of controversy. Hyperinflation will certainly create a mechanical disadvantage: the volume to ventilate is larger and the efficiency of inspiratory muscles is decreased, because of the more horizontal position of the ribs in the thoracic cage. However, this disadvantage is counted somewhat by an easier air flow through the bronchial system because of lower gas density. For example, it has been shown that maximum ventilatory capacity is of the same magnitude in high-altitude natives as in sea-level natives (Velásquez, 1966, 1972).

It has been assumed that there is a direct relationship between hyperinflation of the lung and its diffusing capacity (Bates et al., 1955; Verzar, 1951). This assumption has been demonstrated neither at sea level nor at altitude. However, in addition to the actual measurement of the maximum diffusing capacity in high-altitude natives (Velásquez, 1956), there are some facts that might justify this assumption. Hyperinflation is homogeneously distributed but is more accentuated in the apices (Campos and Iglesias, 1957); alveolar ventilation is greater, as will be discussed later; and there are no signs of maldistribution of air (Velásquez, unpublished data on nitrogen-elimination curves). Thus, at any given metabolic rate in highlanders, the alveolar surface in contact with air is greater than at sea level. This finding is, of course, not evidence that there is an enlarged active diffusing surface unless the active capillary bed is also enlarged.

In high-altitude natives the pulmonary vascular tree is wider and the capillaries are congested (Hurtado, 1932a; Campos and Iglesias, 1957); normal cardiac output with an expanded vascular system results in a slow pulmonary blood flow, improving the transfer of oxygen; and higher pulmonary arterial pressure (Rotta et al., 1956; Peñaloza et al., 1963; Grover, 1965; Hultgren et al., 1965) provides a better perfusion of the lung, especially in the upper part. The increase of $\dot{V}_A/\dot{Q}$ ratio (Hurtado et al., 1956a), with normal dead space (Velásquez, 1972), suggests an hyperaeration of well-perfused alveoli. These are indirect evidences of an enlarged active surface area of alveolar membrane which leads to a more efficient diffusion where lung hyperinflation plays some role. Another function that hyperinflation might serve involves the large functional residual capacity, which provides a larger amount of oxygen at any given time and prevents an excessive drop of its pressure during short periods of apnea and even during expiration, because moderate changes in alveolar oxygen pressure in the steep portion of the oxygen-dissociation curve would affect arterial saturation.

VENTILATION

Ventilation is greater at high altitude than at sea level. This finding is most common and consistent, which is not surprising if it is accounted for by a larger forced respiratory capacity (FRC) and a diminished oxygen concentration in inspired air. In newcomers to high altitude, ventilation increases slowly to reach the highest value within the first week of the sojourn (Douglas et al., 1913; Rahn and Otis, 1949; Chiodi, 1963). Lowlanders acclimatizing for months or years show greater ventilation than native residents (Chiodi, 1957). However, Severinghaus et al. (1966) show the same alveolar ventilation at altitude in sojourners and in natives, although the authors claim that the difference in P_{CO_2} reveals a real difference in ventilation. This claim seems true despite the fact that their values on FRC are very similar to each other, a finding that was probably due to poor methodology. Differences in residual volumes and FRC between lowlanders in process of acclimatization and native highlanders are usually large and could account for differences in P_{CO_2} even when there are little or no differences in ventilation. The larger the FRC, the larger the ventilation necessary to produce the same alveolar P_{CO_2}. We have found in our experiments that the ratio of $\dot{V}_A$ to FRC is 1.5–1.8, both at sea level and at altitude (Velásquez, 1972).

Ventilation in natives is about 30 percent higher per square meter of BSA than in lowlanders (Chiodi et al., 1952; Hurtado et al., 1956; Banchero et al., 1966; Velásquez, 1972). The increase is due mainly to an augmented frequency of breathing rather than deeper inspiration (Chiodi et al., 1952; Hurtado et al., 1956a; Velásquez, 1972) (see Table 12.3). An increment of 30 percent in ventilation, when the FRC is 30 percent larger, is not a proportional increase if the diminished oxygen concentration is accounted for. Thus, the value for alveolar ventilation is less than it should be if oxygen were the

TABLE 12.3   *Ventilation at Sea Level and*
at High Altitude[a]

Measure	Lowlanders at sea level (150 m)	Highlanders at high altitude (4540 m)
No. of subjects	64	96
BSA (m²)	1.69	1.56
f (breaths/min)	11.5	16.0
$\dot{V}_E$ (l/min)	7.2	7.9
$\dot{V}_E$ (l/min/m²)	4.4	5.1
$\dot{V}_A$ (l/min)	4.6	5.3
$\dot{V}_A$ (l/min/m²)	2.7	3.5
MVC (l/min)	189	194
MVC (l/min/m²)	110	124

[a]Data are from Velásquez (1972).

only factor considered. Furthermore, it is already established that fewer air molecules (V_E STPD) are moved in ventilating the lungs at altitude (Grover, 1965).

At 4540 m the alveolar oxygen pressure in native residents is close to 50 torr (Hurtado et al., 1956a; Velásquez, 1972). At altitudes above or below 4500 m, $P_{A_{O_2}}$ is correspondingly higher or lower. Dill et al. (1936) give 46.9 torr at 4700 m and 43.1 torr at 4340 m; Severinghaus et al. (1966) give 50.5 torr at 4330 m; and Lefrancois et al. (1968) give 56 torr at 3660 m and 42 torr at 5200 m; Kreuzer et al. (1964) give a higher value, 56 torr, at 4540 m because of hyperventilation.

These alveolar oxygen pressures are the result of three factors: low inspired oxygen pressure, normal oxygen uptake (Hurtado, 1929; Velásquez, 1946; Picón-Reátegui, 1961; Grover, 1963), and increased alveolar ventilation. If ventilation were to remain the same as at sea level, the oxygen tension would then fall to about 35 torr at 4500 m, a critically low value. On the other hand, if ventilation were to increase to a much higher level, then the oxygen pressure would rise significantly in the alveoli but the P_{CO_2} would drop to an undesirable level. Thus ventilation appears, as a compromise, to maintain the highest possible oxygen pressure in the alveoli with the highest possible P_{CO_2}.

Mechanisms involved in the maintenance of elevated levels of ventilation in high-altitude natives are not well established at present. There are many known facts—some are contradictory to each other and to the classic scheme of the ventilatory control system—but an actual comprehensive knowledge of the problem is still lacking.

Experimentally, O_2 and CO_2 have the same effect on ventilation at high altitude (although quantitatively different) as in sea-level natives. Inhalation of pure oxygen or of oxygen-enriched mixtures at high altitude depresses ventilation during the first minute in about the same magnitude as at sea level (Velásquez, 1966; Lefrancois et al., 1965).

In high-altitude natives, after the first minute of depression, ventilation increases for a few minutes above initial levels and then returns to its normal value. Figure 12.3 summarizes the findings in a group of high-altitude natives tested at 4540 m. It is important to emphasize the twofold reaction of breathing to oxygen inhalation in high-altitude natives: a marked depression during the first minute, indicating that the peripheral chemoreceptors are active in normal breathing; and then the almost immediate restoration of initial ventilation, as if normal oxygen pressure were not playing any role in normal breathing. Changes with hypoxia (16 percent O_2) were nil.

In newcomers, ventilation is continuously depressed by oxygen breathing, suggesting that hyperventilation is maintained by hypoxia. In lowlanders in the process of acclimatization to high altitude, the depression produced by oxygen inhalation is much greater (Dejours et al., 1957; Cerretelli, 1961; Lefrancois et al., 1968); the restoration of sea-level oxygen pressure reduces

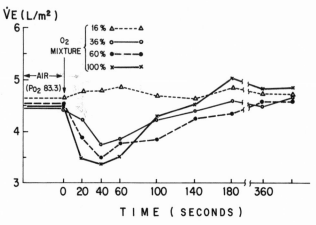

FIGURE 12.3 *Transient effects of hypoxia (pure O_2 and high-concentration mixtures) on ventilation of high-altitude natives. From Velásquez et al. (1968).*

ventilation only during the first minute (Douglas et al., 1913; Houston and Riley, 1947), such that "chemoreceptors' activity is reduced, and thus removal of hypoxia stimulus has little effect upon ventilation" (Rahn and Otis, 1949).

Bjursted (1946), in studies of dogs acclimatizing to hypoxia, concluded that the chemoreflex drive is important during acute exposure but diminishes with acclimatization; the centrogenic response would become supernormal to maintain hyperventilation. The lowering of bicarbonate levels and changes in pH also play an important role in this hypothesis. Oxygen inhalation, for example, reduces ventilation with immediate retention of CO_2, which, in turn, acts as a centrogenic stimulus to produce overventilation. Moreover, the higher "sensitivity" to CO_2, which would appear to be responsible for the sustained hyperventilation, would be only a reflection of the lowered buffering capacity of blood.

As seen in Fig. 12.4, highlanders living at sea level for months or years, show a much lower response, even none at all, to hypoxic drive (Velásquez, 1966; Lahiri et al., 1967). For the study shown in Fig. 12.4, both groups were tested first at 4540 m and then at sea level (at arrival and after 13 and 26 days and 3, 7, and 12 months of stay at sea level). The response to hypoxia was minimal in highlanders and high, as usual, in lowlanders. This finding seems true also when highlanders are tested at altitude (Severinghaus et al., 1966; Lahiri et al., 1969). The fact was described as "blunted sensitivity" (Lahiri et al., 1969) or "loss of sensitivity to hypoxia" (Severinghaus et al., 1966) of chemoreceptors. These results contradict the finding of a sizable ventilatory response to very deep hypoxia; Velásquez (1959) found ventilatory responses of 22.5, 27.3, 39.8, and 61.5 l/min (BTPS) at 8.5, 9.1, 9.8,

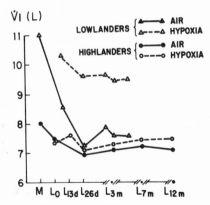

FIGURE 12.4 *Effects of a low-oxygen mixture* (P_{IO_2} = 93 torr) *on ventilation of lowlanders previously acclimatized to altitude (4540 m) for 8 months, and of highlanders native to the same altitude.*

and 10.4 thousand meters, respectively, to breathing air in a low-pressure chamber. Figure 12.5 shows these findings. There is no possibility of comparing these results with those of lowlanders under the same hypoxic stress, since lowlanders would reach unconsciousness before any measurement could be made. On the other hand, the statement of Severinghaus et al. (1966) also contradicts the finding, mentioned above, of the active state of peripheral chemoreceptors during normal breathing as demonstrated by oxygen inhalation.

In other experiments (unpublished data) we have found that high-altitude natives living at sea level for many years have a diminished response to hypoxia, and this response is significantly related to the altitude at which the subjects were born; the higher the birthplace, the lower the response.

High-altitude natives show greater ventilatory responses than lowlanders to inhalation of CO_2 mixtures (Hurtado et al., 1956a; Velásquez, 1966). Chiodi (1957) did not find differences, but his sample is quite small; the marked individual variations at high altitude and at sea level in the response to CO_2 make it very hazardous to deal with small samples, since there are individuals at sea level who do respond to CO_2 with greater ventilation than many highlanders (Velásquez, 1966). Mithoefer (1966) believes that the difference between highlanders and lowlanders must be due to a greater formation of free hydrogen ion per unit rise in P_{CO_2}, in highlanders. Since the degree of carbonic acid dissociation is determined by the initial bicarbonate concentration through its mass-action effect, then in high-altitude natives the hydrogen-ion concentration must be higher for the same P_{CO_2}

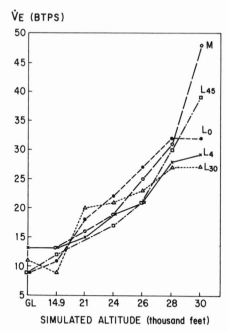

FIGURE 12.5 *Resting ventilation during simulated flights (breathing room air) in a pressure chamber of a group of high-altitude natives tested first at altitude and then during a sojourn of 7 days at sea level. M indicates Morococha, a town at 4540 m; L, Lima, at 150 m; subscripts, the number of days' sojourn in Lima.*

than in sea-level residents, despite the greater buffering capacity of hemoglobin at high altitude. Central receptors of the CO_2 stimulus must receive the action of ion concentration in the extracellular fluid of areas located somewhere near the central surface of the medulla (Mitchell et al., 1963). Severinghaus et al. (1966) postulate that high-altitude natives have a normal medullary respiratory chemoreceptor response but one that is reset proportionally to the prevailing P_{CO_2}. The differences between lowlanders and highlanders must be accounted for by peripheral chemoreceptors. Whatever the mechanisms may be, it seems that breathing CO_2 mixtures produces a greater ventilatory response in high-altitude than in sea-level natives, and an even greater response in lowlanders acclimatizing to high altitude than in both groups.

Studies made in the group of highlanders during acclimatization to sea level have produced some other interesting findings. Figure 12.6 summarizes the values of ventilation at rest and during CO_2 breathing. At altitude (M) CO_2 was mixed with 36 percent O_2 in N_2, so that the mixtures contained 20 torr of P_{CO_2} and 150 torr of P_{O_2}; at sea level (L) CO_2 was mixed with room air (20 torr of CO_2). Subjects were tested 2, 3, 4, and 7 days after arrival. Some facts must be emphasized. First, resting ventilation diminishes from the very beginning, producing an increase in P_{CO_2} (hyperventilation, as expected, does not occur). Second, the response to CO_2 is greater than it is at high altitude, as indicated by the steeper slope of the response curve (as in lowlanders who sojourn at altitude), although the individual variations are wide. Under the concepts already mentioned, there seems to be an increase in "sensitivity" of the central chemoreceptors, such that resting hypoventilation plus CO_2 inhaled would produce a greater concentration of hydrogen ion than at high altitude. But the question arises: Why does resting ventilation decrease despite an increase in P_{CO_2}? Third, at the same P_{CO_2} there are at least two ventilatory values, one at rest and the other during inhalation of CO_2. In both cases, there must be the same hydrogen-ion concentration,

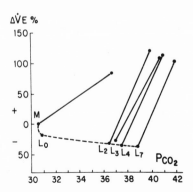

FIGURE 12.6 *Resting ventilation and ventilatory response to CO_2 inhalation (20 torr) in a group of high-altitude natives sojourning at sea level. Subjects were first tested at high altitude (M, Morococha) and then at sea level (L, Lima) during a stay of 1 week. Dashed line joins resting ventilation points; solid lines show the responses to CO_2 inhalation.*

either in blood or in cerebrospinal fluid. Ventilation seems different when CO_2 is inhaled rather than metabolically produced, as observed by Kao et al. (1963) in studying crossed circulation in dogs. The increase in bicarbonate level comes as a result of hypoventilation and retention of CO_2, but not the reverse. This hypoventilation would be contrary to the apparent increase of chemoreceptor sensitivity; the small decrease in the buffering capacity of blood, which is due to better oxygenation of hemoglobin, will not explain the pronounced changes observed.

In summary, the high-altitude native, from the breathing-control standpoint, is as normal as in other aspects of his physiology, and as normal as the sea-level native; his ventilation is perfectly adjusted to the metabolic rate, perhaps even better. In effect, we have found (unpublished data) that the respiratory quotient (RQ) of high-altitude natives in physical exercise remains below 1.0 at different work loads, except during very strenuous exercise, while sea-level subjects' RQs will increase during the course of moderate submaximal work. As an RQ above 1.0 reveals a true hyperventilation, we can state that high-altitude natives hyperventilate less than lowlanders during physical exercise.

It has often been stated, quite incorrectly, that high-altitude natives hyperventilate. If we are to accept the assertion that the total adaptive compensatory mechanism rests upon ventilation, then it is suggested that natives actually hypoventilate. Their ventilation, however, must be considered to be perfectly normal; they will move more air per minute, but this air must ventilate a larger lung volume and counteract the lower concentration of oxygen. Of course the discussion will move into semantics if it is not stated that *normality is different in different environments* and that the use of "hypo" and "hyper" are only relative.

ALVEOLAR–ARTERIAL GRADIENT

Three factors determine the existence of an oxygen-pressure difference between alveolar air and arterial blood: (1) alveolocapillary membrane barrier (diffusion), (2) unequal distribution of air and blood in the lung ($\dot{V}_A/\dot{Q}$ ratio), and (3) right-to-left shunt (true venous admixture). The contribution of each factor to the total gradient at various levels of oxygenation has been analyzed by Farhi and Rahn (1955). The contribution of true venous admixture and of unequal distribution of $\dot{V}_A/\dot{Q}$ ratios becomes nil at low oxygen pressures, whereas each contributes 50 percent of the total gradient at sea-level pressures.

A normal $(A\text{-}a)$ O_2 gradient averages 10 torr (± 5 torr) at sea level. If in acclimatization to altitude, this gradient could be reduced it would save up to 10 torr of O_2 pressure, which is important because oxygen uptake in the lungs occurs at the steeper part of the HbO_2 dissociation curve.

TABLE 12.4   *Alveolar–Arterial Oxygen Gradient in High-Altitude (4540 m) and Sea-Level Natives (torr)*

Condition	N	$P_{aI_{O_2}}$	$P_{A_{O_2}}$	$P_{a_{O_2}}$	$(A\text{-}a)O_2$	$P_{A_{CO_2}}$	$P_{a_{CO_2}}$	$(a\text{-}A)CO_2$
Sea level	22	147.1	102.8	94.0	8.8	38.7	39.8	1.1
Altitude								
At rest	20	83.4	46.3	44.0	2.3	30.2	30.8	0.6
At rest, 36% O_2	14	144.0	105.1	95.3	9.8	29.2	30.2	1.0
At exercise	12	83.4	53.0	43.2	9.7	—	—	—
At exercise, 36% O_2	12	144.0	106.3	91.9	14.5	—	—	—

[a]The oxygen partial pressure in tracheal air (saturated at 37°C).

Dill et al. (1936) found a gradient of 3.4 torr in residents at 4700 m and −0.8 torr at 5340 m; Hurtado et al. (1956a), 0.9 torr at 4540 m; and Severinghaus et al. (1966), 3 torr at 4360 m. Table 12.4 summarizes our findings at 4540 m. Kreuzer et al. (1964), studying the same type of subjects at 4540 m, found values that contradict all the others: 10.5 torr for subjects breathing air and 27 torr for subjects inhaling a mixture containing oxygen at 150 torr. Accentuation of the inequality of distribution of $\dot{V}_A/\dot{Q}$ ratios and increased venous–arterial shunting were claimed to be the causes.

The first question that arises in the analysis of the data of the work by Kreuzer et al. (1964) is the position of the experimental subjects during the test: they were tested in the supine position, while in the other studies the upright position was used. Position introduces a difference because high-altitude natives have approximately 50 percent more blood in the lungs than lowlanders (Monge et al., 1955) and its redistribution will affect the $\dot{V}_A/\dot{Q}$ ratios differently. This is probably the primary reason why arterial oxygen saturation in natives is greatly reduced during mild exercise performed in the supine position (Banchero et al., 1966). In the erect position we have found that harder work has little or no effect on arterial oxygen saturation (unpublished data).

On the other hand, the values of Kreuzer et al. (1964) are too high for alveolar P_{O_2} and too low for alveolar P_{CO_2}, nor are they fully explained by hyperventilation. Errors in alveolar air sampling, however, would account for these values (Severinghaus et al., 1966).

Diffusing Capacity

Decrease of alveolar–arterial gradient does not necessarily lead to a greater diffusing capacity. There must be, in addition, a larger active membrane (as noted above). A gradient within the limits found by Kreuzer et al. (1964) does not preclude the possibility of a larger diffusing capacity at high altitude. The diffusing capacity would not be as great, of course, as it would be without a gradient. Thus if the active membrane is enlarged, the oxygen-diffusing capacity must be greater.

In "acclimatized" lowlanders diffusing capacity for oxygen is decreased at rest (West, 1962). There is no experimental evidence that it is the same in high-altitude native residents, but there is some evidence that it is increased during physical exercise. Indeed, the maximum diffusing capacity is about 50 percent greater in high-altitude natives than in lowlanders (Velásquez, 1956).

Pulmonary Function at Altitude

The purpose of pulmonary function is to provide arterial blood with an adequate amount of oxygen to meet the body's metabolic needs, at the highest possible partial pressure.

We found increased alveolar ventilation with greater functional residual capacity in high-altitude natives. As a result, the alveolar oxygen is greater in quantity and the pressure is larger than it would be if the ventilation were equivalent to sea level, so the pressure gradient between inspired and alveolar air is less. At 4540 m this saving of pressure amounts to 14.9 mm Hg, according to our data. This situation is important for blood saturation since the steeper part of the HbO_2 dissociation curve is involved at these pressures. However, the full compensatory capacity of the ventilation is not used because preventing an excessive loss of CO_2 is as important as increasing O_2 pressure. A diminuation in A-a gradient becomes a natural adjustment to save O_2 pressure with no further loss of CO_2.

A greater diffusing capacity of the lung will allow the delivery of more oxygen to the blood despite the low alveolar oxygen pressure. Evidence has been discussed that suggests that the active surface of alveolar membrane at rest is larger and the finding of greater maximum diffusing capacity has also been acknowledged. Moreover, less plasma volume (Hurtado et al., 1947, 1956b) would diminish the thickness of the membrane, and that slower blood flow (which is due to low values of cardiac output and the enlarged pulmonary vascular tree) will allow a complete pressure equilibration between air and blood. Better diffusing capacity, added to the greater oxygen-transport power of the blood, explains the perfect adequacy of pulmonary function to the metabolic needs of the high-altitude native.

LUNG-TISSUE OXYGEN TRANSPORT

Oxygen is transported from lung to tissue mainly associated with hemoglobin as HbO_2. The quantity of oxygen in physical solution is insufficient to fulfill metabolic needs. Dissolved O_2 depends upon the gas partial pressure: for example, at 100 torr it is 0.3 ml/100 ml of blood and at 50 torr is only half, or 0.15 ml. However, the pressure at which oxygen is dissolved is that which determines the actual saturation of Hb and determines diffusion at the capillary level.

The total quantity of oxygen transported depends upon (1) the amount of the gas taken up in the lung by each liter of blood (which is related to concentration, oxygen saturation, and physicochemical characteristics of the hemoglobin), and (2) the amount of blood delivered to tissues per unit of time (which is a function of the cardiac output).

Concentration of Hemoglobin

Increase in hemoglobin concentration in blood is one of the oldest known characteristics of altitude acclimatization. The hypothesis of an increase of red blood cells as a response to hypoxia was first postulated by Paul Bert in 1878 and confirmed by Viualt (1890) in Morococha residents (4540 m). Douglas et al. (1913) found that not only red blood cells but also hemoglobin was augmented. We know now that the increment of hemoglobin is both relative (concentration) and absolute. Garruto discusses the hematological characteristics of the Andean native in Chapter 13.

In our studies at 4540 m (Hurtado et al., 1956b) we found a mean hemoglobin concentration of 19.7 g/100 ml in high-altitude natives and only 15.2 g/100 ml at sea level; a difference of 29.4 percent. At the accepted capacity of 1.34 ml of oxygen per gram of hemoglobin, the potential carrying capacity of the blood is 26.4 ml of oxygen per 100 ml at high altitude and 20.4 ml/100 ml blood at sea level.

Arterial Oxygen Saturation

Arterial oxygen saturation is determined by the inspired oxygen pressure and the pulmonary function. For these reasons only part of the potential transporting capacity of the blood is actually used: 96.1 percent at sea level and 78.1 percent at 4540 m, according to our data. Table 12.5 shows our values and some others from the literature, at different altitudes.

At these saturations the actual carrying capacity of the blood is 14.61 and 15.39 ml/100 ml at sea level and high altitude, respectively, which means that the arterial blood leaves the lung with more oxygen at high altitude than at sea level, but with lower oxygen pressure: 45.1 and 104.2 torr, respectively.

Affinity of Hemoglobin for Oxygen

Hemoglobin in high-altitude natives seems to have the same structural characteristics as in lowlanders, with an oxygen-dissociation curve of similar shape. (Aste-Salazar, 1966). However, according to Hurtado and Aste-Salazar (1948) and our own data (Hurtado et al., 1956b), the affinity of hemoglobin for oxygen is lower, hence the shifting of the curve to the right.

Barcroft (1925) found that the affinity of hemoglobin for oxygen increased in sojourners at 4330 m; Dill et al. (1931) did not find any change in high-altitude residents (3280 m), although there was a small tendency to decrease in sojourners; Keys et al. (1936) found a decrease of the affinity of Hb for oxygen in sojourners but no change in residents.

TABLE 12.5   *Hemoglobin Concentration (Hb), Arterial Oxygen
Saturation (HbO$_2$), and Cardiac Index in
High-Altitude Natives*

Reference	N	Hb (g/100 ml)	HbO$_2$ saturation (%)	C.I. (l/min/m^2)
Velásquez (1972)				
Sea level	26	16.0	96.1	
4540 m	32	19.7	78.1	
Hurtado and Aste (1948)				
Sea level	38	16.1	96.1	
2390 m	12	17.3	91.7	
3140 m	11	17.9	91.0	
3730 m	15	18.6	87.6	
4540 m	18	21.1	81.1	
4860 m	12	21.7	80.7	
Hurtado et al. (1956a)				
Sea level	80	—	97.9	
4540 m	40	—	81.0	
Rotta et al. (1956)				
Sea level	7	15.4	98.0	3.50
4540 m	7	20.7	79.6	3.33
Hultgren et al. (1965)				
3730 m	21	—	86.0	2.23
Banchero et al. (1966)				
Sea level	22	14.8	95.7	3.97
4540 m	35	19.4	78.4	3.97
Gamboa and Romero (1970)				
4540 m	10	—	81.5	3.20
Moret et al. (1972)				
Sea level	7	15.4	94.2	3.84
3700 m	18	17.7	88.2	3.43
4370 m	9	19.2	83.5	3.87

Lenfant et al. (1971) have demonstrated that in acute exposure to altitude the HbO$_2$ dissociation curve shifts to the right and the magnitude of this deviation is closely related to variations in the erythrocytic concentration of 2,3-diphosphoglycerate. They assume that this factor is the most potent one in the change of hemoglobin affinity for oxygen.

We have found (Hurtado et al., 1956b) that P_{50} (oxygen pressure for half-saturation) is 25.75 torr at sea level and 27.22 torr at 4540 m. This difference is of small physiological significance, but it represents an adaptive mechanism to altitude stress since liberation of oxygen at the tissue level is facilitated. Of course, the oxygen uptake in the lung is slightly reduced, but that is advantageously counteracted by an increase in hemoglobin concentration.

Cardiac Output and Cardiac Index

It is well known that cardiac output ($\dot{Q}$) has a definite but transient increase during acute exposures to altitude (Asmussen and Nielson, 1955; Nagy and Skolnik, 1961; Klausen, 1966; Vogel and Harris, 1967). This increase represents an emergency adjustment of the oxygen-transport system. As the increase in the work load of the heart is not an economical compensation; it is replaced by an increment of hemoglobin concentration. Thus, in high-altitude natives the cardiac output and the cardiac index (C.I.) have been found within sea-level-normal standards, with a tendency to the lower values. We found (Rotta et al., 1956) at sea level a $\dot{Q}$ of 5.91 l/min and a C.I. of 3.50 l/min/m^2, and at high altitude (4540 m) a $\dot{Q}$ of 5.29 l/min and a C.I. of 2.84 l/min/m^2. Other investigators have confirmed these findings (Peñaloza et al., 1962; Banchero et al., 1966).

Oxygen Transport

The amount of oxygen transported from lungs to tissues, per unit of time, can be calculated as follows:

$$Hb_l \times 1.34 \, \frac{Sa}{100} \times \dot{Q} = O_2 \quad ml/min \tag{1}$$

where Hb_l is grams of hemoglobin per liter of blood, Sa/100 the fraction of Hb bound to oxygen, and $\dot{Q}$ the cardiac output. Because of significant differences in body size between sea-level and high-altitude natives, it is better to use the cardiac index in the calculations.

If we apply the data of Table 12.5, the quantity of oxygen transported per minute is 685.1 ml/min/m^2 at sea level and 686.5 ml/min/m^2 at high altitude. However, it will be seen later that capillary blood flow is slower at high altitude, so hemoglobin could be more deprived of oxygen.

Lower arterial oxygen saturation at altitude is then proportionally compensated for by a larger hemoglobin concentration, so any increase in cardiac output, as in exercise, will increase the oxygen transported in the same amount as at sea level. Thus from the point of view of the amount of oxygen available at the capillary level, the respiratory system fulfills its function at any metabolic rate at high altitude.

Since the quantity of oxygen available in the tissue capillaries is of the same magnitude as at sea level, the physiological problem at high altitude is whether the diminished pressure of the gas will be enough to drive it into the cells.

Oxygen diffusion from capillary to tissue is a very complex process; understanding it is difficult because of the multiplicity of interrelated factors involved and the impossibility of calculating a diffusion gradient since tissue P_{O_2} is not accessible for direct measurement. Calculation of P_{O_2} at a given point in the tissue is based on assumptions and models that not only cannot cover all the factors, but might even introduce considerable error in the results.

The simplest assumption is that the capillary has a cylindrical diffusion field, so it could be considered as the axis of a tissue cylinder supplied by that capillary. This model was assumed by Krogh (1917). However, the radial gradient derived from this model does not account for the longitudinal gradient, which could produce a considerable error, and does not take into consideration some known factors, such as the possible intracellular oxygen-transport function of myoglobin (Millikan, 1937) and the slowness of the chemical dissociation HbO_2, which could become an important limiting factor in tissue diffusion (Roughton and Forster, 1957).

Whatever model is chosen, the dimension of the PO_2 gradient between capillary blood and tissue depends upon three main factors: (1) oxygen pressure in the blood, (2) metabolic rate of the tissue, and (3) total amount of tissue supplied by the capillary. If a constancy of the two first factors is assumed, then the PO_2 at any given point in the tissue (and the gradient) depends mainly upon the intercapillary distance, which determines the amount of tissue supplied by each capillary. Effectively, in the analysis of the Krogh–Erland equation (Krogh, 1917), which describes the cylindrical model with radial diffusion, the intercapillary distance becomes a critical factor.

There are, however, other factors that could play a part in altitude acclimatization. Oxygen tension in the tissue will also depend upon the volume of blood contained in the capillary (given by the diameter of the vessel), the velocity of blood flow, the affinity of Hb, and the intensity of the Bohr effect.

The intercapillary distance diminishes when the number of capillaries per unit of tissue volume increases. Valdivia (1956) and Campos and Iglesias (1957) have shown that capillaries in high-altitude natives (animal and man) are more numerous than at sea level. Valdivia found 42 percent more capillaries in high-altitude guinea pigs, with almost no change in the number of muscular fibers; the ratio of capillaries to fibers was 34 percent higher. Campos and Iglesias describe the capillaries of high-altitude native man as "wider and congested." More and larger capillaries mean not only a smaller diffusion pathway but also a greater amount of blood (and oxygen) available at any given time.

On the other hand, we have demonstrated (Rotta et al., 1956) that in high-altitude natives the cardiac-index values are at the lower limits of sea-level normality; thus the capillary blood flow must be slower, allowing greater oxygen extraction. In fact, oxygen saturation of mixed venous blood is lower in high-altitude natives (Rotta et al., 1956). The effect on capillary–venous blood gradient and on capillary oxygen diffusion will be discussed below.

As the blood alkaline buffering is diminished in high-altitude natives, more CO_2 must be carried by hemoglobin, thus enhancing the Bohr effect. Effectively, Hurtado and Aste-Salazar (1948) and Hurtado et al. (1956b) have demonstrated a greater formation of carbamino-CO_2 in high-altitude natives. The loss of the hemoglobin's affinity for oxygen (due to the Bohr effect) means not only a saving of pressure but also a more homogeneous distribution of the gas along the capillary. This follows because the shifting of the dissociation curve increases as blood picks up more and more CO_2 during its movement through the vessel; this is a general physiological function of the Bohr effect but is enhanced at high altitude.

We have found (unpublished data) that during exercise the respiratory quotient is higher in high-altitude natives than in sea-level subjects. Thus, at the same oxygen consumption, more CO_2 is formed in the working muscles; it could be an added factor to heighten the Bohr effect.

TOTAL OXYGEN PRESSURE GRADIENT

The function of the respiratory system is to maintain an optimal oxygen supply to all the body cells, which requires a certain quantity of oxygen at an appropriate pressure in the capillary blood.

When the atmospheric oxygen pressure decreases with increasing altitude, the possibility of maintaining a reliable capillary oxygen pressure is based on the potential capacity of the respiratory system to increase its conductance to transport the gas from atmosphere to mitochondria with the minimum possible pressure loss. Increasing conductance means decreasing the principal resistances to oxygen flow in lung and tissue.

As most of the oxygen in blood is bound to hemoglobin, even at low pressures it could be present in large amounts, if the quantity of Hb increases and if there is an adequate lung-diffusing capacity. We can safely assume that in high-altitude natives performing heavy work loads at high altitudes, the amount of oxygen available per minute in capillary blood is similar to that in lowlanders performing at sea level. Effectively, the aerobic capacity of high-landers performing at altitude and lowlanders performing at sea level is the same (Velásquez, 1972; Elsner et al., 1964; Mazess, 1969a; Baker, 1969).

In regard to the maintenance of high capillary oxygen pressure, it is necessary to examine the total oxygen gradient for the factors that increase conductance of the system and maintain an adequate pressure drop during oxygen transport.

Blood Gradients

From inspired air to arterial blood the oxygen pressure falls from 147.1 to 94.0 torr with a gradient of 53.1 torr at sea level, while at 4540 m of altitude, it falls from 83.4 to 45.2 torr with a gradient of 38.2 torr (Table 12.4). The pressure loss in the transport is 53.1 at sea level and 38.2 at altitude; the difference between these two values is what the pulmonary function saves in terms of oxygen pressure loss: 14.9 torr. In an earlier work (Hurtado et al., 1956a) we found a somewhat larger value: 21.4 torr.

Of those 14.9 torr, 8.9 is the contribution of alveolar ventilation and 6.0 of the alveolar—capillary function (D_{O_2}, venous admixture and $\dot{V}_A/\dot{Q}$ ratio distribution). With the data presented by Kreuzer et al. (1964), the difference in gradients between sea level and altitude is only 10.2 torr; that would be the entire gain in respiratory adaptation to altitude, provided by ventilation alone.

The contribution is much less than its potential capacity would allow. The contribution of $(A\text{-}a)$ O_2 gradient decrease is small because the gradient itself, at sea level, is small. Conversely, its enlarged diffusing capacity partly counteracts the low alveolar P_{O_2} by allowing, at this diminished pressure, the diffusion of large amounts of oxygen into the blood. Rahn (1966) arrives at the same conclusion in his analysis of the conductance of O_2 from the environment to tissues.

However, it must be understood, first, that the alveolar P_{O_2} does not reflect the absolute values of the pulmonary ventilation, because ventilation must be greater to cope with the larger functional residual capacity (the larger the residual space, the higher the ventilation needed to maintain a given $P_{A_{O_2}}$). And, second, the oxygen pressures considered in this analysis are in the steeper part of the HbO_2 dissociation curve, where small changes in pressure will greatly improve the saturation of the blood.

Arterial blood is 78.1 percent saturated at 4540 m and 96.1 percent saturated at sea level (Table 12.5), giving a difference of 18 percent. A change of about 25 percent in hemoglobin concentration will be compensatory if other factors, such as cardiac output, remain unchanged. Table 12.5 shows that Hb, at 4540 m, is 28.7 percent higher than in lowlanders. This small overcompensation will account for the tendency of the cardiac output to low values.

Oxygen Gradients

In the arterial end of tissue capillary the oxygen pressure is the same as in the arterial blood leaving the lungs, so it could be considered constant. Conversely, in venous blood, oxygen pressure is the final result of many interrelated and essentially changeable factors, such as metabolic rate, speed of blood flow, saturation and amount of hemoglobin, and quantity of blood in the capillary. These factors control oxygen diffusion and vary from tissue to tissue. The mean capillary pressure lies between these two limits, so its value, at a given arterial oxygen pressure, depends upon venous P_{O_2}. Barcroft (1925) proposed a simple approach to the calculation of mean capillary pressure ($P\bar{c}_{O_2}$) and results are not very different from those attained by integration:

$$P\bar{c}_{O_2} = P_{V_{O_2}} + \frac{(P_a - P_V)O_2}{3} \tag{2}$$

where $P_{V_{O_2}}$ is oxygen pressure in either venous blood from any organ or tissue or mixed venous blood.

However, when we are dealing with different arterial oxygen pressures, as when comparing sea-level and high-altitude arterial blood samples, the situation changes. Because of the shape of the HbO_2 dissociation curve, the gradient between arterial and mean capillary P_{O_2} is much larger at sea level than at high altitude. This difference reflects the fact that at high oxygen pressures such as those prevailing at lowlands, in the upper, flat part of the curve, diffusion of small amounts of oxygen determines a large decrease in its tension in the blood. In other words, at sea level the P_{O_2} falls much faster at the beginning of the capillary than at high altitude, for the same quantity of oxygen given up. To deliver 2 ml of oxygen from 100 ml of blood containing 20 ml of oxygen at 100 torr (sea-level situation), more than 40 torr is expended. To deliver the same amount of oxygen at an arterial oxygen pressure of 45 torr only expends about 10 torr P_{O_2}.

Thus the shortening of the $(a\text{-}\bar{c})$ O_2 gradient in high-altitude natives is in part due to the factors determining the conditions of venous blood but is mainly due to the shape of the dissociation curve. According to our data (Table 12.6), this gradient is 34.9 torr at sea level and 8.3 at high altitude, a saving of 26.6 torr, greater than that produced by pulmonary function. This mechanism is not one acquired during acclimatization but a natural respiratory adaptation of high-altitude animals.

The oxygen pressure at the venous end of the capillary is the remaining pressure after diffusion. Thus its value depends upon tissue metabolism, amount of tissue served by the capillary, and the other diffusion-controlling factors. If constancy of metabolic rate and diffusion coefficient is assumed, the critical factor governing the oxygen pressure in the tissues (and the diffusion from capillaries to tissues) is the intercapillary distance (or the

TABLE 12.6   *Total Oxygen Gradient in Sea Level and High-Altitude Natives (torr)*

Oxygen pressure	Sea level	Altitude (4540 m)	Gradient difference
$P_{I_{O_2}}$	147.1	83.4	
$P_{A_{O_2}}$	102.8	46.3	
$P_{a_{O_2}}$	94.0	44.0	
$P_{\bar{c}_{O_2}}$	59.4	36.6	
$P_{V_{O_2}}$	42.1	32.9	
$(I\text{-}A)O_2$ grad.	44.3	37.1	7.2
$(A\text{-}a)O_2$ grad.	8.8	2.3	6.5
$(a\text{-}\bar{c})O_2$ grad.	34.6	7.4	27.2
$(\bar{c}\text{-}\bar{V})O_2$ grad.	17.3	3.7	13.6

amount of tissue served by the capillary). Hence it is this factor that is the main determinant of venous P_{O_2}.

If the diffusion pathway is diminished, the pressure needed to drive the oxygen to the farthest cell can be small; the greater number of capillaries in the tissues of high-altitude natives provides an adaptive mechanism to use oxygen at lower pressures. However, by hindering an excessive fall of oxygen pressure and maintaining the highest possible venous P_{O_2} (to preserve a high mean capillary pressure), some other factors are brought into play: a large amount of oxygen in the capillaries (wider capillaries, higher hemoglobin concentration), a greater Bohr effect, and slower capillary-blood-flow rate.

In Table 12.6 the values for capillary–venous oxygen-pressure gradients are 17.5 at sea level and 4.2 at high altitude, with a difference of 13.3 torr. This saving of pressure depends upon the shape of the HbO_2 dissociation curve and the values of venous O_2 pressure.

The actual values of oxygen pressure in mixed venous blood are very significant. At rest they are 41.6 and 32.7 torr in sea-level and high-altitude natives, respectively, a difference of almost 9 torr. At the steeper part of the dissociation curve, this accounts for the liberation of about 2 ml of oxygen from 100 ml of blood containing 15 g of hemoglobin, or just the same quantity that at sea level the blood gives up with a drop of oxygen pressure from 100 to 60 torr.

SUMMARY

In high-altitude natives lung function does not play a major role in preventing oxygen pressure loss but allows the use of low alveolar pressure to diffuse a large quantity of oxygen into blood. Increased hemoglobin concentration will transport this large gas volume to tissues in a fashion so interrelated with cardiac output that the same amount of oxygen will be delivered to tissues per minute in both high-altitude and sea-level natives. The HbO_2 dissociation curve and the shorter diffusing pathway are the main factors responsible for the substantial increase of conductance that allows low oxygen pressures to drive oxygen into the tissues. More oxygen in the capillaries, changes in affinity of hemoglobin for oxygen, and slower capillary blood flow are some of the other important mechanisms employed to maintain high pressure in the capillaries. The net effect of these adaptive mechanisms at high altitude is an efficient and normal oxygen delivery to the tissues.

13

HEMATOLOGY

Ralph M. Garruto

Human populations, subjected to severe environmental stresses over many generations, elicit responses of a complex biocultural nature for the temporary or permanent alleviation of biological strain. The most significant of the primary environmental stresses found at higher elevations is altitude hypoxia, a result of the lowered partial pressure of oxygen. Under conditions of chronic hypoxic stress, primary biological adjustments encompass structural, functional, and biochemical changes, involving the cardiorespiratory system, circulatory dynamics, and tissue utilization of oxygen.

Among the most important physiological processes in the adaptation of native Andean man to his environment are those which serve to minimize tissue hypoxia. Many studies have concluded that altitude polycythemia is one of the principle adaptive mechanisms in man native to high elevations (Hurtado, 1964b; Lenfant and Sullivan, 1971; Merino, 1950; Reynafarje, 1966b). By increasing the total blood volume through an increase in the red cell mass, the hemoglobin concentration and O_2 content of the blood are elevated. These changes are brought about by a negative feedback mechanism acting through a humoral factor, erythropoietin, a glucoprotein formed mainly in the kidneys and liver, which stimulates the bone marrow to increase the rate of red cell production. When the anoxic state in the tissues is alleviated by increasing the O_2 capacity of the blood, erythropoietin levels decrease to trace amounts.

While altitude polycythemia is purported to be adaptive, a number of functional disadvantages could offset the beneficial gains derived from such a response. For example, an increase in erythrocyte concentration increases blood viscosity, thereby increasing blood flow resistance and work load on the heart (Balke, 1964a; Banchero et al., 1966; Smith and Crowell, 1967). While a more extensive development of capillary beds would partially alleviate the resultant rise in blood viscosity (Anthony and Kreider, 1961; Hurtado, 1964b; Lenfant and Sullivan, 1971; Valdivia, 1962), even a modest rise may be causally related to the reported venous inflammations, pulmonary edema, and chronic mountain sickness observed among the Andeans (Monge and Monge, 1966; Quinones, 1968; Roy et al., 1968). The polycythemic responses associated with these pathological conditions clearly do not indicate a physiological advantage under conditions of hypoxic stress.

This chapter summarizes the hematological observations recorded during the course of two separate field investigations between 1969 and 1971 in the southern Peruvian Andean communities of Nuñoa (4000 m) and Macusani (4400 m). The purpose of the investigation was threefold: (1) to assess the degree of altitude polycythemia among permanent highland Quechua and Mestizo adults, (2) to examine peripheral blood changes in Quechua children and adolescents, and (3) to determine the effects of prolonged strenuous physical activity on selected hematological aspects of native Andean man.

SAMPLING AND TESTING PROCEDURES

Because of the theoretical paradox resulting from the suggestion of both physiological advantage and disadvantage in highland residents with polycythemia, a number of specific methodological and procedural controls were developed for the Nuñoa and Macusani studies. By establishing such controls, most of which were not implemented in prior investigations, we were better able to define the basic subset of the population studied while controlling for those factors which might otherwise affect the results.

In Nuñoa and Macusani, healthy volunteers were selected only from those individuals who were determined to be of Quechua heritage (see Chapter 5), while a control sample of Mestizo adults were used to determine whether racial differences in hematological characteristics existed. Healthy children and adolescents, as well as adults, were included in the samples to gain insights into the developmental aspects of hematological change among Andean residents. Nutritional and cultural aspects as well as the biotic environment are described in other chapters of this volume.

Demographic information was collected on all individuals, including date and place of birth, current residence, and work and travel history. Only permanent residents who were born in the highlands and had no travel history to lower altitudes were included in the samples, thus eliminating the effects of short-term or intermittent exposure to hypoxic stress. Furthermore, samples were selected from these communities because of their traditional pre-Columbian horticultural and pastoral way of life. In previous studies a number of volunteers were selected from mining communities and hospital clinics, and often included immigrants from lower altitudes. Also, mining communities in most cases are located at higher altitudes than the highest traditional altiplano communities. A population of such miners surely includes men who already have chronic lung diseases, such as silicosis, which at such high altitudes may have provoked some compensatory polycythemia. Furthermore, mining as an economic activity, rather than the traditional pre-Columbian horticultural and pastoral way of life, while probably not much different in total work output, is culturally a new life style to which the traditional natives may not have developed as efficient work patterns.

The general health status of all subjects was assessed by outward physical appearance, questions about current and past illnesses, and the interpretation of the leucocyte count and differential leucocyte analysis. Known cases of anemia, tuberculosis, silicosis, and polycythemia vera were excluded from the samples; individuals with a history of phlebotomies, blood transfusions, or blood dyscrasias were also omitted. Any abnormalities detected in individuals by urinalyses using Clinisticks (a dipstick method for mass screening of abnormal pH, occult blood, protein, bilirubin, ketones, and glucose; Ames Co.) also resulted in an individual's omission. Individuals who had mild respiratory infections were not eliminated because of the high frequency of these infections among Andean residents.

All blood samples were collected using the microtechnique of finger puncture (capillary blood). Generally, venipuncture posed serious problems because of the reluctance of the Quechua to have their blood taken, and finger punctures became the only practical means of obtaining blood. Deep punctures were made to ensure a free flow of blood with as little admixture of tissue fluid as possible.

Erythrocyte and leucocyte counts as well as hemoglobinometry were performed by two different methods. In the 1969 field expedition, the blood counts for the Macusani sample were performed with a Hausser hemacytometer. The same individual read all counts. Hemoglobins were read on the Lumetron hemoglobinometer, Model 15, employing the oxyhemoglobin method. During the 1971 field expedition, erythrocyte and leucocyte counts for the Nuñoa sample were determined with the Haemacount MK-2 electronic cell counter. This relatively new medical device manufactured by General Science Corporation is the counterpart of the MK-9, a hemoglobinometer employing cyanmethemoglobin. The instruments used in the Nuñoa study were calibrated against the Coulter Counter, Model S, before entering and after leaving Peru. The instrument accuracy of the MK-2 was slightly greater than ±2 percent, while the MK-9 readings were approximately 5–6 percent higher than the Coulter S standard. Hematocrit values for all groups were determined with the Adams microhematocrit centrifuge. Duplicate readings were obtained on all cell counts, hemoglobin concentrations, and hematocrits.

Blood smears for reticulocyte counts were made with a modification of the Osgood Wilhelm technique (Davidsohn and Wells, 1966). Proportional amounts of blood and brilliant cresyl blue dye were mixed together on one corner of the glass slides and allowed to stand for 6 rather than the normal 3 min in a moist, enclosed chamber to prevent the blood-dye mixture from drying before the smears could be made. Reticulocytes were extremely difficult to stain at high altitude with regular procedures; lysing, dye crystallization, and loss of valuable data occurred before the techniques were adequately modified. The effects of low barometric pressure might have resulted in decreased diffusion of stain into the cells. Staining of differential counts for leucocyte analysis and microscopic examination of these cells was conducted according to prescribed methods with one major modification; the staining time, like that for the reticulocytes, was again doubled from 3 to 6 min, and the buffering time increased from 5 to 10 min. In all cases, reticulocyte and differential counts were read by the same individual.

HEMATOLOGICAL RESPONSES

Childhood and Adolescence

At sea level, standard regressions for age-related hematological characteristics are not currently available for comparative purposes. Mean sea-level norms vary from one hospital or laboratory to another, and only scattered composite data from earlier works and reviews are available for general consideration. It has been suggested, however, that a polycythemic condition exists when the red cell count is above 6 million/mm^3 with a corresponding hemoglobin concentration and hematocrit greater than 17.5 g/100 ml and 52 percent, respectively (Page and Culver, 1966).

Previous investigations of highland hematological characteristics have been almost exclusively limited to the postadolescent period. In a report on native Andean residents living at 3800, 4200, and 4500 m, Whittembury and Monge (1972) found, through the use of linear regression analysis, a profound increase in hematocrit with both age and altitude from childhood through middle adulthood. However, the number of subjects in each of their three sample groups was very modest, ranging from 12 to 31 individuals. A more complete study of adolescents, although non-Andean, was performed at 3100 m in Leadville, Colorado, by Treger et al. (1965). They found that boys and girls between 10 and 18 years of age showed the same pattern of change in red cell count, hemoglobin concentration, and hematocrit as their sea-level counterparts, but mean values for all three parameters were 12–17 percent higher. In addition, slight increases were noted in the mean corpuscular volume (MCV) and mean corpuscular hemoglobin (MCH) with age, while the mean corpuscular hemoglobin concentration (MCHC) remained unchanged.

In the highland communities of Nuñoa (4000 m) and Macusani (4400 m) hematological observations were recorded on 251 Quechua boys between the ages of 6 and 22 yr (Garruto, 1973). The means and standard deviations for the red cell counts, hemoglobin concentrations, and hematocrits, as well as the results from the bivariate regression analysis, are summarized in Fig. 13.1 and Tables 13.1–13.3. Overall, an approximate 10 percent increase above sea-level norms was noted in these values, from middle childhood to young adulthood. However, no further increases were thereafter observed as evidenced by mass plots of data for adults (Garruto, 1973). Both Nuñoa and Macusani residents had a similar progression of red cell values, even though there is a 400-m altitudinal difference between the two communities.

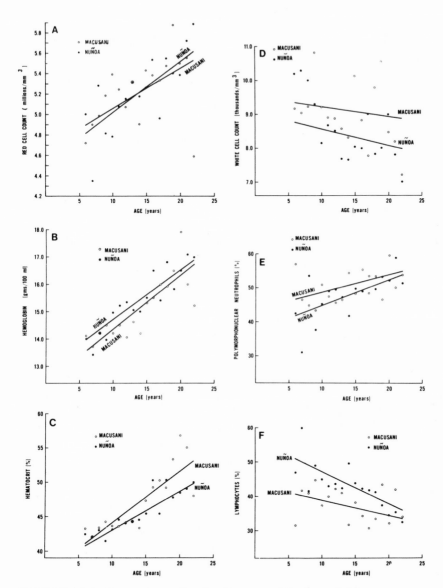

FIGURE 13.1 *Regressions of red cell counts (A), hemoglobin concentrations (B), hematocrit (C), white cell counts (D), polymorphonuclear neutrophils (E), and lymphocytes (F) on age during childhood and adolescence.*

TABLE 13.1 *Linear Regression Equations for Age-Related Hematological Parameters*

Variable	Nuñoa Quechua (4000 m)			Macusani Quechua (4400 m)		
	Regression equation	S.E.	N	Regression equation	S.E.	N
Red cell count	$Y = 4.51 + 0.05x$	0.51	129	$Y = 4.65 + 0.04x$	0.47	100
Hemoglobin concentration	$Y = 12.91 + 0.18x$	1.23	129	$Y = 12.34 + 0.20x$	0.94	114
Hematocrit	$Y = 37.51 + 0.56x$	3.13	131	$Y = 36.39 + 0.76x$	3.48	114
White cell count	$Y = 9.07 - 0.05x$	1.91	136	$Y = 9.53 - 0.03x$	1.80	115
Polymorphonuclear neutrophils	$Y = 37.45 + 0.75x$	11.37	130	$Y = 43.52 + 0.52x$	8.92	115
Lymphocytes	$Y = 55.38 - 0.88x$	10.83	130	$Y = 43.32 - 0.44x$	8.77	115

TABLE 13.2 *Age Distributions for Red Cell Counts,*
Hemoglobin Concentrations, and Hematocrits
Among Nuñoa Boys

	Red cell count (10^6/mm^3)			Hemoglobin (g/100 ml)			Hematocrit (%)		
Age	N	Mean	S.D.	N	Mean	S.D.	N	Mean	S.D.
6	2	5.00	0.03	2	14.0	0.49	2	42.5	0.71
7	1	4.35	–	1	13.4	–	1	42.0	–
8	1	5.28	–	2	14.2	1.56	2	43.0	1.41
9	4	4.81	0.23	4	13.9	1.01	4	41.5	2.08
10	7	4.78	0.32	7	14.9	0.64	7	43.1	2.19
11	11	5.07	0.53	12	15.2	1.04	13	44.5	2.60
12	9	5.15	0.53	8	15.3	1.04	8	44.0	2.20
13	16	5.31	0.47	16	15.1	1.33	16	44.2	2.34
14	12	5.17	0.56	12	15.0	1.41	13	44.5	3.01
15	21	5.26	0.56	19	15.5	1.37	18	45.4	3.13
16	4	5.53	0.82	4	16.5	1.04	4	50.2	3.86
17	8	4.96	0.48	9	15.4	1.20	8	45.4	2.77
18	9	5.55	0.69	8	16.8	1.20	9	50.3	4.42
19	12	5.40	0.44	11	15.8	1.58	12	47.8	3.31
20	8	5.38	0.41	9	16.5	0.94	9	48.4	4.00
21	3	5.72	0.34	3	17.1	0.81	3	49.0	3.61
22	1	5.89	–	2	17.0	2.19	2	50.0	4.24

The ratio of the hemoglobin concentration to the hematocrit is slightly higher in Nuñoa residents than would be expected compared to sea-level values. The apparent reason was that the MK-9 hemoglobinometer gave 5–6 percent higher hemoglobin readouts than the Coulter Counter, Model S. The MK-9 was not used in Macusani.

An increase in reticulocytes (immature red cells) has generally been reported for high-altitude residents, but mean values usually did not exceed 1.0–1.5 percent in the peripheral blood (Hurtado et al., 1947; Hurtado, 1964b; Merino, 1950; Lawrence et al., 1952). While these highland values were approximately 0.5–1.0 percent higher than the sea-level mean, they cannot be considered as indicating a reticulocytosis or any significant increase in effective erythropoiesis (Davidsohn and Wells, 1966; Williams et al., 1972; Wintrobe, 1967). In contrast, reports of bone marrow hyperplasia, increased erthropoietin production, intestinal iron-absorption changes, and increased total blood volume among Morococha residents (4500 m) have suggested a greater erythropoietic activity than that reported for sea-level adults (Merino and Reynafarje, 1949; Reynafarje et al., 1959; Hurtado et al., 1947; Hurtado, 1964a). No reason is apparent for this discrepancy.

An elevated reticulocyte count, representing increased erythropoietic activity, was not found among Nuñoa and Macusani residents (see Table

TABLE 13.3   *Age Distributions of Red Cell Counts,*
Hemoglobin Concentrations, and Hematocrits
Among Macusani Boys

	Red cell count (10^6/mm^3)			Hemoglobin (g/100 ml)			Hematocrit (%)		
Age	N	Mean	S.D.	N	Mean	S.D.	N	Mean	S.D.
6	6	4.72	0.64	6	14.1	0.55	6	43.3	1.75
7	9	4.90	0.41	9	13.7	0.81	9	42.0	2.65
8	8	4.98	0.38	9	14.2	0.50	9	43.3	1.66
9	4	5.18	0.50	6	14.5	0.71	6	44.2	2.23
10	8	5.39	0.42	11	14.2	0.37	11	43.7	2.90
11	5	5.24	0.35	5	14.5	0.84	5	43.6	4.04
12	10	5.07	0.36	10	14.1	0.93	10	44.2	2.10
13	7	5.31	0.52	9	14.6	0.50	9	44.2	2.33
14	6	4.90	0.40	6	14.2	0.43	6	43.3	1.97
15	8	5.43	0.50	9	15.3	1.10	9	47.3	1.80
16	10	5.38	0.51	11	15.5	0.99	11	49.2	3.63
17	4	5.33	0.49	6	16.0	1.26	6	50.2	4.58
18	8	5.47	0.58	8	15.9	0.97	8	49.1	4.36
19	2	5.88	0.08	3	16.5	1.66	3	53.3	8.08
20	3	5.50	0.48	4	17.9	1.54	4	56.8	5.50
21	1	5.58	–	1	16.0	–	1	55.0	–
22	1	4.59	–	1	15.2	–	1	48.0	–

13.4). Moreover, the red cell indices—MCV, MCH, and MCHC—and direct microscopic examination showed the red cells to be normocytic and normochromic. The reticulocyte count and red cell indices were consistent with sea-level norms and were not significantly related to either age or altitude. It should be noted that all red and white cell values for children and adolescents which were not age-related were combined with the adult observations in Table 13.4.

It has been generally accepted that the polycythemia associated with altitude hypoxia is absolute in type, mainly because of an increased red cell mass despite the decreased plasma volume; no corresponding changes have been noted in leucocytes or platelets (Hurtado, 1964b; Merino, 1950; Treger et al., 1965; Sanchez et al., 1970; Prankerd, 1966). A few investigations, however, have reported a slight elevation in the white cell count (Meyer, 1935; Stammers, 1933; Webb, 1913) as well as changes in leucocyte cell types as measured by the differential count, with increased altitude. Specifically, there is evidence of an increase in lymphocytes with a corresponding decrease in polymorphonuclear neutrophils among highland natives when compared with sea-level residents (Stammers, 1933). However, no pertinent changes were reported in monocytes, eosinophils, bands (immature neutrophils), or

TABLE 13.4 *Summary of Hematological Observations Among Men of Nuñoa (4000 m) and Macusani (4400 m)*[a]

Variable	Nuñoa Quechua			Macusani Quechua			Nuñoa Mestizos		
	N	Mean	S.D.	N	Mean	S.D.	N	Mean	S.D.
RBC (10^6/mm^3)	37	5.63	0.57	100	5.53[b]	—	19	5.92	0.4
Hemoglobin (g/100 ml)	38	17.5	1.5	114	16.7[b]	—	20	18.2	1.3
Hematocrit (%)	39	51.4	4.0	114	53.1[b]	—	20	53.6	3.0
Reticulocytes (%)[c]	24	0.78	0.28	117	0.66	0.22	11	0.84	0.3
MCV(μ^3)[c]	157	88.9	7.1	105	88.2	8.1	19	91.4	5.7
MCH (pg)[c]	158	30.2	2.5	105	28.5	2.5	19	31.2	2.2
MCHC (g/100 ml)[c]	158	33.9	1.5	119	32.3	1.7	20	34.0	1.8
WBC (10^3/mm^3)	39	7.88	1.9	115	8.87[b]	—	20	7.30	1.7
Neutrophils (%)									
Polymorphonuclear	41	50.0	12.4	115	55.0[b]	—	18	51.5	10.5
Bands[c]	171	1.5	1.6	120	2.4	2.2	18	1.2	1.3
Lymphocytes (%)	41	37.7	12.6	115	33.6[b]	—	18	40.0	9.8
Monocytes (%)[c]	171	3.0	1.8	120	4.6	2.8	18	2.9	2.2
Eosinophils (%)[c]	171	5.0	4.8	120	4.9	5.1	18	3.8	3.5
Basophils (%)[c]	171	0.4	0.6	120	0.3	0.6	18	0.6	0.7

[a]Mean age for Nuñoa Quechua was 35.7; S.D., 9.9; range, 22–56; for Nuñoa Mestizos it was 30.0; S.D., 11.1; range, 19–52.
[b]Values estimated from regression equations in Table 13.1 for 22-yr-old individuals.
[c]Adult and preadult data combined since variable was not age-related.

basophils (Chiodi, 1950; Hurtado et al., 1947; Hurtado, 1964b; Peterson and Peterson, 1935; Stammers, 1933).

Means, standard deviations, and regression analysis for total white cell, polymorphonuclear neutrophil, and lymphocyte counts in Nuñoa and Macusani boys are summarized in Tables 13.1, 13.5, and 13.6 and Fig. 13.1. The white cell counts decreased from middle childhood to young adulthood, a trend observed in sea-level populations (Albritton, 1952). Yet white cell counts during childhood, especially between 6 and 10 yr of age, appeared to be slightly higher than in sea-level children and may be indicative of the high incidence of respiratory disorders found among Andean children (Buck et al., 1967; Spector, 1971). This finding is especially significant for the Macusani population, which resides at an elevation that is 400 m higher and has a colder and wetter climate than Nuñoa.

Both highland communities demonstrated an increase in polymorphonuclear neutrophils and decrease in lymphocytes with age. While consistent with the trends observed at sea level, the absolute values for lymphocytes were higher, and those for polymorphonuclear neutrophils lower, than would be expected for healthy sea-level children and adolescents (Albritton, 1952). Stammers (1933) has suggested that elevated lymphocyte counts at high

TABLE 13.5 *Age Distributions for Total White Blood Cell*
Counts and Percentage of Polymorphonuclear
Neutrophils and Lymphocytes Among Nuñoa Boys

Age	White cell count ($10^3/mm^3$)			Neutrophils (%)			Lymphocytes (%)		
	N	Mean	S.D.	N	Mean	S.D.	N	Mean	S.D.
6	2	10.2	1.59	2	42.5	14.85	2	47.0	19.80
7	1	10.3	–	1	31.0	–	1	60.0	–
8	2	10.0	3.39	2	53.5	14.85	2	41.5	13.43
9	4	9.29	1.83	4	37.8	9.46	4	49.0	13.49
10	7	8.15	2.23	7	45.1	14.99	7	45.0	13.12
11	13	8.68	2.48	13	49.0	10.29	13	43.0	9.25
12	9	8.51	0.77	9	49.5	13.96	9	43.8	12.46
13	17	7.69	1.34	16	47.2	12.13	16	42.4	13.07
14	13	7.67	1.26	12	41.8	11.60	12	49.6	11.71
15	21	8.04	1.94	20	49.8	12.82	20	43.9	10.59
16	4	7.99	0.65	4	49.0	12.99	4	42.2	10.63
17	9	9.01	1.56	8	48.5	11.34	8	41.8	10.66
18	9	7.82	1.81	9	49.7	8.57	9	41.3	9.72
19	12	8.01	2.37	12	53.2	10.26	12	37.3	11.43
20	9	9.02	3.07	8	52.1	9.26	8	34.4	2.45
21	3	7.80	0.66	3	59.0	3.61	3	35.3	3.06
22	1	7.00	–	2	51.5	0.71	2	32.5	9.19

TABLE 13.6   *Age Distributions for Total White Cell Counts and Percentage of Polymorphonuclear Nuetrophils and Lymphocytes Among Mucusani Boys*

Age	White cell count $(10^3/mm^3)$			Neutrophils (%)			Lymphocytes (%)		
	N	Mean	S.D.	N	Mean	S.D.	N	Mean	S.D.
6	6	9.17	1.47	6	57.0	6.99	6	31.5	6.56
7	9	9.04	1.83	9	46.3	6.22	9	41.7	4.58
8	9	9.23	2.32	9	44.7	7.91	9	41.0	8.12
9	6	10.82	1.94	6	43.3	7.37	6	44.8	12.02
10	11	9.23	1.07	11	51.3	9.24	11	37.2	9.90
11	5	8.90	0.48	5	47.4	7.20	5	40.0	5.43
12	10	8.88	1.36	10	45.8	8.88	10	42.1	8.81
13	9	8.58	1.24	9	46.6	6.84	9	41.0	6.96
14	6	8.30	1.59	6	54.5	7.61	6	31.7	9.67
15	9	10.13	2.40	9	48.4	8.11	9	38.2	7.51
16	12	8.81	1.27	12	55.4	6.36	12	34.2	6.07
17	6	7.77	0.86	6	53.7	9.40	6	30.7	9.79
18	8	9.79	2.83	8	53.6	12.37	8	33.6	9.70
19	3	10.57	3.14	3	46.7	3.21	3	43.3	3.22
20	4	8.47	1.82	4	59.8	16.88	4	32.0	14.33
21	1	8.20	–	1	50.0	–	1	42.0	–
22	1	7.20	–	1	54.0	–	1	34.0	–

altitude may be a product of increased intensity of ultraviolet radiation and increased exposure to it. The high incidence of chronic respiratory infections could also contribute to these changes, but presently no definitive evidence accounts for this condition.

Other white cell types—monocytes, eosinophils, bands (immature neutrophils), and basophils—were neither age- nor altitude-related, and mean values were generally consistent with those of healthy sea-level residents (Table 13.4). The slightly higher eosinophil counts, however, may have indicated the presence of mild parasitic infections or allergies in these populations.

Adulthood

In contrast to the paucity of information available for highland children and adolescents, numerous studies of peripheral-blood responses to chronic hypoxic stress have been reported for adult populations; the more complete studies are summarized in Table 13.7.

Most investigations above 4000 m were conducted in the mining community of Morococha, located at 4500 m in the central Peruvian Andes. Mean red cell counts between 6.0 and 6.7 million/mm^3, as well as corresponding hemoglobin concentrations and hematocrits greater than 20 g/100 ml and 59 percent, respectively, were reported, indicating the presence of a severe polycythemia in the population. In some recent investigations, however, at altitudes between 3700 and 4300 m, the 25–30 percent increases observed in earlier studies have not been found, but rather values which are consistent with or only slightly above those for sea-level residents (Moulin, 1971; Reynafarje et al., 1966; Salguero-Silva, 1971). For example, Moulin (1971) in a study of Aymara and Quechua Indians of the altiplano area near Lake Titicaca found that individual red cell counts were seldom above 6 million/ mm^3 with a majority of values between 5.3 and 5.8 million/mm^3. Based on his observations at different altitude gradients, Moulin (1971) concluded that the red cell count and corresponding hemoglobin concentration and hemato- crit, while slowly increasing with altitude, did not demonstrate the rather dramatic changes noted previously. Moulin's results were confirmed by Salguero-Silva (1971) on populations near La Paz, Bolivia.

Among Nuñoa Quechua men, the mean red cell count was found (Gar- ruto, 1973) to be approximately 5.6 million/mm^3, with a corresponding hemoglobin concentration and hematocrit of 17.5 g/100 ml and 51.4 percent, respectively (Table 13.4). These values represent a 10–12 percent increase above the means established for sea level, Lima residents (Table 13.7) and reflect at most only a slight polycythemic response to hypoxic stress. In Macusani, no samples were obtained from adults over 22 because of the resistance encountered against the taking of blood specimens; therefore, the red and white cell values for Macusani Quechua adults were estimated from the regression equations for 22-year-old individuals, the oldest age for which there are actual data (Table 13.1). These estimated adult values, summarized in Table 13.4, are comparable to those of the Nuñoa Quechua. In contrast to the Quechua samples, the Nuñoa Mestizos demonstrated values about 15–17 percent higher than those for Lima residents, indicating a moderate poly- cythemic response to altitude hypoxia (Table 13.4).

The distribution of the red cell counts, hemoglobin concentrations and hematocrits among Nuñoa Quechua and Mestizo adults is shown in Table 13.8. The Lima sea-level range (Hurtado, 1964b) is RBC, 4.4–5.8 million/ mm^3; hemoglobin concentration, 14.0–17.3 g/100 ml; hematocrit, 41.8–51.4 percent. The U.S. sea-level range (Albritton, 1952; Altman and Dittmer, 1961; Wintrobe, 1967) is RBC, 4.6–6.2 million/mm^3; hemoglobin concentra- tion, 14–18 g/100 ml; hematocrit, 40–54 percent. Between 42 and 78 percent of the Quechua and between 35 and 68 percent of the Mestizos fall within the Lima sea-level ranges established for 95 percent of the sample (Hurtado, 1964b). When U.S. sea-level ranges for male adults are compared, between 52 and 93 percent of the Quechua and between 40 and 84 percent of the Mestizos fall within the established limits (Albritton, 1952; Altman and Dittmer, 1961; Wintrobe, 1967). It is not known whether the differences between highland Quechua and Mestizos are biologically based or just the compound effects of cultural differences complicated by a modest Mestizo sample size.

TABLE 13.7 *Hematological Findings Among Adult Men Resident at Various Altitudes (Mean Values)*

Reference	Altitude (m)	Sample size	RBC (10^6/mm^3)	Hgb (g/100 ml)	HCT (%)	Retics (%)	MCV (μ^3)	MCH (pg)	MCHC (g/100 ml)	WBC (10^3/mm^3)	PMN[a] (%)	Lymphs (%)	Monos (%)	Eos (%)	Bands (%)	Basos (%)
Hurtado (1932b)	4500	25–132	6.7	15.9[b]	71.1		96.2	24.4		5.2	69.0	24.5	6.1	0.3	<0.1	<0.1
Hurtado et al. (1947)	4500	32	6.2	20.8	59.9	1.5	97.5	33.9	34.7	6.9	49.9	39.4	5.5	2.2	3.0	0.2
Chiodi (1950)	4500	66–84	6.5	19.4	59.5		92.4	29.9	32.7	6.7	44.1	35.6	10.2	2.9	6.3	0.8
Lawrence et al. (1952)[c]	4500	11	6.7	19.3	57.0	1.7	85.1	28.8	33.9	7.7	58.0	35.0	5.0	2.0	0.1	7.5
Hurtado (1964b)[c]	4500	72–83	6.4	20.1	59.5	1.0	93.0	31.4	33.6	7.0	51.3	35.8	5.7	3.3	4.1	0–3
Reynafarje (1966b)	4500	50	6.5	20.2	60.0		92.0	31.8	33.7[c]							
Salguero-Silva (1971)[c]	3700		5.3	16.5	47.7		90.0	31.1	34.6							
Hurtado et al. (1947)	3700	40	5.7	18.8	54.1	0.8	95.2	33.0	34.8	6.5	52.8	34.8	4.9	2.5	5.0	0.1
Okin et al. (1966)	3100	65	5.4	17.7	49.0		92.6	32.7	35.1							
Treger et al. (1965)	3100	15	5.5	17.2	49.4		90.5	31.6	34.9							
Anderson and Mugrage (1936)	1600	40	5.4	16.5	48.4		89.2	30.5	34.2							
Okin et al. (1966)	1600	95	5.3	16.6	48.5		91.1	31.0	34.7							
Hurtado et al. (1947)	S.L. (Lima)	175	5.1	16.0	46.8	0.5	90.2	31.2	34.1	6.8	55.1	29.8	7.2	4.2	2.6	0.6
Hurtado (1964b)[c]	S.L. (Lima)	250	5.1	15.6	46.6	0.4	91.4	30.6	33.5	6.7	52.7	32.4	6.4	4.1	4.0	0–4
Albritton (1952)	S.L. (U.S.)		5.4	15.8	47.0	1.5	87.0	29.0	33.5	7.4	56.0	34.0	4.0	2.7	3.0	0.5
Wintrobe (1967)	S.L. (U.S.)		5.4	16.4	47.0		87.0	29.0	34.0	7.0	54–62	25–33	3–7	1–3	3–5	0–0.75
Williams et al. (1972)	S.L. (U.S.)	186	5.1	15.5	46.0		90.1	30.2	33.9	7.2	56.0	34.0	4.0	2.7	3.0	0.5

[a]Polymorphonuclear neutrophils.
[b]Value reported by Hurtado to be incorrect.
[c]MCV, MCH, MCHC were computed from the mean red cell count, hemoglobin, and hematocrit given in the published reports.

TABLE 13.8   *Distribution of Red*
Cell Values Among
Nuñoa Quechua and
Mestizo Adults

Variable	Quechua		Mestizos	
	N	f (%)	N	f (%)
RBC (10^6/mm^3)				
≤4.4	1	2.7	0	0
4.5–4.9	6	16.2	0	0
5.0–5.4	6	16.2	1	5.3
5.5–5.9	16	43.2	12	63.2
6.0–6.4	6	16.2	3	15.8
≥6.5	2	5.4	3	15.8
Total	37		19	
Hemoglobin (g/100 ml)				
≤14.9	2	5.3	0	0
15.0–15.9	3	7.9	0	0
16.0–16.9	9	23.7	6	30.0
17.0–17.9	6	15.8	2	10.0
18.0–18.9	12	31.6	3	15.0
19.0–19.9	4	10.5	7	35.0
≥20.0	2	5.3	2	10.0
Total	38		20	
Hematocrit (%)				
≤44	0	0	0	0
45–48	10	25.6	1	5.0
49–52	18	46.1	5	25.0
53–56	8	20.5	11	55.0
57–60	2	5.1	3	15.0
≥61	1	2.6	0	0
Total	39		20	

The peripheral blood smears indicated no reticulocytosis among the adult samples, although the higher counts were found among the Mestizos. Like the reticulocyte count, the red cell indices—MCV, MCH, and MCHC—were not age-related and, in Table 13.4, were combined with the preadult data. The indices, within the range for healthy sea-level residents, were generally consistent with the observations of previous investigators (Table 13.7). Finally, the peripheral blood smears and red cell indices indicated no evidence of anemia; thus the suggestion that abnormal red cell and hemoglobin production in the face of an iron or protein deficiency would result in a relative anemia masking the adaptive polycythemia is not tenable.

Summarized in Table 13.4 are the mean leucocyte cell counts and mean values for the differential leucocyte cell types. Consistent with the observations of previous investigators of highland populations, the white cell counts were within the normal sea-level range with the exception of those of a few individuals who were suffering from common respiratory infections. In general, mean polymorphonuclear neutrophil counts were lower and lymphocyte counts higher than those expected for healthy sea-level residents; values for monocytes, eosinophils, bands, and basophils were within the normal sea-level range. These observations concur with observations on preadults.

PERIPHERAL BLOOD CHANGES DURING STRENUOUS PHYSICAL ACTIVITY

The association between physical activity and hematological change has primarily been studied among low-altitude residents. Such studies at sea level help to provide information on whether the increased rate of tissue oxygen utilization during strenuous physical activity is met by an elevation in blood oxygenation through an absolute increase in the red cell mass and hemoglobin concentration of the blood. Among highland residents the oxygen-consumption demands of the tissues may be critically intensified by prolonged strenuous physical activity.

Berry et al. (1949) in a study of 147 Olympic athletes at sea level discovered no significant differences in hemoglobin concentration between athletes involved in events demanding strength and endurance and athletes in skill events. In addition, both groups had a mean hemoglobin concentration of approximately 16 g/100 ml, a value consistent with sea-level norms. Astrand (1952) also found that the hemoglobin concentration was not increased by athletic training, while Kjellberg et al. (1949) concluded that physical work capacity was directly related to total body hemoglobin levels.

During a study of short-term responses to intense exercise levels among healthy sea-level policemen, Nylin (1947) found a decrease in total blood volume with a corresponding increase in the hematocrit. He attributed the results to a loss in plasma volume, thus suggesting that hemoconcentration had taken place. Nylin's study was supported by Holmgren (1956), who found that hemoconcentration took place during intense exercise periods, with no evidence to support emptying of the blood reservoirs. In contrast to these studies, Davis and Brewer (1935) found that, in dogs subjected to controlled nutritional and exercise conditions, there was a true increase in hemoglobin concentration, red cell count, total circulating hemoglobin, and red cell mass. During 2 months of prolonged physical activity, initial responses showed a hemoconcentration, but after the first week, the total blood volume increased with a corresponding increase in hemoglobin and red cell mass. Davis and Brewer, therefore, suggested that the O_2 debt of prolonged physical exercise was the stimulus to increased blood formation. The sea-level data thus far remain conflicting.

Grover et al. (1967) has compared high-altitude native athletes of Leadville, Colorado (3100 m), to sea-level athletes. They demonstrated that the performance of the high-altitude athletes either at high altitude or sea level was not statistically different from that of lowland athletes. Furthermore, mean hemoglobin concentration, hematocrit, and red-cell-count values for Leadville athletes were the same as those found in the general Leadville population. There is, however, a general lack of information on the relationship between hematological change and prolonged physical activity among native highlanders living in their natural environment.

In the study reported by Garruto (1973), highland Quechua men from Nuñoa (4000 m) were selected for a 4-week study of hematological responses to strenuous physical activity. By studying selected hematological responses in individuals over an extended period of time, it is possible to eliminate the initial effects of hemoconcentration as well as to detect any changes in blood values that could not be accounted for solely by normal diurnal or weekly variation.

Complete work histories for a 3-month period preceding the investigation were obtained from each individual. Blood specimens were collected prior to the study and at the end of each of 3 successive weeks of monitored work loads. The fourth and final week was limited to tasks involving only light physical activity. The type of strenuous physical work imposed included preparing the chacra for planting, as well as other traditional tasks normally performed by the highland Quechua. All individuals were required to live at the Nuñoa high-altitude research laboratory for the duration of the investigation, to control such factors as nutrition, sleep, and activity levels.

The individual red cell counts, hemoglobin concentrations, and hematocrits are summarized in Table 13.9 and represented in Figs. 13.2–13.4. At least two individuals, Subjects 1152 and 1156, had values consistent with sea-level norms prior to the start of the investigation, while the remaining five individuals showed various degrees of polycythemia. The work histories for these five individuals indicated that they were involved in strenuous physical activities during the 3 months prior to the investigation, and the other two subjects were not. In addition, Subject 1153, a 48-yr-old man, did not expend nearly as much energy as did the others during this 4-week study. The daily assessment of individual energy expenditure was qualitative rather than quantitative; therefore, the individual daily work outputs during the 4 weeks may not be comparable with one another.

Individual red cell counts, hemoglobin concentrations, and hematocrits fluctuated inconsistently during the first 3 weeks of strenuous physical

TABLE 13.9 *Individual Weekly Hematological Responses Among Seven Nuñoa Quechua Indians During Strenuous Physical Activity*

Subject	Before study	Week 1	Week 2	Week 3	Week 4
		RBC (10^6/mm^3)			
1152	5.14	5.15	5.13	5.51	5.17
1153	5.75	5.36	5.13	5.28	4.86
1154	6.40	6.47	6.83	6.14	6.14
1155	5.81	5.64	5.51	5.43	5.55
1156	4.81	4.87	5.19	5.64	4.93
1157	6.18	6.38	6.21	6.29	5.89
1158	5.88	6.50	6.25	6.34	5.88
		Hemoglobin (g/100 ml)			
1152	16.2	16.4	17.3	17.5	16.7
1153	18.5	17.0	16.5	17.2	16.4
1154	–	20.2	21.8	20.6	19.2
1155	18.7	18.1	17.1	16.2	17.1
1156	15.2	15.0	15.2	16.0	15.3
1157	17.5	18.3	17.5	17.6	16.4
1158	18.7	18.5	20.1	19.2	18.5
		Hematocrit (%)			
1152	47	46	50	51	48
1153	53	48	46	49	48
1154	56	55	57	55	55
1155	52	47	48	48	48
1156	42	42	43	46	44
1157	50	50	52	51	47
1158	54	53	55	53	51

activity, with some individuals showing increases and other decreases from one week to the next. No discernible patterns were noted. During the fourth and final week, however, when the imposed activity levels were decreased from strenuous to light, there was an overall decrease in the red cell count, hemoglobin concentration, and hematocrit. In five of the individuals, values were consistent with the normal sea-level range; one was a borderline polycythemic, and one a definite polycythemic.

Although it is difficult to assess the fluctuations that occurred in these values during the first 3 weeks of strenuous work activity, the results do indicate a consistent decrease during the final week. The inconsistent changes during the first 3 weeks might have been the result of differential work output, since physical activity was not quantitatively measured. The weekly sample means, as a statistical measure of central tendency, should therefore

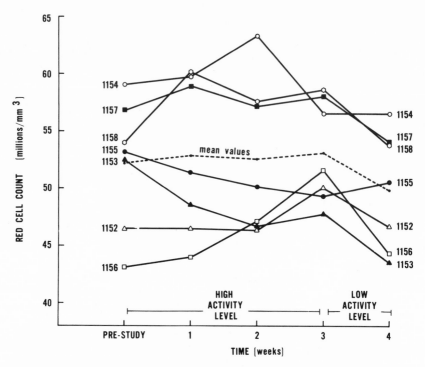

FIGURE 13.2 *Individual and mean weekly red cell counts during strenuous physical activity among Nuñoa highland Indians.*

be viewed cautiously (Table 13.10). In addition, the changes in these hematological values noted during this time period might have been the direct result of diurnal or weekly variation, while the consistency with which the individual red cell counts, hemoglobin concentrations, and hematocrits decreased during the final week may be indicative of the decreased work load, from strenuous to light.

Table 13.10 also summarizes the changes noted in the mean reticulocyte counts during the 4-week study period. There was an increase in the reticulocyte counts, from a mean pre-study value of 0.68 percent, to 1.18 percent at the end of the third week, which decreased slightly to 1.12 percent at the end of the final week. These changes appear to reflect a slight increase in bone marrow activity. The red cell indices of MCV, MCH, and MCHC, while changing slightly throughout the testing period, were, overall, equivalent to normal sea-level values.

Mean weekly changes in the white cell counts did not indicate any particular significance; values increased and decreased throughout the 4-week period. All mean values, however, were at the middle to upper limits of the normal range. Clinical respiratory symptoms were particularly noticeable in

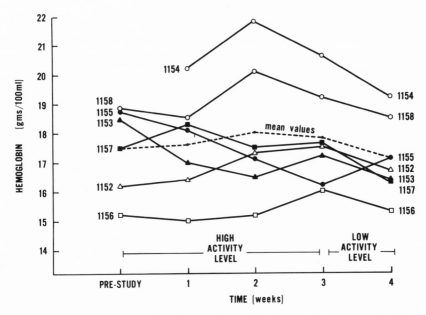

FIGURE 13.3 *Individual and mean weekly hemoglobin concentrations during strenuous physical activity among Nuñoa highland Indians.*

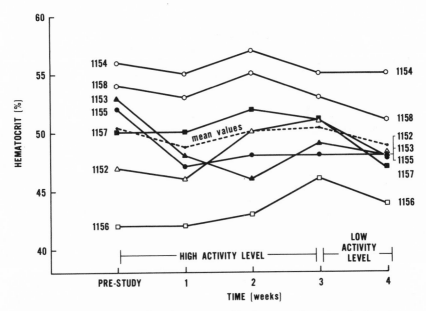

FIGURE 13.4 *Individual and mean weekly hematocrit ratios during strenuous physical activity among Nuñoa highland Indians.*

TABLE 13.10 *Mean Weekly Changes in Erythrocyte and Leucocyte Values During Strenuous Physical Activity Among Seven Nuñoa Quechua Indians*

Variable	Before study		Week 1		Week 2		Week 3		Week 4	
	Mean	S.D.	Mean	S.D.	Mean	S.D.	Mean	S.D.	Mean	S.D.
RBC (10^6/mm³)	5.72	0.56	5.77	0.68	5.75	0.68	5.80	0.43	5.49	0.51
Hemoglobin (g/100 ml)	17.5[a]	1.5	17.6	1.7	18.0	2.2	17.8	1.6	17.1	1.3
Hematocrit (%)	50.4	4.7	48.7	4.4	50.1	4.9	50.4	3.0	48.7	3.4
Reticulocytes (%)	0.68[b]	0.14	0.70[c]	0.20	0.73[d]	0.20	1.18[c]	0.36	1.12[a]	0.70
MCV (μ^3)	88.3	3.6	84.7	4.1	87.4	5.0	87.3	5.0	89.1	5.9
MCH (pg)	31.3	1.6	30.7	1.6	31.3	2.0	30.7	2.4	31.1	1.8
MCHC (g/100 ml)	35.3	0.8	36.4	1.4	36.0	1.4	35.1	1.0	35.1	0.7
WBC (10^3/mm³)	8.43	2.25	9.12	1.54	8.35	1.69	7.99	1.7	9.62	1.81
Neutrophils (%)										
Polymorphonuclear	51.7	11.7	42.1	11.1	48.4	10.4	54.4	12.8	58.0	6.9
Bands	1.7	0.9	0.7	0.9	1.3	0.9	2.8	1.6	2.1	1.5
Lymphocytes (%)	33.8	11.6	43.6	6.6	37.6	7.4	31.0	10.7	29.0	8.0
Monocytes (%)	2.8	1.6	3.4	1.4	1.8	1.9	1.6	2.1	2.3	1.7
Eosinophils (%)	9.8	6.1	9.7	6.0	10.7	7.8	9.7	7.0	8.4	8.7
Basophils (%)	0.0	—	0.4	0.8	0.1	0.3	0.4	0.8	0.0	—

[a]Based on six cases.
[b]Based on four cases.
[c]Based on five cases.
[d]Based on three cases.

individuals 1154 and 1156; at times their individual counts were greater than 12,000/mm^3, thus affecting the represented mean values considerably (Garruto, 1973). The weekly changes noted in the polymorphonuclear neutrophil, lymphocyte, and monocyte counts may reflect the noted respiratory infections observed in some individuals as well as the result of the imposed physical activity. Eosinophil counts were twice as high as the mean for the general adult Nuñoa population; the eosinophilia might be the direct result of some parasitic infection or allergic reaction. However, no substantive conclusions could be drawn from the leucocyte data.

OVERVIEW

This study, on peripheral blood responses to chronic hypoxic stress among highland Quechua Indians who live a traditional life as subsistence farmers and herders, has established baseline hematological data on children and adolescents of native highland Quechua populations as well as providing additional data on highland adults. Observations on hematological change during strenuous physical activity are still inconclusive. Nuñoa and Macusani residents probably still require the physiological adaptation of a low level of polycythemia, albeit by no means as severe a polycythemia as has been generally proposed in earlier works and reviews.

While the concept of ecological and evolutionary adaptation to the environment provides a unified framework for the study of biological variability within and between human populations, many difficulties arise in assessing adaptational responses to environmental stressors, at both population and individual levels. Most, if not all, field studies among human populations are hindered by the lack of controlled conditions. Specifically, controlling for such parameters as age, sex, race, disease, nutritional status, physical activity, stress intensity, and exposure time, as well as a whole host of other cultural, biological, and environmental factors, becomes a major task. Therefore, it is not surprising that many studies are in general disagreement, having, at times, greatly divergent conclusions.

In assessing the degree to which biological responses are adaptive, empirical observations as well as core data have suggested the presence of optimal, and also critical physiological levels in native Andean populations. If these levels are narrowly defined, then the highland native may be precariously adapted to chronic hypoxic stress. A different or increased load on the physiological system, upsetting the tight balance that may exist, could potentially negate the benefits derived from adaptational responses. For example, at barometric pressures two-thirds to one-half that of sea level, increasing the O$_2$ content of arterial blood by increasing the red cell mass would appear to help alleviate a tissue oxygen deficit. In severe polycythemia, however, the adaptive benefits may be minimized because the resultant increase in blood viscosity increases the work load on the cardiopulmonary system. An additional example is cited by Lenfant and Sullivan (1971). They point out that among highland populations a shift to the right in the oxygen–hemoglobin dissociation curve, favoring the release of oxygen from the blood to the tissues through an increase in red-cell 2,3-diphosphoglycerate, may not have absolute importance, as once thought. When the arterial oxygen pressure greatly declines, the increased unloading of oxygen in the tissue is offset by the decreased binding of oxygen to hemoglobin in lungs. Below 3500 m, Lenfant and Sullivan claim a substantial advantage, while at higher altitudes the advantage is minimal. Optimal and critical physiological levels, therefore, present limits beyond which loss of efficiency and frank pathological conditions may ensue. The overall importance of such mechanisms to increased tissue oxygenation, at least under certain conditions, is questionable, and the net positive effect is very small.

Finally, and possibly most important, is the problem of selecting and studying only certain processes of an interrelated biological system and deriving conclusions about adaptation solely on those aspects studied. It is apparent that the study of polycythemia as an adaptive response to hypoxic stress is only one part of a coordinated biological system in the functional adaptation of human populations to chronic hypoxic stress. While it becomes difficult and occasionally impossible to study all the mechanisms involved, and to incorporate them into a single research program, it is imperative to analyze the responses observed in one part of the system in relation to the other parts. Thus a substantial increase in the number of circulating red cells may be of little or no advantage in tissue oxygenation without a corresponding increase in capillarity. The obvious point, then, is that the parts of any coordinated biological system are interrelated and that conclusions about adaptational processes should be made only after considering the effects of all the interrelated physiological mechanisms.

Moreover, other questions concerning the necessity for increased tissue vascularization, the effects of decreased plasma volume, the view that altitude polycythemia is a chronic state rather than an intermittent or short-term condition, and the extent to which such factors as strenuous physical activity, sleep, and metabolism provoke a polycythemic response need to be answered. Further study in Nuñoa and Macusani is needed, especially in the area of erythrokinetics. We may find that assessing adaptational responses in terms of degree and kind is less profitable than defining Andean man in terms of his biological and cultural efficiency within his environment.

14

WORK PERFORMANCE OF NEWCOMERS TO THE PERUVIAN HIGHLANDS

Elsworth R. Buskirk

Performance capacity is difficult to assess. Nevertheless, it has been known for many years that at high altitude, physical performance capacity is lower for the newcomer than the acclimatized native (Dill et al., 1964; Hurtado, 1932a, 1964a, 1964b, 1966). Of particular concern to investigators exploring the physical-performance-capacity problem is understanding not only the impact of hypoxia on the organism, but also the differential impact on groups of subjects who vary in important ways—genetic background, physical conditioning, and previous environmental exposure to hypoxia.

As part of the integrated study of man's acclimatization and adaptation to the habitable highland region of Peru, it was possible to evaluate the effect of upward terrestrial movement by various groups including: relatively sedentary faculty, staff, and graduate students from The Pennsylvania State University; well-conditioned, middle-distance track athletes from The Pennsylvania State University; Quechua native to Peru who were moved from the lowlands to the highlands (Mazess, personal communication); and Quechua who resided on the altiplano. The studies reported in this chapter comprised one of the initial efforts (1965) utilizing the newly constructed laboratory at Nuñoa, Peru. In fact, one of the first tasks of those in the party who performed the initial work-capacity evaluations was to finish the construction of the laboratory, including the electrical system, and to install the equipment and apparatus that would serve the several investigators who followed.

Perhaps more information is available on the physiological consequences of upward movement—that is, from low to high altitude, than for any other aspect of altitude physiology (Consolazio et al., 1966; Dill et al., 1964; Hansen et al., 1966). Thus, the present treatment complements the related information in the literature, largely by treatment of special groups: athletes, sedentary whites, sedentary natives, and so on. Perhaps one of best-documented features related to the applied physiology of upwardly mobile man is the reduction in aerobic capacity at altitude. And his aerobic capacity remains depressed even with acclimatization periods as long as several months or years. The reduction in aerobic capacity is indeed associated with hypoxia, but the physiological correlates remain poorly explained. Comparison with aerobic capacity data from natives residing at high altitude provide a reference base for interpreting data on upward migrants or newcomers to altitude. An earlier interpretation indicated that high-altitude Quechua achieved sea-level values for aerobic capacity (Velásquez, 1964), thus suggesting complete acclimatization to their altitude of residence. During the investigations reported here, the assumption was made that short-term acclimatization to high altitude will not produce in lowlanders the same aerobic capacity as that of native highland Quechua. The assumption was also made that the reduction in aerobic capacity was brought about largely by the environmental hypoxia and the associated reduction in the oxygen content of arterial blood supplying working muscle.

SUBJECTS, METHODS, AND PROCEDURES

In the initial series of experiments, six trained runners and six nonathletic personnel (U.S. white, sedentary) from The Pennsylvania State University (Penn State), together with eight Quechua native to Nuñoa, Peru, participated as subjects in maximal and submaximal exercise tests at 4000 m (actual elevation 3992 m). The barometric oxygen was 90 torr. The subjects' physical characteristics are presented in Table 14.1. All the runners, with the exception of one, had been regular competitors in cross-country as well as participants in events one-half mile (800 m) or longer; the exception was a quarter-miler (400 m). They had just completed their spring track season and each had won points for the Penn State team prior to participating in the study. One of the runners served as the coach and conducted regular training sessions in each environment in which the subjects stayed.

Separate portions of the work partially reported in abbreviated form here have been reported elsewhere by Buskirk and his colleagues (Baker, 1969; Buskirk, 1969, 1971; Buskirk et al., 1967a, 1967b; Buskirk and Mendez, 1967; Kollias and Buskirk, 1974; Kollias et al., 1968), and related work has been reported by Mazess (1969a, 1969b, 1970; Mazess et al., 1968).

The schedule of travel for the six runners and several of the nonathletic personnel is shown in Fig. 14.1. Travel between altitudes was as rapid as possible, although an unavoidable delay was experienced in Lima, Peru, because of problems associated with clearing equipment through Peruvian customs and making arrangements for transshipment to the highlands. Travel was by air to Cuzco, by train to Santa Rosa, and by truck to Nuñoa. On day 49 at altitude, three of the runners and one of the nonathletic personnel left Nuñoa and journeyed to Mt. Evans, Colorado, where they remained for 6 days. They then traveled to Alamosa, Colorado, and stayed there for 6 days before traveling through Denver back to Penn State. The remaining three runners remained in Nuñoa for 61 days before returning to Penn State. Two of the nonathletic personnel accompanied them. The data obtained after leaving Nuñoa are not reported here. The physical activities of the nonathletic

TABLE 14.1 *Physical Characteristics of Subjects in Exercise Tests*

Subjects	N	Age (yr)		Height (cm)		Weight (kg)		BSA (m²)	
		Mean	Range	Mean	Range	Mean	Range	Mean	Range
Kollias et al. (1968)									
Runners	6	20	19–22	178.7	170.9–184.3	71.5	64.1–75.6	1.88	1.73–1.96
U.S. whites, sedentary	6	30	22–40	182.9	173.7–193.6	79.4	65.9–91.8	2.00	1.86–2.20
Quechua	8	25	21–40	158.9	153.8–164.3	57.3	47.7–73.7	1.57	1.43–1.77
Mazess (personal communication)									
U.S. whites, sedentary	4	23	20–28	183.9	186.4–176.9	79.2	73.2–86.8	2.01	1.39–2.04
Sea-level Quechua	10	22	17–29	159.8	148.3–172.7	62.4	47.3–90.4	1.64	1.90–2.08

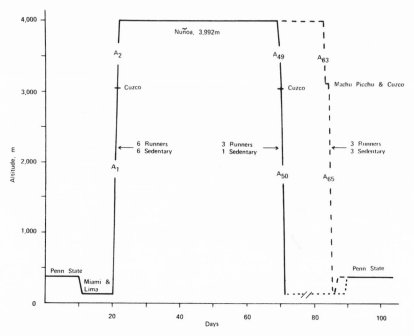

FIGURE 14.1 *Schematic schedule of travel and residence for the six U.S. white runners and six sedentary subjects.*

personnel remained comparable to their normal routines at sea level. The nonathletes occasionally played volleyball or went hiking for short distances. The occupations of the Quechua included pastoral herding, hand farming, or other general labor. Their recreation included soccer and walking long distances to visit others or to participate in fiestas. All the Quechua could ride a bicycle, but only one used a bicycle as a regular means of travel. It should be mentioned that bicycling in the area was difficult, for there were no paved highways but only gravel roads and dirt tracks.

All ergometric tests were conducted with a Monark bicycle ergometer. The maximal work test was designed to exhaust the subject in 10 min or less. After a 5-min warm-up ride of 3 kp (1080 kpm/min) at a pedaling frequency of 60 rpm and a 1- to 2-min rest, the initial load was retained for the first 2 min. Each minute thereafter, the load was increased 0.5 kp (180 kpm) until the subject could no longer maintain the pedaling frequency of 60 rpm (see Fig. 14.2). The highest oxygen consumption ($\dot{V}_{O_2}$) measured during the ride was recorded as the maximum oxygen intake ($\dot{V}_{O_2}$ max).

Two submaximal work tests were performed. The first consisted of riding the bicycle ergometer for 5 min at 3.0 kp and 60 rpm (1080 kpm/min). For the runners, the second submaximal test consisted of riding the bicycle ergometer for 30 min at the same work load, but the nonathletic U.S. whites and the Quechua rode at 2.5 kp and 60 rpm (900 kpm). Each of the submaximal tests required a $\dot{V}_{O_2}$ of at least 70 percent $\dot{V}_{O_2}$ max for all subjects.

A 10-min cumulative $\dot{V}_{O_2}$ measurement was made during the recovery period following the 5-min ride, and a 5-min cumulative $\dot{V}_{O_2}$ measurement after the 30-min ride. Measurements were routinely taken during the last minute of each submaximal ride.

Pace was facilitated during each ergometer ride by use of a metronome, but it was not always maintained, and the subjects were regularly reminded to keep pace. Despite such reminders, workloads did vary slightly because of pace irregularities. Since total pedal revolutions were counted, average pace could be calculated and actual calculated workloads are entered in the tables where appropriate.

Heart rate was measured with bipolar ECG telemetry or by stethoscopic auscultation over the apex of the heart. Each subject breathed through a low-resistance Collins Triple-J valve and expired through a short length of large-bore, low-resistance tubing into a mainfold system connected to a series

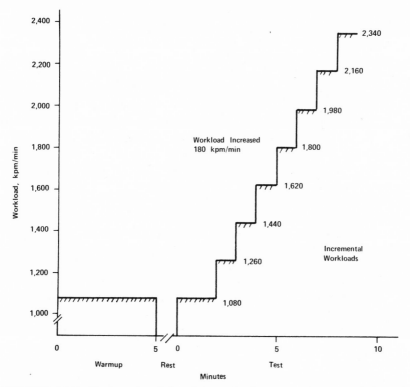

FIGURE 14.2 *Test protocol for the maximal test on the Monark bicycle ergometer.*

of Douglas bags. Upon completion of a test, the contents of each bag were allowed to come to room temperature and mixed. As the contents of each bag was evaluated through a low-resistance dry-gas meter to determine the volume of gas in the bag, a measured amount was drawn off, dried, and pumped through a paramagnetic oxygen analyzer (Beckman E-2) and an infrared carbon dioxide analyzer (Mine Safety Alliance, Lira Model 300). Thus, measurements of $\dot{V}_E$, $\dot{V}_{O_2}$, and $\dot{V}_{CO_2}$ were obtained and R was calculated.

The work-performance experiments could not have been carried out without the collaboration of E. Picón-Reátegui and T. Velásquez.

RESULTS

Maximal Work Capacity

The reduction in aerobic capacity at altitude as measured by the progressive maximal oxygen intake on the bicycle ergometer is presented in Table 14.2. Data are shown for the U.S. white sedentary men, the U.S. white runners, sea-level Quechua, and the *altiplano* Quechua residing at Nuñoa (Baker, 1969). An important feature of the comparison is a lesser percentage reduction in $\dot{V}_{O_2}$ max in the sea-level Quechua tested at 3992 m (see Fig. 14.3). The sea-level Quechua, on the basis of the $\dot{V}_{O_2}$ max criterion, appeared to be partially acclimatized to high altitude (even though they had not lived at high altitude), whereas the U.S. white sedentary subjects and runners were apparently not so acclimatized. If the ventilatory response ($\dot{V}_E$ max) measured during the $\dot{V}_{O_2}$ max test is used as the criterion for acclimatization, results appear comparable among all groups brought to and tested at 3992 m. Although differences among groups are suggested in Table 14.2 for the ventilatory equivalent for oxygen ($\dot{V}_E/\dot{V}_{O_2}$), these differences were not significant. In the newcomers, according to both $\dot{V}_E$ max and $\dot{V}_E/\dot{V}_{O_2}$, acclimatization to altitude appears to be incomplete—that is, both $\dot{V}_E$ and $\dot{V}_E/\dot{V}_{O_2}$ appear to be lower in the highland Quechua. Heart rate (HR max) at 3992 m showed no great change from heart rate at sea level measured at the level of work producing $\dot{V}_{O_2}$ max. A slight reduction in HR max occurred only in the U.S. white sedentary subjects. The data for oxygen pulse ($\dot{V}_{O_2}$ max/HR max) indicated lower values among all groups tested at altitude, in the direction approaching the value extant in the highland Quechua. When body size is taken into account among groups, the role of delivering oxygen to working muscles is reemphasized, for the highland Quechua delivered more oxygen per heart beat to each kilogram of body weight and presumably each kilogram of working muscle. At sea level the trained runner, because of his enhanced physical condition and greater ability to deliver oxygen to working muscles, had a much larger $\dot{V}_{O_2}$ max/HR max. The highland Quechua showed this same feature at altitude, for their unique altitude acclimatization

TABLE 14.2 *Mean Maximum Oxygen Utilization and Mean Related Measurements for Different Groups at Nuñoa, Peru (Altitude 4000 Meters)*

Subjects	Altitude of test (m)	Weeks at altitude	N	Age (yr)	Height (cm)	Weight (kg)	$\dot{V}_{O_2}$ max (l/min)	$\dot{V}_{O_2}$ max (cc/kg-min)	$\dot{V}_E$ max (l/min, STPD)	$\dot{V}_E$ max / $\dot{V}_{O_2}$ max	HR max	$\dot{V}_{O_2}$ max / HR max (cc/beat)
U.S. whites, sedentary	373	—	6	30	183	79	3.92	50.4	131	33.7	185	21.2
	4000	4	12	27	181	75	2.78	38.1	91	32.7	173	16.6
Decrement							1.14 (29%)	12.3 (14%)	40 (31%)	1.0 (3%)	12 (6%)	4.6 (22%)
U.S. whites, runners	373	—	6	20	179	71	4.58	64.2	131	28.8	175	26.5
	4000	4	6	20	179	71	3.14	46.6	105	33.7	172	19.4
Decrement							1.44 (31%)	17.6 (27%)	26 (20%)	4.9 (17%)	3 (2%)	7.1 (27%)
Sea-level Quechua	100	—	10	22	160	62	3.01	49.3	108	36.2	187	16.7
	4000	4	10	22	160	62	2.67	44.5	87	33.4	190	14.5
Decrement							0.34 (11%)	4.8 (10%)	21 (19%)	2.8 (8%)	3[a] (2%)	2.2 (13%)
Nuñoa Quechua	4000	Life	25	25	160	57	2.77	49.1	75	27.3	171	16.0

[a]Increment.

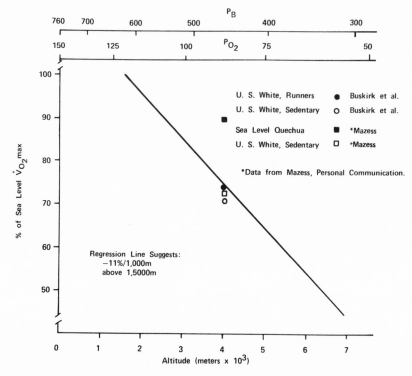

FIGURE 14.3 *Mean percentage reduction in maximal oxygen utilization ($\dot{V}_{O_2}$ max) from sea-level values for groups abruptly exposed to altitude of 4000 m at Nuñoa, Peru.*

yielded values for "oxygen pulse" quantitatively comparable to those of the well-trained athletes.

Ancillary information on $\dot{V}_{O_2}$ max and related physiological measurements for U.S. white sedentary subjects and sea-level Quechua tested both at sea level and altitude is provided in Table 14.3. The data were collected by Richard Mazess. The greater reduction in $\dot{V}_{O_2}$ max at high altitude in the U.S. white group is apparent. Other results are comparable, with the exception that the U.S. white subjects increased their $\dot{V}_E$ at high altitude largely through an increase in respiratory frequency (f) rather than through an increase in tidal volume (TV).

Maximal bicycle-riding time during performance of the $\dot{V}_{O_2}$ max test at 3992 m, shown in Fig. 14.4, provides one measure of work capacity. Note that the smaller highland Quechua rode the bicycle almost the same length of time as did the U.S. white sedentary subjects. The well-conditioned runners could achieve higher work loads and longer riding times than the other groups.

TABLE 14.3 *Mean Maximal Oxygen Utilization and Related Measurements in Ten Quechua and Four U.S. White Subjects Abruptly Moved to Nuñoa, Peru (Altitude 4000 Meters)*

Variable	Sea level		Altitude, 24–25 days		Decrement	
	Quechua	U.S. white	Quechua	U.S. white	Quechua	U.S. white
$\dot{V}O_2$ max (l/min)	3.01	3.67	2.67	2.96	0.34	0.71
$\dot{V}O_2$ max (cc/kg·min)	49.3	46.4	44.5	39.7	4.8	6.7
HR (beats/min)	187	196	190	189	3[a]	7
$\dot{V}_E$ max (l/min, STPD)	108.3	132.6	87.5	97.4	20.8	35.2
$\dot{V}_E$ max (l/min, BTPS)	131.0	160.4	177.1	197.1	46.1[a]	36.7[a]
$\dot{V}_E$ max/$\dot{V}O_2$ max (STPD)	36.0	36.1	32.8	32.9	3.2	3.2
$\dot{V}O_2$ max/HR max (cc/beat)	16.1	18.7	14.01	15.7	2.1	3.0

[a]Increment.

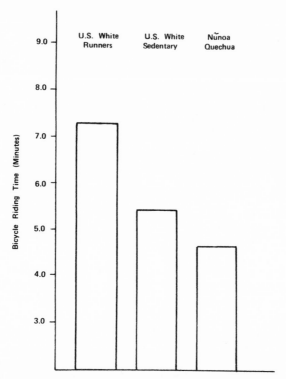

FIGURE 14.4 *Mean and range for maximal bicycle-riding time, in minutes, during the maximal work test used to elicit maximal oxygen intake. [Adapted from Kollias et al. (1968).]*

Submaximal Work

A summary of oxygen-consumption results during 5 min of hard submaximal work is shown in Fig. 14.5. Note that the results for the Quechua (both sea-level and highland groups) fall above those for the U.S. white subjects. The approximate mean difference between regression lines was 13 cm/kg-min. This difference has been interpreted to mean that the Quechua were less efficient on the bicycle ergometer at very high submaximal work loads. In Table 14.4 note that the Quechua were working at 91 percent of their $\dot{V}_{O_2}$ max, whereas the U.S. whites were working at 76 percent (Mazess, personal communication). This difference in relative work intensity was also reflected by the higher ventilation in the Quechua. Most other results during the performance of submaximal exercise were roughly comparable among the various groups.

During the performance of a slightly lower level of submaximal bicycle exercise, oxygen consumption was slightly higher on a body-weight basis in

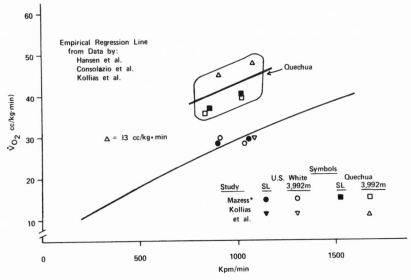

FIGURE 14.5 *Oxygen consumption per kilogram of body weight in young men who performed different work loads on the bicycle ergometer at sea level or an altitude of 4000 m.*

the Quechua than in the U.S. whites (see Table 14.4). Again the exercise ventilation in the Quechua as well as the relative workload was higher, even though their absolute work load was lower.

Oxygen utilization during a 10-min recovery period following 30 min of submaximal exercise is shown in Figure 14.6 in relation to the relative workload on the bicycle ergometer. Because the Quechua were working at a higher relative work load, their recovery oxygen consumption was also higher. A single regression line appears to fit all the data. Note the larger scatter of results for the Quechua, with the highland Quechua having much larger oxygen debts than the other two. Again a comparable absolute work load produced large differences in relative work load between the U.S. whites and the Quechua.

Mean total oxygen consumption per unit work load in relation to percent $\dot{V}_{O_2}$ max is shown in Figure 14.7. Note that the curvilinear empirical regression line appears to fit the data from all groups. The total oxygen requirement per unit work load is higher for the resident Quechua than for the U.S. whites.

Ventilation During Bicycle Exercise

The relationships between pulmonary ventilation during exercise and oxygen consumption among the various groups are shown in Fig. 14.8. The

TABLE 14.4 *Mean Submaximal Work-Load and Physiological Measurements During Work Periods at Sea Level and at 4000 Meters in Ten Quechua and Four U.S. White Subjects*

Variable	Sea level		Altitude, 24–25 days		Decrement	
	Quechua	U.S. white	Quechua	U.S. white	Quechua	U.S. white
	During the Last Minute of a 5-min Work Period					
Absolute kpm/min	1022	1057	1027	1035	5[a]	22
Relative $\dot{V}_{O_2}$ max (%)	85	68	91	76	6[a]	8[a]
$\dot{V}_{O_2}$ (l/min)	2.53	2.48	2.44	2.23	0.09	0.25
$\dot{V}_{O_2}$/kg (cc/kg-min)	40.8	29.6	39.6	28.8	1.2	0.8
HR (beats/min)	170	148	173	158	3[a]	10[a]
$\dot{V}_E$ (l/min, STPD)	78.1	62.1	69.1	57.7	9.0	4.4
$\dot{V}_E$ (l/min, BTPS)	94.5	75.1	139.9	116.8	45.4[a]	41.7[a]
$\dot{V}_E/\dot{V}_{O_2}$ (STPD)	30.8	25.1	28.4	26.0	2.4	0.9[a]
$\dot{V}_{O_2}$/HR (cc/beat)	14.9	16.8	14.1	14.1	0.8	2.7
	During a 30-min Work Period					
Absolute kpm/min	854	900	837	906	17	6[a]
Relative $\dot{V}_{O_2}$ max (%)	75	61	80	75	5[a]	14[a]
$\dot{V}_{O_2}$ (l/min)	2.25	2.22	2.16	2.22	0.09	0
$\dot{V}_{O_2}$/kg (cc/kg-min)	37.2	28.1	36.1	29.8	1.1	1.7[a]
HR (beats/min)	171	151	174	164	3[a]	13[a]
$\dot{V}_E$ (l/min, STPD)	67.4	54.2	61.0	55.8	6.4	1.6[a]
$\dot{V}_E$ (l/min, BTPS)	81.6	65.6	123.5	112.9	41.9[a]	47.3[a]
$\dot{V}_E/\dot{V}_{O_2}$ (STPD)	29.9	24.5	28.4	25.1	1.5	0.6[a]
$\dot{V}_{O_2}$/HR (cc/beat)	13.3	14.7	12.4	13.5	0.9	1.2

[a] Increment.

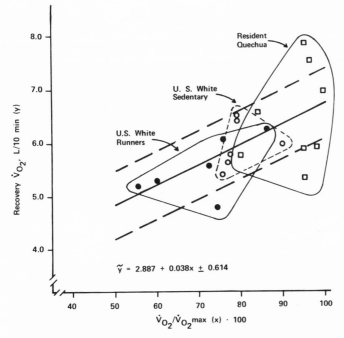

$$\tilde{y} = 2.887 + 0.038x \pm 0.614$$

FIGURE 14.6 *Oxygen utilization during recovery (10 min) in relation to relative oxygen intake (proportion of maximal oxygen intake) for U.S. white groups abruptly exposed to altitude of 4000 m at Nuñoa, Peru, and resident Quechua group. [Adapted from Kollias et al. (1968).]*

largest increments in ventilation per unit work load expressed in terms of oxygen utilization per kilogram of body weight were found in the U.S. whites, the smallest in the highland Quechua, and intermediate values in the sea-level Quechua. Thus, the respiratory drive occurring with hypoxia and exercise shows, perhaps, relatively poor adaptation in the U.S. whites and intermediate adaptation in the sea-level Quechua.

DISCUSSION

The prominent effects of hypoxia are readily apparent during the performance of hard work under hypoxic conditions (Figure 14.3). Newcomers to the highlands showed the common findings of reduced aerobic capacity and greater relative physiological strain at fixed work loads under hypoxic than under normoxic conditions. Study of resident highland Quechua shows that chronic acclimatization involving the growth and developmental years serves to reduce physiological strain. Nevertheless, the selection of comparable work

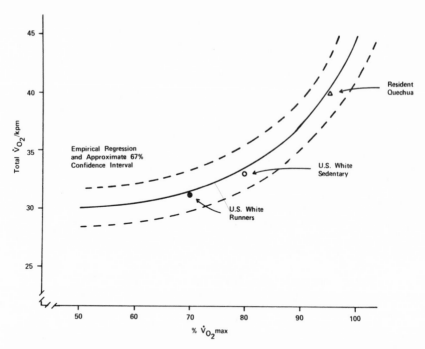

FIGURE 14.7 *Mean total oxygen consumption per unit work load ($\dot{V}_{O_2}/$ kpm) during work and 10-min recovery period in relation to mean relative work load expressed as percentage of maximal oxygen intake (% $\dot{V}_{O_2}$ max) for U.S. white groups abruptly exposed to altitude of 4000 m at Nuñoa, Peru, and resident Quechua group. [Adapted from Kollias et al. (1968).]*

loads to assess strain among different groups is difficult—for example, the simple assignment of fixed, supposedly submaximal work loads on a bicycle ergometer actually provides quite different relative work loads and associated physiological strains. Similarly, the important role of physical conditioning cannot be overlooked, since superior physical condition for dynamic work provides the organism with sufficient reserve to cope with considerable hypoxic stress. Thus, the increase in work performance developed through physical conditioning is useful, for those with highly developed aerobic capacities can carry out routine tasks at a relatively low fraction of their aerobic capacity even at moderately high altitude.

The aerobic capacity of sea-level Quechua was reduced less when they were tested at 4000 m than was the aerobic capacity for the U.S. whites. In Fig. 14.3, aerobic-capacity data in relation to the degree of hypoxia fall on the regression lines prepared from a variety of studies on newcomers. The data from the sea-level Quechua clearly fall above the regression line. Nevertheless, the sea-level Quechua failed to achieve the same aerobic capacity as

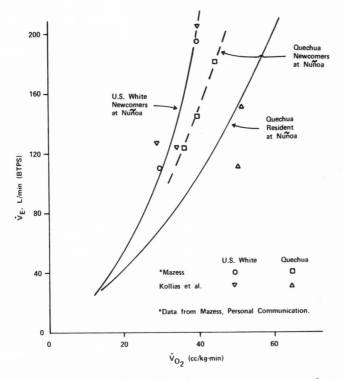

FIGURE 14.8 *Relationship between exercise ventilation* ($\dot{V}_E$) *and oxygen consumption* ($\dot{V}_{O_2}$) *in Quechua and U.S. white subjects abruptly moved to Nuñoa, Peru, and in Quechua who resided at 4000 m.*

the Quechua resident at 4000 m. The suggestion might well be made that a genetic factor of unknown origin modified the impact of hypoxia on the sea-level Quechua.

Although not clearly indicated here, the greatest reduction in aerobic capacity with hypoxia in newcomers occurs within the first few days; a slow, small increase occurs thereafter during sustained residence at moderately high altitude. There is little evidence to suggest that this small increase represents enhanced oxygen distribution to, and extraction and utilization by, working muscle, despite the fact that the acid–base balance has satisfactorily adjusted to the hyperpnea of hypoxia. Low aerobic-capacity values obtained during the first few days of exposure to hypoxia probably reflect the adverse effects of acute mountain sickness, however mild those effects might be.

Aerobic capacity is an integrated measure of oxygen uptake, transport, and utilization capacity. Any step in these processes can be limiting, and not all the contributing variables or limiting factors have been studied under conditions associated with normoxia, let alone hypoxia. There is the possibility, however, that a progressive fall in arterial oxygen saturation may occur with hypoxia despite a rise in alveolar oxygen partial pressure as the exercise level increases. There may well be group differences in this phenomenon, associated with extent of acclimatization. It is known that pulmonary diffusion capacity is improved with physical conditioning and perhaps with acclimatization to hypoxia. The less the pulmonary diffusing capacity for oxygen, the less the oxygen saturation in arterial blood and the lower the aerobic capacity. Whether differences in diffusing capacity played a role in the group differences reported here remains a question. Fortunately, the arterial partial pressure of oxygen ($P_{a_{O_2}}$) decreases less than the alveolar partial pressure (Buskirk et al., 1967b),[2] and this relative preservation of $P_{a_{O_2}}$ must be brought about by increased blood perfusion through pulmonary capillaries, either by flow through formerly unopened capillaries or by increased flow through those that are open.

Despite what might be regarded as lower efficiencies in the Quechua during the performance of hard submaximal work on the bicycle ergometer, the unfamiliar work task they performed must be considered of consequence. Presumably, pedaling the bicycle ergometer requires considerable leg strength, and perhaps accessory muscles are recruited at high work loads by those not thoroughly familiar with the machine. The smaller Quechua might have had lesser leg strength, and might also have utilized accessory muscles at high relative work loads they were asked to perform for 5–30 min. In any event, their aerobic demands, although higher, still fell on the same relative work curve plotted in Fig. 14.6. A fairer work test for the Quechua—that is, for people used to walking and climbing, might well be grade walking on the treadmill. The greater work efficiency of the Indians in Morococha studied by Hurtado (1966), who used a treadmill, might well reflect such a work-test difference.

None of the data reported here collected at 4000 m appear to indicate an important reduction in cardiac output under conditions that yield aerobic capacity. Mean reductions of 3–12 beats per minute for maximal heart rate in the U.S. whites indicate a possible slight reduction in cardiac output that would only partially explain the reduction in aerobic capacity with hypoxia. The sea-level Quechua, however, when tested at 4000 m had a maximal heart rate 3 bpm higher than when tested at sea level. Their aerobic capacity was less influenced by hypoxia and perhaps they maintained their maximal cardiac output at a relatively higher level than did the U.S. whites.

A significant reduction in plasma volume and an associated reduction in blood volume with increased hematocrit was found in the U.S. white runners (Buskirk et al., 1967b). This reduction in circulatory blood volume could limit venous return, stroke volume, and even pulmonary perfusion. Reduction in venous return and stroke volume would tend to reduce maximal cardiac output, and reduction in pulmonary perfusion would reduce arterial oxygen content. The proportional reduction in arterial oxygen content with greater hypoxia results in smaller arteriovenous oxygen differences under exercise conditions eliciting aerobic capacity. It is assumed that oxygen extraction by working muscle is virtually complete and venous oxygen content in blood draining the muscles approximates zero. With the lowering of arterial oxygen content and with minimum venous content, even the same cardiac output results in a reduced aerobic capacity. If cardiac output is reduced as well, the reduction in aerobic capacity may be substantial.

An additional feature of hypoxia is the relative hyperpnea induced. Support for hyperpnea requires oxygen utilization, and the increased oxygen requirements brought about by hyperpnea and hyperventilation occur at the expense of oxygen delivery to the working muscle. On a per-kilogram-body-weight basis, the natives resident at high altitude had relatively high aerobic capacities. The reason may reside in the relatively good physical condition of the Quechua studied as well as in their large volume of circulating hemoglobin, which in turn facilitates a comparatively high arterial oxygen content. The rightward shift of the oxygen dissociation curve of the resident Quechua, compared to that of newcomers, indicates facilitated oxygen unloading capabilities in the tissues—that is, that the shift from arterial to venous blood takes place on a steeper portion of the oxygen-dissociation curve (Hurtado, 1964a, 1964b, 1966). For a fixed drop in oxygen tension, more oxygen is presumably extracted by working muscle. This unloading would be favored by a suspected greater 2,3-diphosphoglycerate (DPG) concentration in the red blood cells of the highland resident. Thus the resident Quechua has favorably acclimatized if he is in a more favorable physiological position for oxygen provision to working muscle during exercise under conditions of hypoxia.

Anaerobic mechanisms, that is, those associated with the development of an oxygen debt, appear to be unaffected at high altitude. Blood pH during exhausting work at high altitude fell to very low values in the U.S. whites despite their relative hyperventilation (Buskirk et al., 1967b). To what extent the low pH reflected greater anaerobic metabolism is unknown.

With increasing work loads, pulmonary ventilation increases out of proportion to oxygen consumption, and much more at high altitudes than at sea level. The increased ventilation may be a source of respiratory as well as generalized fatigue. The differences among groups in pulmonary ventilation when related to oxygen consumption per kilogram of body weight were revealing but remain unexplained.

15

WORK PERFORMANCE OF HIGHLAND NATIVES

Paul T. Baker

Newcomers to the high areas of the Andes have always been impressed with the high level of physical fitness and work capacity of the native. Early attempts to document this capacity showed that the native was probably much more capable of sustained high work outputs than even the more fit newcomers (Barcroft et al., 1923; Herrera and Vergara, 1899). With further developments in the field of exercise physiology, oxygen-consumption capabilities were recognized as prime indicators of sustained (aerobic) work capacities, and efforts were made to determine not only the comparative physical performance of highland natives versus newcomers but also such measures as individual maximal oxygen-consumption capacities ($\dot{V}_{O_2}$ max), so that accurate quantitative comparisons could be made with other world populations. Although measurement techniques had not been completely standardized by the 1950s, those measurements which could be compared suggested that the highland native had a work capacity very similar to that of fit young men at sea level (Velásquez, 1964). In sharp contrast, newcomers to such elevations (4000–5000 m) showed substantially lower $\dot{V}_{O_2}$ max in response to the lowered atmospheric oxygen pressure.

EARLIER STUDIES

The most comprehensive of the early studies tested subjects from a high-altitude mining community (Hurtado, 1964b), and therefore, as noted in Chapter 1, there remained some question as to how well the sample represented the work capacity of the more typical highland man. As Buskirk demonstrated in Chapter 14, representative Nuñoa men also have $\dot{V}_{O_2}$ max which indicate a high level of physical fitness. These values were matched among newcomers only by highly selected and trained sea-level athletes. Donoso et al. (1971) further confirmed the high aerobic capacity of the Andean native with his study of Aymara natives.

In Table 15.1 the aerobic capacities of the high-Andean natives are compared with some representative values for low-altitude populations. For comparability, all $\dot{V}_{O_2}$ max values are expressed on a per-kilogram-of-body-weight basis. The comparison clearly suggests that highland natives have a quite high aerobic capacity. Indeed, their $\dot{V}_{O_2}$ max is not only higher than

TABLE 15.1   *Aerobic Capacity of Young Men From Various Populations and Environments*

Reference group	Fitness level	Test altitude (m)	N	Mean age	Mean aerobic capacity, O_2 (ml/kg-min) (STPD)
Nuñoa natives	Average	4000	25	25	49.1
Donoso et al. (1971)					
Aymara natives	Average	3650	37	29	46.4
Velásquez (1966)					
Peruvian natives	Average	4500	28	—	51.2
Coudert and Zamora (1970)					
Bolivian high-altitude athletes	Very high	3700	29	23	57.7
Weitz (1973)					
Sherpa	Average or below	3400	13	25	45.2
Sherpa	Above average	3400	11	25	50.4
Sherpa	Below average	1400	10	24	42.2
Buskirk and Taylor (1957)					
U.S. males	Below average	S.L.	39	23	44.6
U.S. males	Above average	S.L.	12	24	54.1
Davies et al. (1972)					
Inactive Yoruba	Below average	S.L.	33	26	45.9
Active Yoruba	Above average	S.L.	23	25	55.5
Rennie et al. (1970)					
Eskimos[a]	Average	S.L.	17	30	45.0

[a]Estimated from graphs.

that of newcomers to high altitude but exceeds representative samples from many low-altitude populations.

V_{O_2} max and Work Capacity

From studies of European-derived individuals near sea level, the relationship between $\dot{V}_{O_2}$ max and sustained work capacity has been well established. However, this relationship is empirically derived and theoretically need not apply to all populations and situations. Indeed, it is known that trained individuals can sustain work loads nearer their $\dot{V}_{O_2}$ max for a longer time than untrained individuals (Åstrand and Rodahl, 1970). As Buskirk indicates, early studies in Nuñoa suggested another problem in interpreting work capacity, since it appeared that mechanical efficiency might be lower in natives than in sea-level groups brought to high altitude. In contrast, other Peruvian studies have suggested that mechanical efficiency was greater

(Hurtado, 1966). In a still later study Mazess reported mechanical efficiencies similar to sea-level values (Mazess, 1969a). The technique for determining work output versus oxygen consumption appears an important variable in these conflicting results. A treadmill was used in the studies reporting elevated mechanical efficiencies; a bicycle ergometer was used in the other studies. In Chapter 14 Buskirk suggests that differences in body structure between Nuñoa Indians and the larger European individuals may account for the apparently lower Nuñoa Indian work outputs. I agree with this suggestion but would further note that almost all the Nuñoa natives were completely relatively unfamiliar with bicycle riding and might have expended considerable energy in unrecorded muscle actions associated with balance and muscle-action conflict. If so, it would explain why Mazess, using the bicycle ergometer, found standard mechanical efficiencies when studying more acculturated and urbanized highlanders.

Cardiovascular and Ventilatory Responses

In other features, such as cardiac function and respiration, highlanders appear to be similar to lowlanders when tested in maximal or submaximal work situations. The natives, of course, show a high oxygen delivery per heart beat (oxygen pulse) and low ventilation equivalent, compared with newcomers at high altitude, but the values fall near expected ranges for men tested at low altitude.

PROJECT HYPOTHESES

Given that the work capacity of high-Andean natives is significantly greater than that of all newcomers to high altitude except selected and trained athletes, and similar to that of quite-fit populations at low altitude, many studies have been devoted to determining how this capacity is achieved. Explanations have been offered at two levels. Most research has been devoted to a determination of the anatomical and physiological features that may contribute to the native oxygen extraction and transport ability (see Chapter 12). In search of the more basic processes, several hypotheses have been developed suggesting genetic and environmental causes for the high native capacities. Several of the studies in the present project were devoted to exploring the validity of these suggestions. Generally, no single or simple cause has been suggested for the differences; rather, four underlying factors would appear to explain the differences between native and newcomers:

1. Since the level of physical conditioning of an individual correlates with his work capacity, and since selected and trained lowland athletes can match native work capacity, it has been suggested that highland natives achieve their high work capacity in part by a high degree of physical training (Monge, 1948).

2. Relatively short-term exposure to a variety of physiological stresses produces acclimatizational responses which reduce strain. Certain changes in the physiology of the newcomer suggest that work capacity should increase with exposure to hypoxia. While short-term changes after the first few days have not been shown to increase work capacity substantially, it is claimed that longer-term (1-month to 1-yr) acclimatizational processes produce near-native work capacities in adult lowland migrants to high altitudes (Balke, 1964b).

3. A number of structural and physiological differences have been noted between individuals born and raised at high altitude and adult migrants, such as an enlarged right (heart) ventricle, a depressed hypoxic drive, and increased skeletal muscle vascularity in the highland natives. It has thus been suggested that birth and growth at altitude produce a developmental acclimatization which allows high adult work capacities.

4. Finally, some investigators have felt that the evidence for acclimatizational effects and physical training are not sufficient to explain the difference. They have therefore suggested a possible genetic difference (Monge, 1948; Baker, 1969). No specific genetic associations have been established, but one investigator claims to have found a genetically based shift in the Bohr effect which would enhance oxygen transport and has a genetic base (Morpurgo et al., 1970, 1972).

PROJECT RESULTS

Physical Fitness

Determining the habitual amount of exercise within a population is, indeed, an almost impossible task. However, several types of information collected in Nuñoa provide good indicators of habitual exercise level. Recreation probably plays a minor role in exercise levels. The two primary recreational activities which produce significant exercise are dancing and soccer. Dancing, which is limited to ceremonial occasions, can provide strenuous exercise because it is extended over protracted time periods (2–3 days). However, it is sporadic and seems unlikely to provide a substantial input into physical fitness. Soccer is the only organized sport. Most male adolescents and young adults participate occasionally in the sport, but it does not form a regular and organized behavior for most individuals. Walking, sometimes for considerable distances, probably constitutes the most regular exercise.

Nuñoa is, of course, a peasant society, and it might be imagined that subsistence activities require a high exercise level from both adults and children. However, Thomas's (1973) detailed analysis does not support this hypothesis. He does show that almost all members of the Indian community are involved in physical work and that even young children are contributors to subsistence activities. But hard physical labor is only occasionally demanded during the yearly activity cycle, and the sedentary herding behavior of adolescents does not suggest high exercise levels.

To me the most convincing evidence for a modest exercise level in the population is provided by the nutritional assessments. As noted in Chapter 11, there are some inconsistencies between the various nutritional studies on the average caloric intakes in the Nuñoa area. However, even the more generous estimates suggest caloric intakes for male adolescents and adults that would support only a modest activity level. If these estimates, as shown in Table 15.2, are compared with those for males of similar ages and sizes in different occupational categories, it appears that the habitual exercise levels are indeed modest. This conclusion could be modified if caloric requirements were affected by hypoxia, but there seems no evidence to support such an idea. Based on the monograph published by Buskirk and Mendez (1967), the male Nuñoa's typical day would provide sufficient calories for only restful to light work.

In an attempt to determine the contribution of exercise level to highland native work capacity, Mazess studied a group of university students at high

TABLE 15.2 *Average Caloric Intake for Male Samples of Various Populations and Occupations*

Sample and study	Occupation	Sample	Age range	Weight (kg)	Mean (kcal/day)
Gursky (1969)					
Nuñoa	Pastoralists and day labor	13	18–55	57	2833[a]
Nuñoa	Pastoralists	14	10–18	36	1945[a]
Thomas (1973)					
Nuñoa	Pastoralists	7 families	20–40	—	2125[b]
Picón-Reátegui (Chap. 11)					
Nuñoa	Pastoralists	—	Adult	—	2719
Durnin and Passmore (1967)					
Scotland	Office workers	"10–30"	Adult	—	2520
Scotland	Students	"10–30"	Adult	—	2930
Scotland	Farmers	"10–30"	Adult	—	3550
India	Laboratory technicians	—	Adult	60	2070
India	Mill workers	—	Adult	47	3050
India	Rickshaw pullers	—	Adult	64	4880
Edholm et al. (1970)					
England	Soldiers	64	18–24	59	3849

[a]Measured intake.
[b]Estimate.

TABLE 15.3 *Physical Characteristics and Responses of Trained and Untrained Students During Exercise at High Altitude[a,b]*

	Untrained students		Trained students	
	White (13)	Indian (10)	Lowland (7)	Highland (9)
Physical Characteristics				
Age (yr)	23.5	23.8	21.3	21.1
Stature (cm)	169	162	165	167
Weight (kg)	61.2	59.8	60.2	63.0
Hemoglobin (g/100 ml)	18.4	18.2	18.2	19.1
Hematocrit (%)	51.7	49.7	51.2	51.1
Forced vital capacity (ml)	4744	4655	4878	5242
Max. V.V. (l/min)	180	169	206	214
Responses to Maximal Work				
Maximal oxygen intake (l/min)	2.62	2.79	2.78	3.03
Aerobic capacity (ml/kg min)	42.8	46.8	46.2	48.2
Maximal heart beat (beats/min)	186	188	194	193
Maximal ventilation (l/min)	146	143	165	162
Ventilation equivalent	55.9	51.2	59.3	53.6
Oxygen pulse (ml/beat)	14.1	14.8	14.3	15.7

[a]Modified from Mazess (1969a).

[b]Hemoglobin and hematocrit were determined on peripheral-blood samples (finger puncture); forced vital capacity and 15-sec maximal voluntary ventilation (max. V.V.) were measured on the Jones Pulmonar dry spirometer.

altitude (Puno, Peru) and compared them with students who were enrolled in an institute for physical-education teachers located at the same altitude in southern Peru (Mazess 1968a, 1969a). His university-student sample consisted of 10 students who were judged from morphology to be primarily of European genetic origin and 13 who were morphologically Indian. Exercise levels prior to testing at 3830 m were apparently not precisely recorded, but he indicates that the Indian sample was involved in athletic activities to a greater extent than were the white students. The physical-education-institute group consisted of 7 students of lowland and 9 of highland origin, both with mixed European–Indian ancestry. The highland sample had spent their lives at high altitude, while the lowland sample had come from altitude below 2500 m. Mazess does not indicate how long the lowland sample had been at high altitude but notes that both of these groups, before testing at 4000 m, had been in residence and training at the institute for at least 8 months.

Some results from this study are shown in Table 15.3. The effect of planned physical training is not impressive. Mazess does not report the statistical significance of the differences, but it appears that the major difference between the trained and untrained is in maximal ventilation. $\dot{V}_{O_2}$

max differences are small and, somewhat surprisingly, the trained individuals have $\dot{V}_{O_2}$ maximums slightly lower than those found for the representative sample of male Nuñoans.

In a related study on Nepalese high-altitude natives, Weitz (1973) was able to demonstrate that among the Sherpa the level of work capacity achieved appeared to bear the same relationship to habitual exercise levels as it does in low-altitude populations tested at low altitude. He concluded that the high aerobic capacity of high-altitude Sherpa, compared with that of newcomers, could not be attributed in significant part to a superior level of physical fitness. I feel that the information presently available supports a similar conclusion in relation to the work capacity of the Andean native.

Short-Term Acclimatization

Several studies of short-term exposure to high altitude suggested that physically conditioned individuals may with time increase their $\dot{V}_{O_2}$ max (Balke et al., 1956, 1965, 1966). In two studies, lowland individuals who were not conditioned spent nearly 1 yr at altitude. $\dot{V}_{O_2}$ max for these groups rose to nearly the same value shown by the same individuals prior to upward

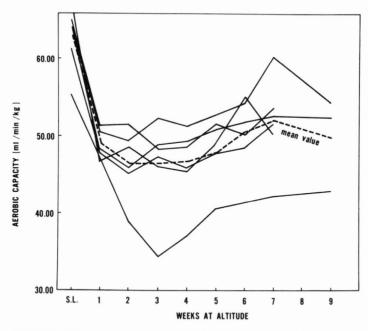

FIGURE 15.1 *Aerobic capacity changes in U.S. athletes during continuous exposure to a 4000-m altitude. The dashed line is the running average of all individuals. Thin lines represent individual changes.*

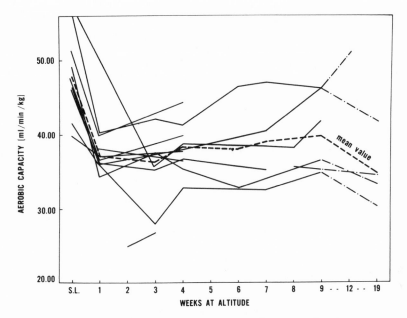

FIGURE 15.2 *Aerobic capacity in untrained U.S. males during continuous exposure to a 4000-m altitude. The dashed line is the running average. Thin lines represent individual changes.*

migration (Velásquez, 1964; Malhotra et al., 1968). What appears to be acclimatization has been suggested as the product of increased exercise levels after upward migration (Kollias and Buskirk, 1974). If exercise level did rise, the level of work capacity would of course be expected to rise as well. Whether this explanation is appropriate for these changes in the $\dot{V}_{O_2}$ max of untrained individuals has not been tested, but in several studies of selected and trained athletes, where exercise level was controlled, no recovery in $\dot{V}_{O_2}$ max levels was found with exposures to high altitude for as long as 2 months (Buskirk et al., 1967b; Faulkner et al., 1968; Nicholas et al., 1968).

In our studies of both physically untrained investigators and trained athletes taken to 4000 m, no significant shifts in average maximal oxygen capacities occurred during periods up to 3 months. As shown in Figs. 15.1 and 15.2, individuals did appear to show both increased and decreased $\dot{V}_{O_2}$ max over time; but whether these individual changes were the results of idiosyneratic behavior and stochastic processes or indicate that some individuals show acclimatizational changes in relation to $\dot{V}_{O_2}$ while others do not could not be determined from their data. Both the athletes and the investigators suffered a greater than normal incidence of respiratory and gastrointestinal diseases during the test period because of the changes in environment; thus levels of habitual exercise might have fallen during the time at altitude.

So it appeared, and more for the athletes than the investigators, in spite of the fact that the athletes attempted to maintain a normal training schedule.

Although most recent studies have failed to show any significant improvement in $\dot{V}_{O_2}$ max as a consequence of acclimatization to altitude, some improved individual performances in activities such as running have been observed. In the absence of a physiological explanation, Kollias and Buskirk (1974) have attributed these improvements to learning and other psychological adjustments.

In summary, our studies in conjunction with others suggest that short-term acclimatizational processes do not contribute significantly to the elevated work capacity in highland natives as compared with that of newcomers from low altitude. This conclusion is subject to modification if future studies indicate that acclimatization to altitude has an impact on individuals trained to near their physiological limits of oxygen consumption, which is different from its impact on those capable of significant increases with training.

Developmental Acclimatization

Whether even longer-term exposure to altitude for adults would produce improvements in work capacity is not known. One of the recent findings which suggest that long-term exposure to hypoxia may alter respiratory function is the blunted hypoxic drive of high-altitude natives, suggested as improving work capacity (Lefrancois et al., 1969). How long an exposure is required to produce a response similar to the native is not known. It has been claimed that early growth under hypoxic conditions is required (Severinghaus et al., 1966), but others have suggested that the capacity may be genetically controlled, or that it may require only an extended hypoxic experience (see Chapter 12). In any case, it is not possible at present to show that this unusual respiratory response is related directly to work capacity. The study by Mazess of the physical-education students (see Table 15.2) suggested that lowland immigrants might achieve aerobic capacities similar to native high-altitude values in a relatively short time, but one must assume that young men choosing to attend a physical-education institute are not typical of lowland males, and the degree to which they had recovered their low-altitude work capacity was not known since values at low altitude were not obtained.

Perhaps exposure to high altitude during infancy and childhood enhances the work capacity of the adult. The support for this suggestion has been indirect, since the work capacity of children has not been directly measured.

However, a number of differences have been noted when the oxygen-transport system of the high-altitude native is compared to sea-level individuals. In addition to the differences in hypoxic drive just discussed, highland natives have greater heart size, with probably greater stroke volume. The blood flow may be redistributed among organs and across working muscle beds (Finch and Lenfant, 1972). Finally, a number of blood enzymes vary in possibly adaptive directions. These include 2,3-diphosphoglycerate (Lenfant et al., 1968), pyruvate-kinase (PK), glucose-6-phosphate dehydrogenase

(G6PD), and hexokinase (HK) (Mandelbaum et al., 1973). These differences, not observed during short-time acclimatization, further support the hypothesis that developmental exposure to high altitude may enhance adult performance.

As part of the overall effort in the present IBP project, a study performed in Cuzco, Peru (3400 m) was undertaken to help assess the effect of growth at high altitude on adult work capacity (Frisancho et al., 1973b). $\dot{V}_{O_2}$ max was determined on four samples of individuals. These samples were natives from the highlands above 3000 m, Peruvian newcomers from near sea level, newcomer whites from the lowland parts of the United States, and a group of Peruvian migrants who had been born below 1000 m but during childhood had migrated with their parents to high altitude. The results for the U.S. newcomers need not be reported here since they almost exactly duplicate the findings of the U.S. investigators who were studied in Nuñoa. It is, nevertheless, somewhat surprising that these individuals did not have work capacities higher than those of the investigator group, who were older, had been at high altitude a shorter time, and were measured at a significantly higher altitude.

The physical characteristics and physiological responses of the remaining three samples are shown in Table 15.4. The samples were generally quite

TABLE 15.4 *Physical Characteristics and Physiological Responses of Peruvian Subjects During Work on a Bicycle Ergometer at 3400 m (Means ± S.D.)* [a]

Variable	Highland controls (20)	Lowland migrants (23)	Lowland newcomers (10)
Physical Characteristics			
Age (yr)	23.4 ± 1.7	21.5 ± 2.3	23.0 ± 3.0
Height (cm)	164.6 ± 5.2	166.7 ± 6.0	164.0 ± 6.5
Weight (kg)	58.6 ± 4.6	60.8 ± 7.7	58.6 ± 7.9
Fat-free weight (kg)	53.1 ± 5.0	55.2 ± 4.8	51.7 ± 6.1
Percentage of fat (%)	8.6 ± 4.5	8.8 ± 5.4	11.8 ± 6.5
Sum skinfolds (mm)	42.9 ± 17.7	44.7 ± 24.7	63.7 ± 24.5[a]
Skin reflectance (%)			
Red filter	42.5 ± 3.6	56.2 ± 3.5[a]	45.1 ± 2.5
Blue filter	16.1 ± 2.0	26.3 ± 3.9	17.0 ± 2.0
Physiological Responses			
$\dot{V}_{O_2}$ max			
ml/kg-min	46.3 ± 5.0	46.0 ± 6.3	38.0 ± 5.2[b]
ml/kg-min[c]	51.2 ± 5.8	50.1 ± 5.4	42.3 ± 5.0[b]
$\dot{V}_E$ max (BTPS) (l/min)	138.5 ± 22.4	139.7 ± 17.9	165.0 ± 17.2[b]
$\dot{V}_E / \dot{V}_{O_2}$	51.3 ± 6.5	50.7 ± 5.4	64.4 ± 7.2[b]
HR max	196.1 ± 6.6	193.2 ± 6.5	192.6 ± 6.0[b]
O_2 pulse (ml/beat)	13.9 ± 1.8	14.4 ± 1.7	11.1 ± 0.6

[a]Modified from Frisancho et al. (1973b).
[b]Significantly different from highland controls, at $p < 0.01$ level.
[c]$\dot{V}_{O_2}$ max related to fat-free weight.

similar, but the lowland newcomers were slightly fatter. The migrants appear, from the skin-color data, to contain a much higher admixture of European genes than the other groups, whose skin color approximates that of relatively unadmixed highland Indians.

The migrant and native samples are nearly identical in their work capacity (Table 15.4), while the newcomer sample shows the expected rather low oxygen consumption capacity in spite of a higher ventilation. The $\dot{V}_{O_2}$ maximums are the same as those Mazess reported for the university students who appeared to be Indian in ancestry, but the values for newcomers are much lower than he reported for the lowland students in the physical-education institute. It should be noted that all three samples in the Cuzco study were of university students, and that the subjects labeled "newcomers" had, in fact, been at high altitude for periods ranging from 2 to 3½ yr.

The data clearly suggest that childhood development at high altitude enhances adult work capacity. However, a close examination of the data shows some possible problems in interpretation. Figure 15.3 indicates the relationship between the age at migration and the $\dot{V}_{O_2}$ max achieved as a young adult. This association suggests that the age at which the individual migrated had a strong negative association with adult $\dot{V}_{O_2}$ max, and a linear regression appears justified. For individuals who migrated in the late teens, the regression prediction agrees nicely with results on newcomers who moved to high altitude as adults. Indeed, the predicted value of $\dot{V}_{O_2}$ max for migrants at age 16 is the same as those reported as an average for newcomers.

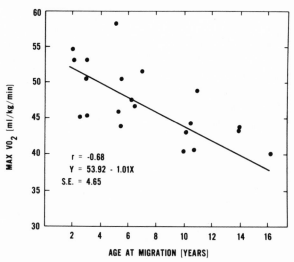

FIGURE 15.3 *Relationship between adult* $\dot{V}_{O_2}$ *max at 3400 m and the age at which the individual migrated from low to high altitude.* [Modified from Frisancho et al. (1973b).]

However, for individuals who migrate as young children, the regression predicts unusually high values. For those who migrate at age 2, it predicts a value not only more than 1 standard deviation above the "native" value in this study, but more than any reported for native men. At least two explanations may be offered for the rather high predicted $\dot{V}_{O_2}$ max for young migrants:

1. The sample size is small, and it may well be that a curvilinear regression would be found on a large sample. If such is the case, it may be that there is a critical age at which migration must occur, or a critical duration of exposure to high altitude.

2. It is possible that the sample of migrants who arrived at younger ages contained a few unusually fit individuals, giving the regression a slope steeper than valid on a population basis.

In any case the data are highly provocative and give strong support to the hypothesis that there may be a developmental acclimatization to high altitude which contributes to the relatively high work capacity of the high-altitude native when compared with newcomers to high altitude. Further studies on this topic seem well justified.

Genetic Factors

The arguments in favor of a genetic basis for a higher work capacity in highland natives than in lowlanders has been primarily supported by historical evidence. It has also been suggested that other explanations based on acclimatization, that is, human genetic plasticity, have not provided satisfactory answers. Thus it has been pointed out that in the Western Hemisphere European and African migrants virtually replaced the native Indian in all areas except the high Andes (Baker, 1969; Monge, 1948). Furthermore, with the exception of the Cuzco study just discussed (Frisancho et al., 1973b), no published data have shown the work capacity of the upward migrant to be as high as that of the native. No specific genetic model has been proposed in support of this hypothesis, although several biochemical and morphological differences between highlanders and lowlanders have been found that may alter work capacity at high altitude and may have a genetic basis: chest and lung characteristics (Hurtado, 1932a, 1964b; Hoff, 1972b) and differences in the oxygen-dissociation curve (Morpurgo et al., 1970).

Lacking any specific genetic association, some indication of possible genetic differences can be obtained from the various studies conducted as part of the present project. One method applied was the exploration of possible population differences in response. The value of this approach is discussed in Chapter 1. Mazess's study of Puno university students was one effort in this direction, the results of which are shown in Table 15.3. In this study he used all the standard morphological features available in order to select two samples of students who represented individuals of European versus Indian heritage. His results indicated a small but statistically significant difference between the groups, and he indicated in his complete report on this study that corrections for factors such as size did not eliminate the significance of the difference (Mazess, 1967). Later, Mazess indicated his belief that the difference might be associated with a higher regular exercise level on the part of the Indians (Mazess, 1969b).

The study by Frisancho et al. (1973b) also provides some population comparison data, since, as noted, the upward migrant sample was much lighter in skin color than the other two groups, presumably indicating a much higher admixture of European genes. Comparison in this study was compounded by the variability in length of exposure to altitude. Nevertheless, it failed to provide any indication of a population difference.

For population-comparison purposes neither study is completely satisfactory because of the sampling problems. Europeans have been in the high-altitude region for nearly 500 yr. Population admixture has been continuous, and while the population identified as Indian seems to have a very low admixture, those who morphologically appear European in genetic heritage are rare and probably contain substantial Indian admixture.

In Chapter 14 Buskirk provides data on a slightly different population-comparison approach. In his study, individuals of highland Indian heritage who had been born or had spent most of their childhood at low altitude were brought to 4000 m, and their work capacity was compared at the two altitudes. As Buskirk notes, the loss in $\dot{V}_{O_2}$ max was much less than it was for either the athletes or the investigators from the United States. Thus, the data suggest some kind of population adaptation that reduces the impact of hypoxic stress on work capacity. Unfortunately, the sample size was small and some of the individuals had spent their early childhood at high altitude. One cannot therefore rule out an explanation based on developmental acclimatization and stochastic processes.

A final test that may be applied to the data on work capacity in reference to a genetic hypothesis is an examination of the variances. If selection operated on a preexisting gene or gene complex affecting this parameter, one might expect a reduction in genotypic variance. On the other hand, if new mutant genes arose which conferred adaptive advantage, then genotypic variance might increase at least during the time this gene or set of genes were part of a transient polymorphism. For example, if a gene or gene complex conferring better oxygen consumption capacity on highland Indians had been selected for, one would not necessarily expect them to be present in the whole population (i.e., selection might still be in operation). Under these conditions the relative contribution of the genetic variance component to the variance in aerobic capacity (h^2) might be higher in native lowlanders than in lowlanders tested under the same conditions. At this point it may be interesting to point out that one study of the h^2 of maximal aerobic capacity of Caucasian twins at low altitude has produced an exceptionally high value (0.934) for this group (Klissouras, 1971).

TABLE 15.5 *Within-Group Standard Deviations of Aerobic Work Capacity for Some Native and Newcomer Samples Tested at High Altitude*

Sample and study	Test altitude (m)	Time at altitude	N	Weight (kg)	S.D. of V_{O_2} max (l/kg-min)
Baker et al. (1968)					
Sea-level Quechua	4000	4 wk	10	61	6.6
Nuñoa natives	4000	Life	25	56	5.8
U.S. athletes	4000	7 wk	6	68	6.5
U.S. athletes	4000	2 wk	6	68	4.7
U.S. investigators	4000	1 wk	11	74	4.2
Frisancho et al. (1973b)					
Lowland Peruvians	3400	2–20 yr	23	61	6.3
Lowland Peruvians	3400	2–4 yr	10	59	5.2
Cuzco natives	3400	Life	20	57	5.0
Mazess (1967)					
Highland "Indians"	3800	Life	10	60	4.6
Highland "whites"	3800	Life	13	61	3.6

As the variances in Table 15.5 show, our studies do not provide any immediate support for either of the two genetic hypotheses stated above. Since it is known that nongenetic factors such as the degree of physical fitness and age heavily influence aerobic capacity, it may be that nongenetic factors are the primary sources for the differences among these variances. Any attempt to demonstrate genetic effects on differences in work capacity at altitude would require larger samples, very tight control over background variables, and, at the very least, an estimate of h^2 for the Quechua population.

In essence, then, the data collected as part of this project offer very little, positively or negatively, to the hypothesis that genetic differences contribute significantly to the high work capacity of the Andean native.

EVALUATION

The typical man of the highland Andes does have a work capacity which equals that of fit lowland males. This capacity would not be unusual if it were not for the reduced oxygen pressure of these high-altitude regions, which produce substantial reductions in the work capacity of newcomers. The basic causes for this high work capacity have been only partially explained by our series of studies. To me the results suggest the following:

1. While native Andean populations are physically fit, there is no evidence of a superior level of fitness, which would explain the high work capacities in the presence of reduced oxygen pressure.

2. The data do not support the idea that in groups of comparable physical condition acclimatization to hypoxia for even up to 1 year will produce in lowland men of European heritage aerobic capacities similar to those of highland natives.

3. A childhood spent at high altitude appears to improve adult work capacity as compared with that of newcomers. Whether the effect on individuals of European heritage differs from the effect on highland native heritage remains to be explored.

4. The possible existence of genetic factors that contribute to the high native work capacity remains unresolved. Data from this project both support and question this hypothesis.

16

NATURAL EXPOSURE
TO COLD

Joel M. Hanna

By most standards the altiplano in the Nuñoa region of southern Peru is cool. The mean annual temperature is only 8.3°C, which is well below the thermally neutral zone for humans. The mean monthly temperature ranges from 10°C in the warmest month—November—to 5.5°C in the coldest month (Baker et al., 1968). Daily temperatures throughout the year are thus lower than those considered comfortable for most populations.

The climate comprises two annual types, as in other monsoon regions: a dry season and a wet season. The dry season extends through about half of the year, reaching a peak in June, July, and August. Over half of the days are completely free of clouds. The days are pleasant with warm afternoons and high solar radiation. The nights are clear and cold because of the long-wave radiation cooling that takes place after sundown. Most of the nights have temperatures below freezing, and a low of -8°C has been recorded for this period. The wet season is characterized by daily thunderstorm activity that produces heavy local precipitation and gusty winds. The clouds reduce solar radiation and temperatures fall, usually to about 5°C. Rain, hail, sleet, and snow may accompany these minimum temperatures. Snow may accumulate up to 3 cm but is quickly melted with sunshine. Daytimes are less pleasant than in the dry season because of the heavy cloud cover, which reduces solar radiation. From December through March heavy cloud cover is recorded for 46 percent of the days. Ambient daytime temperatures are higher when it is clear because of the greater angle of the sunlight. Nights are warmer because the clouds reduce the loss of heat through long-wave radiation. Periods of cloudiness and precipitation are uncomfortable because of the gusty winds that accompany the thunderstorms.

From the viewpoint of the human population those temperatures are cool. The coolness is accentuated because of the lack of fuel for heating of houses; thus, the population is potentially exposed to cool temperatures without respite. Indeed, the only heat sources available are solar radiation and metabolic heat production.

COLD STRESS
IN THE DRY SEASON

During the dry period mean monthly temperature is at its lowest point for the year, but more significantly, nighttime temperatures also fall. In the months of June, July, and August the normal nighttime value is somewhere below freezing. Days are warm and normal outdoor activity continues, but with sundown most people retreat to their homes to escape the intense cold. Those who venture into the night usually clothe themselves in heavy ponchos and cover their heads with stocking caps. Scarves are wrapped about the face for additional protection.

The potential for cold stress during this season is of two types—local exposure of the extremities to the cold as one ventures forth in the night, and total body cooling in unheated houses at night. The first does not appear to be very serious but merits some consideration. The cooling is likely to be of the hands, feet, and face, since these are exposed to varying degrees. The hands can be brought beneath the clothing and remain in a relatively warm environment. The face is wrapped in a scarf, and the air trapped between the scarf and the face is warmed by the expired breath, creating a warmer microenvironment. The feet, on the other hand, are exposed to considerable cold. The only footgear normally used is rubber-tire sandals, but they afford little protection against subfreezing temperatures. The actual potential for cold injury to the feet at this time cannot be estimated, but cold and wind-chill factors are probably not great enough to produce injury (Burton and Edholm, 1955; Wilson and Goldman, 1970). It is noteworthy that Quechua are particularly well adapted to ward off cold injury to the feet (Little, 1968, 1969). While cold injury is probably not important, the Quechua's high foot temperature is wasteful of body heat and if exposure is for an extended period, the foot may provide a significant avenue for loss of body heat.

Another period of potential cold stress occurs during the nights of the dry season. Quechua houses in the Nuñoa region are relatively ineffectively insulated against cold; hence the potential for internal temperatures to fall below freezing is great, and could provide for considerable cold stress in sleeping Indians.

Baker (1966b) has reported measurements of the microclimate in the houses of sleeping families for this period. Nighttime temperatures for 18 adult men, 10 adult women, and 28 children of both sexes were recorded as they slept. Surface temperatures and rectal temperatures were regularly measured as they slept over an 8-hr period. The results suggest that the population is not greatly cold-stressed at this time, even though the interior house temperature falls within a degree or two of freezing. Average indoor temperatures were only 3.6°C. Both men and women maintained similar rectal temperatures throughout the 8-h sleeping period. There was a gradual temperature decline over the first 5 h, followed by a slight upturn for the final 3 h (Fig. 16.1). Women always maintained slightly higher values, and the differential between them and the men increased as the night progressed. Children manifested a distinct pattern of central cooling. They experienced a rapid fall in rectal temperature for the first hour and then attained a certain equilibrium for the remainder of the night. The equilibrium value (36.39°C) is lower than the adults' value (36.6°C), but not dangerously so. In children there is also an interesting relationship between rectal temperature and age. At the beginning of the night it is strong and positive, but as the night progresses the relationship becomes weaker.

Measured skin temperatures of the sleeping Nuñoan residents do not differ appreciably among men, women, and children. The exception is toe temperature, which shows significant differences in an order inverse to that of rectal temperatures. Children now have the highest values and women the lowest. Neither rectal nor skin temperatures reach uncomfortably low values, and thus little real cold stress seems to be experienced at this time (Fig. 16.1).

The temperature differentials that Baker observed during the night are compatible with anticipated group differences in body-tissue insulation. Women have more subcutaneous fat than men or children and are thus able to provide greater insulation for the core. Children have the least fat and are smaller in size (as reflected in Baker's use of age); thus, they produce less insulation and experience a greater fall in core temperature as heat flows to the peripheral regions. The suggestion here is that the cold stress during the night in Nuñoa is related to loss in body heat stores, and that smaller and leaner individuals are more susceptible to cold.

Sleeping behavior during Baker's observations also suggests attempts to limit heat loss. The family frequently slept together in groups of 2 or 4. All

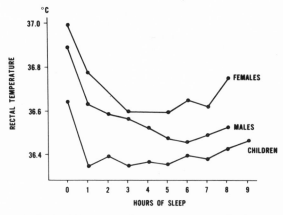

FIGURE 16.1 *Rectal temperature of sleeping Quechua Indians. [Adapted from Baker (1966b).]*

slept in a fetal position even though covered with blankets, sheepskins, and clothing.

Larsen (1973) has recently reported another dry-season study in Nuñoa. He studied four families on a day-long basis. The results are generally compatible with those reported by Baker. During the night the actual cold stress experienced by men, women, and children was minor. The children did tend toward slightly greater heat loss, but not so much as to produce discomfort.

Throughout the day ambient temperature ranged from $-6°C$ at 6 A.M. to $20°C$ at 1 P.M. Despite this great range, the mean exterior clothing temperatures only fluctuated from $20°C$ to $30°C$. Mean temperature beneath clothing was a remarkably constant $32°C$. Larsen found that women lived in the warmest environment, men in a slightly cooler one, and children in the coolest. The children's mean skin temperature fell to only $29.5°C$, which is not very stressful.

He reported two periods of potential stress, which especially affected children: the early morning just after rising, and the evening, before retiring. Baker anticipated the latter period as stressful, as he noted that the children in his sample began sleeping in a cooler thermal state than did the adults.

In sum, dry-season cold stress is largely nighttime cold stress. It may be experienced by those who remain outdoors after dark, but it is not likely to result in local cold injury, and such injury should be prevented by the characteristic high peripheral temperatures of the Quechua. The high heat flow might occasion significant heat loss and result in mild hypothermia, but studies suggest that it is not likely to be consequential with even minimal clothing (Mazess and Larsen, 1972; Hanna, 1970a). A more significant degree of cold stress seems to be experienced by children, who show a considerable reduction in rectal temperature during the night (Figure 16.1). This reduction results from exposure prior to retiring (Larsen, 1973; Baker, 1966b).

COLD STRESS
IN THE RAINY SEASON

The rains begin in late October or early November, when planting begins. Precipitation falls in the afternoon when cloudiness, wind, and thunderstorms lead to increased potential for cooling. Since the Quechua are usually out-doors at this time—in the fields or tending the herds—the potential for becoming soaked and cold-stressed is rather high. The rain, snow, sleet, and hail that fall daily are driven by high winds. Since this is also the growing season, crops must be tended and exposure cannot be avoided.

The daily exposure to cold of several Indian families representing both herding and agriculture ecozones have been studied by Hanna (1968, 1970a). Individual members of 10 families were observed throughout the day as they performed their normal activities in the wet season. Climate conditions, rectal temperature, and surface temperature were monitored regularly. Skin surface temperatures were measured on standing, fully clothed individuals at the following sites: forehead, chest, hand, finger, leg, foot, and toe. Rectal or oral temperature measurements depended upon subject acceptance; most adults accepted with no problem. A single family was studied per day.

The investigators arrived before breakfast, while most of the family members were still asleep. First measurements were made after the meal, as individuals were preparing to go about daily tasks. Observations continued all day at 2-h intervals and were terminated after the evening meal when the families went to bed. Table 16.1 summarizes the climatic data for the period of the study.

Over the 10 days of study, 355 observations were made on 62 different individuals. Ages ranged from 3 to 80, and both sexes were included. Observations were made at two different altitudes representing the herding and the agricultural complexes, which Thomas (1972) has shown to occasion different activity patterns. With different activity patterns, there must be different potentials for exposure.

Over the course of the study, activity patterns for the participants were noted at 2-h intervals. In the low-altitude region, where mixed herding and agriculture were practiced, agricultural activities were not observed. This period was just before the harvest, and little agricultural work needed to be done. As such, the activity of the agriculturalists was mostly herding. Thomas has shown that metabolic heat production during herding is considerably lower than for most other agricultural activities, so the agriculturalists must have been producing less heat than they normally do throughout the day. This instance probably represents the period of maximum cold stress experienced during this season.

TABLE 16.1 *Summary of Climate Data During Wet-Season Studies*

Day	Temperature (°C) Max.	Min.	Mean (12 readings)	Humidity (%)	Precipitation
1	15	2.2	8.3	84.5	None
2	12.8	1.4	8.1	86.4	Frost
3	15.6	1.7	9.8	81.9	Sleet
4	13.4	1.1	9.0	84.7	Frost
5	14.5	5.0	9.9	89.6	None
6	18.3	5.0	12.7	85.5	Frost
7	18.3	5.6	10.1	89.9	Frost
8	14.5	3.4	11.1	85.9	Rain
9	18.9	2.9	11.2	85.6	Rain

In both regions men and children over 5 did most of the herding while women remained near the houses. Thus women and infants could usually find refuge from precipitation by seeking shelter indoors. When the sky was clear they usually sat about the house—outdoors. The children with the herds were usually in play groups of 2–5, and were active much of the time. Men frequently went with the children but also visited neighbors and chased stray animals. In the agricultural regions most of the men also visited the fields to check on crop maturation. Thomas (1972) has discussed these activities in detail and should be consulted for additional information. One of his observations is that herding is a relatively inactive occupation requiring minimal energy expenditure. During the present study about 80 percent of the herding time was spent in sedentary pursuits, although small children tended to move about more than adults.

Table 16.2 summarizes the data for 58 individuals whose temperatures were taken at various sites throughout the day; five measurements were taken at 2-h intervals. It is evident that the surface temperatures are not very low; indeed, the values approximate those of a thermally neutral environment rather than an exposure to cold (Mazess and Larsen, 1972). Hand and foot temperatures are lowest but are always above 20°C. If these findings are representative of average exposure during the rainy season, the cold stress is not severe. The rectal temperatures are also at comfortable levels in all groups. Some children would not accept rectal thermometers, so oral temperature was taken. Simultaneous rectal and oral temperatures on eight young boys and girls showed rectal to be 0.3°C higher; this correction was made. The adult women had slightly lower rectal temperatures than the other groups, but that probably reflects their relative inactivity while they remained

TABLE 16.2 *Mean Temperature Responses of 58 Nuñoa Residents During the Rainy Season (°C)[a]*

Site	Children (3–15)		Adults (15–80)	
	Boys	Girls	Men	Women
Forehead	31.6	31.3	31.7	31.7
Chest	33.4	33.5	33.5	33.7
Arm	30.3	29.9	32.7	31.5
Hand	26.4	24.9	28.7	28.3
Finger	22.3	21.5	24.7	26.0
Leg	29.0	26.6	30.9	28.5
Foot	26.4	23.5	28.4	27.3
Toe	21.7	20.2	22.6	22.5
Rectal	37.4	37.3	37.2	36.8
Corresponding environment	11.4	11.2	10.8	11.7

[a]Rectal temperatures were based on 10 readings; all others, on 13.

TABLE 16.3 *Mean Temperature Responses*
24 Matched Pairs of Subjects
at Chillihua (4300 Meters)
and Sincata (4050 Meters)
Field Sites (°C)

Site	Sincata	Chilihua
Forehead	31.97	30.34
Chest	34.06	32.79
Arm	31.42	30.53
Hand	27.72	26.13
Finger	25.31	21.55
Leg	29.59	27.83
Foot	26.65	25.76
Toe	22.80	20.17
Corresponding environment	12.37	10.05

near the house. The relationships of temperatures and altitude were investigated by comparing skin temperatures at 4300 m and in the agriculture region (4050 m) for 24 pairs of subjects matched for age and sex (Table 16.3). It is clear that skin surface temperatures, reflecting microclimate, closely reflect differential environmental temperatures, but again none of the values in the table is sufficiently low to suggest chronic cold stress.

To study the greatest cold stress observed, an analysis of temperature responses during the coldest part of each day was undertaken. From hourly climatic data the lowest dry-bulb value was selected. The average for the 10 days was 6.2°C. This low usually occurred at midafternoon and was accompanied by gusty winds, a humidity of at least 90 percent, and cloudiness. Some form of precipitation was also associated with this low—either it was falling at the time or the ground was already wet. A summary of these observations is presented in Table 16.4.

These values are somewhat lower than the daily mean responses. Toe and finger temperatures are lowest but still far above any potentially injurious level. The mean rectal temperature is quite high, 37.15°C, suggesting that a general body heat loss did not occur frequently and that superficial cooling was a greater problem. Table 16.4 also lists the minimal temperatures recorded at each site, and again no dangerously low values are observed. The rectal low value is probably an underestimate, because some of the subjects were adult women who were sitting inside houses at the time and were not exposed to wind or cooling. Their low rectal temperatures, 35.8–36.0°C, reflect a long period of inactivity rather than environmentally produced cooling. The lowest observed value for an exposed individual was 36.4°C. Larsen (1973) has reported a similar relationship between inactivity and mean temperature in Nuñoa women. During the dry season the lowest rectal

TABLE 16.4   *Temperature of Various Sites (54 Subjects) Measured When Daily Dry-Bulb Temperatures Were Lowest (°C)*

Site	Mean	S.D.	Minimum
Head	29.61	3.3	21
Chest	32.29	2.4	27.3
Forearm	29.14	3.2	20.5
Hand	22.50	4.6	13.1
Finger	18.83	6.1	10.0
Leg	27.12	3.6	22.0
Foot	20.92	4.9	13.4
Toe	16.54	5.2	7.7
Rectal[a]	37.15	0.65	36.0
Corresponding environment[b]	6.47	1.92	3.3

[a]Measured on 40 subjects. For the remaining 14 (all children) oral temperature was measured and 0.3°C added.
[b]Based on nine readings.

temperatures were also found in adult women who had been sitting inside their houses all day.

In the nighttime studies already described there was a relationship between age and rectal temperature at the beginning of the sleeping period. This finding suggests greater and more rapid cooling in younger, less massive individuals. In the minimum-temperature sample a similar regression analysis was performed, except that body weight in kilograms rather than age was regressed on rectal temperature. The correlation coefficient was not statistically significant ($r = -0.05$). Thus, it appears that size and body temperature are not strongly related during the daytime cold.

Table 16.4 shows that toe temperature fell to the lowest levels during maximum cold. An area of maximum stress is suggested. Toe temperature may also be size-dependent, because Little (1968) has demonstrated that foot temperature is partially dependent upon foot size. On regression analysis of body weight against toe temperature, the correlation coefficient was statistically significant ($r = 0.37$; 58 pairs of observations). The regression relationship is described by: minimum toe temperature equals 0.049 (body weight) plus 12.52. Thus, it appears that during the daytime cold exposure, body size is an important variable in determination of toe temperature, and that the smaller individuals experience the greater toe cooling.

The absence of a significant relationship between weight and rectal temperature and the significant relationship between weight and toe temperature further underlines a point made earlier. The cooling experienced during the daytime exposure to cold is peripheral in nature. Peripheral temperatures fall and show Newtonian cooling, but core or rectal temperature is not greatly influenced, as Tables 16.2–16.4 clearly illustrate. Further, the regression intercept at weight zero is 12.52°C, which is far above the potential point of cold injury. The inference is that under the conditions measured in this study, not even the smallest individual would normally experience any great cooling of the toes. In none of these minimal temperature observations was there snow on the ground, so the most extreme conditions may not be accurately represented. Still, on many occasions the ground was wet with sleet or rain, which should give some approximation of snow.

In summary, studies of the natural levels of exposure to cold in Nuñoa show that the climate is sufficiently severe to provide a potential for cold stress. Such was not observed, however. Neither at night during the dry season nor by day during the wet season is there any indication of severe cooling. At night all measured rectal and peripheral temperatures remain within tolerable limits. During the wet season, even at the coldest part of the day, there seems to be little real cooling, although foot and toe temperatures do decline somewhat. The absence of real body cooling in adults must result from the effectiveness of the centuries-old Quechua technology, which is capable of dealing with even the most severe conditions measured.

TECHNOLOGICAL APPROACHES

By Western standards the technological protection against cold that is utilized by Nuñoa residents is simple and primitive. Still, given the limitations of the altiplano, the population remains well protected. Most importantly, the technology is effective in reducing cold stress and does not require additional calories in the form of fuel.

Shelter

In Nuñoa the most conspicuous cultural protection against cold is the houses. Since the absence of fuel for heating precludes warming them, their effectiveness in moderation of microclimate in cold periods is of some interest.

One of the two dominant forms of houses in Nuñoa is constructed of adobe or sod bricks, sometimes covered with a mud or plaster stucco (Fig. 16.2). This type has a rectangular floor plan, 5 m wide and 10 m long. The roof is gabled and rises about 5 m at the peak. The smaller and less pretentious houses may have only a single opening, a door in one of the long sides; the larger houses, usually found in town, may have several glass windows. The roof may be grass or straw, or occasionally corrugated metal. There is usually a wooden door loosely fitted to a frame, frequently with large cracks around the door that allow air to flow through. The door is always small, perhaps 1 m high, and has a high sill to prevent drafts. A wooden floor may be installed. Interior accommodations vary with function

FIGURE 16.2   *House types in Nuñoa. Adobe buildings in the town of Nuñoa (upper photo). A settlement of stone structures; note the kitchen (cocina) hut with darkened thatch roof in the background (lower photo). (Photos by M. A. Little.)*

(Little, 1968), but if the house is used for sleeping, there is always a raised dirt platform.

The effectiveness of adobe houses as protection against cold has been described by Baker (1966a). Under climatic conditions similar to those found in Nuñoa during the dry season, adobe houses were found to maintain interior temperatures more than 10°C above the ambient outdoor temperature. During the coldest part of the year, when nighttime temperatures fell below freezing, the average minimum of these adobe houses was 7°C. The sleeping Indians had covered themselves with bedding and seemed little stressed by the cold. Since the houses were not heated, their chief function seems to have been the reduction of heat loss through radiation and convection.

The second and more frequent house form in Nuñoa is a small structure with piled stone walls (Fig. 16.2). The floor plan is circular and may be up to 7 m in diameter. The roof is always of grass with a single peak in the center, 2–3 m above the floor. There is a single entryway, about 1 m high and covered with a wooden door or in some cases a poncho. Frequently the walls are bare, but sometimes the cracks between stones may be filled with mud. In most cases the larger cracks remain open so that the occupant can see outside.

The effectiveness of these stone houses in Nuñoa has been reported by Baker (1966b). After all-night studies of 21 such houses, the average indoor–outdoor differential was found to be only 3.7°C. Thus the interior of these houses must approach freezing almost every night during the cold nights of the dry season. Heating from cooking fires may partially warm the interior, but there is nothing in Baker's data to suggest that such heating has any great effect upon the occupants.

The stone houses are constructed in a few hours (LaBarre, 1948) and represent no great investment of energy or time. The material can be picked up from any field in the Nuñoa region, so there is no great economic investment. As the protection they offer against the cold is not great, their value should probably be assessed in terms of protection against precipitation and provision of a safe and unexposed place for storage of goods. Most of these stone dwellings are seen in rural regions and at higher elevations, while the adobe variety is usually confined to town or major hacienda buildings. It thus seems possible that there is a socioeconomic and ecological differential in the protection afforded by houses. More affluent members of the community tend to live in town or in haciendas and thus have permanent, adobe buildings. Less affluent families are less sedentary and more rural, and hence utilize the cheaper stone houses.

Larsen (1973) has recently reported additional observations on Nuñoa dwellings. He compared daily temperature characteristics of four stone and three adobe dormitories as well as several *cocinas,* or kitchens. All dwellings were below ambient temperature throughout most of the day. There was some difference in microclimate, with the stone dwellings remaining cooler through most of the day.

As noted, Baker's (1966a) observations suggest that adobe is more insulative than stone. The apparent discrepancy between these observations and these of Larsen may result from differences in quality of construction or period of the year. Adobe buildings are more valuable and frequently fitted with windows, better doors, and metal roofs with ceilings, which along with their wall construction would yield a more draft-free dwelling. If Larsen's study was conducted during a calm period, these advantages would not be apparent. Similarly, if the adobe structure was not in good repair, its qualities could not be appreciated.

Larsen also describes the thermal effects of small cooking fires by studying dormitories and cocinas at the same time. Cocina temperatures were somewhat elevated when meal preparation was in progress. This finding could be important, for early morning and late evening—the times of meal preparation—are also the periods of greatest cold stress for children.

Stone houses also tend to be found at higher elevations, since constant movement of herds dictates that the most economical structure be constructed. Since temperature is related to elevation, it might be suggested that herders are exposed to a colder microclimate than sedentary farmers in the valley.

Bedding

If houses offer little thermal protection and yet the sleeping Quechua experience little cold stress, their bedding materials must be especially effective. Mazess and Larsen (1972) have recently studied aspects of the potential for thermal protection offered by Quechua bedding under laboratory conditions. They recruited six young Quechua men to sleep overnight (8 h) under three different conditions: in a light woolen sleeping bag at 23°C, in the same light bag at 4°C, and with their own bedding at 4°C. The latter temperature is equal to that reported by Baker (1966a) in his study of house temperatures. The chief differences between this and natural sleeping behavior, as Mazess and Larsen note, is that no clothing was permitted and there was no bundling (sleeping together). Over the 8 h of the night, various surface temperatures, rectal temperature, and oxygen uptake were periodically measured.

In general, surface and rectal temperatures remained near their thermally neutral (23°C) control values when native bedding was used. Most notable exceptions were finger, foot, and toe temperatures, which showed a gradual, but marked, decline. Greatest fall in temperature was in the toes, which approached the cold bag (4°C) rather than thermally neutral (23°C) exposure levels. Metabolic rate showed cyclic elevation, indicating bouts of shivering, but not so severe as to awaken the sleeping subjects. Mazess and Larsen note that if clothing were utilized, as is the native practice, a lesser drop in temperature should be anticipated.

This study clearly illustrates that native bedding is adequate to meet the requirements of sleep at minimum temperature levels. It also suggests that the practice of sleeping in one's clothing is also necessary for maintenance of a comfortable, shiver-free sleep.

Clothing

Like other cold-exposed groups, the Quechua must rely upon clothing as a primary barrier between themselves and a cold environment. Clothing is called upon to act as a barrier to heat flow and as a producer of a warm and portable microclimate.

Most of the Indian population in Nuñoa wears traditional homespun clothing. It is heavy and generally made from alpaca or llama wool. When worn in layers it should provide considerable protection against heat loss.

The design of the traditional costume dates from the middle of the last century and represents a mixture of native and Spanish dress (Adams, 1959; Kubler, 1946). The pattern of clothing prior to that time seems to have been more Indigenous and consisted of a single woolen tunic utilized by men and women. The Nuñoa design is typical of the basic Andean dress pattern found throughout the altiplano. The man wears homemade underwear, usually white, which consists of long pants and a long-sleeved shirt. Over these he places one or more layers consisting of a homemade or store-bought shirt, vest, and jacket. Homemade pants are held up with a brightly colored cloth belt, a *faja*. This outfit is topped off with a colorful poncho, a felt hat, and perhaps a *chullu* or stocking cap. There is generally no hand covering, and the feet may be bare or covered with rubber-tire sandals. The women wear several mid-calf-length woolen skirts, a white wool blouse, and a brightly colored jacket. A carrying cloth may be wrapped around the upper body like a shawl. On their heads they wear hats like the men or in some cases the more traditional mortarboard type. They, too, may go barefoot or use sandals. The children dress like their parents from about age 5. Figure 3.1 illustrates clothing styles of several Nuñoa families.

Clothing tends to be worn in layers, sometimes five or six deep. The outer layers may be either black or some bright color—usually blue or red. Men's suits are always black, but the poncho may be almost any color.

The hands and feet are not covered by clothing nor is there any attempt to provide protection for them in the cold. The hands may be drawn inside the poncho or shawl, but gloves are seldom seen. The lower extremities are usually unprotected from the mid-calf down.

The clothing of infants is described in Chapter 4.

The design of Quechua clothing suggests the application of a traditionally derived scheme which approximates several general principles for cold-weather clothing developed by the U.S. Army (Kennedy, 1961). A first principle is to entrap air and enhance the insulative value of the garment. The homespun materials utilized in Nuñoa are made of wool. Wool is a most desirable cold-weather material because the resilience of its fiber maintains the original volume of trapped air (Windslow and Harrington, 1949). Wool fiber also resists crushing and retains its insulative qualities even with continued use. The Nuñoa residents realize a further advantage by using a coarse weave for interior garments. Thus still more air is retained in a "dead" space near the body.

The trapped air is of value only if it is protected from convective heat loss, for which the wind is chiefly responsible. This protection is achieved by utilizing outer clothing of a tight weave, in some cases so tight that the surface is water-resistant. When commercially manufactured clothing is used, it is usually worn on the surface over traditional clothes, further enhancing the impermeability of the clothing to wind.

Another principle applied by the U.S. Army and also observed in Quechua design is the use of several layers rather than a single bulky garment. This design is related to the need for heat loss and sweat evaporation during exercise. The greatest threat to the loss of the insulative quality of clothing is that the air spaces will fill with water, which would enhance the conduction of heat to the surface as well as reduce temperature through evaporation. The most likely source of water in the air spaces is perspiration. Thus when a man begins to work he removes several layers of shirts and pants. With only one or two coarsely woven, but porous layers present there is a quick evaporation of sweat. When the work is complete, he replaces the several layers of dry clothing he put aside earlier.

The Andean peoples have also established another principle not emphasized in army research. Surface clothing is usually in dark colors for maximum absorption of solar radiation. When the sun is shining and temperatures are above 10°C, the men's suits or women's skirts and jackets are sufficient protection. These are usually dark in color. Since a black garment will absorb about 95 percent of the ambient radiation while a white one will absorb only 30 percent, a considerable thermal advantage is enjoyed. This addition of heat could reverse a negative heat flow in some circumstances. Even on cloudy days some heat gain could be anticipated if clothing surface colors are darker than the environment.

The lower air density of high altitude also should operate to enhance the efficacy of the Indian clothing design (Belding, 1949), in three ways: (1) since the density of air is lower than at sea level, fewer calories are required to warm the same air space; (2) the insulative value of the air itself will increase as the density decreases; (3) the lower air density will reduce convective heat loss since convective currents will be less consequential. Since convective heat loss is thought to be responsible for about 80 percent of the total heat lost through clothing, the advantages of altitude are clear (Belding, 1949, p. 359). Finally, the solar heat gain should be greater at altitude because the atmosphere is less screened.

The efficacy of Nuñoa Quechua traditional clothing has been investigated by Hanna (1968, 1970a). A group of Quechua men and women residents of Nuñoa were recruited for an exposure to cold. They were exposed to a standard cold stress of 10°C for 2 h on two different days. One day they wore a minimal amount of clothing, athletic shorts for men and brief smocks for women. On the other day they used traditional clothing, without ponchos, shawls, or headgear. Over the 2-h exposure, surface temperatures, rectal temperatures, and oxygen uptake were measured.

As might be anticipated, the clothing reduced the cold stress considerably. There was a considerable reduction in oxygen uptake, reflecting a reduction in metabolic heat production. Surface temperatures were higher at all sites, including peripheral areas not covered by clothing. Microclimate temperature as measured at the skin surface under the clothing was increased 4°C, and the caloric saving was 139 and 107 for men and women, respectively.

There were some interesting relationships between temperature response and the use of clothing in each sex. Upper-extremity temperatures were similar in both sexes without clothing, but with its addition the women experienced a far greater increase in surface temperature than did the men. Similarly, lower-extremity temperatures were similar when the subjects were unclothed, but clothing led to greater increases in calf and toe temperatures in men than in women.

These differential increases in temperature are probably a reflection of differences between the sexes in daily patterns of exposure to cold. Specifically, men spend a greater portion of their time in the fields and with the herds, which leads to reduced foot temperatures and local acclimatization. Women, on the other hand, spend a greater proportion of their time washing and cooking; hence their hands are exposed to cold water more frequently. These daily exposure differences are not evident when total-body exposure to cold dictates massive vasoconstriction for heat conservation, but when the stress is milder and body heat content is not a serious problem, the local vascular adaptations become more evident.

The insulative value of Quechua clothing in clo units (1 clo unit is equivalent to an ordinary man's business suit of clothing) was assessed for the final half-hour of the 2-h exposure. Men's clothing without the poncho or hat was 1.21 clo units and women's clothing, again without the shawl or hat, was 1.43 clo units. These values compare favorably with values for other cool-climate clothing. The addition of outer garments should increase the insulation even more.

Why don't the people of the Andes wear footgear? The Indigenous technology could have produced leather or skin boots or shoes which would provide some protection for the feet. During the rainy season, however, they would have become hopelessly waterlogged and under those circumstances actually enhance extremity cooling and body heat loss. Rubber boots are now available in Nuñoa but are not popular. They would overcome the watersoaking problem, but because of their impermeability to sweat they too would become a detriment after periods of activity. In this context the practice of walking barefoot or with sandals is more understandable. If the feet become wet they will not become watersoaked and will dry rapidly. Field studies have shown that their normal temperatures are high enough to avoid injury, so bare feet seem to be the most economical solution to foot-cooling problems.

It is noteworthy that some adaptation to the cool temperatures must take place early in life, and once that is accomplished low foot temperatures are no longer a hardship.

CONCLUSIONS

Despite the cool ambient temperatures, precipitation, and the great potential for exposure to cold, the Quechua of Nuñoa do not seem to be greatly cold-stressed. The studies summarized here have considered all periods of the year when the apparent potential for cold is greatest, yet there is no clear indication that actual stress does occur. It seems likely that some individuals are stressed under some conditions, but the picture of severe cold affecting all the population must be modified.

The apparent avoidance of cold by Nuñoa residents results from their effective technological protection. The most important single item of technology is clothing. Regardless of observed ambient conditions, native clothing provides a comfortable thermally neutral environment over most of the body surface. So important is clothing that it is used during sleep, apparently because bedding alone is inadequate to maintain thermoneutrality. The central role played by clothing is of some interest because the contemporary native costume is not aboriginal. Except for the poncho, the design is a copy of European styles and has evolved only during the last century and a half. Prior to that, an Incaic tunic seems to have been used. How this costume would have influenced cold stress or the biological pattern of response to cold can only be conjectured. It does seem, however, that a short, armless tunic offers less protection than the present design. Here are some important implications for understanding present patterns of response to cold, especially if a genetic component is involved.

Native houses seem to be of minor importance in the thermal sense. Indoor temperatures are not much different from ambient temperatures for most of the day; indeed, they seem to be below ambient temperatures much of the time. Even during meal preparation the thermal advantage of being indoors is of short duration and seems closely related to distance from the stove (Larsen, 1973). The only obvious thermal benefit from housing is in reduction of long-wave radiation heat loss at night and perhaps in reduction of wind chill. Major functions of houses, then, are probably as much protection from precipitation and storage of food and goods as to gain thermal advantage.

The technological protection seems to be minimal at two points. Larsen has shown that early-morning and late-evening exposure to cold is severe, at least for children, but the absolute exposure that he measured was not great and recovery was rapid. The second period of cold stress not well mitigated by technology is exposure of extremities. Since the feet are not covered normally, there is a great potential for cooling. The wet-season studies suggest that maximum cooling of the feet is really quite mild, and temperatures remains far above those required to produce tissue injury. Prolonged exposure of the lower extremities could lead to heat loss, but there is no evidence to suggest that as a serious problem.

Most Nuñoa residents thus seem to escape major cold stress. The centuries-old technology seems adequate to protect them from most cold conditions which have been presently identified and studied. If cold is an important selective factor in an evolutionary sense, it must have operated prior to the recent clothing design changes, or it might operate among infants and young children. Clearly, these questions must be studied to definitely eliminate it from consideration.

17

PHYSIOLOGICAL RESPONSES
TO COLD

Michael A. Little

BACKGROUND TO COLD STUDIES IN PERU

In the study begun in 1964 in the district of Nuñoa, cold tolerance was just one component of a broad spectrum of investigations designed to explore the patterns of adaptation of the native Andean community to a high-altitude environment. Earlier studies in the same general area had produced findings that were difficult to interpret, largely because of sampling and technical problems inherent in those studies' designs.

Note on Terminology

Several terms used here are frequently confused and misused in the literature: "adaptation," "acclimatization," and other terms from fields of environmental biology. The terminology here follows that recommended by Eagan (1963a) and elaborated upon by Folk (1974). "Adaptation" should be used as a general, all-inclusive term to refer to a relatively advantageous adjustment that is beneficial to the survival and well-being of an organism in a specific environment. A *genetic adaptation* is one that is part of the hereditary makeup of the organism. "Acclimatization" refers to a phenotypic adjustment to environmental conditions that may or may not be reversible. *Short-term, long-term, seasonal,* and *developmental acclimatization,* then, describe such adjustment in terms of the time periods necessary for specific adaptive changes to occur. Other terms not used in this chapter are "acclimation," referring to adjustments made over a period of time to a single environmental stress, usually under controlled laboratory conditions, and "habituation," generally defined as a diminuation of sensation associated with repeated stimuli. Finally, *cross-acclimatization* or *cross-adaptation* refer to an adjustment to a particular stress that may positively or negatively influence adjustment to another stress (Hale, 1970).

Earlier Studies

The first study to explore cold tolerance of Andean Indians under field-laboratory conditions was conducted in 1960 by Elsner and Bolstad

(1963) in the town of La Raya, Peru (elevation, 4200 m). They used a procedure designed by Scholander and others (1958), where subjects spent a night sleeping under near-freezing conditions enclosed only in a wool blanket-bag with an insulative value of about 1 clo. [A clo is a unit of insulation roughly equivalent to a man's ordinary business clothing (Newburgh, 1949, p. 445).] Rectal temperature, skin temperatures at selected sites, and metabolic heat production were recorded during the full 8-h period of exposure. Based upon the results of this study and results from similar tests performed on Eskimos, Laplanders, Australian aborigines, and other native groups who are chronically exposed to cold, Hammel (1963, 1964) postulated three distinct native patterns of response to whole-body moderate cold exposure when compared with unacclimatized white controls.

Metabolic acclimatization typifies the responses of Alacaluf Indians from Tierra del Fuego and, to a lesser extent, Eskimos and Arctic Indians. In this case, individuals begin the 8-h test with an elevated metabolic rate which may increase slightly, while at the same time enabling body heat content to be maintained with only slight declines in rectal and skin temperatures.

Insulative-hypothermic acclimatization is characteristic of the responses of Central Australian aborigines and other arid-zone dwellers. The Central Australian aborigine begins the exposure with a metabolic rate that is close to the basal levels for whites. Metabolic rate and rectal and skin temperatures then decline throughout the test to relatively low values, permitting a lower body conductance and less heat loss from the core as a result of generalized vasoconstriction.

Hypothermic acclimatization is identified by Hammel as characteristic of Andean Indians. Here, the individual begins the test with a near-basal metabolic rate that increases slightly throughout the test, but also shows a marked heat loss from the surface by generalized vasodilation, accompanied by a drop in rectal temperature.

Each of the three patterns of response can be contrasted with that of the unacclimatized white who, during the same 8-h test, begins at a basal metabolic level and increases heat production by bouts of violent shivering as well as experiences a fall in body temperature.

Additional studies began in 1962 to examine the physiological responses to cold of the Quechua-speaking Indians of highland Peru (see Fig. 17.1 for sites of all studies to date). The pilot program was initiated in the village of Chinchero (elevation, 3750 m), a small, largely native community about 25 km northwest of the highland city of Cuzco. Two series of cold tests were performed on several groups of young men: a whole-body cooling test of 2 h duration at 14°C, in which subjects rested on cots and were clothed only in shorts (Baker, 1966a), and a test of finger immersion in water at 0°C for a period of 1 h (Hanna, 1965; Baker, 1966a). Both tests were designed to simulate the exposure conditions that Andean natives are likely to experience during day-to-day living. In an attempt to partition out the effects of genetic

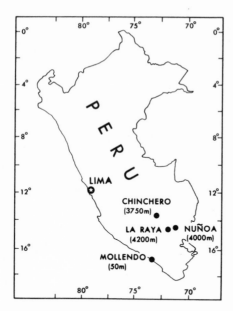

FIGURE 17.1 *Sites in Peru where cold tolerance tests were performed on native subjects. Mollendo Indians were tested in Nuñoa.*

adaptation and acclimatization to cold, four groups of subjects were selected to be tested: (1) Chinchero Indians living in native fashion, (2) Indians from the University of Cuzco, (3) whites from the University of Cuzco, and (4) a small number of United States whites who had been resident in Cuzco for at least 6 weeks. The group of U.S. whites was not included in the test of finger immersion, although data were collected on a more adequate sample in the United States the following year.

The Chinchero research was designed to explore relationships between body size and composition parameters which might indicate the presence of anatomical adaptation to cold, and to compare physiological responses of genetically similar and dissimilar groups of subjects as well as groups with different histories of exposure to cold. For example, differences between the Chinchero Indians and the university Indians in their responses to cold would suggest an acclimatizational basis of adjustment; similar responses would suggest a genetic mode of adaptation. Conversely, differences between the two groups of university students would suggest genetic adaptation; similarities would imply acclimatization.

Results of the whole-body cooling tests performed in Chinchero indicated that although U.S. whites maintained higher rectal temperatures than all the other groups, they had the lowest skin temperatures, especially on the surfaces of the limbs. The two groups of university students were quite similar in all responses, having the lowest rectal temperatures yet falling midway between Chinchero Indians and U.S. whites for most measures of skin temperature. Evidence from these tests points to an acclimatizational mode of increased tolerance to cold among Andean natives. There were, however, several procedural and technical problems associated with the study that limit definitive conclusions to be drawn.

Although metabolic heat production was inferred from rectal or core temperature, it was not measured directly. It has become clear from later investigations (Baker et al., 1967) that core temperature is not a good indicator of metabolic rate during whole-body cooling because of the rapid changes in metabolism resulting from shivering and the sluggish response of core temperature to such changes. A second problem concerned controls on room temperatures during the period of cold exposure. Because air temperatures in the testing room were not controlled, room air temperatures rose as much as 6°C during the 2-h exposure. Finally, subjects were not in an equivalent state of thermal equilibrium at the beginning of the test. Thus, there are questions of comparability of the four groups tested. Unfortunately, each of these problems could not be avoided in light of the conditions under which these early studies were conducted. In fact, any physiological investigation of peasant or primitive peoples in their native habitat is subject to unique technical problems not encountered in the usual laboratory.

Results of the finger-immersion tests are somewhat difficult to interpret, again as the result of some technical problems associated with field studies in the Andes. For example, when the Indian and white university students were compared with the Chincero Indians, both Indian groups appeared to show more flexible and warmer responses of the immersed finger. Yet, when white male and female students were tested in the United States, both responded with temperatures as high as or higher than the three highland Peruvian groups. Two explanations may be offered to account for these disparate results. First, since body thermal state influences peripheral temperatures and since groups of subjects were tested at three localities (the village of Chinchero, the University of Cuzco, and The Pennsylvania State University), some subjects might have been in a mildly chilled state and not responding optimally. Second, ice-water immersion of the fingers is an extraordinarily severe exposure to cold and simply may not elicit responses that are good measures of peripheral cold tolerance.

Current Studies

With these two pilot investigations as a background, a program of further studies of cold tolerance was initiated in 1964 in the district of Nuñoa, Peru. It was hoped that more information could be derived from these studies by

TABLE 17.1 *Laboratory Cold-Exposure Tests Conducted in Nuñoa*

Reference	Test	Subjects				Conditions		
		Sample	Sex	N	Mean age (yr)	Cooling medium	Temp. (C°)	Duration (h)
Baker et al. (1967, 1968), Weitz (1969)	Whole-body cooling (nude)	Nuñoa Indian	M	26	25.8	Air	10	2
		Mollendo Indian	M	9	22.2			
		White	M	15	25.1			
Baker et al. (1967)	Whole-body cooling (nude)	Nuñoa Indian	M	26	25.8	Air	15.5	2
		White	M	4	29.5			
Hanna (1970a)	Whole-body cooling (nude and clothed)	Nuñoa Indian	M	18	29.7	Air	10	2
		Nuñoa Indian	F	18	26.3			
Mazess and Larsen (1972)	Whole-body cooling (blanket-bag and native bedding)	Nuñoa Indian	M	6	25.2	Air	4	8

Thomas (n.d.)	Whole-body cooling (clothed)	Nuñoa Indian	M	12	31.7	Air	11	7
Little (1969), Little et al. (1971)	Foot cooling	Nuñoa Indian	M	30	31.6	Air	0	1
		White[a]	M	26	27.0			
		Nuñoa Indian	M	29	14.0			
		White[a]	M	28	12.9			
		White	M	7	24.4			
		White	F	3	24.3			
Little (1969)	Foot cooling	Nuñoa Indian	M	12	24.4	Water	5, 10, 15	½
		White[a]	M	12	26.2			
Little et al. (1971)	Hand cooling	Nuñoa Indian	M	41	25.4	Air	0	1
		Mollendo Indian	M	10	22.1			
		White	M	8	26.9			
Little et al. (1973)	Hand cooling	Nuñoa Indian	M	17	31.6	Water	4	⅓
		Nuñoa Indian	F	15	30.8			
		White	M	6	28.5			

[a]These subjects were tested at sea level; all other subjects were tested at 4000 m.

exercising greater controls during cold-tolerance tests in the laboratory and the field. Four principal objectives were identified in the Nuñoa program of adaptation to high-altitude cold stress.

1. There was a need to examine the buffering effects of material culture, social and economic practices, activity patterns, nutritional intake, drugs, and other factors on actual exposure to cold. Some of these studies have been discussed in the preceding chapters.

2. Attempts were made to explore problems associated with the covariant stresses of cold and hypoxia. This task proved difficult, since increases in altitude are invariably accompanied by colder environmental temperatures and more severe hypoxic stress.

3. In order to define the patterns of biological adaptation to cold stress, an effort was made to partition out various forms of adjustment, including short-term and developmental acclimatization and genetic adaptation.

4. Finally, some of the studies focused upon physiological mechanisms associated with the process of adaptation to cold.

This chapter deals only with those studies that were carried out under reasonably controlled experimental conditions at the laboratory in Nuñoa, Peru (elevation, 4000 m). In reality, what were studied were responses to cold of physiological systems of temperature regulation. However, inferences on the adaptive value of these responses were drawn at the individual and population levels in this human community.

LABORATORY PROCEDURES

The nine studies conducted at the Nuñoa laboratory are summarized in Table 17.1. Five dealt with whole-body exposures to cold under different conditions; the remaining four studies involved exposure of the extremities to either cold air or cold water.

Test Subjects and Laboratory Facilities

Quechua Indian subjects were recruited from the town and outlying countryside. Attempts were made to include only those individuals who manifested physical characteristics associated with Indian heritage and who had been lifelong residents at high altitude. All Indian subjects received payment for their services as laboratory subjects. White subjects who were tested in Nuñoa were drawn from the research team; as a result, sampling was limited. Tests on U.S. researchers were performed only after individuals had resided at high altitude for a minimum of 4 weeks, although several had spent more than 6 months in the Andes. Indian subjects from the coastal town of Mollendo were transported to Nuñoa and then tested after a 2-week sojourn at altitude. Mollendo natives were either born and reared at sea level or born at altitude and reared from an early age at sea level. Mollendo has a considerably warmer climate than Nuñoa; thus, although cultural practices and ancestry of the high-altitude and coastal groups were similar, the Mollendo Indians had experienced essentially no cold stress in a lifetime of coastal residence. The two foot-cooling investigations included white subjects who were tested at close to sea level in the United States.

The laboratory in Nuñoa, which was constructed of adobe bricks, included two rooms that were used for all tests of cold tolerance. An outer room was designed for preparation and equilibration of subjects, and a Styrofoam-insulated constant-temperature room was used for actual testing. The constant-temperature room contained a generator-powered cooling unit that was enclosed by a small styrofoam chamber used for extremity-cooling experiments. Thus, the entire room could be cooled for whole-body exposures, or cold air could be recycled through the smaller chamber for extremity exposures while the room was heated to a comfortable level. Air temperatures both in the small chamber and in the room could be maintained within ±1.0°C. All temperatures were recorded by means of thermocouples and a Honeywell potentiometer or thermistors and a battery-operated Yellow Springs telethermometer. Temperatures could be read to the nearest 0.05°C, and cumulative errors were estimated to be no greater than 3 percent.

Whole-Body Exposure to Cold

The whole-body exposures to cold air can be conveniently divided into those tests in which subjects were exposed nude (men wore cotton shorts, women wore cotton shorts and halter) at 10 or 15.5°C for 2 h and tests of longer duration (7 or 8 h) in which subjects were insulated with clothing or sleeping covers (see Table 17.1). Prior to all tests, measurements were taken of body dimensions and composition, temperature sensors were attached, and subjects rested for no less than 1 h at 24–28°C in order to achieve thermal equilibrium. Rectal temperature, skin temperature at several sites, and metabolic rate were measured before and during most tests. Metabolic rate was determined by oxygen consumption and carbon dioxide production monitored from a continuous effluent flow system of air (51.4 l/min) through a plastic hood surrounding the head and neck of each subject. In cases where carbon dioxide analysis was not possible, oxygen consumption was calculated on the basis of oxygen extraction, and a correction was applied for RQ (respiratory quotient). Formulas for derived temperature variables are listed below:

Mean weighted skin temperature ($\overline{T}_s$):

$$\overline{T}_s = 0.3 \text{ chest} + 0.2 \text{ forehead} + 0.175 \text{ arm} + 0.05 \text{ finger} \\ + 0.15 \text{ thigh} + 0.075 \text{ calf} + 0.05 \text{ toe temperatures} \tag{1}$$

Mean body temperature (T_b):

$$T_b = 0.33\overline{T}_s + 0.67T_{re} \tag{2}$$

where T_{re} is rectal temperature. The equation is modified from that of Burton (1935).

Extremity Exposure to Cold

Experiments to test local tolerance to cold of both the hands and the feet were conducted with air or water as the medium. Since cold water tends to act as a "heat sink" when contrasted with cold air, comparisons could be made between the responses to a moderate exposure to cold air and to the more acute exposure to cold water. During all tests, subjects were seated and fully clothed except for the hand or foot. Room temperatures were maintained at comfortable levels—usually 24°C. The period of equilibration for the extremity cooling tests amounted to about 1 h. For both whole-body and extremity cooling, testing began at least 2 h after the subjects had eaten. Skin temperatures were measured at the dorsal surface of the hand, the pad of the third finger, the dorsal surface of the foot, and the pads of the first and fifth toes. Although rectal temperatures were not monitored during these local exposures to cold, oral temperatures were taken before the test to assure comparability of samples in body thermal state and to eliminate subjects who were febrile on the day of testing.

One test was designed to measure heat loss from the foot indirectly by temperature changes in a known volume of water (calorimetry). Based upon the principle that 1 kcal of heat is required to raise the temperature of 1 kg of water 1°C, the following formula was applied:

$$H_{loss} = T_w V_w \qquad (3)$$

where H_{loss} is the heat given off by the immersed foot (kcal), T_w the change in water temperature (°C), and V_w the volume of water (liters). In order to control for group differences in foot size, heat loss was equated to a given volume of foot tissue according to the following:

$$H_{loss}/100 \text{ ml foot tissue} = T_w V_w (100)/V_{foot} \qquad (4)$$

where V_{foot} is the foot volume (ml). All hand and foot volume determinations were made by water displacement.

COLD RESPONSES
OF THE ANDEAN NATIVE

Responses to Whole-Body Cooling

The two types of whole-body cold tests—all-night blanket-bag and 2-h nude—were distinguishable in terms of both the induced stresses and elicited responses to these stresses. In a sense, the blanket-bag test simulated more closely the subacute chilling that the Andean Indian frequently experiences during his lifetime, while the 2-h nude exposure can be considered an acute stress that would be experienced only rarely. Comparisons of the 2-h tests of nude subjects exposed to between 10 and 16°C air temperatures will be dealt with first.

Figure 17.2 illustrates the responses of Chinchero, Mollendo, and Nuñoa adult Indian males during nude whole-body exposure to cold. Independent samples of Nuñoa Indians were tested under nearly identical conditions on two occasions, and Mollendo Indians from the coast were brought to Nuñoa for testing. Although this chapter focuses upon the work conducted in Nuñoa, the Chinchero sample is included for comparative purposes. All subjects, with the exception of the Nuñoa Indians tested by Hanna (1970a), are represented by values that are averages of two exposures to cold. Rectal (T_{re}), mean weighted ($\overline{T}_s$), and toe (T_t) temperatures, and metabolic rate (MR) are given as representative responses. There are striking variations in responses of the three Indian groups. The Chinchero group differed slightly from the Nuñoa groups, probably since Chinchero Indians were tested at somewhat warmer ambient temperatures (12–16°C), as well as the fact that the Chinchero sample was drawn from a village about 250 km northwest of Nuñoa. The disparate results of the two Nuñoa studies are paradoxical; they might be attributed to the exceptionally high core temperatures reported by Hanna (1970a).

Despite the marked variation among the Indian samples, there are some consistent patterns of differences between the Indians and whites. Rectal temperatures of Indians were higher than those of whites throughout the test. The declines in T_{re} of the four Indian groups were 1.0, 0.7, 0.4, and 0.3°C, respectively, while whites only dropped 0.15°C. Indians also showed higher $\overline{T}_s$; however, these Indian–white differences were largely attributable to the elevated extremity temperatures of the Indians: Note the skin-temperature changes at the toe site (Fig. 17.2). Skin temperatures at sites on the head and trunk showed minimal or no differences among the four groups. Metabolic rates were only determined on Mollendo and one sample of Nuñoa Indians and the group of whites. Metabolic heat production, corrected for surface area, was significantly higher among the Indians during most of the first hour. During the second hour, whites substantially increased heat production by intensified shivering to bring their rates up to those of the Indians. The initial elevated metabolism of the Nuñoa Indians conforms with the findings of Mazess and others (1969) that members of this population tend to show a basal metabolism about 5 percent higher than standards established for whites at sea level. Mollendo Indians had high core temperatures, relatively low surface temperatures, and a metabolic rate that was intermediate during the first hour. The responses of these coastal Indians will be discussed in a later section.

Indians, therefore, began the test with a higher resting heat production and higher heat storage levels than whites. However, the elevated surface

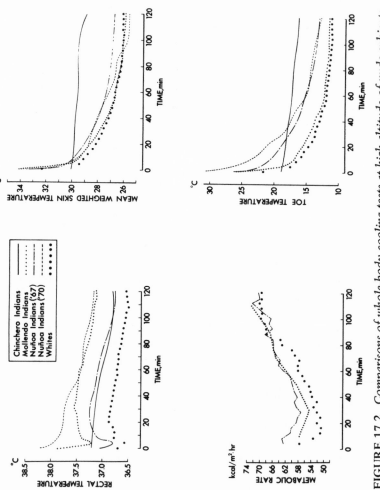

FIGURE 17.2 *Comparisons of whole-body cooling tests at high altitude of nude subjects exposed to 10°C air temperature for 2 h. Nuñoa Indians (1967), N = 26; Nuñoa Indians (1970), N = 18; Chinchero Indians, N = 24; Mollendo Indians, N = 9; whites, N = 15. [Adapted from Baker (1966a), Baker et al. (1967), Hanna (1970a), and Weitz (1969).]*

TABLE 17.2 *Mean Body Temperatures (T_b) of Chinchero Indians, Mollendo Indians, Two Samples of Nuñoa Indians, and U.S. Whites Prior to (T_{b_0}) and at the End of (T_{b_2}) a 2-Hour Nude Exposure to Cold Air[a]*

Subjects	N	T_{b_0} (°C)	T_{b_2} (°C)	$T_{b_0} - T_{b_2}$ (°C)
Chinchero Indians	24	34.86	34.19	0.67
Mollendo Indians	9	36.64	33.45	3.19
Nuñoa Indians	18	36.81	33.35	3.46
Nuñoa Indians	26	35.83	33.47	2.36
Whites	15	35.25	33.10	2.15

[a]Means are calculated from average values of $\bar{T}_s$ and T_{re} for each group.

temperatures of the Indians permitted a greater heat loss than whites had during the first hour of the test. This loss, then, stimulated increased heat production (shivering thermogenesis) in the Nuñoa Indians during the second hour, while at the same time enabling heat losses from the surface to continue at the same or even higher levels. Comparison of the four samples for mean body temperatures (T_b) before and at the end of the test (Table 17.2) shows the greater fall of T_b in Nuñoa Indians. (Chinchero Indians' responses may not be representative, since initial T_b was low, suggesting that these subjects were chilled somewhat before the test began.)

The results of all-night blanket-bag tests at about 4°C for two samples of highland Indians (La Raya and Nuñoa) and a sample of whites tested at sea level are shown in Fig. 17.3. As in the 2-h nude exposures, there were marked differences between the Indian samples in core temperatures. The La Raya sample, tested by Elsner and Bolstad (1963), had a pronounced drop in T_{re}, whereas the Nuñoa sample, as reported by Mazess and Larsen (1972), did not. La Raya Indians, as Hammel (1963, 1964) suggested, did respond to all-night exposure in a hypothermic fashion.

Nuñoan Indians' responses would clearly be identified as "normothermic" and are comparable to those expressed by the group of sea-level whites. Both Indian groups showed about equal declines in T_{re} during the first 3 h of the test. Yet, despite the increased metabolic heat production of the La Raya Indians after the second hour of the test, they were unable to elevate core temperature above 35.2°C. Nuñoa Indians began the test with a higher resting metabolism than the La Raya group, but La Raya increases produced equivalence after the third hour. Rates of heat production of whites and La Raya Indians were similar throughout the test. Mean weighted skin temperatures were variable during the 8 h of the test, with little consistency in group differences. Foot temperatures of whites, however, were lower than those of

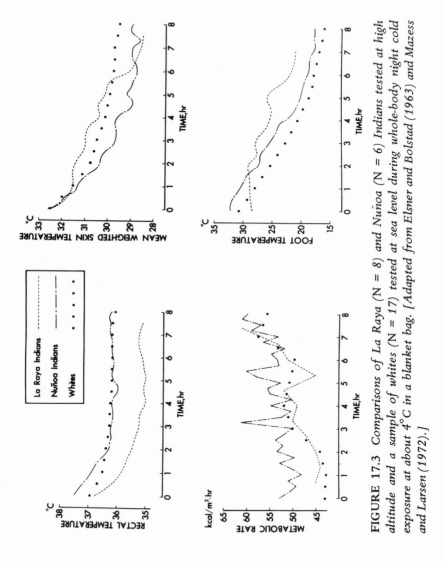

FIGURE 17.3 Comparisons of La Raya (N = 8) and Nuñoa (N = 6) Indians tested at high altitude and a sample of whites (N = 17) tested at sea level during whole-body night cold exposure at about 4°C in a blanket bag. [Adapted from Elsner and Bolstad (1963) and Mazess and Larsen (1972).]

344

TABLE 17.3 *Mean Body Temperatures (Tb) of La Raya and Nuñoa Indians and Whites Tested at Sea Level Prior to (Tb₀) and After 7 Hours (Tb₇) of an All-Night Blanket-Bag Exposure to Cold Air[a]*

Subjects	N	T_{b_0} (°C)	T_{b_7} (°C)	$T_{b_0} - T_{b_7}$ (°C)
La Raya Indians	8	35.33	32.97	2.36
Nuñoa Indians	6	35.88	33.79	2.09
Whites	17	35.68	33.92	1.76

[a]Means are calculated from average values of $\overline{T}_s$ and T_{re} for each group.

both Indian groups after the first hour. Values for mean body temperature are given in Table 17.3. Nuñoa Indians and whites showed lesser declines in T_b, with the more pronounced decline of the La Raya Indians largely reflecting the change in core temperature.

Conclusions that can be drawn from whole-body cold exposure tests are:

1. Andean Indians do not appear to respond to whole-body cooling by hypothermic acclimatization, as first suggested by Hammel (1963, 1964).

2. Nuñoa Indians show both a slightly elevated resting metabolism and core temperature that must enhance thermal comfort during cold exposures of short duration.

3. All Andean Indian groups maintain high levels of heat loss via elevated blood flow to the surface of the extremities.

Responses to Extremity Cooling

The experiments performed to test responses to cold of the hands and feet of Nuñoa Indians have given relatively consistent findings. When comparisons were made between native Andean subjects and subjects of European origin, tested both at sea level and at high altitude, native subjects uniformly maintained peripheral temperatures at higher levels. Figure 17.4 illustrates surface temperature changes at two sites on the foot during local exposure of the foot at 0°C for 1 h. Differences between Nuñoa Indians and whites were about 9°C at the toe site and 6°C at the dorsum site. When the hand was tested under the same exposure conditions (Fig. 17.5), Indians again maintained warmer surface temperatures, although the Indian—white differences were not as pronounced as those observed for the foot. Indians maintained substantially warmer foot than hand temperatures, whereas among whites, the finger was warmer than the toe, and dorsal surfaces of the hand and foot cooled at the same rate (Fig. 17.6). It was suggested that since the lower extremities are somewhat more cold-stressed during normal activities than the upper extremities among Nuñoa Indians, the observed variation in hand and

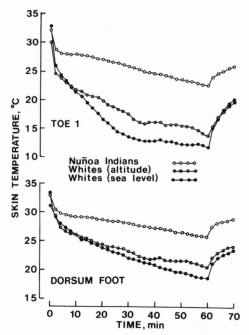

FIGURE 17.4 *Surface temperatures of the foot of Nuñoa Indians (N = 30) and whites (N = 7) at altitude and whites at sea level (N = 26) during 60-min limb exposure to 0°C air and 10-min recovery at 24°C. [Adapted from Little (1968, 1969).]*

foot temperatures might be an expression of differential local acclimatization of the extremities (Little et al., 1971).

In the more acute tests of hand and foot exposure to cold water, Indian subjects still had warmer surface temperatures, yet group differences were not as marked as in the exposures to cold air. For example, Indian–white differences for the surface temperatures of the toe at the end of 60 min exposure to cold air were about 10°C; group differences at the same surface site at the end of 10 min exposure to cold water at 5, 10, or 15°C were <2.0°C. The results of foot calorimetry illustrate these decreases in mean group differences with increasingly severe cold exposure (Fig. 17.7). The variation between 0 and 5 min in Fig. 17.7 can be discounted since most of the heat output during this period is derived from "stored heat." Heat output from 5 to 30 min is largely "circulatory heat." At 5°C water exposure there were no differences between Nuñoa Indians and whites in heat output from the surface. At warmer exposure temperatures, however, Indians had higher skin temperatures and correspondingly greater heat output from the surface

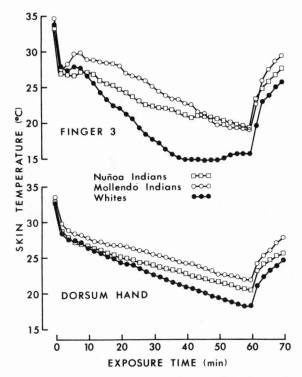

FIGURE 17.5   *Surface temperatures of the hand of Nuñoa (N = 41) and Mollendo (N = 10) Indians, and whites (N = 8) tested at high altitude during 60-min limb exposure to 0°C air and 10-min recovery at 24°C. [Reprinted from Little et al. (1971).]*

than whites. These differences were statistically significant. It was suggested from these findings that, although the Nuñoa Indian still has a thermal advantage during acute exposures of the limbs to cold, his vasomotor system may operate most effectively under conditions of more moderate cold exposure (Little, 1969).

The physiological mechanisms that enable Andean Indians to maintain elevated extremity temperatures during exposures of the limbs and the whole body to cold have not been fully defined. It is clear, however, that the microcirculation is somehow involved, such that blood flow to the surface of the extremities persists under conditions that would routinely produce a pronounced vasoconstriction in unacclimatized whites. During some of the experiments conducted in Nuñoa, measures of circulatory response were estimated from surface temperature changes. For example, the cold-induced vasodilation (CIVD) reaction is a measure of the involvement of arteriovenous

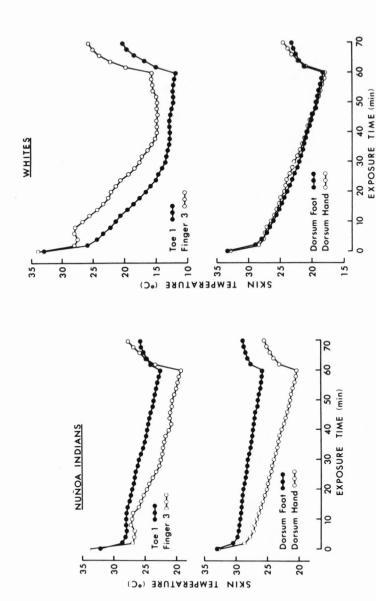

FIGURE 17.6 *Comparisons of hand and foot surface temperatures of Nuñoa Indians (hand N = 41, foot N = 30) and whites (hand N = 8, foot N = 26) during 60-min limb exposure to 0°C air and 10-min recovery at 24°C. [Reprinted from Little et al. (1971).]*

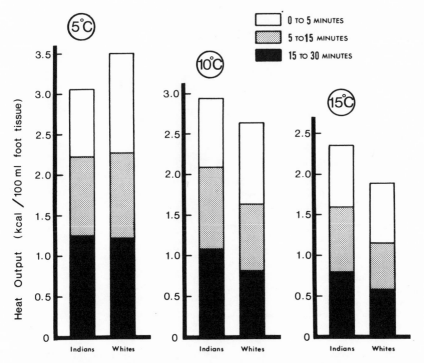

FIGURE 17.7 *Heat output from the foot of Nuñoa Indians (N = 12) and whites (N = 12) during 30-min cold exposures to water at 5, 10, and 15°C. [Reprinted from Little (1969).]*

anastomoses or shunts, vessels which are able rapidly to shunt blood between arterioles and venules, thus rewarming the surface of the skin. Such shunts are found in greatest density in the dermal layers of the skin of the fingers, toes, face, and ears (Nelms, 1963) and are thought to play a "compromise" thermoregulatory role in the extremities by conserving heat, while at the same time preventing severe cooling and associated tissue injury (Lewis, 1930). In general, a greater proportion of Indian subjects displayed CIVD reactions, and with an earlier onset of the rewarming and at higher skin temperatures than whites. However, at least during foot exposure to cold air, the CIVD reaction was not solely responsible for the elevated toe temperatures of Indians. It can be seen from Table 17.4 that although both Indians and whites who reacted had warmer skin temperatures than those who did not, nevertheless, those Indians who did not show the CIVD reaction still maintained warmer skin temperatures than whites who did react.

In later studies of hand exposure to cold water (Little et al., 1973), CIVD, reactive hyperemia (increase in blood flow following arterial occlusion), and recovery responses were inspected to define more adequately the

TABLE 17.4 *Comparisons of 60-*
Minute Mean Toe
Temperatures (°C)
Among Nuñoa
Indians and Whites
Who Reacted or
Did Not React with
Cold-Induced
Vasodilation
(CIVD) During
Foot Exposure to
0°C Air (Averages
of Two Exposures)

Subjects	N	Mean	S.D.
Indians, CIVD	45	27.5	4.9
Indians, no CIVD	15	20.3	5.9
Whites, CIVD	37	17.6	5.0
Whites, no CIVD	15	11.1	1.7

role of arteriovenous anastomoses in the maintenance of digit skin temperatures. It was concluded from this and other work that under conditions of moderate cold stress to the extremities (cold air), CIVD reactions are of minor importance, with warmer surface temperatures resulting from a reduction in peripheral vasoconstriction. In other words, the generalized constriction of peripheral blood vessels (largely arterioles) that is customary in unacclimatized subjects when exposed to cold is not as pronounced in Andean natives. Yet, during exposure of the extremities of Andean natives to a more severe cold stress (cold water), rapid vasoconstriction does occur with correspondingly greater involvement of arteriovenous shunt activity and CIVD.

Variations by Age and Sex

Several studies in the general literature suggest that developmental acclimatization to cold occurs in natives who are chronically cold-stressed. Yoshimura and Iida (1952) compared young and adult Japanese, Chinese, Manchurian Mongols, and nomadic Orochons from the Khingan mountains in an ice-water finger-immersion test. According to their measures of cold tolerance, only among the nomadic Orochons did finger responses to cold improve with age. Among New-World native groups, Miller and Irving (1962) found, when the hands of Alaskan Eskimo children and adults were exposed to cold air, that adults maintained warmer hands than children, but also that Eskimo children responded as well as unacclimated adult whites. The same general age effect appears with Athapascan Indians, where older children show a greater tolerance of the hand to cold than do younger children (Williams et al., 1969).

The results of studies performed on Andean Indians in Nuñoa are in accord with those observed for Orochons, Eskimos, and Athapascan Indians. Figure 17.8 summarizes the findings of a 60-min exposure of the foot to cold air by comparing young and adult responses within samples of Nuñoa Indians and U.S. whites. The young–adult differences recorded for the Indians were not present for the whites, suggesting that developmental acclimatization is one factor contributing to the elevated extremity temperatures of Andean Indians. Among whites, the lack of an age relationship probably reflects the relative absence of cold stress during the developmental period as well as the adult period of life.

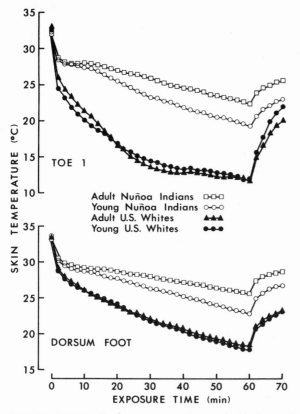

FIGURE 17.8 *Surface temperatures of the foot of Nuñoa Indian adults (N = 30) and youths (N = 29), and white adults (N = 26) and youths (N = 28) during 60-min limb exposure to 0°C air and 10-min recover at 24°C. [Reprinted from Little et al. (1971).]*

Some differences between adult males and females in responses to whole-body and local exposures to cold have been noted for Nuñoa natives. Tests of nude Indian men and women during exposure to air at 10°C showed that women were able to maintain warmer T_{re} and $\overline{T}_s$ than men of comparable ages (Fig. 17.9). Although women had higher values for $\overline{T}_s$, surface temperatures were not uniformly high; women had warmer finger temperatures but men had warmer toe temperatures. Similar sex differences were recorded during an acute exposure of the hand to cold water (Fig. 17.10). In this test, Indian women began with slightly warmer resting surface temperatures of the hand than Indian men, maintained the difference throughout the cold-water immersion period, and increased the temperature differences after removal of the hand from the water. Indian women also showed lesser increases in systolic cold pressor response and heart rate during immersion. Male–female differences in the same direction were also found among whites tested in Nuñoa during foot exposure to cold air (Fig. 17.11). These latter results should be interpreted with some degree of caution because of the small sample sizes of the two groups.

Greater cold tolerance of Indian women, as reflected by warmer core and surface temperatures, may be attributed to the thicker subcutaneous fat deposits and consequent greater tissue insulation characteristic of women (Hardy et al., 1941; Kim et al., 1964). The elevated core temperatures, but

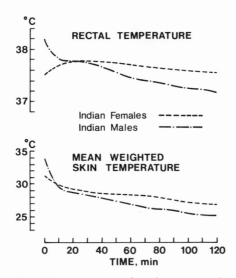

FIGURE 17.9 *Rectal and mean weighted skin temperatures of Nuñoa Indian men (N = 18) and women (N = 18) during whole-body exposure for 2 h at 10°C air. [Adapted from Hanna (1970a).]*

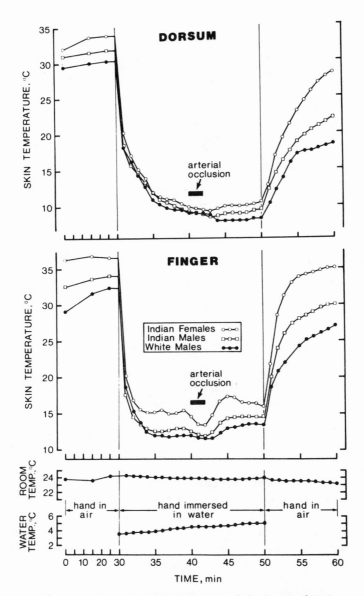

FIGURE 17.10 *Surface temperatures of the hand of Nuñoa Indian men (N = 15) and women (N = 17) and whites (N = 6) during hand immersion in water at 4°C for 20-min and 10-min recovery at 24°C. [Reprinted from Little et al. (1973).]*

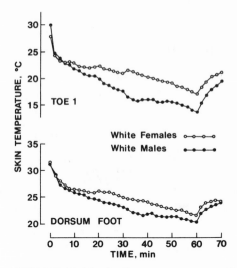

FIGURE 17.11 *Surface temperatures of the foot of white men (N = 7) and white women (N = 3) during 60-min limb exposure to 0°C air and 10-min recovery at 24°C. All subjects tested at high altitude.*

not skin temperatures, of the women should be a function of greater adiposity. The causes for variation by sex in extremity cold tolerance are less clear, although such differences are frequently documented in the literature. For example, among native Ainu and Japanese, women have shown greater cold tolerance than men during ice-water immersion of the fingers (Kondo, 1969; Suzuki, 1969) and lower cold pressor responses during hand immersion in cold water (Itoh et al., 1968). New World native women, including Greenland and Canadian Eskimos (Lund-Larsen et al., 1970; Krog and Wika, 1971–1972) and Canadian Athapascan Indians (Williams et al., 1969), lose more heat from the hands during various tests of cold-water immersion than do native men. These sex differences in local tolerance to cold are less likely to be related to body composition or limb-size dimorphism than, probably, to variation in responses of the microcirculation.

Influence of Body Size and Composition

Heat is transferred from the core of the body to the peripheral areas and surface of the body through the circulatory system and by conduction through various tissues. Carlson and his colleagues (1953; Carlson, 1954) describe the body as consisting of a *core* of central, heat-generating organs and a *shell*, including the limbs, subcutaneous, adipose tissue, and other peripheral structures. Under conditions of cold stress, the core retreats and the shell expands as the result of peripheral circulatory constriction, thus allowing heat to be transferred largely by the slower process of conduction. Under the converse conditions of warm ambient temperatures, exercise, or fever, the core expands through peripheral circulatory dilation, thereby transferring heat to the surface by more rapid means. One of the principal components of the body, adipose tissue or fat, can serve a very important function in temperature regulation by acting as an insulative barrier to conductive heat flow during peripheral vasoconstriction. This value of subcutaneous fat has been demonstrated in several studies where subjects were exposed to standardized cold tests (Baker and Daniels, 1956; Buskirk et al., 1963; Daniels and Baker, 1961; LeBlanc, 1954).

The two whole-body cooling studies conducted in Peru, in which tests of association between body composition variables and thermal response variables were made, were of Chinchero Indians (Baker, 1963b) and Nuñoa Indians (Weitz, 1969). Both studies found suggestive evidence for a relationship between cold tolerance and body-fat content. In the earlier Chinchero study, age was found to be negatively associated with T_{re} and $\overline{T}_s$, suggesting that cold tolerance declines with increasing years. The only other statistically significant correlations were between T_{re} and the sum of six skinfolds (SSF); these relationships were in agreement with previous investigations. Table 17.5 summarizes results of the two studies. If direction of the relationship is considered, as opposed to statistical significance, then T_{re} vs. age and T_{re} vs. SSF appear to be the two consistently related pairs of variables, with $\overline{T}_s$ vs. SSF as a possible relationship. The implication is that the Indian with greater adipose tissue stores shows less drop in T_{re} during whole-body cooling via

TABLE 17.5 *Statistical Significances of Relationships Between* T_{re} *and* $\overline{T}_s$ *with Age, Sum of Skinfolds (SSF), and Lean Body Mass (LBM) in Chinchero (N = 24) and Nuñoa (N = 26) Indians During Whole-Body Exposures to Cold of 2 Hours (Baker, 1963b; Weitz, 1969)[a]*

	Chinchero Indians		Nuñoa Indians	
	60th min	120th min	60th min	120th min
Age vs. T_{re}	<0.01 (−)	<0.01 (−)	N.S. (−)	N.S. (−)
Age vs. T_s	N.S. (−)	<0.05 (−)	N.S. (o)	N.S. (o)
SSF vs. T_{re}	<0.05 (+)	<0.05 (+)	<0.05 (+)	<0.05 (+)
SSF vs. T_s	N.S. (−)	N.S. (o)	N.S. (−)	N.S. (−)
LBM vs. T_{re}	N.S. (+)	N.S. (+)	N.S. (−)	N.S. (−)
LBM vs. $\overline{T}_s$	N.S. (o)	N.S. (o)	N.S. (o)	N.S. (o)

[a]Plus and minus signs indicate direction of relationship.

reduced tissue conductance, while at the same time showing a greater decline in T_s. Despite the relationships between T_{re}, $\overline{T}_s$, and adipose tissue within Indian and white samples, whites with their substantially greater adiposity generally show greater declines in T_{re} than Indians. Hence, although the lower $\overline{T}_s$ values displayed by whites during whole-body cooling may in part be related to abundant fat stores, bivariate correlations indicate that only about 10–20 percent of the variance can be explained by adiposity and consequent reduced heat conductance alone.

There are no theoretical grounds upon which a prediction can be based relating body composition to cold tolerance during local exposure of the extremities. Hands and feet have little metabolically active tissue, muscle, and subcutaneous fat, and heat flow is regulated principally by vasomotor action. The only consistent relationships that appeared during hand and foot exposures to cold air and cold water were scattered positive correlations of age with surface temperatures and measures of adiposity with surface temperatures. The positive relationships between the sum of skinfolds and skin temperatures may reflect the influence of T_{re} upon limb temperatures, since subcutaneous fat is associated with higher T_{re}, and higher T_{re} is known to produce elevated extremity temperatures during local exposure to cold (Blaisdell, 1951; Keatinge, 1957). SSF vs. limb temperature relationships occurred only in white subjects and may have resulted from the high coefficient of variation in whites (54 percent) and low coefficient in Indians (22 percent) for SSF. The possibility also exists that sex differences in response to local cooling of the extremities are related to dimorphism in fat deposition.

Miscellaneous Influences on Cold Tolerance

There are many factors which influence cold tolerance by improving responses or actually aggravating the effects of cold. These include drugs (see Chapter 18), nutritional and health status, absorptive state, physical fitness level, and seasonal and daily (circadian) variations in thermal state of the body. In addition to the studies of drug effects, two such factors were explored during the course of the laboratory work on cold tolerance of Nuñoa natives. The first was the fortuitous discovery of a circadian periodicity in extremity temperature responses to cold stress. Replicate studies of all Nuñoa Indians and U.S. whites were conducted of foot exposure to cold air in the morning and afternoon of the same day (Little, 1969). A consistent pattern among nearly all subjects was evident in which skin temperatures during the morning exposures were lower than during the afternoon exposures. Explanations of anxiety or acclimatization effects were rejected on the grounds that the test was a mild one, that subjects appeared to show no distress, and that any change attributable to acclimatization requires several weeks to appear. Figure 17.12 illustrates the results of three morning and afternoon tests of one experienced subject (M.A.L.) in which the responses

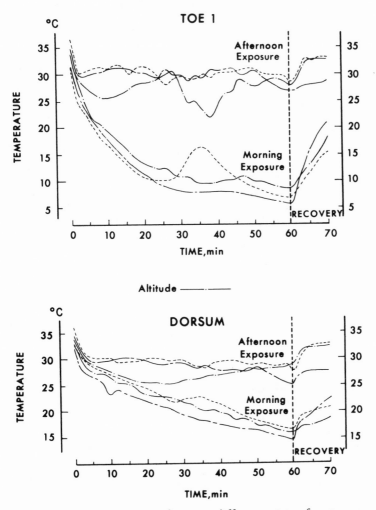

FIGURE 17.12 *Morning–afternoon differences in surface temper-atures of the foot of one individual who was tested on three occasions during limb exposure of 0°C air and 10-min recovery at 24°C.*

were quite uniform, despite an interval of 18 months between the first (at altitude) and two subsequent tests (at sea level). It is likely that the morning–afternoon differences observed under these resting conditions reflect parallel circadian variations in core temperature (Aschoff and Heise, 1972). Despite the persistence of a typical circadian core temperature pattern during normal activities of Nuñoa Indians, surface temperatures appear to be more highly dependent upon ambient temperature variation (Larsen, 1973).

A second factor known to influence the thermal state of the body is the immediate and short-term effect of food intake during meals. Kreider and Buskirk (1957), for example, found that supplemental feeding (600–1200 kcal) prior to sleeping in the cold at night elevated rectal and limb temperatures and metabolic heat production, which in turn contributed to a more restful sleep. A cold study, designed to simulate natural conditions, was conducted on Nuñoa Indian men dressed in customary native clothing. Skin and rectal temperatures and metabolic rate were determined both indoors (warm conditions) and out-of-doors (cold conditions) during a 7-h period covering the late afternoon and evening. A typical hot *masamora* (porridge of flour, potatoes, meat, and onions) was served to the subjects at about the third hour of the test while temperature and metabolic responses were continually being monitored. The influence of the hot meal on hand and foot temperatures is shown in Fig. 17.13. Dorsal surfaces of the hand and foot were elevated 2.6°C and 4.7°C, respectively, above pre-meal levels and the

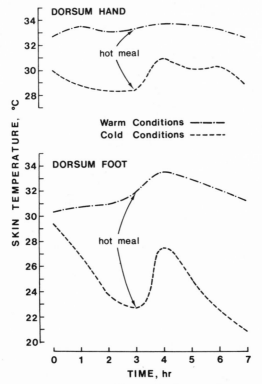

FIGURE 17.13 *Effects of a hot meal on extremity surface temperatures of clothed Nuñoa Indian men (N = 12) who were tested under warm (22°C) and cold (11°C) conditions. [Data from Thomas (n.d.).]*

thermal effect persisted for between 2½ and 4 h. These observations suggest that cold stress in Nuñoa natives is likely to be diminished by the warming effect of a meal taken shortly before retiring for the night.

Altitude and Cold

Much of the information from studies of man that bears upon the bivariate stresses of altitude and cold, and cross-adaptation to these stresses, is indirect and inferential. Studies of rats have demonstrated negative cross-adaptation to altitude and cold (Fregly, 1954; Hale, 1970), whereas the few studies conducted to date on man have produced equivocal results. For example, there appears to be a variable effect of hypoxia on extremity blood flow and consequent surface temperature. Numerous investigators have shown an increase in blood flow or skin temperature under conditions of reduced oxygen pressure (Frank and Wezler, 1948; Kottke et al., 1948; Newman and Cipriano, 1974; Schneider and Sisco, 1914); while others have failed to observe consistent increases and found decreases as well (Abramson et al., 1941, 1943; Durand et al., 1969; Freeman et al., 1936; Gelhorn and Steck, 1938; Jouck, 1944; Lim and Luft, 1960, 1963). A portion of the disparity may be related to the short duration of hypoxic exposure and the "overshoot effect" characteristic of so many adaptive changes (Hale, 1970; Prosser, 1964). The overshoot effect may be related also to the increased shivering and decline in rectal temperature associated with brief exposures to hypoxia (Girling and Topliff, 1966; Kottke et al., 1948; Newman and Cipriano, 1974).

Some research designed to explore problems of cross-adaptation to altitude and cold during exposures of longer duration has been conducted in India and Peru. Nair and associates (Nair and George, 1972; Nair et al., 1973) took young men from sea level to 3300 m, where they remained for 6 weeks before returning again to sea level. During the first 3 weeks, one group of subjects lived under thermoneutral conditions (25–28°C), while a second group was exposed to cold ambient temperatures (6–11°C) for 6 h each day: during the second 3-week period, conditions were reversed for the two groups. In the first experiment (Nair and George, 1972), early-morning oral temperatures were measured under thermoneutral conditions during the entire sojourn at altitude. There were no differences between the two groups, but oral temperatures dropped about 0.62°C up to the fourth week, after which they began rising. Since the experiments were terminated at the end of the sixth week, there is no way of knowing whether recovery would have been complete. The same basic design was followed during the second experiment (Nair et al., 1973), while weekly hand immersion tests of 30 min duration in water at 4°C were conducted. Exposure to hypoxia alone produced no change in heat output from the hand during cold-water immersion. The covariant stresses of cold and hypoxia, however, produced a decrease in heat output that persisted at least into the third week of the experiments. These results suggest that there is a negative cross-tolerance of general cold acclimatization and hypoxia during extremity cold exposure, but no effect of hypoxia alone. If the findings are to be accepted, then it is curious that other studies have noted either an increase or no change in extremity tolerance to cold in subjects who were acclimatized to general or whole-body cooling (Eagen, 1963b; Hellstrøm, 1965). Moreover, Blatteis (1966) observed an increase in skin temperature at the end of 6 weeks' acclimatization to altitude in the Andes when compared with sea-level values during whole-body exposure to cold air. Blatteis also recorded a decrease in O_2 consumption at altitude during whole-body cooling when contrasted with results of the same exposure test at sea level.

The investigations of cold tolerance conducted in Nuñoa were not designed to test the effects of cross-adaptation to altitude and cold. Nevertheless, some comparisons were made between whites tested at sea level and at altitude, and between coastal and Andean natives tested at altitude. For example, Fig. 17.4 illustrates responses of whites during foot cooling in air, in tests conducted at sea level in the United States and in Nuñoa at 4000 m. The slight differences observed in skin temperatures were not statistically significant, suggesting that hypoxia had minimal effects on extremity responses to cold. Responses of a single subject tested in the same procedure at sea level and altitude (Fig. 17.12) similarly showed an absence of altitude effects. The disagreement between these results and those which have demonstrated an elevation of extremity surface temperatures during short-term hypoxic stress (Kottke et al., 1948; Newman and Cipriano, 1974) may be related to the duration of time white subjects spent at altitude in Nuñoa prior to being tested. Generally, all whites had been resident at 4000 m for at least 5 weeks before participating in any tests, a period of time by which most individuals will achieve some degree of acclimatization to hypoxia by erythropoietic, respiratory, cardiovascular, and other changes.

The joint effects of altitude and cold were also evaluated by bringing a group of natives from the coastal town of Mollendo to Nuñoa for whole-body cold (Fig. 17.2) and extremity cold (Fig. 17.5) exposures. Lowland Indians were intermediate between highland Indians and whites in core temperature and metabolic responses, but similar to whites in surface temperature responses during whole-body cooling (Fig. 17.2). Yet during local exposure to cold of the hand, lowland Indians maintained warmer skin temperatures than both whites and highland Indians (Fig. 17.5). Thus, despite a life-long residence at sea level under normoxic and more temperate conditions, lowland Indians responded more favorably to cold at altitude than did whites with similar life histories of exposure.

DISCUSSION

The Andean Indian is able to combat the cold ambient temperatures at altitude both by the efficient use of homespun wool clothing and adequate bedding materials, and through the operation of several physiological mechanisms. Wool from the alpaca, llama, and sheep is spun, woven, and tailored into clothing that insulates the trunk and upper parts of the limbs quite adequately, leaving only the hands, feet, and face exposed during much of the time. At night, the native sleeps between numerous layers of animal hides and wool blankets that generally enable him to achieve adequate thermal comfort despite low night-time ambient temperatures and poorly insulated sleeping structures (Baker, 1966b; Mazess and Larsen, 1972; Larsen, 1973).

There appear to be at least three physiological mechanisms of cold adaptation that set Andean Indians apart from the whites with whom they were compared at altitude and at sea level. First, there is suggestive evidence that highland natives have a slightly elevated basal and resting metabolism. This was observed during two whole-body cooling experiments (Baker et al., 1967; Mazess and Larsen, 1972) and a test of basal metabolism (Mazess et al., 1969). Apprehension as a cause for the elevated metabolism can probably be discounted on the grounds that most natives who were tested in these experiments were seasoned subjects and there were no signs of distress such as increased heart rate or blood pressure. Second, in association with the elevated metabolism, natives have a slightly warmer core temperature than whites. However, both the elevated metabolism and warmer core temperature give the native a thermal advantage only during cold exposures of short duration, a pattern that is similar to the *metabolic acclimatization* exemplified by Alacaluf and Arctic Indians and Alaskan Eskimos (Hammel, 1964). Third, in tests of whole-body as well as local extremity exposure to cold, the Andean Indian maintains high levels of blood flow to the extremities, resulting in warm limb surfaces and correspondingly greater heat loss than whites. Despite the persistent finding of elevated extremity temperatures during cold stress, definitive evidence for a genetic capability among the Andean Indian is lacking.

There may be, however, compelling reasons for the high-altitude native to maintain warm limb temperatures, because of the shift in position of the oxygen-dissociation curve of hemoglobin at different blood temperatures. At lower temperatures, the curve shifts to the left, permitting less oxygen to be delivered to tissues at any given P_{O_2} value greater than about 30 torr. Figure 17.14 illustrates these temperature effects by comparing the arteriovenous P_{O_2} gradient of Morococha natives at 4540 m (38°C) with an estimated effect of the same gradient at a lower temperature (20°C). About twice as much oxygen should be delivered at 38°C as at 20°C, and at lower temperatures, the effect is even more pronounced. For example, Comroe (1965, p. 163) has noted that "blood at 10°C may give up no O_2 even at a P_{O_2} as low as 25 mm Hg." Baker (1969) has suggested, with this information in mind, that the warm extremity temperatures of the Andean native may be an adaptive response to both cold and hypoxia. On the other hand, Chiodi (1966) speculates that peripheral vasodilation at altitude would shunt blood

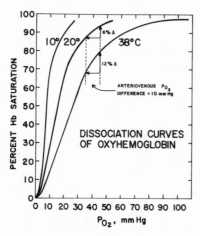

FIGURE 17.14 *Effect of temperature on the oxygen-dissociation curve of hemoglobin (from Comroe, 1965). Arteriovenous P_{O_2} difference of Peruvian natives at Morococha (4540 m) extrapolated from 38°C (Hurtado, 1964b) to 20°C.*

away from the central organs, and thus might increase hypoxia in the core of the body. Finally, it should be emphasized that there is no experimental evidence available to test these hypotheses. Indeed, peripheral tissue hypoxia may be a minor problem to the high-altitude native because of the abundant capillary network present in the surfaces of the hands and feet that principally serves a thermoregulatory function (Abramson, 1967, p. 130; Greenfield, 1963).

18

DRUG USE

Joel M. Hanna

In Nuñoa, as in other parts of the world, the population regularly utilizes a variety of drugs. As elsewhere, tobacco and alcohol are popular. In addition, coca leaves are used frequently. The middle-class Mestizos prefer tobacco and alcohol, while totally rejecting coca. The Indígena population prefers coca and alcohol but uses tobacco occasionally.

Of the three substances, only alcohol is produced locally; however, the preferred alcoholic drinks are those produced elsewhere and brought to Nuñoa by local merchants. All three substances are government-regulated and subject to tax.

The purpose of this chapter is to describe some aspects of the use of these three drugs in Nuñoa and to tie certain aspects of their use to the hypoxic, cold, hypocaloric environment of the altiplano. Much of the material on coca in this chapter is taken from Hanna (1974).

COCA LEAF USE IN NUÑOA

In Nuñoa, as in the rest of Andean America, coca leaves are chewed by a large percentage of the Indian population. The practice superficially resembles tobacco chewing. A wad of leaves is placed in the mouth and chewed until a compact quid is formed. The quid is then packed in one cheek and periodically rechewed. Coca chewing differs from tobacco chewing in that the coca leaves are chewed with a bit of alkali (llipta), which users claim sweetens the quid. A portion of the leaves and all of the juice is swallowed.

The alkaloid—cocaine—in the leaves is thus liberated and passed along the oral mucosa and the rest of the gastrointestinal tract, where it is absorbed (Montesinos, 1965). The extractive process is efficient, with about 80 percent of the available cocaine removed (Cuiffardi, 1948). Although various authors have claimed that the cocaine so acquired is addicting and numbing to the mind (Guitérrez-Noriega, 1949b; Wolff, 1952), there is no evidence of any adverse response or physical dependence in residents of Nuñoa. During almost 2 yr of observations I cannot report any cases of hyperactivity or actual dependence which might be attributed to coca use. Other observers have made similar reports for high-altitude communities (Monge, 1952; Mortimer, 1901; Cardenas, 1952). While using coca in large quantities, I never experienced any psychological aberrations nor any tendency toward dependence.

The only noticeable effect was a mild anesthesia about the lips and mouth, similar to that produced by dental novocaine.

Studies from other parts of Peru have suggested some relationship between frequency of use and altitude of residence. In one such study, Buck et al. (1968) surveyed four villages in southern Peru. In the altiplano at 3500 m, 72 percent of the adults used coca on a regular basis; 28 percent used it at 1700 m, 29 percent at 1050 m, and 3 percent at sea level. In Nuñoa, coca use appears nearly universal among adult Indians. Indeed, it was almost impossible to recruit young adult subjects who did not chew coca regularly—despite a government campaign to end its use.

Asked why they use coca, users frequently reply that it enhances working ability, reduces hunger, reduces fatigue, and promotes a feeling of warmth in the cold (Mortimer, 1901; Little, 1970). Since these are some of the stresses most pervasive in the Nuñoa environment, some causal relationship can be anticipated. To investigate this possibility, three separate studies were undertaken: one to study the quantity of leaves normally consumed, one to examine the effects upon working ability, and one to examine the effects upon tolerance of cold and hunger.

Habitual Consumption

The quantity of coca leaves normally used by habitual users at high altitude has frequently been estimated but seldom measured. The consumption of habitual users was estimated by Gutiérrez-Noriega (1949a) as 20–50 g/day and by Buck et al. (1968, p. 99) as 35–50 g/day. Baker and Mazess (1963) surveyed 39 households in the Nuñoa region and found daily consumption to be 25–75 g (and llipta consumption to be 2–4 g/day). Hence, it would appear that 50 g/day is a mean estimate of daily coca consumption.

The initial study was undertaken to estimate the daily consumption by habitual users. During a dietary study, families with members who habitually used coca leaves were given one plastic bag containing 50 g of leaves for each member who was a habitual user. In addition, each was given a bit of llipta which had been weighed. They were instructed to chew only as much as they normally used and extra bags were available upon request. The next day the bags were collected and the remaining coca leaves and llipta weighed. The average daily coca consumption of the 22 participants is noted in Table 18.1.

The mean daily coca consumption was 58 g per adult, with men chewing slightly more than women. There is some danger that this is an overestimate (subjects taking advantage of free coca), but the quantity is within the range reported by Baker and Mazess (1963) for the same area. The weight of the llipta consumed is slightly higher than that observed by Baker and Mazess.

The amount of cocaine potentially involved at this level of coca consumption is surprising. Cuiffardi (1948) found that 30 g of coca leaves contained an average of 181.5 mg of alkaloids, of which 86 percent was extracted through chewing and 80 percent of that was cocaine. Hence in the present

TABLE 18.1   *Daily Coca Leaf and Llipta*
Consumption in 10 Male and 12
Female Members of 10 Nuñoa
Families

Subjects	Age (yr)	Height (cm)	Weight (kg)	Coca (g/day)	Llipta (g/day)
Men					
Mean	39	151	51	62.5	5.9
S.D.	19	10	10	23.2	4.2
Women					
Mean	40	115	45	54.1	6.4
S.D.	18	4	8	23.3	4.6

study, with a consumption of about 60 g of leaves, the total cocaine available should be about 250 mg. This amount is more than double the recommended dosage for local anesthetic effects, and borders on lethality (Traunt and Takman, 1965). As the total cocaine available should thus be adequate to produce some physiological responses, the following experiment was undertaken.

From a group of 20 applicants with varying degrees of coca addiction, 6 habitually heavy users and 5 occasional users (less than once per week) were selected. Each group chewed coca for a full day and abstained on another. Order of presentation was alternated; half of the subjects abstained from use on the first day and the other half chewed coca on the first day. On their coca-chewing days, habitual users (average age, 30 yr) were given any quantity of coca which they requested, while nonhabitual users (average age, 23 yr) were given 50 g and requested to chew all of it. Llipta was given to be used with coca. During a day of abstention, 3 of the habitual users were required to remain in the laboratory overnight, to prevent access to coca outside the study. Tests were repeated for 3 nonhabitual and 4 habitual users, both with and without coca. Thus there was a total of 18 trials equally divided between habitual and nonhabitual users.

One day after coca was given (or after abstaining from its use), the subjects reported to the laboratory. They were asked to sit quietly for an hour, during which time they continued to chew coca if it was their day to do so. At the end of the hour they were conducted to an experimental room and sat quietly upon a bicycle ergometer for 10 min, after which oxygen intake, heart rate, and blood pressure were measured. Table 18.2 presents the results of these measurements.

None of the differences between coca and noncoca trials is statistically significant for either habitual or nonhabitual users. The limited influence of coca use is thus in contrast with that described in the sea-level laboratory, where considerable physiological and psychological response was found with

TABLE 18.2 *Rsponses of Six Habitual (Three Retested) and Five Nonhabitual (Four Retested) Coca Users After 24 hours of Chewing or Abstaining from Coca*

| | Habitual users | | | | Nonhabitual users | | | |
| | Coca | | No coca | | Coca | | No coca | |
Variable	Mean	S.D.	Mean	S.D.	Mean	S.D.	Mean	S.D.
Oxygen intake (l/min)	0.31	0.1	0.32	0.01	0.30	0.0	0.30	0.0
Heart rate (beats/min)	81	10	80	12	78	10	77	7
Blood pressure (torr)								
Systolic	119	9	122	14	115	11	110	8
Diastolic	83	6	83	10	77	6	83	7

its use (Zapata Ortíz, 1944; Risemberg, 1944; Gutiérrez-Noriega, 1949a). In further contrast, none of the subjects reported fantasies or other psychological phenomena. Disequilibrium, which characterizes cocaine use and had been reported for coca use (Zapata Ortíz, 1944) was not observed, although the subjects sat upon a bicycle ergometer which requires some balancing. None of the habitual users manifested or reported any withdrawal symptoms. Thus there seem to be no overt responses to coca when chewed in habitual quantities.

The absence of responses is probably the result of continual intake of small quantities rather than the intake of 60 g at once. Earlier investigators typically administered larger quantities at one sitting (up to 100 g) and reported pronounced responses. By chewing coca in small quantities, Nuñoa residents seem to avoid undesirable side effects. It is easily imagined that elevated metabolism and hyperactivity as reported by Zapata Ortíz (1944) would increase dietary food requirements while fantasies or other cocaine-induced psychological phenomena would be undesirable to the community at large. The ingestion of small, readily metabolized quantities of cocaine may also avoid habituation. In addition to the slow ingestion of small quantities of leaves, the amount of cocaine available is also small. Only the cocaine absorbed directly through the oral mucosa enters into systemic circulation unchanged. That which passes into the gastrointestinal tract is modified (Montesinos, 1965), thus reducing the actual amount even more.

Coca Use and Working Ability

Because coca use was shown to have little measurable effect in resting subjects, the benefits claimed during work were considered.

Low oxygen tensions should become serious during work at high altitude and could impose considerable stress. It is during this period that coca users claim benefits from chewing coca leaves. To determine if any physiological basis for these claims exist, the following experiments were undertaken (Hanna, 1971a).

After the 1-h rest period described above, 7 occasionally users and 5 habitual users were asked to perform an exercise test. Of these, 1 nonhabitual and 3 habitual users were tested twice, thus yielding a total of 16 "subjects." They were tested after 1 h of rest on 2 days, one day not using coca and the other day using it (any desired quantity for habitual users; about 50 g for nonhabitual users).

Exercise was performed on a Monark bicycle ergometer. The test was progressive, consisting of 3 min of effort at each of four increasing workloads. The final load was about 80 percent of maximal effort. Three subjects did not complete all four levels, so the basic statistical analysis was computed only over levels 1–3. Variables considered were oxygen intake, ventilation, heart rate, and blood pressure.

Blood pressure and ventilation were not statistically different between trials when tested with an analysis of variance. Values for oxygen consumption and heart rates are shown in Fig. 18.1. There is no apparent difference in oxygen consumption, analysis of variance over the first three levels showing no statistical difference between trials. Apparently, coca use did not modify working efficiency, nor did it change the energy requirement for a given task. Heart rates (Fig. 18.1) are statistically different between trials ($0.01 < p < 0.05$). While increased heart rate should have little influence upon actual work performance, it is possibly indicative of some underlying stimulatory effect, such as is generally attributed to cocaine (Truant and Takman, 1965).

The data from this experiment were broken into two groups, based upon 5 subjects who were habitual chewers (4 individual subjects and 1 retest) and the 5 nonhabitual users who most closely matched them in height and weight. A multiple analysis of variance was performed on these 10 subjects; some of

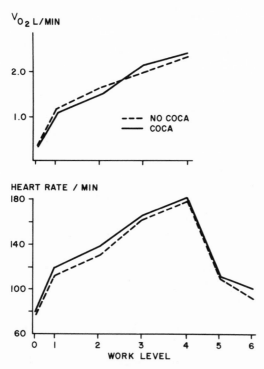

FIGURE 18.1 *Results of coca use on oxygen intake ($\dot{V}_{O_2}$) and heart rate. Work levels 1–4 are 350, 525, 875, and 1150 kg-m/min, respectively. Levels 5 and 6 are heart rate 4 and 30 min, respectively, after cessation of work.* [*From Hanna (1974).*]

TABLE 18.3 *Physical Characteristics of Five Matched Pairs of Subjects: Nonhabitual vs. Habitual Coca Users*

Variable	Nonhabitual users	Habitual users
Age (yr)	24.8	26.2
Height (cm)	155.4	152.2
Weight (kg)	53.8	52.4
Oxygen intake (l/min)[a]	1.64	1.61
Heart rate (beats/min)[a]	139.9	141.5

[a]For the first three levels of work.

the findings are presented in Table 18.3. None of the group differences were statistically significant (paired *t*-tests were used for age, height, and weight); hence there was no difference between habitual and nonhabitual users in any of the parameters measured. It seems that the accelerated heart rate previously noted is not simply related to habitual use.

The final exercise test was an examination of maximal working ability. This test compared 4 habitual users with 4 nonhabitual users after the same pretrial regimen. The test was again conducted on a bicycle ergometer; however, the workload was set at a high level and was increased each minute until the subject was completely exhausted. Maximal oxygen intake and maximal heart rate during the trial were recorded, as were blood pressures before and after the trial (Table 18.4). None of the differences are statistically significant at 5 percent or better. A paired-samples *t*-test with 7 df was used. For duration, $0.01 < p < 0.05$ at maximal workload. However, during the coca-use trials there was a propensity toward a longer riding time, about

TABLE 18.4 *Resting and Maximum Values for Maximal Working Test*

Variable	Rest		Maximal	
	No coca	Coca	No coca	Coca
Oxygen intake (l/min)	0.31	0.33	2.56	2.58
Aerobic capacity (cc/kg/min)	—	—	46.8	46.2
Heart rate (beats/min)	82.7	80.8	183.6	182.5
Blood pressure (torr)				
Systolic	118.2	119.4	152.9	115.7
Diastolic	80.7	83.1	88.9	89.2
Duration (min)	—	—	5.2	5.6

20 sec (0.01 < p < 0.05). This finding is in agreement with observations of Gutiérrez-Noriega (1944), who found that dogs run to exhaustion were able to continue longer if first given cocaine.

Coca use during work performance thus seems to operate in two areas: it produces an accelerated heart rate during submaximal effort, and it may promote increased endurance time. When taken together, these two results suggest how coca chewing may benefit work performance. The most likely factor involved would seem to be cocaine, for both responses have been reported after administration of cocaine hydrochloride (Gutiérrez-Noriega, 1949b). If it is actually cocaine, consideration of other psychostimulants—amphetamines and caffeine—offers some suggestion as to actual advantage gained. Amphetamines produce central stimulation, as does cocaine, and lead to enhanced athletic performance (Weiss and Laties, 1962). Amphetamines also reduce fatigue and lead to longer endurance at maximal effort on the bicycle ergometer (Wyndham et al., 1971), as observed here for coca. The actual mechanisms involved are not known, but under the influence of such drugs the worker feels "peppy" and is less sensitive to fatigue. Both of these responses to coca should be most welcome to the worker in a high-altitude environment.

Coca Use and Cold Stress

When asked about the effect of coca use on response to cold, 75 percent of the Indians questioned by Little (1970) reported using more coca during the cold season than during the warm one. A second study was undertaken to determine if coca use does modify response to cold stress (Hanna, 1971b, 1973).

Fourteen Quechua men, of whom 9 were habitual coca users, served as subjects. As in the exercise study, they chewed coca in accustomed amounts on one day and abstained from use on a second day; they were tested on both days. Before exposure to cold, the men, who were dressed only in athletic shorts, reclined on canvas-covered metal cots and were covered with blankets. After 1 h they were uncovered and exposed to 15.5°C for 2 h. Six surface temperatures, rectal temperature, and oxygen intake were measured during the exposure to cold. They continued to chew coca during both the rest and the exposure periods on the appropriate test day.

Finger, toe, and rectal temperatures during the 2-h exposure are shown in Fig. 18.2. Finger and toe temperatures were significantly lower, by analysis of variance, after coca use. During the second hour of exposure, the coca users showed a lesser decline in rectal temperature, which was also statistically significant. There were no differences in oxygen consumption.

It appears that coca use during exposure to cold produces a mild vasoconstriction which is observed as lower finger and toe temperatures (see also Little, 1970). The result is a reduced heat loss from these areas, and the heat conserved enables the coca user to maintain a higher core temperature.

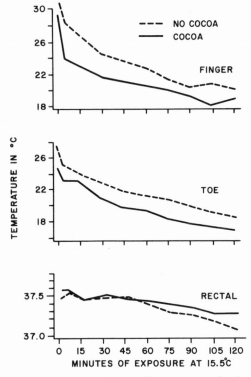

FIGURE 18.2 *Effects of coca use on body temperature.* [*From Hanna (1974).*]

The advantages of increasing heat retention are obvious when observations of day-long routines are considered. Thomas (1972) has determined that over 96 percent of the 24-h period of a Nuñoa man is spent in sedentary activities. Even during the work day (8 A.M. to 4 P.M.), 75 percent of the herding period is spent in sedentary activity. This pattern represents a most beneficial adjustment to hypoxia or caloric stress, but does not produce much heat for maintenance of body thermal balance. Continual use of coca should reduce heat loss throughout the day and provide partial compensation. The absence of external heat sources throughout the Andean region would also favor such passive mechanisms of heat conservation.

Comment

In a biological context, four aspects of coca leaf chewing appear evident.

1. When coca is used in habitual quantities by habitual users, there are none of the profound physiological or psychological disturbances that have been reported in laboratory studies, perhaps because small quantities of leaves are used throughout the day rather than large quantities at only a few times.

2. Physiological responses at rest and at work of a limited number of habitual users and nonhabitual users reveals no appreciable difference that can be related to coca habituation. None of the habitual users reported withdrawal symptoms when they abstained from coca use.

3. During work performance, coca leaf chewing elevates heart rate, which suggests some stimulatory effect. The effect may be similar to that of caffeine or other psychostimulants, and may give the user a feeling of greater well-being. Similarly, during maximal effort, coca leaves—like cocaine—seem to prolong performance, probably through reducing perception of fatigue. Both of these functions should make arduous tasks more bearable for the coca user.

4. Coca leaf chewing aids in conservation of body heat, a most desirable quality in an area where caloric availability (food) is limited.

Coca Use and Nutrition

A biological aspect of coca use which has yet to be studied is its relation to nutrition. Proponents of abolition have claimed that coca use dulls hunger pains in a chronically hungry population (Gutiérrez-Noriega, 1949a; Wolff, 1952). These arguments are based upon the recognized capacity of cocaine to reduce hunger, but adequate information for evaluating this argument is not available. Gutiérrez-Noriega quotes a broad correlation between annual per capita coca consumption and daily food intake. Using average daily food consumption in Lima as a base (100 percent), he reports a 44 percent deficit in grams of food per day per individual in "the southern Peruvian Andes," where annual per capita coca use is highest; a 27 percent deficit in the northern Andes, where consumption is intermediate; and a 13 percent deficit where coca is not used. These imprecise correlations can be questioned on two points: (1) the Lima population is a Mestizo population, which probably tends toward a greater body size, and hence has greater food requirements than does the Andean Indian population; and (2) subsequent dietary studies in the northern (Collazos et al., 1954) and southern Andes (Mazess and Baker, 1964; Picón-Reátegui, 1962) have indicated that the Indian population is probably not greatly hypocaloric. Thus, chronic hunger is probably not the "main cause of the coca habit," as Gutiérrez-Noriega (1949a) has claimed.

Given a hunger-suppressing property in coca leaves, it would be surprising if the user did not use it to his advantage during periods of acute hunger. Martin (1970) quotes Weddel's observations, which seem to support this view: "the Indians who accompanied me in my voyages chewed, in effect, the coca during the entire day; but when evening arrived they replenished their stomachs like starved men and I can assure that I have seen them ingest at one meal as much food as I would consume in two days."

The actual food value of coca leaves is probably small; however, they may aid in vitamin and mineral supplementation. Martin (1970) claims that coca leaves contain vitamin B_1, riboflavin, and vitamin C. He states that "chewing approximately two ounces of coca leaves daily (an average dose) will supply almost a daily vitamin requirement." Baker and Mazess (1963) have noted that the alkali llipta normally used with coca leaves is an important source of calcium in the calcium-deficient Andean populations.

The exact relationship between coca chewing and nutrition has not been established, but caloric deficiency does not seem to be the driving force in its use—except possibly during periods of acute hunger. Some vitamin and mineral value may also accrue from daily coca use.

Economic Aspects of Coca Use

Coca is produced in the foothills on the eastern slopes of the Andes, only a few score miles from the altiplano, where coca consumption is highest (Gutiérrez-Noriega, 1949b). However, the extreme ruggedness of the terrain makes communication between the two regions very difficult. The problem is compounded by the number of valleys that descend from the Andes to the Amazon. These deep canyons with boiling rivers make lateral communication along the foothills difficult. In ancient times, as now, communication was mostly vertical, by means of foot trails from the altiplano to the jungle, with little contact between valleys. More recently, roads have penetrated some valleys, but frequent landslides make their passage problematic (Drewes and Drewes, 1957). Communication with neighboring valleys via the roads is still difficult.

In the coca-producing region, there are two major producing plantation types: large commercial operations and small individual holdings. The larger, more extensive plantations are generally owned by upper-class families who live in cities, and are under the supervision of an administrator. They represent a large investment, but because of the constant demand for coca, a certain return is assured. The large investment by the upper classes and the demand by the lower classes have welded an unlikely union which has resisted all attempts to end the use of coca. Most of the coca plantations are small and their owners may derive all their income from the sale of coca (J. Murra, personal communication). Their operation will be described presently.

There is also a formal distribution network which has been carefully controlled by the national government at various levels, including licensing of local dealers. Taxes and distribution costs are passed on to the ultimate consumer, thus increasing the price somewhat.

Coca leaves in Nuñoa, after passing through the formal network, are not excessively expensive. During my stay the cost of 225 g (½ lb) varied between 10 and 12 Soles ($0.20–0.25 U.S.). Users' preferences were generally based upon the quality of the leaves: the more green leaves and the fewer yellow, the higher the quality.

An Indian laborer doing the most menial task could earn about 35 Soles each day; hence 1 day's work would suffice for over a week's supply of leaves, and 3–4 days' work per month would keep the user in constant supply. With an average daily consumption of 58 g, the annual consumption is about 21,170 g at the cost of 1125 Soles. This amount represents the yearly wool production of 9 alpacas or of 53 sheep (Thomas, 1972), a considerable cost for most families. Fortunately, all the coca used in Nuñoa does not come from the store. The typical farmer receives quantities of coca along with his wages when he is working in town (or for a hacienda). Unfortunately, there is no available estimate of the quantity received from these sources. There is also coca available from fellow farmers, given in return for agricultural assistance and derived from an unofficial network.

Perhaps the most economic manner to acquire coca is to circumvent the formal network by making direct contact with one of the smaller coca producers in the foothills. Each year some men (sometimes with their families) travel to the foothills, taking with them animals, meat, potatoes, and cereals from the altiplano. They trade for coca as well as other tropical products to be used and sold when they return to Nuñoa. In some cases, the traveler may remain and aid in cultivation of fields in these coca-producing regions. The system is viable because it avoids the more costly distribution network and its taxes, but more importantly, the individual farmer can realize a multiplier effect on the materials that he transports. The meat and potatoes could be sold to a local Nuñoa store, but they are worth far more after they have been taken to lower altitudes. Similarly, coca and other products of the foothills are more valuable when taken to Nuñoa. The traveler thus receives a double advantage; a multiplier operates on the goods he takes to the jungle and on the products he brings home to the altiplano.

Burchard (1971) has recently described the functioning of such a system in northern Peru. He reports that strong economic and social alliances are built between individuals in the altiplano and in the coca-producing regions. The high-altitude resident annually descends to the foothills to help his counterpart with cultivation of his fields. Even compadrazco (godparent) relationships may be established. During years of crop failure in the Andes, the farmer can take his small potato crop to his counterpart and trade it for a disproportionately large quantity of coca, which he then takes home and trades for food. Under ideal conditions, an eightfold increase in food can be so obtained. While normally less than an eightfold increase can be expected, even a lesser multiplier is economically helpful.

This reciprocal-exchange network is a form of an ancient one that has been in operation since the Incaic period. During the precontact and Colonial periods, some political divisions owned lands in both the altiplano and foothills. Residents of Andean villages then cultivated both areas on a regular basis because there was only a slight overlap in the agricultural cycles (J. Murra, personal communication). South of Nuñoa there are still a few districts which maintain their own coca plantations (Schaedel, 1959, p. 47).

An important economic consequence of the flow of coca up the eastern slopes is a regional economic integration. Because travel between the high-lands and foothills is so difficult in the absence of some driving force such as coca exchange, it seems most likely that the foothills region would play a less important role in the regional and national economy.

In the altiplano, coca leaf chewing has another salient economic consequence. The Nuñoa region is predominately Indian in cultural and economic makeup. The Indian community tends to be self-sufficient, making or growing almost everything it uses. The Indians are then potentially outside the greater regional and national economic system. If the Indian community would not participate in the regular exchange of goods, a large number of actual and potential consumers would be lost to the economy. The continual use of coca brings large numbers of potential consumers into the town, where they are introduced to the products of other regions and other parts of the world. The potential consumer is thus introduced into the workings of the cash economy and is familiarized with products of which he is not aware. Stores will normally exchange raw materials, meat, potatoes, or wool for coca at fixed rates; thus lack of cash does not constitute a barrier. It would be difficult to underestimate the importance of this economic function in enlargement of the consumer pool and in stimulating the farmers to produce an agricultural surplus to be exchanged for coca or consumer goods.

The isolated Indian family also derives considerable noneconomic benefit from the regular need to procure coca. Since each family group is potentially self-sufficient, it is possible for far-flung and isolated families to spend several months without seeing other people. The coca requirement brings them into contact with other Indians or larger communities on a regular basis.

Finally, as has been noted previously, coca leaves are in some cases a substitute currency. In stores and other situations, a fixed rate of exchange may be established. Part or all of the wages for various tasks may be given in coca. Indeed, coca seems to perform the same economic function as has tobacco and salt in other situations.

ALCOHOL USE IN NUÑOA

The second most popular drug in Nuñoa is alcohol. Both the upper- and middle-class Mestizo community as well as the lower-class Indígena drink it on occasion.

The cost of drinking alcohol in Nuñoa is variable and is largely dependent upon the type of beverage. Most expensive are imported products whose cost is excessive for the lower classes; hence their consumption is limited to the upper-class families. So limited is the demand that currently no Nuñoa store stocks imported liquors. Nationally produced spirits are considerably cheaper and fit all price ranges. Rum, gin, cognac, pisco, anis, and beer can be found in most of the major stores. The non-Indian population favors pisco, a grape brandy, and beer, while the Indígena prefer agua ardiente (sugar-cane whiskey) or chicha (corn beer). The former is about 40 proof and is the only drink available in many stores.

Responses to drinking alcohol in Nuñoa residents have been studied by

Mazess et al. (1968). They compared the responses of a group of altitude-newcomers of European ancestry with those of a group of acclimated residents, three whites and five Indians. The newcomer group showed no appreciable response to a moderate dose of alcohol (0.6 cm^3/kg of body weight) either at rest or at work. The acclimatized group, on the other hand, showed marked increase in ventilation, heart rate, and oxygen uptake. Mazess et al. suggested a differential rate of metabolism based on acclimatization.

An alternative possibility is suggested by recent studies of ethnic differences in alcohol metabolism. Fenna et al. (1971) compared the rate of blood alcohol clearance in groups of Eskimos, American Indians, and Canadians of Caucasian ancestry. They found that the Indians and Eskimos showed a much slower decline in blood alcohol level than did the Caucasians. A differential rate of metabolism is suggested. Also of interest in a recent report by Wolff (1972) that peoples of Oriental ancestry show facial flushing and increased heart rate at levels of alcohol intakes which do not produce such responses in whites. Considering the recent data as well as the composition of the acclimatized group—five Indians, three whites—a differential rate of alcohol metabolism is also suggested for Nuñoa Indians.

If Nuñoa Indians are more sensitive to alcohol than whites and take longer to metabolize it, an interesting problem is presented. For some time it has been known that blood-alcohol clearance and metabolism are slower at altitude than at sea level (McFarland and Forbes, 1936). There is thus the possibility that Nuñoa residents and others living in the altiplano have the slowest known rate of alcohol metabolism in man. LaBarre (1948) has observed that the neighboring Aymara are a notoriously drunken group. He notes that typical fiestas last 3 days and 3 nights, during which time the participants remain highly intoxicated. Such behavior is also seen in Nuñoa and seems compatible with a persistence of high blood-alcohol levels.

In an ecological context alcohol use in Nuñoa is anomalous. Alcohol produces peripheral vasodilation, which enhances heat loss from the extremities. Little (1970) demonstrated that Nuñoa Indians show significant increases in foot temperatures after taking alcohol, in both thermoneutral (25°C) and cold (0°C) environments. Little proposed that some transient increase in comfort would be appreciated but that over a long period considerable heat loss would result. The latter process should be potentiated by ethnic and altitude-produced variables already discussed. Thus, it is difficult to see any ecological benefit accruing from drinking by Nuñoa Indians.

TOBACCO USE IN NUÑOA

All social classes in Nuñoa use tobacco to some extent, but regular use is limited to the upper- and middle-class Mestizos. The only form in which it is available is in cigarettes, all of which are produced nationally. The milder varieties are most expensive and thus limited to the more affluent classes. The lower-class Indígena usually smoke the strong but cheap varieties.

In cigarette smoke there is a variety of chemical substances, but two—nicotine and carbon monoxide—seem most relevant to the high-altitude environment. Nicotine is a stimulant to sympathetic activity and leads to increases in heart rate, vasoconstriction, and pupillary dilation (Mathers et al., 1949). Carbon monoxide results from incomplete combustion of organic matter. It is absorbed if the smoke is inhaled into the lungs. In the blood, carbon monoxide forms a stable bond with hemoglobin and reduces the quantity of oxygen that can be carried. Such an effect would increase the hypoxia already present at the cellular level as well as stimulating an increase in respiratory rate (Traunt and Takman, 1965).

The parallel in systemic effects between tobacco for non-Indians and coca for Indians is evident. Both provide some cardiovascular stimulation, reduce heat loss through peripheral vasoconstriction, and seem to dull hunger. Perhaps they serve the same functions for the different segments of the population.

DRUG INTERACTIONS

A typical Indian social situation may involve smoking, chewing coca, and drinking agua ardiente. The interaction of tobacco with the coca or alcohol produces relatively mild effects. Alcohol—coca interactions are somewhat stronger, and hence of greater consequence.

One of the more usual responses to joint use of coca and alcohol was experienced by the author. With coca chewing the stomach is partially anesthetized so that normal gastric cues as to alcohol content are blocked. These cues, which cause the drinker to reduce his rate of drinking, or promote regurgitation, are not evident. As a result, the drinker continues to consume alcohol beyond the usual level and alcoholic unconsciousness results. Here is a possible explanation for the frequency with which drunks are observed "sleeping it off" in the streets of Nuñoa. If the vasodilation of the alcohol continues to predominate, considerable heat loss could be anticipated.

Another coca—alcohol interaction might be expected to increase the response to alcohol somewhat. As has been noted, cocaine potentiates the influence of catecholamines. The exercise study suggest that coca, too, has this effect. Catecholamine potentials might be expected to decrease blood flow through the muscle mass and redirect it to the core. As such flow to the brain is increased, alcohol content of the brain rises selectively while that of the muscle remains low (Hine and Turkel, 1966, p. 48). Thus, a rapid and powerful interaction might be anticipated.

CONCLUSIONS

In Nuñoa all regularly used drugs are imported from other zones; hence some return for their expense might be anticipated. Coca leaf chewing may be relevant to some aspects of life at high altitude: thermal and economic functions may be involved, along with alleviation of hunger and fatigue. Alcohol seems to play no apparent ecological role. Its intoxicating social role seems to be fully exploited in Nuñoa; Nuñoa residents may be the most alcohol-sensitive people known in the world. Tobacco may have the same functions in the upper classes as coca has in the lower ones, but that remains to be investigated.

19

ENERGY FLOW
AT HIGH ALTITUDE

R. Brooke Thomas

Characteristics of the altiplano physical and biotic environment are discussed in detail in Chapter 2 and can be briefly summarized here. There is persistent and intense stress associated with reduced atmospheric pressure; fluctuating temperature and precipitation with regular diurnal and seasonal cycles, respectively; nonregular climatic events capable of considerably disrupting the biota; and a patchy, finely scaled mosaic of environmental conditions that change in both time and space. These characteristics, in turn, are reflected in a limited and fluctuating productivity spread over wide regions, and affecting energy flow throughout the biotic community. All life forms in this high-altitude region must either adjust to these conditions or avoid them, in order to persist. Andean human groups are no different in this regard from other plant and animal populations. Where they do differ, and differ significantly, is in the range and combined effectiveness of their biobehavioral responses to environmental constraints.

In previous chapters considerable attention has been given to responses of Andean groups to two environmental constraints: hypoxia and cold stress. A third major constraint is energy flow.

While adaptation to the flow of energy has long been a concern of plant and animal ecologists, the application of this concept to human groups has, until recently, received relatively little attention, despite rather extensive data on the components of human flow systems. Thus, although information on energy production, consumption, and expenditure is available for a number of groups, these components have been generally interpreted as distinct units. Consequently, adaptive pathways employed by groups, and their role in structuring related phenomena, remain largely unexplored.

Given the paucity of existing information, the altiplano region of southern Peru appears well suited for investigating human adaptation to a relatively closed energy-flow system. Especially well suited is the high *puna*, ecozone where groups are more isolated from the national culture and environmental factors that disrupt energy flow are more severe than elsewhere. Rural populations residing in this ecozone are primarily reliant upon either their own or animal energy sources (work) for subsistence activities. Available food energy is limited by a low level of net primary production at higher elevations, as well as a low capacity to replace the natural flora with more productive cultigens. Further limitations on available energy are imposed by the unstable nature of the high puna climate, which results in an irregular rate of energy flow from year to year.

The long-term presence of Andean populations in the altiplano region suggests that successful responses to the energy-flow system have been made, responses effective in maintaining adequate consumption levels despite such environmental conditions. In examining these responses it seems important to consider groups that have established an approximate ecological balance with their environment.

This condition appears to be met in the rural sections of the Nuñoa district. The location of Nuñoa in the high wet puna, surrounded on three sides by a series of ranges, makes it one of the more remote areas within the altiplano region. As a consequence of having little contact with the national culture, most of the rural population (over 95 percent Quechua Indians) has remained highly dependent upon the immediate area for its support.

Although the Nuñoa population is not totally isolated (substantial exchange and trade does take place with lower zones and in markets), it is possible to consider the district as an ecosystem in which the human population operates as an important primary and dominant secondary consumer through horticulture and pastoralism. Such a functional role has been achieved by replacing less productive natural plant and animal populations with predominantly locally derived domesticates. A greater portion of the energy flowing through the ecosystem is captured by the human population because of this modification of the biotic community.

Beyond the capture or acquisition of energy, its distribution to group members becomes important; for this information one must turn to the social environment. As Escobar M. has pointed out in Chapter 3, the Nuñoa district at the time of the study (before agrarian reform) was largely composed of haciendas. Rural families who lived on hacienda lands were obligated to herd and cultivate for the owner, as well as for themselves. Thus, the family did not have access to a considerable amount of goods that it directly produced. Such a condition poses an additional constraint on the flow of energy into the Nuñoa rural population.

The study reported here focused upon: (1) determination of the amount of energy flowing through the Nuñoa human population, (2) assessment of the adequacy of this flow, and (3) identification of the principal biological and behavioral responses that have enabled the population successfully to adapt to the energy-flow system.

METHODS AND CONCEPTS

Three key variables form a basis of the energy-flow study: energy production, consumption, and expenditure. Their principal value lies not only in providing estimates of the amount of energy passing through a group, but also in assessing the manner in which it is utilized. Estimates of *energy production*, for instance, indicate the quantity of energy extracted from other animal and plant populations (or acquired from other human groups) which is available for distribution. *Energy consumption* provides a measurement of the energy flowing through group members, and consequently points out the manner by which energy sources are distributed to segments of the group. Finally, *energy expenditure* values indicate how the consumed energy is utilized; of particular importance is the extent to which utilization is related to subsistence activities or, more directly, to the acquisition of new energy sources. Information on production and expenditure provides a means of examining adjustments to the energy-flow system.

Measurement of Energy Flow

Measurement of these components involved a variety of techniques borrowed from human nutrition, work physiology, and agricultural science (Table 19.1). Basically, different techniques are employed to reach the same information, cross-checking each other's accuracy. For energy expenditure, the cost of frequently relied-upon subsistence activities was measured by indirect calorimetric techniques for all participating sex-age groups. Indicators of physiological strain on participants were also measured, allowing for a sex-age group's ability to perform strenuous and prolonged activities. Finally, all measurements of energy were reported in kilogram-calories (kcal). For a detailed description of methods employed in data collection and in estimates of energy consumption, production, and expenditure, see Thomas (1973).

Adaptation to the Flow System

If a group is to maintain itself in an area, energy production or acquisition (food) must exceed the total energy expended by its members. Thus, for each unit of energy expended, somewhat greater than one energy unit must be acquired. This ratio of energy production over energy expenditure has been referred to by Brody (1945) as "energetic efficiency." It serves as a convenient base for: (1) assessing the overall adaptiveness of a group to the energy-flow system(s), and (2) identifying specific responses that contribute to this adapted state.

Energy availability in the Nuñoa ecosystem may operate as a limiting factor on the human group. Although such a situation is rather extreme and atypical, it is worth studying, for several reasons. How different buffering or response systems operate and are integrated with one another can be seen most clearly when energy is the limiting factor. Additionally, most of the generalizations about energy flow apply equally well to situations in which other processes operate as limiting factors. Energy flow rather than nitrogen or carbon cycling is studied because it is easier to measure in man.

TABLE 19.1   *Methods and Procedures Used in Measuring and*
Analyzing Energy Flow

I. Energy production
   A. Collection of data
      1. Regional survey of production
      2. Questionnaires and conversations concerning production techniques
      3. Direct measurement
         a. of production per land unit of animal, per time unit
         b. of food stores
         c. of wastage and loss preceding consumption
         d. in experimentation with productive techniques
   B. Conversion of caloric values
   C. Evaluation of the measurement period
      1. Representativeness of annual production
      2. Annual variability in production
II. Energy consumption
   A. Collection of data
      1. Weighing of food consumed
      2. Questionnaires concerning food use
      3. Daily recording of food items consumed
   B. Conversion to caloric values
   C. Establishment of consumption by sex–age group
   D. Evaluation of the adequacy of energy consumption
      1. Comparison with international standards
      2. Presence of deficiency-related symptoms
      3. Indicators of caloric balance
III. Energy expenditure
   A. Survey of daily activity pattern
   B. Determination of key activities
      1. Importance in subsistence pattern
      2. Extent to which activity is relied on
      3. Performance effort necessary
   C. Testing procedures based on indirect calorimetry
      1. In field measurements
      2. Under standardized testing conditions
   D. Estimation of the energy cost of activities not examined
   E. Time–motion studies
   F. Assessment of physiological strain in performing activities

The concept of "adaptation to the flow system" suggests that hypocaloric stress is effectively counteracted and that energy produced is being utilized in an efficient manner. It is therefore possible to regard adaptation under limiting conditions as a strategy that attempts to minimize the risk of serious disruption in flow and to maximize long-term energetic efficiency (energy production/energy expenditure). The assessment of specific adjustments to energy flow may be approached in the same way. If alternative responses or strategies are available to a group, those with the highest long-term energetic efficiency may be regarded as the most adaptive, since higher energetic efficiency generally makes serious hypocaloric stress less likely. Such a definition does not imply causation, simply a functional relationship.

This rather specific definition of adaptation is an attempt to avoid the ambiguities inherent with a broader usage of the term, such as responses that meet a group's goals or maintain its values. In choosing a more restricted definition, I realize that any response is the result of a complex interplay of past and present events, constraints, and values. The validation of energy as a limiting factor, and the importance of its efficient utilization as a general adaptive response, will be borne out by the extent to which a wide range of responses can be identified as adaptive.

ENERGY FLOW
THROUGH THE NUÑOA POPULATION

The Annual Cycle

Economies which are dependent upon seasonal production of energy sources must regulate the annual utilization of energy so that the performance of crucial subsistence activities will not be impaired nor the resulting production of caloric resources seriously reduced. An examination of seasonal variation in energy flow through the Nuñoa population consequently allows insights into the process of energy utilization in the course of the annual cycle.

The population has attached itself to the energy-flow system primarily through the cultivation of Andean tubers and cereals (quinoa and cañihua) and pastoralism. Activities associated with these subsistence patterns can be grouped into four periods with the annual cycle (see Fig. 19.1); the timing of these periods varies somewhat within the ecosystem. The four periods are (1) the planting–shearing period (September–November), (2) the growing–lambing period (December–February), (3) the harvest period (March–May), and (4) the post-harvest slaughter period (June–August).

During the planting and wool-shearing period, work levels are generally high. Preparation and planting of the Andean cereals fields begins near the end of August and continues into the first half of September. With the onset of rains in mid-September, potatoes are planted, sometimes until late November. Shearing begins in mid-November and extends into December. While food stores are, obviously, not as high as in the preceding post-harvest period, consumption values do not indicate a marked reduction during this period.

In the growing and lambing period, principal activities consist of selling wool, weeding and ridging potato fields, and supervising lambing. These activities do not require high work levels. Foods purchased with money received from wool sales are added during late December and early January, and meat derived from neonatal herd mortality becomes available in January. Despite the addition of these energy sources, food reserves during this period, especially in February and early March, are at their lowest.

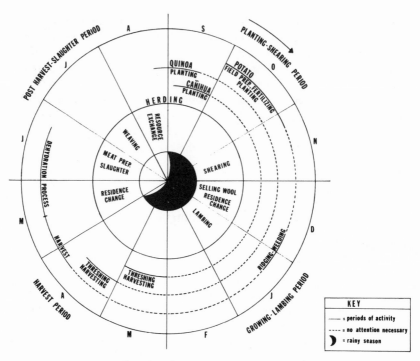

FIGURE 19.1 *Annual cycle of major subsistence activities.*

During the following period all major cultigens are harvested and a portion (10–20 percent) of the herd is slaughtered. This is a time of hard work for most of the population. Since food energy is being produced throughout the period, consumption levels would be expected to increase progressively. Energy consumption during the first 2 months of this period, however, appears to be quite low, despite the availability of Andean cereals. With the commencement of the potato harvest in May, the availability of food energy sources increases rapidly and consumption approximates that of June.

In the post-harvest period, energy reserves are at an annual maximum and work levels remain generally light; caloric consumption is relatively high.

Energy Consumption

Several studies have attempted to assess the dietary status of the human population in Nuñoa (see Chapter 11). Results are variable but suggest that a delicate, but adequate balance exists between nutritional resources and needs during years of normal food production. Such conclusions, however, are based primarily upon data for the post-harvest period, a time when food resources are generally quite high. Clearly, information is needed for other periods in the annual cycle.

In order to obtain such estimates, food consumption surveys were carried out at three locations within the ecosystems during April, June, and October. These dates correspond to three of the four aforementioned periods within the annual cycle. Missing is the growing–lambing period, during which high waters prevented access to the complete sample, and it is during this period that energy consumption is presumed to be lowest (Hanna, 1968). Consequently, annual consumption estimates reported may be somewhat high, owing to this omission of data. Survey location, sample, and methods are similar to those employed by Gursky (1969); however, sample sizes smaller.

From seasonal information on energy consumption, sex–age specific estimates of annual consumption were calculated (Table 19.2), following guidelines set up by FAO (1957). Table 19.3 shows the caloric intake of different segments of the population. Nearly 12 million kcal is consumed by the Nuñoa population each day. Thus, over 4 billion kcal must be produced

TABLE 19.2 *Mean Daily and Annual Caloric Consumption Estimates for Nuñoa, by Age and Sex*

Age (yr)	Males kcal/day	Males kcal/yr	Females kcal/day	Females kcal/yr
Below 1	1120	408,800	1120	408,800
1	604	220,460	724	264,260
2	725	264,625	856	312,440
3	888	324,120	918	335,070
4	919	335,435	992	362,080
5	1009	368,285	1038	378,870
6	1189	433,985	1137	415,005
7	1305	476,325	1245	454,425
8	1393	508,445	1290	470,850
9	1482	540,930	1331	485,815
10	1516	553,340	1398	510,270
11	1578	575,970	1414	516,110
12	1599	583,635	1497	546,405
13	1689	616,485	1511	551,515
14	1777	648,605	1563	570,495
15	1857	677,805	1602	584,730
16	1924	702,260	1623	592,395
17	2019	736,935	1645	600,425
18	2070	755,550	1653	603,345
19	2092	763,580	1667	608,455
20–29	2122	744,530	1677	612,105
30–39	2128	776,720	1677	612,105
40–49	2064	753,360	1627	593,855
50–59	2000	730,000	1576	575,240
60–64	1840	671,600	1451	529,615
65 and over	1575	575,875	1241	452,965

TABLE 19.3   *Sex–Age Composition and Caloric Consumption
Estimates for the Nuñoa Population*

Age group (yr)	N	Population percentage	Daily intake (kcal)	Group intake (kcal)	Total intake percentage
			Males		
0–4	692	18.5	851	588,892	9.6
5–9	618	16.5	1296	800,928	13.1
10–14	449	12.0	1632	732,768	12.0
15–19	337	9.0	1992	671,304	11.0
20–39	921	24.6	2125	1,957,125	31.9
40–64	543	14.5	1968	1,068,624	17.4
65 and over	183	4.9	1575	307,623	5.0
Subtotal	3743	100.0	—	6,127,264	100.0
			Females		
0–4	645	16.1	922	594,690	10.4
5–9	605	15.1	1208	730,840	12.8
10–14	393	9.8	1477	580,461	10.2
15–19	325	8.1	1638	532,350	9.4
20–39	1150	28.7	1677	1,928,550	33.9
40–64	665	16.6	1571	1,044,715	18.4
65 and over	224	5.6	1241	277,984	4.9
Subtotal	4007	100.0	—	5,689,590	100.0
Total	7750	—	—	11,816,854	—

or acquired by the population each year. With regard to individual requirements, dietary surveys indicate that caloric consumption is considerably
below FAO (1957) recommendations. In the course of a normal annual cycle,
Nuñoan young men and women consume an estimated 2100 and 1600
kcal/day, respectively, or about 75 percent of FAO (1957) values. The
percentage appears to be even lower for children. Findings of low caloric
intake in the population, especially among children, are consistent with
results obtained by Gursky (1969) during the post-harvest slaughter period.

Picón-Reátegui (Chapter 11) is critical of the low values reported by both
studies, suggesting that a more reasonable consumption range would be
between 2300 and 3100 kcal/day. Extrapolating from the FAO "standard
man" he adds that an active Nuñoa man and woman would require approximately 2930 and 2136 kcal/day, respectively. A note of caution is needed at
this point. The fact that estimates of caloric intake in the Nuñoa population
fall below an international recommended standard by no means indicates the
existence of a chronic negative caloric balance in this group. It suggests only

that caloric consumption is below that expected, and that further indicators of dietary status and activity patterns must be examined. FAO energy requirements have frequently been criticized as being set too high (Passmore, 1964), as borne out by their recent downward revision (FAO, 1973).

The consumption values noted above refer to a year of normal food production. In such a marginal agricultural zone, however, both local and regional climatic disruptions affecting crop yield are common. In the event of crop failure, energy expended on cultivation is lost. Frost, snow, hail, too much rain, and insects pose a continuous threat to cultigens during vulnerable periods of their development. Likewise, prolonged droughts such as occurred in 1939–1940 and 1956–1957, or dynamic frosts may severely reduce both plant and animal production on a regional scale (see Chapter 2). And such disruptions would cause further reduced caloric intakes for periods of up to 2 years.

Low energy availability consequently appears as an important limiting factor on the Nuñoa population. Stated differently, the amount of human biomass maintained within the ecosystem is restricted by the rate of energy flowing into the group, and its distribution to group members. In this respect, low energy availability differs from hypoxia and cold in that the intensity of these stressors is independent of characteristics of the population. Energy can, therefore, be described as a limiting factor, which by definition is a potentially density-dependent stressor.

Indirect evidence indicates that a high-Andean subsistence pattern based on mixed agriculture and herding has supported human populations in the altiplano for over 3000 years (Lanning, 1967). In the Nuñoa ecosystem superficial archaeological surveys show that a similar pattern has been utilized since at least 1000 A.D., and there is reason to believe that this date should be considerably earlier. Thus the population is apparently able to adjust to potential hypocaloric stress; the persistence of the same subsistence base through time suggests that its employment has enabled Nuñoa populations to achieve an energy balance with the other plant and animal populations composing the biotic community.

More direct evidence of a continued adaptation to the energy-flow system is provided by the health status of the present population. Despite reported low levels of energy consumption, health surveys have not noted widespread deficiency diseases (Baker, 1969; Way, 1972). Further evidence that the Nuñoa population is operating in approximate caloric balance during normal years is provided by Picón-Reátegui; in fact, results from all nutritional studies carried out in the ecosystem are in agreement. It is therefore possible to make an a priori assumption that a successful adjustment has been made to the limited and frequently inconsistent flow of energy through this high puna ecosystem. Thus, in spite of a Mestizo- and Cholo-dominated economic organization, the subsistence base employed by the Indigenous population appears to constitute a basic adaptation to high-Andean ecology which has persisted through time, and which European and national influence has not significantly been able to alter.

Energy Production and Expenditure

In human groups where group cooperation is an essential part of the subsistence pattern, the food procurement or productive unit generally exceeds the individual. Most of the food is produced by young and middle-aged adults and is distributed to less-productive segments of the family and population. Consequently, an individual's energy consumption to a large extent is dependent upon the group's productive capacity.

In response to an ecosystem of fluctuating, and to some extent unpredictable, environmental conditions, the Nuñoa population has relied upon a multiple-subsistence base of horticulture and herding (Table 19.4). Principal cultigens and domesticates are of Andean origin and include the potato, Andean cereals, and the llama and alpaca. Although Old World food sources appear in the region, they are, with the exception of sheep, both limited and restricted to lower altitudes in the ecosystem.

The nuclear family is the basic productive and consumption unit. Decisions about selection of resources directly affect its social viability, and to a large extent the biological survival of its members. While some nuclear families are solely dependent upon either agriculture or herding, they are by no means common. Even families residing in the town, where grazing land is scarce, frequently own animals, kept by relatives or friends in rural areas. Likewise, families inhabiting the highest areas of the ecosystem, where only herding is possible, have access to agricultural lands.

In terms of energetics, energy production and expenditure values for a typical Nuñoa family have been summarized in Fig. 19.2. Symbols used are those recommended by Odum (1971). The flow diagram shows two foci: the sun, from which all energy flowing through the system originates, and the family, which functions as both a primary and a secondary consumer in acquiring and dispensing energy.

A total of 595,000 kcal is produced from cultigens and 760,000 kcal in edible animal products from the herd. Of the latter, only 222,000 kcal is consumed by the family, the remainder being exchanged. From foods produced by the family and foods acquired through exchange, a total of 3,461,000 kcal becomes available to the family per year for consumption. This value corresponds with the estimated caloric intakes discussed above (based upon a family of six members). Of the energy consumed approximately 13 percent (436,000 kcal) is expended directly on energy-producing tasks. Over five times more energy is expended on the herds than on crops, and most of it goes into the task of daily herding.

Energy inputs of specific subsistence tasks are indicated by narrow vertical arrows. The broad horizontal arrows labeled as workgates consist of points in the flow system where relatively small energy or material inputs can

TABLE 19.4   *Domesticated Food Sources in the Nuñoa Ecosystem*

Food source	Reliance	Altitude limit (m)	Conditions of production
			Cultigens
Andean tubers			
Potato (amarga)	High	4450	In general, planted on ridged fields with fertilizer.
Potato (dulce)	High	4250	Potatoes are the hardiest; the amarga has a greater
Oca	Low	4200	yield than the dulce. Rains after planting allow
Isaño	Low	4200	young plants to grow rapidly and large enough to
Ulluca	Low	4200	prevent frost damage. With too much rain late in
			the growing season, potato worms increase.
Andean cereals			
Cañihua	High	4450	Planted on last year's potato field. Litte prepara-
Quinoa	High	4250	tion and no fertilizer needed. Since quinoa grows
			best in wetter, and cañihua in drier seasons, these
			grains are frequently planted together. Cañihua is
			less affected by snow and withstand harsher
			conditions.
Old-World grains			
Barley	Mod.	4200	More susceptible than Andean cereals to frost,
Oats	Low	4100	hail, and snow. Generally grown in sheltered
Wheat	Low	4100	areas. Seed must be obtained in lower ecozones.
			Barley, the most successful, is frequently used as a
			food supplement for livestock.
Other			
Onions	Low	4100	Grown in sheltered areas in the lower parts of the
Beans	Low	4100	ecosystem. Affected by frost; thus limited. Wild
Leafy vegetables	Low	4100	plants are frequently relied upon for leafy vege-
			tables and fruits.
			Domesticates
Andean camelids			
Llama	Mod.	5000	Alpaca, sheep, and llama are the primary herd
Alpaca	High	5000	animals, since all can utilize the shorter pasture
Sheep	High	5000	at higher elevations. Cattle are more restricted
Cattle	Low	4500	to lower areas. Oxen are rarely used for plowing.
Pigs	Low	4500	Pigs and chickens are usually not kept by rural
Guinea pigs	Mod.	5000	families who migrate seasonally.
Chickens	Low	4500	

regulate high rates of flow. Precipitation, time spent in preparation of the potato field, or the amount of fertilizer applied to it, for instance, each constitutes a point at which energy flow into the family can be affected.

A final symbol on Fig. 19.2 which requires explanation is a "strategy decision," indicated by a "black box." This is a point in the flow system where two or more alternating strategies are available to the family. For example, resource-selection decisions must be made as to the relative depen-

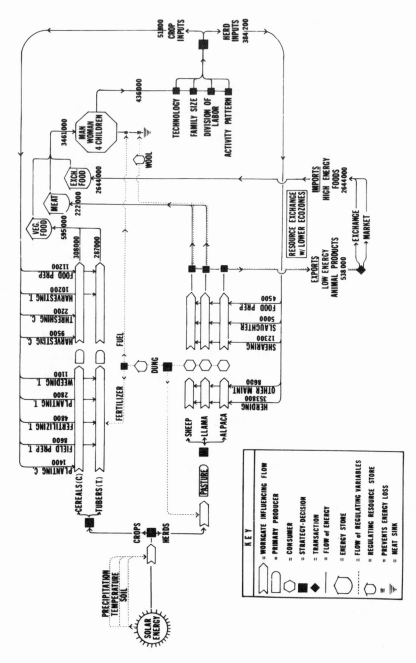

FIGURE 19.2 Annual energy flow through a typical Nuñoan family. Values are presented in kilocalories produced, expended, and consumed in the course of a normal year by a couple with four children, 2–17 yr of age.

dence on cultivation or herding, the mix of cultigens or herd animals, and whether directly to consume or to exchange food items. Likewise, strategy decisions regarding production techniques are also required. It is these alternative responses and how often they are relied upon that will be examined in an effort to assess their adaptiveness.

In assessing overall adaptiveness of a response system, it is important to understand the capabilities and limitations of individual strategies. Of course, strategies employed do not operate independently from one another, but instead contribute to an independent adaptive complex. To be effective, strategies must be available to respond to or to avoid the range of environmental conditions countered.

ADAPTIVE RESPONSES
TO THE ENERGY-FLOW SYSTEM

In counteracting hypocaloric stress a number of adaptive alternatives exist. These alternatives include: (1) avoidance of the stress (i.e., migration), (2) modification of stress-producing conditions (i.e., altering the biotic community), (3) modification of the stress before it influences the organism (i.e., borrowing food), and (4) reduction of physiological strain elicited when the stressor upsets homeostatic processes (i.e., relying on endogenous energy reserves). The alternatives which are ultimately employed will depend largely on both the characteristics of the stress and the efficacy of the various buffering systems.

Among buffering or response systems available to the human group, three broad categories are proposed which differ in the manner and degree to which they counteract hypocaloric stress: the behavioral (including material culture), biological, and demographic buffering systems. While demographic systems obviously consist of biological and cultural components, they nevertheless appear to operate on a different level from the other two, and hence are considered as a separate category.

Behavioral Responses

Adaptive behavioral responses concerning resource selection and production which appear to be the most important in terms of energetics are: (1) a spatially dispersed, multiple-resource base of energetically efficient crops and domestic animals, (2) a system of interzonal exchange whereby surplus resources produced in Nuñoa are exchanged for high-energy foods from lower regions, (3) a division of labor heavily reliant upon child participation, and (4) an activity pattern in which a large portion of the day is spent performing sedentary subsistence tasks.

Multiple Resource Base. As a result of climatic conditions, which are neither constant nor consistent, a series of spacially and temporarily distributed microclimates exists within the Nuñoa ecosystem, as is apparent from the altitude-related distributions of both cultigens and domestic animals noted in Table 19.4. Frequently a microclimate is resource-specific, restricted in land area, and somewhat inconsistent in its annual yield. Consequently, Nuñoa residents attempt to utilize a number of microclimates with the hope that most will be productive in a given year.

The same strategy of dispersed production appears when reliance on trophic levels is considered. Horticulture (the producer trophic level) during normal years will yield a high energetic efficiency (11.5) relative to animal food sources (2.0). Stated differently, for every kilocalorie expended, over 11 kcal is produced from horticultural activities, whereas for herding the energetic return is only about twice the investment. However, it is a long-term energetic efficiency which is of adaptive relevance and not simply the results from a single year. As partial, and occasionally complete, crop failure is not uncommon, dependence upon agriculture entails both a higher potential productivity and higher risk. Pastoralism (the primary consumer trophic level) appears as an alternative subsistence pattern involving low risk, which could supplement agricultural production and buffer nutritional stress in the event of crop failure. Although it would conceivably be possible for Nuñoa residents to become entirely dependent upon pastoralism, such a singular subsistence base does not appear to maximize the acquisition of available energy nor ensure rapid recovery in event of substantial herd losses. Agriculture for a given area fixes much more energy than herding. Thus, it is clearly the most productive subsistence pattern for the limited areas in Nuñoa where it can be performed.

Table 19.5 indicates crop alternatives utilized in Nuñoa, shown as first-year and second-year crops because of their different, yet complementary requirements. Considerable time and energy is spent preparing the new fields for tuber cultivation, including application of a dung fertilizer. These operations are not required for the second-year crops, which produce adequately under poor soil conditions, an important factor for the cultivator who is working under time and labor constraints in preparing a new field at a different location. Relatively high energetic ratios for the second-year crops result in part from the field's having been prepared the year before. Comparing these ratios with the percentage of families growing a given crop shows that high efficiency corresponds with high reliance. Additionally, an association appears between environmental tolerance and scheduling compatibility. For barley, the harvest period overlaps and thus conflicts with the end of the quinoa and beginning of the potato harvest.

High dependence on the Andean camelids as opposed to other livestock is supported by their greater energetic productivity and resistance to adverse climatic conditions in Nuñoa. Products derived from the alpaca constitute principal exchange items for goods produced outside the ecosystem. The value of the llama lies in its multiple utility as a pack animal and as a

TABLE 19.5 *Assessing the Adaptiveness of a Strategy Decision*

	Crop alternatives	Energy ratio (expenditure: production)	Percentage of families growing crops	Environmental tolerance	Production schedule	
					Plant	Harvest
Tubers (St.D.) (1st-yr crop)	potato	1:8	92	High	October	May
	oca	1:4[a]	5	Intermediate	October	May
	ulluco	1:3[a]	9	Intermediate	October	May
	isaño	1:3[a]	18	Intermediate	October	May
Cereals (St.D.) (2nd-yr crop)	quinoa	1:22	98	High	September	April
	cañihua	1:15	64	High	September	March–April
	barley	1:8[a]	24	Low	September	May–April

Strategy decision (St.D.)

[a]Estimated from responses to questionnaires.

secondary wool and meat source. While limited data suggest that sheep have a slightly lower resistance to altitude and caloric production per unit of weight, their products are of greater utility to the nuclear family. Sheep wool is the primary fiber used for clothing. Because an average Nuñoa sheep is about one-third the weight of an alpaca, there is less wastage from meat spoilage. With this exception, other Old World herd animals are not extensively relied upon by the Indigenous population. Cattle are infrequently owned and oxen are rarely used as draft animals. Nonherd animals (i.e., pigs) which cannot be moved with facility are not numerous in the rural areas. Although one or two horses are owned by many families, their principal utility is as transporters of heavy cargoes. Therefore, in view of the domestic animals which are present or could be introduced into the Nuñoa ecosystem, a heavy reliance on the alpaca, llama, and sheep appears as that combination which results in high energetic efficiency as well as economic gain.

A complex pattern of complementation and interdependency exists between primary food sources. Complementation has been suggested by differences in environmental tolerance, recovery rate, requirements, and scheduling between various crops and herd animals (see Fig. 19.1). The interdependency of cultivation and pastoralism is best illustrated by the fertilizer requirement of the tubers. Winterhalder et al. (1974) have pointed out that herds channel a widely dispersed and low-rate primary productivity from the range, into a concentrated and reconstituted form usable as fertilizer or fuel. Nuñoa soils have consistent deficiencies of nitrogen, phosphorus, and organic matter. These elements and others increase substantially when a standard application of dung is added to the field (900 kg/500 m^2). Sheep dung, which is used in preference to that of the camelids, is somewhat superior in nitrogen and has higher concentrations of magnesium, calcium, and potassium.

Camelid dung, on the other hand, has 10 percent more potential energy than that of sheep and is preferred as a fuel. It is estimated that almost 11,000 kg of dung is used per year for this purpose by each family. While a dung fire has a limited effect on heating the hut at night, unpublished results suggest that the energy one needs to produce to keep warm (thermogenesis) is reduced through the effects of a hot meal. Wool in the form of clothing or bedding has a similar effect (see Fig. 19.2).

When fertilizer and fuel requirements are considered together, a family needs access to approximately 12,000 kg/year. Based on the estimate that 40 percent of the animals' dung is defecated in the night-time corral and can be easily collected, a minimum of 25 sheep and 75 llamas are needed by a family to provide sufficient fertilizer and fuel. As no other fertilizer or fuel is available, dung therefore appears to be an essential resource, especially in horticulture as a regulating variable on energy flow into the human group. As such, it provides a crucial link between extensive herding and intensive horticulture.

High mobility of people and resources in a patchy environment is desirable in order to utilize widely dispersed resources. But such mobility entails a considerable energy cost. Energetically adaptive responses would therefore be those that result in a low cost per distance covered. One such response has been to reduce the weight of items transported. Materials goods to be moved with residence changes are not extensive. Freeze-drying of potatoes (chuño) and meats (charqui) reduces their weight by 66–75 percent, as well as preserving them for long periods.

Among transportation alternatives, the llama can carry up to 68 kg (150 lb) for short distances and 45 kg (100 lb) on long treks. This function is of considerable import to Nuñoa families who exploit dispersed microenvironments within the ecosystem and exchange their surplus with other regions. Without such pack animals it is difficult to imagine an effective agricultural subsistence base. A considerable amount of dung must be moved from corrals in the high pastures in order to fertilize the potato fields. Also, at harvest, over 200 kg of potatoes and 90 kg of grain must be transported from the fields to the family dwelling. While members of a family could transport these loads, it would require a considerable expenditure of human energy. Finally, food produced, as well as family belongings, must be moved in transhumant residence changes.

Exchange between regions would be seriously impaired without a suitable pack animal. A survey of loads carried by long-distance travelers has indicated that packs carried rarely exceed 20 kg. Because high-puna products (charqui, chuño, etc.) are bulky, interzonal trade reliant on human transporters would be unproductive. For example, a man carrying 40 kg of charqui and expending 3500 kcal/day would consume the caloric equivalent of his burden within a month. In contrast, the same individual using 11 llamas could transport a 500 kg of charqui to the same destination at a similar or somewhat lower energy cost to himself.

Clearly, a pack animal is needed, but why the llama? Old World pack animals (the horse, mule, and donkey), all of which can carry heavier loads, are present in Nuñoa. Nevertheless, the llama is relied upon primarily. The horse, for example, can be ridden or can carry up to 68 kg for long distances; however, a family will only own one or two horses. In terms of energetics, considerable human energy can be saved by riding a horse as opposed to walking. And energy expended by the animal in locomotion is derived from sources inedible to men. The energy-expenditure rate of horseback riding, derived from a lowland study (Geldrich, 1927), is 3 kcal/min while the horse is walking. Travel on foot (5 kph) with a light load has been estimated at 5.5 kcal/min in Nuñoa. Assuming the walking rate of a horse is 1.5 times that of a man, a given distance can be covered in two-thirds the time. This means that the total energy cost of traveling 10 km is 420 cal (64 percent) greater on foot than on horseback.

Reasons underlying the greater dependence on the llama are, of course, numerous. Gade (1969) has stated that the llama is used because of its superiority at very high elevations, and because the Indians live in isolated areas. While the survival and reproduction potential of the llama appears to be greater than that of the horse in the high puna, other factors also seem to favor its retention. As Gade mentions, the llama can be utilized as a secondary wool and meat source. Additional products, such as hides and dung (not provided by the horse), which the high Andean peoples have traditionally relied upon must also be considered. Furthermore, the degree to which a pack animal is utilized becomes important. Except for the planting and harvest season, residence change, and trade outside the region, the pack animal grazes with the rest of the herds. Horses, being nonruminants, are reported (O. Barreda, personal communication) to consume 4—5 times as much pasture as a llama and therefore reduce the herbivore-carrying capacity for a given area. Thus horses are primarily useful for transporting heavy loads that cannot be distributed among several llamas (i.e., a rider). For cargoes below 45 kg, it is more economical to use a pack animal that produces wool, meat, and a superior-quality dung as well. Energetically, the llama reduces human energy expenditure related to transport, and eventually may be utilized as a food-energy source.

Interzonal Exchange. As suggested from the energetic efficiency of pastoralism, food energy that can be extracted from the high puna flow system is not sufficient to meet consumption requirements of a substantial segment of the Nuñoa population. When animal resources (wool, hides, meat, etc.) produced in this ecosystem, however, are exchanged for high-calorie foods grown at lower elevations, adequate energy levels become available (see Fig. 19.2). Estimates indicate that if all animal resources produced by a typical family were exchanged for wheat flour, energy production derived from pastoralism could be increased as much as five times, for an overall energetic efficiency of 10.0, almost identical to that from agriculture during a normal year. A critical interdependency therefore exists between ecozones, which if disrupted could seriously affect the ability of the Nuñoa population to support itself. The value of controlling ecozones, as a means by which pre-Columbian Andean groups have gained rights to a wide variety of resources, has been reviewed by Murra (1968, 1972). While many contemporary Andean communities no longer have such rights, resource exchange is nonetheless important (Nachtigall, 1965, 1966; Flores Ochoa, 1968; Mayer, 1971; Fonseca, 1972; Custred, 1973; Browman, 1974). The essential nature of such an interchange appears to be emphasized in the Nuñoa population, where it serves as a basic adaptation to the energy-flow system.

Division of Labor. The division of labor in the rural areas of Nuñoa appears to be generally unstructured. There are very few tasks which a family member would or could not perform unless limited physically. Such an arrangement appears beneficial in a dispersed-settlement pattern, since it ensures that subsistence activities can be carried out even though a family

TABLE 19.6   *Comparison of Energy Expended in*
Herding (8-Hour Period) by a 12-Year-Old
30-kg Boy and a 54-kg Man in Nuñoa

Activity (min/period)	Energy expenditure (kcal/min)		Energy cost (kcal)	
	Boy	Man	Boy	Man
Lying (2)	0.9	1.2	1.8	2.4
Sitting (343)	1.0	1.3	343.0	445.9
Standing (20)	1.0	1.5	20.0	30.0
Squatting with arm motion (2)	1.5	1.9	3.0	3.8
Walking slowly (59)	2.3	3.3	135.7	194.7
Walking moderately (11)	2.7	4.5	29.7	49.5
Walking with light load (18)	3.3	5.5	59.4	99.0
Walking up–down hills (20)	3.5	6.0	70.0	120.0
Running (5)	4.5	7.5	22.5	37.5
Total (480)			685.1	982.8

member may be away from home. However, certain tasks are performed more frequently by a given sex–age group. In terms of energetic efficiency, body weight appears as an appropriate basis for assigning tasks since it is highly associated with the energy cost of most nonsedentary activities in Nuñoa. Thus it is hypothesized that the most energetically efficient sex–age group to engage in a given task would be the lightest group which could effectively perform it. This principle seems to apply to participants engaged in a variety of agricultural activities as well as long-distance walking. It is most apparent in daily herding, an activity for which the greatest amount of energy associated with subsistence activities is expended. Since herding involves only light and moderate work levels, a wide range of sex–age groups could effectively participate. Children expend less energy in herding than adults, and by 12 yr of age can complete approximately the same amount of work per day (if herd size is less than 100 animals). A 12-yr-old boy, for instance, will spend about 30 percent fewer calories per day herding than his father (see Table 19.6). In the course of a year, a saving results of well over 100,000 kcal for the family. It therefore appears that the high degree of child participation in daily herding contributes significantly to an energetically efficient division of labor.

Activity Patterns. Within the daily activity pattern, which normally centers around herding, tasks of low energy cost seem to predominate. Stated differently, when it is not necessary to carry out subsistence activities of higher energy cost (i.e., moving the herd from time to time and agricultural tasks), sedentary tasks are generally engaged in. Estimates have indicated that over 75 percent of the herding period is spent in a stationary position. After

TABLE 19.7   *Time and Energy Expended by a Sedentary Nuñoa Man over a 24-Hour Period*

Activity	Energy expenditure (kcal/min)	Time expenditure		Energy cost	
		(min/day)	%	(kcal/day)	%
Sleeping	1.0	480	33.3	480.0	24.2
Lying	1.2	150	10.4	180.0	9.1
Sitting	1.3	565	39.2	734.5	37.0
Standing	1.5	22	1.5	33.0	1.7
Squatting with arm motion	1.9	175	12.2	332.5	16.8
Walking slowly	3.3	17	1.2	56.1	2.8
Walking moderately	4.5	10	0.7	45.0	2.3
Walking with light load	5.5	6	0.4	33.0	1.7
Walking up–down hills	6.0	15	1.0	90.0	4.5
Total		1440	100.0	1984.1	100.0

the slaughter in June, adults frequently stay at home while their children herd, and it is common to record as much as 96 percent of a 24-hr period spent in sedentary activities (see Table 19.7). These findings suggest that the strenuous nature of Andean life assumed by a number of investigators (Monge 1948, Hurtado 1964b) might be somewhat overemphasized, although, obviously, a number of difficult tasks must be performed in the course of the year. Baker (1966a) has indicated that a low activity level in highland natives would serve as a behavioral adjustment to hypoxic stress. It would also reduce energy expenditure and thereby act as an adaptive response to low energy availability as well. In spite of the sedentary nature of herding and related tasks, productive activities take up most of the daylight hours. The daily activity pattern therefore is viewed as an adjustment which increases the overall energetic efficiency of the nuclear family, and consequently operates as an additional behavioral adjustment to the energy-flow system of the high puna.

Biological Responses

Biological adjustments to the energy-flow system constitute a second adaptive pathway available to the Nuñoa population. Worth attention are responses capable of reducing the organism's metabolic demands, and resulting in both a higher energetic efficiency and higher buffering potential against hypocaloric stress. While a number of biological responses operate in this manner, possibly the best documented and easiest to investigate is a reduction in body size. Numerous studies have demonstrated a positive relationship between human size and energy expenditure over a range of submaximal activities (Mahadeva et al., 1953; Sargent, 1961, 1962; Malhotra et al., 1962; Durnin and Passmore, 1967; Brasel, 1968). The maintenance of small body size in the Nuñoa population may be of adaptive value in minimizing energy requirements.

In examining the slow and prolonged growth pattern reported for Nuñoa children in such a context (Frisancho, 1969b), the following responses would be expected. Since the rate of growth per year is reduced, less energy would be required to maintain growth processes; this amount, however, is probably negligible (FAO, 1973). A smaller body size, nevertheless, would result in a reduced energy requirement at a given age. And an extended growth period would prolong the attainment of both adult body size and the higher energy-consumption levels associated with it.

When a more advanced growth pattern (one that proceeds at a faster rate and terminates earlier) is hypothesized for Nuñoans, conservative estimates indicate that between ages 15 and 20 an adolescent would consume an average of 121 kcal more per day, or over 44,000 additional kcal/yr. In terms of crop yield, a nuclear family would need to increase its annual production by almost 18 kg of potatoes plus 8 kg of Andean grains per year over a 6-yr period for each child in the late teens (see Table 19.8). Under normal agricultural conditions, approximately 88 additional square meters would have to be cultivated to meet this increased production. Such a growth pattern, dependent upon greater energy utilization over a shorter period of time, may not be adaptive to a population inhabiting an environment where these demands frequently cannot be met. This hypothesis has been advanced

TABLE 19.8 *Mean Increases in Consumption and Production Necessary to Sustain an "Advanced" Growth Pattern in 15- to 20-year-Old Nuñoans*

	Increase in consumption (kcal)	
Measure	Per child	All children ($N = 794$)
kcal/day	121	96,074
kcal/year	44,165	35,067,010
Potatoes (kg/yr)	18	14,292
Andean grains (kg/yr)	8	6,352
Cultivated land (m²)	88	69,872

by Thompson (1966), Garrow and Pike (1967), Malcolm (1969, 1970), Stini (1972a, 1972b), Garn et al. (1972), and Frisancho et al. (1973a). While a comparison of this sort is obviously limited, it does serve as a general model to point out the energetic consequences of substantial deviation from the normal Nuñoa growth pattern. In addition, it suggests that individuals demonstrating a more advanced pattern might be exposed to higher stress levels during periods of very low energy availability. The extent to which selection would operate against these individuals remains unclear.

Small adult body size in the Nuñoa population conforms to that of other Andean Indigenous groups. Smaller Nuñoa men (1) expend less energy and (2) show less physiological strain while performing a wide range of work levels than do larger men (Thomas, 1970). These conclusions are based primarily on a sample of men whose range of body weight exceed ±1 S.D. of the population mean. Lighter men from Nuñoa were more efficient in carrying out subsistence activities. Studies performed on lowland samples suggest that, had a wider weight range been tested, smaller individuals would have shown a greater physiological strain at high work levels (Wyndham et al., 1963). On this evidence, it is hypothesized that small body size is adaptive as long as the capacity to perform essential subsistence activities is not significantly impaired. Such activities would include strenuous prolonged tasks (i.e., foot plowing) in which the greater physiological strain incurred by a very small person would lower endurance and seriously affect performance. It therefore appears that the smallest and the largest members of the adult population may be at some disadvantage, since they would carry out subsistence activities at a lower energetic efficiency. The extent to which differences in energetic efficiency influence selective pressures and, in turn, maintain the present small body size of Nuñoa residents is not known.

An indirect approach to this question has been attempted by determining the energetic consequences of increasing the mean body size of the Nuñoa adult population. Rough estimates have been established from linear relationships between body weight and caloric intake as established by FAO (1957). In Nuñoa, men and women would need to agument their daily consumption by 130 and 111 kcal, respectively, per 5-kg increase in body weight. In terms of the annual cycle, a couple would require an additional 89,000 kcal/yr (47,450 kcal for the man and 40,515 for the woman). This amount is equivalent to approximately 36 kg of potatoes plus 16 kg of Andean grains, and would necessitate over a 175-m^2 increase in cultivated land under normal agricultural conditions.

The entire adult population of the region—1649 men and 2039 women (Republica del Peru, 1965)—would require over 160 million kcal (78,150,150 for the men and 82,610,085 for the women), the equivalent of 66,000 kg of potatoes plus 28,000 kg of Andean grains per year in excess of current production. (For these estimates, adjustments were made for deviation of the Nuñoa adult intake from FAO recommendations, and mean age of the population.) Thus, discounting possible problems encountered by individual nuclear families in the timing of agricultural activities, increased caloric demands would place considerable pressure on the limited arable land available in the Nuñoa district as well as the number of years land could be left fallow. It is estimated that additional requirements of arable land would amont to over 316,000 m^2. Such demands on the ecozone could disrupt the rather delicate balance that exists between the human population and the energy-flow system of this high-Andean area. And these estimates consider only an increase in body size of adults, who are less than 45 percent of the entire Nuñoa population.

The consequences of a higher body weight would be especially apparent in years when crops failed and caloric requirements could not be met. During such periods, larger adults would be under greater physiological strain resulting from hypocaloric stress.

Demographic Responses

A third group of adaptations to the energy-flow system is demographic in nature. The age at which a child becomes a productive asset to the family, although difficult to estimate, seems to occur at about 6 yr in Nuñoa as well as in other communities (Webster, 1973). Consequently from 6 to 18 yr, or two-thirds of the period the child resides at home, his or her production exceeds consumption. It is, therefore, to a couple's advantage to produce a large family. High fertility is both desired and attempted, as suggested by serial monogamy and maximal pregnancy risk for a woman in her late thirties (Baker and Dutt, 1972). A mean completed fertility of 6.7 children has been reported for Nuñoa women despite altitude-related factors, which may lower reproductive performance (Hoff, 1968).

While high fertility appears adaptive in terms of the family, it poses a potential threat to population stability. Unless limited, population growth would rapidly exceed the human-carrying capacity of the Nuñoa flow system. High mortality, especially at very young ages, is seen as an environmental block to such a threat. From the standpoint of energetics, peak child mortality below 1 yr of age results in a relatively low energy investment per child before death occurs, an investment that would be considerably greater if deaths were concentrated at a later age. The caloric investment in a 1-yr-old child is 408,800 kcal; if the same child were to die at age 5, an investment of 1,229,320 kcal is lost. During the child's productive years, from ages 6 to 18, the mortality rate is less than during the first 4 yr, and considerably below that of any other comparable period of life.

Emigration serves as an additional mechanism for maintaining population stability. In a similar sense, it appears as an adaptive response to fluctuating levels of energy flow in the Nuñoa ecosystem. In the case of a prolonged drought, when energy flow is severely reduced, temporary emigration to lower zones provides an effective escape from such conditions. Seasonal migration is viewed in more positive terms but essentially follows the same principle. At the end of the dry season, men, accompanied by their older sons, frequently engage in interzonal resource exchange. By their doing so, a significant human biomass exits from the ecosystem, and does not draw on local energy reserves for the duration of its absence. If a father and his 15-yr-old son were to leave Nuñoa for 3 weeks, a saving would result of over 83,000 kcal for the family. Furthermore, at this season, food production in Nuñoa would not be affected.

DISCUSSION

While behavioral, biological, and demographic responses interact in such a way as to allow the Nuñoa population to adjust to a limited and frequently disrupted energy-flow system, they do appear to function somewhat differently. Behavioral adaptations operate primarily as energetically efficient patterns of modifying the environment. Such a modification, for example, would be replacing the natural flora and fauna of the ecosystem with higher-yielding domesticates. Behavioral adaptations also include technological patterns associated with energy production, consumption, and expenditure. Conversely, biological responses appear most effective when behavioral adaptations fail. In the case of crop loss, adaptations connected with cultivation have a negligible buffering capacity. Principal biological adjustments are therefore morphological or physiological responses of an organism which reduce potential stress levels by decreasing its energy requirements: this may be achieved either by phenotypic adjustment or genetic adaptation. Unlike behavioral and biological responses, which function as buffers under different conditions, demographic adaptations primarily influence the buffering capacity of these responses. The energetic efficiency of a family engaged in mixed agriculture and pastoralism appears to be dependent on the number of children over 6 years of age. While behavioral adaptations employed by a small and a large family may be quite similar, the latter will generally utilize them more effectively. Similarly, the capacity of biological responses to sustain an organism over a stress period will depend on the amount of food available, in turn influenced by population density and the degree of temporary emigration which has taken place. In view of the different functions and efficacies of behavioral, biological, and demographic pathways, it seems essential to consider them as an entity when examining adaptation to an energy-flow system. To deal only with cultural or biological parameters is not profitable, since it does not permit assessment of the overall interaction of adaptive responses which enable the population to channel sufficient energy to its members.

While the focus of the present investigation has been on aspects of human adaptation, the interpretation of results need not be restricted to this context alone. Adjustments to the energy-flow system constitute a basic adaptation that a group must make to its environment. Adjustments, therefore, may be regarded as an organizational framework capable of influencing the structure and function of other biological and cultural phenomena of the group. The extent of this influence is suggested by the range of biocultural phenomena directly associated with energy production, consumption, and expenditure activities. In Nuñoa, access to energy sources may operate as a limiting factor on the population. The fact that a dispersed-settlement pattern is effective for herding, and that most of the daylight hours are devoted to subsistence activities, places clear limitations on the degree to which political and religious institutions can be developed in a seminomadic community (Webster, 1973). Social and economic ties, on the other hand, would exert an important influence on extrafamilial interaction. In this report, socioeconomic units larger than the nuclear family have been neglected. Thus little has been said about differences in exchange between ritual kinsmen, trading partners, and the market. Moreover, the hacienda, which gets access to about an additional 1,000,000 kcal produced by the family, has not been discussed. Such production costs the family over 40,000 kcal. Neither of these values appear on Fig. 19.2.

The long-term presence of human populations in high-altitude regions of the Andes suggests a successful adaptation to one of the most stressful regions inhabited by man. Adaptive responses to this multiply constrained environment may be regarded as a complex interaction of biocultural adjustments which together buffer the respective stressors to levels tolerable to most members of a group. Hence these responses constitute basic adaptations which (1) are necessary if a group is to survive for an extended period of time, and (2) if altered might affect its capacity to cope with environmental challenges. Unfortunately, our present understanding of many basic adaptations to the high Andes remains unclear.

At present, highland groups are undergoing significant changes in their traditional relationships with the environment, some of which could disrupt the effectiveness of their adaptive responses. In the essentially Andean subsistence pattern, a diversified resource base serves as an effective adaptation against a harsh and frequently unpredictable climate, and interzonal exchange is crucial to energy balance. Consequently, interfering with such exchange or promoting dependency on a single resource (especially cultigens) would probably not benefit this or other high-puna groups. Compulsory education for all children would severely reduce their apparently essential participation in the division of labor; labor alternatives do not appear available at this time. A final concern deals with changes capable of significantly increasing the human biomass supported by the ecosystem. Such an effect might very well result from the introduction of public-health facilities that could substantially decrease mortality without affecting present attitudes toward fertility. Also, an extensive and effective nutritional supplementation program conceivably could influence the rate of growth and, hence, the body size of children and adults. The danger of increasing the human biomass is especially acute in the high-puna ecozone where arable land is limited, and overgrazing will lead to a rapid and irreversible degradation of the biotic community and energy-flow system.

In view of these possible consequences, it is the obligation of community leaders, politicians, and scientists who are committed to change in the highlands to carefully weigh the long-term effects of their programs on basic Andean adaptations. To neglect and to seriously disrupt these adaptations will most likely result in a final blow to the Andean way of life—a way of life that less than 500 yr ago flourished as a major civilization.

20

ENVIRONMENTAL ADAPTATIONS AND PERSPECTIVES

Michael A. Little and Paul T. Baker

In our efforts to understand how Andean people had adapted to their environment, we felt that an approach using many disciplines with their specialized methods and techniques was a necessity. As noted in Chapter 1, the disciplinary efforts were structured by a loose set of objectives and a rather generalized set of research designs derived from evolutionary theory and normative research. Although most of the contributors to this volume were formally trained as biological anthropologists, the scientific disciplines finally represented in the study included a broad variety of the human biological, natural, and social sciences.

The major criticism of multidisciplinary studies has been that while the distinct disciplinary efforts are sound and useful within themselves, the findings often cannot be integrated. We had rather hoped at the beginning of the study that by this stage of effort a unifying principle or model of adaptation might be apparent, based on evolutionary or ecological theory. Such a unifying model is not readily apparent to us at this time, even though several types of system models beyond the energy-flow one discussed in Chapter 19 might be developed if our data were more complete.

Despite our inability to integrate all the findings at this time, we feel that many altitude-adaptation problems have been resolved because of the multidisciplinary approach. It seems appropriate to us to highlight these findings, along with our best guesses on what the next steps would be for understanding how the Andean native has survived and prospered in this area of complex and difficult environmental stresses.

MAJOR AREAS OF CONTRIBUTION

Several research areas gave greater returns when a multidisciplinary approach was followed. The investigation of population structure and dynamics, for example, required the joint methods of demography, genetics, ethnology, and medical science. Growth and development studies cross-cut such fields as physiology, demography, nutritional science, and psychological anthropology. Studies of health and morbidity could not have been conducted outside the cultural and demographic spheres. The work in environ-

405

mental physiology benefited from information on cultural practices, native drug use, nutrition, growth, and population energetics. Finally, the study of the district as an altiplano ecosystem required input from and integration of all the topical areas investigated as subproblems of the Nuñoa project. What follow are capsule reviews of these major areas with brief notes on achieved and still-potential levels of integration.

Population Structure and Dynamics

DeJong (1970) and Baker and Dutt (1972) have observed that national census data are of very limited utility for the study in human populations of biological adaptation to altitude. Inevitably, a standard census does not contain the depth of information required for detailed analysis of highland population structures. As an alternative, DeJong (1970) suggested a conceptual framework that, to a large degree, has been followed in the Nuñoa work (Fig. 20.1). In this structure, three interacting sets of variables were proposed so that demographic variables could be considered as altitude-dependent in one type of approach. A modification and elaboration of DeJong's framework (Fig. 20.2) represents a closer schematic approximation of the framework of the Nuñoa population analyses. The figure illustrates structural

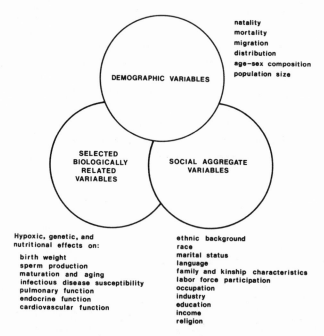

FIGURE 20.1 *Conceptual framework for demographic and biologically related research in high-altitude populations. [From DeJong (1970).]*

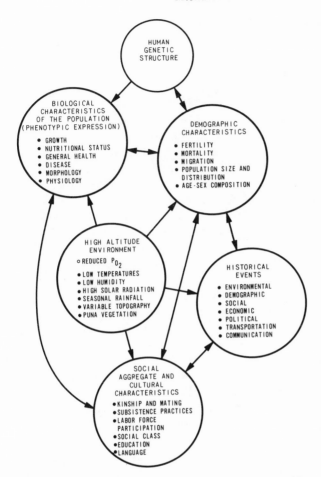

FIGURE 20.2 *Interacting categories of variables investigated as part of the Nuñoa research.*

categories of variables that can be investigated within a population framework, some of which were dealt with in Nuñoa. Two-way arrows signify categories that can act as dependent or independent variables; one-way arrows point in the direction of dependent variables.

For example, both high-altitude stresses and historical events may directly influence the demographic structure of a population, which may in turn modify the gene pool as well. Alternatively, high-altitude stresses may have such an impact upon historical events as to alter the demographic structure of the population. A case in point is the likely fecundity impairment of Europeans at altitude and their low population numbers in the Andes today (Baker and Dutt, 1972; and Chapter 7).

There is a great deal of direct and indirect evidence that altitude can influence the two fundamental demographic parameters—fertility and mortality. This evidence was reviewed by Baker and Dutt (1972), Hoff and Abelson (Chapter 7), and Way (Chapter 8).

Fertility. As described in Chapter 7, effects of altitude on reproductive potential have been documented for both sojourners and Quechua natives. The effects are more acute among sea-level residents who sojourn for brief periods at high altitude. Male sea-level residents who travel to the highlands show temporary decreases in sperm count and urinary testosterone, and females show menstrual-cycle disturbances. No corresponding effects are present among high-altitude natives. There is some indirect evidence that fetal wastage is high in sojourners but quite low in natives, even by sea-level standards. Low fetal wastage among natives might explain the high sex ratio at birth in Nuñoa (about 111 males/100 females). A low prenatal mortality would imply that fewer male fetuses were dying (male mortality is normally higher at all stages of gestation), and thus the increase in the sex ratio at birth.

Birth weights of highland native babies are low by worldwide standards (Meredith, 1970). Newborn babies from Cerro de Pasco (4340 m elevation), Puno (3870 m), and Cuzco (3416 m) average between 2700 and 3100 g, while newborns from Tacna (568 m) and Lima (203 m) range between 3200 and 3600 g (see Chapter 9). Despite the low birth weights at high altitude, placental weights for natives are high, which produces an increase in the placental weight/birth weight ratio.

The fertility history of women beyond menopause (completed fertility) in Nuñoa gives an average of 6.7 births per woman. Although this value may seem high compared with that of industralized populations, it is relatively low when compared with that of other peasant populations where fertility is maximized. The contention that fertility is reduced at high altitude in Quechua natives is strengthened by studies of downward migrants from the altiplano to the coastal Tambo valley (see Chapter 7). Among downward migrants, total fertility is slightly greater than 8 births per woman; parity interval, which at high altitude ranges from 3.1 to 5 (according to the method calculated), drops to 2.7 years at sea level. The total fertility of downward migrants at sea level is, in fact, slightly greater than that of coastal-born residents. The suggestion is that release from hypoxic stress while fertility continues to be socially maximized can lead to an increase in reproductive performance.

Despite the abundant evidence for an hypoxic influence on fecundity, it is not possible to define the precise influence of hypoxia on highland fertility since our study of the sociocultural variables was incomplete. Table 20.1 shows a systematic framework for fertility analysis that was developed by Davis and Blake (1956), with information from the Nuñoa population. Obviously, some of the data required for a complete analysis of these

TABLE 20.1 *Application of the Analytic Framework of Davis and Black (1956) to the Fertility of Nuñoa*

Intermediate variables	Nuñoa Quechua population
I. Factors affecting exposure to intercourse	
A. Formation and dissolution of unions	
1. Age of entry in sexual unions	1. Mean age of first pregnancy, 19.5 yr
2. Permanent celibacy	[a]2. Very rare
3. Amount of reproductive period spent after or between unions	[a]3. Likely to be minimal, but not really known
	[a]4. Minimal, but may occur because of grazing herds at some distance from household, trading activities, and seasonal work migration
B. Within unions	[a]5. Not known (see Chapter 8)
4. Voluntary abstinence	[a]6. Not known
5. Involuntary (impotence, illness, etc.)	7. Probable reduction of fecundity by hypoxia; infants breast-fed for 20 months
6. Coital frequency	[a]8. No or minimal use
II. Factors affecting exposure to conception	[a]9. No practices known
7. Fecundity as affected by involuntary causes	10. Low values for spontaneous abortion reported
8. Use of contraception	11. None that are known
9. Fecundity as affected by voluntary causes (sterilization, subincision, etc.)	
III. Factors affecting gestation and successful parturition	
10. Fetal mortality from involuntary causes	
11. Fetal mortality from voluntary causes	

[a] Areas with incomplete data.

intermediate variables are extremely difficult to gather. Yet, more information, particularly on "factors affecting exposure to intercourse," on both high-altitude and downward-migrant populations should further illuminate the relationship between altitude and fertility.

Mortality.   Although residents of the district of Nuñoa are able to maximize fertility to compensate for the effects of hypoxia, their control of disease-related mortality is limited to folk medicine. In Nuñoa, the poor health-care facilities and lack of sanitation complicate any analysis of altitude effects on mortality. In all of Peru, altitude is negatively related to health care and sanitation. For example, in 1959 there were half as many hospital beds and one-fourth as many physicians per unit population in the Andes than on the coast of Peru (Direccion Nacional de Estadistica y Censos, 1961).

Mazess (1965) found higher neonatal death rates in Peruvian highland departments than lowland departments. After statistical control for postneonatal death rate and crude death rate (associated with health care), a highly significant positive relationship persisted for neonatal mortality and altitude. Moreover, the proportion of neonatal to postneonatal deaths in the highlands was nearly 50 percent greater than in the low-altitude zone. Neonatal and postneonatal mortality in Nuñoa are compared in Table 20.2 with values from other areas in Peru. In spite of the likelihood of underenumeration (Baker and Dutt, 1972), the neonatal mortality values are very high and contribute nearly half the mortality rate during the first year of life.

Mortality is between 13 and 16 percent by age 1 year and about 30 percent by age 5 yr in Nuñoa. Death rates continue to decline up to about age 14, after which they increase (see Chapter 8). Life tables were not constructed for the district of Nuñoa because the accuracy of assessing age is very low in the older individuals. Even so, we found no indication that residents of Nuñoa enjoy the pronounced longevity suggested by Leaf (1973) for some high-altitude populations.

Genetic and Demographic Relationships.   Knowledge of the demographic characteristics of a population is essential to the understanding of genetic structure and process. Changes in gene frequencies from generation to generation occur through the processes of differential fertility, differential mortality, and migration of people and gene movement within and between populations.

The district of Nuñoa can be considered a relatively isolated breeding population comprised of Mestizo and Indian elements which are, in turn, relatively isolated biologically from one another. Studies of gene markers in both these populations have roughly quantified these differences (see Chapter 5). In the Indian population resident within the district, mating patterns indicate that district endogamy accounts for about 87 percent of the unions (13 percent gene flow into the district), and internal gene flow is high (see Chapter 6). Gene flow in and out of the district is somewhat more difficult to quantify. For example, exposure to intercourse increases at markets and

TABLE 20.2 *Neonatal and Postneonatal Mortality in Selected Regions of Peru*

| Deaths per 1000 births | Peru, 1958–1959[a] | | Lima department, 1958–1959 | Puno department, 1958–1959 | Nuñoa district, 1950–1968 |
	12 lowland departments	12 highland departments	Lowland[a]	Highland[a]	Highland[b]
Neonatal (0–28 days)	28.4	52.0	25.7	49.7	66.7
Postneonatal (29 days–1 yr)	54.7	71.0	54.6	67.0	68.7
Neonatal/postneonatal (%)	51.9	73.2	47.1	74.2	97.1

[a]Calculated from Mazess (1965).
[b]Calculated from Spector (1971).

fiestas in Nuñoa and in neighboring districts when casual sexual liaisons may be formed, often after high alcohol consumption by both sexes. Gene flow out of the district (out-migration) has been calculated (see Chapter 6) by comparing rates of predicted population increase, from crude birth and death rates, with census enumeration of actual change in population size. These calculations on data from 1940 to 1961 indicate that out-migration was occurring at an average rate of about 2.5 percent of the population per year. Based upon births and deaths, predicted population growth during this period was greater than 3 percent per year. Thus the real population growth of less than 1 percent per year results from the buffering effect of out-migration on relatively high rates of natural increase. Historical evidence suggests that gene flow into the Nuñoa district was greater prior to 1870, when transportation and commerce routes shifted from the district. Gene flow out of the district appears to be on the increase at present because of population pressure on the available land, and for other socioeconomic reasons (see Chapter 3). As discussed in Chapter 3, educational processes help channel the out-migration flow, but we cannot determine from present data the potential effect on the genetic structure of the population.

Random or stochastic changes in the gene pool (i.e., genetic drift) of Nuñoa are considered minimal because the population is not totally isolated and its effective breeding population is relatively large (see Chapters 5 and 6).

Fertility and mortality data from Nuñoa were applied to indices of postnatal "opportunity for selection" developed by Crow (1958; see Chapter 5). The fertility index (based upon mean family size and population variance) for Nuñoa is very low and the mortality index (based upon the percentage of the population that survives to reproductive age) is moderately high. The magnitudes of these indices point to the importance of differential mortality as a mode of postnatal selection in Nuñoa. However, the low index for fertility indicates that differential fertility plays a smaller role in selection opportunity than differential mortality, largely because of the small variance in family size in Nuñoa. In fact, this evidence supports the argument that fertility is maximized behaviorally in Nuñoa, since most societies that maximize fertility (i.e., Hutterites, rural Quebec) have equally low indices.

Growth and Development

Whereas most studies concerned with environmental stress and the biology of adaptation have focused upon young adults, few have dealt with the more complex adaptation during the developmental period. Growth is clearly an adaptive process in its own light, and the imposition of additional stresses from the external environment requires even more compensatory adjustment.

The bulk of the work on growth in Nuñoa and other parts of Peru has focused upon (1) a description of normal growth patterns at high altitude, and (2) comparisons of high-altitude and low-altitude growth patterns in order to partition out the effects of hypoxia and other environmental parameters that can modify human growth. Additional work has been conducted for (3) a determination of the importance of developmental acclimatization to hypoxia and cold.

Growth in Nuñoa. The physical growth (height, weight, skeletal development) of Nuñoa Indians is slow, prolonged through to ages in the early 20s, and characterized by a moderately to poorly defined adolescent growth spurt (see Chapter 10). Associated with these growth patterns are late sexual maturation and late development of sexual dimorphism (adipose tissue, muscle, and bone deposition). For example, sexual dimorphism in deposition of adipose tissues does not begin to occur until about the age of 14 yr, and sexual dimorphism in deposition of muscle does not appear until after 16 years of age. In Nuñoa, infant growth is characterized by smaller body size, lower weight, less adipose tissue, and slower skeletal development than in corresponding Indian populations of the lowlands (see Chapter 9).

Influence on Growth at Altitude. Various research designs were employed to factor out the effects of altitude, socioeconomic status, rural–urban residence, race, and sex on growth patterns.

Within the district of Nuñoa, comparisons were made of children who resided in either rural (haciendas and estancias) or urban (the town) parts of the district and who resided at higher (>4300 m) or lower (<4300 m) elevations. Rural Indian youths tended to be leaner at all ages than youths from the town, but both groups were similar in all other growth parameters. Altitude comparisons indicated that although the two samples were also generally similar, adolescent growth was somewhat slower in the higher-altitude sample and chest circumference somewhat greater in relation to size. Since chest circumference is highly correlated with lung capacity, the differences may be related to hypoxia. Determination of other pulmonary-function variables reinforced this altitude relationship (see Chapters 10 and 12).

The study of infant growth (birth to 2 yr of age) begun in 1965 in Nuñoa was substantially expanded to include one additional sample from the urban highlands and several lowland samples (both downward migrants and residents). By careful statistical manipulation of the data, Haas (Chapter 9) was able to demonstrate the growth-retarding effects of nutrition and poor health care, lower socioeconomic status, and high altitude. The rural Nuñoa Quechua infants had the greatest retardation in physical growth and skeletal development when compared with highland urban (Puno) and lowland rural (Cocachacra) Quechua Indians. Altitude was found to be the primary contributor to retardation in the physical growth of infants in Nuñoa and other highland areas. On the other hand, slow psychomotor development appeared more closely linked to ethnic affiliation and socioeconomic status, at least beyond 12 months of age, than to high altitude. For example, late support skills such as walking alone and walking backward were achieved in the highlands at the median ages of 15.9 and 17.3 months, respectively, with only a few days' difference between these and lowland values.

Not all physical growth at altitude was slowed. Two characteristics that may be related to altitude hypoxia—chest size and size of the marrow cavity of long bones—were advanced over norms for U.S. children.

Developmental Acclimatization to Hypoxia and Cold.   As noted in Chapter 1, many of the responses to altitude stress that were originally hypothesized as under simple genetic control now appear to be related to developmental acclimatization as well.

From two lines of evidence it appears that the increased chest size and elevated pulmonary capacity of highlanders are at least in part developmental responses to hypoxia. (1) The altitudinal differences in chest size found within the district of Nuñoa by Frisancho (Chapter 10) suggest that greater hypoxic exposure during growth leads to increased chest size. (2) Frisancho and others (1973c) demonstrated that individuals who were born at sea level, but who migrated to high altitude (Cuzco) as children, achieved values for forced vital capacity that were equal to those of high-altitude natives. Forced vital capacity of those born at sea level who migrated to altitude as adults was about 7 percent lower.

Aerobic work capacity is another response at high altitude that seems to be structured by lifelong exposure to hypoxic stress (see Chapter 15). Frisancho et al. (1973b) found, among those who migrated to altitudes above 3000 m between the ages of 2 and 16 yr, that the length of residence at high altitude was positively related to maximal oxygen consumption (aerobic capacity).

Developmental acclimatization to cold stress on the lower extremities was suggested by the cold-tolerance tests of adults and children from Nuñoa and the United States (Little et al., 1971; and Chapter 17). In these tests of foot exposure to cold air, Nuñoa Indian adults maintained warmer skin temperatures than Indian children, and both Indian groups (young and adult) had warmer temperatures than U.S. subjects. The U.S. studies did not show any age differences in thermal responses.

Multiple Altitude Stresses and Growth.   Human growth at high altitude requires that the young accommodate at all ages to a variety of environmental stresses. These stresses can be either reduced or intensified by the cultural system within which the young are socialized and later interact as adults. Moreover, the stresses or pressures of hypoxia, cold, disease, and inadequate nutrition that accompany the day-to-day experience of growing up may be exacerbated by the less frequent events of crop failure, epidemic, and severe cold spells. Some of these pressures which influence growth can be buffered by the cultural system, at least partially, while others depend upon biological modes of adaptation.

A diagrammatic representation of some stresses at high altitude that can influence biological growth processes is given in Fig. 20.3. At a very simple level, intrinsic or genetically programmed growth is modified by each of the four primary stresses imposed upon the Andean Indian (hypoxia, disease, low

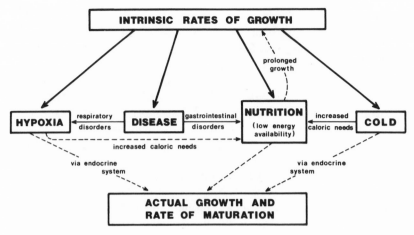

FIGURE 20.3 *Influences of altitude stresses on growth in the Peruvian altiplano.*

energy availability, and cold). As discussed in Chapter 4, culture tends to have a greater impact on cold and nutritional stresses through clothing, shelter, and subsistence practices than on disease and hypoxia. In addition, each of the four stresses interact at the individual and population levels, which results in an intensification of some of the stresses. Cold temperatures, for example, increase caloric needs—even at the infant stage as Glass et al. (1968, 1969) have demonstrated. In the absence of caloric supplementation in the cold, calories may be diverted from growth to heat production. Gastrointestinal diseases can also modify nutritional needs by slowing down or limiting absorption (Scrimshaw and Béhar, 1964). Although infant and childhood diarrhea are not as common at high altitude as in tropical sea-level zones (Buck et al., 1968; and Chapter 8) the growth-inhibiting effect of a disease—nutrition interaction at high altitude cannot be completely discounted.

A perhaps more germane relationship at high altitude is that between respiratory diseases and hypoxia. Respiratory diseases such as tuberculosis, bronchitis, and pneumonia are major causes of death at high altitude (Frisancho and Yañez, 1971; and Chapter 8). These and less acute respiratory diseases are likely to affect growth by increasing hypoxic stress and reducing oxygen transport to the tissues. Finally, hypoxia and cold may influence growth by altering hormone output from the endocrine glands. Although many of the endocrine changes observed with hypoxic and cold stress are transient (Siri et al., 1969; Selye, 1956), the growth inhibitors cortisol and ACTH may be slightly elevated in highland Indians (Moncloa, 1966; Surks, 1969). Inferences about the potential effect of hypoxia and cold on human growth via the endocrine system are quite speculative at this time and await verification in the future.

General Health

Sojourners.   Sea-level residents who rapidly ascend to altitudes of 3000 m or above are likely to suffer some ill effects of hypoxia or even acute altitude sickness for several days or longer. Symptoms include headache, shortness of breath, Cheyne–Stokes breathing (especially while sleeping), dizziness, nausea, anorexia, flatulence, and generalized malaise. The higher the altitude, the greater the proportion of sojourners who will experience some or most of these symptoms. Other more serious conditions may arise in the sojourners. Pulmonary edema, characterized by fluid in the alveoli of the lungs, may occur, but with low frequency among sojourners. Roy (1969) in studies of rapid movements of sea-level soldiers in India to elevations between 3500 and 5500 m in the Himalayas noted an incidence of 3–15 percent altitude-induced pulmonary edema. Chronic mountain sickness or chronic soroche, characterized by cerebral edema, tissue hypoxia, and polycythemia, is a condition that can affect both sojourners and native Quechua highlanders (Monge and Monge, 1966).

Of the more than 50 sea-level residents from the United States who participated in the Nuñoa project between 1964 and 1969, there were two cases of altitude-induced pulmonary edema (treated by retreat to lower altitude), and one case of chronic soroche, including an acute bout with classical symptoms of mental aberrations, migraine crisis, loss of volitional control, and photophobia (spontaneous recovery). Aside from these episodes, illness upon first arriving at high altitude, and minor complaints of respiratory and gastrointestinal disorders, the health of the research workers was generally good.

Highland Quechua Indians.   No systematic survey by medical examinations was conducted in the district of Nuñoa. Moreover, there are no medical records kept in the district capital. Nevertheless, a variety of data was gathered that bears upon the health of the Nuñoa population. For example, health questionnaires were administered and survey data were collected on pulmonary function, blood pressure, hematology, and dental characteristics. Nutritional status and fitness were assessed for smaller samples.

Nuñoa Indians are physically fit, with aerobic capacity values equal to or exceeding those of sea-level native peasants (Andersen, 1967) and high-altitude native peasants (Andersen, 1972; Weitz, 1973) from other parts of the world (see Chapters 14 and 15). From survey data it appears that dental health is excellent, with incidences of caries and missing teeth extraordinarily low. As Picón-Reátegui notes (Chapter 11), nutritional status is fair to good when locally produced food makes up the bulk of the diet. However, there is some doubt that protein and calories are sufficient to meet the additional needs in some individuals for pregnancy, lactation, and growth. From the nutritional surveys, caloric intake of children seemed to be between 15 and 25 percent lower than recommended allowances. Although no frank symptoms of protein, mineral, or vitamin deficiencies were observed, vitamin A and vitamin C intakes appear to be seasonally low. It is clear, from the surveys in the district of Nuñoa, that there is substantial seasonal variation and within-district variation in dietary intake.

Casual observations of children in Nuñoa uncovered one case of congenital syphilis, one case of polydactyly, and one case, in an infant, of what appeared to be cataracts or pterygium. Polydactyly was also observed among the Bolivian Aymara (Buechler and Buechler, 1971), and a high incidence of pterygium is associated with intense solar radiation (Forsius et al., 1970); however, our observations were not comprehensive and hence not particularly revealing. There is no information from Nuñoa on patent ductus arteriosus and other congenital heart defects that are reported to be in higher frequency at altitude (see Chapter 8). Based on predictive curves, patent ductus arteriosus should have an incidence of less than 1 percent at the highest elevations surveyed (Baker, 1971). This specific congenital heart disease has been attributed largely to pulmonary hypertension, which is characteristic of highland natives (Marticorena et al., 1967).

An exceptionally high incidence of respiratory diseases has been documented for Andean populations (Hellriegel, 1967). In Nuñoa, where respiratory diseases account for nearly 60 percent of all deaths, they are particularly acute among infants and children (see Chapter 8). These findings are somewhat unusual in that gastrointestinal disease and infant diarrhea is usually a major cause of death in most nonwestern peasant populations. In Nuñoa gastrointestinal disease accounts for less than 7 percent of all deaths. The elevated lymphocyte counts observed by Garruto (Chapter 13) in the Nuñoa population may reflect the high incidence of respiratory ailments. Respiratory diseases were also more common in migrants from high altitude to the coast than either in coastal natives or in those who migrated from one coastal area to another (Beall, 1972; and Chapter 8). At present, these differences are unexplained, but the respiratory-ailment frequency of downward migrants may somehow be a residual effect of residence at high altitude.

Cardiovascular Disease and Altitude. With the exception of the congenital heart defects noted above, cardiovascular disease among highland Indians has a very low incidence. Aneurysms and arteriosclerosis are rare (Hellriegel, 1967), and hypertensive and coronary diseases are two to three times lower at high altitude than at sea level (Marticorena et al., 1967).

One of the best-documented relationships with high altitude is low blood pressure (Buck et al., 1968; Marticorena et al., 1967; and Chapter 8). Figure 20.4 illustrates systolic and diastolic blood-pressure changes with age for the United States and Nuñoa. In the United States and other industralized nations, systolic pressure shows a gradual mean increase in adults, whereby hypertensive levels are frequently reached by ages in the late 50s and 60s. Nuñoa adults had minimal or nonsignificant increases with age. Even among the more acculturated residents of the district, changes with age were slight and did not reach hypertensive levels. Baker (in press b) has concluded, on

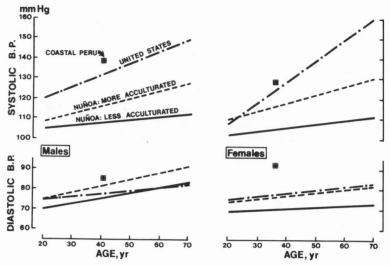

FIGURE 20.4 *Blood-pressure changes with age in the United States, coastal Peru, and Nuñoa. [Adapted from Baker (1969).]*

the basis of low blood pressures among downward migrants who have resided at sea level for many years, that a childhood spent at high altitude may confer a permanent resistence to hypertension. It is clear that nonwestern life styles with associated moderate physical fitness and low-fat dietary intakes reduce the risk of hypertension (Huizinga, 1972; see comparison of acculturated and nonacculturated Nuñoa residents in Fig. 20.4). However, there does appear to be an altitude effect in addition, since sea-level natives living at high altitude show lower systolic blood pressures after a prolonged residence at altitude (Peñaloza, 1966).

Environmental Physiology

In order to survive in the high-altitude environment of the altiplano, the Quechua Indian must combat both behaviorally and physiologically the stresses of hypoxia and cold while maintaining the activity levels necessary for subsistence. Although the technology and culturally structured behavior of the highland Indian does much to buffer altitude stresses, this protection is seldom totally effective and biological modes of adaptation must be employed.

Three major questions were explored in dealing with physiological adaptation to altitude.

1. What is the extent and duration of exposure of the highland Indian to the altitude stresses of hypoxia and cold?

2. How does culture (behavior, technology, subsistence patterns, etc.) reduce or intensify these stresses?

3. What physiological responses act to reduce the impact of altitude stresses, and how do these responses differ from those of other populations?

In attempts to answer these questions, data were gathered on Nuñoa Indians (1) by observation and measurement while individuals were engaged in normal activities, (2) by simulating normal activities under quasicontrolled conditions, and (3) by standardized testing of individuals in the laboratory where conditions could be better controlled.

Native Activity Patterns in Nuñoa. For the Indian in Nuñoa, physical activities, which increase hypoxic stress, vary by age, by sex, and by primary modes of subsistence (at lower elevations, mixed herding and agriculture; at higher elevations, herding only). As Thomas points out (1973; and Chapter 19), much of the physical activity involves the performance of sedentary subsistence tasks, and the energetically more efficient children often perform tasks that would require more work if done by adults. Children frequently engage in active running play, and the subjective impression is that they do not seem to be constrained by hypoxia. Pastoral activities require far less work than agricultural pursuits, although herding of llamas, alpacas, and sheep requires walking over steep terrain and occasional running after stray animals. Agricultural field preparation, planting, and harvesting are the most strenuous subsistence activities performed. Thomas (1973) reports that a man preparing a potato field by use of the foot plow may work at between 60 and 77 percent of his maximal aerobic capacity. A woman assisting in field preparation will seldom exceed 60 percent of her maximal aerobic capacity.

Other activities where moderate to strenuous exercise is performed include walking to markets at a distance of up to 30 km or more, dancing and marching during fiestas, and seasonal movement of herds to distant pastures. Despite the amount of time spent in relatively sedentary subsistence activities, the physical work performed by the adult Indian of either sex probably exceeds that of the average American.

Exposure to cold of the Indian in Nuñoa (see Chapter 16) is reduced somewhat by the effective insulation of homespun wool clothing and bedding materials, shelter, and certain patterns of behavior (minimal bathing; sedentary activities during warm periods of the day). Cold stress may be intensified, on the other hand, by the requirements of subsistence under a variety of weather conditions, especially when children participate. Seasonal and diurnal variations in air temperature, wind chill, and precipitation (rain, snow, sleet, and hail) produce differential stress by sex and age categories. During the height of the dry season, when diurnal temperature ranges often reach 25°C (-5 to 20°C), children and adults may be chilled in the early morning and early evening hours. Children also suffer some degree of cold stress for a few hours after retiring for the night, and although neonates and young infants appear to be reasonably well protected from the cold (see Chapter 4), they may be cold-stressed on occasion. Animal herds are moved out to graze by 8:00 A.M. and are returned by 6:00 P.M. This schedule implies exposure during the dry season when air temperatures are between 0 and 10°C. The early part of the wet season, characterized by rain, snow, and strong winds, coincides with preparation of agricultural plots and planting. These tasks must be carried out within a given time period, despite weather conditions.

Cold stress of the extremities is experienced by men during repair of dams and irrigation ditches and by women during food preparation and clothes washing. Cold spells, blizzards, and prolonged rains, which would produce acute stress, occur at 3- or 4-yr intervals. In general, the climatic conditions that exist in Nuñoa should be stressful to the Indian relying upon his native technology and material culture. The conclusion drawn in Chapter 16 that cold stress is slight or absent in Nuñoa is based largely upon the warm surface temperatures of the Indian, which, in fact, may reflect physiological adjustments that have already been made to the high-altitude cold environment.

Physiological Responses to Altitude: Work Capacity. Exercise or work aggravates the problems associated with delivery of oxygen to the tissues at altitude. Work-capacity tests performed on Quechua Indian men in Nuñoa indicated that they have a high aerobic capacity, low maximal ventilation, low ventilation equivalent ($\dot{V}_E$ max/$\dot{V}_{O_2}$ max), and high oxygen pulse ($\dot{V}_{O_2}$ max/HR max) when these measurements are controlled for body weight (see Chapters 14 and 15). Thus, high-altitude Indians were able to deliver more oxygen to working muscle per unit ventilatory and heart rates than sea-level residents exercised at high altitude. When sea-level sedentary whites and white athletes were tested at Nuñoa, aerobic capacity and oxygen pulse were markedly lower than sea-level values, but with athletes showing the higher values. Quechua Indians from low altitude when tested at high altitude also showed a reduction in oxygen-consumption capacity, but the loss was much less than it was for the white samples. Corresponding values for Nuñoa Indians were higher than those of the three sea-level groups tested at high altitude, suggesting that the highland native has achieved a marked degree of adaptation to the altitude-induced physiological strain of hypoxia during work.

Although genetic factors contributing to the adaptive advantage of the highland Indian cannot be discounted, two sources of evidence suggest that at least a part of this advantage in oxygen transport during work derives from a lifetime spent at high altitude. Mazess (1969a) tested Indians and whites in the city of Puno (3800 m) who were lifelong residents at high altitude. He found that the Indians' aerobic capacity was greater than that of the whites but that the difference was only about 7 percent; this value is less than the 10 percent decrement in aerobic capacity of sea-level Indians between low- and high-altitude tests. As noted earlier, Frisancho and others (1973b), in their study of upward migrants to the city of Cuzco (3400 m), found that aerobic capacity of those who migrated to altitude prior to adolescence was equal to that of Cuzco-born and -reared Indians. Despite this evidence, the question of the relative influence of developmental acclimatization and genetic adaptation on work performance of the Andean Indian is still open, since the people tested were of mixed Indian and European backgrounds, and the controls on physical conditioning, nutrition, and other developmental—environmental variables were incomplete.

Physiological Responses to Altitude: Exposure to Cold. When compared with whites at sea level and high altitude, Nuñoa Indians tested under a variety of laboratory conditions appeared to respond to cold by several physiological modes of adaptation (see Chapter 17). Basal heat production (BMR) of Nuñoa Indians was about 5 percent higher than U.S. standards (Boothby et al., 1936), and body-core temperatures were slightly warmer at the onset of whole-body cooling tests than in whites. Both characteristics should be advantageous to the native during the short bouts of chilling that customarily occur in the morning and evening hours. The most persistent finding was that of elevated surface temperatures and increased blood flow of the hand and the foot during both local-extremity and whole-body exposures to cold. For extremities, temperature differences between Indians and whites were greatest during moderate exposures to cold air, yet these differences persisted even during acute exposures to cold water. Maintenance of warm extremities requires heat transfer from the rest of the body. In Nuñoa Indians, this heat loss is partially offset by elevated metabolism, but the Indians certainly require increased caloric intake to compensate for the higher metabolism.

Several microcirculatory mechanisms seem to be responsible for the high blood flow in the Indians' hands and feet during exposure to cold. Under moderate cold stress, there is a release of vasoconstrictor tone (probably of arterioles or precapillary sphincters) which perfuses a large number of capillaries at the surface of the extremities. Under more intense cold stress, cold-induced vasodilation occurs by perfusion of arteriovenous shunts that bypass the capillary networks. Extremity responses to cold of the Andean Indian may result from local (hand and foot) habituation to cold, or may reflect a more generalized response to cold. In any case, there are real advantages to Andean Indians in their consistent maintenance of warm extremities, despite the greater heat loss it produces. This statement holds, since it is well established that chronic vasoconstriction can produce tissue injury in members of other populations at ambient temperatures as high as $15°C$, and certainly at $8°C$ (Rodahl and Issekutz, 1965).

Work, Hypoxia, and Cold. The high-altitude environment stresses of hypoxia and cold, combined with the additional stress of physical work, can interact to produce both positive and negative cross-adaptational effects. A diagrammatic representation of some potential cross-adaptations is shown in Fig. 20.5. Listed separately, in Fig. 20.5 are several short-term and long-term acclimatizations that generally occur when healthy individuals are exposed independently to each of the stresses. Of course, disease and nutritional stresses will modify these relationships. With the exception of physical

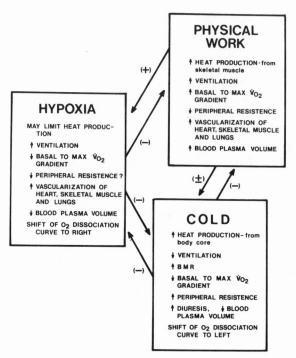

FIGURE 20.5 *Cross-adaptations and cross-maladaptations of hypoxia, physical work, and cold. [Adapted from Weihe (1966).]*

conditioning acting to preadapt the individual to hypoxia (Weihe, 1966), and immediate activity acting to reduce cold stress, the acclimatizational changes that take place for each of the stresses are generally antagonistic.

For example, heat production increases during both work and exposure to cold, yet hypoxia may limit heat production (Hemingway and Nahas, 1952; Girling and Topliff, 1966), at least in newcomers to high altitude. Another potentially antagonistic relationship is in the shifts in the dissociation curve of oxyhemoglobin (Fig. 20.6). The shift to the right at high altitude has been documented by Hurtado (1964b) for Morococha Indians, the shift to the left would depend upon sufficient cold stress to lower blood temperature (see Chapter 17). Further, adaptations of the pulmonary and cardiovascular systems might interfere with one another for each of the three stresses. In general, we have very few experimental data on antagonistic and synergistic responses to multiple stresses.

Ecological Systems Approaches

Ecology of the Puna Zone. High-altitude regions are particularly appropriate for studies of human ecology. In central and southern Peru, ecosystem

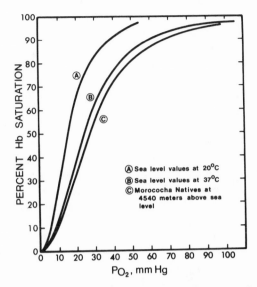

FIGURE 20.6 *Effect of temperature and altitude on the oxygen-dissociation curve of hemoglobin. [Adapted from Comroe (1965) and Hurtado (1964b).]*

changes are dependent upon slight variations in elevation which produce a wide variety of ecosystems within the same latitudinal belt. Associated with this diversity of ecosystems is corresponding variation in human subsistence modes and patterns of vertical trade and exchange among the human populations inhabiting these different zones. There are limiting factors that characterize each ecozone: cold, hypoxia, and energy availability become progressively important limiting factors with increasing altitude, while protein availability appears to be limiting at lower altitudes. Finally, the dry puna grasslands of the altiplano have been exploited for hundreds of years by natives utilizing a relatively simple technology. While the basic subsistence patterns have thus been constant over a very long period, two major perturbations have disturbed the system. The first occurred because of the Spanish conquest. We consider the second to be the highland population explosion of the past 50 yr.

Thomas and Winterhalder (see Chapters 2 and 19) have outlined in some detail the environmental characteristics of the Nuñoa puna zone. In Nuñoa, there are three major trophic levels of primary concern to the resident human population. The first level includes puna grasses and cultivated crops, comprising the bulk of the producers. The second level consists of the domestic herbivores (consumers), including the camelids (alpacas and llamas), sheep, cattle, and horses. The human population can be considered the only component of the third level (higher-order consumers), since carnivores are virtually absent from the region. Figure 20.7 is a simplified diagrammatic representation of the food web of the four main components of biomass in the Nuñoa district. Puna grasses and occasionally domestic grains provide forage for the livestock, which in turn provide meat, milk, dung, wool, and hides, and transport for the native population. Cultivated grains and tubers provide the staples of the native's diet, while livestock provide small, but essential, amounts of protein.

Most of the Nuñoa Indians' needs (including homespun clothing and food) are products of basic subsistence activities. However, as Escobar (Chapter 3) and Thomas (Chapter 19) note, economic exchanges, both within the district and with districts at lower elevations, play an important role in providing food and other commodities. Much of this trade takes place through commercial exchanges. Figure 20.8 illustrates sources of income and products that are purchased by the Nuñoa Indian families. Thus, in addition to the complex interdependency that exists among the Indian population, natural puna grassland vegetation, cultivated crops, and domestic herds, there is also a vertical-zone interdependency based upon trade. The puna zone of Nuñoa provides meat and other animal products and surplus tubers and grains in exchange for coca, cane alcohol, and high-energy foods from lower zones. Perhaps because of the sharp population increase of recent decades, the balance of the interdependencies is now quite delicate and could be easily disrupted. Such disruption would have serious consequences to the welfare of both the environment and the population.

Energy Flow in Nuñoa. The Indian population of Nuñoa today exists within a tight energy budget (see Chapter 19), in which productivity is maximized by a diversified pattern of subsistence. Agricultural productivity of Andean tubers (potato, oca, añu) and chenopods (quinoa and cañihua) is

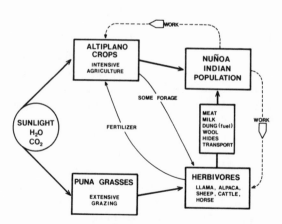

FIGURE 20.7 *Simplified diagram of the food web of the Nuñoa Indian population. [Adapted from Winterhalder et al. (1974).]*

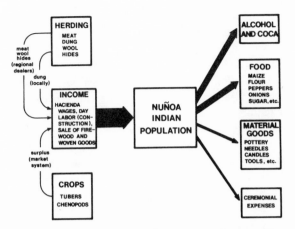

FIGURE 20.8 *Sources of income and expenditures associated with subsistence and vertical-zone exchange.*

high, giving an energetic efficiency of 11.5 (food energy produced/human energy expended). Compared to an energetic efficiency of about 2.0 for animal-herding activity, crops would appear to be a better choice in any native strategy decision regarding production. There are, however, a variety of reasons why a mixed agricultural/herding economy is an optimal pattern for puna grasslands, and may, in fact, serve as a model for such a managed ecosystem.

Crops grown in the high-altitude puna zone are vulnerable, and crop failure is a recurring phenomenon, owing to variation in seasonal rainfall patterns, drought, frost, and rare cold spells. Although techniques for the preservation of tubers and grains tend to reduce the acute affects of crop failure, livestock are a more stable commodity that serve as a stored source of energy to carry the population through crisis periods. In addition to providing a more stable source of stored energy, domestic camelids and sheep act as energy converters by producing dung that can be utilized as fuel or fertilizer (Winterhalder et al., 1974). Hence, agricultural productivity is dependent upon dung production. Thus the energetic efficiency of herding is raised and the efficiency of cultivation is lowered when fertilizer is added to a energy-balance model of the system. The two modes of subsistence achieve an even greater level of equality when animal products from the puna zone are traded for food produced in lower zones. The caloric return in exchanges of meat, hides, and wool for maize, flour, and other foods raises the energetic efficiency of herding (for trade) to a value comparable to that of agriculture (about 10.0). Finally, since less than 2 percent of the land in the district of Nuñoa is suitable for agriculture (Thomas, 1973), grazing of domestic herds is the only viable method of food production from much of the land area. Furthermore, the replacement of wild camelids (quanaco and vicuña), which grazed puna lands in large numbers prior to animal domestication in the Andes, by domestic forms serves to maintain the state of ecosystem equilibrium that existed before human settlement.

In addition to the cultural adaptations discussed above, Thomas (Chapter 19) notes several other population responses to the limited energy resources in Nuñoa. Within the behavioral realm, low-body-mass children (with concomitantly low energy requirements) are extensively used as pastoralists, and much of the subsistence tasks of adults involve low levels of physical activity. Thomas also suggests that the prolonged period of child and adolescent growth and small adult body size are biological responses to limited availability of energy.

As presently structured, it appears that the system is energetically near its maximum support for the population. Even as presently structured, continuous adult out-migration is required to balance the system. An outside force such as the introduction of fertilizer or a change in meat and wool prices could increase the population-carrying capacity of the energy-flow system, but it is difficult to conceive of how an internal restructuring could increase the energy yield.

FUTURE PERSPECTIVES

Despite the vast literature that has accumulated on adaptation of natives and sojourners to high terrestrial altitudes within the past 30 yr, there still appear to us three major directions of research which could enhance our understanding of man's adaptation to this ecozone.

1. Much research, for example, has focused upon the single stresses of altitude, such as hypoxia, cold, disease, and nutritional inadequacy, each treated as an independent parameter. Little research, beyond work with experimental laboratory animals, has been attempted on the difficult problem of human responses to the multiple stresses experienced at high altitude or problems associated with generalized (nonspecific) stress resistance.

2. Another fruitful area of investigation, one with considerable social, economic, and biological import, relates to worldwide human migrations into new environments. Mountain zones are no exception; most migration is in a downward direction.

3. Modeling and simulation of highland ecosystems with human populations as an integral component is a third area that should be developed. At present we have sufficient information to construct simple models that could be refined as new data are generated.

Brief comments on these three areas of new and potential research follow.

Multiple and Cross-Adaptations

Infectious-disease vectors, limited nutrient availability, intense solar radiation, low humidity, cold temperatures, and reduced oxygen tension are the most easily identified stresses to which Andean Indians are exposed. When adaptation to one of these stresses influences the ability to adapt to another (either positively or negatively) it is known as cross-adaptation (Fregly, 1970). Cross-resistance (a positive interaction) and cross-sensitivity (a negative interaction) to the stresses present in the high-altitude environment of the Andean Indian are generally not known.

Laboratory studies of cross-adaptation on human subjects cannot be extrapolated easily to the natural high-altitude conditions of the native, for several reasons. It is clear that transient and intermittent exposures to stress elicit different patterns of adaptation than do continuous exposures. For example, in some cases positive cross-adaptation may be limited to early phases of the adaptation process (Hale, 1970). Brief exposures to single or multiple stresses usually produce an "overshoot" effect which only simulates an adaptive response (Prosser, 1964).

Some of the implications of cross-adaptation to high-altitude stresses have been touched upon in this volume. More hypotheses than answers have been generated, and this area of research may prove to be the most challenging one facing environmental physiologists in regard to adaptation to high altitude.

Migration and Environmental Change

Upward and downward migration of people provides a natural laboratory for studies of the effects of environmental change (Harrison, 1966; Baker, in press a). As noted in Chapter 1, comparisons of samples of upward and downward migrants, lateral migrants at high and low altitudes, and non-migrants should give us information on the persistence of stress tolerance and on the role of developmental acclimatization. Several studies have already utilized samples of migrants, with high degrees of success (Abelson et al., 1974; Baker, in press b; Frisancho et al., 1973b, 1973c). From this work, effects of environmental change (through migration) on fertility, growth, health, pulmonary function, and exercise capacity have been documented. Studies of transient migrants may even be employed to gather information on cross-adaptation and nonspecific stress resistance.

Systems Modeling

The ultimate objective in ecological studies is to develop predictive models of ecosystem dynamics and processes. Mathematical modeling and simulation of Andean ecosystems is a complex but logical next step for human investigations at high altitude. The research results covered in this book are certainly adequate for the development of preliminary demographic and population biology models. Thomas's (1973) efforts at energy-flow modeling are indicative of what can be done to study man's relationship with his environment, and such work should be further developed.

The advantages of a modeling approach for studies of human adaptation are manifold. For example, problem areas and data gaps can be recognized more easily; data can be gathered more selectively, as opposed to the "shotgun" approach frequently required for pilot studies; and long-range objectives can be identified to rationally limit the scope of a research project. Finally, predictive models of population growth and ecosystem change are needed by government officials and decision makers in order intelligently to exploit and manage mountain zones and to maintain or improve the delicate balance that exists at the present.

REFERENCES

Abelson, A. E. 1972. Altitude, migration and fertility in Peru. M.A. thesis. Pennsylvania State Univ., University Park, Pa.

——, T. S. Baker, and P. T. Baker. 1974. Altitude, migration and fertility. Soc. Biol. *21:* 12-27.

Abramson, D. I. 1967. Circulation in the extremities. Academic Press, New York.

——, H. Landt, and J. E. Benjamin. 1941. Peripheral vascular responses to general anoxia. Proc. Soc. Exp. Biol. Med. *48:* 214-216.

——, H. Landt, and J. E. Benjamin. 1943. Peripheral vascular response to acute anoxia. Arch. Int. Med. *71:* 583-593.

Acosta Chavez, M. H. 1964. Algunos aspectos del niño primaturo en las alturas: estudio clínico—estadístico realizado en el Hospital de Huarón a 4750 metros de altura sobre el nivel del mar. Tesis 3886, Facultad de Medicina, Lima, Peru.

Adams, R. N. 1959. A community in the Andes. Univ. Washington Press, Seattle.

Albó, J. 1972. Esposos, suegros y padrinos entre los Aymaras. Symposium on Andean Kinship and Marriage, American Anthropological Association, Toronto.

Albritton, E. C. 1952. Standard values in blood. Saunders, Philadelphia.

Alers, J. O. 1965. Population and development in a Peruvian community. J. Int. Am. Stud. *7:* 423-428.

Allen, F. H., Jr. 1959. Summary of blood group phenotypes in some Aboriginal Americans. Am. J. Phys. Anthrop. *17:* 86.

Altland, P. D. 1949a. Breeding performance of rats exposed repeatedly to 18,000 feet simulated altitude. Physiol. Zool. *22:* 235-246.

——. 1949b. Effects of discontinuous exposure to 25,000 feet simulated altitude on growth and reproduction of the albino rat. J. Exp. Zool. *110:* 1-18.

——, and E. Allen. 1952. Studies on degenerating sex cells in immature mammals, III. J. Morphol. *91:* 541-553.

——, and B. Highman. 1968. Sex organ changes and breeding performance of male rats exposed to altitude: effects of exercise and physical training. J. Reprod. Fert. *15:* 215-222.

——, and B. Highman. 1971. Effects of polycythemia and altitude hypoxia on rat heart and exercise tolerance. Am. J. Physiol. *221:* 388-393.

Altman, P. L., and D. S. Dittmer. 1961. Blood and other body fluids.

Federation of American Societies for Experimental Biology, Washington, D.C.

Alzamora, V., A. Rotta, and G. Battilana. 1953. On the possible influence of great altitudes on the determination of certain cardiovascular anomalies. Pediatrics *12:* 259-262.

Andersen, K. L. 1967. Work capacity of selected world populations, pp. 66-90. *In* P. T. Baker and J. S. Weiner (eds.), The biology of human adaptability. Oxford Univ. Press, Oxford.

———. 1972. The effect of altitude variation on the physical performance capacity of Ethiopian men, pp. 154-163. *In* D. J. M. Vorster (ed.), Human biology of environmental change. International Biological Programme, London.

Anderson, M. E., and E. R. Mugrage. 1936. Red blood cell values for normal men and women. Arch. Int. Med. *58:* 136-146.

Anthony, A., and J. Krieder. 1961. Blood volume changes in rodents exposed to simulated high altitude. Am. J. Physiol. *200:* 523-526.

Archivo General de Indias. 1558. Contaduría 1824, 4-0, Manuscript.

Arias-Stella, J., and S. Recavarren. 1962. Right ventricular hypertrophy in native children living at high altitude. Am. J. Pathol. *41:* 54-64.

Aschoff, J., and A. Heise. 1972. Thermal conductance in man: its dependence on time of day and on ambient temperature, pp. 334-348. *In* S. Itoh, K. Ogata, and H. Yoshimura (eds.), Advances in climatic physiology. Springer-Verlag, Berlin.

Asmussen, E., and M. Nielsen. 1955. The cardiac output in rest and work at low and high oxygen pressures. Acta Physiol. Scand. *35:* 73-83.

Aste-Salazar, H. 1966. Diferenciación de hemoglobinas humanas en las grandes alturas. Acta Cient. Venezolana *17:* 117-121.

Åstrand, P. O. 1952. Experimental studies of physical working capacity in relation to sex and age. Munksgaard, Copenhagen.

———, and K. Rodahl. 1970. Textbook of work physiology. McGraw-Hill, New York.

Baker, P. T. 1958. Racial difference in heat tolerance. Am. J. Phys. Anthrop. *16:* 287-305.

———. 1960. Climate, culture and evolution, pp. 3-16. *In* G. Lasker (ed.), The processes of ongoing human evolution. Wayne State Univ. Press, Detroit, Mich.

———. 1963a. Adaptation to high altitude cold in the Andes. Annual Progress Report. Surgeon General Contract DA-49-193-MD-2260. Pennsylvania State Univ., University Park, Pa.

———. 1963b. The influence of body characteristics on human temperature responses to high altitude cold. Progress Report, Nov. 3, 1963, Contract DA-49-193-MD-2260. Office of the Surgeon General, Washington, D.C.

———. 1965a. Multidisciplinary studies of human adaptability: theoretical justification and method. *In* J. S. Weiner (ed.), International biological programme: a guide to the human adaptability proposals. Handbook IBP 1. ICSU Special Committee for the International Biological Programme.

———. 1965b. The biological and cultural structure of a high altitude Peruvian population. Report on Surgeon General Contract DA-49-193-MD-2260. Pennsylvania State Univ., University Park, Pa.

———. 1966a. Ecological and physiological adaptations in Indigenous South Americans, pp. 275-304. *In* P. T. Baker and J. S. Weiner (eds.), The biology of human adaptability. Oxford Univ. Press, Oxford.

———. 1966b. Micro-environment cold in a high altitude Peruvian population, pp. 67-77. *In* H. Yoshimura and J. S. Weiner (eds.), Human adaptability and its methodology. Japan Society for the Promotion of Sciences, Tokyo.

———. 1968. Multidisciplinary studies of human adaptability: theoretical justification and method. Mater. Pr. Antropol. *75:* 321-332. Wroclaw, Poland.

———. 1969. Human adaptation to high altitude. Science *163:* 1149-1156.

———. 1971. Adaptation problems in Andean human populations, pp. 475-507. *In* F. M. Salzano (ed.), The ongoing evolution of Latin American populations. Charles C Thomas, Springfield, Ill.

———. In press a. Research strategies in population biology and environmental stress. *In* E. Giles and J. Friedlaender (eds.), The measures of man: methodologies in human biology. Schenkman Publishing Co., Cambridge, Mass.

———. In press b. Un estudio de los aspectos biológicos y sociales de la migración andina. Archivos del Instituto de Biología Andina, Lima, Peru.

———, and F. Daniels, Jr. 1956. Relationship between skinfold thickness and body cooling for two hours at 15°C. J. Appl. Physiol. *8:* 409-416.

———, and J. S. Dutt. 1972. Demographic variables as measures of biological adaptation: a case study of high altitude human populations, pp. 352-378. *In* G. A. Harrison and A. J. Boyce (eds.), The structure of human populations. Clarendon Press, Oxford.

———, and R. Mazess. 1963. Calcium: unusual sources in the highland Peruvian diet. Science *142:* 1466-1467.

———, and J. S. Weiner (eds.). 1966. The biology of human adaptability. Clarendon Press, Oxford.

———, E. E. Hunt, and S. T. Sen. 1958. The growth and interrelations of skinfolds and brachial tissues in man. Am. J. Phys. Anthrop. *16:* 39-58.

———, A. R. Frisancho, M. A. Little, R. B. Mazess, and R. B. Thomas. 1965. A preliminary study of the cultural and biological characteristics of a Peruvian highland population. Annual Progress Report U.S. Army Surgeon General. Contract DA-49-193-MD-2260.

———, E. R. Buskirk, E. Picón-Reátegui, J. Kollias, R. B. Mazess, R. F. Akers, A. R. Frisancho, M. A. Little, E. K. Prokop, R. B. Thomas, and A. B. Way. 1966a. Micro-environment cold in a high altitude Peruvian population. *In* Altitude and cold: a study of the cold exposure and thermoregulatory responses of high altitude Quechua Indians. Annual Progress Report. Grant DA-49-193-MD-2260. Pennsylvania State Univ., University Park, Pa.

——, A. R. Frisancho, and R. B. Thomas. 1966b. A preliminary analysis of human growth in the Peruvian Andes, pp. 259-269. *In* M. S. Malhotra (ed.), Human adaptability in environments and physical fitness. Defence Institute of Physiology and Allied Sciences. Madras—3, Research and Development Organization, Ministry of Defence, Government of India.

——, E. R. Buskirk, J. Kollias, and R. B. Mazess. 1967. Temperature regulation at high altitude: Quechua Indians and U.S. whites during total body cold exposure. Hum. Biol. *39:* 155-169.

——, G. Escobar, G. DeJong, C. J. Hoff, R. B. Mazess, J. M. Hanna, M. A. Little, and E. Picón-Reátegui. 1968. High altitude adaptation in a Peruvian community. Occasional Papers in Anthropology 1. Pennsylvania State Univ., University Park, Pa.

Baker, T. S. 1966. Quechua marriage: some ecological determinants of marriage patterns in the southern highlands of Peru. M.S. thesis. Pennsylvania State Univ., University Park, Pa.

——, A. V. Little, and P. T. Baker. 1967a. First report on early development at high altitude. PHS Grant 1 RO1 HD-01756-01. Department of Anthropology, Pennsylvania State Univ., University Park, Pa.

——, A. V. Little, and A. R. Frisancho. 1967b. Infant growth in a high altitude population. Am. J. Phys. Anthrop. *27:* 248 (abstract).

Baldwin, E. de F., A. Cournand, and D. W. Richards, Jr. 1948. Pulmonary insufficiency: I. Methods of analysis, physiologic classification, standard values in normal subjects. Medicine (Baltimore) *27:* 243-278.

Balke, B. 1964a. Cardiac performance in relation to altitude. Am. J. Cardiol. *14:* 796-810.

——. 1964b. Work capacity and its limiting factors at high altitude, pp. 233-240. *In* W. H. Weihe (ed.), The physiological effects of high altitude. Macmillan, New York.

——, J. G. Wells, and J. P. Ellis. 1956. Effects of altitude acclimatization on work capacity. Fed. Proc. *15:* 7.

——, F. J. Nagle, and J. Daniels. 1965. Altitude and maximum performance in work and sports activity. J. Am. Med. Assoc. *194:* 646.

——, J. A. Faulkner, and J. T. Daniels. 1966. Maximum performance capacity at sea level and at moderate altitude before and after training at altitude. Schweiz. Z. Sportmed. *14:* 106.

Banchero, N., F. Sime, D. Peñaloza, J. Cruz, R. Gamboa, and E. Marticorena. 1966. Pulmonary pressure, cardiac output and arterial oxygen saturation during exercise at high altitude and at sea level. Circulation *33:* 249-262.

Barcroft, J. 1925. The respiratory function of the blood: 1. Lessons from high altitudes. Cambridge Univ. Press, Cambridge.

——. 1936. Fetal circulation and respiration. Physiol. Rev. *16:* 103-128.

——, C. A. Binger, A. V. Bock, J. H. Doggart, H. S. Forbes, G. Harrop, J. C. Meakins, and A. C. Redfield. 1923. Observations upon the effect of high altitude on the physiological processes of the human body, carried out in the Peruvian Andes, chiefly at Cerro de Pasco. Phil. Trans. Roy. Soc. Lond., *B211:* 351-480.

Barron, D. H., J. Metcalf, G. Meschia, W. Huckabee, A. Hellegers, and H. Prystowsky. 1964. Adaptation of pregnant ewes and their fetuses to altitude. *In* W. H. Weihe (ed.), The physiological effects of high altitude. Macmillan, New York.

Barry, H. A., M. K. Bacon, and I. Child. 1959. Relation of child training to subsistence economy. Am. Anthrop. *61:* 51-63.

Bartlett, D. 1972. Postnatal development of the mammalian lung. *In* R. Goss (ed.), Regulation of organ and tissue growth. Academic Press, New York.

Bartlett, D., Jr., and J. E. Remmers. 1971. Effects of high altitude exposure on the lungs of young rats. Respir. Physiol. *13:* 116-125.

Bates, D. B., N. G. Boucot, and A. E. Dorner. 1955. Pulmonary diffusing capacity in normal subjects. J. Physiol. (Lond.) *129:* 237-252.

Baum, J. A. 1967. Estudio sobre la educación rural en el Perú: los núcleos escolares campesinos. United States Agency for International Development, Mexico, D.F.

Bayley, N. 1969. Manual for the Bayley scales of infant development. Psychological Corp., New York.

Beall, C. M. 1972. Respiratory disease in migrant populations living in a Peruvian coastal valley. M. A. thesis. Pennsylvania State Univ., University Park, Pa.

Beals, E. 1969. Vegetational change along altitudinal gradients. Science *165:* 981-985.

Belding, H. S. 1949. Protection against dry cold, p. 351-367. *In* L. Newburgh (ed.), The physiology of heat regulation and the science of clothing. Saunders, Philadelphia.

Bennett, W. C. 1946. The Andean highlands. *In* J. H. Steward (ed.), The Andean civilizations. Handbook of South American Indians, Smithsonian Institution, Washington, D.C. *2:* 1-60.

Berry, L., R. B. Mitchell, and D. Rubenstein. 1955. Effects of acclimatization to altitude on susceptibility of mice to influenza a virus infection. Proc. Soc. Exp. Biol. Med. *88:* 543-548.

Berry, W. T., J. B. Bever, E. R. Bransby, A. K. Chalmers, B. M. Needham, H. E. Magee, H. S. Townsend, and C. G. Daubney. 1949. The diet, hemoglobin values and blood pressures of Olympic athletes. Br. Med. J. *1:* 300-304.

Billings, W. D. 1973. Arctic and alpine vegetations: similarities, differences, and susceptibility to disturbance. Bio Science *23:* 697-704.

Bjure, J. 1963. Sperometric studies in normal subjects: IV. Ventilatory capacities in healthy children 7–17 years of age. Acta Paediatr. *52:* 232-240.

Bjurstedt, A. G. 1946. Interaction of centrogenic and chemoreflex control of breathing during oxygen deficiency at rest. Acta Physiol. Scand. *12* (Suppl. 39): 1-88.

Blaisdell, R. K. 1951. Effect of body thermal state on cold-induced cyclic vasodilatation in the finger. Environmental Protection Report 177. Quartermaster Climatic Research Laboratory, Natick, Mass.

Blatteis, C. 1966. Comments following a presentation by H. Chiodi, pp. 474-475. *In* The physiology of work in cold and altitude. Proceedings of the Sixth Symposium on Arctic Biology and Medicine. Arctic Aeromedical Laboratory, Ft. Wainwright, Alaska.

Bolton, C., and R. Bolton. 1972. Techniques of socialization among the Qolla. Paper delivered at the 40th International Congress of Americanists, Sept. 3–10, 1972, Rome.

Bolton, R. 1972. The marriage pattern of the Qolla. Symposium on Andean Kinship and Marriage, American Anthropological Association, Toronto.

Boothby, W. M., J. Berkson, and H. L. Dunn. 1936. Studies of the energy metabolism of normal individuals: a standard for basal metabolism with a nomogram for clinical application. Am. J. Physiol. *116:* 468-484.

Boren, H. G., R. C. Kory, and J. C. Syner. 1966. The lung volume and its subdivisions in normal men. Am. J. Med. *41:* 96-114.

Bouloux, C. J. 1968. Contribution à L'étude biologique des phénomènes pubertaires en très haute altitude (La Paz). Centre d'Hématypologie du Centre National de la Recherche Scientifique. Centre Régional de Transfusion Sanguine et d'Hémalogie, Toulouse, France.

Boyce, A. J., J. S. J. Haight, D. B. Rimmer, and G. A. Harrison. 1974. Respiratory function in Peruvian Quechua Indians. Hum. Biol. *1:* 144-152.

Bradshaw, B. S. 1969. Fertility differences in Peru: a reconsideration. Pop. Stud. *23:* 5-19.

Brasel, J. A. 1968. Oxygen consumption and growth. *In* D. B. Cheek (ed.), Human growth, body composition, cell growth, energy, and intelligence. Lea & Febiger, Philadelphia.

Braselton, T. B., J. S. Robey, and G. A. Collier. 1969. Infant development in the Zinacanteco Indians of Southern Mexico. Pediatrics *44:* 274.

Brody, S. 1945. Bioenergetics and growth. Van Nostrand Reinhold, New York.

Browman, D. L. 1970. Early Peruvian peasants: the culture history of a central highlands valley. Unpublished Ph.D. dissertation. Harvard Univ., Cambridge, Mass.

———. 1974. Pastoral nomadism in the Andes. Current Anthrop. *15:* 188-196.

Brožek, J. 1961. Body measurements including skinfold thickness as indicator of body composition. *In* J. Brožek and A. Henschel (eds.), Techniques for measuring body composition. National Academy of Sciences—National Research Council, Washington, D.C.

Buck, A. A., T. T. Sasaki, R. I. Anderson, J. C. Hitchcock, and G. R. Leigh. 1967. Comprehensive epidemiological studies of four contrasting Peruvian villages. Geographic Epidemiology Unit, Johns Hopkins Univ., Baltimore, Md.

———, T. T. Sasaki, and R. I. Anderson. 1968. Health and disease in four Peruvian villages: contrasts in epidemiology. Johns Hopkins Press, Baltimore, Md.

Budowski, G. 1968. La influencia humana en la vegetación natural de montañas tropicales americanas. *In* E. J. Fittkau et al. (eds.), Biogeography and ecology in South America. Dr. W. Junk, Publishers, The Hague.

Buechler, H. C., and J.-M. Buechler. 1971. The Bolivian Aymara. Holt, Rinehart and Winston, New York.

Bueno, Cosme. 1951. Descripción del virreinato del Peru (1763–1778). Lima, Peru.

Bullard, R. W. 1972. Vertebrates at altitudes, pp. 209-225. *In* Yousef, Horvath and Bullard (eds.), Physiological adaptations: desert and mountain. Academic Press, New York.

Burchard, R. E. 1971. Coca and food exchanges in Andean Peru. Paper read at 70th Anniversary Meeting of American Anthropology Association, New York.

Burri, P. H., and E. R. Weibel. 1971a. Morphometric estimation of pulmonary diffusion capacity: II. Effect of PO_2 on the growing lung. Adaptation of the growing rat lung to hypoxia and hyperhypoxia. Respir. Physiol. *11:* 247-264.

———, and E. R. Weibel. 1971b. Morphometric evaluation of changes in lung structure due to high altitude. *In* R. Porter and J. Knight (eds.), High altitude physiology. Cardiac and respiratory aspects. Churchill Livingstone, Edinburgh.

Burton, A. C. 1935. Human calorimetry: II. The average temperature of the tissues of the body. J. Nutr. *9:* 261-280.

———, and O. G. Edholm. 1955. Man in a cold environment: physiological and pathological effects of exposure to low temperatures. Edward Arnold, London.

Buskirk, E. R. 1969. Decrease in physical working capacity at high altitude, pp. 204-222. *In* A. H. Hegnauer (ed.), Proceedings of the symposium on biomedicine problems of high terrestrial elevations. U.S. Army Research Institute of Environmental Medicine, Natick, Mass.

———. 1971. Work and fatigue in high altitude, pp. 312-322. *In* E. Simonson (ed.), Physiology of work capacity and fatigue. Charles C Thomas, Springfield, Ill.

———, and J. Mendez. 1967. Nutrition, environment and work performance with special reference to altitude. Fed. Proc. *26:* 1760-1767.

———, and H. L. Taylor. 1957. Maximal oxygen intake and its relation to body composition, with special reference to chronic physical activity and obesity. J. Appl. Physiol. *11:* 72.

——, R. H. Thomson, and G. D. Whedon. 1963. Metabolic response to cooling in the human: role of body composition and particularly of body fat, pp. 429-442. *In* J. D. Hardy (ed.), Temperature, its measurement and control in science and industry, Vol. 3, Pt. 3. Van Nostrand Reinhold, New York.

——, J. Kollias, R. F. Akers, E. K. Prokop, and E. Picón-Reátegui. 1967a. Maximal performance at altitude and on return from altitude in conditioned runners. J. Appl. Phyiol. *23:* 259-266.

——, J. Kollias, E. Picón-Reátegui, R. Akers, E. Prokop, and P. T. Baker. 1967b. Physiology and performance of track athletes at various altitudes in the United States and Peru, pp. 233-247. *In* R. F. Goddard (ed.), The effects of altitude on physical performance. Lovelace Foundation, Albuquerque, N.M.

Cabrera, A. L. 1968. Ecología vegetal de la puna. *In* C. Troll (ed.), Geoecology of the mountainous regions of the tropical Americas. Ferd. Dümmlers Verlag, Bonn.

Calderón, L., A. Llerena, L. Munive, and F. Kruger. 1966. Intravenous glucose tolerance test in pregnancy in women living in chronic hypoxia. Diabetes *15:* 130-132.

Campos, R. de C., J., and B. Iglesias. 1957. Observaciones anatomopatológicas en 49 personas normales, nativos y residentes de la altura, muertas en accidentes. Rev. Lat. Am. Anat. Patol. *1:* 109-130.

Cancian, F. 1965. Economics and prestige in a Maya community: the religious cargo system in Zinacantan. Stanford Univ. Press, Stanford, Calif.

Cardenas, M. 1952. Psychological aspects of coca addiction. Bull. Narcotics *42:* 6-9.

Carlson, L. D. 1954. Man in a cold environment: a study in physiology. Arctic Aeromedical Laboratory, Ladd Air Force Base, Fairbanks, Alaska.

——, H. L. Burns, T. H. Holmes, and P. P. Webb. 1953. Adaptive changes during exposure to cold. J. Appl. Physiol. *5:* 672-676.

Carson, R. P., W. O. Evans, J. S. Shields, and J. P. Hannon. 1969. Symptomatology, pathophysiology, and treatment of acute mountain sickness. Fed. Proc. *28:* 1085-1091.

Carter, W. E. 1972. Trial marriage in the Andes? Symposium on Andean Kinship and Marriage, American Anthropological Association, Toronto.

Cavalli-Sforza, L. L., and W. F. Bodmer. 1971. The genetics of human populations. W. H. Freeman, San Francisco.

——, and A. W. F. Edwards. 1967. Phylogenetic analysis: models and estimation procedures. Am. J. Hum. Genet. *19:* 233-257.

Cerretelli, P. 1961. Some aspects of the respiratory function in man acclimatized to high altitude (the Himalayas). Int. Z. Angew. Physiol. Einschl. Arbeitsphysiol. *18:* 386-392.

Chagnon, N. A. 1974. Studying the Yanomamo. Holt, Rinehart and Winston, New York.

Chambochumbi, M. N. 1949. Efectos de la coca sobre el metabolismo basal en sujectos no habituados. Rev. Farmacol. Med. Expt. *1:* 216-231.

Cheek, D., J. A. Graystone, and R. A. Rowe. 1969. Hypoxia and malnutrition in newborn rats: effects on RNA, DNA and protein tissues. Am. J. Physiol. *217:* 642-645.

Chervin, A. 1907. Anthropologie bolivienne, 3 vols. Tome II, Anthropométrie, p. 435, Paris.

Chiodi, H. 1950. Blood picture at high altitude. J. Appl. Physiol. *2:* 431-436.

———. 1957. Respiratory adaptations to chronic high altitude hypoxia. J. Appl. Physiol. *10:* 81-87.

———. 1963. Respiratory adaptation to high altitude, pp. 363-378. *In* J. S. Haldane (ed.), The regulation of human respiration. F. A. Davis, Philadelphia.

———. 1964. Action of high altitude chronic hypoxia on newborn animals, pp. 97-112. *In* W. H. Weihe (ed.), The physiological effects of high altitude. Macmillan, New York.

———. 1966. Blood tissue changes during high altitude and cold acclimatization, pp. 453-479. *In* The physiology of work in cold and altitude. Proceedings of the Sixth Symposium on Arctic Biology and Medicine. Arctic Aeromedical Laboratory, Ft. Wainwright, Alaska.

———. 1970–1971. Comparative study of the blood gas transport in high altitude and sea level camelidae and goats. Respir. Physiol. *11:* 84-93.

———, L. Otero-Calderón, and J. R. Suarez. 1952. La sensibilidad del centro respiratorio en la altura. Cienc. Invest. (B. Aires) *8:* 446-469.

Ciocco, A. 1938. The masculinity of stillbirths and abortions in relation to the duration of uterogestation and to stated causes of fetal mortality. Hum. Biol. *10:* 235-250.

CISM. 1968. Encuesta de fecundidad en la ciudad de Cerro de Pasco. Centro de Investigaciones Sociales por Muestro and the Ministerio de Trabajo y Comunidades del Perú, Lima, Peru.

Clegg, E. J., and G. A. Harrison. 1971. Reproduction in human high altitude populations. Hormones *2:* 13-25.

———, G. A. Harrison, and P. T. Baker. 1970. The impact of high altitude on human populations. Hum. Biol. *42:* 486-518.

———, I. G. Pawson, E. H. Ashton, and R. M. Flinn. 1972. The growth of children at different altitudes in Ethiopia. Phil. Trans. Roy. Soc. Lond. *264:* 403-437.

Cobo, Bernabe de. 1956. Historia del Nuevo Mundo, Vol. 2. Biblioteca de Autores Españoles 92, Madrid, Atlas.

Collazos, C., H. S. White, R. L. Huenemann, E. Reh, P. L. White, A. Castellanos, R. Benites, Y. Bravo, A. Loo, I. Moscoso, C. Caceres, and A. Dieseldorf. 1954. Dietary surveys in Peru: III. Chacan and Vicos, rural communities in the Peruvian Andes. J. Am. Dietet. Assoc. *30*: 1222-1248.

——, P. L. White, H. S. White, E. Viñas, T. E. Alvistur, R. Urquieta, J. Vasquez, C. Diaz, A. Quiroz, A. Roca, D. M. Hegsted, and R. B. Bradfield. 1957. La composición de los alimentos peruanos. An. Fac. Med. (Lima) *40*: 232-266.

——, I. Moscoso, Y. Bravo, A. Castellanos, C. Caceres, A. Roca, and R. B. Bradfield. 1960. La alimentación y el estado de nutrición en el Perú. An. Fac. Med. (Lima) *43*: 7-297.

Comas, J. 1971. Anthropometric studies in Latin America Indian populations. *In* F. Salzano (ed.), The ongoing evolution of Latin American populations. Charles C Thomas, Springfield, Ill.

Comroe, J. H. 1965. Physiology of respiration. Year Book Medical Publishers, Chicago.

——, R. E. Forster, A. B. Dubois, W. A. Briscoe, and E. Carlsen. 1955. The lung: clinical physiology and pulmonary function tests. Year Book Medical Publishers, Chicago.

Consolazio, C. F., R. E. Johnson, and L. T. Peccora. 1963. The physiological measurement of metabolic function in man. McGraw-Hill, New York.

——, R. Nelson, L. O. Matoush, and J. E. Hansen. 1966. Energy metabolism at high altitude (3475 m). J. Appl. Physiol. *21*: 1732-1740.

——, L. O. Matoush, H. L. Johnson, and T. A. Daws. 1968. Protein and water balances of young adults during prolonged exposure to high altitude (4300 m). Am. J. Clin. Nutr. *21*: 154-161.

Conway, D. L., and P. T. Baker. 1972. Skin reflectance of Quechua Indians: the effects of genetic admixture, sex, and age. Am. J. Phys. Anthrop. *36*: 267-282.

Coope, E., and D. F. Roberts. 1971. Dermatoglyphic studies of populations in Latin America, pp. 405-453. *In* F. M. Salzano (ed.), The ongoing evolution of Latin American populations. Charles C Thomas, Springfield, Ill.

Cotes, J. E. 1965. Lung function. Blackwell Scientific, Oxford.

Coudert, J., and M. P. Zamora. 1970. Estudio del consumo de oxigeno en La Paz (3700 m) sobre un grupo de atletas nativos de la altura. Instituto Boliviano de Biología de Altura Anuario *1970*: 109-113.

Crow, J. F. 1958. Some possibilities for measuring selection intensities in man. Hum. Biol. *30*: 1-13.

Crowe, P. R. 1971. Concepts in climatology. St. Martin's Press, New York.

Cruxent, J. M. 1968. Theses for meditation on the origin and dispersion of man in South America. *In* Biomedical challenges presented by the American Indian. Pan Am. Health Org. Sci. Publ. 165, pp. 11-16. Washington, D.C.

Cruz-Coke, R. 1967. Genetic characteristics of high altitude populations in Chile. Paper presented at PAHO/WHO/IBP Meeting of Investigators on Population Biology of Altitude, Nov. 13–17. Washington, D.C.

——, A. P. Cristoffanini, M. Aspillaga, and F. Biancani. 1966. Evolutionary forces in human populations in an environmental gradiant in Arica, Chile. Hum. Biol. *38:* 421-438.

Cuiffardi T., E. 1948. Dosis de alcaloides que ingieren los habituados a la coca. Rev. Farmacol. Med. Expt. *1:* 216-231.

——. 1949. Contribución a la química del cocaísmo. Rev. Farmacol. Med. Expt. *2:* 18-93.

Cummins, H., and C. Midlo. 1943. Fingerprints, palms and soles: an introduction to dermatoglyphics. Blakiston, New York.

Custred, G. 1973. Symbols and control in a high altitude Andean community. Unpublished Ph.D. dissertation. Indiana Univ., Bloomington, Ind.

Daniels, F., Jr., and P. T. Baker. 1961. Relationship between body fat and shivering in air at $15°C$. J. Appl. Physiol. *16:* 421-425.

Darden, T. R. 1972. Respiratory adaptations of a fossorial mammal, the pocket gopher (*Thomomys bottae*). J. Comp. Physiol. *78:* 121-137.

Darlington, P. J., Jr. 1965. The biogeography of the southern end of the world. Harvard Univ. Press, Cambridge, Mass.

Da Rocha, F. 1971. Antropometria em indigenas brasileiros. Ph.D. dissertation, Federal University of Rio Grande Do Sul, Instituto de Biociencias, Publication 2, Pôrto Alegre, Brazil.

Davidsohn, I., and B. Wells. 1966. Todd-Sanford clinical diagnosis by laboratory methods. Saunders, Philadelphia.

Davies, C. T. M., C. Barnes, R. H. Fox, R. O. Ojikutu, and A. S. Samueloff. 1972. Ethnic differences in physical working capacity. J. Appl. Physiol. *33:* 726.

Davis, J. E., and N. Brewer. 1935. Effect of physical training on blood volume, hemoglobin, alkali reserve and osmotic resistance of erythrocytes. Am. J. Physiol. *113:* 586-591.

Davis, K., and J. Blake. 1956. Social structure and fertility: an analytic framework. Econ. Dev. Cult. Change *4:* 211-235.

DeJong, G. 1967. The population of Nuñoa, a preliminary report. Unpublished manuscript. Pennsylvania State Univ., University Park, Pa.

——. 1970. Demography and research with high altitude populations. Soc. Biol. *17:* 114-119.

Dejours, P., F. Girard, Y. Labrousse, R. Molimard, and A. Teillac. 1957. Existence d'un stimulus oxygène de la ventilation après acclimatation à l'altitude de 3613 m, chez l'homme. C. R. Acad. Sci. (Paris) *245:* 2534-2536.

Delaquerriere-Richardson, L., E. S. Forbes, and E. Valdivia. 1965. Effect of simulated high altitude on the growth rate of albino guinea pigs. J. Appl. Physiol. *20:* 1022-1025.

Deustua J., L. 1971. Organización de una hacienda ganadera en Puno. Ministerio de Agricultura, Informe 28, Peru.

Diez de San Miguel, G. 1567 (1964). Visita hecha a la provincia de Chucuito por Garci Diez de San Miguel en el año 1567. Documentos Regionales para la Ethnohistoria Andina 1. Casa de la Cultura del Perú, Lima, Peru.

Dill, D. B., H. T. Edwards, A. Folling, S. A. Oberg, A. M. Pappenheimer, Jr., and H. Talbott. 1931. Adaptations of the organism to changes in oxygen pressure. J. Physiol. (Lond.) *71:* 45-63.

————, E. H. Christensen, and H. T. Edwards. 1936. Gas equilibria in the lungs at high altitude. Am. J. Physiol. *115:* 530-538.

————, E. F. Adolph, and C. G. Wilber (eds.). 1964. Handbook of physiology: adaptation to the environment. American Physiological Society, Washington, D.C.

Dirección Nacional de Estadística y Censos. 1961. Boletín de estadística peruana. Ministerio de Hacienda y Comercio, Lima, Peru.

Dobyns, H. F. 1964. The social matrix of Peruvian Indigenous communities. Cornell-Peru Project Monographs. Cornell Univ., Ithaca, N.Y.

Dobzhansky, T. 1955. Evolution, genetics and man. Wiley, New York.

Donayre, J. 1966. Population growth and fertility at high altitude. *In* Life at high altitudes. Pan Am. Health Org. Sci. Publ. 140, pp. 74-79. Washington, D.C.

————, R. Guerra-Garcia, F. Moncloa, and L. A. Sobrevilla. 1968. Endocrine studies at altitude: IV. Changes in the semen of men. J. Reprod. Fert. *16:* 55-58.

Donoso P., H., E. Apud, M. C. Sanudo, and R. Santolaya. 1971. Capacidad aeróbica como índice de adecuadad física en muestras de poblaciones (urbanas y nativas de la altura) y en un grupo de atletas de selección. Rev. Med. Chile *99:* 719-731.

Douglas, C. G., J. S. Haldane, Y. Henderson, and E. C. Schneider. 1913. Physiological observations made on Pike's Peak, Colorado, with special reference to adaptation to low barometric pressures. Phil. Trans. Roy. Soc. Lond. *B203:* 185-318.

Dourojeanni, M. 1972. Flora y fauna del Perú: importancia de su conservación. El Serrano 272.

Drewes, W., and A. Drewes. 1957. Climate and related phenomena of the eastern Andean slopes of Central Peru. Syracuse Univ. Research Institute, Syracuse, N.Y.

Dubos, René. 1965. Man adapting. Yale Univ. Press, New Haven, Conn.

Dunnill, M. S. 1962. Postnatal growth of the lung. Thorax *17:* 329-333.

Durand, J., J.-M. Verpillat, M. Pradel, and J.-P Martineaud. 1969. Influence of altitude on the cutaneous circulation of residents and newcomers. Fed. Proc. *28:* 1124-1128.

Durnin, J. V. G. A., and R. Passmore. 1967. Energy, work and leisure. Heinemann, London.

Dutt, J. S. 1969. Population movement and its effect on gene flow in a highland Peruvian Quechua community. M.A. thesis. Pennsylvania State Univ., University Park, Pa.

Eagan, C. J. 1963a. Introduction and terminology to panel session H: habituation and peripheral tissue adaptations. Fed. Proc. *22:* 930-932.

———. 1963b. Resistance to finger cooling related to physical fitness. Nature *200:* 851-852.

Edholm, O. G., J. M. Adam, M. J. R. Healy, H. S. Wolff, R. Goldsmith, and T. W. Best. 1970. Food intake and energy expenditure of army recruits. Br. J. Nutr. *24:* 1091-1107.

Ehrenreich, P. M. A. 1897. Anthropologische Studien uber die Urbewohner Brasiliens vornemlich der Staaten Mato Grosso, Goyaz und Amazonas. F. Vieweg & Sohn, Braunschweig. 165 pp.

Ehrlich, R., and R. J. Mieszkuc. 1962. Effects of space cabin environment on resistance to infection: I. Effect of 18,000 feet altitude on resistance to respiratory infection. J. Infect. Dis. *110:* 278-281.

Eidt, R. C. 1968. The climatology of South America. *In* E. J. Fittkau et al. (eds.), Biogeography and ecology in South America. Dr. W. Junk, Publishers, The Hague.

Ellenberg, H. 1958. Wald oder Steppe? Die naturliche Pflanzendecke der Anden Perus: I and II. Umschau.

Elsner, R. W. 1963. Comparisons of Australian Aborigines, Alafaluf Indians, and Andean Indians. Fed. Proc. *22:* 840-845.

———, and A. Bolstad. 1963. Thermal and metabolic responses to cold of Peruvian Indians native to high altitudes. Tech. Rep. AAL-TDR-62-64, Arctic Aeromedical Laboratory, Ft. Wainwright, Alaska.

———, A. Bolstad, and C. Forno. 1964. Maximum oxygen consumption of Peruvian Indians native to altitude, pp. 217-223. In W. H. Weihe (ed.), Physiological effects of high altitude. Macmillan, New York.

Engel, F. 1960. Un groupe humain datant de 5000 ans à Paracas, Peru. J. Soc. Americanistes *49:* 7-35.

———. 1971. Exploration of the Chilca canyon. Current Anthrop. *12:* 55-58.

Epstein, Erwin H. 1971. Education and Peruanidad: internal colonialism in the Peruvian highlands. Comp. Educ. Rev. June 1971: 188-201.

Escobar M., G. 1959. El distrito de Asillo, Puno. Manuscript.

———. 1967. Organización social y cultural del sur del Perú. Serie Antropología Social 7. Instituto Indigenista Interamericano, Mexico, D.F.

———. 1968. Sicaya: problems of cultural change in a community in the central Andes of Peru. University Microfilms, Ann Arbor, Mich.

———. 1969. The role of sports in the penetration of urban culture to the rural areas of Peru, p. 72-81. Kroeber Anthropological Society Paper 40, Berkeley, Calif.

———. 1972. A preliminary descriptive analysis of the kin and family structure of the middle class population of the city of Cuzco, Peru. Symposium on Andean Kinship and Marriage, American Anthropological Association, Toronto.

FAO/WHO. 1957. Calorie requirements. Second Committee on Calorie Requirements, FAO Nutrition Studies 15, Rome.

———. 1973. Energy and protein requirements. WHO Tech. Rep. Ser. 522, Geneva.

Farabee, W. C. 1922. Indian tribes of eastern Peru. Papers of the Peabody Museum of American Archaeology and Ethnology, Harvard Univ. 10: 1-194.

Farhi, E. L., and H. Rahn. 1955. A theoretical analysis of the alveolar–arterial difference with special reference to the distribution effect. J. Appl. Physiol. 7: 699-703.

Faulkner, J. A., J. Kollias, C. B. Favour, E. R. Buskirk, and B. Balke. 1968. Maximum aerobic capacity and running performance at altitude. J. Appl. Physiol. 24: 685.

Fenna, D., L. Mix, O. Schaefer, and J. Gilbert. 1971. Ethanol metabolism in various racial groups. Can. Med. Assoc. J. 105: 472-475.

Fernandez-Cano, L. 1959. The effects of increase or decrease of body temperature or of hypoxia on ovulation and pregnancy in the rat, pp. 97-106. In C. W. Lloyd (ed.), Recent progress in the endocrinology of reproduction. Academic Press, New York.

Ferris, H. B. 1916. The Indians of Cuzco and the Apurimac. Mem. Am. Anthrop. Assoc. 3: 56-148.

Finch, C. A., and C. Lenfant. 1972. Oxygen transport in man. New England J. Med. 286: 407-415.

Fisher, R. A. 1958. The genetical theory of natural selection, 2nd ed. Dover, New York.

Fitch, W., and J. Neel. 1969. The phylogenetic relationships of some Indian tribes of Central and South America. Am. J. Hum. Gen. 21: 384-397.

Fittkau, E. J. 1968. The fauna of South America. In E. J. Fittkau et al. (eds.), Biogeography and ecology in South America. Dr. W. Junk, Publishers, The Hague.

Flores Ochoa, J. A. 1968. Los pastores de partía: una introducción a su estudio. Social 10. Instituto Indigenista Interamericano, Mexico, D.F. Serie Antropología

Folk, G. E., Jr. 1974. Textbook of environmental physiology, 2nd ed. Lea & Febiger, Philadelphia.

Fonseca Martel, C. 1972. Sistemas económicas en las comunidades campesinas del Perú. Unpublished Ph.D. dissertation. Univ. Nacional Mayor de San Marcos, Lima, Peru.

Food and Nutrition Board, N.R.C.–N.A.S. 1968. Recommended dietary allowances. National Research Council–National Academy of Sciences, Washington, D.C.

Forbes, W. H. 1936. Blood sugar and glucose tolerance at high altitudes. Am. J. Physiol. 116: 309-316.

Forsius, H., A. W. Eriksson, and H. Luukka. 1970. Ophthalmological characteristics of Eskimos in Augpilagtok. Arctic Anthrop. 7(1): 9-16.

Fortes, Meyer. 1938. Social and psychological aspects of education in Taleland. Africa 2(4).

Forwand, S. A., and M. Landowne. 1968. Effect of acetazolamide on acute mountain sickness. New Eng. J. Med. *279:* 839-845.

Frank, E., and K. Wezler. 1948. Physikalishe Warmeregulation gegen Kälte und Hitze im Sauerstoffmangel. Pflügers Arch. *250:* 598-622.

Freedman, R. 1961-62. The sociology of human fertility. Current Soc. *10/11:* 35-121.

Freeman, N. E., J. L. Shaw, and J. C. Snyder. 1936. Peripheral blood flow in surgical shock: reduction in circulation through the hand resulting from pain, fear, cold, and asphyxia, with quantitative measurements of the volume flow of blood in clinical cases of surgical shock. J. Clin. Invest. *15:* 651-664.

Fregly, M. J. 1954. Cross acclimatization between cold and altitude in rats. Am. J. Physiol. *176:* 267-274.

——. 1970. Comments on cross-adaptation, pp. 170-176. *In* D. H. K. Lee and D. Minard (eds.), Physiology, environment and man. Academic Press, New York.

Frisancho, A. R. 1966. Human growth in a high altitude Peruvian population. M. A. thesis. Pennsylvania State Univ., University Park, Pa.

——. 1969a. Human growth and pulmonary function of a high altitude Peruvian Quechua population. Hum. Biol. *41:* 365-379.

——. 1969b. Growth, physique and pulmonary function at high altitude: a field study of a Peruvian Quechua population. Ph.D. dissertation. Pennsylvania State Univ., University Park, Pa.

——. 1970. Developmental responses to high altitude hypoxia. Am. J. Phys. Anthrop. *32:* 401-408.

——, and P. T. Baker. 1970. Altitude and growth: a study of the patterns of physical growth of a high altitude Peruvian Quechua population. Am. J. Phys. Anthrop. *32:* 279-292.

——, and J. Cossman. 1970. Secular trends in neonatal mortality in the mountain states. Am. J. Phys. Anthrop. *33:* 103-106.

——, S. M. Garn, and W. Ascoli. 1970. Childhood retardation resulting in reduction of adult body size due to lesser adolescent skeletal delay. Am. J. Phys. Anthrop. *33:* 325-336.

——, J. Sanchez, D. Pallardel, and L. Yañez. 1973a. Adaptive significance of small body size under poor socio-economic conditions in southern Peru. Am. J. Phys. Anthrop. *39:* 255-262.

——, C. Martinez, T. Velásquez, J. Sanchez, and H. Montoye. 1973b. Influence of developmental adaptation on aerobic capacity at high altitude. J. Appl. Physiol. *34:* 176-180.

——, T. Velásquez, and J. Sanchez. 1973c. Influences of developmental adaptation on lung function at high altitude. Hum. Biol. *45:* 583-594.

——, and L. Yañez. 1971. Características de la mortalidad infantil en la altura, pp. 39-53. *In* A. R. Frisancho (ed.), Adaptación biológica a la altura. Center for Human Growth and Development and Department of Anthropology, Univ. Michigan, Ann Arbor, Mich.

Gade, D. W. 1969. The llama, alpaca and vincuña: fact vs. fiction. J. Geog. *58:* 339-343.

Garbell, M. A. 1947. Tropical and equatorial meterology. Pitman, New York.

Garn, S. M., and J. A. Haskell. 1960. Fat thickness and developmental status in childhood and adolescence. J. Dis. Child. *99:* 746-751.

——, J. M. Nagy, A. K. Poznanski, and M. B. McCann. 1972. Size reduction associated with brachymesophalangia-5: a possible selective advantage. Am. J. Phys. Anthrop. *33:* 325-336.

Garrido-Klinge, G., and L. Peña. 1959. The gastroduodenal ulcer in high altitudes (Peruvian Andes). Gastroenterology *37:* 390-400.

Garrow, J. S., and M. C. Pike. 1967. The long-term prognosis of severe infantile malnutrition. Lancet *1:* 1-4.

Garruto, R. M. 1969. Pulmonary function and body morphology. Selected relationships studied at high altitudes. M. A. thesis. Pennsylvania State Univ., University Park, Pa.

——. 1970. Pulmonary function and body morphology: selected relationships studied at high altitude. Am. J. Phys. Anthrop. *33:* 130 (abstract).

——. 1973. Polycythemia as an adaptive response to chronic hypoxic stress. Ph.D. thesis. Pennsylvania State Univ., University Park, Pa.

——, C. J. Hoff, P. T. Baker, and H. J. Jacobi. 1975. Phenotypic variation in ABO and Rh blood groups, PTC tasting ability and lingual rotation among southern Peruvian Quechua Indians. Hum. Biol 47: 193–199.

Geldrich, J. 1927. Über den Energieverbrauch beim Reitem. Biochem. Z. *188:* 1.

Gelhorn, E., and I. E. Steck. 1938. Effect of the inhalation of gases with a low oxygen and increased carbon dioxide tension in the peripheral blood flow in man. Am. J. Physiol. *124:* 735-741.

Gillin, J. 1941. The Quechua-speaking Indians of the Province of Imbabura (Ecuador) and their anthropometric relations with the living populations of the Andean Region. Bull. Bur. Am. Ethnol. *128:* 167-228.

Girling, F., and E. D. L. Topliff. 1966. The effect of breathing 15%, 21% and 100% oxygen on the shivering response of nude human subjects at 10°C. Can. J. Physiol. Pharmacol. *44:* 495-499.

Glass, L., W. A. Silverman, and J. C. Sinclair. 1968. Effect of the thermal environment on cold resistance and growth of small infants after the first week of life. Pediatrics *41:* 1033-1046.

——, W. A. Silverman, and J. C. Sinclair. 1969. Relationships of thermal environment and calorie intake to growth and resting metabolism in the late neonatal period. Biol. Neonat. *14:* 324-340.

Glenn, W. G. 1959. Preliminary study of human sera in subjects exposed to simulated altitude. Aerospace Med. *30:* 576-579.

Goldberg, D. 1959. The fertility of two generation urbanites. Pop. Stud. *12:* 214-222.

Gordon, A., F. J. Zornetta, S. A. D'Angelo, and H. A. Charipper. 1943.

Effects of atmospheric pressure on the activity of the thyroid, reproductive system and anterior lobe of the pituitary in the rat. Endocrinology *33:* 366-383.

Grahn, D., and J. Kratchman. 1963. Variation in neonatal death rate and birth weight in the United States and possible relations to environmental radiation, geology and altitude. Am. J. Hum. Genet. *15:* 329-352.

Greenfield, A. D. M. 1963. The circulation through the skin, pp. 1325-3151. *In* W. F. Hamilton and P. Dow (eds.), Handbook of physiology. Sec. 2, Circulation, Vol. II. American Physiological Society, Washington, D.C.

Greulich, W. W. 1957. A comparison of the physical growth and development of American-born and native Japanese children. Am. J. Phys. Anthrop. *15:* 489-515.

——, and S. I. Pyle. 1959. Radiographic atlas of skeletal development of the hand and wrist, 2nd ed. Stanford Univ. Press, Stanford, Calif.

Grimby, G., and B. Soderholm. 1963. Spirometric studies in normal subjects: III. Static lung volumes and maximum voluntary ventilation in adults with a note on physical fitness. Acta Med. Scand. *173:* 199-206.

Grover, R. F. 1963. Basal oxygen uptake of man at high altitude. J. Appl. Physiol. *18:* 909-912.

——. 1965. Pulmonary circulation in animals and man at high altitudes. Ann. N.Y. Acad. Sci. *127:* 632-639.

——, J. T. Reeves, E. B. Grover, and J. E. Leathers. 1967. Muscular exercise in young men native to 3100 m altitude. J. Appl. Physiol. *22:* 555-564.

Guerra-Garcia, R. 1971. Testosterone metabolism in men exposed to high altitude. Acta Endocrinol. Panam. *2:* 55-62.

——, A. Velasquez, and J. Whittembury. 1965. Urinary testosterone in high altitude natives. Steroids *6:* 351-355.

Gursky, M. 1969. A dietary survey of three Peruvian highland communities. M.A. thesis. Pennsylvania State Univ., University Park, Pa.

Gutiérrez-Noriega, C. 1944. Acción de la cocaína sobre la resistencia a la fatiga en el perro. Rev. Med. Expt. *3:* 239-243.

——. 1949a. El hábito de la coca en el Perú. Am. Indigena *9:* 143-154.

——. 1949b. Errores sobre la interpretación del cocaísmo en las grandes alturas. Rev. Farmacol. Med. Expt. *1:* 100-123.

Haas, J. D. 1972. Physical growth and development of Peruvian infants at high and low altitude. Am. J. Phys. Anthrop. *37:* 438-439 (abstract).

——. 1973a. Altitudinal variation and infant growth and development in Peru. Ph.D. dissertation. Pennsylvania State Univ., University Park, Pa.

——. 1973b. The development of motor function in Peruvian Indian and mestizo infants. Paper read at the 42nd Annual Meeting of the American Association of Physical Anthropologists, April 12–14, 1973, Dallas.

Hale, H. B. 1970. Cross-adaptation, pp. 158-169. *In* D. H. K. Lee and D. Minard (eds.), Physiology, environment and man. Academic Press, New York.

——, R. B. Mefferd, G. Waters, G. E. Forster, and D. Criscuolo. 1959. Influence of long-term exposure to adverse environments on organ weights and histology. Am. J. Physiol. *196:* 520-524.

Hammel, H. T. 1963. Effect of race on response to cold. Fed. Proc. *22:* 795-800.

——. 1964. Terrestrial animals in cold: recent studies of primitive man, pp. 413-434. *In* D. B. Dill, E. F. Adolph, and C. G. Wilber (eds.), Handbook of physiology, Sec. 4, Adaptation to the environment. American Physiological Society, Washington, D.C.

Hanna, J. M. 1965. Biological and cultural factors in peripheral blood flow at low temperatures. M. A. thesis. Pennsylvania State Univ., University Park, Pa.

——. 1968. Cold stress and micro climate in the Quechua Indians of Peru. *In* High altitude adaptation in a Peruvian community. Occasional Papers in Ahthropology 1, Department of Anthropology, Pennsylvania State Univ., University Park, Pa.

——. 1970a. A comparison of laboratory and field studies of cold response. Am. J. Phys. Anthrop. *32:* 227-232.

——. 1970b. The effects of coca chewing on exercise in the Quechua of Peru. Hum. Biol. *42:* 1-11.

——. 1971a. Further studies on the effects of coca chewing on exercise. Hum. Biol. *43:* 200-209.

——. 1971b. Responses of Quechua Indians to coca ingestion during cold exposure. Am. J. Phys. Anthrop. *34:* 274-278.

——. In press. Reacciones que experimentan los indios Quechuas a la coca durante la exposición al frío. Archivos del Instituto de Biología Andina, Lima, Peru.

——. 1974. Coca leaf use in southern Peru: some biological aspects. Am. Anthrop. *76:* 281-296.

Hansen, J. E., J. A. Vogel, G. P. Steller, and C. F. Consolazio. 1966. Oxygen uptake in man during rest, exhaustive work and recovery at 4300 m. U.S. Army MRNL Report 292, Denver, Colo.

Hardy, J. D., A. T. Milhorat, and E. F. DuBois. 1941. Basal metabolism and heat loss of young women at temperatures from 22°C to 35°C. J. Nutr. *21:* 383-404.

Harris, A. S. 1945. Inspiratory tonus in anoxia. Am. J. Physiol. *143:* 140-147.

Harris, C. W., J. L. Shields, and J. P. Hannon. 1966. Acute altitude sickness in females. Aerospace Med. *37:* 1163-1167.

Harris, R. S. 1945. An approach to the nutritional problems of other nations. Science *102:* 42.

Harrison, G. A. 1966. Human adaptation with reference to the IBP proposals for high altitude research, pp. 509-519. *In* P. T. Baker and J. S. Weiner (eds.), The biology of human adaptability. Oxford Univ. Press, Oxford.

——, C. F. Kuchemann, M. A. S. Moore, A. J. Boyce, T. Baju, A. E.

Mourant, M. J. Godber, B. G. Glasgow, A. C. Kopec, D. Tills, and E. J. Clegg. 1969. The effects of altitude variation in Ethiopian populations. Phil. Trans. Roy. Soc. Lond. *256:* 147-182.

Hart, M. C., M. M. Orsalesi, and C. D. Cook. 1963. Relation between anatomic respiratory dead space and body size and lung volume. J. Appl. Physiol. *18:* 519-522.

Hawthorn, G. 1970. The sociology of fertility. Macmillan, London.

Hecht, H. H. 1967. Certain vascular adjustments and maladjustments at altitude, p. 189. *In* R. Margaria (ed.), Exercise at altitude.

Heer, D. M. 1964. Fertility differences between Indian and Spanish speaking parts of Andean countries. Pop. Stud. *18:* 71-84.

———. 1967. Fertility differences in Andean countries: a reply to W. H. James. Pop. Stud. *21:* 71-73.

Hegsted, D. M., A. G. Tsongas, D. B. Abbot, and F. J. Stare. 1946. Protein requirements of adults. J. Lab. Clin. Med. *31:* 261-284.

———, I. Moscoso, and C. Collazos. 1952. A study of the minimum calcium requirements of adult men. J. Nutr. *46:* 181-201.

Heimendinger, J. 1958. Die Ergebnisse von Küpermessungen an 5000 Basler Kindern von 0 bis 18 Jahren. Schweiz. Med. Wochenschr. *88:* 785-787, 807-813.

Hellriegel, K. O. 1967. Health problems at altitude. Paper presented at the WHO/PAHO/IBP Meeting of Investigators on Population Biology of Altitude, Nov. 13–17, Washington, D.C.

Hellstrøm, B. 1965. Local effects of acclimatization to cold in man. Norwegian Research Council for Science and the Humanities, Oslo.

Hemingway, A., and G. G. Nahas. 1952. Effect of hypoxia on the metabolic response to cold. J. Appl. Physiol. *5:* 267-272.

Henry, L. 1961. Some data on natural fertility. Eug. Quart. *8:* 81-91.

Herrera, A. L., and L. D. Vergara. 1899. La Vie sur les hauts plateaux. Imprimerie de I. Escalante, Mexico, D.F.

Highman, B., and P. D. Altland. 1964. Immunity and resistance to pathogenic bacteria at high altitude, pp. 177-180. *In* W. H. Weihe (ed.), The physiological effects of high altitude. Macmillan, New York.

Hilger, Sister Inez. 1950. Arapaho child life and its cultural background. Smithsonian Institution, Bureau of American Ethnology, Bull. 148. Washington, D.C.

Hine, C. H., and H. Turkel. 1966. Research on the scientific literature and reports on the effects on man of alcohol alone and in combination with other drugs. AAL-TR-63-22. Arctic Aeromedical Laboratory, Ft. Wainwright, Alaska.

Hodge, W. H. 1946. Cusion plants of the Peruvian puna. J. N.Y. Bot. Garden *47*(558): 133-141.

Hoff, C. J. 1968. Reproduction and viability in a highland Peruvian Indian population. *In* High altitude adaptation in a Peruvian community. Occasional Papers in Anthropology 1, Department of Anthropology, Pennsylvania State Univ., University Park, Pa.

———. 1972a. Altitude variations in the physical growth of Peruvian Quechua Indians. Am. J. Phys. Anthrop. *37:* 441 (abstract).

———. 1972b. Preliminary observations on altitudinal variations in the physical growth and development of Peruvian Quechua. Ph.D. dissertation. Pennsylvania State Univ., University Park, Pa.

Holdridge, L. R. 1957. Life zone ecology. Tropical Science Center, San José, Costa Rica.

Holmgren, A. 1956. Hemoglobin concentration during muscular exercise. Scand. J. Clin. Lab. Invest. (Suppl. 24) *8:* 60-65.

Holt, S. B. 1968. The genetics of dermal ridges. Charles C Thomas, Springfield, Ill.

Houston, C. S., and R. L. Riley. 1947. Respiratory and circulatory changes during acclimatization to high altitude. Am. J. Physiol. *149:* 565-588.

Howard, R. C., P. D. Bruns, and J. A. Lichty. 1957. Studies of babies born at high altitude: III. Arterial oxygen saturation and haematocrit values at birth. Am. J. Dis. Child. *93:* 674-677.

Huizinga, J. 1972. Casual blood pressure in populations, pp. 164-169. *In* D. J. M. Vorster (ed.), Human biology of environmental change. International Biological Programme, London.

Hultgren, H., and W. Spickard. 1960. Medical experiences in Peru. Stanford Med. Bull. *18:* 76-95.

———, J. Kelly, and H. Miller. 1965. Pulmonary circulation in acclimatized man at high altitudes. J. Appl. Physiol. *20:* 213-238.

Hultquist, B. 1956. Studies on naturally occurring ionizing radiation. Kungl-Svenska Vetenskapsakademiens Handlinger, Vol. 6.

Hunt, R., and H. Schraer. 1965. Skeletal response of rats exposed to reduced barometric pressure. Am. J. Physiol. *208:* 1217-1221.

Hurtado, A. 1928. Sobre el volumen del tórax, la capacidad vital y el metabolismo básico en la altura. An. Fac. Med. (Lima) *1-2:* 266.

———. 1929. Estudios sobre el soldado peruano. Metabolismo basal en el soldado peruano. Rev. Sanidad Mil. (Lima) *2:* 9-24.

———. 1932a. Respiratory adaptation in the Indian native of the Peruvian Andes. Am. J. Phys. Anthrop. *17:* 137-165.

———. 1932b. Studies at high altitude: blood observations on the Indian natives of the Peruvian Andes. Am. J. Physiol. *100:* 487-505.

———. 1937. Aspectos fisiológicos y patológicos de la vida en la altura. Acad. Nac. Med. Lima, Peru. Ed. Empresa Rimac S.A.

———. 1955. Pathological aspects of life at high altitudes. Mil. Med. *117:* 272-284.

———. 1960. Some clinical aspects of life at high altitudes. Ann. Int. Med. *53:* 247-258.

——. 1964a. Acclimatization to high altitudes. *In* W. H. Weihe (ed.), The physiological effects of high altitude. Macmillan, New York.

——. 1964b. Animals in high altitudes: resident man, pp. 843-860. *In* D. B. Dill, E. F. Adolph, and C. G. Wilber (eds.), Handbook of physiology, Sec. 4, Adaptation to the environment. American Physiological Society, Washington, D.C.

——. 1966. Natural acclimatization to high altitudes. *In* Life at high altitudes. Pan Am. Health Org. Sci. Publ. 140, pp. 7-8. Washington, D.C.

——. 1969. Introduction, pp. 1-6. *In* A. H. Hegnauer (ed.), Biomedicine problems of high terrestrial elevations. U.S. Army Research Institute of Environmental Medicine, Natick, Mass.

——, and H. Aste-Salazar. 1948. Arterial blood gases and acid–base balance at sea level and at high altitude. J. Appl. Physiol. *1:* 304-325.

——, and A. Guzmán-Barrón. 1934. Estudios antropométricos en 100 indios peruanos de los departamentos centrales del Perú. Rev. Sanidad Mil. (Lima) *7:* 113-138.

——, N. Kaltreider, and W. S. McCann. 1934. Respiratory adaptation to anoxemia. Am. J. Physiol. *109:* 626-637.

——, C. F. Merino, and E. Delgado. 1947. Influence of anoxemia on hemopoietic activity. Arch. Int. Med. *75:* 284-323.

——, T. Velásquez, C. Reynafarje, R. Lozano, R. Chávez, H. Aste-Salazar, B. Reynafarje, C. Sánchez, and J. Muñoz. 1956a. Mechanisms of natural acclimatization: studies on the native resident of Morococha, Peru, at an altitude of 14,500 feet. AF SAM Report 56-1, U.S. Air Force School of Aviation Medicine, Randolph Field, Tex.

——, T. Velásquez, C. Reynafarje, and H. Aste-Salazar. 1956b. Blood gas transport and acid-base balance at sea level and at high altitude. AF SAM Report 56-104, U.S. Air Force School of Aviation Medicine, Randolph Field, Tex.

Hytten, F. E., and I. Leitch. 1971. The physiology of human pregnancy. Blackwell Scientific, Oxford.

ICNND. 1959. Nutrition survey of the armed forces: Peru. A Report of the Interdepartmental Committee on Nutrition for National Defense. Department of Defense, Washington, D.C.

INCAP-ICNND. 1961. Food composition tables for use in Latin America. INCAP-ICNND, National Institutes of Health, Bethesda, Md.

Instituto de Nutrición, Institutos Nacionales de Salud. 1973. Cuotas de calorías y proteínas. Lima, Peru.

Instituto Nacional de Planification. 1964. Sexto censo nacional de población. Resultados de primera prioridad. Dirección Nacional de Estadística y Censos, Lima, Peru.

Itoh, S., H. Shirato, and A. Kuroshima. 1968. Cold pressor response of the Ainu. J. Physiol. Soc. Japan *30:* 49-50.

Iutaka, S., E. W. Bock, and W. G. Varnes. 1971. Factors affecting fertility in natives and migrants in urban Brazil. Pop. Stud. *25:* 55-82.

James, W. H. 1966. The effect of high altitude on fertility in Andean countries. Pop. Stud. *20:* 87-101.

Jelliffe, D. B. 1968. Infant nutrition in the subtropic and tropics. World Health Organization Monograph Series 24. WHO, Geneva.

Jenks, W. F. 1956. Peru. *In* W. F. Jenks (ed.), Handbook of South American geology (Geological Society of America Memoir 65). Waverly Press, Baltimore, Md.

Johnson, D., and P. D. Roofe. 1965. Blood constituents of normal newborn rats and those exposed to low oxygen tension during gestation: weight of newborn and litter size also considered. Anat. Rec. *153:* 303-309.

Johnston, F. E., and K. M. Kensinger. 1971. Fertility and mortality differentials and their implications for microevolutionary change among the Cashinahua. Hum. Biol. *43:* 356-364.

———, and R. M. Malina. 1966. Age changes in the composition of the upper arm in Philadelphia children. Hum. Biol. *38:* 1-21.

———, P. S. Gindhart, R. L. Jantz, K. M. Kensinger, and G. F. Walker. 1971. The anthropometric determination of body composition among the Peruvian Cashinahua. Am. J. Phys. Anthrop. *34:* 409-416.

Jouck, K. T. 1944. Über Sauerstoffverbrauch und Wärmehaushalt im Sauerstoffmangel. Luftfahrtmedizin *9:* 26-32.

Kao, F. F., C. C. Mitchel, S. S. Mei, and W. K. Li. 1963. Somatic afferent influence on respiration, pp. 696-711. *In* G. G. Nahas (ed.), Regulation of respiration. Ann. N.Y. Acad. Sci.: *10.*

Karlberg, P. 1955. Nord. Med. *54:* 1477.

Keatinge, W. R. 1957. The effect of general chilling on the vasodilator response to cold. J. Physiol. (Lond.) *139:* 497-507.

Kennedy, S. J. 1961. Clothing and personal protection, pp. 56-67. *In* F. Fisher (ed.), Man living in the arctic. National Research Council, Washington, D.C.

Kerwing, A. J. 1944. Observations on the heart size of natives living at high altitude. Am. Heart J. *28:* 69.

Keys, A., F. G. Hall, and E. Guzmán-Barrón. 1936. The position of the oxygen dissociation curve of human blood at high altitude. Am. J. Physiol. *115:* 292-307.

Kim, P. K., B. S. Kang, S. H. Song, S. K. Hong, and D. W. Rennie. 1964. Differences in the physical insulation of Korean men and women, pp. 69-74. *In* H. Rahn, S. K. Hong, and D. W. Rennie (eds.), Korean sea women. State Univ. N.Y. at Buffalo and Yonse Univ. College of Medicine, Seoul, Korea.

Kjellberg, S. R., V. Rudge, and T. Sjostrand. 1949. The relation of the cardiac volume to the weight and surface area of the body, the blood volume and the physical capacity for work. Acta Radiol. *31:* 113-122.

Klausen, K. 1966. Cardiac output in man at rest and work during and after acclimatization to 3800 m. J. Appl. Physiol. *21:* 609-616.

Klissouras, V. 1971. Heritability of adaptive variation. J. Appl. Physiol. *31:* 338-344.

Koford, C. 1957. The vicuña and the puna. Ecol. Monogr.: *27*(2).

Kollias, J., and E. R. Buskirk. 1974. Exercise and altitude, pp. 211-227. *In* W. R. Johnson and E. R. Buskirk (eds.), Medicine and science of exercise and sport, 2nd ed. Harper & Row, New York.

——, E. R. Buskirk, R. F. Akers, E. K. Prokop, P. T. Baker, and E. Picón-Reátegui. 1968. Work capacity of long time residents and newcomers to altitude. J. Appl. Physiol. *24:* 792-799.

Kondo, S. 1969. A study on acclimatization of the Ainu and the Japanese with reference to hunting temperature reaction. J. Fac. Sci. Tokyo Univ., Sec. 5, *3:* 253-265.

Kory, R. C., R. Callahan, H. G. Boren, and J. C. Syner. 1961. Clinical spirometry in normal men. Am. J. Med. *30:* 243-258.

Kottke, F. J., J. S. Phalen, C. B. Taylor, M. B. Visscher, and G. T. Evans. 1948. Effect of hypoxia upon temperature regulation of mice, dogs, and man. Am. J. Physiol. *153:* 10-15.

Kreider, M. B., and E. R. Buskirk. 1957. Supplemental feeding and thermal comfort during sleep in the cold. J. Appl. Physiol. *11:* 339-343.

Kreuzer, F., S. M. Tenney, J. C. Mithoefer, and J. Remmers. 1964. Alveolar arterial oxygen gradient in Andean natives at high altitude. J. Appl. Physiol. *19:* 13-16.

Krog, J., and M. Wika. 1971-1972. Studies of the peripheral circulation in the hand of the Igloolik Eskimo, pp. 173-181. *In* International biological program, human adaptability project (Igloolik, N.W.T.), Annual Report 4. Anthropological Series 11, Univ. Toronto, Ontario.

Krogh, A. 1917. The number and distribution of capillaries in muscles with calculation of the oxygen pressure head necessary for supplying the tissues. J. Physiol. (Lond.) *52:* 409-415.

Krüger, H., and J. Arias-Stella. 1964. Malignant tumors in high altitude people. Cancer *17:* 1340-1347.

——, and J. Arias-Stella. 1970. The placenta and the newborn infant at high altitude. Am. J. Obstet. Gynec. *106:* 486-451.

Krum, A. A. 1957. Reproduction and growth of laboratory rats and mice at altitude. Ph.D. dissertation. University of California, Berkeley, Calif.

Kubler, G. 1946. The Quechua in the colonial world. *In* J. H. Steward (ed.), The Andean civilizations. Handbook of South American Indians, Smithsonian Institution, Washington, D.C. 2: 331-410.

LaBarre, W. 1948. The Aymara Indians of the Lake Titicaca Plateau, Bolivia. Memoir 68, American Anthropological Association, Menosha, Wis.

Lahiri, S., F. F. Kao, T. Velásquez, C. Martinez, and W. Pezzia. 1967.

Constancy of P_{O_2} parameters of respiration in highlanders and lowlanders. Proc. Can. Fed. Biol. Soc. *10:* 149.

——, F. Kao, T. Velásquez, C. Martinez, and W. Pezzia. 1969. Irreversible blunted respiratory sensitivity to hypoxia in high altitude natives. Respir. Physiol. *6:* 360-374.

Lanning, E. P. 1967. Peru before the Incas. Prentice-Hall, Englewood Cliffs, N.J.

Larsen, R. M. 1973. The thermal microenvironment of a highland Quechua population; biocultural adjustment to the cold. M.A. thesis. University of Wisconsin, Madison, Wis.

Lasker, G. 1953. The age factor in bodily measurements of adult male and female Mexicans. Hum. Biol. *25:* 50.

——. 1954. Human evolution in contemporary communities. Southwestern J. Anthrop. *10:* 353-365.

——. 1962. Differences in anthropometric measurements within and between three communities in Peru. Hum. Biol. *34:* 63-70.

Lasker, G. W., and B. Kaplan. 1964. The coefficient of breeding isolation. Hum. Biol. *39:* 327-338.

Lathrop, D. W. 1969. Review of "Peru before the Incas," by E. P. Lanning. Am. Antiquity *34:* 341-345.

Lawrence, J. H., R. L. Huff, W. Siri, L. R. Wasserman, and T. G. Hennessy. 1952. A physiological study in the Peruvian Andes. Acta Med. Scand. *142:* 117-130.

Leaf, A. 1973. Getting old. Sci. Am. *229*(3): 44-52.

LeBlanc, J. 1954. Subcutaneous fat and skin temperature. Can. J. Biochem. Physiol. *32:* 354-358.

Lee, R. B., and I. DeVore (eds.). 1968. Man the hunter. Aldine, Chicago.

Lefrancois, R., H. Gautier, and P. Pasquis. 1965. Ventilatory oxygen drive in high altitude natives. Proc. 23rd Int. Congr. Physiol. Sciences, Tokyo, No. 434.

——, H. Gautier, and P. Pasquis. 1968. Ventilatory oxygen drive in acute and chronic hypoxia. Respir. Physiol. *4:* 217-228.

——, H. Gautier, P. Pasquis, and E. Vargas. 1969. Factors controlling respiration during muscular exercise at altitude. Fed. Proc. *28:* 1296-1300.

Lenfant, C., and K. Sullivan. 1971. Adaptation to high altitude. New Eng. J. Med. *284:* 1298-1309.

——, J. Torrance, E. English, C. A. Finch, C. Reynafarje, J. Ramos, and J. Faura. 1968. Effect of altitude on oxygen binding by hemoglobin and on organic phosphate levels. J. Clin. Invest. *47:* 2652.

——, J. D. Torrance, and C. Reynafarje. 1971. Shift of O_2-Hb dissociation curve at altitude: mechanism and effect. J. Appl. Physiol. *30:* 625-631.

Lewis, T. 1930. Observations upon the reactions of the vessels of the human skin to cold. Heart *15:* 177-208.

Lichty, J. A., R. Y. Ting, P. D. Bruns, and E. Dyar. 1957. Studies of babies born at high altitude. Am. Med. Assoc. J. Dis. Child. *93:* 666-667.

Lieth, H. 1973. Primary production: terrestrial ecosystems. Hum. Ecol. *1*(4): 303-332.

Li, C. C. 1955. Population genetics. University of Chicago Press, Chicago.

Lim, T. P. K., and U. C. Luft. 1960. Body temperature regulation in hypoxia. Physiologist *3:* 105.

——, and U. C. Luft. 1963. The effect of induced hypoxia on thermoregulation and cardiopulmonary function. Tech. Rep. AAL-TDR-62-19. Arctic Aeromedical Laboratory, Ft. Wainwright, Alaska.

Little, M. A. 1968. Racial and developmental factors in foot cooling: Quechua Indians and U.S. whites. *In* High altitude adaptation in a Peruvian community. Occasional Papers in Anthropology 1, Department of Anthropology, Pennsylvania State Univ., University Park, Pa.

——. 1969. Temperature regulation at high altitude: Quechua Indians and U.S. whites during foot exposure to cold water and cold air. Hum. Biol. *41:* 519-535.

——. 1970. Effects of alcohol and coca on foot temperature responses of highland Peruvians during a localized cold exposure. Am. J. Phys. Anthrop. *32:* 233-242.

——, R. B. Thomas, R. B. Mazess, and P. T. Baker. 1971. Population differences and developmental changes in extremity temperature responses to cold among Andean Indians. Hum. Biol. *43:* 70-91.

——, R. B. Thomas, and J. W. Larrick. 1973. Skin temperature and cold pressor responses of Andean Indians during hand immersion in water at 4°C. Hum. Biol. *45:* 643-662.

Livingstone, F. B. 1958. Anthropological implications of sickle cell gene distribution in West Africa. Am. Anthrop. *60:* 533-562.

Llerena, L. A. 1973. Determinación de hormona luteinizante por radioinmunoensayo. Variaciones fisiológicas y por efecto de la altura. Tésis doctoral, Universidad Peruana Cayetano Heredia, Instituto de Investigaciones de Altura, Lima, Peru.

Lloyd, J. K., O. H. Wolff, and S. Whelen. 1961. Childhood obesity. A long term study of height and weight. Br. Med. J. *15:* 145-148.

Lund-Larsen, K., M. Wika, and J. Krog. 1970. Circulatory responses of the hand of Greenlanders to local cold stimulation. Arctic Anthrop. 7(1): 21-25.

MacNeish, R. S. 1971. Early man in the Andes. Sci. Am. 224: 34-46.

Mahadeva, K., R. Passmon, and B. Woolf. 1953. Individual variations in metabolic cost of standardized exercises: food, age, sex, race. J. Physiol. (Lond.) *121:* 225.

Malcolm, L. A. 1969. Growth and development of the Kaiapit children of the Markham Valley, New Guinea. Am. J. Phys. Anthrop. *31:* 39-51.

——. 1970. Growth and development of the Bundi child of the New Guinea highlands. Hum. Biol. *42:* 293-328.

Malhotra, M. S., S. S. Ramaswamy, and S. N. Ray. 1962. Influence of body weights on energy expenditure. J. Appl. Physiol. 17: 433.

——, S. S. Ramaswamy, G. L. Dua, and J. Sengupta. 1968. Physical work capacity as influenced by age. In A. Wanke (ed.), International biological programme: problems in human adaptability. Mater. Pr. Antropol. 75: 149-162.

Malina, R. M. 1973. Ethnic and cultural factors in the development of motor abilities and strengths in American children. In G. W. Rareck (ed.), Physical activity, human growth and development. Academic Press, New York.

Mandelbaum, I. M., P. Fondu, Ch. Heyder-Bruckner, A. Van Steirteghem, and S. Kabeya-Mudiay. 1973. Erythrocyte enzymes and altitude. Biomedicine 19: 517-520.

Mann, G. 1968. Okosysteme Sudamerikas. In E. J. Fittkau et al. (eds.), Biogeography and ecology in South America. Dr. W. Junk, Publishers, The Hague.

Marticorena, E. A., J. Severino, and H. N. Hultgren. 1967. I. Cardiopulmonary pathology at high altitude. II. How the people became old at high altitude. III. Treatment of high altitude acute pulmonary edema by bed rest alone. Paper presented at the WHO/PAHO/IBP Meeting of Investigators on Population Biology of Altitude, Nov. 13–17, Washington, D.C.

Martin, R. T. 1970. The role of coca in the history, religion and medicine of South American Indians. Econ. Bot. 24: 422-437.

Mathers, J. A. L., M. Patterson, and R. Levy. 1949. Some effects on the circulation of smoking cigarettes with varying nicotine content. Am. Heart J. 37: 612-618.

Matienzo, J. de. 1967. Gobierno del Perú (1567). Travaux de L'Institut Français d'Études Andines, Tome XI, Paris-Lima.

Matson, G., H. Sutton, J. Swanson, and A. Robinson. 1966. Distribution of hereditary blood groups among Indians of South America. Am. J. Phys. Anthrop. 24: 325-350.

Mayer, E. 1971. Un carnero por un saco de papas: aspectos de trueque en la zona de Chaupiwaranga: Pasco. Actas y Memorias del XXXIX Congreso Internacional de Americanistas, Lima, Peru.

Mazess, R. B. 1965. Neonatal mortality and altitude in Peru. Am. J. Phys. Anthrop. 23: 209-213.

——. 1967. Group differences in exercise performance at high altitude (3830 m). Ph.D. dissertation. Univ. Wisconsin, Madison, Wis.

——. 1968a. Exercise performance and altitude adaptation, p. 213-223. In Proceedings of the 37th International Congress of Americanists, Buenos Aires.

——. 1968b. Hot—cold food beliefs among Andean peasants. J. Am. Diet. Assoc. 53(2): 109-113.

——. 1968c. The oxygen cost of breathing in man: effects of altitude, training and race. Am. J. Phys. Anthrop. 29: 365-375.

———. 1969a. Exercise performance at high altitude in Peru. Fed. Proc. *28:* 1301-1306.

———. 1969b. Exercise performance of Indian and white high altitude residents. Hum. Biol. *41:* 494-518.

———. 1970. Cardiorespiratory characteristics and adaptation to high altitudes. Am. J. Phys. Anthrop. *32:* 267-278.

———, and P. T. Baker. 1964. Diet of Quechua Indians living at high altitude: Nuñoa, Peru. Am. J. Clin. Nutr. *15:* 341-351.

———, and R. Larsen. 1972. Responses of Andean highlanders to night cold. Int. J. Biometeor. *16:* 181-192.

———, E. Picón-Reátegui, R. B. Thomas, and M. A. Little. 1968. Effects of alcohol and altitude on man during rest and work. Aerospace Med. *39:* 403-406.

———, E. Picón-Reátegui, R. B. Thomas, and M. A. Little. 1969. Oxygen intake and body temperature of basal and sleeping Andean Indians at high altitude. Aerospace Med. *40:* 6-9.

McClung, J. P. 1969. Effects of high altitude on human birth. Harvard Univ. Press, Cambridge, Mass.

McFarland, R. A. 1952. Anoxia: its effects on the physiology and biochemistry of the brain and on behavior. *In* The biology of mental health and disease. Hoeber, New York.

———, and W. H. Forbes. 1936. The metabolism of alcohol in man at high altitude. Hum. Biol. *8:* 387-398.

McGarvey, S. 1974. A follow-up study on the biological and social status of Quechua infants. M.A. thesis. Pennsylvania State Univ., University Park, Pa.

Mejia Valera, J. 1963. Sumario sobre factores sociales en la migración interna, pp. 184-187. *In* H. F. Dobyns and M. C. Vasquez (eds.), Migración e integración en el Peru. Monografias Andinas 2, Lima, Peru.

Menon, N. D. 1965. High-altitude pulmonary edema: a clinical study. New Eng. J. Med. *273:* 55-73.

Meredith, H. V. 1970. Body weight at birth of viable human infants: a worldwide comparative treatise. Hum. Biol. *42:* 217-264.

Merino, C. F. 1950. Studies on blood formation and destruction in the polycythemia of high altitude. Blood *5:* 1-31.

———, and C. Reynafarje. 1949. Bone marrow studies in polycythemia of high altitude. J. Lab. Clin. Med. *34:* 637-647.

Meschia, G., H. Prystowsky, A. Hellegers, W. Huckabee, J. Metcalf, and D. H. Barron. 1960. Observations of the oxygen supply to the fetal llama. Quart J. Exp. Physiol. *45:* 284-291.

Metropolitan Life Insurance Company. 1943. Ideal weights for men. Stat. Bull. *24:* 6.

Meyer, O. O., M. H. Seevers, and S. R. Beatty. 1935. The effect of reduced atmospheric pressure on the leucocyte count. Am. J. Physiol. *113:* 166-174.

M.H.C. n.d. Ministerio de Hacienda y Comercio del Perú, Lima. Unpublished data from the sixth national census.

M.H.C. 1942. Censo nacional de población. Ministerio de Hacienda y Comercio del Perú, Lima, Peru.

——. 1965. Censo nacional de población, tomo 1. Ministerio de Hacienda y Comercio del Perú, Lima, Peru.

Miall, W. E., M. T. Ashcroft, H. G. Lovell, and F. Moore. 1964. A longitudinal study of the decline of adult height and age in two Welsh communities. Hum. Biol. 36: 445.

Miller, L. K., and L. Irving. 1962. Local reactions to air cooling in an Eskimo population. J. Appl. Physiol. 17: 449-455.

Millikan, C. A. 1937. Experiments on muscle hemoglobin in vivo; the instantaneous measurement of muscle metabolism. Proc. Roy. Soc. Lond. B123: 218-241.

Mishkin, B. 1946. The contemporary Quechua, pp. 411-470. In J. H. Steward (ed.), Handbook of South American Indians, Vol. 2 (Bulletin 43). Bureau of American Ethnology, Washington, D.C.

Mitchell, R. A., H. H. Loeschcke, J. W. Severinghaus, B. W. Richardson, and W. H. Massion. 1963. Regions of respiratory chemoresensitivity on the surface of the medulla. Ann. N.Y. Acad. Sci. 109: 661-681.

Mithoefer, J. C. 1966. Physiological patterns: the respiration of Andean natives. In Life at high altitudes (proceedings of the special session held during the Fifth Meeting of the PAHO Advisory Committee on Medical Research). Pan Am. Health Org. Sci. Publ. 140, pp. 21-26. Washington, D.C.

Moncloa, F. 1966. Physiological patterns: endocrine factors. In Life at high altitudes. Pan Am. Health Org. Sci. Publ. 140, pp. 36-39. Washington, D.C.

Monge C., C., A. Cazorla, G. Wittembury, Y. Sakata and C. Rizo-Patrón. 1955. A description of the circulatory dynamics in the heart and lung of people at sea level and at high altitude, by means of the dye dilution technique. Acta Physiol. Latinoam. 5: 198-210.

Monge M., C. 1937. High altitude diseases. Arch. Int. Med. 59: 32-40.

——. 1948. Acclimatization in the Andes. Johns Hopkins Press, Baltimore, Md.

——. 1952. The need for studying the problem of coca leaf chewing. Bull. Narcotics 4(4): 13-15.

——, and C. Monge C. 1966. High altitude diseases: mechanism and management. Charles C Thomas, Springfield, Ill.

——, and P. Mori-Chavez. 1942. Fisiología de la reproducción en la altura. An. Fac. Med. (Lima) 25: 34.

Montesinos, A. F. 1965. Metabolism of cocaine. Bull. Narcotics 17: 11-17.

Moore, C. R., and D. Price. 1948. A study at high altitude of reproduction, growth, sexual maturity, and organ weights. J. Exp. Zool. 108: 171-216.

Moret, P., E. Cobarrubias, J. Coudert, and F. Duchosal. 1972. Cardiocirculatory adaptation to chronic hypoxia: III. Comparative study of C.O., pulmonary and sistemic circulation between sea level and high altitude residents. Acta Cardiol. 27(fasc. 5): 596-619.

Morpurgo, G., P. Battaglia, L. Bernini, A. M. Paolucci, and G. Modiano. 1970. Higher Bohr effect in the Indian natives of Peruvian highlands as compared with the Europeans. Nature 227: 387-388.

——, P. Battaglia, N. D. Carter, G. Modiano, and S. Passi. 1972. The Bohr effect and the red cell 2,3-DPG and Hb content in Sherpas and Europeans at low and at high altitude. Experientia 28: 1280-1283.

Morrison, P. R. 1962. Temperature regulation in animals native to tropical and high altitude environments, pp. 381-413. *In* Hannon and Viereck (eds.), Comparative physiology of temperature regulation. Proc. 2nd Symp. Arctic Biol. Med.

Mortimer, W. 1901. Peru, history of coca, "the divine plant" of the Incas. J. H. Vail, New York.

Morton, W. E. 1966. Altitude and rheumatic fever in Colorado. Am. J. Epidemiol. 83: 250-254.

——, D. J. Davids, and J. A. Lichty. 1964. Mortality from heart disease at high altitude: the effects of high altitude on mortality from arteriosclerotic and hypertensive heart disease. Arch. Environ. Health 9: 21-24.

Moulin, J. 1971. Hématimétrie et cytologie en milieu tropical de l'Amérique du Sud. Ph.D. dissertation. Université Paul-Sabatier, Toulouse.

M.S.P.A.S. 1965. Nacimientos, defunciones y defuciones fetales. Oficina de Planificación, División de Estadísticas de Salud, Lima, Peru.

Murra, J. V. 1968. An Aymara kingdom in 1567. Ethnohistory 15: 115-151.

——. 1970. Current research and prospects in Andean ethnohistory. Latin Am. Res. Rev. 5: 3-36.

——. 1972. El "control vertical" de un máximo de pisos ecológicos en la económica de las sociedades andinas. *In* Visita de la Provincia de León de Huanuco (1562), Inigo Ortiz de Zuniga, Visitador. Univ. Hermilio Valdizán, Huanuco, Peru.

Nachtigall, H. 1965. Beitrage zur Kultur der Indianischen Lama-züchter der Puna de Atacama (Cnordwest-Argentinien). Z. Ethnol. 90: 184-218.

——. 1966. Indianischen Fischer, Feldbauer und Viehzüchter. Beitrage zur Peruanischen Volkerkunde. Marburger Studien zur Volkerkunde 2.

Naeye, R. L. 1966. Organ and cellular development in mice growing at simulated high altitude. Lab. Invest. 15: 700-706.

Nagy, Z., and J. Skolnik. 1961. The mechanism by which cardiac output increases in hypoxia. Lancet 1(7187): 1146-1147.

Nair, C. S., and S. George. 1972. The effect of altitude and cold on body temperature during acclimatization of man at 3300 m. Int. J. Biometeor. 16: 79-84.

——, M. S. Malhotra, and O. P. Tiwari. 1973. Heat output from the hand of men during acclimatization to altitude and cold. Int. J. Biometeor. *17:* 95-101.

N.A.S. 1970. Maternal nutrition and the course of pregnancy. National Academy of Sciences, Washington, D.C.

Nayak, N. C., S. Roy, and T. K. Narayanan. 1964. Pathologic features of altitude sickness. Am. J. Pathol. *45:* 381-391.

Needham, C. D., M. C. Rogan, and I. McDonald. 1954. Normal standards for lung volumes, intrapulmonary gas-mixing, and maximum breathing capacity. Thorax *9:* 313-325.

Neel, J. V. 1951. The population genetics of two inherited blood dyscrasias in man. Cold Spring Harbor Symp. Quant. Biol. *15:* 141-158.

——, and N. A. Chagnon. 1968. The demography of two tribes of primitive, relatively unacculturated American Indians. Proc. Nat. Acad. Sci. *59:* 680-689.

Nelms, J. D. 1963. Functional anatomy of skin related to temperature regulation. Fed. Proc. *22:* 933-936.

Nelson, D., and M. W. Burril. 1944. Repeated exposure to simulated high altitude: estrus cycle and fertility of white rats. Fed. Proc. *3:* 34.

Newburgh, L. H. (ed.). 1949. Physiology of heat regulation and the science of clothing. Saunders, Philadelphia.

——, F. H. Wiley, and F. H. Lashmet. 1931. A method for the determination of heat production over long periods of time. J. Clin. Invest. *10:* 703-721.

Newman, M. T. 1953. The application of ecological rules to the racial anthropology of the aboriginal New World. Am. Anthrop. *55:* 311-327.

——. 1974. Palm and fingerprints of Quechua Indians from the North Central Peruvian sierra. Hum. Biol. *46:* 519-530.

Newman, R. W., and L. F. Cipriano. 1974. Effect of hypoxia on temperature regulation of men exposed to 10°C air temperature. Am. J. Phys. Anthrop. *40:* 146 (abstract).

Nicholas, W. C., J. Kollias, E. R. Buskirk, and M. J. Tershak. 1968. Prophylactic use of succinylsulfathiozole and performance capacities. J. Am. Med. Assoc. *205:* 757.

Niswander, J. D., F. Keiter, and J. V. Neel. 1967. Some anthropometric, dermatoglyphic and nonquantitative morphological traits of the Xavantes of Simoes Lopes. Am. J. Hum. Genet. *19:* 490-501.

Nylin, G. 1947. The effect of heavy muscular work on the volume of circulating red corpuscles in man. Am. J. Physiol. *148:* 180-184.

Oberg, K. 1954. Culture shock. Bobbs-Merrill, New York.

Odum, H. T. 1971. Environment, power and society. Wiley, New York.

Okin, J. T., A. Treger, H. R. Overy, J. V. Weil, and R. F. Grover. 1966. Hematological response to medium altitude. Rocky Mt. Med. J. *63:* 44-47.

Olrog, C. C. 1968. Birds of South America. *In* E. J. Fittkau et al. (eds.), Biogeography and ecology in South America. Dr. W. Junk, Publishers, The Hague.

ONERN/CORPUNO. 1965. Programa de inventario y evaluación de los recursos naturales del departamento de Puno, Sector de Prioridad I, 6 vols. Lima, Peru.

Page, L. B., and P. J. Culver. 1966. Laboratory examinations in clinical diagnosis. Harvard Univ. Press, Cambridge, Mass.

Palomino F., S. 1971. La dualidad en la organización socio-cultural de algunos pueblos del área andina. Rev. Museo Nac. (Lima) *37*: 231-260.

Papadakis, J. 1969. Soils of the world. American Elsevier, New York.

Passmore, R. 1964. An assessment of the report of the second committee on calorie requirements (FAO, 1957). FAO/WHO, Rome.

Paulston, R. G. 1971. Education and community development in Peru: problems at the cultural interface. Council Anthrop. Educ. Newslett. *2*(2).

Pawson, I. G. 1972. Growth and development in a Himalayan population. Am. J. Phys. Anthrop. *37*: 447-488 (abstract).

Pearson, O. P. 1951. Mammals in the highlands of southern Peru. Bull. Mus. Comp. Zool. *106*(3).

———. 1959. Biology of the subterranean rodents ctenomys in Peru. Memorias del Museo de Historia Natural "Javier Prado," No. 9. Univ. Nacional Mayor de San Marcos, Lima, Peru.

———, and C. P. Ralph. In press. The diversity and abundance of vertebrates along an altitudinal gradient in Peru.

Peñaloza, D. 1966. Physiological patterns: cardiovascular characteristics of healthy man. *In* Life at high altitudes. Pan Am. Health Org. Sci. Publ. 140, pp. 27-31. Washington, D.C.

———, R. Gamboa, J. Dyer, M. Echevarria, and E. Marticorena. 1960. The influence of high altitudes on the electrical activity of the heart: I. Electrocardiographic observations in the newborn, infants and children. Am. Heart J. *59:* 11.

———, F. Sime, N. Banchero, and R. Gamboa. 1962. Pulmonary hypertension in healthy man born and living at high altitude. Med. Thorac. *19:* 449-460.

———, F. Sime, N. Banchero, R. Gamboa, J. Cruz, and E. Marticornea. 1963. Pulmonary hypertension in healthy man born and living at high altitudes. Am. J. Cardiol. *11:* 150.

Peñaloza, J. B. 1971. Crecimiento y desarrollo sexual del adolescente andino. Tesis doctoral. Univ. Nacional Mayor de San Marcos, Lima, Peru.

Penrose, L. S. 1961. Genetics of growth and development of the factors. *In* L. S. Penrose (ed.), Recent advances in human genetics. J. & A. Churchill, London.

Peterson, R. F., and W. G. Peterson. 1935. The differential count at high altitudes. J. Lab. Clin. Med. *20:* 723-726.

Pett, L. B., and G. F. Ogilvie. 1956. The Canadian weight-height survey, pp. 67-78. *In* J. Brožek (ed.), Body measurements and human nutrition. Wayne State Univ. Press, Detroit, Mich.

Picón-Reátegui, E. 1961. Basal metabolic rate and body composition at high altitude. J. Appl. Physiol. *16:* 431-434.

———. 1962. Studies on the metabolism of carbohydrates at sea level and at high altitudes. Metabolism *11:* 1148-1154.

———. 1963. Intravenous glucose tolerance test at sea level and at high altitudes. J. Clin. Endocrinol. Metab. *23:* 1256-1261.

———. 1968. The effect of coca chewing on metabolic balance in Peruvian high altitude natives. *In* High altitude adaptation in a Peruvian community. Occasional Papers in Anthropology 1, Department of Anthropology, Pennsylvania State Univ., University Park, Pa.

———, E. R. Buskirk, and P. T. Baker. 1970. Blood glucose in high altitude natives and during acclimatization to altitude. J. Appl. Physiol. *29:* 560-563.

Pinson, E. A. 1942. Evaporation from human skin with sweat glands inactivated. Am. J. Physiol. *137:* 492-503.

Plato, C. C. 1970. Polymorphism in the C line of palmar dermatoglyphics with a new classification of the C line terminations. Am. J. Phys. Anthrop. *33:* 413-420.

———. In press. Variation and distribution of the dermatoglyphic features in different populations. *In* W. Hirsch (ed.), Proceedings of the Penrose memorial colloquium.

———, and Wertelecki. 1972. A method for subclassifying the interdigital patterns: a comparative study of palmar dermatoglyphics. Am. J. Phys. Anthrop. *37:* 97-110.

———, P. Brown, and D. C. Gajdusek. 1972. Dermatoglyphics of the Micronesians from the outer islands of Yap. Z. Morph. Anthrop. *64:* 29-44.

———, R. M. Garruto, C. Hoff, and P. T. Baker. 1974a. Digital and palmar dermatoglyphic patterns among southern Peruvian Quechua. Hum. Biol. *46:* 495-518.

———, M. T. Newman, and R. M. Garruto. 1974b. A survey of population differences in dermatoglyphic patterns of Eskimo and North, Central and South American Indian groups. (In preparation.)

Prankerd, T. A. J. 1966. Polycythemia. Proc. Roy. Soc. Med. *59:* 51-53.

Preto, J. C., and M. Calderon. 1947. Estudios bioantropométricos en los escolares Peruanos. Boletín del Instituto Psicopedaggógico Nacional 2. Lima, Peru.

Price, B. J. 1971. Prehispanic irrigation agriculture in nuclear America. Latin Am. Res. Rev. *6:* 3-60.

Prosser, C. L. 1964. Perspectives of adaptation: theoretical aspects, pp. 11-25. *In* D. B. Dill, E. F. Adolph, and C. G. Wilber (eds.), Handbook of physiology, Sec. 4, Adaptation to the environment. American Physiological Society, Washington, D.C.

Puffer, R. R., and C. V. Serrano. 1973. Patterns of mortality in childhood: report of the inter-American investigation of mortality in childhood. Pan Am. Health Org. Sci. Publ. 262. Washington, D.C.

Pugh, L. G. C. E. 1962. Physiological and medical aspects of the Himalayan scientific and mountaineering expedition, 1960–1961. Br. Med. J.: 621-627.

———. 1964. Animals in high altitudes: man above 5000 meters—mountain exploration, pp. 861-868. *In* D. B. Dill, E. F. Adolph, and C. G. Wilber (eds.), Handbook of physiology, Sec. 4, Adaptation to the Environment. American Physiological Society, Washington, D.C.

Putzer, H. 1968. Überlick über die geologische Entwicklung Sudamerikas. *In* E. J. Fittkau et al. (eds.), Biogeography and ecology in South America. Dr. W. Junk, Publishers, The Hague.

Quevedo A., S. 1949. Crecimiento y alimentación de los aborígines de Anta. H. G. Rozas Sucs., Cuzco, Peru.

———. 1961. Antropología del indígena cuzqueno. Rev. Univ. (Cuzco) *120:* 159-270.

Quilici, J. 1968. Les altiplanides du corridor intérandin: étude hémotypologique. Centre d'Hémotypologie du Centre National de la Recherche Scientifique, Toulouse, France.

Quinones, M. E. 1968. La enfermedad varicosa en la altura. Arch. Inst. Biol. Andina *2:* 274-275.

Rahn, H. 1966. Conductance of oxygen from the environment to the tissues. *In* Life at high altitudes. Pan Am. Health Org. Sci. Publ. 140, pp. 2-6. Washington, D.C.

———, and A. B. Otis. 1949. Man's respiratory response during and after acclimatization to high altitude. Am. J. Physiol. *157:* 445-462.

Recommendations concerning body measurements for the characterization of nutritional status. 1956. Hum. Biol. *28:* 111-123.

Rennie, D. W., P. Di Prampero, R. W. Fitts, and L. Sinclair. 1970. Physical fitness and respiratory function of Eskimos of Wainwright, Alaska. Arctic Anthrop. 7(1): 73-82.

Republica del Peru. 1965. Censo nacional de población, tomo 1, Lima, Peru.

Reynafarje, B., E. Marticorena, J. Guillen, and A. Arrarte. 1966. Contenido pigmentario y enzimático del músculo esquelético humano a nivel del mar y en la altura. Arch. Inst. Biol. Andina *1:* 170-178.

Reynafarje, C. 1966a. Iron metabolism during and after altitude exposure in man and in adapted animals (Camelids). Fed. Proc. *25:* 1240-1242.

———. 1966b. Physiological patterns: hematological aspects. *In* Life at high altitudes. Pan Am. Health Org. Sci. Publ. 140. Washington, D.C.

———, R. Lozano, and J. Valdivieso. 1959. The polycythemia of high altitudes: iron metabolism and related aspects. Blood *14:* 433-455.

Reynolds, E. L. 1960. The distribution of subcutaneous fat in childhood and adolescence. Monogr. Soc. Res. Child. Develop. *15:* 189.

Risemberg, M. F. 1944. Acción de la coca y la cocaína en sujetos habituados. Rev. Med. Expt. *3:* 317-328.

Ritchie, J. M., P. J. Cohen, and R. D. Dripps. 1966. Cocaine, procaine and other synthetic local anesthetics, p. 367. *In* L. S. Goodman and A.

Gilman (eds.), The pharmacological basis of therapeutics, 3rd ed. Macmillan, New York.

Roberts, D. F. 1953. Body weight, race and climate. Am. J. Phys. Anthrop. *11:* 533-538.

———. 1956. A demographic study of a Dinka village. Hum. Biol. *28:* 323-349.

———. 1969. Race, genetics and growth. J. Biosoc. Sci. (Suppl. 1): 43-67.

Robinson, W. C. 1963. Urbanization and fertility: the non-western experience. Milbank Mem. Fund Quart. *41:* 291-308.

Rodahl, K., and B. Issekutz, Jr. 1965. Nutritional effects on human performance in the cold, pp. 7-47. *In* Nutritional requirements for survival in the cold and at altitude. Proceedings of the Fifth Symposium on Arctic Biology and Medicine. Arctic Aeromedical Laboratory, Ft. Wainwright, Alaska.

Rodríguez S. S., A. 1958. Nuñoa, notas de campo. Plan del Sur, Cuzco, Peru.

Romero, E. 1928. Monografía del departamento de Puno. Lima, Peru.

Rothammer, F., and R. Spielman. 1972. Anthropometric variation in the Aymara: genetic, geographic and topographic contributions. Am. J. Hum. Genet. *24:* 371-380.

Rotta, A. 1947. Physiological condition of the heart in natives living at high altitude. Am. Heart J. *33:* 669.

———, A. D. Cánepa, A. Hurtado, T., Velásquez, and R. Chávez. 1956. Pulmonary circulation at sea level and at high altitude. J. Appl. Physiol. *9:* 328-336.

Roughton, F. J. W., and R. E. Forster. 1957. Relative importance of diffusion and chemical reaction rates in determining rate of exchange of gases in the human lung, with special reference to true diffusing capacity of pulmonary membrane and volume of blood in the lung capillaries. J. Appl. Physiol. *11:* 291-302.

Rowe, J. H. 1946. Inca culture at the time of the Spanish conquest, pp. 183-330. *In* J. H. Steward (ed.), The handbook of South American Indians, Vol. 2, Bureau of American Ethnology Bulletin 143, Smithsonian Institution, Washington, D.C.

Roy, S. 1969. General discussion. Panel, high altitude pulmonary edema, p. 121. *In* A. H. Hegnauer (ed.), Biomedicine problems of high terrestrial elevations. U.S. Army Research Institute of Environmental Medicine, Natick, Mass.

Roy, S. B., and I. Singh. 1969. Acute mountain sickness in Himalayan terrain: clinical and physiological studies, pp. 32-41. *In* A. H. Hegnauer (ed.), Biomedicine problems of high terrestrial elevations. U.S. Army Research Institute of Environmental Medicine, Natick, Mass.

———, J. S. Guleria, K. Khanna, J. R. Talwar, S. C. Manchada, J. N. Pande, V. S. Kaushik, P. S. Subba, and J. E. Wood. 1968. Immediate circulatory response to high altitude hypoxia in man. Nature *217:* 1177-1178.

Ruiz-Carillo, L. 1973. Epidemiología de la hipertensión arterial y de la cardiopatía isquémica en las grandes alturas: prevalencia y factores relevantes a su historia natural. Doctoral thesis. Univ. Peruana Cayetano Heredia, Lima, Peru.

Sacchetti, A. 1964. Capacidad respiratoria y aclimatación en las razas andinas. Ensayo de antropología fisioauxológica. J. Soc. Americanistes *53:* 9-83.

Salguero-Silva, H. 1971. Índices hematoicos normales en La Paz. Unpublished manuscript, Instituto Nacional de Salud Ocupacional, La Paz, Bolivia.

Salzano, F. M. 1972. Genetic aspects of the demography of American Indians and Eskimos, pp. 234-251. *In* G. A. Harrison and A. J. Boyce (eds.), The structure of human populations. Clarendon Press, Oxford.

Sanchez, C., C. Merino, and M. Figallo. 1970. Simultaneous measurement of plasma volume and cell mass in polycythemia of high altitude. J. Appl. Physiol. *28:* 775-778.

Sargent, D. W. 1961. An evaluation of basal metabolic data for children and youth in the United States. Home Economics Research Report 14. U.S. Department of Agriculture, Washington, D.C.

———. 1962. An evaluation of basal metabolic data for infants in the United States. Home Economics Research Report 18. U.S. Department of Agriculture, Washington, D.C.

Schaedel, R. P. 1959. Los recursos humanos del departamento de Puno, Vol. 5. Plan para el desarrollo del sur del Perú, Lima, Peru.

———. 1967. La demografía y los recursos humanos del sur del Peru. Serie Antropología Social 8. Instituto Indigenista Interamericano, Mexico, D.F.

Schneider, E. C., and D. L. Sisco. 1914. The circulation of the blood in man at high altitudes: II. The rate of blood flow and the influence of oxygen on the pulse rate and blood flow. Am. J. Physiol. *34:* 29-47.

Scholander, P. F., H. T. Hammel, J. S. Hart, D. H. LeMessurier, and J. Steen. 1958. Cold adaptation in Australian aborigines. J. Appl. Physiol. *13:* 211-218.

Schraer, H., and M. T. Newman. 1958. Quantitative roentgenography of skeletal mineralization in malnourished Quechua Indian boys. Science *128:* 476.

Schreider, E. 1957. Ecological rules and body-heat regulation in man. Nature *179:* 915-916.

Schull, W. J., and J. W. MacCluer. 1968. Human genetics: structure of populations. Am. Rev. Genet. *2:* 278-304.

Schwabe, G. H. 1968. Towards an ecological characterization of the South American continent. *In* E. J. Fittkau et al. (eds.), Biogeography and ecology in South America. Dr. W. Junk, Publishers, The Hague.

Scribner, S., and M. Cole. 1973. Cognitive consequences of formal and informal education. Science *182:* 553-559.

Scrimshaw, N. S., and M. Béhar. 1964. Causes and prevention of malnutrition, pp. 385-434. *In* G. H. Beaton and E. W. McHenry (eds.), Nutrition:

a comprehensive treatise, Vol. II, Vitamins, nutrient requirements, and food selection. Academic Press, New York.

Selye, H. 1956. The stress of life. McGraw-Hill, New York.

Sever, J. L. 1966. Prenatal infections affecting the developing fetus and newborn. *In* The prevention of mental retardation through control of infectious diseases. U.S. Public Health Service Publ. 1762, Washington, D.C.

Severinghaus, J. W., C. R. Baiton, and A. Carcelén. 1966. Respiratory insensitivity to hypoxia in chronically hypoxic man. Respir. Physiol. *1:* 338-354.

Shields, J. L., J. P. Hannon, R. P. Carson, K. S. K. Chinn, and W. O. Evans. 1969. Pathophysiology of acute mountain sickness, pp. 9-23. *In* A. H. Hegnauer (ed.), Biomedicine problems of high terrestrial elevations. U. S. Army Research Institute of Environmental Medicine, Natick, Mass.

Sick, W.-D. 1968. Geographical substance. *In* E. J. Fittkau et al. (eds.), Biogeography and ecology in South America. Dr. W. Junk, Publishers, The Hague.

Simpson, G. 1949. The meaning of evolution. Yale Univ. Press, New Haven, Conn.

Siri, W. E., A. S. Cleveland, and P. Blanche. 1969. Adrenal gland activity in Mt. Everest climbers. Fed. Proc. *28:* 1251-1256.

Smith, C. T. 1970. Depopulation in the Central Andes in the 16th century. Current Anthrop. *11:* 453-464.

Smith, E. E., and J. W. Crowell. 1967. Role of an increased hematocrit in altitude acclimatization. Aerospace Med. *38:* 39-43.

Sobrevilla, L. A. 1967. Fertility at high altitude. Paper presented at PAHO/WHO/IBP Meeting of Investigators on Population Biology of Altitude, Nov. 13–17, Washington, D.C.

———. 1971. Nacer en los Andes: estudios fisiológicos sobre el embarazo y parto en la altura. Doctoral thesis. Univ. Peruana Cayetano Heredia, Lima, Peru.

———, I. Romero, F. Kruger, and J. Whittembury. 1968. Low oestrogen excretion during pregnancy at high altitude. Am. J. Obstet. Gynec. *102:* 823-833.

Sokal, R. R., and P. H. A. Sneath. 1963. Principles of numerical taxonomy. W. H. Freeman, San Francisco.

Solon, L. R., W. M. Lowder, A. Shambon, and H. Blatz. 1960. Investigations of natural environmental radiation. Science *131:* 903-906.

Spector, R. M. 1971. Mortality characteristics of a high altitude Peruvian population. M.A. thesis. Pennsylvania State Univ., University Park, Pa.

Spuhler, J. N. 1962. Empirical studies on quantitative human genetics, pp. 241-250. *In* The use of vital and health statistics for genetic and radiation studies. WHO, Geneva.

Stammers, A. D. 1933. The polymorphonuclear-lymphocyte ratio at an altitude of 5750 feet. J. Physiol. (Lond.) *78:* 335-338.

Stein, Z., and M. Susser. 1973. Letter. Science *180:* 135-136.

Steward, J., and L. Faron. 1959. Native peoples of South America. McGraw-Hill, New York.

Stiglich, G. 1918. Almanaque de "La Crónica" y diccionario geográfico del Perú. Lima, Peru.

Stini, W. A. 1969. Nutritional stress and growth: sex differences in adaptive responses. Am. J. Phys. Anthrop. *31:* 417-426.

——. 1972[a]. Reduced sexual dimorphism in upper arm muscle circumference associated with protein-deficient diet in a South American population. Am. J. Phys. Anthrop. *36:* 341-352.

——. 1972[b]. Malnutrition, body size and proportion. Ecol. Food Nutr. *1:* 121-126.

Stoudt, H. W., A. Damon, and R. A. McFarland. 1960. Heights and weights of white Americans. Hum. Biol. *28:* 111-123.

Stuart, H. C., S. S. Stevenson, M. J. E. Senn, A. E. Hansen, J. B. Bartram, and T. E. Shaffer. 1956. Tablas de valores normales empleados como patrones de referencia en la valoración de las medidas corporales. *In* W. E. Nelson (ed.), Tratado de pediatría, 3rd ed. Salvat, Barcelona.

Sturtevant, A. H. 1940. A new inherited character in man. Proc. Nat. Acad. Sci. U.S. *26:* 100-102.

Stycos, J. M. 1963. Culture and differential fertility in Peru. Pop. Stud. *16:* 257-270.

Sundstroem, E. S., and G. Michaels. 1942. The adrenal cortex in adaptation to altitude, climate, and cancer. Mem. Univ. Calif. *12.*

Surks, M. I. 1969. Endocrine adaptations to high altitude exposure, pp. 186-203. *In* A. H. Hegnauer (ed.), Biomedicine problems of high terrestrial elevations. U.S. Army Research Institute of Environmental Medicine, Natick, Mass.

Suzuki, M. 1969. Peripheral response to cold. J. Anthrop. Soc. Nippon *77:* 213-223.

Swaminathan, M. 1967. Availability of plant proteins. *In* A. A. Albanese (ed.), Newer methods of nutrition biochemistry with applications and interpretations, Vol. III. Academic Press, New York.

Tanner, J. M. 1962. Growth at adolescence, 2nd ed. Blackwell Scientific, Oxford.

Tengerdy, R. P., and T. Kramer. 1968. Immune response of rabbits during short term exposure to high altitude. Nature *217:* 367-369.

Tenney, S. M., H. Rahn, R. C. Stroud, and J. C. Mithoefer. 1953. Adaptation to high altitude: changes in lung volume during the first seven days at Mt. Evans, Colorado. J. Appl. Physiol. *5:* 607-613.

Ten-State Nutrition Survey. 1968-1970. 1972. I. Historical development. II.

Demographic Data. Atlanta. U.S. Department of Health, Education, and Welfare, Center for Disease Control Publ. HSM 72-8131. Washington, D.C.

Thomas, R. B. n.d. Energy expenditure of Andean Indians during exposures to ambient temperatures of 22°C and 11°C. (In preparation.)

———. 1970. El tamaño pequeño del cuerpo como forma de adaptación de una población Quechua a la altura. Actas y Memorias del XXXIX Congreso Internacional de Americanistas, Lima, Peru.

———. 1972. Human adaptation to energy flow in a high Andes. Ph.D. dissertation. Pennsylvania State Univ., University Park, Pa.

———. 1973. Human adaptation to a high Andean energy flow system. Occasional Papers in Anthropology 7, Department of Anthropology, Pennsylvania State Univ., University Park, Pa.

Thompson, A. M. 1966. Adult stature. In J. J. Van der Werff, T. Bosch, and A. Hask (eds.), Somatic growth of the child. Charles C Thomas, Springfield, Ill.

Timiras, P. S. 1964. Comparison of growth and development of the rat at high altitude and at sea level, pp. 21-30. In W. H. Weihe (ed.), The physiological effects of high altitude. Macmillan, New York.

———. 1965. High altitude studies. In W. I. Gay (ed.), Methods of animal experimentation, Vol. 2. Academic Press, New York.

———, and D. E. Wooley. 1966. Functional and morphological development of brain and other organs at high altitude. Fed. Proc. 25: 1312-1320.

Trapani, I. 1966. Altitude, temperature and the immune response. Fed. Proc. 25: 1254-1259.

———. 1969. Environment, infection, and immunoglobin synthesis. Fed. Proc. 28: 1104-1106.

Traunt, A., and B. Takman. 1965. Local anesthetics, pp. 133-156. In J. DiPalma (ed.), Drill's pharmacology in medicine, 3rd ed. McGraw-Hill, New York.

Treger, A., D. B. Shaw, and R. F. Grover. 1965. Secondary polycythemia in adolescents at high altitude. J. Lab. Clin. Med. 66: 304-314.

Troll, C. C. 1968. The Cordilleras of the tropical Americas; aspects of climate, phytogeographical and agrarian ecology. In C. Troll (ed.), Geo-ecology of the mountainous regions of the tropical Americas. Ferd. Dümmlers Verlag, Bonn.

Valdivia, E. 1956. Mechanisms of natural acclimatization: capillary studies at high altitude. Report 56-101, School of Aviation Medicine, Randolph Field, Tex.

———. 1962. Total capillary bed of myocardium in chronic hypoxia. Fed. Am. Soc. Exp. Biol. 21: 221-225.

Van Liere, E. J., and J. C. Stickney. 1963. Hypoxia. Univ. Chicago Press, Chicago.

Vasquez de Espinosa, A. 1942. Compendium and description of the West Indies. Smithsonian Misc. Coll. *102.*

——. 1948. Compendio y descripción de las Indias Occidentales. Smithsonian Misc. Coll. *108.*

Vayda, A. P. (ed.). 1969. Environment and cultural behavior. Doubleday, Garden City. N.Y.

Velásquez, T. 1946. Metabolismo basal en la altura. Thesis for Bachelor of Medicine. Univ. Nacional Mayor de San Marcos, Lima, Peru.

——. 1956. Maximal diffusing capacity of the lungs at high altitude. AF SAM Report 56-108. U.S. Air Force School of Aviation Medicine, Randolph Field, Tex.

——. 1959. Tolerance to acute anoxia in high altitude natives. J. Appl. Physiol. *14:* 357-362.

——. 1964. Response to physical activity during adaptation to altitude, pp. 289-299. *In* W. H. Weihe (ed.), The physiological effects of high altitude. Macmillan, New York.

——. 1966. Acquired acclimatization: to sea level. *In* Life at high altitudes. Proceedings of the special session held during the Fifth Meeting of the PAHO Advisory Committee on Medical Research. Pan Am. Health Org. Sci. Publ. 140, pp. 58-63. Washington, D.C.

——. 1972. Análisis de la función respiratoria en la adaptación a la altitud. Medical Doctor thesis. Univ. Nacional Mayor de San Marcos, Lima, Peru, Ed. Programa Académico de Medicina Humana.

——, C. Martinez, W. Pezzia, and N. Gallardo. 1968. Ventilatory effects of oxygen in high altitude natives. Respir. Physiol. *5:* 211-220.

Vellard, J. 1961. Populations indigènes des hauts plateaux andins: II. Les Aymaras. Trav. Inst. Français d'Études Andines (Lima) *8:* 1-32.

——. 1972. Études analytiques des populations du Perou et de la Bolivie. *In* J. C. Quilici (ed.), Définition et analyse biologique des populations Amérindiennes: étude de leur environnement. Centre d'Hémotypalogie, C.H.U. de Purpan, Toulouse, France.

Verzar, F. 1951. Dauer-akklimatization an grosse Höhen. Bull. Schweiz. Akad. Med. Wiss. *7:* 26.

Viault, F. 1890. Sur l'augmentation considérable du nombre des globules rouges dans le sang chez les habitants des hauts-plateaux de l'Amérique du Sud. C. R. Acad. Sci. (Paris) *111:* 917-918.

Vogel, J. A., and C. W. Harris. 1967. Cardiopulmonary responses of resting man during early exposure to high altitude. J. Appl. Physiol. *22:* 1124-1128.

Wade, N. E. 1974. Bottle-feeding: adverse effects of a western technology. Science *184:* 45-47.

Watt, E. W., E. Picón-Reátegui, H. E. Gehagan, and E. R. Buskirk. 1973. Serum lipids, body fat, and blood pressure of high altitude and downward migrant Peruvian Quechua. Paper presented at the Federation of American Societies of Experimental Biology Intersociety Meetings, Atherosclerosis II, Atlantic City, N.J.

Way, A. B. 1972. Health, exercise capacity and effective fertility aspects of migration to sea level by high altitude Peruvian Quechua Indians. Ph.D. dissertation. Univ. Wisconsin, Madison, Wis.

Webb, G. B. 1913. The effect of altitude on the white blood cells. Phil. Trans. Roy. Soc. *203:* 312-315.

Weberbauer, A. 1936. Phytogeography of the Peruvian Andes. *In* J. F. MacBride (ed.), Flora of Peru: I. Field Museum of Natural History, Botanical Series, Publication 351, Vol. 13, Chicago.

———. 1945. El mundo vegetal de los Andes peruanos. Ministerio de Agricultura, Lima, Peru.

Webster, S. 1973. Native pastoralism in the south Andes. Ethnology *12* 115-133.

Weihe, W. H. 1964. Some examples of endocrine and metabolic functions in rats during acclimatization to high altitude, pp. 33-42. *In* W. H. Weihe (ed.), The physiological effects of altitude. Macmillan, New York.

———. 1966. General adjustments of acclimatized and unacclimatized man to cold, work, and altitude, pp. 481-524. *In* The physiology of work in cold and altitude. Proceedings of the Sixth Symposium on Arctic Biology and Medicine. Arctic Aeromedical Laboratory, Ft. Wainwright, Alaska.

Weiner, J. S. 1965. A guide to the human adaptability proposals. Blackwell Scientific, Oxford.

———, and J. A. Lourie. 1969. Human biology: a guide to field methods. F. A. Davis, Philadelphia.

Weir, J. A. 1953. Association of blood pH with sex ratio in mice. J. Hered. *44:* 133-138.

———. 1955. Male influence on sex ratio of offspring in high and low blood pH lines of mice. J. Hered. *46:* 277-283.

Weiss, B., and V. Laties. 1962. Enhancement of human performance by caffeine and amphetamines. Pharmacol. Rev. *14:* 1-36.

Weitz, C. A. 1969. Morphological factors affecting responses to total body cooling among three human populations tested at high altitude. M.A. thesis. Pennsylvania State Univ., University Park, Pa.

———. 1973. The effects of aging and habitual activity pattern on exercise performance among a high altitude Nepalese population. Ph.D. dissertation. Pennsylvania State Univ., University Park, Pa.

West, H. F. 1920. A comparison of various standards for the normal vital capacity of the lungs. Arch. Int. Med. *25:* 306-316.

West, J. B. 1962. Diffusing capacity of the lung for carbon monoxide at altitude. J. Appl. Physiol. *17:* 421-426.

Whitehead, L. 1968. Altitude, fertility and mortality in Andean countries. Pop. Stud. *22:* 335-346.

Whiting, J. W. M. 1964. Effects of climate on certain cultural practices, pp. 511-544. *In* W. H. Goodenough (ed.), Explorations in cultural anthropology. McGraw-Hill, New York.

——, I. L. Child, and W. W. Lambert. 1966. Field guide for the study of socialization. Wiley, New York.

Whittembury, J. and C. Monge. 1972. High altitude, haematocrit and age. Nature *238:* 278-279.

WHO. 1961. Public health aspects of low birth weight. World Health Organization Tech. Rep. Ser. 217. WHO, Geneva.

——. 1964. Research in population genetics of primitive groups. World Health Organization Tech. Rep. Ser. 279. WHO, Geneva.

——. 1965. WHO expert committee on nutrition in pregnancy and lactation. WHO Tech. Rep. Ser. 302. WHO, Geneva.

——. 1968. Research on human population genetics. World Health Organization Tech. Rep. Ser. 387. WHO, Geneva.

——. 1970. The prevention of perinatal mortality and morbidity. World Health Organization Tech. Rep. Ser. 457. WHO, Geneva.

——. 1971. Joint FAO/WHO expert committee on nutrition: eight report. World Health Organization Tech. Rep. Ser. 477. WHO, Geneva.

Wickes, D. R., and W. C. Lowdermilk. 1938. Soil conservation in ancient Peru. Soil Conserv. *4:* 91-94.

Wilder, R. M. 1941. A primer for diabetic patients. Saunders, Philadelphia.

Williams, D. D., J. H. Petajan, and S. B. Lee. 1969. Summer and winter hand calorimetry of children in the village of Old Crow. Int. J. Biometeor. *13* (Pt. II, Suppl.): 11 (abstract).

Williams, W. J., E. Beutler, A. J. Erslev, and R. W. Rundles. 1972. Hematology. McGraw-Hill, New York.

Wilson, O., and R. Goldman. 1970. Role of air temperature and wind in time necessary for a finger to freeze. J. Appl. Physiol. *29:* 658-664.

Wilson, P. J., and J. Buettner-Janusch. 1961. Demography and evolution in Columbia. Am. Anthrop. *63:* 940-953.

Windslow, C-E. A., and L. Harrington. 1949. Temperature and human life. Princeton Univ. Press, Princeton, N.J.

Winterhalder, B., R. Larsen, and R. B. Thomas. 1974. Dung as an essential resource in a highland Peruvian community. Hum. Ecol. *2:* 89-104.

Wintrobe, M. M. 1967. Clinical hematology. Lea & Febiger, Philadelphia.

Wolf, E. R. 1966. Peasants. Prentice-Hall, Englewood Cliffs, N.J.

Wolff, P. O. 1952. General considerations on the problem of coca leaf chewing. Bull. Narcotics *4:* 2-5.

——. 1972. Ethnic differences in alcohol sensitivity. Science *175:* 449-450.

Wright, S. 1931. Evolution in Mendelian populations. Genetics *16:* 97-159.

——. 1943. Isolation by distance. Genetics *28:* 114-138.

——. 1948. On the roles of directed and random changes in gene frequency in the genetics of populations. Evolution *2:* 279-295.

——. 1951. The genetical structure of populations. Ann. Eugen. *15:* 323-354.

Wulff, L. Y., I. A. Braden, F. H. Shilliot, and J. F. Tomashefski. 1968. Physiological factors relating to terrestrial altitudes: a bibliography. Ohio State Univ. Libraries Publ. 3, Ohio State Univ. Press, Columbus, Ohio.

Wyndham, C. H., N. B. Strydom, J. F. Morrison, C. G. Williams, G. Bredell, J. Peter, H. M. Cooke, and A. Joffe. 1963. The influence of gross body weight on oxygen consumption and on physical working capacity of manual labours. Ergonomics *6:* 275.

——, G. Rogers, A. Benade, and N. Strydom. 1971. Physiological effects of the amphetamines during exercise. S. Afr. Med. J. *45:* 247-252.

Yoshimura, H., and T. Iida. 1952. Studies on the reactivity of skin vessels to extreme cold: II. Factors concerning the individual difference of the reactivity, or the resistance against frostbite. Jap. J. Physiol. *2:* 177-185.

Zapata Ortíz, B. 1944. Modificaciones psicológicas y fisiológicas producidas por la coca y la cocaína en los coqueros. Rev. Med. Expt. *5:* 132-162.

APPENDIX:
LIST OF SYMBOLS

Metabolism and Thermoregulation

RMR	resting metabolic rate
BMR	basal metabolic rate
T_{re}	rectal temperature (a measure of core temperature)
$\bar{T}_s$	mean weighted skin temperature
T_b	mean body temperature
kcal	kilogram calorie or kilocalorie
watt	kcal/h $\times$ 1.163

Pulmonary Function, Circulation, and Exercise

VC	vital capacity
TLC	total lung capacity
RV	residual volume
MVC	maximum ventilatory capacity
FRC	functional residual capacity
$\dot{V}_{O_2}$	oxygen consumption
$\dot{V}_{CO_2}$	carbon dioxide production
$\dot{V}_E$	ventilation
$\dot{V}_A$	alveolar ventilation
P_{O_2}	partial pressure of oxygen
P_{CO_2}	partial pressure of carbon dioxide
$P_{I_{O_2}}$	partial pressure of O_2 in inspired air
$P_{A_{O_2}}$	partial pressure of O_2 in alveolar air
$P_{a_{O_2}}$	partial pressure of O_2 in arterial blood
$(A\text{-}a)O_2$	alveolar–arterial O_2 gradient
$(a\text{-}A)CO_2$	arterial–alveolar CO_2 gradient
R	respiration exchange ratio
RQ	respiratory quotient
STPD	standard temperature and pressure, dry ($0°C$, 760 torr)
BTPS	body temperature and pressure, saturated with water vapor
ATPS	ambient temperature and pressure, saturated with water vapor
HR	heart rate
$\dot{Q}$	cardiac output
TBV	thoracic blood volume

kpm   kilogram-meter of work at 1 gravity (1 kpm/min = 0.1635 W)

$\dot{V}_E$ max/$\dot{V}_{O_2}$ max   ventilation equivalent (at conditions producing $\dot{V}_{O_2}$ max)

$\dot{V}_{O_2}$ max/HR max   oxygen pulse (heart rate at conditions producing $\dot{V}_{O_2}$ max)

Hematology

RBC	red blood count
WBC	white blood count
Hb or Hgb	hemoglobin concentration
Hct	hematocrit
MCV	mean corpuscular volume
MCH	mean corpuscular hemoglobin
MCHC	mean corpuscular hemoglobin concentration
Retics	reticulocytes
Neutros	neutrophils, segmented
Lymphs	lymphocytes
Monos	monocytes
Eosinos	eosinophils
Basos	basophils

Demography

CBR	crude birth rate (live births/1000 population/yr)
NRR	net reproduction rate (sum of the product of female age specific fertility rates and proportion of women surviving to that age)
SSR	secondary sex ratio (number of males born per 100 females born in a population)

Miscellaneous

SA or BSA	body surface area
SSF	sum of skinfolds
FFW	fat-free weight

INDEX

ABO blood groups, 107-109, 115-116
Acclimatization, 3, 5
  developmental, 5, 14, 332, 338, 351
  energy flow, 402
  hypothermic, 333
  metabolic, 333
  pulmonary function, 237-260
  short-term, 332, 338
  work capacity, 295-296
Acculturation, 82-84
  disease, effect on, 100, 156
  educational effect on, 84, 95-96
  Nuñoa project effect on, 83
  sports, effect on, 84
  transportation, 83
Adaptation, 2-3, 147 (*See also* Acclimatization)
  energy flow, 382, 402
  genetic, 2, 158, 332
  multiple and cross adaptation, 426-427
  physiological, 2
  stress interaction, 410-411, 414-415, 421-422
Adaptation to high altitude, 2-3
  historical evidence, 3
  low-altitude populations, 2
  mammals, 2
  native populations, 2-3, 158
  pulmonary function, 237-260
Agrarian reform (1969), 75, 84
Agriculture, 57
  energy flow, 383
  Nunoa, 68
Alcohol, 375-376
  altitude and response to, 376

ecological benefits, 376
  ethnic differences in response to, 376
  metabolism of, 376
Altiplano
  definition, 22
  description, 22-36
  topography, 23
Altitude
  domestic animals, effect on, 44-45, 57-58
  fecundity, effect on, 4
  growth, effect on, 162-179
  horticulture, effect on, 56
  migration patterns, 117, 119
  mortality, effect on, 4
  parturition, effect on, 4
  pulmonary function, 237-260
  temperature, effect on, 27
Anthropometry, 181, 200-207
Atmospheric pressure, 33

Child care, 88-92
  bathing practices, 88
  clothing, infant, 88, 90
  disease
    infectious, 89-90
    nutritional deficiency, 89-90
  folk remedies, 89-91
  medical care, 89-90, 91
  medication, modern, 89, 91
  morbidity, infant, 85
  nursing practices, 89-91
  nutrition, 88-89
  sanitation, 89-90, 91-92
  sleeping arrangements, 88, 90
  thermoregulation, 16, 88-90
  toilet training, 90
  weaning, 89

Child-care studies, methodology,
    86-87
  ethnographic observation, 87
  mother recall questionnaire, 87
  Whiting's maintenance systems
    approach, 86
Child training, 92-97
  cultural continuity, 92, 95-96
  division of labor, 92-94
  formal education, 94-95
    acculturation, 95-96
    curriculum, 95
    legal requirements in Peru,
      94-95
    teaching, 94
  informal training, 92-94
    socializing agents, com-
      padrazgo, 92
    socializing agents, extended
      family, 92, 95
    socializing agents, nuclear
      family, 92, 95
  observational learning, 94
  residence patterns, 92
  sex roles, 92-94
Cholo, 67
  gene flow, role in, 126
Circulation, peripheral, 15
Climate, 23-26, 50
  air circulation patterns, 24
  factors affecting, 25
  frost
    dynamic, 31-32
    static, 31
  humidity, 33
  precipitation, 25-27, 31, 50
  radiation, 36
  temperature, 27-33, 50
    altitude effects, 27
    annual cycle, 27
    diurnal cycle, 27, 316, 318,
      326-330
Clothing, infant, 88-90 (see also
    Microclimate, Nuñoa)
Coca leaf, 228, 233-234
  cardiopulmonary response, 368,
    372
  chemical content, 363
  cold stress, 370-372

  consumption patterns, 364-367
  digestion, 363
  dose, 367, 371
  hunger suppression, 372
  nutrition, 4, 372-373
  preparation, 363
  psychological effects, 367, 371
  socioeconomic aspects, 373-375
  temperature regulation, 16, 372
  withdrawal, 367, 372
  work performance, 367-370, 372
Coefficient of breeding isolation,
    120
Compadrazgo, 66, 92
Crafts, Nuñoa, 68

Deforestation, 85
Demography, 406-412 (see also
    Fertility; Migration patterns;
    Mortality)
Dermatoglyphics, 100-107
Development, 161-179, 412-415
    (see also Growth)
  adolescent growth spurt, 182,
    195, 199
  altitude, effect on, 177-178, 183,
    193
  child care, 178
  ethnic differences, 177-178
  fertility, effect of, 135-137
  hormone levels, female, 195
  infant growth spurt, 161
  menarche, 195
  Mestizo, 163, 165, 167, 171
  motor skills, 176-178
  sexual maturation, secondary,
    195
  skeletal maturation, 174, 190,
    199
  skin color, 199
  socioeconomic factors, 177-178
  tooth eruption, 174
Diet (see Nutrition)
Digital interlocking patterns,
    107-109
Disease, 146-150, 155-160 (see also
    Medical practices; Morbidity)
  acute illness, 148
  altitude, effect on, 148-150

chronic illness, 147-149
infectious disease, 149-150
in children, 89-90
nutritional deficiency in infants,
89-90
perceived causes, 89-90
respiratory infections, 149-150
Drug use, 363-378 (*see also*
Alcohol; Coca leaf; Tobacco)

Ecology, theory, 15
Economy, Nuñoa, 67-75
barter, 72
commerce, 72-74
division of labor, 68, 71
energy flow, 379-404
gene flow, effect on, 116-117
reciprocity, 71-72
Effective population size, Nuñoa,
120, 126
Energy flow, 424-425
acclimatization, 402
activity levels, 383, 387, 397-398
adaptive strategies, 389-404
age and procurement, 388
agriculture, 383
annual cycles, 383-384
behavioral responses, 391
body size, 398-401
division of labor, 396
energy
consumption, 379-381,
384-388
expenditure, 379-381
input, 388-389
production, 379-384
sources, 379
fertility, 401
flow diagram, 388, 390
food-procurement unit, 388
genetic adaptation, 402
growth, 399-400
haciendas, 380, 403
hypoxia, 398
interzonal exchange, 396
migration patterns, 395, 401-402
Nuñoa, 379-404
nutrition, 384-388
pastoralism, 383, 392-396

population control, 387
prehistory, 387
primary production, 379
research design, 380-383
seasonal production, 383
sex and procurement, 388
trophic levels, 392
Estancias, land tenure, 70
Ethnohistory, 61-65
colonial period, Nuñoa, 62, 63,
124-126
Incaic period, Nuñoa, 62, 124
linguistics, 124
prehistory, Nuñoa, 61-62, 124,
387
republican period, Nuñoa, 64-65

Family size, 401
desired, 138
Nuñoa, 138, 146
socioeconomic implications,
138-140
Fauna
domestic, 57-58
hypoxic effect on, 44-45
wild, 41-42, 43-45, 56-57
Fecundity (*see* Fertility)
Fertility, 112-113, 128-146, 147,
408-410
altitude, effect on, 133-145
birth
intervals, 145, 146
rates, 132
census studies, 133, 134
child/woman ratio, 134
cold stress, effect on, 138
completed fertility, 138, 141,
408
contraception, 135, 141
crude birth rates, 135
cultural factors, 128, 133, 137,
141, 144, 146
demographic structures, 133
desired family size, 138
educational status, 141
environmental effect on, 4, 15
Ethiopian populations, 135
growth and development, effect
on, 135-137

Fertility—*continued*
  historical evidence, 128, 131
  hypoxia, effect on, 128-133 (*see also* Hypoxia)
  linguistic associations, 133
  marriage patterns, 135, 141
  menarche, 135
  menopause, 137
  migration patterns, 134, 135, 140, 141-145
  Nuñoa, 137-138
  nutritional effect on, 136-137
  reproductive span, 137, 141, 146
  rituals, Nuñoa, 79-80
  sex ratio
    adult, 133
    secondary, 131
  socioeconomic factors, 133, 137, 141, 144
  vital statistics data, 134-137
Fiestas, 81
  mating patterns, effect of, 118, 123
Flora
  domestic, 55
  wild, 41-42, 50-51, 54

Gene flow, 112-114, 115, 410-412 (*see also* Marriage patterns; Mating patterns; Migration patterns)
  dermatoglyphics, 107-109
  ethnohistory, 123-126
  Nuñoa
    and other districts, 115-127
    isolation of population, 115-117, 118, 121, 126
    rate in, 117-120, 126
    within, 121, 126
  Nuñoa urban center, effect of, 123
  research design, 115-116
  southern Peru, 107-109
Gene markers, 107-109, 115-127, 410
Genetic distance in southern Peru, 109-111
  research design, 100

Genetic-distance test, 109
Genetic drift, 112-114, 120-121
  Nuñoa, 120, 123, 126
Genetic history, Quechua, 98-99
  ethnohistory, 98-99, 123-126
  gene flow, 123-126
  research design, 99-100
Genetic homogeneity, 114
Geology
  altiplano, 23
  central Andes, 21-23
Growth, 161-179, 412-415 (*see also* Development)
  activity level, 193
  adolescent growth spurt, 182, 195, 199
  altitude, effect of, 162-179, 183, 193, 197
  birth weights, 162-165
  body composition, 188-190
  cardiac growth, 200
  critical periods, 161
  developmental acclimatization, 165
  environmental stresses, 14, 161, 165, 180
  ethnic differences, 163, 165, 167, 171-172
  genetic factors, 161, 165, 196-197, 199
  hematopoeitic function, 198, 200
  hypoxia, effect of, 164-165, 174, 178, 193-200
  infant, 161, 165-179
  infant growth spurt, 161
  intrauterine environment, 161
  maternal adaptation, 163, 179
  medical care, 174-176
  Mestizo, 163, 165, 167, 171
  motor skills, effect on, 178
  neonatal mortality, 165
  nutrition, effect of, 174-176, 192-193, 195, 199
  patterns, 181-185
  postnatal, 165-176
  prenatal, 161-165
  pulmonary function, 185-188, 197, 200

rates, 170-176, 199
sex differences, 163, 170, 176,
181-182, 199
socioeconomic factors, 164, 167,
171, 182-183, 193, 197, 199
work performance, 309

Hacienda
community membership, 74
energy flow, 380, 403
land tenure, 70-71
Health, Nuñoa, 416-418 (*see also*
Disease; Medical practices;
Morbidity)
Hemaglobin, oxygen transport,
252-257
Hematology, 261-282
activity levels, effect of, 275-281
adults, 271-275
age differences, 264-267, 270-271
altitude effects, 261-282
anemia, 274
blood counts, 263-268
children and adolescents, 262-271
developmental trends, 264-267
high-altitude native, 15
hypoxia, effect of, 261-282
oxygen debt, 276, 299
oxygen dissociation curve, 282
plasma volume, 268
polycythemia, 261, 272, 282
research design, 262-263
respiratory infections, effect of,
271
work performance, 298
Herding, Nuñoa, 68
Hypoxia, 420-422
birth weights, effect on, 131-132,
162-163
conception, effect on, 131
fertility, effect of, 128-133
high-altitude natives, 130
low-altitude natives, 130
gametogenesis, effect on, 128-130
gestation, effect on, 130-133, 146
menstrual cycle, effect on,
129-130
miscarriage, effect on, 131, 146

parturition, effect on, 130-133
placenta, effect on, 131, 146
polycythemia, 261
prezygotic selection, effect on,
131
ventilation, effect on, 245-247
vital capacity, effect on, 240
work performance, 283

Inbreeding, 112
Indigenas, 67
International Biological Program, 1,
11, 309

Kinship system 65-66
ceremonial kinship (com-
padrazgo), 66
socioeconomic factors, 138-140

Land tenure systems, 69-71
estancias, 70
haciendas, 70
Indian tenure, 70, 74
land distribution, 69
peasant tenure, 69
Land use, nutrition, 212
Lingual rotation, 107-109
Lung volume
body morphology, relationship
with, 241-242
hyperinflation, 243
lung capacity, 237
Quechua Indians, 237
racial variation, 238, 239
residual volume, 237, 238, 242,
243
thoracic growth, 237, 238, 241
vital capacity, 237-239, 242

Marriage patterns, 66
assortative mating, 122
gene flow, effect on, 123
Mestizo, 118
Nuñoa, 138
Quechua marriage system, 123
Mating patterns
environmental factors, 121
fiestas, effect on, 118, 123

Mating patterns—*continued*
  gene flow, effect on, 118, 123
  Mestizo, 118
  number of mates, 123
  Nuñoa, 138
  Nuñoa urban center, effect on,
    123
  serial monogamy, 137-138
  socioeconomic factors, 123, 126,
    140
Medical practices (*see also* Disease;
    Morbidity)
  folk curers, 80
  folk remedies, 89-91
  medication, modern, 89, 91
Menarche, 136
Mestizo, 67
  gene flow, role in, 126
  growth and development, 163,
    165, 167, 171
  marriage patterns, 118
  mating patterns, 118
Microclimate, Nuñoa, 315-319,
    323-326, 338
  bedding, 326
  clothing, 316, 318, 326-330
  fuel, 315, 323
  housing, 323-326
  posture, 318
  sleeping arrangements, 316-318
  socioeconomic differences,
    318-319
Migration patterns, 427
  age structure, 86, 96-97, 117
  altitude, 117, 119
  cultural effect on, 116-117, 126
  disease, effect on, 150
  economy, effect of, 117, 119,
    126
  emigration, 116-117, 118-119,
    126
  energy flow, 395, 401-402
  environmental effect on, 116
  fertility, effect on, 134, 135, 140,
    141-145
  gene flow, effect on, 116-117
  genetic homogeneity, 119-120

  immigration patterns, 117, 120,
    126
  Nuñoa, 116-127
    ethnohistoric, 123-126
    isolation in, 115-117, 118,
      126-127
    transportation, 116, 126
  social structure, effect on,
    116-117
Morbidity, 147-160 (*see also*
    Disease; Mortality)
  acute illness, 148
  altitude and, 148-149, 157-159
  cardiovascular disease, 156
  childbirth, 157
  chronic illness, 147-149
  degenerative disease, 156-157
  gastrointestinal disease, 155-156
  infant, causes, 85
  infectious disease, 149-150,
    155-156
  migration patterns, effect on,
    150, 155
  respiratory infections, 149-150,
    156-157
Morphology, 200-207 (*see also*
    Development; Growth)
  adult, 200-207
Mortality, 112-113, 147, 410
  altitude, effect on, 148, 150-151
  death rates, 135
  health care and, 159
  infant, 85, 132, 134, 154
    hypoxia, effect on, 132
    medical facilities, 132
    sex differences, 132
  infanticide, 137
  neonatal, 132, 154, 165
  Nuñoa, 150-155
    age-specific rates, 152-153
    crude death rates, 148, 150
    seasonal variations, 151
    sex-specific rates, 152-155
    survivorship curves, 153
  pastoralists, 154, 157
  postneonatal, 147
Multidisciplinary studies, 405-428

Natural selection
  differential fertility, 412
  differential mortality, 412
  selection intensity, postnatal,
    112-114
  selection pressures, Nuñoa, 127
Nuñoa (*see also specific topic*)
  description, 6, 46-58
  district of, 9, 115, 121
  ethnohistory, 61-65, 123-126
  location, 6, 46
  map, 6
  population, 9, 10, 118-119, 120,
    125
  social structure, 11, 12
  town, 10
  transportation, 9
Nuñoa ecosystem
  animal-to-land ratios, 58
  deforestation, 45
  description, 46-58, 121, 379-380
  food zones, 208
  land distribution, 69
  location, 46
  overgrazing, 45
  valley and river systems, 46
Nuñoa project
  methodological modifications,
    13-14, 16-20
  normative data, 15
  objectives, 15
  population selection, 6-10
  research design, 1-20
  sampling, 11, 12
  theoretical background, 2-4
  theoretical modifications, 14-16
  timetable, 10
Nutrition
  activity levels
    diurnal, 208-209
    seasonal, 222
  alcohol consumption, 209
  animal products, 21-22
  ascorbic acid, 232-233
  calcium, 228-229
  caloric intake, 215-226
    age differences, 217, 224

  altitude, effect on, 224
  basal metabolic rate, 224
  body weight, 217, 222
  community differences,
    216-217
  dietary source, 215
  sex differences, 217, 218
  skinfolds, 217-222
  carbohydrates, 214-215
  child care, 88-89
  coca-leaf chewing, 4, 228, 233,
    234
  community differences, 235
  deficiency disease, 222
  energy
    expenditure, 208-209, 223
    flow, 384-388
  fat intake, 214-215, 227-228
    community differences, 227
    dietary sources, 227
    hypoxia, effect of, 227
  fertility, effect on, 136-137
  food
    preparation, 212-214, 228
    preservation, 212-214, 232-233
  growth, 174-176, 192-193, 195,
    199, 225, 227, 235
  high-altitude surveys, 4, 5
  hypoxia, effect of, 215
  imported foodstuffs, 209-211,
    215, 235
  iron, 229-230
  locally produced foods, 209-211,
    215, 235
  meal scheduling, 208, 213
  meat consumption, 211-212,
    227-228
  metabolic balance study, Nuñoa,
    226, 227, 229, 230
  niacin, 231
  pastoralism, 211
  phosphorus, 229
  pregnancy and lactation, stress of,
    225-227, 235
  protein intake, 214-215, 226-227
    dietary sources, 226
    digestibility coefficient, 226

Nutrition—*continued*
nitrogen balance, 226
recommended allowances,
222-233, 235
riboflavin, 231
thiamine, 231
vitamin A, 230
vitamin D, 236
work performance, 304
Overgrazing, 45
Oxygen dissociation curve, 243,
253, 254, 286, 288, 296-299,
361
Oxygen pressure (*see also* Hypoxia)
alveolar, 245
capillary, 237
inspired air, 253
tissue, 237
Oxygen transport, 237-260
alveolar-arterial gradient, 250-252
blood levels, 252-253, 257
capillary-tissue gradient, 255,
258-260
cardiac
index, 255
output, 255
hemoglobin, 252, 258, 282
high-altitude native, 3
oxygen conductance, 237
rate, 255
studies of, 6
total oxygen pressure gradient,
257-260, 282

Pastoralism, 57
alpaca, 57
gene flow, effect on, 117
llama, 57
nutrition, 211
sheep, 57
Political system, Nuñoa, 76-79
ideology, 77-79
national-level participation, 75
PTC (phenylthiocarbamide) tasting,
107-109
Public works, Nuñoa, 77-78
Pulmonary function, 237-260 (*see
also* Hypoxia; Lung volume;

Oxygen pressure; Oxygen
transport; Ventilation)
diffusing capacity, 251-252
growth, 185-188, 197, 200
high-altitude native, 237-260
low-altitude native, 237-260
work performance, 298
Puna
description, 21-23, 422-424
food zones, 200
Puna ecozone (*see* Nuñoa
ecosystem)

Quechua Indian
biological characteristics, 5
ethnohistory, 61-65, 123-126
genetic history, 98-99, 123-126
growth and development,
163-164, 167
health, 416-417
lung volume, 237-238
physiological testing, 5, 418-419
respiratory quotient, 250, 257
studies of, 4
work performance, 286, 288,
296-299

Religion
Catholicism, 80-81
folk, 79-80
nativistic, 82
Nuñoa, 79-80
ritual celebration, 81
Research design
child-care-studies methodology,
86-87
energy flow, 380-383
fertility studies, 128-145
gene flow, 115-116
genetic distance in southern Peru,
100
genetic history, Quechua, 99-100
hematology, 262-263
migration and fertility, 140
multidisciplinary studies, 405-428
multiple stress—multiple
population model, 19
Nuñoa project, 1-20

single stress—multiple population model, 19
systems model, 17, 427-428
temperature regulation, 319, 333, 338-340
work performance, 284-288
RH blood group, 107-109, 115-116

Selection (*see* Natural selection)
Settlement patterns, 403
Sex ratio
  adult, 133
  secondary, 131
Sincata, 65, 122-126, 211
Social structure
  colonial period, 64
  mobility, 67
  Nuñoa, 65-67
    gene flow, effect on, 116-117
  stratification, 66-67
Soils, altiplano, 36
Sports, Nuñoa, 77
Stress, environmental, 2
  effect on adaptation, 36-37

Tambo Valley, fertility, 140-145
Technology, Nuñoa, 67-68
  fertilizer, 394
  fuel, 315, 323, 394
  housing, 323-326
Temperature regulation, 315-362, 421-422
  activity levels, 317-322
  age differences, 317, 318, 350-354
  alcohol, effect on, 16
  altitude effects, 359-362
  basal metabolic rate, 361
  bedding, 326
  body size, 322, 334, 354-356
  circadian rhythms, 356
  coca-leaf chewing, effect on, 16, 234, 372
  cold response, 4, 5, 332-338
  core temperature, 323, 335, 338, 339-340, 345, 361
  cultural factors, 315-331, 338

diurnal temperature cycles, environmental, 318, 330
drugs, 356
fat insulation, 317, 352, 355-356
high-altitude native, 340-345
hypothermic acclimatization, 333
hypoxia, effect on, 338, 359-362
infants and children, 88-90
metabolic acclimatization, 333
nutrition, 356
peripheral temperature, 322-323, 335, 338, 340, 345-350
research design, 319, 333, 338-340
resting metabolic rate, 341, 345, 361
sex differences, 317, 320, 322, 327, 329, 350-354, 356
shivering, 343, 359
socioeconomic differences, 318-319
thermally neutral zone, 315, 335, 359
tobacco consumption, 377
vasoconstriction, 350
vasodilation, 347
Tobacco
  cardiovascular effects, 377
  hunger suppression, 377
  hypoxia, effect on, 377
  social class and consumption, 376
  temperature regulation, 377
Topography, altiplano, 23
Transportation, Nuñoa, 9, 395-396
  gene flow, effect on, 116
Trophic levels, 392

Ventilation, 244-250
  hyperventilation, 249-250
  hypoventilation, 250
  work capacity, 293-295, 299

Work performance, 420-421
  acclimatization, 295-296, 303, 306
  aerobic capacity, 283, 288, 296-299, 306
  body morphology, 298, 302

Work performance—*continued*
cardiovascular response, 302
conditioning, 296, 302-306, 313
developmental acclimatization,
    303, 308-309, 310, 314
genetic factors, 297, 303,
    311-314
growth, effect of, 309
hematology, 298-299
highland natives, 300-314
hypoxia, effect on, 283, 297-299,
    308
low-altitude natives, 283, 299
maximal work capacity, 288
migrants, 307, 310-311
Nepal, 306
nutrition, 304
oxygen debt, 299
pulmonary function, 298-299
research design, 284-288
submaximal work, 292
U.S. athletes, 283-299
ventilation, 293-295, 299, 302,
    305